VOLUME XL

SOCIETY
of
ACTUARIES

Transactions

The work of science is to substitute facts for appearances and demonstrations for impressions. —RUSKIN

PART II

1988

MANUFACTURED FOR THE SOCIETY BY IMPERIAL PRINTING COMPANY,
ST. JOSEPH, MICHIGAN

PRINTED IN THE UNITED STATES OF AMERICA

ISBN 0-938959-09-3

The *Transactions* are published annually by the Society of Actuaries, successor to the Actuarial Society of America and the American Institute of Actuaries, in lieu of *Transactions* and the *Record*, respectively, heretofore published by the two former organizations.

NOTICE

The Society assumes no responsiblity for statements made or opinions expressed in the articles, criticisms, and discussions published in these *Transactions*.

CONTENTS OF VOLUME XL, PART II

Samuel N. Ain
Morgan Hanlon Alvord
Albert William Anderson
Edward Charles Benham
Edmund Callis Berkeley
John Allen Bradford
Alexander Thomson Brooks
Joseph A. Budinger
Alden Thomson Bunyan
Joseph Andrew Christman
Barrett N. Coates, Jr.
Harvey H. Conklin, Jr.

Thomas Kilburn Dodd
Francis Thomas Driscoll
Robert Donald Drisko
Maurice Howard Farrant
Carl Hahn Fischer
George R. Fraser
Joseph B. Glenn
George William Keith Grange
Henry Strong Huntington, III
Robert James Kirton
Myron Henry Margolin
William Craig McCarter
Joseph Trevor McNeely
John Haynes Miller
Harry D. Morgan
Bennet Bronson Murdock
Thomas John Norris
Melvin C. Pryce
Anthony J. Savasta
Michael C. Schlussel
Edward James Seligman
Phillip John Shore
Charles W. Southern
Margaret Walker
Harold Graham Walton
Max S. Weinstein
Charlie Thomas Whitley
William Shelly York

SOCIETY OF ACTUARIES
475 N. MARTINGALE ROAD, SCHAUMBURG, ILLINOIS 60173
OCTOBER 1988

BOARD OF GOVERNORS

OFFICE OF THE SOCIETY

JOHN E. O'CONNOR, JR., *Executive Director*
BERNARD A. BARTELS, *Registrar*
RICHARD BILISOLY, F.S.A., *Education Actuary*
RACHEL L. BRODY, *Director of Operations*
BARBARA M. CHOYKE, *Director of Continuing Education*
LINDEN N. COLE, F.S.A., *Education Actuary*
LINDA M. DELGADILLO, *Director of Communications*
MARK G. DOHERTY, *Director of Research*
MARTA L. HOLMBERG, Ph.D., *Education Executive*
WILLIAM KEPRAIOS, C.P.A., *Director of Finance*
WARREN R. LUCKNER, F.S.A., *Research Actuary*
JOHN A. (JACK) LUFF, F.S.A., F.C.I.A., *Experience Studies Actuary*
RICHARD MATTISON, F.S.A., *Education Actuary*
JAMES WEISS, *Director of Information Services Center*

Editorial Board—The *Transactions*
  Douglas A. Eckley, Editor

Society of Actuaries Staff Editor
  Barbara A. Simmons

SOURCE OF EARNINGS ANALYSIS FOR FLEXIBLE PREMIUM AND INTEREST-SENSITIVE LIFE AND ANNUITY PRODUCTS

ROBERT W. STEIN AND JOSEPH H. TAN

ABSTRACT

Although source of earnings analysis procedures are well defined for traditional life insurance products, it is difficult to apply such procedures to the nontraditional flexible premium and interest-sensitive life and annuity products, because of the dynamic nature of the nontraditional products. This paper provides a solution to this problem by presenting formulas that define a comparable source of earnings analysis for examining the contributions to the income of these nontraditional products. A simple example illustrates the application of the described methodology.

INTRODUCTION

This paper describes the application of source of earnings (SOE) analysis methodology to the reported pretax GAAP income of universal life and other interest-sensitive life and annuity products. SOE analysis procedures have been defined for traditional products, primarily in Richard G. Horn's paper, "Life Insurance Earnings and the Release from Risk Policy Reserve System" (*TSA* XXIII (1971):391). However, the dynamic aspects of flexible premium and interest-sensitive products have made it difficult to readily apply existing analytical procedures to these new products. This paper presents formulas that define a comparable SOE analysis for examining the contributions to income of flexible premium and interest-sensitive products. The described methodology is illustrated through the use of a simple example.

The methodology presented can be used to better understand the earnings reported under GAAP accounting methods that are premium-based. However, the specific methodology can be generalized to apply to situations in which the accounting approach is account value-based. Premium-based methods are prospective; these include the methods commonly referred to as full percent of premium, traditional GAAP, composite, and prospective deposit, all of which vary only by the magnitude of the provisions for adverse deviation included in reserve assumptions. Account value-based methods are retrospective and rely on the policy's account value as a measure of the reserve liability. Approaches included here are the actuarial retrospective deposit and the FASB retrospective deposit methods. We believe that the described methodology can be useful under present and expected future accounting requirements.

TRADITIONAL PRODUCT ANALYSES

The ability to analyze GAAP earnings by source was demonstrated in Richard G. Horn's landmark paper, which first presented the "release from risk" concept. Although the paper was primarily intended to support the development of a rational approach to GAAP for traditional fixed premium/fixed benefit life products, it also provided a means by which the actual income of a block of business could be examined and attributed to its underlying source. In this context, gain or loss can be associated with:

- The expected GAAP profit margin (that is, the difference between the gross premium and the net GAAP premium)
- The release of provisions for adverse deviation included in reserve assumptions (that is, the difference between "most likely experience" and GAAP reserve assumptions)
- The variation of experience from "most likely" assumptions.

These "sources" of gain and loss can be computed for each experience element used in the calculation of benefit and expense reserves. Thus, the reconciliation of expected and actual income identifies amounts attributable to experience with respect to policy lapse or surrender, death, interest earnings, and expense levels. Variations in results caused by policy parameters (for example, premiums, death benefits, cash values, etc.) were nonexistent, as traditional products' experience could not vary from reserve assumptions. Mr. Horn's paper defines the reported GAAP income of a traditional product by this formula:

Actual Income:

$$
\begin{aligned}
&= (GP - NP)(1 + i^a) && \text{[loading gain]} \\
&+ (q^e - q^a)(1 - V) && \text{[gain from mortality]} \\
&+ (w^e - w^a)(CV - V) && \text{[gain from withdrawal]} \\
&+ (\text{Expected Cost} - \text{Actual Cost})(1 + i^a) && \text{[gain from expense]} \\
&+ (i^a - i^e)(V + NP - \text{Expected Cost}) && \text{[gain from interest]}
\end{aligned}
$$

or

Actual Income:
$$= (GP - NP)(1 + i^e)$$
$$+ (q^e - q^a)(1 - V)$$
$$+ (w^e - w^a)(CV - V)$$
$$+ (\text{Expected Cost} - \text{Actual Cost})(1 + i^e)$$
$$+ (i^a - i^e)(V + GP - \text{Actual Cost})$$

A later section of this paper extends this approach to both the experience elements and the policy parameters of flexible premium/interest-sensitive life and annuity products.

Broadening the applicability of this methodology is considered an important step in developing a better means of evaluating and understanding the financial performance of new-generation products. Thus, a means of reconciling actual and expected results that focuses on the variation of experience and policy parameters inherent in the accounting system will provide critical information with respect to the financial consequences of not achieving anticipated experience. This will not only "explain" results, but also allow management to concentrate on areas of performance that most affect financial results. Also, it is believed that this information can support better, more informed product management and pricing decisions. From this perspective, the data can be used to evaluate the reasonableness of key pricing assumptions, leading to improved initial and subsequent pricing of the major variables under such contracts. Thus, implementation of the methodology described can enhance the company's ability to manage the future performance of existing business and future production.

UNIVERSAL LIFE AND FLEXIBLE PREMIUM ANNUITY ANALYSES

Application to New Products

Because of the fixed nature of the traditional life product, the SOE analysis for this product is relatively simple. However, such is not the case with universal life (UL). Death benefits, future premiums, cash values, interest spreads, mortality and expense charges, and reserve factors are all subject to change. Clearly, all such changes affect current and future earnings and their sources. Moreover, an SOE analysis for such products is complicated by the interdependency of the various sources of earnings. To a lesser extent, such complications also exist in the flexible premium annuity (FPA) SOE analysis.

For example, let us take the case of a deviation in the current year's earned rate from the original expectation. Ideally, the company will modify its credited rate to obtain the same interest spread. However, depending on the GAAP methodology used (both benefit reserve and DAC), maintaining the same interest spread can result in GAAP profits for the current year that vary from originally expected income levels. Also, a change in the current year's credited rate will affect the account balance, which will have a domino effect on the various sources of earnings; it will affect current and future years' cash values, reserves, death benefits, expense and mortality charges, and interest gains. How can we analyze the effects of such earned and credited rate changes on the current and the future years' sources of earnings? Can we develop a procedure for calculating the credited rate so as to maintain the original expected GAAP profit?

A similar situation exists whenever a company revises its expense charges because of variation of actual expenses from assumed expenses. Any changes in current year's expense or mortality charges affect the account balance, which in turn affects current and future years' sources of earnings.

Perhaps the most significant variation, and the most common, is the deviation of actual premium received from assumed premium income. Clearly, such premium variations affect the loading gain (the percent of premium profit). Also, premium variations affect the account balance and charges and expenses, which vary with premium. Because of such changes, the original profit expectations and the sources of such profits will be completely different. How can we measure the effects of such premium variations on current and future years' GAAP profits and on the sources of such profits?

Impact of Reserve Methods

The relative magnitude of the various sources of earnings depends on the GAAP methodology used. That is, GAAP reserve assumptions and experience variations from them will differ for each of the traditional, retrospective, prospective, or composite GAAP methods. Also, an analysis of the sources of actual GAAP profits depends on how the net GAAP reserve is made "dynamic" with respect to actual experience, that is, how the GAAP reserve is adjusted based on the emergence of actual experience. Approaches for making UL and FPA GAAP reserves dynamic currently include the following:

1. Perhaps the most common technique for making GAAP reserves dynamic with respect to actual experience is by adjusting the reserve based on the amount of insurance in force. This is the approach used for traditional life business and is best illustrated when the expense reserve factors are

expressed as amounts per thousand in force, or when dynamic DAC amortization schedules are used. For level premium/level face amount plans (which account for most traditional life business), adjustments based on face amount are the same as adjustments based on premium. Perhaps because of the simplicity and the prevalence of the method in traditional life business, some companies also are making their UL GAAP reserves (mainly DAC) dynamic through the use of in-force amount.

However, adjustments based on the amount of insurance or premium in force make the valuation sensitive only to surrender and mortality experience. This is sufficient for fixed premium/fixed benefit products, but does not recognize the flexible premium/flexible benefits of the new, interest-sensitive products. In general, then, additional or different procedures are necessary to ensure that both the benefit and expense (DAC) reserve valuations appropriately reflect the emerging characteristics of these flexible products.

2. The most popular approach for adjusting benefit and/or expense reserves for interest-sensitive products is to relate reserves to account balances. That is, the GAAP reserve is made dynamic by adjusting the expected reserve by the ratio of actual to expected account balances. Such an approach is widely used because:
   - It is simple and easy to apply.
   - It is a disciplined approach for adjusting reserves based on actual experience (that is, no subjective judgment is involved in the adjustment).
   - It generally gives accurate results when actual policy parameters are reasonably close to expected. Even if actual policy parameters deviate from expected, this approach will still yield reserve close to the "true" reserve (that is, the reserve based on repricing/revaluation using revised assumptions) if the same profit margin is maintained when the mortality and expense charges are revised and when interest crediting rates are determined.
   - It has advantages compared to an adjustment based on premims received to date because:
     (i) Account balance data are more readily available than premium history.
     (ii) Unlike the premium history, the account balance takes into account other policy parameters that may affect profit, such as interest credits and actual mortality and expense charges.

However, making the reserves dynamic to account balances also has drawbacks:
   - It may not produce sufficiently accurate results if the mortality gain is the main or only source of profit. In such cases, it may be more appropriate to adjust the reserve (or DAC) based on the in-force amount.

- The existence of large dump-in (or nonrecurring) premiums makes the pure application of the actual to expected account balance ratio inappropriate. For this reason, most companies have introduced either one or both of the following refinements:
  - (i) Different GAAP reserve per-account-balance factors are separately used for account balances resulting from dump-in versus non-dump-in premiums.
  - (ii) Each UL plan is modeled by using several premium classes with different premium assumptions and different GAAP reserve to account balance factors. Policies grouped in the same premium class should be homogeneous and should possess the same expected premium pattern.
3. The most cumbersome method is that proposed by the recent FASB Statement on Universal Life Accounting. In this approach, the DAC reflects actual cumulative experience by regularly evaluating the original amortization schedule and revising the schedule if evidence suggests that the earlier estimate of gross profit needs revision. Although such a dynamic DAC approach has its strengths, it also has the following limitations:
   - It is tedious and cumbersome to implement.
   - Such an approach can lead to manipulation of earnings, because the determination of when the schedule should be revised is subjective.

   With regard to benefit reserves, the FASB statement has made it completely reactive to the account balance by equating it to the account balance. Although the account balance is often sufficient to provide for future benefits, it could be inadequate for some UL plans. For example:
   - (i) Some UL policies may guarantee that mortality charges will stay level or decline over the life of the policy, while the actual mortality cost should increase over time.
   - (ii) Some UL policies may offer persistency bonuses in the form of extra interest credits or lower expense and mortality charges for policies persisting beyond a given year.

In each of the above UL policies, the account balance for the early durations may not be sufficient to mature all future obligations.

UNIVERSAL LIFE SOURCE OF EARNINGS ANALYSIS
FOR RESERVE METHODS BASED ON ACCOUNT BALANCES

The remainder of this paper provides a UL SOE analysis useful when the reserve methodology adjusts GAAP reserves according to the actual to expected account balance ratio. As stated earlier, the reserve adjustment based on account balances has appeal and is perhaps the most popular dynamic approach used for UL reserve computations. The SOE analysis shown below can be applied to all premium-based UL reserve methods, including traditional, prospective, and composite GAAP methods. With some modifications, the approach also can be applied to account value-based approaches such as the retrospective method.

Assumptions

To aid in understanding the procedure and to simplify the results, the following assumptions have been made:
1. An annual case is assumed, with premiums, expenses, and policy charges occurring at the beginning of the policy year (BOY) and deaths and withdrawals occurring at the end of the policy year (EOY).
2. Expenses and policy charges are expressed in two forms only: per-inforce amount and percentage of premium. Per-policy expenses and expense charges can be easily translated to per-in-force amount or percentage of premium forms through the use of an average size assumption. Mortality charges also can be converted into a charge per in-force amount, which varies by duration.
3. Taxes and interest on surplus are ignored.

The SOE formulas shown below could be easily extended to the situation where some or all of the simplifying assumptions are not used.

Definition of Symbols

For the numerical examples in this paper, primed notation symbolizes expected values, and unprimed notation symbolizes actual values.

Where applicable, all the following values are per amount in force at time t:

t = Time t
GP = Gross premium
V = Net GAAP reserve
E^o = Non % premium expense (including commission)
$E^\%$ = % premium expense (including commission)
DB = Death benefit
CV = Cash surrender value
AB = Account balance
q^d = Mortality rate
q^w = Withdrawal rate
i^E = Interest earned rate

i^c = Interest credited rate
NP = GAAP net premium
C^o = Non % premium charge (including mortality charge)
$C\%$ = % premium charge
BP = Book profit
$\%Pf$ = % premium profit

To aid in the presentation of results, the following symbols are also used:
1. An asterisk is used to denote "adjusted" expected value, defined as the expected value (primed notation) multiplied by the ratio of actual to expected account balances at the beginning of year t (that is, at time $t - 1$). For instance,
   (*i*) "Adjusted" expected GP,

$$GP_t^* = GP_t' \, (A_{t-1})$$

where $A_{t-1} = AB_{t-1}/AB'_{t-1}$

(*ii*) "Adjusted" expected reserve V,

$$V_t^* = V_t' \, (A_{t-1})$$

Because the reserve is made dynamic by using the ratio of actual to expected account balances, the ratio at the beginning of the year will have an impact on the current year's sources of earning. For instance, if the ratio (A_{t-1}) is 95%, then it might be anticipated that the end of the year GAAP reserve also would be 95% of the originally expected reserve. That is, we would have "adjusted" the original expectation by 95%. Hence, the "adjusted" expected reserve

$$V_t^* = V_t' \, (A_{t-1}) = 95\% \; V_t'.$$

Note that if actual experience is close to expected, the ratio is approximately one, and hence

$$V_t^* = V_t.$$

That is, there is no need to "adjust" our expectation.
2. We will use G to denote the ratio of the GAAP reserve to the account balance. In other words, G is the GAAP reserve factor, expressed per dollar of account balance, not per amount in force. We see that

$$G_t = \frac{V_t'}{AB_t'} = \frac{V_t}{AB_t}.$$

Derivation of Formulas

Starting with the familiar book profit equation,

$$BP_t = GP_t$$
$$+ i_t^E [V_{t-1} + GP_t - E_t^o - E_t^\% GP_t]$$
$$- DB_t q_{t-1}^d$$
$$- AB_t q_{t-1}^w$$
$$- [V_t' A_t (1 - q_{t-1}^d - q_{t-1}^w) - V_{t-1}' A_{t-1}]$$
$$- [E_t^o + E_t^\% GP_t]$$

where $A_t = \dfrac{AB_t}{AB_t'}$ and $V_t = V_t' A_t$, we substitute three expressions,

$$V_{t-1}' = V_t' (1 - q_{t-1}^{d'} - q_{t-1}^{w'}) - V_{t-1}' i_t^{E'} - NP_t' (1 + i_t^{E'})$$
$$+ DB_t' q_{t-1}^{d'} + CV_t' q_{t-1}^{w'} + (E_t^{o'} + E_t^{\%'} GP_t') (1 + i_t^{E'})$$
$$AB_t' = AB_{t-1}' + i_t^{c'} AB_{t-1}' + GP_t' - GP_t' C_t^{\%'}$$
$$+ i_t^{c'} GP_t' - i_t^{c'} GP_t' C_t^{\%'} - C_t^{o'} - C_t^{o'} i_t^{c'}$$

and

$$AB_t = AB_{t-1} + i_t^c AB_{t-1} + GP_t - GP_t C_t^\%$$
$$+ i_t^c GP_t - i_t^c GP_t C_t^\% - C_t^o - C_t^o i_t^c$$

After simplifying and collecting related terms, we have the SOE formulas shown below. Those interested in the complete derivation should contact Joe Tan at his *Yearbook* address.

UL SOE Formulas and Interpretations

To aid in understanding the UL SOE formulas, we have classified all the terms of the formula into two groups: terms similar to the traditional life SOE analysis and terms peculiar to UL policies. The latter, as one might expect, are due to the flexible nature of the UL contracts (for example, premium, death benefit, cash value, interest credit) and the effect of the actual to expected account balance ratio on the various sources of earnings.

1. *Terms Similar to Traditional Life SOE Formula*

   Gain from loading (% of premium profit):

$$GP_t \, (\%Pf) \, (1 + i_t^{E'}) \tag{1.1}$$

   Gain from interest earning:

$$(i_t^E - i_t^{E'}) \, [V_{t-1} + GP_t - (E_t^o + E_t^{\%} \, GP_t)] \tag{1.2}$$

   Gain from mortality:

$$(q_{t-1}^{d'} - q_{t-1}^d) \, (DB_t - V_t) \tag{1.3}$$

   Gain from withdrawal:

$$(q_{t-1}^{w'} - q_{t-1}^w) \, (CV_t - V_t) \tag{1.4}$$

   Gain from non % premium expense:

$$(E_t^{o'} - E_t^o) \, (1 + i_t^{E'}) \tag{1.5}$$

   Gain from % premium expense:

$$(E_t^{\%'} - E_t^{\%}) \, GP_t \, (1 + i_t^{E'}) \tag{1.6}$$

The derivation and interpretation of these terms can easily be found in the actuarial literature (for example, Mr. Larry Warnock's Study Note on GAAP Reserves, 1972) and are not repeated here. The interest-earning item found in terms (1.1), (1.5), and (1.6) stems from the assumption of the BOY occurrence for premium and expenses.

2. *Terms Peculiar to UL*

   Gain from interest crediting:

$$(i_t^{c'} - i_t^c) \, G_t \, [AB_{t-1} + GP_t - (C_t^o + C_t^{\%} \, GP_t)] \tag{2.1}$$

For UL, the interest gain depends on the interest spread. In addition to the difference in actual and expected earned rates, term (1.2), the difference in actual and expected credited rates is a source of earnings. However, the difference in credited rates does not flow through current year's income at 100%, but only at G_t%.

Recall that:

(*i*) G is the ratio of the expected GAAP reserve to the expected account balance (*AB*), and

(*ii*) The product of G and the actual *AB* equals the actual (or reported) GAAP reserve.

When a company declares a lower credited rate than originally expected, the only impact on the current year's GAAP profit is through a lesser increase in the GAAP reserve, which results from the lesser increase in account balance. For the gain from interest *earnings*, term (1.2), the difference in the actual and expected rate results in an interest *earnings* differential based on BOY assets (which equals BOY reserve in our formulation) and cash flow occurring at BOY (that is, premium and expenses). In comparison, the difference in actual and expected *credited* rates results in an interest crediting differential based on BOY AB and the net flow of money into the AB occurring at BOY (that is, premiums less charges).

Additional mortality loss:

$$-q^{d'}_{t-1} [(DB_t - V_t) - (DB^*_t - V^*_t)] \qquad (2.2)$$

This additional mortality element results from the difference between the actual and the adjusted expected net amount at risk (that is, $DB - V$). Recall that the adjusted expected value (dsignated by an asterisk) stands for the expected value at time t "adjusted" by the actual to expected AB at BOY t. We can rewrite the above expression as the sum of two pieces, (2.2.1) and (2.2.2):

$$-q^{d'}_{t-1} (NAR'_t) (1 - A_{t-1}) \qquad (2.2.1)$$

$$-q^{d'}_{t-1} (NAR_t - NAR'_t) \qquad (2.2.2)$$

where NAR = net amount at risk = $DB - V$.

Note that (2.2.1) is negative (that is, giving rise to additional mortality loss) whenever the actual AB at BOY t is less than originally expected. Such an AB could come about, for example, when:

- The actual premiums received in the first $t - 1$ years are less than expected.
- The actual interest credited in the first $t - 1$ years is less than expected.
- The actual mortality and expense charges deducted in the first $t - 1$ years are higher than expected.

This is an example of how the actual experience of the first $t - 1$ years affects the tth year profit.

Similarly, term (2.2.1) is positive (that is, it gives rise to additional mortality gain) whenever the actual AB at BOY is higher than originally expected. And term (2.2.1) is zero whenever actual AB at BOY t is equal to expected.

Observing term (2.2.2), we see that additional mortality loss will result whenever the actual *NAR* at time t is higher than expected. Such an *NAR* occurs, for example, when:

- The actual *DB* is higher than expected due to elective or automatic death benefit increases.
- For those UL policyholders who elected the face plus account balance death benefit option, actual *DB* could be higher due to higher than expected *AB* increases.
- The actual reserve released at death for time t could be lower than expected.

Additional withdrawal loss:

$$-q^w_{t-1} \left[(CV_t - V_t) - (CV^*_t - V^*_t) \right] \qquad (2.3)$$

Similar to the net amount at risk (that is, $DB - V$), we can define the net amount at surrender (*NAS*) as $CV - V$. Following (2.2), we can rewrite (2.3) as the sum of:

$$-q^w_{t-1} (NAS'_t)(1 - A_{t-1}) \qquad (2.3.1)$$

and

$$-q^w_{t-1} (NAS_t - NAS'_t) \qquad (2.3.2)$$

The analysis shown in (2.2) could easily be extended here by substituting cash surrender value for death benefit and withdrawal rate for mortality rate.

Gain from non % premium charge:

$$G_t (C^o_t - C^{o'}_t)(1 + i^c_t) \qquad (2.4)$$

This term parallels term (1.5), gain from non % premium expense. However, unlike term (1.5), this gain results from the excess of actual charges over expected, not expected expenses over actual. This term results from the difference between actual and expected non % premium mortality and expense charges deducted from the *AB*, which affect current year's GAAP profit by increasing or reducing the GAAP reserve. As explained in (2.1), this increase or reduction in reserves is not at 100%, but at $G\%$, where G is the ratio of the expected reserve to the expected *AB*.

In other words, when the actual mortality or the expense charges deducted are higher than expected, the actual *AB* would be lower, which would reduce the actual reserve by $G\%$ of such excess of actual over expected mortality/expense charges. The BOY assumption of the charges also leads to an interest credit for a year.

While some ability to change policy expense charges may be present, in general it is unlikely that such gains or losses would develop. That is, actual and expected expense charges will normally be indentical. However, to the extent this item reflects mortality charges, there frequently will be an impact.

Gain from % premium charge:

$$G_t \, (C_t^{\%} - C_t^{\%'}) \, GP_t \, (1 + i_t^{c'}) \tag{2.5}$$

This term parallels term (1.6), gain from % premium expense. Just as in term (2.4), the excess of actual over expected charges, with interest thereon, gives rise to a $G\%$ current year's bottom-line effect.

Additional loss from non % premium expense:

$$-E_t^{o'} \, (1 - A_{t-1}) \, (1 + i_t^{E'}) \tag{2.6}$$

This additional expense loss will result whenever actual AB at BOY t is less than expected. The loss disappears whenever the account balance at BOY t matches the expected amount. Because of the BOY expense assumption, there is a one-year interest effect.

Additional gain from non % premium charge:

$$G_t \, (C_t^{o'}) \, (1 - A_{t-1}) \, (1 + i_t^{c'}) \tag{2.7}$$

Just as an additional non % premium expense loss, term (2.6), results whenever actual AB at BOY t is lower than expected, an additional non % premium charge gain, term (2.7), also results whenever actual AB is lower than expected. Because the impact of mortality and expense charges on income is indirectly through AB (which affects the reserve), such impact carries with it a year interest credit effect and only a $G\%$ (unlike expense, which is at 100%) magnitude.

In addition to terms (2.6) and (2.7) (which are non % premium), there also is an additional loss from % premium expense and an additional gain from % premium charge. However, we have included the latter two with the next term, premium persistency gain, as the gain/loss arising from actual versus expected premium persistency is partially offset by such % premium expenses/charges.

Premium persistency gain:

$$(GP_t - GP_t^*) [(1 - E_t^{\%'} - \%Pf)$$

$$(1 + i_t^{E'}) - G_t (1 - C_t^{\%'})(1 + i_t^{c'})] \quad (2.8)$$

Because of the variable premium nature of UL, a policy could stay in force for years even if the actual premiums paid are less than assumed. This discrepancy is often referred to as actual versus assumed premium persistency, whose bottom-line effect is measured by term (2.8).

Looking at the formula, we see that the base from which we are measuring the premium deviation is the adjusted expected GP. Note that

$$GP_t - GP_t^* = (GP_t - GP_t') + GP_t' (1 - A_{t-1});$$

that is, the premium discrepancy is caused by (*i*) the difference between actual and expected premiums and (*ii*) the ratio of the actual AB at BOY t to the expected AB.

The bottom-line effect of such a premium discrepancy is equal to the magnitude of the discrepancy multiplied by (A) − (B), where (A) and (B) represent the expressions within the brackets, respectively. Because of the BOY premium assumption, (A) shows that the premium discrepancy earns one year of interest. (A) also shows that the premium discrepancy is partially offset by the % premium expense and % premium profit. The effect of % premium expense is obvious. Regarding the % premium profit term, its appearance here is due to the manner we chose to write term (1.1), gain from loading. Term (1.1) says that for every dollar of premium the company collects, it will increase its bottom line by % Pf times one dollar, which is clearly not true. Because of the reserve methodology used, the % premium profit is earned only on the portion of premium up to the adjusted expected premium. Hence, we see that if we remove the % Pf item from term (2.8) and combine it with term (1.1), term (1.1) will become

$$GP_t^* (\%Pf) (1 + i_t^{E'}).$$

Nevertheless, we chose to show term (1.1) the way it is because we prefer to show term (1.1) as a familiar term of the traditional life SOE formula.

(B) shows that the amount of premium persistency discrepancy flows directly into the account balance, after reduction by the % premium charge. Then, with a year's interest credit, such premium discrepancy affects AB, which increases or reduces the reserve by $G\%$ of the AB.

Combining (A) and (B), we see that the bottom line effect of $GP - GP^*$ is:

(i) Offset by the % premium expense and the % premium profit included in term (1.1)

(ii) Increased by a year of interest earnings (because of the BOY premium and expense assumptions)

(iii) Offset by the amount of increase in reserves caused by such premium discrepancy, which comes about from the effect of such premium discrepancy on AB.

Some Questions Answered by Our SOE Formulas

The different terms of the SOE formulas given in the preceding section are organized in a manner that is easy to understand and interpret and that shows how the total profit comprises the various sources of profit. By re-arranging the various terms of the formulas, we also can answer some of the intriguing UL and FPA questions that are often asked of actuaries. Some examples follow.

1. *How is the current year's GAAP profit affected when actual BOY* AB *deviates from expected?*

From the formulas presented above, it is clear that the ratio of actual to expected BOY AB has a tremendous impact on GAAP profits. Specifically, each of the following gain or loss items emerges when A_{t-1} is not equal to 1:

- Term (2.2.1), which is part of the additional mortality loss, term (2.2).
- Term (2.3.1), which is part of the additional withdrawal loss, term (2.3).
- Term (2.6), additional loss from non % premium expense.
- Term (2.7), additional gain from non % premium charge.
- A portion of term (2.8), the premium persistency gain. This portion is equal to

$$GP'_t (1 - A_{t-1}) [(1 - E_t^{\%'} - \%Pf) (1 + i_t^{E'}) - G_t (1 - C_t^{\%'}) (1 + i_t^{c'})].$$

In addition to the above effects, there are some other less obvious gains and losses whenever actual BOY AB deviates from expected. These less obvious gains and losses are likely to be smaller than those mentioned above, and they result from those terms that are functions of BOY AB. For example:

- Term (2.1) and term (1.2) (because V depends on AB). These terms will have no effect if actual rates equal expected.
- Terms (1.3) and (2.2.2), because the amount of BOY AB can affect the EOY DB and V. If the actual mortality rate equals expected, term (1.3) will have no effect.

- Terms (1.4) and (2.3.2), due to the effect of the actual BOY *AB* on EOY *CV* and *V*. No effect will result from term (1.4) if the actual withdrawal rate equals expected.

2. *Knowing that policyholders pay lower premiums than assumed, can we estimate the bottom-line impact?*

This question is answered by term (1.1) (% premium profit) and term (2.8) (premium persistency gain). The effect on term (1.1) is obvious; for term (2.8), please refer to that section for an explanation of the effect.

Also, lower premium paid will result in lower EOY *AB*, which will affect

- Current year's terms (2.2) and (2.3), due to the EOY assumption of deaths and withdrawals, and
- Future years' earnings. An analysis similar to that for question 1 can be made to determine the earnings impact and sources.

3. *If the actual earned rate turns out to be 2% lower than expected, can we maintain the same current and future years' GAAP profits by declaring a credited rate 2% lower than the expected credited rate?*

We can answer this question by comparing terms (1.2) and (2.1). Note that term (2.1) can be rewritten as the sum of:

- Term (2.1.1) = $(i_t^{c'} - i_t^c) \left[\dfrac{G_t}{G_{t-1}} (V_{t-1}) \right]$.

and

- Term (2.1.2) = $(i_t^{c'} - i_t^c) G_t [GP_t - (C_t^o + C_t^\% GP_t)]$.

Similarly, term (1.2) can be rewritten as the sum of:

- Term (1.2.1) = $(i_t^E - i_t^{E'}) V_{t-1}$

and

- Term (1.2.2) = $(i_t^E - i_t^{E'}) [GP_t - (E_t^o + E_t^\% GP_t)]$.

Comparing terms (2.1.1) and (1.2.1), we see that the current year's interest gain or loss due to BOY reserve *V* is minimal because the two terms more or less offset each other. The only difference in the two terms is that the gain due to a 2% reduction in credited rate is grossed by the ratio of *G* at EOY to *G* at BOY. Recalling that *G* is the ratio of *V* to *AB*, we expect *G* to increase from BOY to EOY. Hence, the gain due to a 2% reduction in credited rate will more than offset the loss due to a 2% reduction in earned rate. That is, a minimal current year's gain will result from interest effect on BOY reserve V.

Comparing terms (2.1.2) and (1.2.2), we note that current year's profit will be different when both earned and credited rates are reduced 2%. This is caused by the following differences in terms (2.1.2) and (1.2.2):

- % and non % charges versus expenses. For early durations, expenses are likely to be higher than charges, primarily due to high acquisition cost. For later durations, unless substantial expense escalation occurs (for example, high inflation rate), the opposite is generally true, since mortality charge increases with duration.
- G% in term (2.1.2) versus 100% in term (1.2.2). G is smaller than 100%; hence the loss due to lower earned rate on *premium and expenses*, term (1.2.2), will more than offset the gain due to lower credited rate on *premium and charges*, term (2.1.1).

Because lower credited rate will result in lower EOY AB, terms that depend on AB also will be affected. The analysis similar to the last part of question 2 can be repeated here.

4. *Knowing that the company's actual expenses are higher than expected, how can we adjust expense charges to maintain essentially the same bottom line?*

The income effect of an expense variance (that is, actual versus expected) is represented by term (1.5) (gain from non % premium expense) and term (1.6) (gain from % premium expense). To offset this income variance, expense charges can be increased. Looking at terms (2.4) and (2.5), we note that to maintain the same bottom line, the increase in expense charge has to be larger than the increase in expense. This amount is roughly equal to the expense variance divided by G. Also, if we consider the interest effect, the above quantity has to be grossed up by the following factor (which is greater than 1):

$$(1 + i_t^{E'})/(1 + i_t^{c'}).$$

Also, any increase in current year's expense charge will decrease the EOY AB, which will affect future earnings (and their sources). The analysis used in the last part of question 2 can be repeated here.

Examples

In this section, we illustrate the above methodology with a typical UL policy issued at age 45 to a nonsmoker male. The values shown are for the first 20 policy years. The following assumptions are made:

Mortality rate (q^d): as shown in Appendix 1.A.
Withdrawal rate (q^w): 20%, 15%, 10%, 5% thereafter.
Gross premium (*GP*): $1,000 per year.
% Premium charge ($C^\%$): 5%.
Non % premium charge (C^o): $50 per year.
% Premium expense ($E^\%$): 80%, 5% thereafter.
Non % premium expense (E^o): $75, $25 thereafter.
Death benefit (*DB*): $50,000 all years.
Earned rate (i^E): 10% all years.
Credited rate (i^c): 8% all years.
Surrender charges (*SC*): Used in the computation of *CV* and expressed as a % of total premium paid since issue:

Year	SC
1	90%
2	80
3	70
4	60
5	50
6	40
7	30
8	20
9	10
10+	0

Expected net GAAP reserve (*V*): Based on traditional GAAP method with no provision for adverse deviation. This gives rise to a net GAAP premium of $965.38 per year.

We illustrate with five examples. The first example is the case in which actual experience equals expected, and the last four correspond to the four questions raised above. These five examples are shown in Appendices 1 to 5. For each example, three tables are shown:

1. The assumptions and policy values used (for example, Appendix 1.A).
2. The regular income statement (for example, Appendix 1.B).
3. The SOE statement (for example, Appendix 1.C).

Example 1: Actual Experience Equals Expected

Using the assumptions and policy values shown in Appendix 1.A and assuming that actual experience emerges as expected, Appendices 1.B and 1.C were derived. We see that the only profit is the % premium profit. That is, with the exception of term (1.1), all the terms of our SOE formula are zero. The % premium profit can be computed as:

$$\$1,000 \left(1 - \frac{965.38}{1,000}\right) (1 + .10)$$

where the middle quantity is the % profit.

Example 2: Lower Than Expected AB

In this example, we consider a lower than expected increase in AB by assuming that the interest credited rate decreased by 50 basis points in year 2 and 100 basis points in years 3 to 20. Appendix 2.A shows the resulting policy values.

Comparing Appendix 2.B with Appendix 1.B, we see that as the credited rate decreased, GAAP profit increased. As expected, the increase in profit compounds year after year, resulting in a large profit in year 20. What are the sources of such profits? Appendix 2.C provides the answer.

First, we would expect a gain due to the lower interest credited rate starting in year 2 (the first year when the credited rate is reduced). As shown in Appendix 2.C, this gain amounts to $4.92, term (2.1). Because of the decrease in EOY AB for year 2, additional gain and loss items also emerge due to terms (2.3.2) and (2.2.2), respectively. For instance, term (2.3.2) shows that the additional withdrawal loss in year 2 is

$$- q_1^{w} \left[(CV_2 - V_2) - (CV_2' - V_2')\right]$$
$$= -.15 \left[(412.40 - 1057.75) - (421.76 - 1062.67)\right] = 0.67$$

Because of our EOY assumption for deaths and withdrawals, additional mortality and withdrawal losses due to terms (2.2.2) and (2.3.2) always appear in the year when the EOY AB is changed. In reality, however, the effects of terms (2.2.2) and (2.3.2) are less, because deaths and withdrawals can occur any time during the year.

Starting in year 3, because the BOY AB is lower than expected, more sources of profit emerge. From the analysis given for question 1 above, we realize that aside from the % premium profit, other sources of profit are present in year 3:

Source	Term	Amount
Gain from interest crediting	2.1	$20.11
Additional mortality loss.	2.2	− 0.42
Additional withdrawal loss	2.3	1.73
Additional loss from non % premium expense	2.6	− 0.13
Additional gain from non % premium charge	2.7	0.17
Premium persistency gain.	2.8	1.38
Gain from interest earning	1.2	0*
Gain from mortality	1.3	0*
Gain from withdrawal.	1.4	0*

*This is zero because actual rate (e.g., mortality rate) equals expected.

Example 3: Actual Premiums Less Than Expected

This example assumes that actual premium is lower than expected starting year 2:

$950 for year 2
$900 for year 3
$850 for year 4
$800 thereafter

Appendix 3.A shows the corresponding policy values.

For the first year when actual premium differs from expected (for example, year 2), the sources of profit affected are:

1. % of premium profit term (1.1). This is decreased by the amount of premium reduction multiplied by the % profit, compounded with a year's interest earnings. That is,

$$\$50 \ (3.46\%) \ (1 + .1) = \$1.90.$$

2. Premium persistency gain, term (2.8). This amounts to

$$(\$950 - 1 * \$1,000) \left[(1 - .05 - .0346) \ (1 + .1) \right.$$
$$\left. - \frac{1062.67}{2021.76} \ (1 - .05) \ (1 + .08) \right] = - \$23.38.$$

3. Terms that depend on EOY AB for year 2 [$ − 0.04 for term (2.2.2) and $ − 2.35 for term (2.3.2)]. The analysis here is the same as for example 2 above.

For years 3 and beyond, because the BOY AB is lower than expected, other sources of profit also emerge. Analysis similar to example 2 can be made. Again, if actual rates (for example, mortality rate) equal expected, some terms will have no effect. Hence, terms (1.2), (1.3), (1.4), and (2.1) turned out to be zero.

Example 4: 2% Reduction in Both Earned and Credited Rates

Appendix 4.A shows the resulting policy values when we reduce both earned and credited rates by 2% starting year 3. The analysis for this example is as shown in question 3.

For year 3, we have

BOY $G = 0.5256$.
EOY $G = 0.6906$.
$E\% = C\% = 5\%$.
$E^o = \$25$.
$C^o = \$50$.

Hence:

$$\text{Term (2.1.1)} = 2\% * \left[\frac{0.6906}{0.5256}\right] * 1062.67 = 27.93.$$

$$\text{Term (2.1.2)} = 2\% * 0.6906 * [1{,}000 - (50 + .05 * 1{,}000)] = 12.43.$$

$$\text{Term (1.2.1)} = -2\% * 1062.67 = -21.25.$$

$$\text{Term (1.2.2)} = -2\% * [1{,}000 - (25 + .05 * 1{,}000] = -18.50.$$

Regarding the interest spread on BOY reserve V, term (1.2.1) versus term (2.1.1), we see that because the ratio of G's is 1.314, a gain amounting to $6.68 arises. Regarding the effect of the interest spread on premium, expenses, and charges, term (1.2.2) versus term (2.1.2), we see that there is a loss of $6.07. This is due to the G value of 0.6906 (less than 1) and to the non % premium expense being lower than the non % premium charge. The net gain of $0.61 ($6.68 − $6.07) equals the sum of terms (1.2) and (2.1) of Appendix 4.C.

Because the credited rate affects EOY AB, terms (2.2.2) and (2.3.2) also are affected in year 3. They amount to $−0.07 and $1.81. The analysis here is the same as for example 2. It should be emphasized that in reality, the effects of terms (2.2.2) and (2.3.2) are less, because deaths and withdrawals can occur any time during the year.

For years 4 and beyond, because BOY AB's are changed, terms that depend on BOY AB also contribute additional gains or losses. Analysis similar to example 2 can be applied here.

Example 5: Increasing the Expense Charge Due to the Increase in Actual Expenses

In this example, we assume that the non % premium expense increases by $10 starting in year 5. To overcome this expense problem, the insurance company decides to increase the mortality charge (which is treated as a type of non % premium charge in our formulation). The question is, how much should the increase be?

According to question 4 above, if we wish to completely offset the loss due to the increased expense by the gain due to the increased charge in year 5, the charge has to be increased by

$$\frac{E_t^o - E_t^{o'}}{G_t} * \frac{(1 + i_t^{E'})}{(1 + i_t^{c'})}$$

Appendix 5.A shows the resulting policy values when such a change is introduced.

Appendix 5.B shows that, contrary to our expectation, the resulting fifth year GAAP profit is higher than the original expected profit of $38.09. Why? Turning to Appendix 5.C, we find the answer. Even though term (2.4) offsets term (1.5) dollar for dollar, additional gains and losses emerge due to terms (2.2.2) and (2.3.2). These gains and losses emerge because the fifth year EOY AB decreased due to increased mortality charges. This phenomenon should have been expected, because it occurs in all previous examples. In reality, however, the magnitude of terms (2.2.2) and (2.3.2) in year 5 will likely be reduced by half. This is because in reality, mortality charges are levied monthly, and on the average, deaths and withdrawals occur at the middle of the year. (Note that the midyear assumption is more realistic than our simplified EOY assumption.)

For years 6 and beyond, because BOY AB's are changed, more terms are affected and analysis similar to that for example 2 should be used.

Consider another question. Knowing that terms (2.2.2) and (2.3.2) also contribute additional gains and losses in the fifth year, how much should the mortality charges be increased to yield the original \$38.09 expected profit?

It can be shown algebraically that under our EOY assumption, the increase in mortality charge is equal to the above formula, but with G_t replaced by

$$G_t + q^{w'}_{t-1} (1 - G_t) - q^{d'}_{t-1} G_t.$$

If such an increase in mortality charges is implemented instead, the resulting policy values and income statement will be as shown in Appendix 5.D and 5.E, respectively. As Appendix 5.F shows (the resulting SOE statement), the sum of terms (2.2), (2.3) and (2.4) exactly offsets the loss due to term (1.5) in year 5.

CONCLUSION

In this paper we have stressed the importance of SOE analysis. We also have presented the difficulties involved in performing such an analysis on UL and other interest-sensitive products. The primary difficulty lies in the variability of the account balance and its effects on policy values and reserves.

The main contribution of this paper is in the extension of the traditional source of earnings analysis to Universal Life and other interest-sensitive products. The sources of earnings (and their magnitudes) depend on the reserve methodology and the manner in which the reserve is made dynamic with respect to actual experience. The procedure illustrated in the paper is for a reserve methodology that is premium-based (that is, full percent of premium, traditional GAAP, composite, and prospective deposit), and made dynamic with the use of the account balance. We believe that the procedure can be generalized to apply to account value-based reserve methods and other reserve methodologies. The difficulty of the generalization will depend on the methodology used. Nonetheless, the illustrated procedure will be useful because it promotes an understanding of how the different parameters and policy values of an interest-sensitive product are interrelated and how they contribute to income. Also, the results of a premium-based method can approximate the results of an account value-based method. (This is because the two methods are inherently interrelated. For example, by choosing the assumptions appropriately, we can easily derive the profit pattern of the retrospective deposit method by using the composite method.) Thus, this analysis technique should prove to be an important step toward understanding how profits emerge from UL and other interest-sensitive products.

ACKNOWLEDGMENT

We thank Mr. Anthony J. Tokarz, ASA, who helped prepared the illustrative examples.

APPENDIX 1.A

ACTUAL EXPERIENCE ASSUMPTIONS

t	C°	C%	E°	E%	GP	i^c	i^e	q^d	q^w	DB	AB	CV	A	V	NP
1	50.00	.0500000	75.00	.8000000	1,000	.0800000	.1000000	.0009533	.2000000	50,000	972.00	72.00	1.00000	46.74	965.38
2	50.00	.0500000	25.00	.0500000	1,000	.0800000	.1000000	.0013138	.1500000	50,000	2,021.76	421.76	1.00000	1,062.67	965.38
3	50.00	.0500000	25.00	.0500000	1,000	.0800000	.1000000	.0017038	.1000000	50,000	3,155.50	1,055.50	1.00000	2,179.25	965.38
4	50.00	.0500000	25.00	.0500000	1,000	.0800000	.1000000	.0020238	.0500000	50,000	4,379.94	1,979.94	1.00000	3,350.72	965.38
5	50.00	.0500000	25.00	.0500000	1,000	.0800000	.1000000	.0023441	.0500000	50,000	5,702.34	3,202.34	1.00000	4,630.24	965.38
6	50.00	.0500000	25.00	.0500000	1,000	.0800000	.1000000	.0027494	.0500000	50,000	7,130.52	4,730.52	1.00000	6,016.03	965.38
7	50.00	.0500000	25.00	.0500000	1,000	.0800000	.1000000	.0031915	.0500000	50,000	8,672.96	6,572.96	1.00000	7,508.19	965.38
8	50.00	.0500000	25.00	.0500000	1,000	.0800000	.1000000	.0035453	.0500000	50,000	10,338.80	8,738.80	1.00000	9,112.14	965.38
9	50.00	.0500000	25.00	.0500000	1,000	.0800000	.1000000	.0038401	.0500000	50,000	12,137.91	11,237.91	1.00000	10,832.06	965.38
10	50.00	.0500000	25.00	.0500000	1,000	.0800000	.1000000	.0042098	.0500000	50,000	14,080.94	14,080.94	1.00000	12,666.81	965.38
11	50.00	.0500000	25.00	.0500000	1,000	.0800000	.1000000	.0047339	.0500000	50,000	16,179.41	16,179.41	1.00000	14,670.19	965.38
12	50.00	.0500000	25.00	.0500000	1,000	.0800000	.1000000	.0053938	.0500000	50,000	18,445.77	18,445.77	1.00000	16,858.50	965.38
13	50.00	.0500000	25.00	.0500000	1,000	.0800000	.1000000	.0062972	.0500000	50,000	20,893.43	20,893.43	1.00000	19,247.83	965.38
14	50.00	.0500000	25.00	.0500000	1,000	.0800000	.1000000	.0072644	.0500000	50,000	23,536.90	23,536.90	1.00000	21,863.99	965.38
15	50.00	.0500000	25.00	.0500000	1,000	.0800000	.1000000	.0082652	.0500000	50,000	26,391.85	26,391.85	1.00000	24,738.33	965.38
16	50.00	.0500000	25.00	.0500000	1,000	.0800000	.1000000	.0099000	.0500000	50,000	29,475.20	29,475.20	1.00000	27,893.65	965.38
17	50.00	.0500000	25.00	.0500000	1,000	.0800000	.1000000	.0108060	.0500000	50,000	32,805.22	32,805.22	1.00000	31,390.60	965.38
18	50.00	.0500000	25.00	.0500000	1,000	.0800000	.1000000	.0118140	.0500000	50,000	36,401.64	36,401.64	1.00000	35,279.04	965.38
19	50.00	.0500000	25.00	.0500000	1,000	.0800000	.1000000	.0129780	.0500000	50,000	40,285.77	40,285.77	1.00000	39,618.24	965.38
20	50.00	.0500000	25.00	.0500000	1,000	.0800000	.1000000	.0142860	.0500000	50,000	44,480.63	44,480.63	1.00000	44,480.63	965.38

APPENDIX 1.B

INCOME STATEMENT

Year	Premium	Inv Inc	Exps	Dth Ben	Sur Ben	Chg-Res	Total Income
1	1,000.00	12.50	875.00	47.67	14.40	37.35	38.09
2	1,000.00	97.17	75.00	65.69	63.26	855.14	38.09
3	1,000.00	198.77	75.00	85.19	105.55	894.94	38.09
4	1,000.00	310.42	75.00	101.19	99.00	997.15	38.09
5	1,000.00	427.57	75.00	117.21	160.12	1,037.16	38.09
6	1,000.00	555.52	75.00	137.47	236.53	1,068.44	38.09
7	1,000.00	694.10	75.00	159.57	328.65	1,092.79	38.09
8	1,000.00	843.32	75.00	177.26	436.94	1,116.03	38.09
9	1,000.00	1,003.71	75.00	192.01	561.90	1,136.73	38.09
10	1,000.00	1,175.71	75.00	210.49	704.05	1,148.08	38.09
11	1,000.00	1,359.18	75.00	236.70	808.97	1,200.43	38.09
12	1,000.00	1,559.52	75.00	269.69	922.29	1,254.45	38.09
13	1,000.00	1,778.35	75.00	314.86	1,044.67	1,305.73	38.09
14	1,000.00	2,017.28	75.00	363.22	1,176.85	1,364.13	38.09
15	1,000.00	2,278.90	75.00	413.26	1,319.59	1,432.96	38.09
16	1,000.00	2,566.33	75.00	495.00	1,473.76	1,484.49	38.09
17	1,000.00	2,881.87	75.00	540.30	1,640.26	1,588.22	38.09
18	1,000.00	3,231.56	75.00	590.70	1,820.08	1,707.69	38.09
19	1,000.00	3,620.40	75.00	648.90	2,014.29	1,844.13	38.09
20	1,000.00	4,054.32	75.00	714.30	2,224.03	2,002.91	38.09

APPENDIX 1.C

SOE Income

Year	Gain 1.1	Gain 1.2	Gain 1.3	Gain 1.4	Gain 1.5	Gain 1.6	Gain 2.1	Gain 2.2	Gain 2.3	Gain 2.4	Gain 2.5	Gain 2.6	Gain 2.7	Gain 2.8	Total Income
1	38.09	.00	.00	.00	.00	.00	.00	.00	.00	.00	.00	.00	.00	.00	38.09
2	38.09	.00	.00	.00	.00	.00	.00	.00	.00	.00	.00	.00	.00	.00	38.09
3	38.09	.00	.00	.00	.00	.00	.00	.00	.00	.00	.00	.00	.00	.00	38.09
4	38.09	.00	.00	.00	.00	.00	.00	.00	.00	.00	.00	.00	.00	.00	38.09
5	38.09	.00	.00	.00	.00	.00	.00	.00	.00	.00	.00	.00	.00	.00	38.09
6	38.09	.00	.00	.00	.00	.00	.00	.00	.00	.00	.00	.00	.00	.00	38.09
7	38.09	.00	.00	.00	.00	.00	.00	.00	.00	.00	.00	.00	.00	.00	38.09
8	38.09	.00	.00	.00	.00	.00	.00	.00	.00	.00	.00	.00	.00	.00	38.09
9	38.09	.00	.00	.00	.00	.00	.00	.00	.00	.00	.00	.00	.00	.00	38.09
10	38.09	.00	.00	.00	.00	.00	.00	.00	.00	.00	.00	.00	.00	.00	38.09
11	38.09	.00	.00	.00	.00	.00	.00	.00	.00	.00	.00	.00	.00	.00	38.09
12	38.09	.00	.00	.00	.00	.00	.00	.00	.00	.00	.00	.00	.00	.00	38.09
13	38.09	.00	.00	.00	.00	.00	.00	.00	.00	.00	.00	.00	.00	.00	38.09
14	38.09	.00	.00	.00	.00	.00	.00	.00	.00	.00	.00	.00	.00	.00	38.09
15	38.09	.00	.00	.00	.00	.00	.00	.00	.00	.00	.00	.00	.00	.00	38.09
16	38.09	.00	.00	.00	.00	.00	.00	.00	.00	.00	.00	.00	.00	.00	38.09
17	38.09	.00	.00	.00	.00	.00	.00	.00	.00	.00	.00	.00	.00	.00	38.09
18	38.09	.00	.00	.00	.00	.00	.00	.00	.00	.00	.00	.00	.00	.00	38.09
19	38.09	.00	.00	.00	.00	.00	.00	.00	.00	.00	.00	.00	.00	.00	38.09
20	38.09	.00	.00	.00	.00	.00	.00	.00	.00	.00	.00	.00	.00	.00	38.09

Gain 1.1 = gain from loading (% of premium profit)
Gain 1.2 = gain from earned interest
Gain 1.3 = gain from mortality
Gain 1.4 = gain from withdrawal
Gain 1.5 = gain from non % premium expenses
Gain 1.6 = gain from % premium expenses
Gain 2.1 = gain from credited interest

Gain 2.2 = additional mortality loss
Gain 2.3 = additional withdrawal loss
Gain 2.4 = gain from non % premium charge
Gain 2.5 = gain from % premium charge
Gain 2.6 = additional loss from non % premium expense
Gain 2.7 = additional gain from non % of premium charge
Gain 2.8 = premium persistency gain

APPENDIX 2.A

ACTUAL EXPERIENCE ASSUMPTIONS

t	C^o	$C\%$	E^o	$E\%$	GP	i^c	i^e	q^d	q^w	DB	AB	CV	A	V	NP
1	50.00	.0500000	75.00	.8000000	1,000	.0800000	.1000000	.0009533	.2000000	50,000	972.00	72.00	1.00000	46.74	965.38
2	50.00	.0500000	25.00	.0500000	1,000	.0750000	.1000000	.0013138	.1500000	50,000	2,012.40	412.40	.99537	1,057.75	965.38
3	50.00	.0500000	25.00	.0500000	1,000	.0700000	.1000000	.0017038	.1000000	50,000	3,116.27	1,016.27	.98757	2,152.15	965.38
4	50.00	.0500000	25.00	.0500000	1,000	.0700000	.1000000	.0020238	.0500000	50,000	4,297.41	1,897.41	.98116	3,287.58	965.38
5	50.00	.0500000	25.00	.0500000	1,000	.0700000	.1000000	.0023441	.0500000	50,000	5,561.23	3,061.23	.97525	4,515.66	965.38
6	50.00	.0500000	25.00	.0500000	1,000	.0700000	.1000000	.0027494	.0500000	50,000	6,913.51	4,513.51	.96957	5,832.93	965.38
7	50.00	.0500000	25.00	.0500000	1,000	.0700000	.1000000	.0031915	.0500000	50,000	8,360.46	6,260.46	.96397	7,237.66	965.38
8	50.00	.0500000	25.00	.0500000	1,000	.0700000	.1000000	.0035453	.0500000	50,000	9,908.69	8,308.69	.95840	8,733.05	965.38
9	50.00	.0500000	25.00	.0500000	1,000	.0700000	.1000000	.0038401	.0500000	50,000	11,565.30	10,665.30	.95282	10,321.05	965.38
10	50.00	.0500000	25.00	.0500000	1,000	.0700000	.1000000	.0042098	.0500000	50,000	13,337.87	13,337.87	.94723	11,998.36	965.38
11	50.00	.0500000	25.00	.0500000	1,000	.0700000	.1000000	.0047339	.0500000	50,000	15,234.52	15,234.52	.94160	13,813.43	965.38
12	50.00	.0500000	25.00	.0500000	1,000	.0700000	.1000000	.0053938	.0500000	50,000	17,263.93	17,263.93	.93593	15,778.36	965.38
13	50.00	.0500000	25.00	.0500000	1,000	.0700000	.1000000	.0062972	.0500000	50,000	19,435.41	19,435.41	.93022	17,904.65	965.38
14	50.00	.0500000	25.00	.0500000	1,000	.0700000	.1000000	.0072644	.0500000	50,000	21,758.89	21,758.89	.92446	20,212.35	965.38
15	50.00	.0500000	25.00	.0500000	1,000	.0700000	.1000000	.0082652	.0500000	50,000	24,245.01	24,245.01	.91866	22,726.00	965.38
16	50.00	.0500000	25.00	.0500000	1,000	.0700000	.1000000	.0099000	.0500000	50,000	26,905.16	26,905.16	.91281	25,461.51	965.38
17	50.00	.0500000	25.00	.0500000	1,000	.0700000	.1000000	.0108060	.0500000	50,000	29,751.52	29,751.52	.90691	28,468.59	965.38
18	50.00	.0500000	25.00	.0500000	1,000	.0700000	.1000000	.0118140	.0500000	50,000	32,797.13	32,797.13	.90098	31,785.69	965.38
19	50.00	.0500000	25.00	.0500000	1,000	.0700000	.1000000	.0129780	.0500000	50,000	36,055.93	36,055.93	.89500	35,458.49	965.38
20	50.00	.0500000	25.00	.0500000	1,000	.0700000	.1000000	.0142860	.0500000	50,000	39,542.84	39,542.84	.88899	39,542.84	965.38

APPENDIX 2.B

INCOME STATEMENT

Year	Premium	Inv Inc	Exps	Dth Ben	Sur Ben	Chg-Res	Total Income
1	1,000	12.50	875.00	47.67	14.40	37.35	38.09
2	1,000	97.17	75.00	65.69	61.86	850.96	43.67
3	1,000	198.28	75.00	85.19	101.63	875.52	60.94
4	1,000	307.72	75.00	101.19	94.87	964.39	72.26
5	1,000	421.26	75.00	117.21	153.06	991.72	84.27
6	1,000	544.07	75.00	137.47	225.68	1,009.59	96.33
7	1,000	675.79	75.00	159.57	313.02	1,019.74	108.46
8	1,000	816.27	75.00	177.26	415.43	1,027.78	120.78
9	1,000	965.81	75.00	192.01	533.26	1,032.31	133.22
10	1,000	1,124.61	75.00	210.49	666.89	1,026.88	145.34
11	1,000	1,292.34	75.00	236.70	761.73	1,059.01	159.90
12	1,000	1,473.84	75.00	269.69	863.20	1,090.91	175.05
13	1,000	1,670.34	75.00	314.86	971.77	1,118.30	190.40
14	1,000	1,882.96	75.00	363.22	1,087.94	1,150.25	206.55
15	1,000	2,113.74	75.00	413.26	1,212.25	1,189.51	223.71
16	1,000	2,365.10	75.00	495.00	1,345.26	1,210.37	239.47
17	1,000	2,638.65	75.00	540.30	1,487.58	1,276.02	259.76
18	1,000	2,939.36	75.00	590.70	1,639.86	1,352.30	281.50
19	1,000	3,271.07	75.00	648.90	1,802.80	1,439.70	304.68
20	1,000	3,638.35	75.00	714.30	1,977.14	1,542.30	329.60

APPENDIX 2.C

SOE INCOME

Year	Gain 1.1	Gain 1.2	Gain 1.3	Gain 1.4	Gain 1.5	Gain 1.6	Gain 2.1	Gain 2.2	Gain 2.3	Gain 2.4	Gain 2.5	Gain 2.6	Gain 2.7	Gain 2.8	Total Income
1	38.09	.00	.00	.00	.00	.00	.00	.00	.00	.00	.00	.00	.00	.00	38.09
2	38.09	.00	.00	.00	.00	.00	4.92	−0.01	0.67	.00	.00	.00	.00	.00	43.67
3	38.09	.00	.00	.00	.00	.00	20.11	−0.42	1.73	.00	.00	−0.13	0.17	1.38	60.94
4	38.09	.00	.00	.00	.00	.00	30.73	−1.30	1.82	.00	.00	−0.34	0.51	2.76	72.26
5	38.09	.00	.00	.00	.00	.00	42.20	−2.27	2.67	.00	.00	−0.52	0.83	3.28	84.27
6	38.09	.00	.00	.00	.00	.00	54.51	−3.50	3.29	.00	.00	−0.68	1.13	3.50	96.33
7	38.09	.00	.00	.00	.00	.00	67.64	−4.99	3.52	.00	.00	−0.84	1.42	3.61	108.46
8	38.09	.00	.00	.00	.00	.00	81.62	−6.57	3.22	.00	.00	−0.99	1.71	3.70	120.78
9	38.09	.00	.00	.00	.00	.00	96.46	−8.22	2.24	.00	.00	−1.14	2.00	3.80	133.22
10	38.09	.00	.00	.00	.00	.00	112.13	−10.23	0.40	.00	.00	−1.30	2.29	3.96	145.34
11	38.09	.00	.00	.00	.00	.00	129.10	−12.88	0.42	.00	.00	−1.45	2.58	4.04	159.90
12	38.09	.00	.00	.00	.00	.00	147.46	−16.27	0.45	.00	.00	−1.61	2.88	4.04	175.05
13	38.09	.00	.00	.00	.00	.00	167.33	−20.87	0.47	.00	.00	−1.76	3.19	3.95	190.40
14	38.09	.00	.00	.00	.00	.00	188.90	−26.26	0.48	.00	.00	−1.92	3.50	3.76	206.55
15	38.09	.00	.00	.00	.00	.00	212.39	−32.40	0.48	.00	.00	−2.08	3.82	3.41	223.71
16	38.09	.00	.00	.00	.00	.00	237.96	−41.88	0.46	.00	.00	−2.24	4.16	2.93	239.47
17	38.09	.00	.00	.00	.00	.00	266.06	−49.11	0.42	.00	.00	−2.40	4.51	2.19	259.76
18	38.09	.00	.00	.00	.00	.00	297.06	−57.46	0.33	.00	.00	−2.56	4.87	1.17	281.50
19	38.09	.00	.00	.00	.00	.00	331.39	−67.33	0.20	.00	.00	−2.72	5.25	−0.21	304.68
20	38.09	.00	.00	.00	.00	.00	369.56	−78.82	0.00	.00	.00	−2.89	5.67	−2.00	329.60

Gain 1.1 = gain from loading (% of premium profit)
Gain 1.2 = gain from earned interest
Gain 1.3 = gain from mortality
Gain 1.4 = gain from withdrawal
Gain 1.5 = gain from non % premium expenses
Gain 1.6 = gain from % premium expenses
Gain 2.1 = gain from credited interest

Gain 2.2 = additional mortality loss
Gain 2.3 = additional withdrawal loss
Gain 2.4 = gain from non % premium charge
Gain 2.5 = gain from % premium charge
Gain 2.6 = additional loss from non % premium expense
Gain 2.7 = additional gain from non % of premium charge
Gain 2.8 = premium persistency gain

APPENDIX 3.A

ACTUAL EXPERIENCE ASSUMPTIONS

t	C^c	$C\%$	E^o	$E\%$	GP	i^c	i^e	q^d	q^w	DB	AB	CV	A	V	NP
1	50.00	.0500000	75.00	.8000000	1,000	.0800000	.1000000	.0009533	.2000000	50,000	972.00	72.00	1.00000	46.74	965.38
2	50.00	.0500000	25.00	.0500000	950	.0800000	.1000000	.0013138	.1500000	50,000	1,970.46	410.46	.97463	1,035.71	965.38
3	50.00	.0500000	25.00	.0500000	900	.0800000	.1000000	.0017038	.0500000	50,000	2,997.50	1,002.50	.94993	2,070.13	965.38
4	50.00	.0500000	25.00	.0500000	850	.0800000	.1000000	.0020238	.0500000	50,000	4,055.40	1,835.40	.92590	3,102.44	965.38
5	50.00	.0500000	25.00	.0500000	800	.0800000	.1000000	.0023441	.0500000	50,000	5,146.63	2,896.63	.90255	4,179.01	965.38
6	50.00	.0500000	25.00	.0500000	800	.0800000	.1000000	.0027494	.0500000	50,000	6,325.16	4,205.16	.88705	5,336.54	965.38
7	50.00	.0500000	25.00	.0500000	800	.0800000	.1000000	.0031915	.0500000	50,000	7,597.97	5,767.97	.87605	6,577.57	965.38
8	50.00	.0500000	25.00	.0500000	800	.0800000	.1000000	.0035453	.0500000	50,000	8,972.61	7,592.61	.86786	7,908.04	965.38
9	50.00	.0500000	25.00	.0500000	800	.0800000	.1000000	.0038401	.0500000	50,000	10,457.22	9,687.22	.86153	9,332.19	965.38
10	50.00	.0500000	25.00	.0500000	800	.0800000	.1000000	.0042098	.0500000	50,000	12,060.60	12,060.60	.85652	10,849.36	965.38
11	50.00	.0500000	25.00	.0500000	800	.0800000	.1000000	.0047339	.0500000	50,000	13,792.24	13,792.24	.85246	12,505.70	965.38
12	50.00	.0500000	25.00	.0500000	800	.0800000	.1000000	.0053938	.0500000	50,000	15,662.42	15,662.42	.84911	14,314.66	965.38
13	50.00	.0500000	25.00	.0500000	800	.0800000	.1000000	.0062972	.0500000	50,000	17,682.22	17,682.22	.84631	16,289.54	965.38
14	50.00	.0500000	25.00	.0500000	800	.0800000	.1000000	.0072644	.0500000	50,000	19,863.59	19,863.59	.84393	18,451.77	965.38
15	50.00	.0500000	25.00	.0500000	800	.0800000	.1000000	.0082652	.0500000	50,000	22,219.48	22,219.48	.84191	20,827.37	965.38
16	50.00	.0500000	25.00	.0500000	800	.0800000	.1000000	.0099000	.0500000	50,000	24,763.84	24,763.84	.84016	23,435.08	965.38
17	50.00	.0500000	25.00	.0500000	800	.0800000	.1000000	.0108060	.0500000	50,000	27,511.75	27,511.75	.83864	26,325.39	965.38
18	50.00	.0500000	25.00	.0500000	800	.0800000	.1000000	.0118140	.0500000	50,000	30,479.49	30,479.49	.83731	29,539.52	965.38
19	50.00	.0500000	25.00	.0500000	800	.0800000	.1000000	.0129780	.0500000	50,000	33,684.64	33,684.64	.83614	33,126.50	965.38
20	50.00	.0500000	25.00	.0500000	800	.0800000	.1000000	.0142860	.0500000	50,000	37,146.22	37,146.22	.83511	37,146.22	965.38

APPENDIX 3.B

INCOME STATEMENT

Year	Premium	Inv Inc	Exps	Dth Ben	Sur Ben	Chg-Res	Total Income
1	1,000.00	12.50	875.00	47.67	14.40	37.35	38.09
2	950.00	92.42	72.50	65.69	61.57	832.25	10.42
3	900.00	186.57	70.00	85.19	100.25	823.88	7.25
4	850.00	285.26	67.50	101.19	91.77	870.91	3.90
5	800.00	383.74	65.00	117.21	144.83	857.83	−1.13
6	800.00	491.40	65.00	137.47	210.26	876.03	2.65
7	800.00	607.15	65.00	159.57	288.40	891.16	3.02
8	800.00	731.26	65.00	177.26	379.63	907.03	2.34
9	800.00	864.30	65.00	192.01	484.36	921.70	1.23
10	800.00	1,006.72	65.00	210.49	603.03	929.03	−0.84
11	800.00	1,158.44	65.00	236.70	689.61	971.85	−4.72
12	800.00	1,324.07	65.00	269.69	783.12	1,016.02	−9.77
13	800.00	1,504.97	65.00	314.86	884.11	1,057.82	−16.82
14	800.00	1,702.45	65.00	363.22	993.18	1,105.60	−24.54
15	800.00	1,918.68	65.00	413.26	1,110.97	1,162.09	−32.65
16	800.00	2,156.24	65.00	495.00	1,238.19	1,203.95	−45.91
17	800.00	2,417.01	65.00	540.30	1,375.59	1,289.57	−53.45
18	800.00	2,706.04	65.00	590.70	1,523.97	1,388.17	−61.80
19	800.00	3,027.45	65.00	648.90	1,684.23	1,500.74	−71.42
20	800.00	3,386.15	65.00	714.30	1,857.31	1,631.74	−82.20

APPENDIX 3.C

SOE Income

Year	Gain 1.1	Gain 1.2	Gain 1.3	Gain 1.4	Gain 1.5	Gain 1.6	Gain 2.1	Gain 2.2	Gain 2.3	Gain 2.4	Gain 2.5	Gain 2.6	Gain 2.7	Gain 2.8	Total Income
1	38.09	.00	.00	.00	.00	.00	.00	.00	.00	.00	.00	.00	.00	.00	38.09
2	36.18	.00	.00	.00	.00	.00	.00	−0.04	−2.35	.00	.00	.00	.00	−23.38	10.42
3	34.28	.00	.00	.00	.00	.00	.00	−2.25	−2.76	.00	.00	−0.70	0.95	−22.26	7.25
4	32.37	.00	.00	.00	.00	.00	.00	−5.23	−1.75	.00	.00	−1.38	2.07	−22.18	3.90
5	30.47	.00	.00	.00	.00	.00	.00	−8.94	−1.99	.00	.00	−2.04	3.25	−21.88	−1.13
6	30.47	.00	.00	.00	.00	.00	.00	−13.65	−1.44	.00	.00	−2.68	4.44	−14.49	2.65
7	30.47	.00	.00	.00	.00	.00	.00	−18.29	−1.00	.00	.00	−3.11	5.28	−10.33	3.02
8	30.47	.00	.00	.00	.00	.00	.00	−22.24	−0.58	.00	.00	−3.41	5.90	−7.81	2.34
9	30.47	.00	.00	.00	.00	.00	.00	−25.64	−0.14	.00	.00	−3.63	6.37	−6.20	1.23
10	30.47	.00	.00	.00	.00	.00	.00	−29.41	0.35	.00	.00	−3.81	6.73	−5.17	−0.84
11	30.47	.00	.00	.00	.00	.00	.00	−34.24	0.31	.00	.00	−3.95	7.03	−4.33	−4.72
12	30.47	.00	.00	.00	.00	.00	.00	−40.10	0.27	.00	.00	−4.06	7.28	−3.63	−9.77
13	30.47	.00	.00	.00	.00	.00	.00	−47.85	0.23	.00	.00	−4.15	7.51	−3.03	−16.82
14	30.47	.00	.00	.00	.00	.00	.00	−56.20	0.20	.00	.00	−4.23	7.71	−2.49	−24.54
15	30.47	.00	.00	.00	.00	.00	.00	−64.91	0.17	.00	.00	−4.29	7.90	−1.99	−32.65
16	30.47	.00	.00	.00	.00	.00	.00	−78.74	0.14	.00	.00	−4.35	8.08	−1.51	−45.91
17	30.47	.00	.00	.00	.00	.00	.00	−86.88	0.11	.00	.00	−4.40	8.26	−1.01	−53.45
18	30.47	.00	.00	.00	.00	.00	.00	−95.87	0.07	.00	.00	−4.44	8.44	−0.49	−61.80
19	30.47	.00	.00	.00	.00	.00	.00	−106.17	0.04	.00	.00	−4.47	8.64	0.08	−71.42
20	30.47	.00	.00	.00	.00	.00	.00	−117.70	0.00	.00	.00	−4.51	8.85	0.69	−82.20

Gain 1.1 = gain from loading (% of premium profit)
Gain 1.2 = gain from earned interest
Gain 1.3 = gain from mortality
Gain 1.4 = gain from withdrawal
Gain 1.5 = gain from non % premium expenses
Gain 1.6 = gain from premium expenses
Gain 2.1 = gain from credited interest

Gain 2.2 = additional mortality loss
Gain 2.3 = additional withdrawal loss
Gain 2.4 = gain from non % premium charge
Gain 2.5 = gain from % premium charge
Gain 2.6 = additional loss from non % premium expense
Gain 2.7 = additional gain from non % of premium charge
Gain 2.8 = premium persistency gain

APPENDIX 4.A

ACTUAL EXPERIENCE ASSUMPTIONS

t	C	C%	E°	E%	GP	i^c	i^e	q^d	q^w	DB	AB	CV	A	V	NP
1	50.00	.0500000	75.00	.8000000	1,000	.0800000	.1000000	.0009533	.2000000	50,000	972.00	72.00	1.00000	46.74	965.38
2	50.00	.0500000	25.00	.0500000	1,000	.0800000	.1000000	.0013138	.1500000	50,000	2,021.76	421.76	1.00000	1,062.67	965.38
3	50.00	.0500000	25.00	.0500000	1,000	.0600000	.0800000	.0017038	.1000000	50,000	3,097.07	997.07	.98148	2,138.89	965.38
4	50.00	.0500000	25.00	.0500000	1,000	.0600000	.0800000	.0020238	.0500000	50,000	4,236.89	1,836.89	.96734	3,241.28	965.38
5	50.00	.0500000	25.00	.0500000	1,000	.0600000	.0800000	.0023441	.0500000	50,000	5,445.10	2,945.10	.95489	4,421.37	965.38
6	50.00	.0500000	25.00	.0500000	1,000	.0600000	.0800000	.0027494	.0500000	50,000	6,725.81	4,325.81	.94324	5,674.57	965.38
7	50.00	.0500000	25.00	.0500000	1,000	.0600000	.0800000	.0031915	.0500000	50,000	8,083.36	5,983.36	.93202	6,997.77	965.38
8	50.00	.0500000	25.00	.0500000	1,000	.0600000	.0800000	.0035453	.0500000	50,000	9,522.36	7,922.36	.92103	8,392.56	965.38
9	50.00	.0500000	25.00	.0500000	1,000	.0600000	.0800000	.0038401	.0500000	50,000	11,047.70	10,147.70	.91018	9,859.14	965.38
10	50.00	.0500000	25.00	.0500000	1,000	.0600000	.0800000	.0042098	.0500000	50,000	12,664.56	12,664.56	.89941	11,392.68	965.38
11	50.00	.0500000	25.00	.0500000	1,000	.0600000	.0800000	.0047339	.0500000	50,000	14,378.44	14,378.44	.88869	13,037.21	965.38
12	50.00	.0500000	25.00	.0500000	1,000	.0600000	.0800000	.0053938	.0500000	50,000	16,195.14	16,195.14	.87799	14,801.54	965.38
13	50.00	.0500000	25.00	.0500000	1,000	.0600000	.0800000	.0062972	.0500000	50,000	18,120.85	18,120.85	.86730	16,693.63	965.38
14	50.00	.0500000	25.00	.0500000	1,000	.0600000	.0800000	.0072644	.0500000	50,000	20,162.10	20,162.10	.85662	18,729.06	965.38
15	50.00	.0500000	25.00	.0500000	1,000	.0600000	.0800000	.0082652	.0500000	50,000	22,325.83	22,325.83	.84594	20,927.06	965.38
16	50.00	.0500000	25.00	.0500000	1,000	.0600000	.0800000	.0099000	.0500000	50,000	24,619.38	24,619.38	.83526	23,298.37	965.38
17	50.00	.0500000	25.00	.0500000	1,000	.0600000	.0800000	.0108060	.0500000	50,000	27,050.54	27,050.54	.82458	25,884.08	965.38
18	50.00	.0500000	25.00	.0500000	1,000	.0600000	.0800000	.0118140	.0500000	50,000	29,627.57	29,627.57	.81391	28,713.88	965.38
19	50.00	.0500000	25.00	.0500000	1,000	.0600000	.0800000	.0129780	.0500000	50,000	32,359.23	32,359.23	.80324	31,823.04	965.38
20	50.00	.0500000	25.00	.0500000	1,000	.0600000	.0800000	.0142860	.0500000	50,000	35,254.78	35,254.78	.79259	35,254.78	965.38

APPENDIX 4.B

INCOME STATEMENT

Year	Premium	Inv Inc	Exps	Dth Ben	Sur Ben	Chg-Res	Total Income
1	1,000.00	12.50	875.00	47.67	14.40	37.35	38.09
2	1,000.00	97.17	75.00	65.69	63.26	855.14	38.09
3	1,000.00	159.01	75.00	85.19	99.71	858.69	40.43
4	1,000.00	245.11	75.00	101.19	91.84	933.76	43.31
5	1,000.00	333.30	75.00	117.21	147.26	948.66	45.18
6	1,000.00	427.71	75.00	137.47	216.29	953.87	45.08
7	1,000.00	527.97	75.00	159.57	299.17	950.98	43.25
8	1,000.00	633.82	75.00	177.26	396.12	945.41	40.03
9	1,000.00	745.40	75.00	192.01	507.39	935.77	35.25
10	1,000.00	862.73	75.00	210.49	633.23	915.94	28.07
11	1,000.00	985.41	75.00	236.70	718.92	930.96	23.84
12	1,000.00	1,116.98	75.00	269.69	809.76	944.42	18.11
13	1,000.00	1,258.12	75.00	314.86	906.04	952.28	9.94
14	1,000.00	1,409.49	75.00	363.22	1,008.11	962.92	0.24
15	1,000.00	1,572.32	75.00	413.26	1,116.29	978.68	−10.90
16	1,000.00	1,748.16	75.00	495.00	1,230.97	975.75	−28.55
17	1,000.00	1,937.87	75.00	540.30	1,352.53	1,011.80	−41.75
18	1,000.00	2,144.73	75.00	590.70	1,481.38	1,054.88	−57.23
19	1,000.00	2,371.11	75.00	648.90	1,617.96	1,105.01	−75.76
20	1,000.00	2,619.84	75.00	714.30	1,762.74	1,165.35	−97.55

644

APPENDIX 4.C

SOE INCOME

Year	Gain 1.1	Gain 1.2	Gain 1.3	Gain 1.4	Gain 1.5	Gain 1.6	Gain 2.1	Gain 2.2	Gain 2.3	Gain 2.4	Gain 2.5	Gain 2.6	Gain 2.7	Gain 2.8	Total Income
1	38.09	.00	.00	.00	.00	.00	.00	.00	.00	.00	.00	.00	.00	.00	38.09
2	38.09	.00	.00	.00	.00	.00	.00	.00	.00	.00	.00	.00	.00	.00	38.09
3	38.09	−39.75	.00	.00	.00	.00	40.36	−0.07	1.81	.00	.00	.00	.00	.00	40.43
4	38.09	−61.28	.00	.00	.00	.00	61.16	−1.97	2.95	.00	.00	−0.51	0.77	4.11	43.31
5	38.09	−83.33	.00	.00	.00	.00	83.42	−3.96	4.75	.00	.00	−0.90	1.43	5.68	45.18
6	38.09	−106.93	.00	.00	.00	.00	107.07	−6.39	6.06	.00	.00	−1.24	2.06	6.37	45.08
7	38.09	−131.99	.00	.00	.00	.00	132.03	−9.33	6.61	.00	.00	−1.56	2.65	6.74	43.25
8	38.09	−158.46	.00	.00	.00	.00	158.35	−12.41	6.11	.00	.00	−1.87	3.24	6.98	40.03
9	38.09	−186.35	.00	.00	.00	.00	186.02	−15.61	4.26	.00	.00	−2.17	3.81	7.21	35.25
10	38.09	−215.68	.00	.00	.00	.00	214.96	−19.48	0.76	.00	.00	−2.47	4.36	7.54	28.07
11	38.09	−246.35	.00	.00	.00	.00	245.99	−24.55	0.81	.00	.00	−2.77	4.93	7.71	23.84
12	38.09	−279.24	.00	.00	.00	.00	279.27	−30.99	0.85	.00	.00	−3.06	5.49	7.70	18.11
13	38.09	−314.53	.00	.00	.00	.00	314.97	−39.71	0.88	.00	.00	−3.36	6.07	7.53	9.94
14	38.09	−352.37	.00	.00	.00	.00	353.38	−49.90	0.89	.00	.00	−3.65	6.66	7.14	0.24
15	38.09	−393.08	.00	.00	.00	.00	394.85	−61.44	0.88	.00	.00	−3.94	7.26	6.48	−10.90
16	38.09	−437.04	.00	.00	.00	.00	439.59	−79.21	0.84	.00	.00	−4.24	7.87	5.54	−28.55
17	38.09	−484.47	.00	.00	.00	.00	488.38	−92.63	0.76	.00	.00	−4.53	8.51	4.14	−41.75
18	38.09	−536.18	.00	.00	.00	.00	541.77	−108.07	0.60	.00	.00	−4.82	9.18	2.20	−57.23
19	38.09	−592.78	.00	.00	.00	.00	600.43	−126.24	0.36	.00	.00	−5.12	9.88	−0.39	−75.76
20	38.09	−654.96	.00	.00	.00	.00	665.18	−147.31	0.00	.00	.00	−5.41	10.62	−3.76	−97.55

Gain 1.1 = gain from loading (% of premium profit)
Gain 1.2 = gain from earned interest
Gain 1.3 = gain from mortality
Gain 1.4 = gain from withdrawal
Gain 1.5 = gain from non % premium expenses
Gain 1.6 = gain from % premium expenses
Gain 2.1 = gain from credited interest

Gain 2.2 = additional mortality loss
Gain 2.3 = additional withdrawal loss
Gain 2.4 = gain from non % premium charge
Gain 2.5 = gain from % premium charge
Gain 2.6 = additional loss from non % premium expense
Gain 2.7 = additional gain from non % of premium charge
Gain 2.8 = premium persistency gain

APPENDIX 5.A

ACTUAL EXPERIENCE ASSUMPTIONS

t	C	C%	E°	E%	GP	i^e	i^c	q^d	q^w	DB	AB	CV	A	V	NP
1	50.00	.0500000	75.00	.8000000	1,000.00	.0800000	.1000000	.0009533	.2000000	50,000.00	972.00	72.00	1.00000	46.74	965.38
2	50.00	.0500000	25.00	.0500000	1,000.00	.0800000	.1000000	.0013138	.1500000	50,000.00	2,021.76	421.76	1.00000	1,062.67	965.38
3	50.00	.0500000	25.00	.0500000	1,000.00	.0800000	.1000000	.0017038	.1000000	50,000.00	3,155.50	1,055.50	1.00000	2,179.25	965.38
4	50.00	.0500000	25.00	.0500000	1,000.00	.0800000	.1000000	.0020238	.0500000	50,000.00	4,379.94	1,979.94	1.00000	3,350.72	965.38
5	62.54	.0500000	35.00	.0500000	1,000.00	.0800000	.1000000	.0023441	.0500000	50,000.00	5,688.79	3,188.79	.99762	4,619.24	965.38
6	62.07	.0500000	35.00	.0500000	1,000.00	.0800000	.1000000	.0027494	.0500000	50,000.00	7,102.85	4,702.85	.99612	5,992.68	965.38
7	61.77	.0500000	35.00	.0500000	1,000.00	.0800000	.1000000	.0031915	.0500000	50,000.00	8,630.38	6,530.38	.99509	7,471.33	965.38
8	61.56	.0500000	35.00	.0500000	1,000.00	.0800000	.1000000	.0035453	.0500000	50,000.00	10,280.33	8,680.33	.99434	9,060.60	965.38
9	61.41	.0500000	35.00	.0500000	1,000.00	.0800000	.1000000	.0038401	.0500000	50,000.00	12,062.43	11,162.43	.99378	10,764.70	965.38
10	61.32	.0500000	35.00	.0500000	1,000.00	.0800000	.1000000	.0042098	.0500000	50,000.00	13,987.19	13,987.19	.99334	12,582.47	965.38
11	61.23	.0500000	35.00	.0500000	1,000.00	.0800000	.1000000	.0047339	.0500000	50,000.00	16,066.04	16,066.04	.99299	14,567.39	965.38
12	61.14	.0500000	35.00	.0500000	1,000.00	.0800000	.1000000	.0053938	.0500000	50,000.00	18,311.28	18,311.28	.99271	16,735.59	965.38
13	61.06	.0500000	35.00	.0500000	1,000.00	.0800000	.1000000	.0062972	.0500000	50,000.00	20,736.24	20,736.24	.99248	19,103.03	965.38
14	60.96	.0500000	35.00	.0500000	1,000.00	.0800000	.1000000	.0072644	.0500000	50,000.00	23,355.30	23,355.30	.99228	21,695.30	965.38
15	60.87	.0500000	35.00	.0500000	1,000.00	.0800000	.1000000	.0082652	.0500000	50,000.00	26,183.99	26,183.99	.99212	24,543.49	965.38
16	60.76	.0500000	35.00	.0500000	1,000.00	.0800000	.1000000	.0099000	.0500000	50,000.00	29,239.09	29,239.09	.99199	27,670.20	965.38
17	60.64	.0500000	35.00	.0500000	1,000.00	.0800000	.1000000	.0108060	.0500000	50,000.00	32,538.72	32,538.72	.99188	31,135.60	965.38
18	60.51	.0500000	35.00	.0500000	1,000.00	.0800000	.1000000	.0118140	.0500000	50,000.00	36,102.47	36,102.47	.99178	34,989.09	965.38
19	60.36	.0500000	35.00	.0500000	1,000.00	.0800000	.1000000	.0129780	.0500000	50,000.00	39,951.48	39,951.48	.99170	39,289.49	965.38
20	60.19	.0500000	35.00	.0500000	1,000.00	.0800000	.1000000	.0142860	.0500000	50,000.00	44,108.60	44,108.60	.99164	44,108.60	965.38

APPENDIX 5.B

INCOME STATEMENT

Year	Premium	Inv Inc	Exps	Dth Ben	Sur Ben	Chg-Res	Total Income
1	1,000.00	12.50	875.00	47.67	14.40	37.35	38.09
2	1,000.00	97.17	75.00	65.69	63.26	855.14	38.09
3	1,000.00	198.77	75.00	85.19	105.55	894.94	38.09
4	1,000.00	310.42	75.00	101.19	99.00	997.15	38.09
5	1,000.00	426.57	85.00	117.21	159.44	1,026.74	38.19
6	1,000.00	553.42	85.00	137.47	235.14	1,057.33	38.48
7	1,000.00	690.77	85.00	159.57	326.52	1,081.23	38.45
8	1,000.00	938.63	85.00	177.26	434.02	1,104.12	38.23
9	1,000.00	997.56	85.00	192.01	558.12	1,124.53	37.90
10	1,000.00	1,167.97	85.00	210.49	699.36	1,135.68	37.44
11	1,000.00	1,349.75	85.00	236.70	803.30	1,187.58	37.17
12	1,000.00	1,548.24	85.00	269.69	915.56	1,241.15	36.83
13	1,000.00	1,765.06	85.00	314.86	1,036.81	1,291.99	36.39
14	1,000.00	2,001.80	85.00	363.22	1,167.77	1,349.90	35.92
15	1,000.00	2,261.03	85.00	413.26	1,309.20	1,418.17	35.41
16	1,000.00	2,545.85	85.00	495.00	1,461.95	1,469.26	34.63
17	1,000.00	2,658.52	85.00	540.30	1,626.94	1,572.16	34.12
18	1,000.00	3,205.06	85.00	590.70	1,805.12	1,690.68	33.56
19	1,000.00	3,590.41	85.00	648.90	1,997.57	1,826.03	32.91
20	1,000.00	4,020.45	85.00	714.30	2,205.43	1,983.54	32.18

647

APPENDIX 5.C

SOE Income

Year	Gain 1.1	Gain 1.2	Gain 1.3	Gain 1.4	Gain 1.5	Gain 1.6	Gain 2.1	Gain 2.2	Gain 2.3	Gain 2.4	Gain 2.5	Gain 2.6	Gain 2.7	Gain 2.8	Total Income
1	38.09	.00	.00	.00	.00	.00	.00	.00	.00	.00	.00	.00	.00	.00	38.09
2	38.09	.00	.00	.00	.00	.00	.00	.00	.00	.00	.00	.00	.00	.00	38.09
3	38.09	.00	.00	.00	.00	.00	.00	.00	.00	.00	.00	.00	.00	.00	38.09
4	38.09	.00	.00	.00	−11.00	.00	.00	.00	.00	11.00	.00	.00	.00	.00	38.09
5	38.09	.00	.00	.00	−11.00	.00	.00	−0.03	0.13	11.00	.00	.00	.00	.00	38.19
6	38.09	.00	.00	.00	−11.00	.00	.00	−0.35	0.37	11.00	.00	−0.07	0.11	0.34	38.48
7	38.09	.00	.00	.00	−11.00	.00	.00	−0.64	0.47	11.00	.00	−0.11	0.18	0.46	38.45
8	38.09	.00	.00	.00	−11.00	.00	.00	−0.89	0.44	11.00	.00	−0.14	0.23	0.50	38.23
9	38.09	.00	.00	.00	−11.00	.00	.00	−1.11	0.29	11.00	.00	−0.16	0.27	0.52	37.90
10	38.09	.00	.00	.00	−11.00	.00	.00	−1.33	0.03	11.00	.00	−0.17	0.30	0.52	37.44
11	38.09	.00	.00	.00	−11.00	.00	.00	−1.60	0.03	11.00	.00	−0.18	0.33	0.51	37.17
12	38.09	.00	.00	.00	−11.00	.00	.00	−1.92	0.02	11.00	.00	−0.19	0.35	0.48	36.83
13	38.09	.00	.00	.00	−11.00	.00	.00	−2.32	0.02	11.00	.00	−0.20	0.36	0.45	36.39
14	38.09	.00	.00	.00	−11.00	.00	.00	−2.76	0.02	11.00	.00	−0.21	0.38	0.41	35.92
15	38.09	.00	.00	.00	−11.00	.00	.00	−3.22	0.01	11.00	.00	−0.21	0.39	0.35	35.41
16	38.09	.00	.00	.00	−11.00	.00	.00	−3.94	0.01	11.00	.00	−0.22	0.40	0.28	34.63
17	38.09	.00	.00	.00	−11.00	.00	.00	−4.37	0.01	11.00	.00	−0.22	0.41	0.20	34.12
18	38.09	.00	.00	.00	−11.00	.00	.00	−4.84	0.01	11.00	.00	−0.22	0.43	0.10	33.56
19	38.09	.00	.00	.00	−11.00	.00	.00	−5.37	.00	11.00	.00	−0.23	0.44	−0.02	32.91
20	38.09	.00	.00	.00	−11.00	.00	.00	−5.97	.00	11.00	.00	−0.23	0.45	−0.16	32.18

Gain 1.1 = gain from loading (% of premium profit)
Gain 1.2 = gain from earned interest
Gain 1.3 = gain from mortality
Gain 1.4 = gain from withdrawal
Gain 1.5 = gain from non % premium expenses
Gain 1.6 = gain from % premium expenses
Gain 2.1 = gain from credited interest

Gain 2.2 = additional mortality loss
Gain 2.3 = additional withdrawal loss
Gain 2.4 = gain from non % premium charge
Gain 2.5 = gain from % premium charge
Gain 2.6 = additional loss from non % premium expense
Gain 2.7 = additional gain from non % of premium charge
Gain 2.8 = premium persistency gain

APPENDIX 5.D

ACTUAL EXPERIENCE ASSUMPTIONS

t	C°	C%	E°	E%	GP	i^c	i^e	q^d	q^w	DB	AB	CV	A	V	NP
1	50.00	.0500000	75.00	.8000000	1,000	.0800000	.1000000	.0009533	.2000000	50,000	972.00	72.00	1.00000	46.74	965.38
2	50.00	.0500000	25.00	.0500000	1,000	.0800000	.1000000	.0013138	.1500000	50,000	2,021.76	421.76	1.00000	1,062.67	965.38
3	50.00	.0500000	25.00	.0500000	1,000	.0800000	.1000000	.0017038	.1000000	50,000	3,155.50	1,055.50	1.00000	2,179.25	965.38
4	50.00	.0500000	25.00	.0500000	1,000	.0800000	.1000000	.0020238	.0500000	50,000	4,379.94	1,979.94	1.00000	3,350.72	965.38
5	62.43	.0500000	35.00	.0500000	1,000	.0800000	.1000000	.0023441	.0500000	50,000	5,688.91	3,188.91	.99765	4,619.34	965.38
6	61.99	.0500000	35.00	.0500000	1,000	.0800000	.1000000	.0027494	.0500000	50,000	7,103.07	4,703.07	.99615	5,992.87	965.38
7	61.71	.0500000	35.00	.0500000	1,000	.0800000	.1000000	.0031915	.0500000	50,000	8,630.67	6,530.67	.99512	7,471.58	965.38
8	61.52	.0500000	35.00	.0500000	1,000	.0800000	.1000000	.0035453	.0500000	50,000	10,280.68	8,680.68	.99438	9,060.91	965.38
9	61.39	.0500000	35.00	.0500000	1,000	.0800000	.1000000	.0038401	.0500000	50,000	12,062.84	11,162.84	.99382	10,765.07	965.38
10	61.31	.0500000	35.00	.0500000	1,000	.0800000	.1000000	.0042098	.0500000	50,000	13,987.65	13,987.65	.99338	12,582.89	965.38
11	61.23	.0500000	35.00	.0500000	1,000	.0800000	.1000000	.0047339	.0500000	50,000	16,066.54	16,066.54	.99302	14,567.84	965.38
12	61.15	.0500000	35.00	.0500000	1,000	.0800000	.1000000	.0053938	.0500000	50,000	18,311.82	18,311.82	.99274	16,736.08	965.38
13	61.08	.0500000	35.00	.0500000	1,000	.0800000	.1000000	.0062972	.0500000	50,000	20,736.80	20,736.80	.99250	19,103.54	965.38
14	61.00	.0500000	35.00	.0500000	1,000	.0800000	.1000000	.0072644	.0500000	50,000	23,355.86	23,355.86	.99231	21,695.82	965.38
15	60.92	.0500000	35.00	.0500000	1,000	.0800000	.1000000	.0082652	.0500000	50,000	26,184.54	26,184.54	.99214	24,544.00	965.38
16	60.84	.0500000	35.00	.0500000	1,000	.0800000	.1000000	.0099000	.0500000	50,000	29,239.59	29,239.59	.99201	27,670.68	965.38
17	60.74	.0500000	35.00	.0500000	1,000	.0800000	.1000000	.0108060	.0500000	50,000	32,539.16	32,539.16	.99189	31,136.02	965.38
18	60.62	.0500000	35.00	.0500000	1,000	.0800000	.1000000	.0118140	.0500000	50,000	36,102.83	36,102.83	.99179	34,989.44	965.38
19	60.48	.0500000	35.00	.0500000	1,000	.0800000	.1000000	.0129780	.0500000	50,000	39,951.73	39,951.73	.99171	39,289.74	965.38
20	60.33	.0500000	35.00	.0500000	1,000	.0800000	.1000000	.0142860	.0500000	50,000	44,108.71	44,108.71	.99164	44,108.71	965.38

APPENDIX 5.E

INCOME STATMENT

Year	Premium	Inv Inc	Exps	Dth Ben	Sur Ben	Chg-Res	Total Income
1	1,000.00	12.50	875.00	47.67	14.40	37.35	38.09
2	1,000.00	97.17	75.00	65.69	63.26	855.14	38.09
3	1,000.00	198.77	75.00	85.19	105.55	894.94	38.09
4	1,000.00	310.42	75.00	101.19	99.00	997.15	38.09
5	1,000.00	426.57	85.00	117.21	159.45	1,026.83	38.09
6	1,000.00	553.43	85.00	137.47	235.15	1,057.40	38.41
7	1,000.00	690.79	85.00	159.57	326.53	1,081.29	38.39
8	1,000.00	838.66	85.00	177.26	434.03	1,104.16	38.20
9	1,000.00	997.59	85.00	192.01	558.14	1,124.56	37.88
10	1,000.00	1,168.01	85.00	210.49	699.38	1,135.71	37.43
11	1,000.00	1,349.79	85.00	236.70	803.33	1,187.60	37.17
12	1,000.00	1,548.28	85.00	269.69	915.59	1,241.16	36.84
13	1,000.00	1,765.11	85.00	314.86	1,036.84	1,291.99	36.42
14	1,000.00	2,001.85	85.00	363.22	1,167.79	1,349.88	35.96
15	1,000.00	2,261.08	85.00	413.26	1,309.23	1,418.13	35.47
16	1,000.00	2,545.90	85.00	495.00	1,461.98	1,469.20	34.72
17	1,000.00	2,858.57	85.00	540.30	1,626.96	1,572.08	34.23
18	1,000.00	3,205.10	85.00	590.70	1,805.14	1,690.58	33.68
19	1,000.00	3,590.44	85.00	648.90	1,997.59	1,825.91	33.05
20	1,000.00	4,020.47	85.00	714.30	2,205.44	1,983.40	32.34

APPENDIX 5.F

SOE Income

Year	Gain 1.1	Gain 1.2	Gain 1.3	Gain 1.4	Gain 1.5	Gain 1.6	Gain 2.1	Gain 2.2	Gain 2.3	Gain 2.4	Gain 2.5	Gain 2.6	Gain 2.7	Gain 2.8	Total Income
1	38.09	.00	.00	.00	.00	.00	.00	.00	.00	.00	.00	.00	.00	.00	38.09
2	38.09	.00	.00	.00	.00	.00	.00	.00	.00	.00	.00	.00	.00	.00	38.09
3	38.09	.00	.00	.00	.00	.00	.00	.00	.00	.00	.00	.00	.00	.00	38.09
4	38.09	.00	.00	.00	.00	.00	.00	.00	.00	.00	.00	.00	.00	.00	38.09
5	38.09	.00	.00	.00	−11.00	.00	.00	−0.03	0.13	10.90	.00	.00	.00	.00	38.09
6	38.09	.00	.00	.00	−11.00	.00	.00	−0.35	0.37	10.93	.00	−0.06	0.11	0.33	38.41
7	38.09	.00	.00	.00	−11.00	.00	.00	−0.64	0.46	10.95	.00	−0.11	0.18	0.46	38.39
8	38.09	.00	.00	.00	−11.00	.00	.00	−0.89	0.44	10.97	.00	−0.13	0.23	0.50	38.20
9	38.09	.00	.00	.00	−11.00	.00	.00	−1.10	0.29	10.98	.00	−0.15	0.27	0.51	37.88
10	38.09	.00	.00	.00	−11.00	.00	.00	−1.33	0.03	10.98	.00	−0.17	0.30	0.52	37.43
11	38.09	.00	.00	.00	−11.00	.00	.00	−1.59	0.03	11.00	.00	−0.18	0.32	0.51	37.17
12	38.09	.00	.00	.00	−11.00	.00	.00	−1.91	0.02	11.01	.00	−0.19	0.34	0.48	36.84
13	38.09	.00	.00	.00	−11.00	.00	.00	−2.31	0.02	11.02	.00	−0.20	0.36	0.45	36.42
14	38.09	.00	.00	.00	−11.00	.00	.00	−2.75	0.02	11.04	.00	−0.21	0.38	0.40	35.96
15	38.09	.00	.00	.00	−11.00	.00	.00	−3.21	0.01	11.05	.00	−0.21	0.39	0.35	35.47
16	38.09	.00	.00	.00	−11.00	.00	.00	−3.93	0.01	11.08	.00	−0.22	0.40	0.28	34.72
17	38.09	.00	.00	.00	−11.00	.00	.00	−4.36	0.01	11.09	.00	−0.22	0.41	0.20	34.23
18	38.09	.00	.00	.00	−11.00	.00	.00	−4.83	0.01	11.11	.00	−0.22	0.42	0.10	33.68
19	38.09	.00	.00	.00	−11.00	.00	.00	−5.37	.00	11.14	.00	−0.23	0.44	−0.02	33.05
20	38.09	.00	.00	.00	−11.00	.00	.00	−5.97	.00	11.16	.00	−0.23	0.45	−0.16	32.34

Gain 1.1 = gain from loading (% of premium profit)
Gain 1.2 = gain from earned interest
Gain 1.3 = gain from mortality
Gain 1.4 = gain from withdrawal
Gain 1.5 = gain from non % premium expenses
Gain 1.6 = gain from % premium expenses
Gain 2.1 = gain from credited interest

Gain 2.2 = additional mortality loss
Gain 2.3 = additional withdrawal loss
Gain 2.4 = gain from non % premium charge
Gain 2.5 = gain from % premium charge
Gain 2.6 = additional loss from non % premium expense
Gain 2.7 = additional gain from non % of premium charge
Gain 2.8 = premium persistency gain

THE EFFECTS OF MORTALITY ON INDIVIDUAL ANNUITIES

NAFTALI TEITELBAUM

I. INTRODUCTION

The purpose of this paper is to illustrate the effects of mortality on the pricing and valuation of individual immediate annuities. Historical annuity mortality experience gathered from the *Transactions* is reviewed to provide a basis for projecting future annuity mortality improvement. Marginal effects of mortality on the pricing of an idealized model office of immediate annuities issued over a 20-year period are examined.

Considerations in the underwriting of substandard annuities and their effects on pricing and valuation of structured settlement annuities also are presented.

II. HISTORICAL EXPERIENCE

The 1940s

"In order to know where you are going, examine from whence you come" has always been sage advice. A review of the findings on annuity mortality presented in actuarial literature will set the stage for our examination of the effects of variations in mortality experience.

Jenkins and Lew, in their landmark paper "A New Mortality Basis for Annuities" [12], presented the Joint Mortality Committee's experience on immediate nonrefund annuities from 1941 to 1946 anniversaries as the basis for the 1943 Experience Table. This table was the foundation for the construction of the Annuity Table for 1949, which included conservatively estimated changes in mortality between 1943 and 1949. Both tables provide for a one-year select mortality period.

Jenkins and Lew introduced the concept of projecting anticipated future mortality experience in pricing and valuation in order to recognize continuing trends in mortality improvement as well as medical advances that promote longevity. They reviewed principal North American long-term mortality statistics from insurance and population sources to determine average yearly rates of decrease in mortality by decennial age groups, and elicited the informed opinion of many authorities in the fields of population, public health, geriatric medicine, and medical specialists on what could be expected in the future. The results of their work formed the basis for two mortality projection scales.

653

The first scale, Projection Scale A, assumes a continuation of the rates of mortality decrease determined by Jenkins and Lew in their studies. The second scale, Projection Scale B, assumes a prospective viewpoint, reflecting their moderately conservative conclusions on how future mortality improvements will occur, independent of past experience. Jenkins and Lew derived Projection Scale B by assuming smaller rates of decrease in mortality at the younger ages and somewhat higher rates of decrease at ages over 60. Younger-age mortality was assumed to have run its course of improvement, while older-age mortality was assumed to be subject to efforts to reduce mortality from cardiovascular-renal diseases, cancer, and new medical discoveries and techniques.

Using Projection Scale B, Jenkins and Lew derived two forecasted tables, the Annuity Table for 1959 and the Annuity Table for 1979, to represent conservative estimates of annuity mortality that would likely be in effect 10 and 30 years after 1949, respectively. Comparison of mortality rates under the conservatively loaded 1937 Standard Annuity Table with the authors' tables, with and without projection, reveals the change that had been occurring and was projected to occur over the years. Table 1 compares male and female mortality rates from these tables at selected ages.

TABLE 1

COMPARISON OF MORTALITY RATES $(1000q_x)$
FROM 1937 STANDARD ANNUITY, 1943 EXPERIENCE TABLE (ULTIMATE),
AND ANNUITY TABLE FOR 1949 (ULTIMATE)

Age x	1937 Standard Annuity	1943 Experience Table	Annuity Table for 1949	Annuity Table for 1959	Annuity Table for 1979
Male					
15	1.262	0.800	0.537	0.474	0.368
35	2.981	1.779	1.391	1.227	0.954
55	13.554	12.876	10.565	9.316	7.244
75	60.464	60.248	54.501	50.743	43.978
95	248.059	332.413	316.834	316.834	316.834
Female					
15	1.257	0.432	0.278	0.245	0.191
35	2.065	1.266	0.942	0.831	0.646
55	9.288	5.920	4.705	4.149	3.226
75	41.758	41.267	35.829	33.360	28.918
95	177.138	300.501	288.153	288.153	288.153

At ages up to 94, mortality rates under the Annuity Tables for 1959 and 1979 show decreasing improvement when compared to rates under the 1943

Experience Table. At ages 95 and older, mortality rates under the Annuity Tables for 1959 and 1979 were assumed to be the same as those under the Annuity Table for 1949, with grading at ages 88 to 94.

Annuitant mortality can be divided into three groups: ages below 40, ages 40–60, and ages over 60. Jenkins and Lew indicate that for ages below 60, improvement in mortality rates have a relatively minor effect on immediate life annuity values. Therefore, they conclude that mortality improvement at ages 60 and older will have the controlling effect on annuity values, with cardiovascular-renal disease being the major contributor to higher death rates. They show that even partial improvement in this area could produce significant reduction in mortality rates.

Jenkins and Lew proposed Projection Scale B as the most reasonable basis for projecting mortality improvement up to age 90. They assume no future improvement in mortality for ages 90 and over.

Within a year after publication of the Jenkins and Lew paper, Bowerman [3] proposed modifications to the 1949 tables, including lower death rates at ages 89 and older in order not to exceed population and insured life mortality rates for the same time period, and extending the tables to age 120. Bowerman indicates that intercompany annuity data at advanced ages were sparse and population data provided a firmer basis for deriving advanced-age annuity mortality than that used by Jenkins and Lew. An extension of the British A1924–29 insured life experience table was used to extend Bowerman's table beyond age 109 when population figures ran out.

Peterson, in his paper "Group Annuity Mortality" [17], indicates that other actuaries also have questioned the assumption that there will be no further improvement in longevity beyond age 89.

The 1950s

These impressions also were borne out by facts. In 1961, Sternhell and Page presented their paper "The 1960 Modification of the a-1949 Table with Projection—Actuarial Note" [21]. The authors reviewed three intercompany immediate annuities mortality studies prepared by the Committee on Mortality under Ordinary Insurance and Annuities. These studies covered experience between 1946 and 1948, 1948 and 1953, and 1953 and 1958 anniversaries. Aggregate mortality margins in the a-1949 Table had just about disappeared based upon the improved experience exhibited both between 1948 and 1953 anniversaries and 1953 and 1958 anniversaries. Mortality improvement at ages 80 and over in both these studies was evident, especially for females.

Sternhell and Page therefore proposed modification of the a-1949 Table and of Projection Scale B to reflect the latest improvement in mortality and to restore the a-1949 Table margins. Table 2 compares the annual rates of decrease in mortality rates assumed by Jenkins and Lew under Projection Scale B with the 1960 Modification of the a-1949 Table with Projection assumed by Sternhell and Page.

TABLE 2

ANNUAL RATES OF DECREASE IN MORTALITY RATE*

Attained Age	Rate for Projection Scale B	Rate for the 1960 Modification of the a-1949 Table with Projection	Jenkins Suggested Projection Scale
0–50	1.25%	1.25%	1.25%
60	1.20	1.20	1.25
65	1.10	1.10	1.25
70	0.95	0.95	1.25
75	0.75	0.75	1.10
80	0.50	0.50	0.90
85	0.25	0.50	0.70
90	0	0.50	0.50
95	0	0.50	0.30
100	0	0.50	0.15
105–108	0	0.50	0
109	0	0	0

*Rates at intermediate ages are derived by straight-line interpolation.

It is interesting to note Lew's comments in his discussion of the Sternhell and Page paper. Lew shows that the effects of select mortality are more important than the effects of future improvement in mortality, especially past age 70, in computing immediate annuity rates. He also questions the attention given to the ultimate level of mortality rates at attained ages over 80 in view of the nature of the experience data available. In his discussion, Jenkins recommends that Sternhell and Page should have assumed somewhat larger annual rates of mortality improvement at ages 60–85 and somewhat smaller rates at ages 95 and over, as shown in the last column of Table 2. Jenkins points out that projections of future mortality rates are a practical necessity. Without them, rates and reserves will sooner or later produce financial losses that can be sizable.

The 1960s

Lew makes a far-reaching comment [13] in 1969, based upon his review of intercompany experience [7] covering the period from 1963 to 1967 anniversaries. This experience showed further declines in ultimate mortality, which again eliminated margins in the Sternhell and Page modified a-1949 Table. He points out that decreases in annuitant mortality may occur because of a change in the character of our customers.

Further details on the intercompany experience study covering the period from 1963 to 1967 anniversaries are provided by Cherry in his paper "The 1971 Individual Annuity Mortality Table," published in 1971 [6]. The need for this table, to be used for valuing annuities, arose because of surplus strains produced by new money interest rates used in pricing annuities that were higher than the maximum 3-1/2% interest rate permitted for valuation of annuities. A new table, the 1963 Experience Table, was constructed as the basis for the valuation table.

The new 1963 Experience Table was developed by combining the experience under immediate annuities, life income settlements and matured deferred annuities based upon the combined intercompany mortality studies of immediate annuities from 1963 to 1967 anniversaries and of settlement annuities from 1960 to 1965 anniversaries. Lew had commented that annuity mortality is more significantly affected by amounts of annual income than by number of contracts, so the new experience table was derived on this basis.

Mortality rates for males and females under the 1963 Experience Table are less than those under the Annuity Table for 1949. A mixed result appears when rates under the 1963 Experience Table are compared with those under the Annuity Table for 1959. All male rates, except at age 95, are lower under the Annuity Table for 1959 — and would be more so if that table had been projected to 1963. Only female ages around the middle 50s are lower under the Annuity Table for 1959. Settlement option annuity rates exhibit aggregate mortality improvements somewhat larger than those for immediate annuities. Blending them with immediate annuity rates and introducing group annuity mortality at ages 50 and below calls for caution in comparing the 1963 Experience Table with tables generated earlier.

Cherry analyzed average annual rates of decrease in mortality separately on immediate annuities and settlement annuities based upon prior experience studies compared to the present studies. He concludes that Projection Scale B is a fairly good representation of historical improvements and that it also provides a reasonable set of assumptions for projecting future mortality decreases over the next 20 years.

The 1970s

Projection Scale B, originally propounded by Jenkins and Lew in 1949, appeared in 1971 to be a reasonable gauge of future mortality improvement over the next 20 years. But mortality improved at such a pace that in 1980 a committee was formed to again study annuitant mortality and the need for a new valuation table. The results of the committee's work were presented in the *Transactions* as a paper titled "Report of the Committee to Recommend a New Mortality Basis for Individual Annuity Valuation (Derivation of the 1983 Table *a*)," which was published in 1981 [18].

The committee determined from 1971–76 annuity mortality experience that a new valuation table was needed for the 1980s and that recent improvement in mortality at the high ages required replacement of Projection Scale B. Other sources of mortality at the higher ages, such as U.S. population mortality, confirmed this improvement.

The committee came to the same conclusions as the committee preparing the 1971 IAM valuation table: that the 1983 Table *a* for valuation should also be based on:

- The total experience under immediate refund and nonrefund annuities, matured deferred annuities and settlement options (Only pension trust issues were excluded.)
- Amounts of income rather than number of contracts
- Inclusion of all durations in the experience studies, that is, an aggregate table, which would be safer for a valuation table than an ultimate mortality table
- Sex-distinct mortality tables, to avoid the problem of companies having varying male-female business distributions from that assumed in developing the valuation table, either at issue or at a later time
- A limiting age of 115 at which $q_x = 1$
- Mortality rates below age 50 from a source other than the experience studies.

Construction of the 1983 Table *a* first required development of the 1973 Experience Table. Data were compiled based upon the Society's 1971–76 annuity mortality study, yielding usable mortality rates only at ages over 50. Graduation of rates reduced usable rates to ages over 60 only. Therefore, the committee took 1971 IAM Table mortality rates at ages 47 and under, backing out the 10% load factor, which would be added later to rates at all ages under the new experience table, the 1971–76 graduated rates at ages 67 and over, and used a cubic curve to connect the two sets of mortality rates. A regraduation of these rates produced the 1973 Experience Table. Table 3 compares these rates with the 1963 Experience Table rates and includes 1983 Basic Table rates for future discussion.

TABLE 3

COMPARISON OF MORTALITY RATES (1000q_x)

Age x	1963 Experience Table (1000q_x)	1973 Experience Table		1983 Basic Table	
		1000q_x	Ratio to 1963 Experience Table	1000q_x	Ratio to 1973 Experience Table
Males					
7	0.457	0.448	0.980	0.370	0.826
17	0.518	0.507	0.979	0.508	1.002
27	0.775	0.759	0.979	0.756	0.996
37	1.468	1.422	0.969	1.146	0.806
47	4.253	4.155	0.977	3.343	0.805
57	11.817	9.601	0.812	7.658	0.798
67	25.647	21.682	0.845	17.467	0.806
77	61.574	57.261	0.930	47.272	0.826
87	145.608	138.957	0.954	119.894	0.863
97	377.968	281.058	0.744	243.467	0.866
107	734.383	568.770	0.774	518.120	0.911
Females					
7	0.197	0.180	0.914	0.149	0.828
17	0.266	0.240	0.902	0.239	0.996
27	0.475	0.433	0.912	0.431	0.995
37	0.915	0.832	0.909	0.673	0.809
47	2.018	1.850	0.917	1.500	0.811
57	5.981	4.801	0.803	3.832	0.798
67	13.386	12.664	0.946	10.012	0.791
77	40.587	34.574	0.852	28.433	0.822
87	128.843	104.173	0.809	90.907	0.873
97	268.911	254.797	0.948	220.718	0.866
107	499.209	484.418	0.970	451.160	0.931

The committee worked to develop projection factors over the period 1973–1983 that, when applied to the 1973 Experience Table, would produce the 1983 Basic Table. When loaded 10%, this table would be the desired 1983 a valuation table. Suitable data for a projection were unavailable, yet it was recognized that there was a substantial drop in mortality since 1968, especially at older ages, and therefore improvement rates derived from prior annuity experience were inappropriate to apply over the 1973–1983 period. Because U.S. white population improvement rates tended to follow annuity and settlement option experience over the period covered by the 1963 Experience Table data, the committee used this experience, incorporating Medicare experience to some degree, in deriving its own single set of projection factors for males and females for 1973–1983. Sex-distinct projection factors were derived for projecting mortality beyond 1983. The reason for hesitating to use Medicare experience improvement rates at higher ages is that the data were available only for white and nonwhite lives combined.

Table 4 compares the 1973–83 projection factors with those of Projection B developed by Jenkins and Lew as well as a scale later suggested by Jenkins.

TABLE 4

COMPARISON OF IMPROVEMENT FACTORS (INTERPOLATED*)

Age	Projection B	Jenkins' Suggested Scale	1973–1983 Assumed Factors
7................	1.25%	1.25%	2.00%
12–27............	1.25	1.25	0
32................	1.25	1.25	1.00
37–50............	1.25	1.25	2.25
60................	1.20	1.25	2.25
65................	1.10	1.25	2.25
70................	0.95	1.25	2.25
75................	0.75	1.10	2.10
80................	0.50	0.90	1.85
85................	0.25	0.70	1.60
90................	0	0.50	1.60
95................	0	0.30	1.60

*Straight-line interpolation for ages not shown.

Mortality experience has caused prior estimates of improvement rates, which were reasonable based upon medical and social developments around 1950 and 1960, to be woefully inadequate according to such developments over the ensuing 10–20 years. The 1973–1983 Assumed Factors at ages 65 and older are more than double those under Projection B and the 1.60 rate continues beyond age 90, while the Projection B rates assume no improvement for ages 90 and above. Jenkins' suggested scale was an improvement, but the committee's rates exceed twice Jenkins' rates at ages 80 and older.

The 1973–1983 period has resulted in an approximately overall 10–15 percent decrease in mortality rates for both sexes according to the committee's assumptions. The 1963–1973 period resulted in an approximately 10 percent decrease in mortality rates.

The Early 1980s

Controversy abounds regarding the future trend of mortality improvement in the early 1980s for the elderly, although there is agreement that other age-group segments will experience mortality improvement. The committee reviewed literature on the topic of aging with the following results.

- In his article "Aging, Natural Death and the Compression of Mortality" [9], Fries comments that whereas chronic disease may be postponed so that more people live longer to reach the expected length of life (about age 85), the total length of life is fixed for all practical purposes because of the loss of organ reserve with increasing age so the body cannot restore itself after a health threat. We may expect decreases in mortality, but they will lessen with increasing age.

   Yet, recent decreases in U.S. white population mortality and Medicare experience are in contradiction to Fries' viewpoint.

- In their article "The Recent Decline in Mortality of the Extreme Aged: An Analysis of Statistical Data" [19], which relies on intercensal estimates of U.S. population in the 1970s, Rosenwaike, Yaffe and Sagi disagree with the idea that there may only be little improvement in the extremely aged mortality rates.

   The committee questions some of Rosenwaike et al.'s analyses, which were based upon Medicare experience compared with Census Bureau population estimates, thinking that some of the substantial drop in mortality for the over-age-85 group is probably due to age misstatements and other errors.

- The authors above share an opinion that the sharp downturn in cardiovascular disease mortality is due to a single cause: controlling heart disease risk factors, plus more effective emergency, acute and long-term care for patients with cardiovascular disease.

   Another writer, Stallones [20], concludes that there is no single cause or combination of causes that accounts for the decline in ischemic heart disease.

   In his discussion "Mortality Trend in Hypertension, United States, 1950–1976" [2] Borhani comments that "mortality from hypertension and hypertensive heart disease has declined steadily and dramatically since 1950." He believes the underlying cause to be a much increased public awareness of hypertension and an increase in the rate of adequate treatment of this ailment.

- Analysis of the major causes of death among U.S. white population between 1968 and 1978 by the Statistical Bureau of the Metropolitan Life Insurance Company corroborated the opinions on heart and circulatory deaths and also showed substantial decreases for several other causes of death.

   The committee indicates that the distribution by cause of death for annuitants would differ from that of the U.S. population, but no such annuitant analysis is available. Hence, any set of future mortality improvement factors must be based on their relationship to changes by cause of death.

Agreement on future trends in mortality for annuitants is difficult to reach. Conjecture will become more the method of analysis because of an expected paucity of data. Several companies contributing data to the Society's Committee on Mortality under Ordinary Insurance and Annuities have, because of the expense, ceased their contributions. This committee expected to complete a study of annuitant mortality over the 1976–81 period some time during 1987, but a report is still forthcoming.

III. THE PRESENT

The Middle and Later 1980s — Traditional Annuitant Mortality

Our historical review of annuitant mortality has taught us that longevity is inexorably extending. Although one may quibble about the rate of extension and its effect on various age groups, mortality projection factors obviously are a necessity in both the adequate pricing of annuities and their valuation. For valuation, we can use a conservatively constructed static mortality table because reserve strengthening can occur prospectively, but nonparticipating annuity pricing must anticipate mortality improvements dynamically.

Several factors could soon cause a decrease in annuity mortality improvement for fixed-benefit annuities as a group. Heretofore, this group was somewhat homogeneous and was characterized by its ability to antiselect in its purchase of an annuity, thereby outliving insured lives and the general U.S. population of the same age. Such antiselection should not be expected to abate.

Tax laws of the U.S. favor the purchase of deferred annuities as a means by which an individual can defer tax on the interest income declared by the insurer under such an annuity. Insurers have received a very large amount of premium over the last five to six years, and the public continues to purchase this product. Eventually, these amounts will be annuitized with limited antiselection. In addition, the Tax Reform Act of 1986 requires a minimum amount of withdrawal each year from the Individual Retirement Account funds of every person over the age of 70-1/2. Even a small percentage of such withdrawals via annuitization for a life annuity would result in a large group of annuitants who have not antiselected.

Since the early 1980s, a new and burgeoning group of annuity contracts has been characterized by a complete lack of antiselection. The contract usually is the result of a settlement by a casualty insurer in a personal injury case and is known as a structured settlement annuity. A complete description of this line of business is provided by a panel discussion published in the *Record* under the title "Immediate Annuities and Structured Settlements" [11]. Structured settlement annuitants are not deciding to purchase or not to purchase an annuity because of their own feelings about their longevity.

Other economic realities and pressures prevail at the time of settlement with the casualty insurer. The socioeconomic status of such annuitants might be expected to differ from that of an individual electing to purchase an annuity.

The mortality to be expected from structured settlement annuitants would be more akin to the mortality expected from the U.S. population. Unless a separate class for the structured settlement group is established when studying annuitant mortality, an attenuation of the mortality improvement rates exhibited by the combined groups could reasonably be expected. This fact, plus the anticipation that future intercompany annuity mortality studies may not be produced, forces us to base annuity projection factors on some modification of U.S. population mortality improvements when pricing annuities for the last half of the 1980s and beyond. As stated by the committee recommending 1983 Table a for valuation,

"Any set of future improvement rates must take into consideration that there will be periods of retrogression and no improvement in addition to periods of greater than average improvement."

Indeed, the committee developed Projection Scale G for 1983 and beyond for just these reasons.

Projection Scale G assumes that the prime forces affecting annuitant mortality are the same as those affecting the U.S. population; that is, the focus on mortality improvement factors must be based upon their relationship to changes by cause of death, especially because we can reasonably assume that there will be no increasing annuitant antiselection when purchasing annuities. A projection of future U.S. mortality using cause-of-death analyses of the U.S. population by the U.S. Department of Health and Human Services [1] formed the basis of the committee's Projection Scale G development. The committee took these cause-of-death rates and converted them to an all-cause basis to develop Projection Scale G. Since that study in 1980, the Social Security Administration (SSA) has published *Actuarial Study No. 87*, in September 1982 [8]. *Actuarial Study No. 87* not only presents mortality rates of the U.S population for 1980 based upon the latest statistics then available, but also projects mortality out to the year 2050 with a mortality table being developed for the beginning of each decade. In their analysis, the SSA actuaries examined mortality improvements during 1968–78 for ten major groups of causes of death and then considered how new diagnostic and surgical techniques, environmental conditions, improvements in nutrition, incidence of violence, treatment of causes of diseases, prenatal care improvements, incidence of abortion, cigarette smoking, drug misuse, and value of life conception changes would affect future improvements in mortality. The AIDS epidemic was not factored into the projection.

Annual percentage improvements in central death rates by sex and cause of death for the years 2007 and later were postulated. Prior to 2007, mortality improvement was assumed to change gradually from historical improvements observed during 1968–78. Mortality tables for each decade were prepared based upon the projected mortality. Table 5 compares the improvement rates shown in the committee's report under its Table 21 [18, page 719] with the improvement rates shown in the SSA's Study [8, page 15] and with the committee's Projection G factor applicable to the central age.

Note that the annual improvement rates shown in the committee's Table 21 were derived by projecting 1977 U.S. population mortality rates over a ten-year period utilizing the SSA's Alternative II assumptions from *Actuarial Study No. 82*. The annual improvement rates shown in our Table 5 were derived by the SSA actuaries after analyzing improvements in central death rates during 1968–78 by age, sex and cause of death and then developing calendar-year U.S. Life Tables for decennial years beginning with 1990 and ending with 2050.

Table 5 reveals the diversity of results when the SSA improvement rates are compared with those derived by the committee. For males they range from 110 percent, 41 percent, and 62 percent increases at central ages 0, 2, and 7, respectively, to 40 percent and 86 percent increases at central ages 77 and 82, respectively. Other central age increases are more in the 0–25 percent range, with three central ages showing a lower improvement rate under *Actuarial Study No. 87*. Ratios for females are similar but less pronounced; for example, the central ages 0 and 82 ratios are only 88 percent and 23 percent, respectively. Other female central age ratio increases are closer to 10 percent, except for central ages 32 and 37. These ratios indicate a general assumption of greater mortality improvement at almost all ages, especially the youngest and oldest central ages, when the latest study is compared with the previous study, for both sexes.

It is informative to compare the Projection G improvement factors with the other improvement factors shown in Table 5. Mortality improvement rates exhibited at almost all ages in its derived study of U.S. population improvement rates were reduced by the committee, especially at male central ages 12 to 32. The latest SSA study indicates a continuation of mortality improvement in the U.S. population. However, remember that we are dealing with improvement in mortality rates of individual annuitants who already

TABLE 5

Comparison of U.S. Population Annual Mortality Improvement Rates under Social Security Administration's *Actuarial Study No. 87* and the Society's Committee Deriving 1983 Table a

Age	Central Age	Males				Females			
		SSA Actuarial Study No. 87	Committee Deriving 1983 Table a	Ratio*	Projection G	SSA Actuarial Study No. 87	Committee Deriving 1983 Table a	Ratio*	Projection G
0.	0	5.08%	2.42%	2.10	—	4.67%	2.49%	1.88	—
1–4.	2	2.87	2.03	1.41	—	3.45	2.36	1.46	—
5–9.	7	3.28	2.02	1.62	1.50	3.46	2.47	1.40	1.50
10–14.	12	2.16	1.78	1.21	0.25	2.59	2.50	1.04	1.00
15–19.	17	1.40	1.23	1.14	0.20	1.69	1.81	0.93	0.50
20–24.	22	1.44	1.16	1.24	0.10	1.77	1.94	0.91	0.50
25–29.	27	1.11	1.43	0.78	0.10	2.62	2.49	1.05	0.75
30–34.	32	2.21	1.87	1.18	0.75	3.76	2.78	1.35	1.25
35–39.	37	2.66	2.30	1.16	1.00	4.01	2.90	1.38	2.25
40–44.	42	2.69	2.54	1.06	2.00	3.00	2.70	1.11	2.25
45–49.	47	2.38	2.53	0.94	1.75	2.53	2.27	1.11	2.00
50–54.	52	2.16	2.35	0.92	1.75	2.07	1.97	1.05	2.00
55–59.	57	2.55	2.12	1.20	1.50	2.00	1.70	1.18	1.75
60–64.	62	2.00	1.84	1.09	1.50	1.51	1.62	0.93	1.75
65–69.	67	1.58	1.56	1.01	1.50	1.67	1.64	1.02	1.75
70–74.	72	1.51	1.27	1.19	1.25	2.30	1.77	1.30	1.75
75–79.	77	1.43	1.02	1.40	1.25	2.56	1.93	1.33	1.50
80–84.	82	1.54	0.83	1.86	1.25	2.60	2.11	1.23	1.50
85–89.	87	1.56	N.G.	—	1.25	2.43	N.G.	—	1.50
90–94.	92	1.59	N.G.	—	1.00	1.96	N.G.	—	1.25

*SSA *Actuarial Study No. 87* result divided by Committee Deriving 1983 Table a result.
N.G. — not given.

exhibit greater longevity than that of the U.S. population. Hence, as previously discussed, U.S. population rates of mortality improvement can be expected to exceed that of the individual annuity population group.

When a study is produced ten years hence, we will probably find that neither the assumptions under SSA *Actuarial Study No. 87* nor Projection G have been accurate. The question is, how inaccurate will they be? There is no specific answer to this question, especially because the homogeneity of the individual annuity class will change as discussed above. Therefore, I believe, a range of individual annuity mortality improvement projection scales is appropriate, to be represented by Projection I and Projection J. The following assumptions are arbitrary and are intended to indicate the effect on annuities of this range of projection factors.

In deriving these scales, we conservatively assume that, for annuity pricing purposes, both the SSA *Actuarial Study No. 87* and Projection G understate mortality improvement by 10 percent. We further assume that Projection I and Projection J lie between the adjusted aforementioned scales. Projection I is assumed to be equal to Projection G as adjusted plus 15 percent for males and 10 percent for females of the difference between the adjusted scales, except that for male central ages 12 to 32 inclusive the 15 percent factor is 10 percent. Projection J is assumed to be the average of the adjusted scales, except that for central ages 12 to 32 inclusive, Projection J equals Projection G as adjusted plus 20 percent of the difference between the adjusted scales. Projection I and Projection J values are then rounded. Table 6 shows the derivation of Projection I and Projection J. Table 7 compares Projection G with Projection I and Projection J. The resulting ratios imply that these latter two projection scales would produce significantly different effects on a portfolio of issued annuities. However, that may not necessarily be the case, depending upon the certain periods involved in the portfolio of annuities issued.

Other assumptions can obviously be made, and each assumption will produce its own effect on a portfolio of issued annuities. The effects on pricing of assuming Projection Scales I and J are studied later in this paper. We can then see how significantly different the effects on pricing of a Projection Scale J assumption are from the effects on pricing of a Projection Scale I assumption. If, in the opinion of the actuary performing such a study, the resulting premiums are not conservative enough or are too conservative, the actuary can modify the projection scale assumption and apply it in accordance with the procedures discussed in Section IV of this paper to produce gross premiums that incorporate mortality improvement in pricing.

TABLE 6

Derivation of Projection I and Projection J

	Males					

Central Age	(1) 110% of Study No. 87	(2) 110% of Projection G	(3) Projection I 0.15(1) + 0.85 (2)	(4) Projection J 0.5(1) + 0.5(2)	(5) Final Projection I	(6) Final Projection
0	5.59%	0	0.84%	2.80%	0.85%	2.80%
2	3.16	0	0.47	1.58	0.50	1.60
7	3.61	1.65%	1.94	2.63	2.00	2.60
12	2.38	0.28	0.49*	0.70†	0.50	0.70
17	1.54	0.22	0.35*	0.48†	0.35	0.50
22	1.58	0.11	0.26*	0.40†	0.25	0.40
27	1.22	0.11	0.22*	0.33†	0.20	0.35
32	2.43	0.83	0.99*	1.15†	1.00	1.15
37	2.93	2.20	2.31	2.57	2.30	2.60
42	2.96	2.20	2.31	2.58	2.30	2.60
47	2.62	1.93	2.03	2.28	2.00	2.30
52	2.38	1.93	2.00	2.16	2.00	2.20
57	2.81	1.65	1.82	2.23	1.80	2.20
62	2.20	1.65	1.73	1.93	1.75	1.90
67	1.74	1.65	1.66	1.70	1.65	1.75
72	1.66	1.38	1.42	1.52	1.40	1.50
77	1.57	1.38	1.41	1.48	1.40	1.50
82	1.69	1.38	1.43	1.54	1.40	1.50
87	1.72	1.38	1.43	1.55	1.40	1.50
92	1.75	1.10	1.29	1.43	1.30	1.50
97	N.G.	1.10	1.16‡	1.30‡	1.15	1.30

	Females					

Central Age	(1) 110% of Study No. 87	(2) 110% of Projection G	(3) Projection I 0.10(1) + 0.90(2)	(4) Projection J 0.5(1) + 0.5(2)	(5) Final Projection I	(6) Final Projection
0	5.14%	0	0.51%	2.57%	0.50%	2.60%
2	3.80	0	0.38	1.90	0.40	1.90
7	3.81	1.65%	1.87	2.73	1.90	2.75
12	2.85	1.10	1.28	1.45	1.25	1.45
17	1.86	0.55	0.68	0.81	0.70	0.80
22	1.95	0.55	0.69	0.83	0.70	0.80
27	2.88	0.83	1.04	1.24	1.00	1.25
32	4.14	1.38	1.66	1.93	1.65	1.95
37	4.41	2.48	2.67	3.45	2.65	3.45
42	3.30	2.48	2.56	2.89	2.55	2.90
47	2.78	2.20	2.26	2.49	2.25	2.50
52	2.28	2.20	2.21	2.24	2.20	2.25
57	2.20	1.93	1.96	2.07	1.95	2.10
62	1.66	1.93	1.90	1.80	1.90	1.80
67	1.84	1.93	1.92	1.89	1.90	1.90
72	2.53	1.93	1.99	2.23	2.00	2.25
77	2.82	1.65	1.77	2.24	1.75	2.25
82	2.86	1.65	1.77	2.26	1.75	2.25
87	2.67	1.65	1.75	2.16	1.75	2.15
92	2.16	1.38	1.46	1.77	1.45	1.75
97	N.G.	1.38	1.43‡	1.65‡	1.45	1.65

*0.10 × (1) + 0.90 × (2).
†0.20 × (1) + 0.80 × (2).
‡Assumed.
N.G. — not given.

TABLE 7

COMPARISON OF PROJECTION G WITH PROJECTION I AND PROJECTION J

Central Age	Projection			Ratios	
	G	I	J	Proj. I/Proj. G	Proj. J/Proj. G
Males					
0	—	0.85%	2.80%	—	—
2	—	0.50	1.60	—	—
7	1.50%	2.00	2.60	133%	173%
12	0.25	0.50	0.70	200	280
17	0.20	0.35	0.50	175	250
22	0.10	0.25	0.40	250	400
27	0.10	0.20	0.35	200	350
32	0.75	1.00	1.15	133	153
37	2.00	2.30	2.60	115	130
42	2.00	2.30	2.60	115	130
47	1.75	2.00	2.30	114	131
52	1.75	2.00	2.20	114	126
57	1.50	1.80	2.20	120	147
62	1.50	1.75	1.90	117	127
67	1.50	1.65	1.75	110	117
72	1.25	1.40	1.50	112	120
77	1.25	1.40	1.50	112	120
82	1.25	1.40	1.50	112	120
87	1.25	1.40	1.50	112	120
92	1.00	1.30	1.50	130	150
97	1.00	1.15	1.30	115	130
Females					
0	—	0.50%	2.60%	—	—
2	—	0.40	1.90	—	—
7	1.50%	1.90	2.75	127%	183%
12	1.00	1.25	1.45	125	145
17	0.50	0.70	0.80	140	160
22	0.50	0.70	0.80	140	160
27	0.75	1.00	1.25	133	167
32	1.25	1.65	1.95	132	156
37	2.25	2.65	3.45	118	153
42	2.25	2.55	2.90	113	129
47	2.00	2.25	2.50	113	125
52	2.00	2.20	2.25	110	113
57	1.75	1.95	2.10	111	120
62	1.75	1.90	1.80	109	103
67	1.75	1.90	1.90	109	109
72	1.75	2.00	2.25	114	129
77	1.50	1.75	2.25	117	150
82	1.50	1.75	2.25	117	150
87	1.50	1.75	2.15	117	143
92	1.25	1.45	1.75	116	140
97	1.25	1.45	1.65	116	132

The Middle and Later 1980s — U.S. Population Mortality

In view of the dramatic growth in sales of structured settlement annuities, the recent underlying mortality trends of the U.S. population should also be examined.

Table 8 compares the values of $1000q_x$ separately for the all races males and all races females at quinquennial ages under the most recent mortality tables published by the National Center for Health Statistics and the SSA in *Actuarial Study No. 87*. Mortality rates under the "U.S. Decennial Life Tables for 1979–81" were published in 1985 [15] and those under the "Vital Statistics of the United States 1982" Table were published in 1986 [16]. Mortality rates under the 1980 Life Table and 1990 Life Table were taken directly from *Actuarial Study No. 87*. Mortality rates for the 1987 Life Table were calculated by linear interpolation between the 1980 and 1990 Life Tables.

The improvement in U.S. population longevity when comparing the complete U.S. Decennial Life Table for 1979–81 mortality rates with those of the 1980 Life Table can be summarized as shown in Table 9.

Overall, the U.S. Decennial Life Table for 1979–81 shows mortality rates about the same or slightly lower than the mortality rates under the 1980 Life Table, until age 95, after which mortality rates under the former table are significantly lower.

Although Life Tables are based upon a sampling of deaths during the study year, whereas U.S. Decennial Life Tables are based upon the entire decennial census data, this comparison indicates that either type of table mortality rates can be used as a basis for estimating mortality, without materially affecting or masking the emerging improvement in mortality rates.

The Vital Statistics of the United States 1982 Table, when compared to the 1980 Life Table, shows mortality rates at most ages that are significantly lower — from 5 percent to 15 percent — for males and females, mostly 5–10 percent above age 40. This may be contrasted with the generally 1–5 percent reduction under the U.S. Decennial Life Table for 1979–81.

The close range of the ratios in Table 10 for the 1987 Life Table compared to the Vital Statistics of the United States 1982 Table at quinquennial ages seems to confirm the consistency between these tables. That is, the 1987 Life Table reasonably reflects additional expected mortality improvement over the period 1982–1987, and therefore the 1987 Life Table can be used to represent *current* expected mortality of the U.S. population.

TABLE 8

COMPARISON OF $1000q_x$ VALUES

| | Values of $1000q_x$ | | | | | Ratios to 1980 Life Table | | | | |
(1) Age	(2) 1980 Life Table	(3) U.S. Dec. Life Table for 1979–1981	(4) Vital Stat. of the U.S. 1982 Table	(5) 1987 Life Table	(6) 1990 Life Table	(7) (3)/(2)	(8) (4)/(2)	(9) (5)/(2)	(10) (6)/(2)	(11) Age
				Males						
0	14.04	13.93	12.80	11.56	10.49	0.9922	0.9117	0.8234	0.7472	0
5	0.42	0.42	0.40	0.35	0.32	1.0000	0.9524	0.8333	0.7619	5
10	0.21	0.21	0.21	0.18	0.16	1.0000	1.0000	0.8571	0.7619	10
15	1.01	0.96	0.89	0.88	0.82	0.9505	0.8812	0.8713	0.8119	15
20	1.90	1.81	1.61	1.61	1.49	0.9526	0.8474	0.8474	0.7842	20
25	2.04	1.99	1.76	1.87	1.80	0.9755	0.8627	0.9167	0.8824	25
30	1.93	1.91	1.79	1.74	1.66	0.9896	0.9275	0.9016	0.8601	30
35	2.15	2.16	2.02	1.85	1.72	1.0047	0.9395	0.8605	0.8000	35
40	3.04	3.03	2.75	2.60	2.41	0.9967	0.9046	0.8553	0.7928	40
45	4.82	4.76	4.41	4.11	3.81	0.9876	0.9149	0.8527	0.7905	45
50	7.93	7.75	7.31	6.93	6.50	0.9773	0.9218	0.8739	0.8197	50
55	12.39	12.06	11.56	10.57	9.79	0.9734	0.9330	0.8531	0.7902	55
60	18.52	18.46	17.71	16.09	15.05	0.9968	0.9563	0.8688	0.8126	60
65	28.95	28.17	27.20	26.26	25.11	0.9731	0.9396	0.9071	0.8674	65
70	43.28	42.07	40.45	39.58	38.00	0.9720	0.9346	0.9145	0.8780	70
75	63.54	61.67	59.57	57.84	55.40	0.9706	0.9375	0.9103	0.8719	75
80	91.99	90.69	87.27	83.39	79.70	0.9859	0.9487	0.9065	0.8664	80
85	134.97	134.19		123.63	118.77	0.9942		0.9160	0.8800	85
90	192.38	188.48		177.11	170.57	0.9797		0.9206	0.8866	90
95	263.05	261.49		242.27	233.36	0.9941		0.9210	0.8871	95
100	329.11	318.65		303.25	292.16	0.9682		0.9214	0.8877	100
105	400.41	358.45		368.95	355.46	0.8952		0.9214	0.8877	105
110	487.16			448.88	432.47			0.9214	0.8877	110
115	1,000.00			1,000.00	1,000.00			1.0000	1.0000	115

TABLE 8 — *Continued*

| (1) Age | Values of $1000q_x$ | | | | | Ratios to 1980 Life Table | | | | (11) Age |
	(2) 1980 Life Table	(3) U.S. Dec. Life Table for 1979–1981	(4) Vital Stat. of the U.S. 1982 Table	(5) 1987 Life Table	(6) 1990 Life Table	(7) (3)/(2)	(8) (4)/(2)	(9) (5)/(2)	(10) (6)/(2)	
					Females					
0	11.22	11.20	10.23	9.37	8.57	0.9982	0.9118	0.8351	0.7638	0
5	0.30	0.31	0.30	0.24	0.22	1.0333	1.0000	0.8000	0.7333	5
10	0.20	0.18	0.17	0.17	0.15	0.9000	0.8500	0.8500	0.7500	10
15	0.40	0.40	0.37	0.36	0.34	1.0000	0.9250	0.9000	0.8500	15
20	0.58	0.58	0.54	0.52	0.49	1.0000	0.9310	0.8966	0.8448	20
25	0.65	0.65	0.60	0.59	0.56	1.0000	0.9231	0.9077	0.8615	25
30	0.75	0.75	0.71	0.64	0.59	1.0000	0.9467	0.8533	0.7867	30
35	0.98	1.04	0.95	0.78	0.69	1.0612	0.9694	0.7959	0.7041	35
40	1.61	1.63	1.49	1.35	1.24	1.0124	0.9255	0.8385	0.7702	40
45	2.66	2.62	2.45	2.28	2.11	0.9850	0.9211	0.8571	0.7932	45
50	4.13	4.16	3.96	3.63	3.42	1.0073	0.9588	0.8789	0.8281	50
55	6.32	6.27	6.12	5.63	5.33	0.9921	0.9684	0.8908	0.8434	55
60	9.52	9.47	9.33	8.83	8.54	0.9947	0.9800	0.9275	0.8971	60
65	14.55	14.27	14.16	13.60	13.19	0.9808	0.9732	0.9347	0.9065	65
70	22.03	21.69	21.33	19.87	18.94	0.9846	0.9682	0.9020	0.8597	70
75	34.32	33.88	32.99	29.81	27.87	0.9872	0.9612	0.8686	0.8121	75
80	56.15	56.22	52.85	47.87	44.32	1.0012	0.9412	0.8525	0.7893	80
85	93.52	94.09		79.21	73.08	1.0061		0.8470	0.7814	85
90	149.48	146.61		131.56	123.88	0.9808		0.8801	0.8287	90
95	224.28	218.23		207.67	200.55	0.9730		0.9259	0.8942	95
100	297.13	281.76		278.50	270.51	0.9483		0.9373	0.9104	100
105	379.22	328.17		355.44	345.25	0.8654		0.9373	0.9104	105
110	483.99			447.93	432.47			0.9255	0.8936	110
115	1,000.00			1,000.00	1,000.00			1.0000	1.0000	115

TABLE 9

SOCIAL SECURITY ADMINISTRATION'S 1980 LIFE TABLE
VERSUS U.S. DECENNIAL LIFE TABLE FOR 1979–81
COMPARISON OF $1000q_x$ VALUES

Males		Females	
Age Category	Comment	Age Category	Comment
0–14	Almost no difference	0–14	Varying reductions from 4.5% to 14%
15–21	1979–81 Table shows 4%–8% lower rates	15–32	Generally the same rates wavering up or down by 1%–2%
22–49	Almost no difference or at most a 2% reduction in mortality rate	33–41	Increased mortality rates from 1.2% to 8.7%
50–58	2%–4% lower rates under 1979–81 Table	42–92	Generally the same rates or 1.5%–3.5% lower
59–64	Almost no difference	93–100 ...	1.8%–5.2% lower rates
65–80	1.5%–4.5% lower rates under 1979–81 Table	101–109 ...	6.3%–23% lower rates
81–96	Almost no difference		
97–109	A steadily increasing reduction in mortality from 1.5% to 18.9%		

TABLE 10

COMPARISON OF $1000q_x$ VALUES
UNDER THE 1987 LIFE TABLE
WITH THE VITAL STATISTICS
OF THE UNITED STATES 1982 TABLE
AT QUINQUENNIAL AGES

Age	1987 Life Table	
	Male Ratio	Female Ratio
0	0.903	0.916
5	0.875	0.800
10	0.857	1.000
15	0.989	0.973
20	1.000	0.963
25	1.063	0.983
30	0.972	0.901
35	0.916	0.821
40	0.945	0.906
45	0.932	0.931
50	0.948	0.917
55	0.914	0.920
60	0.909	0.946
65	0.965	0.960
70	0.978	0.932
75	0.971	0.904
80	0.956	0.906
84	0.972	0.871

This can be seen more clearly by comparing values of $1000q_x$ under the 1980 Life Table projected two years to 1982 using the mortality improvement rates (MIR) over the period 1980–1990 determined by the formula

$$\text{MIR} = 1 - \left[\frac{1990 \text{ Life Table } 1000q_x \text{ Value}}{1980 \text{ Life Table } 1000q_x \text{ Value}} \right]^{1/10}$$

with values of $1000q_x$ under the Vital Statistics of the United States 1982 Table.

Table 11 shows the $1000q_x$ values under these tables and their ratios. Mortality rates for females at central ages 52 or older are almost identical, with variations of 2–5 percent for younger central ages. Males show variations in rates of 0–4 percent at central ages 52 or older and 0–11 percent at younger central ages.

TABLE 11

Comparison of 1980 Life Table Values of $1000q_x$ Projected to 1982
Using the Mortality Improvement Rate over the Period 1980 to 1990
with $1000q_x$ Values from the Vital Statistics of the United States 1982 Table

Central Age	Males			Females		
	1980 Life Table Projected to 1982	Vital Stat. of the U.S. 1982 Table	Ratio Vital Stat. 1982 Table to Projected 1982 L.T.	1980 Life Table Projected to 1982	Vital Stat. of the U.S. 1982 Table	Ratio Vital Stat. 1982 Table to Projected 1982 L.T.
2....	0.72	0.66	0.917	0.53	0.56	1.057
7....	0.32	0.34	1.063	0.24	0.22	0.917
12....	0.29	0.27	0.931	0.20	0.19	0.950
17....	1.44	1.30	0.903	0.51	0.49	0.961
22....	1.97	1.76	0.893	0.59	0.56	0.949
27....	1.95	1.73	0.887	0.67	0.62	0.925
32....	1.87	1.87	1.000	0.77	0.79	1.026
37....	2.31	2.21	0.957	1.07	1.11	1.037
42....	3.47	3.27	0.942	1.91	1.81	0.948
47....	5.60	5.40	0.964	3.06	2.98	0.974
52....	9.23	8.86	0.960	4.74	4.74	1.000
57....	13.96	13.73	0.984	7.25	7.24	0.999
62....	21.09	20.92	0.992	11.03	11.02	0.999
67....	33.63	32.12	0.955	16.92	16.72	0.988
72....	49.06	47.03	0.959	25.32	25.19	0.995
77....	72.02	69.65	0.967	39.84	39.66	0.995
82....	103.74	101.22	0.996	65.65	65.10	0.992

Of great import is the fact that when these MIR values are applied to the 1980 Life Table to project a 1987 Life Table, thus establishing a connection between the 1980 Life Table, Vital Statistics of the United States 1982 Table and 1987 Life Table, the resulting mortality rates are very close to the linearly interpolated 1987 Life Table values shown in Table 8. Our linearly interpolated morality rates are always higher. Simplicity of calculation, in this case, has not sacrificed accuracy in the resulting rates, although they could have been somewhat more conservative from a pricing viewpoint.

The appropriateness of mortality rates in the 1987 Life Table for advanced ages is confirmed in that the projected mortality experience shown under the 1987 Life Table for ages 66 and older, which reflects expected improvements since 1980, is consistent with the graduated Medicare probabilities of death within one year developed by Wilkin in his 1981 paper "Recent Trends in the Mortality of the Aged" [22]. His tables are based on Medicare data covering the period 1968–78 and present separate mortality scales for each year from 1968 to 1978 (preliminary figures only for 1978).

Table 12 shows a comparison of Wilkin's rates for 1977 with the 1987 Life Table rates, together with the average annual percentage decline over the period 1968–1978 shown in Wilkin's paper and the 1987 Medicare experience mortality rates that would have emerged if his rate of decline continued from 1968–1978 until 1987. Because Wilkin's mortality rates are presented at half-ages, for example, 65.5, 66.5, and so on, we used straight-line interpolation to determine his mortality rates at exact ages, 66, 67, and so on.

TABLE 12

COMPARISON OF MORTALITY RATES
1977 MEDICARE EXPERIENCE VS. 1987 LIFE TABLE

| Age | Medicare Experience | | | $1000q_x$ 1987 Life Table | Ratio Life Tables to Medicare Experience Table 1987 |
	1977 $1000q_x$ Mortality Rate	Average Annual Percent Decline 1968–1978	Projected $1000q_x$ Mortality Rate to 1987		
			Males		
66...........	32.22	1.525%	27.63	28.93	104.7%
71...........	47.76	1.465	41.21	42.66	103.5
76...........	69.57	1.355	60.70	62.48	102.9
81...........	99.86	1.495	85.90	89.67	104.4
86...........	145.06	1.480	124.97	133.69	107.0
91...........	204.39	1.410	177.33	189.03	106.6
96...........	251.94	1.605	214.30	255.56	119.3
			Females		
66...........	15.48	1.460%	13.36	14.80	110.8%
71...........	23.86	2.090	19.32	21.49	111.2
76...........	38.22	2.535	29.57	32.64	110.4
81...........	63.27	2.635	48.44	53.01	109.4
86...........	104.20	2.390	81.81	87.68	107.2
91...........	163.01	1.890	134.69	145.08	107.7
96...........	221.97	1.800	185.10	223.51	120.8

Obviously, we would not expect a projected mortality improvement rate under Medicare experience to operate accurately over a period of almost 20 years. A ratio of approximately 104 percent for males and 109 percent for females, at ages 66–91, when comparing the Life Table for 1987 with projected Medicare mortality rates during these years, nevertheless tends to confirm the agreement in resulting morality rates between these tables. Therefore, we can assume that the projected 1987 Life Table represents current mortality experience of the U.S. population. Ratios of 119–121 percent at age 96 may be the result of a paucity of Medicare data at such advanced age. This does not detract from the overall conclusion reached above.

IV. THE EFFECT OF MORTALITY ON ANNUITY PRICING

Traditional Annuities

An insurer's gain or loss from mortality over the lifetime of a block of nonparticipating immediate annuity issues is locked in at the time of issue. Interest earnings and expenses each contribute their share of the gain or loss as the block of issues ages over time, but can be affected by an insurer's actions over this period. This paper explores the contribution of mortality alone toward the gain or loss on blocks of fixed single-premium, single life immediate annuities that have been issued by a large insurer over the period 1966–1986 inclusive. Such exploration uses historical rates of longevity as well as the projection of such rates into the future, which have been discussed in previous sections. The financial effect of mortality rate variations is then determined.

Theoretically, we would want data from the new annuity issues of each issue year showing date of issue, plan, sex, issue age, modal income, state of issue, and gross single premium. Knowing the date and state of issue generally fixes the rate scale applicable in calculating the gross premium and the rate of any premium tax. One could calculate a "mortality gross premium" by eliminating the expense element, policy fee, and premium tax and assuming the pricing interest rates. Thus, the mortality gross premium equals the present value of benefits discounted at the gross premium pricing scale mortality and interest rates.

What if mortality rates vary from the rates assumed in pricing? If we knew the survival rates experienced each year for all lives in the block of issues, by historical analysis and by assumption of projected mortality from the present we could determine the present value of benefits discounted at the gross premium pricing scale interest rates and the "experience" (at least to the present, and then projected) mortality rates. When subtracted from the present value of benefits under the gross premium mortality pricing basis, such value indicates the gain or loss arising from mortality.

Gains or losses from mortality could be analyzed for specific calendar-year periods or for specific contract durations, if such amounts are significant in the aggregate, by calculating the difference between appropriate portions of the two premiums described above over the periods selected. The effect of variations in assumed experience mortality rates on the mortality gross premium could be calculated for the issue-year blocks. We explore the effect of two sets of experience mortality rate assumptions on such blocks.

As a practical matter, a less-than-optimum amount of the theoretically desirable new annuity issues data was available from this company for the period 1966–1986. This thwarts the idea of data consistency whereby, for example, gross premiums are reasonably related to the annual income benefits for a plan-sex-age cell. The data available were therefore adjusted to eliminate inconsistencies.

The result was plan-sex-age data with premiums consistent with the applicable pricing rate scale and annual income benefits purchased. As a result of the modifications and adjustments, the issue-year data blocks represent a generalized model for the following analyses of the effects of mortality on annuity pricing.

Table A in Appendix I shows the idealized plan-sex-age grouping data of number of contracts, annual income, and adjusted gross single premiums by issue year that make up the model. This table also shows the mortality gross premium at issue corresponding to the adjusted gross single premium at issue. Table B shows the actuarial assumptions for mortality and interest applicable by issue year used to calculate mortality gross premiums. These assumptions, combined with expense assumptions, also are used to calculate adjusted gross premiums for each issue-year block.

We know the attained-age mortality rates assumed to be in effect during any issue year. They are expressed by the pricing mortality table used to calculate the mortality gross premiums for that issue year. A snapshot of attained-age mortality rates that can be assumed to be in effect during 1973 and 1983 is provided by the 1973 Experience Table and 1983 Basic Table mortality rates, some of which are shown in Table 3. Of course, these two tables can be replaced by other experience tables developed by individual companies whose actual annuity mortality experience deviates in a sufficient degree from the intercompany experience. Whichever tables are used, their corresponding rates at any attained age can be used to calculate a yearly mortality improvement factor. These factors, when applied to the preceding table mortality rates, generate a set of mortality tables for each intervening year. Yearly mortality rates for any sex-specific issue age can then be taken as those mortality rates along the diagonal of rates when age and year are advanced one at a time. In this way, any sex-distinct issue age for any issue year is assigned a string of mortality rates from issue.

An example will clarify the principle involved. Consider a 1970 issue to a male age 45. The rates from ages 45–65 under the 1969 Company Modified Annuity Table, the 1973 Experience Table, and the 1983 Basic Table are shown in Table 13.

TABLE 13

Male $1000q_x$ Values under Various Annuity Tables

Attained Age	(1) 1969 Co. Mod. Annuity*	(2) 1973 Experience	(3) 1983 Basic	Mortality Improvement Rates	
				(4) 1973/1969†	(5) 1983/1973‡
45	3.625	3.289	2.657	3.190%	2.111%
46	4.116	3.709	2.988	3.411	2.138
47	4.657	4.155	3.343	3.731	2.151
48	5.246	4.622	3.718	4.133	2.153
49	5.880	5.107	4.110	4.589	2.148
50	6.557	5.613	4.518	5.050	2.147
51	7.111	6.138	4.938	4.786	2.152
52	7.676	6.684	5.370	4.508	2.165
53	8.250	7.250	5.811	4.216	2.188
54	8.829	7.831	6.260	3.920	2.214
55	9.415	8.420	6.718	3.655	2.233
56	10.240	9.012	7.184	4.169	2.242
57	11.103	9.601	7.658	4.729	2.236
58	12.009	10.188	8.146	5.334	2.212
59	12.959	10.810	8.671	5.865	2.181
60	13.957	11.511	9.266	6.221	2.146
61	15.032	12.336	9.961	6.376	2.116
62	16.217	13.328	10.787	6.331	2.093
63	17.525	14.527	11.769	6.062	2.083
64	18.965	15.951	12.920	5.606	2.085
65	20.554	17.610	14.248	5.022	2.096

*Developed by the large company.
†For the period 1970–1973.
‡For the period 1973–1983.

The mortality improvement rates (MIR), also shown in Table 13, were calculated for 1970 issues at each attained age X by using the formulas:

$$\text{MIR} = 1 - \left[\frac{1973 \text{ Table } q_x}{1969 \text{ Table } q_x}\right]^{1/3}$$

and

$$\text{MIR} = 1 - \left[\frac{1983 \text{ Table } q_x}{1973 \text{ Table } q_x} \right]^{1/10}$$

based upon the number of years involved between the tables. Note that this produces a different set of MIR factors by issue year even though the pricing mortality table may not have changed. Thus, a 1969 issue would require an exponent of 1/4 in the first formula and retain an exponent of 1/10 in the second formula. This is consistent with the actuarial pricing assumption that the same mortality table represents current mortality over several issue years. Blending, after issue, into the 1973 or 1983 tables therefore would occur at a faster pace by modifying the exponent as described above.

Applying the MIR factors to the mortality rates shown in columns (1) and (2) of Table 13 produces the mortality tables for years 1970–1983 shown in Table 14. The string of mortality rates covering years 1970–1983 for our 45-year-old male therefore would be taken as those rates shown for age 45 in 1970, age 46 in 1971, age 47 in 1972, until age 58 in 1983, that is, 3.625, 3.976, 4.316, until 8.146.

Future mortality rates beyond 1983 would be determined by a table of projection factors applied to the mortality rates determined to be extant in 1983. For our study of the 1966–1986 issue blocks, we have assumed Projection Scale I and Projection Scale J from Table 7 to represent rates of mortality improvement beyond the year 1983. Table A in Appendix I shows the mortality gross premiums calculated under both these projection scales.

Out of all the issue-year block plan-sex cells in Table A, only two cells show mortality gross premiums based upon a projection scale to be less than the mortality gross premium at issue. Issue years 1966–1979 show, for each issue year, projection scale-based mortality gross premiums for all plan-sex cells combined that exceed the mortality gross premiums at issue by 2.71 percent to 4.85 percent under Projection Scale I and by 2.83 percent to 4.93 percent under Projection Scale J. Plan-sex cells for issue years 1980–1986 show that projection scale-based mortality gross premiums are no more than 1.03 percent greater than the mortality gross premiums at issue. Details by issue year are shown in Table 15, which is an extract from the data of Table A in Appendix I. These results for issue years 1966–1979 are significant and indicate that original pricing did not adequately account for mortality improvement according to the combination of assumptions inherent in the 1973 and 1983 experience mortality tables and in Projection Scales I and J. Thus, unless a company with such a mix of issues consistently maintains an

TABLE 14

Specimen $1000q_x$ Mortality Rates for Issue Year 1970

Attained Age	1970	1971	1972	1973	1974	1975	1976	1977	1978	1979	1980	1981	1982	1983
45	3.625	3.509	3.397	3.289	3.220	3.152	3.085	3.020	2.956	2.894	2.833	2.773	2.714	2.657
46	4.116	3.976	3.840	3.709	3.630	3.552	3.476	3.402	3.329	3.258	3.188	3.120	3.053	2.988
47	4.657	4.483	4.316	4.155	4.066	3.978	3.893	3.809	3.727	3.647	3.568	3.492	3.416	3.343
48	5.246	5.029	4.821	4.622	4.522	4.425	4.330	4.237	4.145	4.056	3.969	3.883	3.800	3.718
49	5.880	5.610	5.353	5.107	4.997	4.890	4.785	4.682	4.581	4.483	4.387	4.292	4.200	4.110
50	6.557	6.226	5.912	5.613	5.493	5.375	5.259	5.146	5.036	4.928	4.822	4.718	4.617	4.518
51	7.111	6.771	6.447	6.138	6.006	5.877	5.750	5.626	5.505	5.387	5.271	5.158	5.047	4.938
52	7.676	7.330	7.000	6.684	6.539	6.398	6.259	6.124	5.991	5.861	5.734	5.610	5.489	5.370
53	8.250	7.902	7.569	7.250	7.091	6.936	6.784	6.636	6.491	6.349	6.210	6.074	5.941	5.811
54	8.829	8.483	8.150	7.831	7.658	7.488	7.322	7.160	7.002	6.847	6.695	6.547	6.402	6.260
55	9.415	9.071	8.739	8.420	8.232	8.048	7.868	7.693	7.521	7.353	7.189	7.028	6.871	6.718
56	10.240	9.813	9.404	9.012	8.810	8.613	8.419	8.231	8.046	7.866	7.690	7.517	7.349	7.184
57	11.103	10.578	10.078	9.601	9.386	9.176	8.971	8.771	8.575	8.383	8.196	8.012	7.833	7.658
58	12.009	11.368	10.762	10.188	9.963	9.742	9.527	9.316	9.110	8.908	8.711	8.519	8.330	8.146

actual-to-expected mortality ratio relative to intercompany mortality of much more than 100 percent, its expected profits will be spent to provide unanticipated benefits to surviving annuitants.

TABLE 15

COMPARISON OF MORTALITY GROSS PREMIUMS
BASED ON PROJECTION SCALES I AND J
WITH SUCH PREMIUMS CHARGED AT ISSUE
TOTAL ALL ISSUES IN ALTERNATE ISSUE YEARS

Issue Year	Mortality Table Year*	(1) Mortality Gross Premium at Issue	(2) Mortality Gross Premium Projection I	(3) Mortality Gross Premium Projection J	(4) Ratio (2)/(1)	(5) Ratio (3)/(1)
1966.....	1965	19,573,461	20,351,457	20,361,920	1.0397	1.0403
1968.....	1965	23,956,252	25,041,288	25,063,669	1.0453	1.0462
1970.....	1969	17,710,693	18,286,843	18,302,070	1.0325	1.0334
1972.....	1969	21,790,082	22,577,135	22,600,281	1.0361	1.0372
1974.....	1974	18,193,370	18,740,831	18,771,039	1.0301	1.0318
1976.....	1974	24,979,968	25,822,745	25,865,913	1.0337	1.0355
1978.....	1974	19,901,731	20,569,055	20,607,095	1.0335	1.0354
1980.....	1979	7,827,423	7,895,868	7,907,867	1.0087	1.0103
1982.....	1981	16,509,576	16,549,083	16,581,833	1.0024	1.0044
1984.....	1981	19,354,998	19,501,118	19,543,675	1.0075	1.0097
1986.....	1981	21,531,495	21,703,278	21,749,738	1.0080	1.0101

*Year of Company Modified Annuity Table used in pricing.

Projection Scale J is apparently similar in its effect on annuity pricing, based upon the issue blocks studied, to Projection Scale I. No meaningful conclusions would be reached under Projection Scale J results that would not be reached by utilizing Projection Scale I results. Note, however, that this result is a function of the distribution of issues within attained-age cells. The bulk of issues in our model are at ages 60–80.

Mortality improvement at attained ages over 80 for issues at ages 60–80 is not as significant as that for attained ages at issue of 50–70, for example. Tables C and D of Appendix I show details at the issue age level that produce the data summarized in Table A. As stated previously, a substitute scale for Projection Scale J, for example, could be utilized in the derivation of mortality gross premiums that show significantly different results from the mortality gross premiums derived under a Projection Scale I assumption. Such an exercise may answer the question, "What degree of mortality improvement, by age bands, produces a meaningful change in mortality gross premiums when compared to Projection Scale I mortality gross premiums?"

The mortality gross premium ratios shown in Table 15, by virtue of their saw-tooth progression, illustrate the effect on pricing of the static mortality table assumption. Use of a static 1965 Company Modified Annuity Table assumption for mortality in pricing during each year from 1966 to 1969 does not adequately recognize mortality improvement. The variance between assumed and actually emerging mortality, according to intercompany mortality experience, becomes greater with each passing year that the 1965 Table is used in pricing. When the 1969 Table is introduced in 1970, the mortality gross premiums for 1970 include provision for that portion of emerging improvement in longevity as is provided for in the static 1969 Table, which will also turn out to be inadequate with the passage of time. A similar situation emerges during the issue-years 1971–1973, with slight exception for 1973, as well as during the issue years of 1975–1979 following the introduction of the 1974 Table in 1974, with exceptions for issue years 1977–1979. Note from Table C of Appendix I that the majority of annual income issued by attained age for all plan-sex cells has shifted to the 70–89 age group for issue years 1977–1979 from the 60–79 age group in prior issue years. The effect on pricing of mortality improvement at attained ages over 80 is less pronounced than for younger attained ages, as previously noted.

Mortality gross premiums for issue years 1980–1986 from Table 15, assuming Projection Scales I or J, are only slightly higher than the corresponding mortality gross premiums at issue. This is because introduction of the static 1979 Table in 1980, and then the static 1981 Table in 1982, contains enough margin to anticipate the mortality improvements inherent in Projection Scales I and J. Table 16 compares male mortality rates at issue age 65 for a 1969 issue and a 1982 issue. The 1969 issue is based upon the static 1965 Table for pricing, and mortality improvement is based upon the 1973 Table, 1983 Table and Projection Scale I. The 1982 issue is based upon the static 1981 Table for pricing, and mortality improvement is based upon the 1983 Table and Projection Scale I.

The proportion that the difference in mortality rates for the 1969 issue bears to the static attained-age rate increases steadily, reaching almost 31 percent of the static rate at age 92. The comparable proportions under the 1982 issue are lower for each attained age except age 66, turn negative at attained ages 83–87, and reach a maximum of 12.4 percent at age 92. Comparisons at other issue ages for issue years prior to 1980 would yield results similar to those shown in Table 16, because the curve of static 1981 table mortality rates is not always higher than the curve of projected mortality

TABLE 16

COMPARISON OF $1000q_x$ VALUES
UNDER STATIC AND MORTALITY IMPROVEMENT BASES
STARTING AT MALE AGE 65
FOR AN ISSUE OF 1969 AND AN ISSUE OF 1982
SHOWING THE PROPORTION THAT THE DIFFERENCE IN RATES
BEARS TO THE ATTAINED AGE STATIC RATE

| | 1969 Issue | | | 1982 Issue | | |
Attained Age	1965 Table	Projection Scale I	Proportion	1981 Table	Projection Scale I	Proportion
65...........	21.182	21.182	0	15.490	15.490	0
68...........	27.161	24.842	0.08538	19.837	18.758	0.05439
71...........	35.146	31.466	0.10471	25.904	24.497	0.05432
74...........	45.780	39.322	0.14107	34.240	31.622	0.07646
77...........	59.889	49.120	0.17982	44.331	41.056	0.07388
80...........	78.519	62.248	0.20722	56.847	54.830	0.03548
83...........	102.955	79.610	0.22675	72.200	73.153	−0.01320
86...........	134.052	100.046	0.25368	92.671	95.903	−0.03488
89...........	172.052	121.773	0.29223	125.388	121.773	0.02883
92...........	219.297	151.517	0.30908	173.019	151.517	0.12428

rates, but rather remains close to or comes below the latter curve at some attained-age groups.

Tables 17 and 18 compare the ratios of mortality gross premiums based on Projection Scales I and J with such premiums charged at issue, separately by plan and sex, so that any variations from or similarities to the ratios shown in Table 15 for all issues combined, as well as separately by sex and by plan, can be noted.

TABLE 17

MORTALITY GROSS PREMIUM RATIOS DERIVED
BY COMPARING SUCH PREMIUMS BASED ON PROJECTION SCALE I
WITH SUCH PREMIUMS CHARGED AT ISSUE

Issue Year	Mortality Table Year	Life Only M and F Combined	10 CC Only M and F Combined	Males Only Life and 10 CC Combined	Females Only Life and 10 CC Combined	All Plans for M and F Combined
1966........	1965	1.0481	1.0361	1.0320	1.0462	1.0397
1968........	1965	1.0551	1.0416	1.0374	1.0499	1.0453
1970........	1969	1.0250	1.0353	1.0260	1.0370	1.0325
1972........	1969	1.0271	1.0385	1.0327	1.0387	1.0361
1974........	1974	1.0256	1.0314	1.0293	1.0307	1.0301
1976........	1974	1.0290	1.0351	1.0346	1.0328	1.0337
1978........	1974	1.0293	1.0350	1.0296	1.0373	1.0335
1980........	1979	1.0044	1.0096	1.0156	1.0021	1.0087
1982........	1981	0.9967	1.0037	1.0004	1.0043	1.0024
1984........	1981	1.0094	1.0072	1.0072	1.0079	1.0075
1986........	1981	1.0118	1.0073	1.0064	1.0090	1.0080

TABLE 18

MORTALITY GROSS PREMIUM RATIOS DERIVED
BY COMPARING SUCH PREMIUMS BASED ON PROJECTION SCALE J
WITH SUCH PREMIUMS CHARGED AT ISSUE

Issue Year	Mortality Table Year	Life Only M and F Combined	10 CC Only M and F Combined	Males Only Life and 10 CC Combined	Females Only Life and 10 CC Combined	All Plans for M and F Combined
1966	1965	1.0490	1.0365	1.0323	1.0469	1.0403
1968	1965	1.0562	1.0425	1.0376	1.0513	1.0462
1970	1969	1.0261	1.0361	1.0265	1.0382	1.0334
1972	1969	1.0283	1.0395	1.0333	1.0401	1.0372
1974	1974	1.0270	1.0331	1.0300	1.0329	1.0318
1976	1974	1.0310	1.0368	1.0357	1.0353	1.0355
1978	1974	1.0317	1.0368	1.0306	1.0402	1.0354
1980	1979	1.0066	1.0110	1.0163	1.0045	1.0103
1982	1981	0.9992	1.0056	1.0017	1.0070	1.0044
1984	1981	1.0128	1.0092	1.0084	1.0110	1.0097
1986	1981	1.0156	1.0092	1.0075	1.0119	1.0101

Life only ratios would be expected to be greater than 10-CC plan ratios because of the accounting for mortality improvement during contract years 1–10. This holds true in Table 17, however, only for issue years 1966–1969 and 1983–1986. Reference to Table C of Appendix I shows that the company has applied age setbacks in the pricing of life only annuities at ages 65 or older during issue years 1970–1979. This anticipation of mortality improvement for life only annuities causes the ratios for a 10-CC plan to exceed those required for a life only annuity, because part of the Projection Scale improved longevity is already included in the static mortality rates used in pricing. The average ratios for years 1980–1986 are so close that differences in central issue ages within the life only and 10-CC plan, coupled with the proximity and intertwining of the mortality curve based upon mortality improvement to the static 1979 and 1981 tables pricing mortality curves, cause the relationship between the life only ratio and the 10-CC ratio to alternate positions between issue years 1980–1982 and 1983–1986.

When life and 10-CC plans are combined, male only ratios would be expected to be lower than the ratios for these plans issued to females, because the Projection Scale I and J factors are so much greater for females. Indeed, except for issue years 1975, 1976, 1980, and 1981, this is the case, as shown in Table 17, thus reflecting the greater mortality improvement for females in proportionately larger mortality gross premiums relative to those premiums at issue than would be required for males. These exception years arise also because of the close interplay between central issue ages and the relationship of the static mortality and projection mortality curves.

From a historical perspective, we can conclude that the profits anticipated on the issue blocks of 1966–1979 have been ephemeral, if annuity mortality experience is similar to the results shown in intercompany experience studies. Use of a static mortality table assumption over a period of time erodes the profits inherent in pricing when there is meaningful improvement in longevity.

The issues of 1980–1986 also show encroachment on anticipated profit margins but not to the degree as that emerging for prior years' issues, only because mortality improvement has not been as dramatic relative to the modifications of the 1971 IAM table adopted by the company and because these recent issue years have not experienced the mortality improvement evidenced in prior years. Will such improvement come about? History can repeat itself. But nonparticipating fixed-income annuities already issued cannot be modified to counter any emerging mortality improvement.

The picture is clear: Mortality improvement must be anticipated to an even greater degree for nonparticipating fixed-income annuities than has been assumed in the past, with limited anticipation of the effects of the AIDS epidemic. To what degree is up to the judgment of the company.

Structured Settlement Annuities

Our analysis of traditional annuities has shown how significant the mortality contribution can be to gains and losses. The mortality effects on pricing structured settlement annuities are even more crucial because of the competitiveness of this marketplace. Margins are squeezed because of the open competitiveness generated by the brokers selling these annuities. Usually, the carrier with the lowest price is awarded the contract as long as that insurer is rated A or better by the A.M. Best Company. Mortality contributions to gains therefore must be reasonable, and investment bailouts should not be expected.

Mortality improvement must be anticipated in pricing structured settlement annuities for the same reasons as traditional annuities. The projected mortality rates of the U.S. population for each decade from 1990 to 2050, as shown in *Actuarial Study No. 87*, show that marked reductions in mortality are expected in the next 20 years, with a slower rate of improvement thereafter. This can be seen from an excerpt of $1000q_x$ values from these tables, as shown in Table 19.

TABLE 19

COMPARISON OF $1000q_x$
UNDER LIFE TABLES FOR THE U.S.: 1980–2050

Calendar Year	1000q_x at Age					
	0	20	40	60	80	100
Males						
1980	14.04	1.90	3.04	18.52	91.99	329.11
1990	10.49	1.49	2.41	15.05	79.70	292.16
2000	9.85	1.38	2.09	13.55	74.65	266.42
2010	9.31	1.36	2.02	13.00	71.52	252.90
2020	8.81	1.36	1.97	12.50	68.58	240.72
2030	8.34	1.35	1.93	12.02	65.82	229.23
2040	7.90	1.35	1.88	11.58	63.21	218.40
2050	7.50	1.34	1.84	11.15	60.75	208.18
Females						
1980	11.22	0.58	1.61	9.52	56.15	297.13
1990	8.57	0.49	1.24	8.54	44.32	270.51
2000	7.92	0.48	1.06	8.03	39.06	247.41
2010	7.46	0.48	1.02	7.72	36.95	233.36
2020	7.03	0.48	0.99	7.42	35.05	220.61
2030	6.64	0.47	0.96	7.13	33.26	208.60
2040	6.27	0.47	0.93	6.86	31.58	197.28
2050	5.93	0.47	0.91	6.60	30.00	186.62

The effect of pricing structured settlement annuities under a current static mortality table, as opposed to using mortality tables that anticipate mortality improvement, is shown in Table 20. To create the tables that assume mortality improvement, we first took the 1980, 1990, and 2000 Life Tables by sex shown in *Actuarial Study No. 87* and derived MIR factors at each attained age x, separately for males and females, by using the formulas:

$$ \text{MIR} = 1 - \left[\frac{\text{'1980 + t' Life Table } q_x}{\text{'1980 + s' Life Table } q_x} \right]^{1/10} $$

where t = 10, 20 and s = 0, 10. MIR values were applied to the respective life tables to produce life tables for each year from 1980 to 1990 and from 1990 to 2000.

Development of a 1987 gross premium scale based upon mortality improvement would assume that mortality rates for a given issue age and sex would be equal to those selected from the life tables of 1980 to 2000, starting with the $1000q_x$ value at the issue age selected in the 1987 Life Table for the appropriate sex and proceeding for successive year $1000q_x$ values by advancing one age and life table at a time for each value selected. For female

TABLE 20

COMPARISON OF STRUCTURED SETTLEMENT
MORTALITY GROSS PREMIUMS
UNDER VARIOUS MORTALITY TABLE ASSUMPTIONS

Issue Age	1980 Life Table	1987 Life Table	1992 Life Table	1997 Life Table	Mortality Improvement		
					1987–2000	1987–2010	1987–2020
Life Annuity—Male							
0	141,000	141,600	141,900	142,100	141,900	141,900	141,900
20	138,000	138,700	139,100	139,300	139,300	139,400	139,500
40	126,400	127,900	128,700	129,200	129,200	129,400	129,500
60	97,000	99,400	100,800	101,700	101,100	101,300	101,300
80	54,700	57,400	59,000	60,000	58,700	58,700	58,700
Life Annuity—Female							
0	142,500	142,900	143,100	143,200	143,000	143,100	143,100
20	141,300	141,700	141,900	142,000	142,100	142,100	142,200
40	132,500	133,500	134,100	134,400	134,400	134,600	134,700
60	109,900	111,900	113,000	113,800	113,800	114,000	114,100
80	65,600	69,900	72,400	74,000	72,200	72,200	72,200
10-Year Certain and Life Annuity—Male							
0	142,200	142,600	142,800	142,900	142,800	142,800	142,900
20	138,700	139,300	139,600	139,800	139,800	139,900	140,000
40	127,700	129,000	129,700	130,100	130,200	130,400	130,500
60	104,600	106,200	107,200	107,800	107,700	107,800	107,900
80	83,700	84,500	85,000	85,400	85,200	85,200	85,200
10-Year Certain and Life Annuity—Female							
0	143,400	143,700	143,800	143,900	143,800	143,800	143,800
20	141,500	141,800	142,000	142,100	142,200	142,300	142,300
40	133,200	134,100	134,600	134,900	135,000	135,100	135,300
60	113,900	115,600	116,600	117,300	117,400	117,700	117,700
80	86,700	88,300	89,300	90,000	89,700	89,700	89,700
20-Year Certain and Life Annuity—Male							
0	142,800	143,100	143,300	143,400	143,400	143,400	143,400
20	139,600	140,100	140,400	140,500	140,600	140,700	140,800
40	130,600	131,500	132,000	132,300	132,500	132,700	132,800
60	118,100	118,800	119,100	119,400	119,400	119,600	119,600
80	114,000	114,100	114,100	114,100	114,100	114,200	114,200
20-Year Certain and Life Annuity—Female							
0	143,900	144,100	144,200	144,200	144,200	144,200	144,200
20	141,800	142,100	142,300	142,400	142,400	142,500	142,600
40	134,800	135,500	135,900	136,100	136,200	136,400	136,500
60	121,800	122,800	123,500	123,900	124,100	124,300	124,400
80	114,100	114,200	114,300	114,400	114,400	114,400	114,400

TABLE 20 — *Continued*

Issue Age	1980 Life Table	1987 Life Table	1992 Life Table	1997 Life Table	Mortality Improvement		
					1987–2000	1987–2010	1987–2020
Life Annuity with Annual 3 Percent Cost-of-Living Adjustment—Male							
0	223,800	225,600	226,400	226,900	226,700	227,000	227,200
20	208,000	210,100	211,200	211,900	212,100	212,600	213,000
40	174,800	178,200	180,000	181,200	181,400	182,000	182,400
60	119,800	123,800	126,000	127,500	126,800	127,200	127,300
80	60,700	64,100	66,100	67,500	65,900	65,900	65,900
Life Annuity with Annual 3 Percent Cost of Living Adjustment—Female							
0	229,600	230,900	231,600	231,900	231,800	232,000	232,200
20	218,000	219,500	220,400	220,900	221,200	221,600	222,000
40	189,700	192,300	193,800	194,800	195,000	195,700	196,200
60	141,100	144,900	147,200	148,600	148,900	149,500	149,800
80	74,300	79,900	83,100	85,300	83,100	83,200	83,200
10-Year Certain and Life Annuity with Annual 3 Percent Cost-of-Living Adjustment—Male							
0	225,100	226,700	227,400	227,900	227,800	228,100	228,300
20	208,800	210,800	211,900	212,600	212,800	213,300	213,600
40	176,400	179,500	181,300	182,400	182,600	183,300	183,700
60	129,000	131,900	133,700	134,800	134,700	135,100	135,200
80	95,000	96,100	96,900	97,400	97,200	97,200	97,200
10-Year Certain and Life Annuity with Annual 3 Percent Cost-of-Living Adjustment—Female							
0	230,700	231,800	232,400	232,700	232,700	232,900	233,100
20	218,300	219,700	220,600	221,100	221,400	221,800	222,100
40	190,600	193,100	194,500	195,400	195,700	196,400	196,900
60	145,900	149,400	151,500	152,800	153,200	153,900	154,200
80	99,300	101,700	103,200	104,400	103,900	104,000	104,000
20-Year Certain and Life Annuity with Annual 3 Percent Cost-of-Living Adjustment—Male							
0	226,200	227,500	228,200	228,600	228,700	228,900	229,100
20	210,200	212,100	213,100	213,700	214,000	214,500	214,800
40	181,100	183,600	185,000	185,800	186,200	186,800	187,200
60	150,000	151,400	152,300	152,900	153,000	153,400	153,500
80	141,300	141,400	141,400	141,500	141,500	141,500	141,500
20-Year Certain and Life Annuity with Annual 3 Percent Cost-of-Living Adjustment—Female							
0	231,500	232,500	233,000	233,300	233,300	233,500	233,700
20	218,800	220,200	221,000	221,500	221,800	222,200	222,500
40	193,100	195,200	196,500	197,300	197,700	198,400	198,900
60	158,200	160,700	162,200	163,200	163,600	164,300	164,500
80	141,500	141,700	141,800	141,900	142,000	142,000	142,000

TABLE 20 — *Continued*

Issue Age	1980 Life Table	1987 Life Table	1992 Life Table	1997 Life Table	Mortality Improvement 1987–2000	Mortality Improvement 1987–2010	Mortality Improvement 1987–2020
Life Annuity with Annual 5 Percent Cost-of-Living Adjustment—Male							
0..........	351,300	356,100	358,600	360,000	360,100	361,100	362,000
20..........	301,400	306,500	309,300	311,000	311,800	313,100	314,300
40..........	229,400	235,500	238,900	241,100	241,600	243,100	244,100
60..........	141,200	146,800	150,000	152,100	151,400	152,100	152,300
80..........	65,400	69,400	71,800	73,400	71,600	71,700	71,700
Life Annuity with Annual 5 Percent Cost-of-Living Adjustment—Female							
0..........	370,200	374,100	376,200	377,500	377,600	378,600	379,500
20..........	326,100	330,300	332,700	334,300	335,200	336,600	337,800
40..........	257,900	263,400	266,500	268,700	269,400	271,100	272,400
60..........	171,800	178,000	181,600	184,000	184,600	185,900	186,400
80..........	81,300	88,000	91,900	94,600	92,100	92,300	92,300
10-Year Certain and Life Annuity with Annual 5 Percent Cost-of-Living Adjustment—Male							
0..........	352,800	357,300	359,700	361,100	361,400	362,300	363,200
20..........	302,300	307,300	310,000	311,700	312,500	313,900	315,000
40..........	231,200	237,000	240,300	242,400	243,100	244,600	245,500
60..........	151,500	156,000	158,600	160,400	160,300	161,000	161,200
80..........	103,700	105,200	106,200	106,900	106,600	106,700	106,700
10-Year Certain and Life Annuity with Annual 5 Percent Cost-of-Living Adjustment—Female							
0..........	371,400	375,100	377,100	378,300	378,600	379,600	380,500
20..........	326,300	330,500	332,900	334,500	335,400	336,800	338,100
40..........	258,900	264,200	267,300	269,400	270,200	271,900	273,200
60..........	177,200	183,000	186,400	188,700	189,500	190,800	191,300
80..........	109,300	112,500	114,500	116,000	115,400	115,600	115,600
20-Year Certain and Life Annuity with Annual 5 Percent Cost-of-Living Adjustment—Male							
0..........	354,500	358,800	361,100	362,400	362,800	363,800	364,700
20..........	304,600	309,400	312,000	313,700	314,500	315,800	317,000
40..........	237,800	242,800	245,700	247,500	248,300	249,700	250,700
60..........	180,200	182,700	184,200	185,200	185,400	186,100	186,300
80..........	165,900	166,000	166,100	166,100	166,200	166,200	166,200
20-Year Certain and Life Annuity with Annual 5 Percent Cost-of-Living Adjustment—Female							
0..........	372,800	376,300	378,200	379,400	379,800	380,800	381,700
20..........	327,400	331,500	333,800	335,400	336,300	337,700	338,900
40..........	262,600	267,500	270,400	272,300	273,200	274,900	276,100
60..........	194,200	198,600	201,300	203,100	203,900	205,200	205,700
80..........	166,200	166,400	166,700	166,900	166,900	167,000	167,000

issue age 40, as an example from Table 21, values of $1000q_x$ for 1987 to
1991 would be 1.34, 1.49, 1.64, 1.76, and 1.90, respectively.

TABLE 21

VALUES FOR FEMALES OF $1000q_x$
UNDER VARIOUS LIFE TABLES

	Female $1000q_x$					
	Life Table for the Year					
Attained Age	1980	1987	1988	1989	1990	1991
40...............	1.61	1.34	1.31	1.27	1.24	1.22
41...............	1.80	1.52	1.49	1.45	1.42	1.40
42...............	2.00	1.71	1.67	1.64	1.60	1.58
43...............	2.21	1.88	1.84	1.80	1.76	1.73
44...............	2.42	2.07	2.02	1.97	1.93	1.90
45...............	2.66	2.26	2.21	2.16	2.11	2.08

Mortality rates during the years 2001 and thereafter can be derived either
by extending this method through the development of 2001 to 2010 Life
Tables or by assuming no further mortality improvement beyond 2000 and
using the 2001 Life Table as an ultimate mortality table. We have taken
both these courses in our analysis.

Table 19 showed that meaningful improvement in mortality rates can still
be anticipated after the year 2000. We have therefore made the following
mortality table assumptions in deriving the mortality gross premiums:

Basis	Mortality Table
A	1980 Life Table
B	1987 Life Table
C	1992 Life Table
D	1997 Life Table
E	Composite 1987–2000, Ultimate 2001 Life Table thereafter
F	Composite 1987–2010, Ultimate 2011 Life Table thereafter
G	Composite 1987–2020, Ultimate 2021 Life Table thereafter

Mortality gross premium rates are derived by using the mortality assumptions above at issue ages 0, 20, 40, 60, 80 for a life only, 10-year certain
and life, and 20-year certain and life annuity providing $1,000 per month
to a male and a female at a 0 percent, 3 percent, and 5 percent annual cost-
of-living adjustment in benefit and the following interest rate assumption:

Cost-of- Living Adjustment	No. of Years Initial 9% Rate Is Guaranteed	Ultimate Interest Rate Thereafter
0%	20	7%
3	17	7
5	15	7

As a practical matter, note that pricing gross premiums would probably be developed by using a static mortality table assumption and of course would include a loading for expenses, contingencies, and profit. If mortality improvement were to be included, the basic characteristic of such premium scale would be that present values calculated under the static table would approximate the present values calculated by using the composite mortality table that recognized mortality improvement, under the same assumption for investment yields. This approximation simplifies gross premium calculation and is similar in concept to a whole life premium replacing a set of yearly renewable term premiums.

Mortality basis A has been included in Table 20 because it approximates the underlying static mortality assumption for structured settlement annuity pricing by a number of companies. If the static mortality assumption had been the 1987 Life Table, meaningful mortality premium increases emerge starting at the ages shown in Table 22. This table also shows the mortality gross premiums and the percentage increases at these ages. Admittedly, the 1 percent benchmark is subjective. However, the results for any reasonably chosen percentage increase in premium will be similar to those of Table 22.

Table 23 shows the ratio of mortality gross premium rates under various mortality assumptions to either the 1980 Life Table or the 1987 Life Table. Consider that a pricing benchmark value of profits on an annuity is often about 4 percent of premium when reviewing the ratios in Table 23.

With ratios at some plan-age cells exceeding 10 percent, and many of them in the 3–4 percent range, the 1980 Life Table is clearly inappropriate today for pricing structured settlement annuities. The 1987 Life Table, although a derived mortality table emanating from the projected 1990 Life Table, would account for past mortality improvement but does not provide for future mortality improvement. We now consider the effects of pricing structured settlement annuities assuming ongoing mortality improvement.

At first, we assume that mortality improves until the year 2000 inclusive and that the 2001 Life Table represents ultimate mortality for each year after 2000. Subsequently, we advance the mortality improvement periods to 2010

TABLE 22

Mortality Gross Premiums and Their Percentage Increase
at Ages for Which the Percentage Increase Is First at Least about 1%
Where Pricing Assumes 1980 Life Table and 1987 Life Table Mortality

COLA	Plan	Age	1980 Life Table	1987 Life Table	Percentage Increase
		Males			
0	Life annuity	40	126,400	127,900	1.19%
0	10-Year certain and life	40	127,700	129,000	1.02
0	20-Year certain and life	None	—	—	—
3%	Life annuity	20	208,000	210,100	1.01
3	10-Year certain and life	20	208,800	210,800	0.96
3	20-Year certain and life	20	210,200	212,100	0.90
5	Life annuity	0	351,300	356,100	1.37
5	10-Year certain and life	0	352,800	357,300	1.28
5	20-Year certain and life	0	354,500	358,800	1.21
		Females			
0	Life annuity	60	109,900	111,900	1.82%
0	10-Year certain and life	60	113,900	115,600	1.49
0	20-Year certain and life	None	—	—	—
3%	Life annuity	40	189,700	192,300	1.37
3	10-Year certain and life	40	190,600	193,100	1.31
3	20-Year certain and life	40	193,100	195,200	1.09
5	Life annuity	0	370,200	374,100	1.05
5	10-Year certain and life	0	371,400	375,100	1.00
5	20-Year certain and life	0	372,800	376,300	0.94

and 2020, with ultimate mortality being assumed to follow the 2011 and 2021 Life Tables in respective subsequent years. We will compare mortality gross premium ratios under these assumptions to 1987 Life Table mortality gross premiums to detect meaningful changes in mortality gross premiums.

Table 24 shows the ages at which meaningful mortality gross premium increases emerge under our 1 percent benchmark together with the mortality gross premiums themselves and the respective percentage increases in premiums at these ages.

The tables show that mortality improvement must be assumed in pricing structured settlement annuities. The only mitigating fact is that structured settlement annuities are more often issued at younger issue ages, with a guarantee period of at least 20 years and no cost-of-living adjustment. Only a model office study by a company would indicate the overall effect on profits of mortality improvement.

The question then remains, how far into the future should we assume that mortality improvement will occur? Analysis of the cells for which structured settlement annuities are usually sold, that is, those involving at least a 20-year guarantee period, reveals that despite competitive forces, which will

TABLE 23

COMPARISON OF STRUCTURED SETTLEMENT
MORTALITY GROSS SINGLE PREMIUM RATIOS
UNDER VARIOUS MORTALITY TABLE ASSUMPTIONS
AND ORIGINAL MORTALITY GROSS SINGLE PREMIUM SCALES

Issue Age	1987 Life Table	1992 Life Table	1997 Life Table	1992 Life Table	1997 Life Table	Mortality Improvement		
						1987–2000	1987–2010	1987–2020
	Compared to 1980 Life Table			Compared to 1987 Life Table		Compared to 1987 Life Table		
Life Annuity — Male								
0	1.0043	1.0064	1.0078	1.0021	1.0035	1.0021	1.0021	1.0021
20	1.0051	1.0080	1.0094	1.0029	1.0043	1.0043	1.0050	1.0058
40	1.0119	1.0182	1.0222	1.0063	1.0102	1.0102	1.0117	1.0125
60	1.0247	1.0392	1.0485	1.0141	1.0231	1.0171	1.0191	1.0191
80	1.0494	1.0786	1.0969	1.0279	1.0453	1.0226	1.0226	1.0226
Life Annuity — Female								
0	1.0028	1.0042	1.0049	1.0014	1.0021	1.0007	1.0014	1.0014
20	1.0028	1.0042	1.0050	1.0014	1.0021	1.0028	1.0028	1.0035
40	1.0075	1.0121	1.0143	1.0045	1.0067	1.0067	1.0082	1.0090
60	1.0182	1.0282	1.0355	1.0096	1.0170	1.0170	1.0188	1.0197
80	1.0655	1.1037	1.1280	1.0358	1.0587	1.0329	1.0329	1.0329
10-Year Certain and Life Annuity — Male								
0	1.0028	1.0042	1.0049	1.0014	1.0021	1.0014	1.0014	1.0021
20	1.0043	1.0065	1.0079	1.0022	1.0036	1.0036	1.0043	1.0050
40	1.0102	1.0157	1.0188	1.0054	1.0085	1.0093	1.0109	1.0116
60	1.0153	1.0249	1.0306	1.0094	1.0151	1.0141	1.0151	1.0160
80	1.0096	1.0155	1.0203	1.0059	1.0107	1.0083	1.0083	1.0083
10-Year Certain and Life Annuity — Female								
0	1.0021	1.0028	1.0035	1.0007	1.0014	1.0007	1.0007	1.0007
20	1.0021	1.0035	1.0042	1.0014	1.0021	1.0028	1.0035	1.0035
40	1.0068	1.0105	1.0128	1.0037	1.0060	1.0067	1.0075	1.0089
60	1.0149	1.0237	1.0299	1.0087	1.0147	1.0156	1.0182	1.0182
80	1.0185	1.0300	1.0381	1.0113	1.0193	1.0159	1.0159	1.0159
20-Year Certain and Life Annuity — Male								
0	1.0021	1.0035	1.0042	1.0014	1.0021	1.0021	1.0021	1.0021
20	1.0036	1.0057	1.0064	1.0021	1.0029	1.0036	1.0043	1.0050
40	1.0069	1.0107	1.0130	1.0038	1.0061	1.0076	1.0091	1.0099
60	1.0059	1.0085	1.0110	1.0025	1.0051	1.0051	1.0067	1.0067
80	1.0009	1.0009	1.0009	1.0000	1.0000	1.0000	1.0009	1.0009
20-Year Certain and Life Annuity — Female								
0	1.0014	1.0021	1.0021	1.0007	1.0007	1.0007	1.0007	1.0007
20	1.0021	1.0035	1.0042	1.0014	1.0021	1.0021	1.0028	1.0035
40	1.0052	1.0082	1.0096	1.0030	1.0044	1.0052	1.0066	1.0074
60	1.0082	1.0140	1.0172	1.0057	1.0090	1.0106	1.0122	1.0130
80	1.0009	1.0018	1.0026	1.0009	1.0018	1.0018	1.0018	1.0018

TABLE 23 — *Continued*

Issue Age	1987 Life Table	1992 Life Table	1997 Life Table	1992 Life Table	1997 Life Table	Mortality Improvement 1987–2000	1987–2010	1987–2020
	Compared to 1980 Life Table			Compared to 1987 Life Table		Compared to 1987 Life Table		
Life Annuity with Annual 3 Percent Cost-of-Living Adjustment — Male								
0	1.0080	1.0116	1.0139	1.0035	1.0058	1.0049	1.0062	1.0071
20	1.0101	1.0154	1.0188	1.0052	1.0086	1.0095	1.0119	1.0138
40	1.0195	1.0297	1.0366	1.0101	1.0168	1.0180	1.0213	1.0236
60	1.0334	1.0518	1.0643	1.0178	1.0299	1.0242	1.0275	1.0283
80	1.0560	1.0890	1.1120	1.0312	1.0530	1.0281	1.0281	1.0281
Life Annuity with Annual 3 Percent Cost-of-Living Adjustment — Female								
0	1.0057	1.0087	1.0100	1.0030	1.0043	1.0039	1.0048	1.0056
20	1.0069	1.0110	1.0133	1.0041	1.0064	1.0077	1.0096	1.0114
40	1.0137	1.0216	1.0269	1.0078	1.0130	1.0140	1.0177	1.0203
60	1.0269	1.0432	1.0532	1.0159	1.0255	1.0276	1.0317	1.0338
80	1.0754	1.1184	1.1480	1.0401	1.0676	1.0401	1.0413	1.0413
10-Year Certain and Life Annuity with Annual 3 Percent Cost-of-Living Adjustment — Male								
0	1.0071	1.0102	1.0124	1.0031	1.0053	1.0049	1.0062	1.0071
20	1.0096	1.0148	1.0182	1.0052	1.0085	1.0095	1.0119	1.0133
40	1.0176	1.0278	1.0340	1.0100	1.0162	1.0173	1.0212	1.0234
60	1.0225	1.0364	1.0450	1.0136	1.0220	1.0212	1.0243	1.0250
80	1.0116	1.0200	1.0253	1.0083	1.0135	1.0114	1.0114	1.0114
10-Year Certain and Life Annuity with Annual 3 Percent Cost-of-Living Adjustment — Female								
0	1.0048	1.0074	1.0087	1.0026	1.0039	1.0039	1.0047	1.0056
20	1.0064	1.0105	1.0128	1.0041	1.0064	1.0077	1.0096	1.0109
40	1.0131	1.0205	1.0252	1.0073	1.0119	1.0135	1.0171	1.0197
60	1.0240	1.0384	1.0473	1.0141	1.0228	1.0254	1.0301	1.0321
80	1.0242	1.0393	1.0514	1.0147	1.0265	1.0216	1.0226	1.0226
20-Year Certain and Life Annuity with Annual 3 Percent Cost-of-Living Adjustment — Male								
0	1.0057	1.0088	1.0106	1.0031	1.0048	1.0053	1.0062	1.0070
20	1.0090	1.0138	1.0167	1.0047	1.0075	1.0090	1.0113	1.0127
40	1.0138	1.0215	1.0260	1.0076	1.0120	1.0142	1.0174	1.0196
60	1.0093	1.0153	1.0193	1.0059	1.0099	1.0106	1.0132	1.0139
80	1.0007	1.0007	1.0014	1.0000	1.0007	1.0007	1.0007	1.0007
20-Year Certain and Life Annuity with Annual 3 Percent Cost-of-Living Adjustment — Female								
0	1.0043	1.0065	1.0078	1.0022	1.0034	1.0034	1.0043	1.0052
20	1.0064	1.0101	1.0123	1.0036	1.0059	1.0073	1.0091	1.0104
40	1.0109	1.0176	1.0218	1.0067	1.0108	1.0128	1.0164	1.0190
60	1.0158	1.0253	1.0316	1.0093	1.0156	1.0180	1.0224	1.0236
80	1.0014	1.0021	1.0028	1.0007	1.0014	1.0021	1.0021	1.0021

TABLE 23 — *Continued*

Issue Age	1987 Life Table	1992 Life Table	1997 Life Table	1992 Life Table	1997 Life Table	Mortality Improvement		
						1987–2000	1987–2010	1987–2020
	Compared to 1980 Life Table			Compared to 1987 Life Table		Compared to 1987 Life Table		
Life Annuity with Annual 5 Percent Cost-of-Living Adjustment — Male								
0	1.0137	1.0208	1.0248	1.0070	1.0110	1.0112	1.0140	1.0166
20	1.0169	1.0262	1.0319	1.0091	1.0147	1.0173	1.0215	1.0254
40	1.0266	1.0414	1.0510	1.0144	1.0238	1.0259	1.0323	1.0365
60	1.0397	1.0623	1.0772	1.0218	1.0361	1.0313	1.0361	1.0375
80	1.0612	1.0979	1.1223	1.0346	1.0576	1.0317	1.0331	1.0331
Life Annuity with Annual 5 Percent Cost-of-Living Adjustment — Female								
0	1.0105	1.0162	1.0197	1.0056	1.0091	1.0094	1.0120	1.0144
20	1.0129	1.0202	1.0251	1.0073	1.0121	1.0148	1.0191	1.0227
40	1.0213	1.0333	1.0419	1.0118	1.0201	1.0228	1.0292	1.0342
60	1.0361	1.0570	1.0710	1.0202	1.0337	1.0371	1.0444	1.0472
80	1.0824	1.1304	1.1636	1.0443	1.0750	1.0466	1.0489	1.0489
10-Year Certain and Life Annuity with Annual 5 Percent Cost-of-Living Adjustment — Male								
0	1.0128	1.0196	1.0235	1.0067	1.0106	1.0115	1.0140	1.0165
20	1.0165	1.0255	1.0311	1.0088	1.0143	1.0169	1.0215	1.0251
40	1.0251	1.0394	1.0484	1.0139	1.0228	1.0257	1.0321	1.0359
60	1.0297	1.0469	1.0587	1.0167	1.0282	1.0276	1.0321	1.0333
80	1.0145	1.0241	1.0309	1.0095	1.0162	1.0133	1.0143	1.0143
10-Year Certain and Life Annuity with Annual 5 Percent Cost-of-Living Adjustment — Female								
0	1.0100	1.0153	1.0186	1.0053	1.0085	1.0093	1.0120	1.0144
20	1.0129	1.0202	1.0251	1.0073	1.0121	1.0148	1.0191	1.0230
40	1.0205	1.0324	1.0406	1.0117	1.0197	1.0227	1.0291	1.0341
60	1.0327	1.0519	1.0649	1.0186	1.0311	1.0355	1.0426	1.0454
80	1.0293	1.0476	1.0613	1.0178	1.0311	1.0258	1.0276	1.0276
20-Year Certain and Life Annuity with Annual 5 Percent Cost-of-Living Adjustment — Male								
0	1.0121	1.0186	1.0223	1.0064	1.0100	1.0111	1.0139	1.0164
20	1.0158	1.0243	1.0299	1.0084	1.0139	1.0165	1.0207	1.0246
40	1.0210	1.0332	1.0408	1.0119	1.0194	1.0227	1.0284	1.0325
60	1.0139	1.0222	1.0277	1.0082	1.0137	1.0148	1.0186	1.0197
80	1.0006	1.0012	1.0012	1.0006	1.0006	1.0012	1.0012	1.0012
20-Year Certain and Life Annuity with Annual 5 Percent Cost-of-Living Adjustment — Female								
0	1.0094	1.0145	1.0177	1.0050	1.0082	1.0093	1.0120	1.0144
20	1.0125	1.0195	1.0244	1.0069	1.0118	1.0145	1.0187	1.0223
40	1.0187	1.0297	1.0369	1.0108	1.0179	1.0213	1.0277	1.0321
60	1.0227	1.0366	1.0458	1.0136	1.0227	1.0267	1.0332	1.0358
80	1.0012	1.0030	1.0042	1.0018	1.0030	1.0030	1.0036	1.0036

TABLE 24

MORTALITY GROSS PREMIUMS AND THEIR PERCENTAGE INCREASE
AT AGES FOR WHICH THE PERCENTAGE INCREASE IS FIRST AT LEAST ABOUT 1%
WHEN PRICING ASSUMES 1987 LIFE TABLE STATIC MORTALITY
AND MORTALITY IMPROVEMENT DURING 1987–2000

COLA	Plan	Age	1987 Life Table	Mortality Improvement 1987–2000	Percentage Increase
		Males			
0	Life annuity	40	127,900	129,200	1.02%
0	10-Year certain and life	40	129,000	130,200	0.93
0	20-Year certain and life	None	—	—	—
3%	Life annuity	20	210,100	212,100	0.95
3	10-Year certain and life	20	210,800	212,800	0.95
3	20-Year certain and life	20*	212,100	214,000	0.90
5	Life annuity	0	356,100	360,100	1.12
5	10-Year certain and life	0	357,300	361,400	1.15
5	20-Year certain and life	0*	358,800	362,800	1.11
		Females			
0	Life annuity	60	111,900	113,800	1.70%
0	10-Year certain and life	60	115,600	117,400	1.56
0	20-Year certain and life	60*	122,800	124,100	1.06
3%	Life annuity	40	192,300	195,000	1.40
3	10-Year certain and life	40	193,100	195,700	1.35
3	20-Year certain and life	40*	195,200	197,700	1.28
5	Life annuity	0	374,100	377,600	0.94
5	10-Year certain and life	0	375,100	378,600	0.93
5	20-Year certain and life	0*	376,300	379,800	0.93

*Percentage increase at some higher age becomes nonmeaningful for this cell, although percentage increase may be rising for some ages before falling.

soon be addressed, it is prudent to assume mortality improvement until the year 2020, inclusive. This is shown in Table 25, which summarizes by plan, sex and age the relationship of the 1987–2010 mortality improvement ratios from Table 23 to the 1987–2000 mortality improvement and 1987–2020 mortality improvement ratios.

Out of the 90 cells in Table 25, 27 show the 1987–2010 mortality improvement ratio to be equal to the 1987–2020 mortality improvement ratio, while for 18 cells they are meaningfully above the average of the 1987–2000 and 1987–2020 mortality improvement ratios. That leaves half the cells with ratios under the 1987–2010 mortality improvement assumption equal to or slightly higher than the average of the ratios under the 1987–2000 and 1987–2020 mortality improvement assumptions.

Out of the 30 cells involving a 20-year certain period, 13 belong in the former category. Thus, the remaining 17 cells, which are at issue ages 0, 20, and 40 (except for two of them), represent the cells at which structured settlement annuities are usually sold. I believe those cells should be priced to reflect mortality improvement out to the year 2020.

For simplicity in pricing structured settlement annuities, especially for purposes of pricing substandard annuities under the age-rating method, it may be desirable to price from a static mortality table assumption. Such a static mortality table should produce gross single premiums that are reasonably close to those produced by an assumption of mortality improvement from 1987 to 2020, inclusive.

TABLE 25

RELATIONSHIP OF PREMIUM RATIOS
UNDER A 1987–2010 MORTALITY IMPROVEMENT ASSUMPTION
TO PREMIUM RATIOS UNDER 1987–2000 MORTALITY IMPROVEMENT
AND 1987–2020 MORTALITY IMPROVEMENT

Issue Age	Plan	Male	Female
	0 Percent Annual Cost-of-Living Adjustment		
0	Life annuity	Same	2010–2020
20	Life annuity	Middle	2000–2010
40	Life annuity	About middle	About middle
60	Life annuity	2010–2020	About middle
80	Life annuity	Same	Same
0	10-Year certain and life	2000–2010	Same
20	10-Year certain and life	Middle	2010–2020
40	10-Year certain and life	About middle	About middle
60	10-Year certain and life	Middle	2010–2020
80	10-Year certain and life	Same	Same
0	20-Year certain and life	Same	Same
20	20-Year certain and life	Middle	Middle
40	20-Year certain and life	About middle	About middle
60	20-Year certain and life	2010–2020	About middle
80	20-Year certain and life	2010–2020	Same
	3 Percent Annual Cost-of-Living Adjustment		
0	Life annuity	About middle	Middle
20	Life annuity	About middle	Middle
40	Life annuity	About middle	About middle
60	Life annuity	Above middle	Above middle
80	Life annuity	Same	2010–2020
0	10-Year certain and life	Middle	Middle
20	10-Year certain and life	About middle	Middle
40	10-Year certain and life	Above middle	Middle
60	10-Year certain and life	Above middle	Above middle
80	10-Year certain and life	Same	2010–2020
0	20-Year certain and life	Middle	Middle
20	20-Year certain and life	About middle	Middle
40	20-Year certain and life	About middle	About middle
60	20-Year certain and life	Above middle	Above middle
80	20-Year certain and life	Same	Same

TABLE 25 — *Continued*

Issue Age	Plan	Male	Female
	5 Percent Cost-of-Living Adjustment		
0	Life annuity	Middle	Middle
20	Life annuity	Middle	Middle
40	Life annuity	Above middle	Above middle
60	Life annuity	Above middle	Above middle
80	Life annuity	2010–2020	2010–2020
0	10-Year certain and life	Middle	Middle
20	10-Year certain and life	Above middle	Middle
40	10-Year certain and life	Above middle	Above middle
60	10-Year certain and life	Above middle	Above middle
80	10-Year certain and life	2010–2020	2010–2020
0	20-Year certain and life	Middle	Middle
20	20-Year certain and life	Middle	Middle
40	20-Year certain and life	Middle	Middle
60	20-Year certain and life	Above middle	Above middle
80	20-Year certain and life	Same	2010–2020

Key:
Same — The ratios under all three mortality improvement assumptions are the same.
Middle — The 1987–2010 mortality improvement ratio equals the average of the 1987–2000 and 1987–2020 mortality improvement ratios.
About middle — The 1987–2010 mortality improvement ratio is slightly higher than the average of the 1987–2000 and 1987–2020 mortality improvement ratios.
Above middle — The 1987–2010 mortality improvement ratio is meaningfully closer to the 1987–2020 mortality improvement ratio than it is to the average of the 1987–2000 and 1987–2020 mortality improvement ratios.
2000–2010 — The 1987–2010 mortality improvement ratio is the same as the 1987–2000 mortality improvement ratio but less than the 1987–2020 mortality ratio.
2010–2020 — The 1987–2010 mortality improvement ratio is the same as the 1987–2020 mortality improvement ratio but greater than the 1987–2000 mortality improvement ratio.

Table 26 compares the mortality gross premiums, before loading, derived under the static mortality assumptions of 1992, 1997, and 2002 Life Tables and mortality improvement from 1987 to 2020, inclusive.

The static 2002 Life Table premiums obviously reproduce the premiums derived assuming 1987–2020 mortality improvement with the greatest fidelity. More than 75 percent of the 90 cells in Table 26 show the 2002 Life Table premium to be the most appropriate.

TABLE 26

MORTALITY GROSS PREMIUMS
UNDER VARIOUS MORTALITY ASSUMPTIONS

Issue Age	COLA	Plan	1992 Life Table	1997 Life Table	2002 Life Table	Mortality Improvement 1987–2020
		Males				
0....	0	Life annuity	141,900	142,100	142,200	141,900
20....	0	Life annuity	139,100	139,300	139,400	139,500
40....	0	Life annuity	128,700	129,200	129,600	129,500
60....	0	Life annuity	100,800	101,700	102,400	101,300
80....	0	Life annuity	59,000	60,000	60,900	58,700
0....	0	10-Year certain and life	142,800	142,900	143,000	142,900
20....	0	10-Year certain and life	139,600	139,800	139,900	140,000
40....	0	10-Year certain and life	129,700	130,100	130,500	130,500
60....	0	10-Year certain and life	107,200	107,800	108,300	107,900
80....	0	10-Year certain and life	85,000	85,400	85,700	85,200
0....	0	20-Year certain and life	143,300	143,400	143,400	143,400
20....	0	20-Year certain and life	140,400	140,500	140,600	140,800
40....	0	20-Year certain and life	132,000	132,300	132,600	132,800
60....	0	20-Year certain and life	119,100	119,400	119,600	119,600
80....	0	20-Year certain and life	114,100	114,100	114,200	114,200
0....	3%	Life annuity	226,400	226,900	227,200	227,200
20....	3	Life annuity	211,200	211,900	212,400	213,000
40....	3	Life annuity	180,000	181,200	182,100	182,400
60....	3	Life annuity	126,000	127,500	128,600	127,300
80....	3	Life annuity	66,100	67,500	68,600	65,900
0....	3	10-Year certain and life	227,400	227,900	228,200	228,300
20....	3	10-Year certain and life	211,900	212,600	213,000	213,600
40....	3	10-Year certain and life	181,300	182,400	183,200	183,700
60....	3	10-Year certain and life	133,700	134,800	135,700	135,200
80....	3	10-Year certain and life	96,900	97,400	97,900	97,200
0....	3	20-Year certain and life	228,200	228,600	228,900	229,100
20....	3	20-Year certain and life	213,100	213,700	214,200	214,800
40....	3	20-Year certain and life	185,000	185,800	186,500	187,200
60....	3	20-Year certain and life	152,300	152,900	153,400	153,500
80....	3	20-Year certain and life	141,400	141,500	141,500	141,500
0....	5%	Life annuity	358,600	360,000	361,100	362,000
20....	5	Life annuity	309,300	311,000	312,400	314,300
40....	5	Life annuity	238,900	241,100	242,800	244,100
60....	5	Life annuity	150,000	152,100	153,800	152,300
80....	5	Life annuity	71,800	73,400	74,800	71,700
0....	5	10-Year certain and life	359,700	361,100	362,100	363,200
20....	5	10-Year certain and life	310,000	311,700	313,100	315,000
40....	5	10-Year certain and life	240,300	242,400	244,100	245,500
60....	5	10-Year certain and life	158,600	160,400	161,800	161,200
80....	5	10-Year certain and life	106,200	106,900	107,600	106,700
0....	5	20-Year certain and life	361,100	362,400	363,400	364,700
20....	5	20-Year certain and life	312,000	313,700	314,900	317,000
40....	5	20-Year certain and life	245,700	247,500	249,000	250,700
60....	5	20-Year certain and life	184,200	185,200	186,000	186,300
80....	5	20-Year certain and life	166,100	166,100	166,200	166,200

TABLE 26 — *Continued*

Issue Age	COLA	Plan	1992 Life Table	1997 Life Table	2002 Life Table	Mortality Improvement 1987–2020
		Females				
0....	0	Life annuity	143,100	143,200	143,300	143,100
20....	0	Life annuity	141,900	142,000	142,100	142,200
40....	0	Life annuity	134,100	134,400	134,700	134,700
60....	0	Life annuity	113,000	113,800	114,400	114,100
80....	0	Life annuity	72,400	74,000	75,300	72,200
0....	0	10-Year certain and life	143,800	143,900	143,900	143,800
20....	0	10-Year certain and life	142,000	142,100	142,200	142,300
40....	0	10-Year certain and life	134,600	134,900	135,100	135,300
60....	0	10-Year certain and life	116,600	117,300	117,800	117,700
80....	0	10-Year certain and life	89,300	90,000	90,600	89,700
0....	0	20-Year certain and life	144,200	144,200	144,300	144,200
20....	0	20-Year certain and life	142,300	142,400	142,500	142,600
40....	0	20-Year certain and life	135,900	136,100	136,300	136,500
60....	0	20-Year certain and life	123,500	123,900	124,200	124,400
80....	0	20-Year certain and life	114,300	114,400	114,400	114,400
0....	3%	Life annuity	231,600	231,900	232,200	232,200
20....	3	Life annuity	220,400	220,900	221,300	222,000
40....	3	Life annuity	193,800	194,800	195,600	196,200
60....	3	Life annuity	147,200	148,600	149,800	149,800
80....	3	Life annuity	83,100	85,300	87,100	83,200
0....	3	10-Year certain and life	232,400	232,700	233,000	233,100
20....	3	10-Year certain and life	220,600	221,100	221,500	222,100
40....	3	10-Year certain and life	194,500	195,400	196,200	196,900
60....	3	10-Year certain and life	151,500	152,800	153,900	154,200
80....	3	10-Year certain and life	103,200	104,400	105,300	104,000
0....	3	20-Year certain and life	233,000	233,300	233,500	233,700
20....	3	20-Year certain and life	221,000	221,500	221,900	222,500
40....	3	20-Year certain and life	196,500	197,300	198,000	198,900
60....	3	20-Year certain and life	162,200	163,200	164,000	164,500
80....	3	20-Year certain and life	141,800	141,900	142,100	142,000
0....	5%	Life annuity	376,200	377,500	378,500	379,500
20....	5	Life annuity	332,700	334,300	335,500	337,800
40....	5	Life annuity	266,500	268,700	270,300	272,400
60....	5	Life annuity	181,600	184,000	186,000	186,400
80....	5	Life annuity	91,900	94,600	96,800	92,300
0....	5	10-Year certain and life	377,100	378,300	379,300	380,500
20....	5	10-Year certain and life	332,900	334,500	335,800	338,100
40....	5	10-Year certain and life	267,300	269,400	271,000	273,200
60....	5	10-Year certain and life	186,400	188,700	190,600	191,300
80....	5	10-Year certain and life	114,500	116,000	117,300	115,600
0....	5	20-Year certain and life	378,200	379,400	380,400	381,700
20....	5	20-Year certain and life	333,800	335,400	336,600	338,900
40....	5	20-Year certain and life	270,400	272,300	273,800	276,100
60....	5	20-Year certain and life	201,300	203,100	204,600	205,700
80....	5	20-Year certain and life	166,700	166,900	167,100	167,000

We now compare the mortality gross single premiums based upon a 2002 Life Table mortality assumption with those based upon a 1987 Life Table mortality assumption. Results are shown in Table 27. Significant premium increases are required for both males and females at almost all ages where a cost-of-living adjustment in benefit is to be provided. This segment of annuity benefit types cannot be ignored.

TABLE 27

PERCENTAGE INCREASE IN MORTALITY GROSS SINGLE PREMIUMS
UNDER A 2002 LIFE TABLE MORTALITY ASSUMPTION
OVER THOSE UNDER A 1987 LIFE TABLE MORTALITY ASSUMPTION

		Ratio of Mortality Gross Premiums				
COLA	Plan	Age 0	Age 20	Age 40	Age 60	Age 80
		Males				
0	Life annuity	0.42%	0.50%	1.33%	3.02%	6.10%
	10-Year certain and life	0.28	0.43	1.16	1.98	1.42
	20-Year certain and life	0.21	0.36	0.84	0.67	0.09
3%	Life annuity	0.71	1.09	2.19	3.88	7.02
	10-Year certain and life	0.66	1.04	2.06	2.88	1.87
	20-Year certain and life	0.62	0.99	1.58	1.32	.07
5%	Life annuity	1.40	1.92	3.10	4.77	7.78
	10-Year certain and life	1.34	1.89	3.00	3.72	2.28
	20-Year certain and life	1.28	1.78	2.55	1.81	0.12
		Females				
0	Life annuity	0.28%	0.28%	0.90%	2.23%	7.73%
	10-Year certain and life	0.14	0.28	0.75	1.90	2.60
	20-Year certain and life	0.14	0.28	0.59	1.14	0.18
3%	Life annuity	0.56	0.82	1.72	3.38	9.01
	10-Year certain and life	0.52	0.82	1.61	3.01	3.54
	20-Year certain and life	0.43	0.77	1.43	2.05	0.28
5%	Life annuity	1.18	1.57	2.62	4.49	10.00
	10-Year certain and life	1.12	1.60	2.57	4.15	4.27
	20-Year certain and life	1.09	1.54	2.36	3.02	0.42

Profit is not the only criterion that determines the resulting gross premium scale promulgated by the company. Competitiveness plays an important part.

We can cite the effects on competitiveness from another study in which actual structured settlement gross premiums were compared with 17 competitor insurance companies' premium scales in effect during April 1987. Although the basic data for the rates tested are not the same as those described in this paper, the relative change in competitive position is informative. Table 28 shows the change in competitive position when gross premiums originally based upon a 1980 Life Table mortality assumption are changed to assume either 1987 Life Table mortality or mortality improvement over the period 1987–2000, inclusive, for a 20-year certain and life annuity issued to a male at standard age 25, 45 or 65. Also shown is the effect of mortality improvement assumptions on pricing COLA annuities and the resulting relatively larger movement in competitive position.

TABLE 28

CHANGE IN RELATIVE COMPETITIVE POSITION DURING APRIL 1987
WHEN 1980 LIFE TABLE MORTALITY IS REPLACED
BY EITHER 1987 LIFE TABLE MORTALITY
OR MORTALITY IMPROVEMENT OVER THE YEARS 1987–2000
UNDER A 20-YEAR CERTAIN AND LIFE ANNUITY

Age	COLA	1987 Life Table	1995 Life Table
25	0	−3	−4
	3%	−3	−3
	6	−1	−1
45	0	−3	−4
	3	−3	−5
	6	−4	−5
65	0	−1	−1
	3	−3	−3
	6	−1	−1

The purchasers of structured settlement annuities maintain that price, that is, lowest premium, is the driving force in the sale of these annuities, coupled with safety and security of the issuing company. These are conflicting forces. Based upon the analyses above, a company's safety and security can be ascertained based upon financial statistics for that company extant today. What will a company's safety and security position be, for example, 20 years from now, however, if it writes a good portion of COLA structured settlement annuities but does not assume mortality improvement? This question, of course, also applies to annuities without COLA benefits.

V. MORTALITY AND UNDERWRITING

Traditional Annuities

Traditional fixed-income annuities are not usually bought by individuals with impaired longevity. Normally, it is the individual who expects to live longer than average who purchases an annuity. Substandard annuities, being relatively rare, have been underwritten by the traditional life underwriter who must exercise a reverse judgment in determining the increased benefit to be paid.

No elaborate underwriting manuals or procedures have been established for the substandard individuals wishing to purchase an annuity. The underwriter would use best judgment in determining a percentage of extra mortality to be experienced by the proposed annuitant, and then a reduced premium for the requested benefit may be calculated by the pricing formula utilizing the lower survival rates, or an age rating system may be used whereby the premium at an older age is used to determine the annuity cost for the proposed annuitant.

This may be an acceptable procedure for traditional fixed-income annuities because of its negligible effect on a company's overall profits. Any cost arising from underestimation of longevity can be viewed as an agency accommodation to the field force who write annuities. This picture has changed in the last five years because of structured settlement annuities.

Structured Settlement Annuities

Structured settlement annuities most often are purchased for the benefit of individuals who have suffered personal injury. A meaningful number of cases are issued on a life with expected substandard mortality.

Although only up to about 5 percent of the structured settlement annuities issued by a company may involve substandard annuitants, a large number of requests to price substandard annuities are usually received. This arises from extensive shopping for the lowest premium by brokers. Consequently, an insurance company that is active today in the structured settlement line of business will find itself with one or more underwriters and possibly a medical director engaged full-time in underwriting substandard annuities.

Procedures for underwriting substandard annuities in structured settlement situations are similar to those for substandard traditional fixed-income annuities. The underwriter evaluates each case subjectively based upon years of experience in underwriting for life insurance coverages. Individual judgment by the underwriter is a key element in the underwriting of each substandard annuity.

Under one method of rating substandard annuities, ratings may be internally expressed as additional mortality percentages for pricing purposes, as discussed under traditional annuities underwriting, but the prevalent method is expressed by using the age rating method. This latter method is practical for use by brokers because it allows them to utilize a company's published standard annuity rate tables.

When the pricing actuary decides on the mortality table to be used in calculating structured settlement annuity rate scales, standard life expectancies by sex based on that table are determined. In evaluating a substandard annuity case, the underwriter estimates the life expectancy and uses the table to determine the attained age, by sex, for which the life expectancy is closest to the estimate. That age is the rated age. Table 29 illustrates a life expectancy table that has been used in substandard structured settlement annuity pricing.

TABLE 29

LIFE EXPECTANCY [14]

Age	Male	Female	Age	Male	Female
0...........	70.2	77.8	45.........	29.1	35.2
5...........	66.3	73.8	50.........	24.8	30.7
10..........	61.5	68.9	55.........	20.8	26.4
15..........	56.5	64.0	60.........	17.2	22.3
20..........	52.0	59.1	65.........	14.0	18.4
25..........	47.5	54.3	70.........	11.1	14.8
30..........	42.8	49.5	75.........	8.6	11.5
35..........	38.2	44.6	80.........	6.7	8.8
40..........	33.6	39.9	85.........	5.3	6.7

Table 30 illustrates the range of age ratings actually quoted by companies for a particular type of injury. Usually the same medical information is furnished to all companies from whom a substandard annuity quote is requested. This author can cite one factual situation, however, in which the original submission of a 1/2-inch-thick set of medical papers resulted in a 5-year rating up of the true age. Subsequently, a single-sheet letter was received on this case. As a result of this one page, the 5-year rating up was changed to a 45-year rating up in age! The figures in Table 30 represent selected quotes for illustration. More than seven companies quoted on these cases, and Company A is not necessarily the same company on each case.

This spread in ages reflects substantial individual judgment on the part of a company's underwriter and/or medical director. The difference in resulting premiums between companies is vast, even allowing for standard pricing differences. Although premiums for substandard annuities are a very small portion of the total structured settlement annuity premiums a company may

TABLE 30

RANGE OF AGE RATINGS
ON SELECTED SUBSTANDARD STRUCTURED SETTLEMENT ANNUITIES
ACTUALLY QUOTED BY DIFFERENT INSURERS

True Age of Proposed Annuitant	Rated Age Quoted by Company							Total Spread in Quoted Ages
	A	B	C	D	E	F	G	
7	7	10	13	13	16	20	26	19 years
9	36	40	45	55	64	66	67	31 years
4	12	20	23	32	38	42	54	42 years
7	11	30	46	50	51	63	64	53 years
8	8	18	37	45	61	65	69	61 years

collect, the potential loss of profits can be great because of the volumes involved in this category of business. Elaboration on the factors considered in underwriting substandard annuities will be revealing. Because this is a sensitive and proprietary area for companies, the dearth of information available precludes a complete examination of this topic.

Substandard structured settlement annuity quotes most often arise from the following causes: brain injuries, mental retardation, and spinal cord injuries. Less often occurring injuries include: birth trauma, burns, cerebral palsy, vascular disease, and vegetative state. Other injuries are classified as miscellaneous because there are so many of them, and each one represents a very small portion of the totality of injury types underwritten. They can include: cancer, cardiovascular problems, diabetes, drug overdose, encephalopathy, psychiatric disorders, pulmonary problems, renal failure, seizures, stroke, and systemic problems.

Life insurance underwriting practices can be introduced in evaluating substandard annuity risks. After criteria to be considered in underwriting are established, a debit system can be utilized to assign to each criterion a range of debits reflecting the gamut of optimum to most adverse situations for the criterion. A range of total debits then would translate into an effect on life expectancy.

Analyzed in Table 31 are the injuries most frequently evaluated in underwriting. The criteria as well as the debits are illustrative. They do not represent the current practice or actual debits of any particular company but show the range of interrelating criteria and the room for subjective interpretation. Often, it may be a combination of information, which cannot be analyzed by individual components, that carries more weight.

TABLE 31

Criterion	Range of Debits and Credits
Brain Injury	
Cause of Injury	
Traumatic accident	−50 to 0
Birth trauma	−25 to 0
Anoxia (oxygen deprivation)	−25 to 0
Type of Injury	
Closed	
Mental retardation	−20 to 0
Concussion	−5 to 0
Fracture (with or without operation)	−20 to 0
Open wound (with or without operation)	−20 to 0
Extent of recovery	
Residual impairments	
Seizures	−15 to −5
Coma level (deep, moderate, vegetative)	−60 to −15
Cognitive deficits	
Walk	−15 to 0
Talk	−5 to 0
Mental level	−50 to 0
Daily living activities	
Wash	−5 to 0
Feed	−10 to 0
Clothe	−5 to 0
Bowel and bladder control	−15 to 0
Catheter need	−10 to −5
Duration Since Injury	−15 to 0
Age at Time of Injury	
0–1 years	−15 to 0
2–5 years	−4 to 0
6–10 years	−3 to 0
11–20 years	−2 to 0
21–50 years	−1 to 0
51 or more years	−9 to 0
Environment	
Good family support	0 to 0*
Noncaring family	−10 to 0
Ward of the state, no family	−20 to 0
Health care facility	0 to 0*
Home care	0 to 0*
Currency of Data from Present Date to Date of History or Onset of Injury†	
More than 1 year old	−5 to 0
Within 6–12 months	−3 to 0
Within 6 months	−1 to 0

Total Debits	Percentage Decrease in Life Expectancy‡
−100 to −80	75%–85%
−79 to −60	60%–75%
−59 to −40	40%–60%
−39 to −25	15%–40%
−24 to −15	10%–15%
−14 to 0	0%–10%

TABLE 31 — *Continued*

Criterion	Range of Debits
Mental Retardation (Expanded Details from Brain Injury Criteria)	
Cause of Injury	
Birth trauma	−25 to 0
Anoxia (oxygen deprivation)	−25 to 0
Duration Since Injury	
Within 6 months	−15 to 0
Within 1 year	−10 to 0
1–2 years	−7 to 0
3–6 years	−5 to 0
Over 6 years	−2 to 0
Age at Time of Injury	
0–1 years	−15 to 0
2–5 years	−4 to 0
6–10 years	−3 to 0
Over 10 years	−2 to 0
Degree of Retardation	
Profound	−20 to −15
Severe	−15 to −10
Moderate	−10 to −5
Mile	−5 to 0
Borderline	−3 to 0
Skill Deprivation	
Walking	−15 to 0
Feeding	−10 to 0
Language	−5 to 0
Ability to work	−5 to 0
Medical Problems	
Microcephaly	−15 to −5
Pneumonias	−15 to −5
Seizures	−10 to 0
Incontinence	−5 to 0
Hydrocephalus shunt	−10 to −5
Gag-reflex	−20 to 0
Environment	
Good family support	0 to 0*
Noncaring family	−10 to 0
Ward of the state, no family	−20 to 0
Health care facility	0 to 0*
Home care	0 to 0*
Works some time	0 to 0*
Currency of Data from Present Date to Date of History or Onset of Injury†	
More than 1 year old	−10 to −5
Within 12 months	−5 to 0

Total Debits	Percentage Decrease in Life Expectancy‡
−100 to −75	80%–90%
−74 to −55	60%–80%
−54 to −40	45%–60%
−39 to −30	35%–45%
−29 to −20	25%–35%
−19 to −10	10%–25%
−9 to 0	0%–10%

TABLE 31 — *Continued*

Criterion	Range of Debits
Spinal Cord Injuries	
Cause of Injury	
Traumatic	−5 to 0
Other	−2 to 0
Type of Injury	
Injured disc	−3 to 0
Quadriparesis	−2 to 0
Quadriplegia	−10 to −3
Paraparesis	−2 to 0
Paraplegia	−5 to −2
Complete paralysis	−5 to −2
Incomplete paralysis	−2 to 0
Operation	
Not required	0 to 0
Required (based on cause and type)	−15 to 0
Medical problems	
Blood pressure/blood clots	−10 to −5
Psychosocial	−3 to 0
Spasticity	−5 to 0
Recurrent ulcers	−10 to 0
Support mechanisms	
Bowels	−10 to 0
Urinary	
Need Foley catheter	−10 to 0
Infections	−15 to −5
Renal	−20 to −10
Breathing	
Need respirator	−15 to 0
Spasticity	−5 to 0
Osteomyelitis/scoliosis	−5 to 0
Duration since injury	
0–1 years	−10 to 0
1–2 years	−8 to 0
2–5 years	−5 to 0
Over 5 years	−1 to 0
Age at Time of Injury	
0–5 years	−10 to 0
6–10 years	−8 to 0
11–20 years	−6 to 0
21–40 years	−10 to 0
Over 40 years	−15 to −5
Environment	
Good family support	0 to 0*
Noncaring family	0 to 0*
Ward of the state, no family	−5 to 0
Health care facility	−2 to −1
Home care	0 to 0*
Currency of Data from Present Date to Date of History	
or Onset of Injury†	
More than 1 year old	−5 to 0
Within 6–12 months	−2 to 0
Within 6 months	−1 to 0

TABLE 31 — *Continued*

Total Debits	Percentage Decrease in Life Expectancy#
− 70 to − 50	40%–50%
− 49 to − 30	30%–40%
− 29 to − 15	20%–30%
− 14 to − 5	10%–20%
− 4 to 0	0%–10%

*Consider in the overall picture but no specific debits or credits.
†Date of onset, age of annuitant, recentness or completeness of data are all considered simultaneously.
‡Total debits may also be expressed as number of years reduction in life expectancy or a multiple mortality rating determined from underwriting manuals used in rating life insurance applicants.

As might be expected, the debits assigned to common criteria between injury types, as well as the percentage decrease in life expectancy for the same range of total debits within injury types, are not the same.

Whether a company has established an underwriting network similar to the examples above or not, the underwriter in effect evaluates each case based upon the relationships in these examples, albeit through mental considerations for the most part. Therefore, the result is also expected: diversity of conclusions by individual underwriters.

A contributing cause to this diversity also can be found in the underlying studies of a particular injury that are available to the underwriter. Because many such injuries would result in a declination of life insurance coverage, the structured settlement annuity line of business is only about five years old, and only about 15–20 companies are writing this business, there are not extensive statistical data. Too often the available statistical data are more than 15 years old and are based upon treatment in the 1940s to 1960s, which does not take into account improved medical care, or the data are based upon a small number of lives.

For example, a paper titled "Survival in Traumatic Spinal Cord Injury" by Geisler, Jousse, Wynne-Jones, and Breithaupt [10] refers to a 1960 and 1973 study of 1,501 traumatic spinal injured patients rehabilitated between 1945 and 1953 and presents an updated 1980 study of 1,478 such patients discharged from a Canadian hospital as of December 31, 1980. On exposure from January 1974 to December 1980, the 1,478 lives accounted for 7,794 life-years and 194 deaths.

According to the 1975–77 Ontario population mortality tables, 75.7 deaths were expected over that time period. These results must be further broken down into subcategories as shown in Table 32.

TABLE 32

RESULTS OF 1980 STUDY OF TRAUMATIC SPINAL INJURED PATIENTS

Category	Complete Tetraplegic	Partial Tetraplegic	Complete Paraplegic	Partial Paraplegic	Total
Lives					
Male	205	336	340	371	1,252
Female	26	60	82	58	226
Total	231	396	422	429	1,478
Total life-years	1,174.5	2,138	2,420	2,064.5	7,797
Total actual deaths	33	48	55	58	194
Total expected deaths	4.3	22.9	17.3	31.2	75.7

Articles providing injury-specific studies are hard to find, and when they do surface, they are based upon what might be termed a dearth of information. From this type of information, underwriting considerations must be formulated and conclusions reached.

The underwriting of substandard annuities today obviously is more of an art than a science. This can greatly affect the profitability of the structured settlement line of business because of the wide ranging results that underwriting can have on the mortality assumption.

VI. MORTALITY AND PRICING SUBSTANDARD ANNUITIES

Two methods of pricing substandard annuities, whether of the traditional or structured settlement type, have been mentioned: rating up the issue age using life expectancies, and using multiple annuity mortality table values of $1000q_x$ at each attained age. As a corollary to the latter method, one may assume additional deaths added to the tabular number of deaths at each attained age before calculating $1000q_x$ values. Of course, the results of these last two methods then can be translated into a corresponding rated issue age for use by the field force in calculating the premium for various annuity forms of benefit. One rated age may be offered for all annuity forms for simplicity of use by the field force.

It is informative to examine the effect on pricing caused by variations in age ratings offered by different insurers. We examine this effect from the viewpoint of a single insurer who offers each of the age ratings used by competing insurers. In that way we can utilize the single insurer's rate tables to note the resulting reduction in price as the rated age increases. In practice, from the viewpoint of the broker quoting prices for the client, variations in price from our results will occur because of the differences in standard premium scales declared by each insurer.

Assume that the broker is seeking a quote for a substandard male age 7 for whom one of the following annuity forms will be purchased: life annuity, 20-year certain and life annuity, 30-year certain and life annuity, at $1000 per month, each with either a 0 percent, 3 percent, or 6 percent cost-of-living adjustment. Suppose further that the insurer receives the age ratings for this individual of ages 18, 29, 40, 51, 62. Table 33 shows the total gross single premiums that this insurer would charge under a gross premium scale that was in use at the time the quote was requested.

TABLE 33

GROSS SINGLE PREMIUM FOR A $1000-PER-MONTH ANNUITY
TO A MALE AGE 7 AT VARIOUS AGE RATINGS UNDER SEVERAL ANNUITY PLANS

	Life Annuity		20-Year Certain and Life		30-Year Certain and Life	
Pricing Age	Gross Premium	Ratio to Standard Age Premium	Gross Premium	Ratio to Standard Age Premium	Gross Premium	Ratio to Standard Age Premium
0 Percent Cost-of-Living Adjustment						
7	$148,800	100.0%	$149,400	100.0%	$149,900	100.0%
18	145,500	97.8	147,200	98.5	148,100	98.8
29	141,400	95.0	143,500	96.1	145,300	96.9
40	132,400	89.0	137,400	92.0	141,600	94.5
51	117,300	78.8	129,900	86.9	138,500	92.4
62	96,200	64.7	123,800	82.9	137,200	91.5
3 Percent Cost-of-Living Adjustment						
7	$227,500	100.0%	$228,400	100.0%	$229,600	100.0%
18	216,600	95.2	219,000	95.9	220,900	96.2
29	202,900	89.2	205,900	90.1	209,800	91.4
40	181,000	79.6	188,300	82.4	197,300	85.9
51	151,400	66.5	169,600	74.3	188,000	81.9
62	116,800	51.3	155,700	68.2	184,400	80.3
6 Percent Cost-of-Living Adjustment						
7	$430,300	100.0%	$431,700	100.0%	$434,300	100.0%
18	382,100	88.8	385,600	89.3	389,700	89.7
29	331,000	76.9	335,400	77.7	343,600	79.1
40	270,800	62.9	281,600	65.2	300,900	69.3
51	207,100	48.1	233,800	54.2	272,800	62.8
62	146,500	34.0	202,700	47.0	262,900	60.5

As expected, the ratio of age-rated gross premiums to standard-age gross premiums decreases with increasing certain period. For COLA plans, the ratio is significantly lower than for corresponding fixed-benefit payment plans. For example, a 20-year certain and life annuity with 0 percent COLA shows a ratio of 92.0 percent at rated age 40. The corresponding 3 percent COLA ratio is 82.4 percent, while for a similar 6 percent COLA annuity, the ratio is 65.2 percent.

Consider 4 percent of gross premium to represent the present value of profits. A 20-year certain and life annuity reaches 96.1 percent of the standard premium at rated age 29 for a 0 percent COLA. A 95.9 percent ratio is reached at rated age 18 for a 3 percent COLA, while a 96.2 percent ratio is reached at rated age 11 for a 6 percent COLA, although this is not shown in Table 33. This implies that age ratings older than these three carry the potential to wipe out expected profits. If Table 29 were used to determine rated ages, our proposed substandard annuitant, according to the rated ages shown in Table 33, would be expected to survive for the number of years shown below:

Issue Age	Life Expectancy (years)
7	64.4
18	53.8
29	43.8
40	33.6
51	24.0
62	15.8

Thus, for example, if a 3 percent COLA 20-year certain and life annuity were purchased, survival beyond the guarantee period under an age 62 age rating would involve greater loss to the company in each year of survival than if survival lasted beyond 24 years under an age 51 rating, because of the larger premium collected at issue age 51.

Although the analysis above is just an example, the conclusion is clear: Unless a high overall confidence level applies, the potential for loss on substandard business is great where very substantial age ratings are offered.

Underwriters and actuaries must be cognizant of the possibility of significant mortality improvement in impaired lives arising from improved medical care or scientific breakthroughs, in addition to projected mortality decreases for standard lives. For example, if persons with spinal cord injuries were to become productive members of society, their longevity would be increased. This is not beyond the realm of imagination with the advent of computers that can be commanded even by quadriplegics. The potential for insurance company loss is great.

VII. MORTALITY AND VALUATION

Standard Lives

Marginal effects on the valuation of both traditional and structured settlement fixed-income annuities generated by substituting the 1983-a mortality table in place of the 1971 IAM mortality table were illustrated in the *Transactions* in 1981 [18]. These effects paled compared to the reduction in valuation reserves for such annuities permitted by increased valuation interest rates described in the 1980 amendments to the NAIC Valuation Law, which has been adopted by all 50 states and the District of Columbia. In view of the effects of mortality improvement on annuity pricing, however, it would perhaps be appropriate to consider the use of projection factors in annuity valuation as well, without further comment in this paper.

However, one aspect of mortality warrants elaborate discussion about its effect on valuation reserves: substandard lives.

Substandard Lives

The burgeoning premium volume for substandard structured settlement annuities can have a material effect on reserves. The five methods used by companies to determine the mortality rates in reserve calculations are listed below, with the first two probably being the most prevalent. Substandard annuity reserves are determined as:

1. The reserve for a standard life at the true age of the substandard life.
2. The reserve for a standard life at the substandard life's rated up age used in pricing the annuity.
3. The reserve at the true age of the substandard life using multiple mortality table q_x values reflecting the underwriter's evaluation of extra mortality to be expected.
4. The reserve at the true age of the substandard life using that constant number of deaths added at each attained age to the valuation mortality table number of deaths that will reproduce the life expectancy of the annuitant used in pricing the annuity.
5. The reserve at the true age of the substandard life using mortality rates graded over a predetermined number of years from the pricing mortality table rate to the standard valuation mortality table rate.

Method 1, the most conservative, makes no allowance at any duration for the greater probability of the substandard annuitant's death. Such a method produces the greatest surplus strain and noncompetitive premiums to pay for additional capital requirements.

Method 2, the least conservative, makes full allowance at all durations of the greater probability of the substandard annuitant's death. This method produces the least surplus strain and adopts the full judgment of the underwriter in assessing future longevity. The extreme situation can arise that the annuitant has outlived the period for which reserves are calculable under the valuation mortality table. Lesser degrees of underreserving at earlier durations also occur under this method.

Consider the child at birth who is assessed a 70-year rate up in age by the underwriter. Reserve factors for issue age 70 would run out after 45 years if the limiting age of the table is taken as 116. Improvement in medical care, excellent home care, or even a misassessment of the seriousness of the injury whether by error or by inappropriate statistical guides could result in the annuitant surviving beyond age 45. Reserve factors during the 45-year period also would be inadequate by failing to account for survival beyond true age 45 for this annuitant.

Method 3 incorporates the underwriter's judgment in assessing the severity of the mortality risk by determining the adjustment factors to standard mortality rates that are needed commencing with the true issue age. Surplus strain is thereby reduced. This method is still subject, however, to the accuracy of the underwriter's assessment and the degree of annuitants' increased longevity above that contemplated by the assessment. To the degree that the multiple mortality table rating correctly assesses the probability of death, reserves released would follow the release of risk. Reserves would be held during the entire lifetime of the annuitant, although their sufficiency may be subject to question.

Method 4 is similar to method 3 except that constant extra deaths are added at each attained age to the tabular number of deaths at such ages, instead of dealing with a multiple of standard mortality rates. Reduction in surplus strain runs off more quickly under method 4 than under method 3. Method 4 also avoids the problem of table runoff, so that the annuitant will not outlive the reserve.

Method 5, a blend of two methods, incorporates the underwriter's judgment in assessing the severity of the mortality risk, by starting with pricing basis mortality rates, thereby alleviating surplus strain. Underwriting liberalizations can be attenuated by grading such mortality rates into the standard valuation table mortality rates over a specified but shorter time period, for example, 5 or 10 years. From a competition viewpoint, this method would not be as appropriate for a company just entering this line of business because the surplus strain would be longer-lasting than if method 2 were used. Yet, some companies may not wish to adopt the least conservative reserving method, method 2.

From a regulatory viewpoint, method 5 represents the ideal way to tailor the reserving method with the confidence attached to underwriting practices as well as other individual company characteristics.

Actual experience, when compared to an underwriter's estimate of expected longevity over the annuitant's lifetime, can have a significant effect on the adequacy of substandard reserves for a company writing a good portion of COLA annuities. A periodic review of the valuation file of structured settlement annuities is a must to ensure that each surviving annuitant's contract has a reasonable reserve established for it, especially for COLA annuities in which relatively large benefit amounts are payable to annuitants who may reach advanced age.

In establishing a substandard reserve basis, a degree of conservatism is warranted because of the skimpy statistical data used in promulgating underwriting guidelines and the competitive nature of this line of business.

VIII. SURVEY OF STRUCTURED SETTLEMENT ANNUITY CHARACTERISTICS

Because structured settlement annuities are relatively new, their characteristics may be vastly different than those of traditional annuities. With this in mind, companies thought to be writing structured settlement annuities were polled to determine specific information on this class of business. Where information may have touched on proprietary topics, the data were requested in such form as to be useful but to protect confidentiality. Responses were received from 15 companies, although not all these companies answered all questions. Appendix II summarizes the responses.

Traditional fixed-income annuities are normally issued to male, female, and joint lives. The proportion of joint life issues may, from traditional annuity experience, be expected to lie in the 20–40 percent range. With 13 out of 15 companies responding that they issue joint life annuities, it is noteworthy that none of these companies has received more than 3.7 percent of its premium involving life contingencies as joint life, and only eight of these companies reported any joint life premium. Five companies did not respond, and the other two companies actually received either less than 0.1 percent of premium for joint life annuities or received no such premium at all. The arithmetic average proportion of joint life premium for those eight companies is closer to 2.5 percent.

As a proportion of total premiums, including premiums not involving life contingencies, the largest proportion is 3.0 percent, and the average for the nine companies reporting is about 1.6 percent. On a number-of-lives basis, the largest proportion of contracts sold as joint life annuities is 2.0 percent, while the average proportion for the ten companies reporting is about 1 percent. Joint life structured settlement annuities represent a very small portion of total sales.

Note from the response to question 2 that males have purchased 43.6–63.0 percent of the structured annuities when measured on a lives basis, for an average of 57.5 percent. On the basis of amount of premiums involving life contingencies, the range becomes 51.2–68.0 percent, for an average of 58.5 percent. If premiums not involving life contingencies are to be included in the calculations, the companies reporting show a range of 50.5–70.0 percent, for an average of 60.7 percent. This 57–61 percent average ratio is in the same range as that for traditional fixed-income annuities, especially if we set that range at 40–80 percent to accommodate the distribution of the larger number of companies that write traditional fixed-income annuities. Even a 50–70 percent range contains the structured annuities proportion sold to males.

Question 3 provides an important piece of information in the consideration of mortality effects on structured settlement annuities. If such annuities are more often than not issued with long certain periods, then the effect of underestimating mortality improvement is greatly mitigated, as previously discussed. On a number-of-lives basis, 13 reporting companies show that between 2 percent and 28.1 percent of their contracts are straight-life annuity forms with no guarantee period. Company B, with the 28.1 percent proportion, and Company C, with 22.0 percent, issue about twice as many pure life annuities than the third-highest reporting company, with a 12.6 percent proportion. The average proportion of life annuities issued is 8.8 percent including Company B and Company C and 5.9 percent if Company B and Company C are excluded.

Annuities certain are about four times as likely to be written with a 10-year guarantee period than with a period of 1–9 years, Company K results excluded. This factor increases to about five if the Company A result is excluded. A guarantee period of 20 years is about six times as likely to be written as a period of 11–19 years. Question 3 also reveals that an average of about 87.0 percent of life contingent annuities have guarantee periods of 10 years or more, while an average of about 66.3 percent of such annuities have guarantee periods of 20 years or more.

Table 34 compares analogous figures derived from question 3 on an amount-of-premium basis with those just indicated on a number-of-lives basis.

TABLE 34

ANALYSIS OF STRUCTURED SETTLEMENT LIFE CONTINGENT ANNUITIES
AND THEIR ANNUITY CERTAIN GUARANTEE PERIODS
BY LIVES AND AMOUNT OF PREMIUM

Basis	Average Proportion of Issues by			
	Number of Lives	Ratio	Amount of Premium	Ratio
Life Only				
All 13 companies	8.8%		7.0%	
Excluding Companies B and C	5.9		4.1	
Certain Period — All 12 Companies				
1–9 years	4.0		2.5	
10 years	15.3	3.8	14.7	5.9
11–19 years	5.5		4.0	
20 years	32.6	6.0	30.7	7.7
10 or more years	87.0		90.4	
20 or more years	66.3		71.7	

The analysis above includes annuity contracts issued to both standard and substandard lives. Examination of the responses to question 4 reveals that for a small number of companies, substandard annuities are a minor portion of their total. Companies J and L are examples when analyzed on the basis of premium income. Companies I and K can be added when analyzed on a number-of-lives basis. Most other companies write a substantial proportion of premium on substandard lives. Examples of these are Companies A, B, D, G, and M. Thus, of the nine companies writing substandard business, four write insignificant amounts of substandard annuity, while five write significant amounts. Company A, for that matter, writes more substandard business than standard: at a 6:1 ratio on an amount-of-premium basis!

Requests to break out the substandard annuity portion by both including and excluding annuity certain and lump-sum benefits not involving life contingencies was intended as an accommodation to those companies unable to break out their data to exclude no life contingency issues.

An extensive amount of shopping via substandard annuity rating requests is the norm in this line of business. Question 5 is intended to reveal success ratios in issuing annuities on the lives of substandard annuitants for whom a rating is offered. Unfortunately, only six companies responded to this question, presumably because many companies do not make the effort to ascertain this information. Except for Company J, a maximum of 6 percent of the rated cases end up as a sold annuity, when considering only life contingent annuities sold. That maximum rate of cases sold is only 4 percent, when all structured settlement annuities sold form the denominator of the ratio. Company J sold 15 percent of the cases for which it rendered a quote — truly extraordinary.

Question 6 is intended to determine the prevalent true issue age categories of the structured settlement annuities sold, whether on a standard or sub-standard basis. Responses are on a number-of-lives and on an amount-of-premium basis, considering life contingent annuities only and separately all structured annuities. The number of companies responding in the format requested is shown in Table 35. Company K was unable to determine the proportion of annuities sold by the requested age categories, so its results for this question are not included in the study.

TABLE 35

NUMBER OF COMPANIES RESPONDING TO QUESTION 6

	Number of Lives	Amount of Premium
Life contingent annuities only	9	10
All structured annuities	11	10

Table 36 shows the proportionate distribution of issues by age groups under each of the four categories, based upon the arithmetic average of the reported proportions in each age grouping cell. More statistically valid methods to analyze these data are not available, in keeping with the concept of maintaining confidentiality.

Considering life contingent annuities only, the following observations can be made:

- Proportions by issue age groups are similar whether measured by number of lives or amount of premiums, until age 60.
- The 20–29 age grouping cell contains the largest group of issues under both methods of measurement.
- At least 85 percent of all issues are below 60.
- More than 50 percent of all issues are at ages below 40 on a number-of-lives basis.
- Just less than 50 percent of all issues are at ages below 30 on an amount-of-premium basis.
- Just about 50 percent of all issues are between the ages of 20 and 50 on a number-of-lives basis.
- More than 55 percent of all issues are between the ages of 20 and 50 on an amount-of-premium basis.
- Only about 5 percent of all issues are at ages 70 or older on a number-of-lives basis.

TABLE 36

ANALYSIS OF STRUCTURED SETTLEMENT ANNUITY
TRUE ISSUE AGE GROUPINGS
BASED ON AVERAGE OF REPORTED PROPORTIONS IN EACH CELL

| | Proportion of Issues in Age Grouping | | | |
| | By Number of Lives | | By Amount of Premium | |
Issue Age Group	Life and C&L Annuities Only	All Annuities Combined	Life and C&L Annuities Only	All Annuities Combined
0–9	9.8%	19.6%	12.7%	14.7%
10–19	13.0	21.2	12.1	14.3
20–29	20.4	16.4	22.9	20.6
30–39	12.0	14.3	16.8	17.3
40–49	17.1	11.9	18.1	15.5
50–59	11.6	9.2	9.5	10.4
60–69	11.0	4.2	5.9	3.9
70–79	3.9	2.2	1.6	2.6
80–89	1.1	0.5	0.4	0.3
90–99	0.1	0	0	0
Unknown	0	0.5	0	0.4
Total	100.0%	100.0%	100.0%	100.0%

- Only about 2 percent of all issues are at ages 70 or older on an amount-of-premium basis.

Considering all annuities combined, the following observations can be made:

- Proportions by issue age groups are similar whether measured by number of lives or amount of premium for all issue age groups except 10–19.
- The 10–19 age grouping cell contains the largest group of issues on a number-of-lives basis, and the 20–29 age grouping cell takes its place on an amount-of-premium basis.
- At least 90 percent of all issues are below age 60.
- More than 50 percent of all issues are at ages below 30 on a number-of-lives basis (more than 70 percent are below age 40).
- Just about 50 percent of all issues are at ages below 30 on an amount-of-premium basis (more than 65 percent are below age 40).
- More than 40 percent of all issues are between the ages of 20 and 50 on a number-of-lives basis.
- More than 50 percent of all issues are between the ages of 20 and 50 on an amount-of-premium basis.
- Only about 3 percent of all issues are at ages 70 or older under both methods of measurement.

Obviously, variations from the average statistics quoted above will be evidenced by individual company data. For example, Company I is the only company to show less than 50 percent of issues to be below age 40. The result is not confirmed by the total of all annuities data for this cell. However, these overall results should be useful benchmarks by which to measure a company's individual experience.

Thirteen companies responded to question 7 by indicating the mortality table basis in their structured settlement annuity pricing. Six companies used some form of the 1979–81 U.S. Population mortality table (one company blended it with the 1971 IAM table and another with 1983 Table a), while two companies used a blend of the 1971 GAM and 1983 GAM tables and two companies used some form of 1971 IAM table without blending. One company used the 1980 U.S. Population table and another used 1983 Table a without blending. The remaining responding company used its own experience table on a select and ultimate basis, mentioning explicitly that mortality improvement was included. Of course, modifications of the tables by the other companies comprise some degree of estimating mortality improvement. Diversity in assumptions for mortality appears to be the norm.

Although five methods of valuing substandard annuities were discussed in Section VII, the 12 companies who responded to question 8 indicated that they used four of those age-mortality bases in pricing such annuities, thereby excluding the constant addition of death at each age method. Nine of these companies price such annuities by using life expectancies determined from a rated age. Simplicity of use for the broker in the field tends to make this the most popular pricing method. Company J determines price based upon the annuitant's true age by using multiple annuity tables. Company N uses rated age in pricing on either a life expectancy basis or by converting from an issue age multiple annuity table calculation, depending upon the decision of the underwriter to determine which method was more appropriate. Company M prices annuities on a rated age basis by converting from an issue age calculation based on either multiple annuity tables or additional deaths added to each age, again depending upon the underwriter's decision.

The underlying mortality table for pricing standard structured settlement annuities also is used to price substandard annuities, as indicated by each of the 13 companies writing such annuities who responded to question 9. A degree of consistency in rates is retained by this choice of underlying mortality table.

The responses to question 10 regarding valuation of substandard annuities are worth noting. Seven of these companies use the method that produces the least surplus strain — standard reserve at pricing age. Only three companies use the method that produces the greatest surplus strain — standard reserve at true age. Companies D and L base reserves on multiple mortality annuity tables at the annuitant's true age. Company J grades mortality over a period that varies by plan from the pricing mortality basis to standard mortality.

Table 37 compares the pricing and valuation basis for each company responding to questions 8 and 10. This table reveals the correlation between pricing by rated age using life expectancies and valuation using standard reserves at the pricing age. Six companies follow this method. Companies D and L use a multiple annuity table at true age instead. Companies A and O use a standard table reserve at true age for valuation. Companies J and M do not use this pricing basis, and Company K did not indicate its pricing basis.

TABLE 37

COMPARISON OF PRICING AND VALUATION BASES
FOR COMPANIES RESPONDING TO QUESTIONS 8 AND 10

| Company | Pricing by Rated Age Using Life Expectancies | Valuation by | | Standard Table Reserve at True Age | Pricing by True* Age Using Multiple Annuity Tables | Valuation by Mortality Graded over a Given Period from Pricing Mortality to Standard Mortality* |
		Standard Reserve at Pricing Age	Multiple Annuity at True Age			
A	X			X		
B	X	X				
C	Not applicable	—				
D	X		X			
E	X	X				
F	X	X				
G	X	X				
H		Not applicable	—			
I	X	X				
J					X	X - years vary
K	N.R.	X				
L	X		X			
M					X	X†
N	X‡	X				
O	X			X		

N.R. = No response to the question.
*Rated age for Company M and Company N.
†Company M also prices on an additional death at each age basis.
‡Company N also prices on a multiple annuity table basis.

Surplus strain for a company writing structured settlement annuities is affected not only by how it values its substandard annuities, but also by how it values lump sum and annuity certain payments that do not involve survivorship, as well as increasing benefit (COLA) plans. Questions 11 and 12 elicited responses on how the above contract provisions were valued. Twelve out of 15 companies responded that they value these benefits as single premium immediate annuities, thus providing for the highest valuation interest rate (9.25 percent in 1986, 8.00 percent in 1987). Immediate annuities provide for commencement of benefit payments within 13 months of the contract's issue or purchase date (under New York State law).

Weighting factors for plan types A, B or C, based upon a guarantee duration that produces interest rates varying between 6-1/2 percent and 8 percent during 1987, must be used for annuities with benefit commencement deferred more than 13 months. The period between the contract date of issue or purchase and the commencement date of benefit payments determines which weighting factor by plan type is applicable.

Valuation interest rates are further affected by increasing benefit payments or lump sum payments in a calendar year whose sum of all benefits exceeds the prior year sum of all benefits by 15 percent if valuation is on an aggregate basis, or by 10 percent for each contract valued on a seriatim basis (under New York State law). Aggregate method refers to a determination of the sum of future benefits payable at each attained age for all lives covered under all contracts, for all issue years combined. The other allowable valuation basis, seriatim, refers to a determination of the sum of future benefits payable at each attained age for each life individually, even though there may be more than one life covered under a single contract and even if there is more than one form of benefit payable to that life. Single-premium immediate annuity valuation interest rates may not be used to value the excess amounts, aggregate or seriatim, if the above percentage excesses apply. Weighting factors must be used in such cases to determine the valuation interest rate applicable to such excess benefit payments.

Companies J, K and O, having indicated that they value annuities certain and lump sums as separate contracts, would have to use the lower interest rates in their statutory valuation of lump sum benefits.

This statutory reserve method for issues of 1984–1987 will require a recalculation for federal tax reserve purposes under Section 807(c) of the 1954 Internal Revenue Code. Section 807(c) requires annuity certain and nonlife contingent lump sum benefit payments tax reserves to equal the present value of future benefits by discounting at an appropriate rate of interest. Quoting from Section 807(c), the

"appropriate rate of interest for any obligation is the higher of the prevailing State assumed interest rate . . . or the rate of interest assumed by the company . . . in determining the guaranteed benefit."

The gross premium interest rate assumption will always exceed the maximum statutory valuation interest rate. Thus, tax reserves for these benefits will always be less than statutory reserves, producing greater surplus strain and lost investment income on funds paid out in income taxes on the difference in increases between these reserves. Statutory provisions require the use of a lower valuation interest rate. From questionnaire responses, apparently more companies use the higher interest rate in statutory valuation. Information regarding tax reserves was not requested in the questionnaire. It is clear from Section 807(c), however, than an even higher interest rate is required for tax reserve calculations.

The Omnibus Budget Reconciliation Act of 1987 (OBRA) affects the federal taxation of annuity issues starting in 1988 by requiring lower tax reserves than those produced under previous tax law. OBRA mandates the use of the CARVM valuation method to determine federal tax reserves, independent of the statutory reserve valuation method used, and prescribes the tax valuation interest rate that must be used. This rate may not be less than the statutory valuation interest rate.

The federal valuation interest rate is defined as the greater of the prevailing interest rate (PIR) and the applicable federal rate (AFR). PIR is the highest interest rate allowed by at least 26 states. AFR is the annual rate determined by averaging the applicable federal mid-term rates at the beginning of each calendar month in the 60-month period immediately preceding the calendar year for which the determintion is made (excluding months before August 1986). This produces a 1988 federal tax valuation interest rate of 7.77 percent. Such a change in federal tax reserves requires prospective repricing of annuities because of its effect on the Gain From Operations.

All companies except Company L treat increasing benefit contracts as level benefit plans, according to their response to question 12. They therefore would use the highest permitted statutory valuation interest rate to value these contracts, subject to the adjustment in interest rates for excess of benefit payments by calendar-year comparison explained above. Company L indicated that it varies its statutory valuation interest rate depending upon the

COLA rate used to determine benefits. Such resulting rates may not exceed the maximum valuation interest rates prescribed by statute.

Underlying the comments in this paper on structured settlement annuities is the fact that this new line of business, with its own characteristics, must be based upon a broader foundation of experience studies — for standard mortality as well as for substandard mortality. Question 13 reveals that only four out of the 15 responding companies are prepared at this time to participate in a mortality study of structured settlement annuities. Participation capabilities of nine other writers of this line of business would be deferred from 1 to 8 years in the future, with two companies being unable at this time to determine when such participation would be possible. Company O would agree to participate if the effort involved was cost-justified.

Such a response is not unexpected. Gearing up for this new line of business by using existing systems or by creating new systems may sometimes be crude or just expedient and require refinement — with possible inability to recapture prior data for inclusion into a more refined system. Suffice it to say that no meaningful studies of the structured settlement annuity line of business can be expected for at least 2 or 3 years if the responding companies are representative of the other companies writing this line of annuities.

Question 14 requested companies to list the 10 most prevalent types of substandard cases for which quotes are requested. All 13 companies writing substandard annuities responded. Each listing reflected a different distribution of injury types, as shown in Appendix II. Although some types were among a company's top 10, the percentage for that company was small enough to warrant listing that injury under "miscellaneous" for purposes of the question 15 summary chart. Some injuries are shown separately because of the meaningful proportion they represent within a company. For example, cerebral palsy could have been combined with birth trauma, as could mental retardation.

The major categories of injury types for all companies combined are discussed in the mortality and underwriting section. Question 14 responses reveal, however, how many categories are described by individual companies as "major" that contain proportions of 10% or less. Of the 73 proportions shown for all 13 companies, there are 36 proportions equal to 10 percent or less. Another approach is to examine the proportions exactly as reported in response to question 14 without regard to labeling specific injury types. Table 38 shows these proportions, specifically identifying the "miscellaneous" or "other" category.

TABLE 38

PROPORTION OF INJURY TYPES BY RESPONDING COMPANY
MOST FREQUENTLY UNDERWRITTEN
FOR SUBSTANDARD STRUCTURED SETTLEMENT ANNUITIES

Company	Proportions Reported in Category											
	1	2	3	4	5	6	7	8	9	10	11	12
A	40%	30%	5%	10%	15%							
B	60	20	10	5	5M							
C	N.A.											
D	N.R.											
E	25	17	14	2	1	41M						
F	5	15	10	15	5	50M						
G	17	13	14	3	20	6	5	2	6	4	2	8M
H	N.A.											
I	20	17	11	8	4	3	3	2	2	2	28M	
J	33	33	10	3	7	7	3	3	1M			
K	70	20	10M									
L	31.3	18.5	10.8	9.2	4.6	3.1	3.1	1.5	1.5	1.0	15.4M	
M	19	18	12	8	7	6	6	5	5	4	10M	
N	50	15	5	30M	5M							
O	28.5	28.5	38	5M								

N.A. = not applicable.
N.R. = No response to the question.
M = Miscellaneous or other.

Of the 76 proportions shown in Table 38 after excluding those 11 coded M for miscellaneous, 44 proportions represent injury types comprising 10% or less of a company's total injury types underwritten. Of the 11 miscellaneous proportions, seven companies show miscellaneous proportions of 10% or more, the highest three percentages being 30 percent, 41 percent and 50 percent! Clearly, this shows the diversity of the types of cases being underwritten.

One may wonder whether reliable statistics can be gathered from such a splintering of information. It may turn out that only the three to four most prevalent injury types could be subject to intercompany study.

Companies B, I and L furnished technical references used to evaluate substandard annuities, as requested by question 16. These sources are shown in Appendix II. The paper "The Medical Underwriting of Substandard Life Annuities" [5] contains a listing of references to papers on this topic. Further references can be found in the paper "The Epidemiology of Severe Injuries in Structured Settlement Applicants" [4], which studied 6,461 cases of individuals applying for substandard structured settlement annuities to describe the epidemiologic characteristics of their injuries.

Five companies requested elaboration on aspects of the structured settlement line that were not covered in the questionnaire, at the invitation of question 17. These requests are shown in Appendix II. The comments below relate to these requests. Those questions not covered here either require discussion beyond the scope of this paper (for example, other than mortality pricing assumptions), relate to proprietary information, or are covered in the text of this paper.

Company B's question on asset/liability matching was submitted prior to the Society of Actuaries meeting in May 1987. A panel of vendors discussed their software packages on asset/liability matching at that meeting. The presentation included a handout paper that compared the salient features of each package.

This author has not heard of any commercially developed software usable for administrative processing in the structured settlement line.

Table 30, which is only illustrative of rated ages being quoted, apparently indicates that there is no real maximum age for substandard ratings. Whatever age rating is warranted by the projected life expectancy according to the medical criteria will be quoted, without "loading" for recoveries and so on.

IX. CONCLUSIONS

Estimation of mortality for annuity pricing purposes took a quantum leap in 1949 with the publication of the Jenkins and Lew paper. Subsequent experience mortality tables have shown that development of mortality improvement factors is still an art rather than a science. This paper has attempted to show that conservative mortality improvement factors are a necessity in pricing annuities, based upon historical events. However, there is no making up for past underestimations of morality in the development of nonparticipating annuity products. Investment income gains can no longer be relied upon to offset mortality losses due to competitive pricing pressures and the potential of losses in this area due to investment complexities.

Structured settlement annuities pricing is subject to intense competitive pressure. Substandard annuities pricing carries the potential to produce mortality losses that may wipe out the gains on a larger block of standard annuity issues. The foundation for including substandard annuity mortality in the pricing process is relatively weak from an actuarial viewpoint. Cautious pricing of this aspect of structured settlement annuities is recommended.

The author hopes that more of the companies writing structured settlement annuities will be able to submit their data to enhance the value of the questionnaire included in this paper, as well as participate in expanding the information available on this line of business.

REFERENCES

1. BAYO, F.R. AND FABER, J.F. "United States Population Projections for OASDI Cost Estimates, 1980," *Actuarial Study No. 82*, SSA Publication No. 11-11529. Washington, D.C.: U.S. Department of Health and Human Services, June 1980.

2. BORHANI, N.D. "Mortality Trend in Hypertension, United States, 1950–1976," In *Proceedings of the Conference on the Decline in Coronary Heart Disease Mortality*, NIH Publication No. 79-1610. Washington, D.C.: U.S. Dept. of Health, Education and Welfare, May 1979.

3. BOWERMAN, W.G. "Annuity Mortality," *TSA* II, Part II (1950): 76–102.

4. BUTZ, R.H. "The Epidemiology of Severe Injuries in Structured Settlement Applicants," *Journal of Insurance Medicine* 18, No. 3 (Summer 1986): 2–15.

5. CHAIT, L. AND TEITELBAUM, N. "The Medical Underwriting of Substandard Life Annuities," *Journal of Insurance Medicine* 14, No. 3 (July–September 1983): 27–29.

6. CHERRY, H. "The 1971 Individual Annuity Mortality Table," *TSA* XXIII, Part I (1971): 475–568.

7. COMMITTEE ON MORTALITY UNDER ORDINARY INSURANCES AND ANNUITIES. "Mortality under Individual Immediate Annuities," *TSA 1969 Reports* No. 2 (1970): 5–62.

8. FABER, J.F. "Life Tables for the United States: 1900–2050," *Actuarial Study No. 87*, SSA Publication No. 11-11534. Washington, D.C.: U.S. Department of Health and Human Services, September 1982.

9. FRIES, J.M. "Aging, Natural Death and the Compression of Mortality," *New England Journal of Medicine* CCCIII, No. 3 (July 17, 1980): 130.

10. GEISLER, W.O., JOUSSE, A.T., MEAGEN, W.J., AND BREITHAUPT, D. "Survival in Traumatic Spinal Cord Injury," *Paraplegia* 21 (1983): 364–373.

11. "Immediate Annuities and Structured Settlements," *Record* II, No. 1 (April 1–2, 1985): 487–520.

12. JENKINS, W.A. AND LEW, E.A. "A New Mortality Basis for Annuities," *TSA* I (1949): 369–498.

13. LEW, E.A. "Recent Mortality under Individual Immediate Annuities," *TSA* XXI, Part II (1969): D547–D549.

14. NATIONAL CENTER FOR HEALTH STATISTICS. "Vital Statistics of the United States, 1978," Vol. II, Sec. 5, Pub. No. PHS-81-1104. Washington, D.C.: U.S. Government Printing Office, 1981.

15. NATIONAL CENTER FOR HEALTH STATISTICS. "U.S. Decennial Life Tables for 1979–81," Vol. 1, Number 1, United States Life Tables, Pub. No. PHS 85-1150-1. Washington, D.C.: U.S. Government Printing Office, 1985.

16. NATIONAL CENTER FOR HEALTH STATISTICS. "Vital Statistics of the United States, 1982," Vol. II, Mortality, Part A, Pub. No. PHS 86-1122. Washington, D.C.: U.S. Government Printing Office, 1986.

17. PETERSON, R.M. "Group Annuity Mortality," TSA IV (1952): 246–307.

18. "Report of the Committee to Recommend a New Mortality Basis for Individual Annuity Valuation (Derivation of the 1983 Table a)," TSA XXXIII (1981): 675–750.

19. ROSENWAIKE, I., YAFFE, N., AND SAGI, P.C. "The Recent Decline in Mortality of the Extremely Aged: An Analysis of Statistical Data," American Journal of Public Health LXX, No. 10 (October 1980): 1074.

20. STALLONES, R.A. "The Rise and Fall of Ischemic Heart Disease," Scientific American XXIV, No. 3 (November 1980): 53.

21. STERNHELL, C.M. AND PAGE, C.H. "The 1960 Modification of the a-1949 Table with Projection," TSA XIII, Part I (1961): 127–168.

22. WILKIN, J.C. "Recent Trends in the Mortality of the Aged," TSA XXXIII (1981): 11–62.

APPENDIX I

TABLE A1

FIXED IMMEDIATE ANNUITIES

MORTALITY GROSS SINGLE PREMIUMS (NO LOADING)

ASSUMING 1965 COMPANY MORTALITY TABLE

WITH MORTALITY IMPROVEMENT BASED ON EXPERIENCE TABLES AND PROJECTION SCALES I AND J

Sex	Plan	Number of Contracts	Annual Income	Annual Income Distribution	Adjusted Single Premium	Mortality Gross Premium		
						At Issue	Projection I	Projection J
For Issues of 1966; with Interest of 4.75 Percent for the First 15 Years and 3.5 Percent Thereafter								
Male	Life	223	306,400	44.6%	2,686,540	2,521,695	2,619,939	2,622,193
Female	Life	296	380,400	55.4	3,609,500	3,388,787	3,575,128	3,577,701
Subtotal		519	686,800	34.1	6,296,040	5,910,482	6,195,067	6,199,894
Male	10 CC	505	630,700	47.5	6,735,212	6,366,039	6,551,999	6,552,682
Female	10 CC	606	697,500	52.5	7,730,105	7,296,940	7,604,391	7,609,344
Subtotal		1,111	1,328,200	65.9	14,465,317	13,662,979	14,156,390	14,162,026
Subtotal male		728	937,100	46.5	9,421,752	8,887,734	9,171,938	9,174,875
Subtotal female		902	1,077,900	53.5	11,339,605	10,685,727	11,179,519	11,187,045
Total all issues		1,630	2,015,000	100.0%	20,761,357	19,573,461	20,351,457	20,361,920
For Issues of 1967; with Interest of 5 Percent for the First 12 Years and 3.75 Percent Thereafter								
Male	Life	204	313,100	41.5%	2,713,390	2,547,103	2,656,673	2,657,774
Female	Life	360	441,700	58.5	4,141,761	3,888,220	4,116,385	4,120,456
Subtotal		564	754,800	30.2	6,855,151	6,435,323	6,773,058	6,778,230
Male	10 CC	477	689,300	39.5	7,263,950	6,872,433	7,089,671	7,092,371
Female	10 CC	953	1,055,900	60.5	11,540,004	10,909,389	11,395,988	11,409,793
Subtotal		1,430	1,745,200	69.8	18,803,954	17,781,822	18,485,659	18,502,164
Subtotal male		681	1,002,400	40.1	9,977,340	9,419,536	9,746,344	9,750,145
Subtotal female		1,313	1,497,600	59.9	15,681,765	14,797,609	15,512,373	15,530,249
Total all issues		1,994	2,500,000	100.0%	25,659,105	24,217,145	25,258,717	25,280,394

TABLE A1 — *Continued*

Sex	Plan	Number of Contracts	Annual Income	Annual Income Distribution	Adjusted Single Premium	At Issue	Mortality Gross Premium	
							Projection I	Projection J
	For Issues of 1968; with Interest of 5.5 Percent for the First 13 Years and 3.75 Percent Thereafter							
Male	Life	220	343,200	43.1%	2,926,251	2,705,952	2,831,261	2,832,557
Female	Life	399	453,300	56.9	4,184,202	3,861,970	4,098,372	4,104,299
Subtotal		619	796,500	31.2	7,110,453	6,567,922	6,929,633	6,936,856
Male	10 CC	473	633,800	36.0	6,490,573	6,125,218	6,330,115	6,330,549
Female	10 CC	1,001	1,126,100	64.0	11,952,867	11,263,112	11,781,540	11,796,264
Subtotal		1,474	1,759,900	68.8	18,443,440	17,388,330	18,111,655	18,126,813
Subtotal male		693	977,000	38.2	9,416,824	8,831,170	9,161,376	9,163,106
Subtotal female		1,400	1,579,400	61.8	16,137,069	15,125,082	15,879,912	15,900,563
Total all issues		2,093	2,556,400	100.0%	25,553,893	23,956,252	25,041,288	25,063,669
	For Issues of 1969; with Interest of 5.7 Percent for the First 13 Years and 3.75 Percent Thereafter							
Male	Life	151	199,800	33.4%	1,684,327	1,557,265	1,635,900	1,636,654
Female	Life	302	398,300	66.6	3,635,007	3,352,915	3,574,621	3,578,292
Subtotal		453	598,100	27.1	5,319,334	4,910,180	5,210,521	5,214,946
Male	10 CC	431	543,900	33.8	5,505,974	5,195,547	5,382,743	5,384,656
Female	10 CC	971	1,066,200	66.2	11,180,024	10,536,255	11,050,720	11,060,547
Subtotal		1,402	1,610,100	72.9	16,685,998	15,731,802	16,433,463	16,445,203
Subtotal male		582	743,700	33.7	7,190,301	6,752,812	7,018,643	7,021,310
Subtotal female		1,273	1,464,500	66.3	14,815,031	13,889,170	14,625,341	14,638,839
Total all issues		1,855	2,208,200	100.0%	22,005,332	20,641,982	21,643,984	21,660,149

TABLE A2

Fixed Immediate Annuities
Mortality Gross Single Premiums (No Loading)
Assuming 1969 Company Mortality Table
With Mortality Improvement Based on Experience Tables and Projection Scales I and J

Sex	Plan	Number of Contracts	Annual Income	Annual Income Distribution	Adjusted Single Premium	At Issue	Mortality Gross Premium	
							Projection I	Projection J
For Issues of 1970; with Interest of 7 Percent for the First 16 Years and 3.25 Percent Thereafter								
Male	Life	144	262,200	42.7%	2,093,306	1,955,147	1,985,827	1,986,749
Female	Life	251	351,400	57.3	3,013,105	2,814,938	2,903,403	2,907,843
Subtotal		395	613,600	30.0	5,106,411	4,770,085	4,889,230	4,894,592
Male	10 CC	375	596,600	41.7	5,660,984	5,286,989	5,444,788	5,447,041
Female	10 CC	679	835,800	58.3	8,195,268	7,653,619	7,952,825	7,960,437
Subtotal		1,054	1,432,400	70.0	13,856,252	12,940,608	13,397,613	13,407,478
Subtotal male		519	858,800	42.0	7,754,290	7,242,136	7,430,615	7,433,790
Subtotal female		930	1,187,200	58.0	11,208,373	10,468,557	10,856,228	10,868,280
Total all issues		1,449	2,046,000	100.0%	18,962,663	17,710,693	18,286,843	18,302,070
For Issues of 1971; with Interest of 7 Percent for the First 16 Years and 3.25 Percent Thereafter								
Male	Life	178	339,300	42.8%	2,813,842	2,628,637	2,693,551	2,694,745
Female	Life	303	453,600	57.2	3,738,795	3,492,285	3,596,322	3,602,053
Subtotal		481	792,900	25.3	6,552,637	6,120,922	6,289,873	6,296,798
Male	10 CC	557	1,117,300	47.6	10,868,516	10,153,842	10,510,411	10,514,787
Female	10 CC	870	1,228,400	52.4	11,413,553	10,659,675	11,059,837	11,070,750
Subtotal		1,427	2,345,700	74.7	22,282,069	20,813,517	21,570,248	21,585,537
Subtotal male		735	1,456,600	46.4	13,682,358	12,782,479	13,203,962	13,209,532
Subtotal female		1,173	1,682,000	53.6	15,152,348	14,151,960	14,656,159	14,672,803
Total all issues		1,908	3,138,600	100.0%	28,834,706	26,934,439	27,860,121	27,882,335

TABLE A2 — Continued

Sex	Plan	Number of Contracts	Annual Income	Annual Income Distribution	Adjusted Single Premium	Mortality Gross Premium		
						At Issue	Projection I	Projection J
			For Issues of 1972; with Interest of 6.75 Percent for the First 16 Years and 3.25 Percent Thereafter					
Male	Life	173	314,700	52.5%	2,535,420	2,368,596	2,422,661	2,424,977
Female	Life	228	284,300	47.5	2,289,540	2,138,568	2,206,626	2,209,784
Subtotal		401	599,000	23.4	4,824,960	4,507,164	4,629,287	4,634,761
Male	10 CC	472	780,200	39.8	7,499,496	7,005,466	7,258,226	7,260,970
Female	10 CC	858	1,182,300	60.2	11,003,317	10,277,452	10,689,622	10,704,550
Subtotal		1,330	1,962,500	76.6	18,502,813	17,282,918	17,947,848	17,965,520
Subtotal male		645	1,094,900	42.7	10,034,916	9,374,062	9,680,887	9,685,947
Subtotal female		1,086	1,466,600	57.3	13,292,857	12,416,020	12,896,248	12,914,334
Total all issues		1,731	2,561,500	100.0%	23,327,773	21,790,082	22,577,135	22,600,281
			For Issues of 1973; with Interest of 7 Percent for the First 16 Years and 3.25 Percent Thereafter					
Male	Life	166	374,200	45.2%	3,063,496	2,862,109	2,950,239	2,952,993
Female	Life	223	453,400	54.8	3,685,089	3,442,569	3,544,521	3,551,259
Subtotal		389	827,600	30.3	6,748,585	6,304,678	6,494,760	6,504,252
Male	10 CC	494	924,800	48.6	8,608,772	8,039,967	8,313,853	8,320,289
Female	10 CC	709	978,400	51.4	8,885,537	8,299,883	8,615,287	8,626,547
Subtotal		1,203	1,903,200	69.7	17,494,309	16,339,850	16,929,140	16,946,836
Subtotal male		660	1,299,000	47.6	11,672,268	10,902,076	11,264,092	11,273,282
Subtotal female		932	1,431,800	52.4	12,570,626	11,742,452	12,159,808	12,177,806
Total all issues		1,592	2,730,800	100.0%	24,242,894	22,644,528	23,423,900	23,451,088

TABLE A3

FIXED IMMEDIATE ANNUITIES
MORTALITY GROSS SINGLE PREMIUMS (NO LOADING)
ASSUMING 1974 COMPANY MORTALITY TABLE
WITH MORTALITY IMPROVEMENT BASED ON EXPERIENCE TABLES AND PROJECTION SCALES I AND J

Sex	Plan	Number of Contracts	Annual Income	Annual Income Distribution	Adjusted Single Premium	Mortality Gross Premium		
						At Issue	Projection I	Projection J
For Issues of 1974; with Interest of 7.5 Percent for the First 14 Years and 5.25 Percent Thereafter								
Male	Life	141	260,900	48.7%	2,029,948	1,897,255	1,942,877	1,943,757
Female	Life	181	274,900	51.3	2,323,905	2,172,041	2,230,502	2,235,526
Subtotal		322	535,800	25.1	4,353,853	4,069,296	4,173,379	4,179,283
Male	10 CC	386	637,300	39.9	5,880,939	5,497,006	5,667,842	5,672,530
Female	10 CC	596	961,900	60.1	9,227,218	8,627,068	8,899,610	8,919,226
Subtotal		982	1,599,200	74.9	15,108,157	14,124,074	14,567,452	14,591,756
Subtotal male		527	898,200	42.1	7,910,887	7,394,261	7,610,719	7,616,287
Subtotal female		777	1,236,800	57.9	11,551,123	10,799,109	11,130,112	11,154,752
Total all issues		1,304	2,135,000	100.0%	19,462,010	18,193,370	18,740,831	18,771,039
For Issues of 1975; with Interest of 7.5 Percent for the First 14 Years and 5.25 Percent Thereafter								
Male	Life	140	344,500	52.7%	2,581,288	2,413,928	2,466,111	2,468,667
Female	Life	189	309,600	47.3	2,328,886	2,179,613	2,227,625	2,232,325
Subtotal		329	654,100	27.6	4,910,174	4,593,541	4,693,736	4,700,992
Male	10 CC	458	823,000	48.0	8,634,566	8,046,284	8,367,463	8,373,744
Female	10 CC	574	890,800	52.0	7,945,813	7,439,196	7,672,569	7,682,912
Subtotal		1,032	1,713,800	72.4	16,580,379	15,485,480	16,040,032	16,056,656
Subtotal male		598	1,167,500	49.3	11,215,854	10,460,212	10,833,574	10,842,411
Subtotal female		763	1,200,400	50.7	10,274,699	9,618,809	9,900,194	9,915,237
Total all isues		1,361	2,367,900	100.0%	21,490,553	20,079,021	20,733,768	20,757,648

TABLE A3 — Continued

Sex	Plan	Number of Contracts	Annual Income	Annual Income Distribution	Adjusted Single Premium	Mortality Gross Premium		
						At Issue	Projection 1	Projection J
For Issues of 1976; with Interest of 7.5 Percent for the First 14 Years and 5.25 Percent Thereafter								
Male	Life	178	395,200	52.4%	3,139,317	2,932,536	3,017,881	3,022,609
Female	Life	215	358,600	47.6	2,874,406	2,687,390	2,764,853	2,771,392
Subtotal		393	753,800	25.3	6,013,723	5,619,926	5,782,734	5,794,001
Male	10 CC	463	1,111,200	50.0	10,574,022	9,875,096	10,233,189	10,241,671
Female	10 CC	612	1,112,000	50.0	10,134,125	9,484,946	9,806,822	9,830,241
Subtotal		1,075	2,223,200	74.7	20,708,147	19,360,042	20,040,011	20,071,912
Subtotal male		641	1,506,400	50.6	13,713,339	12,807,632	13,251,070	13,264,280
Subtotal female		827	1,470,600	49.4	13,008,531	12,172,336	12,571,675	12,601,633
Total all issues		1,468	2,977,000	100.0%	26,721,870	24,979,968	25,822,745	25,865,913
For Issues of 1977; with Interest of 7.5 Percent for the First 14 Years and 5.25 Percent Thereafter								
Male	Life	241	541,614	54.2%	3,640,253	3,405,940	3,451,109	3,454,570
Female	Life	266	458,061	45.8	3,186,489	2,983,875	3,064,575	3,073,148
Subtotal		507	999,675	27.0	6,826,742	6,389,815	6,515,684	6,527,718
Male	10 CC	595	1,351,413	50.0	11,215,239	10,505,027	10,780,973	10,787,060
Female	10 CC	683	1,351,412	50.0	11,388,210	10,672,466	11,018,180	11,033,160
Subtotal		1,278	2,702,825	73.0	22,603,449	21,177,493	21,799,153	21,820,220
Subtotal male		836	1,893,027	51.1	14,855,492	13,910,967	14,232,082	14,241,630
Subtotal female		949	1,809,473	48.9	14,574,699	13,656,341	14,082,755	14,106,308
Total all issues		1,785	3,702,500	100.0%	29,430,191	27,567,308	28,314,837	28,347,938

TABLE A3 — Continued

Sex	Plan	Number of Contracts	Annual Income	Annual Income Distribution	Adjusted Single Premium	Mortality Gross Premium		
						At Issue	Projection I	Projection J
For Issues of 1978; with Interest of 7.5 Percent for the First 14 Years and 5.25 Percent Thereafter								
Male	Life	161	409,600	52.8%	2,756,080	2,578,251	2,633,699	2,636,341
Female	Life	179	366,200	47.2	2,785,018	2,605,847	2,702,318	2,711,861
Subtotal		340	775,800	30.1	5,541,098	5,184,098	5,336,017	5,348,202
Male	10 CC	445	902,900	50.2	7,743,046	7,248,351	7,483,952	7,490,974
Female	10 CC	525	896,700	49.8	7,977,057	7,469,282	7,749,086	7,767,919
Subtotal		970	1,799,600	69.9	15,720,103	14,717,633	15,233,038	15,258,893
Subtotal male		606	1,312,500	51.0	10,499,126	9,826,602	10,117,651	10,127,315
Subtotal female		704	1,262,900	49.0	10,762,075	10,075,129	10,451,404	10,479,780
Total all issues		1,310	2,575,400	100.0%	21,261,201	19,901,731	20,569,055	20,607,095
For Issues of 1979; with Interest of 7.5 Percent for the First 14 Years and 5.25 Percent Thereafter								
Male	Life	79	145,402	57.9%	953,218	891,627	899,596	900,622
Female	Life	101	105,639	42.1	756,512	708,078	728,761	731,492
Subtotal		180	251,041	23.0	1,709,730	1,599,705	1,628,357	1,632,114
Male	10 CC	194	405,096	48.2	3,398,471	3,182,182	3,278,239	3,282,056
Female	10 CC	249	435,349	51.8	3,754,488	3,516,973	3,645,756	3,654,919
Subtotal		443	840,445	77.0	7,152,959	6,699,155	6,923,995	6,936,975
Subtotal male		273	550,498	50.4	4,351,689	4,073,809	4,177,835	4,182,678
Subtotal female		350	540,988	49.6	4,511,000	4,225,051	4,374,517	4,386,411
Total all issues		623	1,091,486	100.0%	8,862,689	8,298,860	8,552,352	8,569,089

TABLE A4

FIXED IMMEDIATE ANNUITIES
MORTALITY GROSS SINGLE PREMIUMS (NO LOADING)
ASSUMING 1979 COMPANY MORTALITY TABLE
WITH MORTALITY IMPROVEMENT BASED ON EXPERIENCE TABLES AND PROJECTION SCALES I AND J

Sex	Plan	Number of Contracts	Annual Income	Annual Income Distribution	Adjusted Single Premium	Mortality Gross Premium		
						At Issue	Projection I	Projection J
For Issues of 1980; with Interest of 9.22 Percent for the First 14 Years and 6.97 Percent Thereafter								
Male	Life	53	122,088	56.0%	728,952	683,954	694,838	695,946
Female	Life	69	95,926	44.0	646,324	606,300	601,079	602,802
Subtotal		122	218,014	19.5	1,375,276	1,290,254	1,295,917	1,298,748
Male	10 CC	171	446,403	49.6	3,374,987	3,167,674	3,216,746	3,218,341
Female	10 CC	220	453,604	50.4	3,589,306	3,369,495	3,383,205	3,390,778
Subtotal		391	900,007	80.5	6,964,293	6,537,169	6,599,951	6,609,119
Subtotal male		224	568,491	50.8	4,103,939	3,851,628	3,911,584	3,914,287
Subtotal female		289	549,530	49.2	4,235,630	3,975,795	3,984,284	3,993,580
Total all issues		513	1,118,021	100.0%	8,339,569	7,827,423	7,895,868	7,907,867
For Issues of 1981; with Interest of 9.22 Percent for the First 14 Years and 6.97 Percent Thereafter								
Male	Life	35	141,565	57.9%	815,326	765,280	759,865	760,989
Female	Life	46	102,848	42.1	660,603	619,758	610,811	613,146
Subtotal		81	244,413	26.8	1,475,929	1,385,038	1,370,676	1,374,135
Male	10 CC	108	320,136	48.0	2,419,051	2,270,562	2,305,402	2,307,937
Female	10 CC	139	346,536	52.0	2,794,094	2,622,350	2,632,730	2,638,211
Subtotal		247	666,672	73.2	5,213,145	4,892,912	4,938,132	4,946,148
Subtotal male		143	461,701	50.7	3,234,377	3,035,842	3,065,267	3,068,926
Subtotal female		185	449,384	49.3	3,454,697	3,242,108	3,243,541	3,251,357
Total all issues		328	911,085	100.0%	6,689,074	6,277,950	6,308,808	6,320,283

TABLE A5

Fixed Immediate Annuities
Mortality Gross Single Premiums (No Loading)
Assuming 1981 Company Mortality Table
with Mortality Improvement Based on Experience Tables and Projection Scales I and J

Sex	Plan	Number of Contracts	Annual Income	Annual Income Distribution	Adjusted Single Premium	Mortality Gross Premium		
						At Issue	Projection I	Projection J
For Issues of 1982; with Interest of 11.45 Percent for the First 14 Years and 9.2 Percent Thereafter								
Male	Life	81	371,128	67.6%	2,168,285	2,027,468	2,011,155	2,014,246
Female	Life	92	177,810	32.4	1,198,867	1,120,165	1,126,182	1,130,956
Subtotal		173	548,938	22.8	3,367,152	3,147,633	3,137,337	3,145,202
Male	10 CC	206	847,246	45.6	6,484,186	6,058,984	6,078,556	6,085,567
Female	10 CC	250	1,011,887	54.4	7,813,013	7,302,959	7,333,190	7,351,064
Subtotal		456	1,859,133	77.2	14,297,199	13,361,943	13,411,746	13,436,631
Subtotal male		287	1,218,374	50.6	8,652,471	8,086,452	8,089,711	8,099,813
Subtotal female		342	1,189,697	49.4	9,011,880	8,423,124	8,459,372	8,482,020
Total all issues		629	2,408,071	100.0%	17,664,351	16,509,576	16,549,083	16,581,833
For Issues of 1983; with Interest of 11.45 Percent for the First 14 Years and 9.2 Percent Thereafter								
Male	Life	67	219,672	49.2%	1,415,657	1,322,097	1,331,875	1,334,383
Female	Life	87	227,085	50.8	1,524,596	1,424,230	1,442,967	1,448,923
Subtotal		154	446,757	15.5	2,940,253	2,746,327	2,774,842	2,783,306
Male	10 CC	246	1,212,740	49.9	9,886,637	9,228,184	9,286,094	9,295,360
Female	10 CC	312	1,218,236	50.1	9,875,695	9,221,334	9,294,614	9,323,994
Subtotal		558	2,430,976	84.5	19,762,332	18,449,518	18,580,708	18,619,354
Subtotal male		313	1,432,412	49.8	11,302,294	10,550,281	10,617,969	10,629,743
Subtotal female		399	1,445,321	50.2	11,400,291	10,645,564	10,737,581	10,772,917
Total all issues		712	2,877,733	100.0%	22,702,585	21,195,845	21,355,550	21,402,660

TABLE A5 — Continued

Sex	Plan	Number of Contracts	Annual Income	Annual Income Distribution	Adjusted Single Premium	Mortality Gross Premium		
						At Issue	Projection I	Projection J
For Issues of 1984; with Interest of 11.45 Percent for the First 14 Years and 9.2 Percent Thereafter								
Male	Life	60	285,383	55.2%	1,745,857	1,631,579	1,645,666	1,649,081
Female	Life	88	231,749	44.8	1,605,435	1,499,814	1,515,309	1,522,337
Subtotal		148	517,132	19.6	3,351,292	3,131,393	3,160,975	3,171,418
Male	10 CC	222	1,017,965	48.0	8,546,158	7,971,687	8,026,834	8,035,124
Female	10 CC	303	1,101,800	52.0	8,835,168	8,251,918	8,313,309	8,337,133
Subtotal		525	2,119,765	80.4	17,381,326	16,223,605	16,340,143	16,372,257
Subtotal male		282	1,303,348	49.4	10,292,015	9,603,266	9,672,500	9,684,205
Subtotal female		391	1,333,549	50.6	10,440,603	9,751,732	9,828,618	9,859,470
Total all issues		673	2,636,897	100.0%	20,732,618	19,354,998	19,501,118	19,543,675
For Issues of 1985; with Interest of 11.45 Percent for the First 14 Years and 9.2 Percent Thereafter								
Male	Life	81	458,909	57.9%	2,740,620	2,561,936	2,581,554	2,586,421
Female	Life	121	333,908	42.1	2,233,317	2,086,371	2,119,153	2,129,545
Subtotal		202	792,817	21.6	4,973,937	4,648,307	4,700,707	4,715,966
Male	10 CC	246	1,323,483	46.0	10,459,775	9,766,557	9,825,207	9,834,061
Female	10 CC	345	1,553,655	54.0	11,794,574	11,023,622	11,113,642	11,149,010
Subtotal		591	2,877,138	78.4	22,254,349	20,790,179	20,938,849	20,983,071
Subtotal male		327	1,782,392	48.6	13,200,395	12,328,493	12,406,761	12,420,482
Subtotal female		466	1,887,563	51.4	14,027,891	13,109,993	13,232,795	13,278,555
Total all issues		793	3,669,955	100.0%	27,228,286	25,438,486	25,639,556	25,699,037

TABLE A5 — *Continued*

Sex	Plan	Number of Contracts	Annual Income	Annual Income Distribution	Adjusted Single Premium	Mortality Gross Premium		
						At Issue	Projection I	Projection J
			For Issues of 1986; with Interest of 11.45 Percent for the First 14 Years and 9.2 Percent Thereafter					
Male	Life	93	271,322	51.6%	1,714,916	1,602,485	1,618,211	1,621,020
Female	Life	94	254,074	48.4	1,761,822	1,645,596	1,668,272	1,677,595
Subtotal		187	525,396	17.3	3,476,738	3,248,081	3,286,483	3,298,615
Male	10 CC	232	941,556	37.6	7,454,777	6,961,527	7,000,535	7,007,313
Female	10 CC	338	1,562,059	62.4	12,113,315	11,321,887	11,416,260	11,443,810
Subtotal		570	2,503,615	82.7	19,568,092	18,283,414	18,416,795	18,451,123
Subtotal male		325	1,212,878	40.0	9,169,693	8,564,012	8,618,746	8,628,333
Subtotal female		432	1,816,133	60.0	13,875,137	12,967,483	13,084,532	13,121,405
Total all issues		757	3,029,011	100.0%	23,044,830	21,531,495	21,703,278	21,749,738

TABLE B

ADJUSTED GROSS PREMIUM AND MORTALITY GROSS PREMIUM
ACTUARIAL ASSUMPTIONS FOR MORTALITY AND INTEREST

Inclusive Issue Years				Interest Rates		
From	To	Mortality Table		Initial Rate	for Years	Rate Thereafter
1966		1965 Company Modified Annuity Table		4.75%	1–15	3.50%
1967		1965 Company Modified Annuity Table		5.00	1–12	3.75
1968		1965 Company Modified Annuity Table		5.50	1–13	3.75
1969		1965 Company Modified Annuity Table		5.70	1–13	3.75
1970	1971	1969 Company Modified Annuity Table		7.00	1–16	3.25
1972		1969 Company Modified Annuity Table		6.75	1–16	3.25
1973		1969 Company Modified Annuity Table		7.00	1–16	3.25
1974	1979	1974 Company Modified Annuity Table		7.50	1–14	5.25
1980	1981	1979 Company Modified Annuity Table		9.22	1–14	6.97
1982	1986	1981 Company Modified Annuity Table		11.45	1–14	9.20

739

TABLE C1

GROSS SINGLE PREMIUMS
ASSUMING 1965 COMPANY MORTALITY TABLE

Sex	Plan	Age True	Age Calc.	Number of Contracts	Annual Income	Load Percent	Factor with Load	Premium With Load	Premium No Load
				For Issues of 1966; with Interest of 4.75 Percent for the First 15 Years and 3.5 Percent Thereafter					
Male	Life	45	45.00	4	5,209	7.50%	2,102	91,244	84,410
Male	Life	55	55.00	11	14,707	7.00	1,738	213,006	198,051
Male	Life	65	65.00	76	104,176	6.00	1,329	1,153,749	1,084,607
Male	Life	75	75.00	92	126,543	6.00	920	970,163	911,822
Male	Life	85	85.00	39	53,927	6.00	556	249,862	234,802
Male	Life	92	92.00	1	1,838	6.00	556	8,516	8,003
Subtotal				223	306,400			2,686,540	2,521,695
Male	10 CC	45	45.00	9	10,722	7.50	2,127	190,047	175,755
Male	10 CC	55	55.00	24	30,274	6.90	1,792	452,092	420,931
Male	10 CC	65	65.00	172	214,438	5.60	1,442	2,576,830	2,431,795
Male	10 CC	75	75.00	208	260,479	5.20	1,166	2,530,988	2,399,885
Male	10 CC	85	85.00	89	111,003	4.80	1,030	952,776	906,762
Male	10 CC	92	92.00	3	3,784	4.80	1,030	32,479	30,911
Subtotal				505	630,700			6,735,212	6,366,039

TABLE C1 — *Continued*

Sex	Plan	Age True	Age Calc.	Number of Contracts	Annual Income	Load Percent	Factor with Load	Premium With Load	Premium No Load
				For Issues of 1966; with Interest of 4.75 Percent for the First 15 Years and 3.5 Percent Thereafter					
Female	Life	45	45.00	4	4,945	7.50%	2,296	94,614	87,505
Female	Life	55	55.00	12	15,216	7.00	1,951	247,387	230,074
Female	Life	65	65.00	79	101,567	6.00	1,518	1,284,823	1,207,623
Female	Life	75	75.00	137	176,125	6.00	1,057	1,551,368	1,457,915
Female	Life	85	85.00	60	77,602	6.00	627	405,470	381,368
Female	Life	92	92.00	4	4,945	6.00	627	25,838	24,302
Subtotal				296	380,400			3,609,500	3,388,787
Female	10 CC	45	45.00	8	9,068	7.50	2,308	174,408	161,315
Female	10 CC	55	55.00	24	27,900	7.00	1,977	459,653	427,526
Female	10 CC	65	65.00	162	186,232	5.80	1,583	2,456,710	2,313,764
Female	10 CC	75	75.00	280	322,942	5.40	1,236	3,325,303	3,147,332
Female	10 CC	85	85.00	124	142,290	5.00	1,041	1,234,366	1,172,294
Female	10 CC	92	92.00	8	9,068	5.00	1,041	78,665	74,709
Subtotal				606	697,500			7,730,105	7,296,940
Subtotal life				519	686,800			6,296,040	5,910,482
Subtotal 10 CC				1,111	1,328,200			14,465,317	13,662,979
Subtotal male				728	937,100			9,421,752	8,887,734
Subtotal female				902	1,077,900			11,339,605	10,685,727
Total all issues				1,630	2,015,000			20,761,357	19,573,461

TABLE C1 — *Continued*

Sex	Plan	Age		Number of Contracts	Annual Income	Load Percent	Factor with Load	Premium	
		True	Calc.					With Load	No Load
				For Issues of 1967; with Interest of 5 Percent for the First 12 Years and 3.75 Percent Thereafter					
Male	Life	45	45.00	4	5,323	7.50%	2,067	91,689	84,829
Male	Life	55	55.00	10	15,029	7.00	1,714	214,664	199,584
Male	Life	65	65.00	69	106,454	6.00	1,313	1,164,784	1,094,904
Male	Life	75	75.00	84	129,310	6.00	910	980,601	921,712
Male	Life	85	85.00	36	55,105	6.00	551	253,024	237,960
Male	Life	92	92.00	1	1,879	6.00	551	8,628	8,114
Subtotal				204	313,100			2,713,390	2,547,103
Male	10 CC	45	45.00	8	11,718	7.50	2,091	204,186	188,899
Male	10 CC	55	55.00	23	33,086	6.90	1,767	487,191	453,626
Male	10 CC	65	65.00	162	234,362	5.35	1,420	2,773,284	2,624,748
Male	10 CC	75	75.00	197	284,681	5.15	1,152	2,732,938	2,591,894
Male	10 CC	85	85.00	84	121,317	4.95	1,020	1,031,195	979,860
Male	10 CC	92	92.00	3	4,136	4.95	1,020	35,156	33,406
Subtotal				477	689,300			7,263,950	6,872,433

TABLE C1 — *Continued*

Sex	Plan	Age True	Age Calc.	Number of Contracts	Annual Income	Load Percent	Factor with Load	Premium With Load	Premium No Load
				For Issues of 1967; with Interest of 5 Percent for the First 12 Years and 3.75 Percent Thereafter					
Female	Life	45	45.00	5	5,742	7.50%	2,254	107,854	99,779
Female	Life	55	55.00	14	17,668	7.00	1,922	282,982	263,205
Female	Life	65	65.00	96	117,934	6.00	1,499	1,473,192	1,384,609
Female	Life	75	75.00	167	204,507	6.00	1,045	1,780,915	1,673,736
Female	Life	85	85.00	73	90,107	6.00	622	467,055	438,921
Female	Life	92	92.00	5	5,742	6.00	622	29,763	27,970
Subtotal				360	441,700			4,141,761	3,888,220
Female	10 CC	45	45.00	12	13,727	7.50	2,266	259,212	239,800
Female	10 CC	55	55.00	38	42,236	7.00	1,948	685,631	637,632
Female	10 CC	65	65.00	255	281,925	5.55	1,558	3,660,326	3,458,105
Female	10 CC	75	75.00	441	488,882	5.20	1,219	4,966,226	4,707,513
Female	10 CC	85	85.00	195	215,403	5.20	1,031	1,850,671	1,754,528
Female	10 CC	92	92.00	12	13,727	5.20	1,031	117,938	111,811
Subtotal				953	1,055,900			11,540,004	10,909,389
Subtotal life				564	754,800			6,855,151	6,435,323
Subtotal 10 CC				1,430	1,745,200			18,803,954	17,781,822
Subtotal male				681	1,002,400			9,977,340	9,419,536
Subtotal female				1,313	1,497,600			15,681,765	14,797,609
Total all issues				1,994	2,500,000			25,659,105	24,217,145

TABLE C1 — *Continued*

Sex	Plan	Age True	Age Calc.	Number of Contracts	Annual Income	Load Percent	Factor with Load	Premium With Load	Premium No Load
				For Issues of 1968; with Interest of 5.5 Percent for the First 13 Years and 3.75 Percent Thereafter					
Male	Life	45	45.00	4	5,834	8.60%	1,997	97,087	88,747
Male	Life	55	55.00	10	16,474	7.75	1,656	227,341	209,752
Male	Life	65	65.00	75	116,688	6.10	1,269	1,233,976	1,158,304
Male	Life	75	75.00	91	141,742	7.60	902	1,065,427	983,940
Male	Life	85	85.00	39	60,403	12.30	581	292,451	256,467
Male	Life	92	92.00	1	2,059	12.30	581	9,969	8,742
Subtotal				220	343,200			2,926,251	2,705,952
Male	10 CC	45	45.00	8	10,775	8.60	2,021	181,469	165,829
Male	10 CC	55	55.00	23	30,422	7.65	1,709	433,260	400,025
Male	10 CC	65	65.00	161	215,492	5.70	1,376	2,470,975	2,329,953
Male	10 CC	75	75.00	195	261,759	5.30	1,122	2,447,447	2,318,669
Male	10 CC	85	85.00	83	111,549	4.90	996	925,857	880,716
Male	10 CC	92	92.00	3	3,803	4.90	996	31,565	30,026
Subtotal				473	633,800			6,490,573	6,125,218

TABLE C1 — *Continued*

Sex	Plan	Age True	Age Calc.	Number of Contracts	Annual Income	Load Percent	Factor with Load	Premium With Load	Premium No Load
				For Issues of 1968; with Interest of 5.5 Percent for the First 13 Years and 3.75 Percent Thereafter					
Female	Life	45	45.00	5	5,893	8.60%	2,174	106,762	97,559
Female	Life	55	55.00	16	18,132	7.75	1,853	279,988	258,311
Female	Life	65	65.00	107	121,031	6.10	1,444	1,456,406	1,367,342
Female	Life	75	75.00	185	209,878	7.60	1,032	1,804,951	1,668,270
Female	Life	85	85.00	81	92,473	12.30	654	503,978	442,302
Female	Life	92	92.00	5	5,893	12.30	654	32,117	28,186
Subtotal				399	453,300			4,184,202	3,861,970
Female	10 CC	45	45.00	13	14,639	8.60	2,185	266,552	243,652
Female	10 CC	55	55.00	40	45,044	7.75	1,878	704,939	650,398
Female	10 CC	65	65.00	267	300,669	5.90	1,506	3,773,396	3,549,728
Female	10 CC	75	75.00	464	521,385	5.50	1,187	5,157,367	4,874,238
Female	10 CC	85	85.00	204	229,724	5.10	1,007	1,927,767	1,828,572
Female	10 CC	92	92.00	13	14,639	5.10	1,007	122,846	116,524
Subtotal				1,001	1,126,100			11,952,867	11,263,112
Subtotal life				619	796,500			7,110,453	6,567,922
Subtotal 10 CC				1,474	1,759,900			18,443,440	17,388,330
Subtotal male				693	977,000			9,416,824	8,831,170
Subtotal female				1,400	1,579,400			16,137,069	15,125,082
Total all issues				2,093	2,556,400			25,553,893	23,956,252

TABLE C1 — *Continued*

| Sex | Plan | Age | | Number of Contracts | Annual Income | Load Percent | Factor with Load | Premium | |
		True	Calc.					With Load	No Load
				For Issues of 1969; with Interest of 5.7 Percent for the First 13 Years and 3.75 Percent Thereafter					
Male	Life	45	45.00	3	3,397	8.60%	1,965	55,626	50,838
Male	Life	55	55.00	7	9,590	7.75	1,632	130,424	120,285
Male	Life	65	65.00	51	67,932	6.10	1,252	708,757	665,653
Male	Life	75	75.00	62	82,517	7.60	893	614,064	567,110
Male	Life	85	85.00	27	35,165	12.60	579	169,671	148,322
Male	Life	92	92.00	1	1,199	12.60	579	5,785	5,057
Subtotal				151	199,800			1,684,327	1,557,265
Male	10 CC	45	45.00	7	9,246	8.60	1,988	153,175	139,994
Male	10 CC	55	55.00	21	26,107	7.65	1,683	366,151	338,197
Male	10 CC	65	65.00	146	184,926	5.70	1,358	2,092,746	1,973,796
Male	10 CC	75	75.00	178	224,631	5.30	1,111	2,079,709	1,968,985
Male	10 CC	85	85.00	76	95,727	4.90	987	787,355	749,043
Male	10 CC	92	92.00	3	3,263	4.90	987	26,838	25,532
Subtotal				431	543,900			5,505,974	5,195,547

TABLE C1 — *Continued*

Sex	Plan	Age True	Age Calc.	Number of Contracts	Annual Income	Load Percent	Factor with Load	Premium With Load	Premium No Load
				For Issues of 1969; with Interest of 5.7 Percent for the First 13 Years and 3.75 Percent Thereafter					
Female	Life	45	45.00	4	5,178	8.60	2,137	92,212	84,282
Female	Life	55	55.00	12	15,932	7.75	1,824	242,166	223,410
Female	Life	65	65.00	81	106,346	6.10	1,424	1,261,973	1,184,858
Female	Life	75	75.00	140	184,413	7.60	1,021	1,569,047	1,449,905
Female	Life	85	85.00	61	81,253	12.60	652	441,475	385,870
Female	Life	92	92.00	4	5,178	12.60	652	28,134	24,590
Subtotal				302	398,300			3,635,007	3,352,915
Female	10 CC	45	45.00	13	13,861	8.60	2,149	248,227	226,830
Female	10 CC	55	55.00	39	42,648	7.75	1,849	657,135	606,166
Female	10 CC	65	65.00	259	284,675	5.90	1,485	3,522,853	3,314,649
Female	10 CC	75	75.00	449	493,650	5.50	1,174	4,829,543	4,563,614
Female	10 CC	85	85.00	198	217,505	5.10	997	1,807,104	1,715,662
Female	10 CC	92	92.00	13	13,861	5.10	997	115,162	109,334
Subtotal				971	1,066,200			11,180,024	10,536,255
Subtotal life				453	598,100			5,319,334	4,910,180
Subtotal 10 CC				1,402	1,610,100			16,685,998	15,731,802
Subtotal male				582	743,700			7,190,301	6,752,812
Subtotal female				1,273	1,464,500			14,815,031	13,889,170
Total all issues				1,855	2,208,200			22,005,332	20,641,982

TABLE C2

Gross Single Premiums
Assuming 1969 Company Mortality Table

Sex	Plan	Age True	Age Calc.	Number of Contracts	Annual Income	Load Percent	Factor with Load	Premium With Load	Premium No Load
				For Issues of 1970; with Interest of 7 Percent for the First 16 Years and 3.25 Percent Thereafter					
Male	Life	45	45.00	2	4,457	6.60%	1,710	63,512	59,333
Male	Life	55	55.00	7	12,586	6.60	1,452	152,291	142,235
Male	Life	65	65.00	49	89,148	6.60	1,158	860,278	803,688
Male	Life	75	74.01	60	108,289	6.60	869	784,193	732,233
Male	Life	85	83.01	25	46,147	6.60	586	225,351	210,483
Male	Life	92	83.01	1	1,573	6.60	586	7,681	7,175
Subtotal				144	262,200			2,093,306	1,955,147
Male	10 CC	45	45.00	6	10,142	6.60	1,731	146,298	136,641
Male	10 CC	55	55.00	18	28,637	6.60	1,499	357,724	334,165
Male	10 CC	65	65.00	128	202,844	6.60	1,259	2,128,172	1,987,758
Male	10 CC	75	75.00	155	246,396	6.60	1,056	2,168,285	2,024,740
Male	10 CC	85	85.00	66	105,001	6.60	951	832,133	777,187
Male	10 CC	92	92.00	2	3,580	6.60	951	28,372	26,498
Subtotal				375	596,600			5,660,984	5,286,989

TABLE C2 — *Continued*

Sex	Plan	Age True	Age Calc.	Number of Contracts	Annual Income	Load Percent	Factor with Load	Premium With Load	Premium No Load
				For Issues of 1970; with Interest of 7 Percent for the First 16 Years and 3.25 Percent Thereafter					
Female	Life	45	45.00	3	4,568	6.60	1,857	70,690	66,024
Female	Life	55	55.00	10	14,056	6.60	1,618	189,522	176,983
Female	Life	65	65.00	67	93,824	6.60	1,312	1,025,809	958,228
Female	Life	75	74.50	117	162,698	6.60	972	1,317,854	1,231,276
Female	Life	85	83.50	51	71,686	6.60	644	384,715	359,518
Female	Life	92	83.50	3	4,568	6.60	644	24,515	22,909
Subtotal				251	351,400			3,013,105	2,814,938
Female	10 CC	45	45.00	9	10,865	6.60	1,867	169,041	157,905
Female	10 CC	55	55.00	27	33,432	6.60	1,639	456,625	426,404
Female	10 CC	65	65.00	181	223,159	6.60	1,367	2,542,153	2,374,525
Female	10 CC	75	75.00	314	386,976	6.60	1,110	3,579,528	3,342,902
Female	10 CC	85	85.00	139	170,503	6.60	958	1,361,182	1,270,897
Female	10 CC	92	92.00	9	10,865	6.60	958	86,739	80,986
Subtotal				679	835,800			8,195,268	7,653,619
Subtotal life				395	613,600			5,106,411	4,770,085
Subtotal 10 CC				1,054	1,432,400			13,856,252	12,940,608
Subtotal male				519	858,800			7,754,290	7,242,136
Subtotal female				930	1,187,200			11,208,373	10,468,557
Total all issues				1,449	2,046,000			18,962,663	17,710,693

TABLE C2 — *Continued*

Sex	Plan	Age True	Age Calc.	Number of Contracts	Annual Income	Load Percent	Factor with Load	Premium With Load	Premium No Load
				For Issues of 1971; with Interest of 7 Percent for the First 16 Years and 3.25 Percent Thereafter					
Male	Life	46	46.00	3	5,768	6.60%	1,685	80,992	75,669
Male	Life	54	54.00	9	16,286	6.60	1,479	200,725	187,507
Male	Life	65	65.00	61	115,362	6.60	1,158	1,113,243	1,040,012
Male	Life	74	73.10	73	140,131	6.60	898	1,048,647	979,714
Male	Life	80	78.50	31	59,717	6.60	724	360,293	336,449
Male	Life	92	83.01	1	2,036	6.60	586	9,942	9,286
Subtotal				178	339,300			2,813,842	2,628,637
Male	10 CC	49	49.00	10	18,994	6.60	1,640	259,585	242,433
Male	10 CC	54	54.00	27	53,630	6.60	1,523	680,654	635,786
Male	10 CC	67	67.00	189	379,882	6.60	1,213	3,839,974	3,587,158
Male	10 CC	70	70.00	230	461,445	6.60	1,148	4,414,491	4,124,454
Male	10 CC	80	80.00	98	196,645	6.60	989	1,620,683	1,514,390
Male	10 CC	92	92.00	3	6,704	6.60	951	53,129	49,621
Subtotal				557	1,117,300			10,868,516	10,153,842

TABLE C2 — *Continued*

Sex	Plan	Age		Number of Contracts	Annual Income	Load Percent	Factor with Load	Premium	
		True	Calc.					With Load	No Load
		For Issues of 1971; with Interest of 7 Percent for the First 16 Years and 3.25 Percent Thereafter							
Female	Life	46	46.00	4	5,897	6.60	1,835	90,175	84,240
Female	Life	58	58.00	12	18,144	6.60	1,534	231,941	216,621
Female	Life	66	65.95	81	121,111	6.60	1,280	1,291,851	1,206,317
Female	Life	79	78.10	140	210,017	6.60	840	1,470,119	1,373,873
Female	Life	80	79.00	62	92,534	6.60	808	623,062	581,659
Female	Life	92	83.50	4	5,897	6.60	644	31,647	29,575
Subtotal				303	453,600			3,738,795	3,492,285
Female	10 CC	46	46.00	11	15,969	6.60	1,846	245,656	229,503
Female	10 CC	58	58.00	35	49,136	6.60	1,561	639,177	596,845
Female	10 CC	68	68.00	232	327,983	6.60	1,284	3,509,418	3,278,675
Female	10 CC	79	79.00	403	568,749	6.60	1,032	4,891,241	4,567,741
Female	10 CC	85	85.00	178	250,594	6.60	958	2,000,575	1,867,881
Female	10 CC	92	92.00	11	15,969	6.60	958	127,486	119,030
Subtotal				870	1,228,400			11,413,553	10,659,675
Subtotal life				481	792,900			6,552,637	6,120,922
Subtotal 10 CC				1,427	2,345,700			22,282,069	20,813,517
Subtotal male				735	1,456,600			13,682,358	12,782,479
Subtotal female				1,173	1,682,000			15,152,348	14,151,960
Total all issues				1,908	3,138,600			28,834,706	26,934,439

TABLE C2 — *Continued*

Sex	Plan	Age True	Age Calc.	Number of Contracts	Annual Income	Load Percent	Factor with Load	Premium With Load	Premium No Load
				For Issues of 1972; with Interest of 6.75 Percent for the First 16 Years and 3.25 Percent Thereafter					
Male	Life	47	47.00	3	5,350	6.60%	1,696	75,613	70,637
Male	Life	56	56.00	8	15,106	6.60	1,452	182,783	170,704
Male	Life	68	67.70	59	106,998	6.60	1,089	971,007	907,188
Male	Life	74	73.10	72	129,971	6.60	910	985,613	920,693
Male	Life	82	80.30	30	55,387	6.60	674	311,090	290,681
Male	Life	92	83.00	1	1,888	6.60	592	9,314	8,693
Subtotal				173	314,700			2,535,420	2,368,596
Male	10 CC	46	46.00	8	13,263	6.60	1,746	192,977	180,202
Male	10 CC	56	56.00	23	37,450	6.60	1,504	469,373	438,306
Male	10 CC	65	65.00	160	265,268	6.60	1,280	2,829,525	2,642,244
Male	10 CC	75	75.00	195	322,223	6.60	1,069	2,870,470	2,682,214
Male	10 CC	85	85.00	83	137,315	6.60	961	1,099,664	1,027,474
Male	10 CC	92	92.00	3	4,681	6.60	961	37,487	35,026
Subtotal				472	780,200			7,499,496	7,005,466

TABLE C2 — *Continued*

Sex	Plan	Age		Number of Contracts	Annual Income	Load Percent	Factor with Load	Premium	
		True	Calc.					With Load	No Load
				For Issues of 1972; with Interest of 6.75 Percent for the First 16 Years and 3.25 Percent Thereafter					
Female	Life	49	49.00	3	3,696	6.60	1,807	55,656	51,990
Female	Life	52	52.00	9	11,372	6.60	1,732	164,136	153,345
Female	Life	67	66.90	61	75,908	6.60	1,268	802,095	749,363
Female	Life	79	78.10	106	131,631	6.60	851	933,483	871,546
Female	Life	85	83.50	46	57,997	6.60	650	314,150	293,613
Female	Life	92	83.50	3	3,696	6.60	650	20,020	18,711
Subtotal				228	284,300			2,289,540	2,138,568
Female	10 CC	47	47.00	11	15,369	6.60	1,867	239,116	223,317
Female	10 CC	56	56.00	10	14,188	6.60	1,647	194,730	181,846
Female	10 CC	67	67.00	189	260,106	6.60	1,334	2,891,512	2,701,024
Female	10 CC	78	78.00	438	602,973	6.60	1,063	5,341,336	4,988,305
Female	10 CC	85	85.00	206	283,752	6.60	968	2,288,933	2,138,406
Female	10 CC	92	92.00	4	5,912	6.60	968	47,690	44,554
Subtotal				858	1,182,300			11,003,317	10,277,452
Subtotal life				401	599,000			4,824,960	4,507,164
Subtotal 10 CC				1,330	1,962,500			18,502,813	17,282,918
Subtotal male				645	1,094,900			10,034,916	9,374,062
Subtotal female				1,086	1,466,600			13,292,857	12,416,020
Total all issues				1,731	2,561,500			23,327,773	21,790,082

TABLE C2 — *Continued*

For Issues of 1973; with Interest of 7 Percent for the First 16 Years and 3.25 Percent Thereafter

| Sex | Plan | Age | | Number of Contracts | Annual Income | Load Percent | Factor with Load | Premium | |
		True	Calc.					With Load	No Load
Male	Life	44	44.00	3	6,362	6.60%	1,735	91,984	85,910
Male	Life	55	55.00	8	17,961	6.60	1,452	217,328	202,979
Male	Life	65	65.00	56	127,228	6.60	1,158	1,227,750	1,146,987
Male	Life	73	72.20	69	154,545	6.60	927	1,193,860	1,115,600
Male	Life	85	83.01	29	65,859	6.60	586	321,611	300,393
Male	Life	92	83.01	1	2,245	6.60	586	10,963	10,240
Subtotal				166	374,200			3,063,496	2,862,109
Male	10 CC	44	44.00	8	15,722	6.60	1,753	229,672	214,560
Male	10 CC	54	54.00	24	44,390	6.60	1,523	563,383	526,245
Male	10 CC	68	68.00	168	314,432	6.60	1,191	3,120,738	2,914,772
Male	10 CC	75	75.00	204	381,942	6.60	1,056	3,361,090	3,138,579
Male	10 CC	85	85.00	87	162,765	6.60	951	1,289,913	1,204,739
Male	10 CC	92	92.00	3	5,549	6.60	951	43,976	41,072
Subtotal				494	924,800			8,608,772	8,039,967

TABLE C2 — *Continued*

Sex	Plan	Age True	Age Calc.	Number of Contracts	Annual Income	Load Percent	Factor with Load	Premium With Load	Premium No Load
				For Issues of 1973; with Interest of 7 Percent for the First 16 Years and 3.25 Percent Thereafter					
Female	Life	46	46.00	3	5,894	6.60%	1,835	90,129	84,198
Female	Life	54	54.00	9	18,136	6.60	1,644	248,463	232,104
Female	Life	66	65.95	60	121,058	6.60	1,280	1,291,285	1,205,789
Female	Life	78	77.20	103	209,924	6.60	873	1,527,197	1,427,045
Female	Life	85	83.50	45	92,494	6.60	644	496,384	463,874
Female	Life	92	83.50	3	5,894	6.60	644	31,631	29,559
Subtotal				223	453,400			3,685,089	3,442,569
Female	10 CC	46	46.00	8	10,762	6.60	1,846	165,555	154,669
Female	10 CC	56	56.00	8	10,762	6.60	1,613	144,659	135,121
Female	10 CC	67	67.00	130	179,047	6.60	1,312	1,957,581	1,827,895
Female	10 CC	78	78.00	390	538,120	6.60	1,049	4,704,066	4,395,452
Female	10 CC	85	85.00	170	234,816	6.60	958	1,874,614	1,750,274
Female	10 CC	92	92.00	3	4,893	6.60	958	39,062	36,472
Subtotal				709	978,400			8,885,537	8,299,883
Subtotal life				389	827,600			6,748,585	6,304,678
Subtotal 10 CC				1,203	1,903,200			17,494,309	16,339,850
Subtotal male				660	1,299,000			11,672,268	10,902,076
Subtotal female				932	1,431,800			12,570,626	11,742,452
Total all issues				1,592	2,730,800			24,242,894	22,644,528

TABLE C3

GROSS SINGLE PREMIUMS
ASSUMING 1974 COMPANY MORTALITY TABLE

Sex	Plan	Age True	Age Calc.	Number of Contracts	Annual Income	Load Percent	Factor with Load	Premium With Load	Premium No Load
				For Issues of 1974; with Interest of 7.5 Percent for the First 14 Years and 5.25 Percent Thereafter					
Male	Life	45	44.85	2	4,435	7.50%	1,605	59,318	54,857
Male	Life	55	54.85	7	12,523	7.20	1,396	145,684	135,235
Male	Life	65	64.85	48	88,706	6.60	1,132	836,793	781,821
Male	Life	75	74.40	58	107,752	6.40	844	757,856	709,464
Male	Life	85	83.00	25	45,919	6.20	582	222,707	208,763
Male	Life	92	83.00	1	1,565	6.20	582	7,590	7,115
Subtotal				141	260,900			2,029,948	1,897,255
Male	10 CC	45	45.00	7	10,834	7.50	1,622	146,440	135,458
Male	10 CC	55	55.00	19	30,590	7.20	1,438	366,570	340,096
Male	10 CC	65	65.00	131	216,682	6.60	1,223	2,208,351	2,062,361
Male	10 CC	75	75.00	159	263,205	6.40	1,032	2,263,563	2,118,695
Male	10 CC	85	85.00	68	112,165	6.20	927	866,475	812,689
Male	10 CC	92	92.00	2	3,824	6.20	927	29,540	27,707
Subtotal				386	637,300			5,880,939	5,497,006

TABLE C3 — *Continued*

Sex	Plan	Age True	Age Calc.	Number of Contracts	Annual Income	Load Percent	Factor with Load	Premium With Load	Premium No Load
				For Issues of 1974; with Interest of 7.5 Percent for the First 14 Years and 5.25 Percent Thereafter					
Female	Life	45	44.85	2	3,574	7.50	1,726	51,406	47,557
Female	Life	55	54.85	7	10,996	7.20	1,553	142,307	132,058
Female	Life	65	64.85	49	73,398	6.60	1,293	790,863	738,456
Female	Life	75	74.70	84	127,278	6.40	967	1,025,649	959,687
Female	Life	85	84.10	37	56,080	6.20	631	294,887	276,652
Female	Life	92	84.10	2	3,574	6.20	631	18,793	17,631
Subtotal				181	274,900			2,323,905	2,172,041
Female	10 CC	45	45.00	8	12,505	7.50	1,734	180,697	167,160
Female	10 CC	55	55.00	24	38,476	7.20	1,568	502,753	466,605
Female	10 CC	65	65.00	159	256,827	6.60	1,335	2,857,200	2,668,247
Female	10 CC	75	75.00	276	445,359	6.40	1,094	4,060,190	3,798,996
Female	10 CC	85	85.00	121	196,228	6.20	935	1,528,943	1,434,635
Female	10 CC	92	92.00	8	12,505	6.20	935	97,435	91,425
Subtotal				596	961,900			9,227,218	8,627,068
Subtotal life				322	535,800			4,353,853	4,069,296
Subtotal 10 CC				982	1,599,200			15,108,157	14,124,074
Subtotal male				527	898,200			7,910,887	7,394,261
Subtotal female				777	1,236,800			11,551,123	10,799,109
Total all issues				1,304	2,135,000			19,462,010	18,193,370

TABLE C3 — Continued

Sex	Plan	Age		Number of Contracts	Annual Income	Load Percent	Factor with Load	Premium	
		True	Calc.					With Load	No Load
		For Issues of 1975; with Interest of 7.5 Percent for the First 14 Years and 5.25 Percent Thereafter							
Male	Life	46	45.85	1	3,858	7.50%	1,586	50,990	47,161
Male	Life	57	56.85	8	18,500	7.08	1,348	207,817	193,046
Male	Life	68	67.73	51	124,399	6.54	1,048	1,086,418	1,015,769
Male	Life	76	75.26	57	141,452	6.38	817	963,052	902,035
Male	Life	85	83.00	21	51,813	6.20	582	251,293	235,559
Male	Life	92	83.00	2	4,478	6.20	582	21,718	20,358
Subtotal				140	344,500			2,581,288	2,413,928
Male	10 CC	42	42.00	34	60,079	7.50	1,670	836,099	773,462
Male	10 CC	53	53.00	78	139,910	7.32	1,478	1,723,225	1,597,177
Male	10 CC	63	63.00	197	353,890	6.72	1,266	3,733,540	3,483,726
Male	10 CC	73	73.00	121	218,095	6.44	1,065	1,935,593	1,811,235
Male	10 CC	81	81.00	27	49,380	6.28	956	393,394	368,758
Male	10 CC	92	92.00	1	1,646	6.20	927	12,715	11,926
Subtotal				458	823,000			8,634,566	8,046,284

TABLE C3 — *Continued*

Sex	Plan	Age True	Age Calc.	Number of Contracts	Annual Income	Load Percent	Factor with Load	Premium With Load	Premium No Load
				For Issues of 1975; with Interest of 7.5 Percent for the First 14 Years and 5.25 Percent Thereafter					
Female	Life	47	46.85	3	3,467	7.50	1,697	49,029	45,355
Female	Life	58	57.85	6	10,434	7.02	1,485	129,121	120,081
Female	Life	69	68.81	45	74,304	6.52	1,168	723,226	676,163
Female	Life	78	77.52	82	133,902	6.34	867	967,442	906,396
Female	Life	85	84.10	49	80,682	6.20	631	424,253	398,018
Female	Life	92	84.10	4	6,811	6.20	631	35,815	33,600
Subtotal				189	309,600			2,328,886	2,179,613
Female	10 CC	48	48.00	4	5,523	7.50	1,692	77,874	72,030
Female	10 CC	57	57.00	23	35,632	7.08	1,526	453,120	421,112
Female	10 CC	68	68.00	98	152,505	6.54	1,260	1,601,303	1,496,549
Female	10 CC	78	78.00	304	472,124	6.34	1,032	4,060,266	3,804,400
Female	10 CC	85	85.00	141	218,335	6.20	935	1,701,194	1,596,260
Female	10 CC	92	92.00	4	6,681	6.20	935	52,056	48,845
Subtotal				574	890,800			7,945,813	7,439,196
Subtotal life				329	654,100			4,910,174	4,593,541
Subtotal 10 CC				1,032	1,713,800			16,580,379	15,485,480
Subtotal male				598	1,167,500			11,215,854	10,460,212
Subtotal female				763	1,200,400			10,274,699	9,618,809
Total all issues				1,361	2,367,900			21,490,553	20,079,021

TABLE C3 — *Continued*

Sex	Plan	Age True	Age Calc.	Number of Contracts	Annual Income	Load Percent	Factor with Load	Premium With Load	Premium No Load
				For Issues of 1976; with Interest of 7.5 Percent for the First 14 Years and 5.25 Percent Thereafter					
Male	Life	48	47.85	8	18,179	7.50%	1,547	234,358	216,811
Male	Life	58	57.85	9	20,946	7.02	1,323	230,930	214,638
Male	Life	64	63.85	62	136,739	6.66	1,161	1,322,950	1,234,937
Male	Life	76	75.26	66	147,014	6.38	817	1,000,920	937,504
Male	Life	85	83.01	31	68,765	6.20	581	332,937	312,482
Male	Life	92	83.01	2	3,557	6.20	581	17,222	16,164
Subtotal				178	395,200			3,139,317	2,932,536
Male	10 CC	47	47.00	21	51,115	7.50	1,588	676,422	625,853
Male	10 CC	54	54.00	25	58,894	7.26	1,458	715,562	663,638
Male	10 CC	63	63.00	160	384,475	6.72	1,266	4,056,211	3,784,807
Male	10 CC	75	75.00	172	413,366	6.40	1,032	3,554,948	3,327,431
Male	10 CC	85	85.00	81	193,349	6.20	927	1,493,621	1,400,905
Male	10 CC	92	92.00	4	10,001	6.20	927	77,258	72,462
Subtotal				463	1,111,200			10,574,022	9,875,096

TABLE C3 — *Continued*

Sex	Plan	Age True	Age Calc.	Number of Contracts	Annual Income	Load Percent	Factor with Load	Premium With Load	Premium No Load
				For Issues of 1976; with Interest of 7.5 Percent for the First 14 Years and 5.25 Percent Thereafter					
Female	Life	49	48.85	3	4,303	7.50	1,666	59,740	55,258
Female	Life	52	51.85	10	16,854	7.38	1,613	226,546	209,849
Female	Life	68	67.82	53	88,574	6.54	1,200	885,740	828,027
Female	Life	77	76.58	105	174,997	6.36	901	1,313,936	1,229,833
Female	Life	85	84.10	40	66,700	6.20	631	350,731	329,042
Female	Life	92	84.10	4	7,172	6.20	631	37,713	35,381
Subtotal				215	358,600			2,874,406	2,687,390
Female	10 CC	45	45.00	2	889	7.50	1,734	12,846	11,884
Female	10 CC	57	57.00	36	65,608	7.08	1,526	834,315	775,379
Female	10 CC	67	67.00	135	245,530	6.56	1,285	2,629,217	2,456,630
Female	10 CC	78	78.00	289	525,309	6.34	1,032	4,517,657	4,232,968
Female	10 CC	85	85.00	147	266,880	6.20	935	2,079,440	1,951,176
Female	10 CC	92	92.00	3	7,784	6.20	935	60,650	56,909
Subtotal				612	1,112,000			10,134,125	9,484,946
Subtotal life				393	753,800			6,013,723	5,619,926
Subtotal 10 CC				1,075	2,223,200			20,708,147	19,360,042
Subtotal male				641	1,506,400			13,713,339	12,807,632
Subtotal female				827	1,470,600			13,008,531	12,172,336
Total all issues				1,468	2,977,000			26,721,870	24,979,968

TABLE C3 — *Continued*

| Sex | Plan | Age | | Number of Contracts | Annual Income | Load Percent | Factor with Load | Premium | |
		True	Calc.					With Load	No Load
		For Issues of 1977; with Interest of 7.5 Percent for the First 14 Years and 5.25 Percent Thereafter							
Male	Life	45	44.85	2	4,333	7.50%	1,605	57,954	53,596
Male	Life	57	56.85	6	12,999	7.08	1,348	146,022	135,644
Male	Life	65	64.85	52	116,447	6.60	1,132	1,098,483	1,026,320
Male	Life	78	76.98	106	237,227	6.34	764	1,510,345	1,414,739
Male	Life	85	83.00	74	165,192	6.20	582	801,181	751,018
Male	Life	92	83.00	1	5,416	6.20	582	26,268	24,623
Subtotal				241	541,614			3,640,253	3,405,940
Male	10 CC	45	45.00	5	10,811	7.50	1,622	146,129	135,171
Male	10 CC	56	56.00	11	24,325	7.14	1,417	287,238	266,708
Male	10 CC	68	68.00	80	182,441	6.54	1,160	1,763,596	1,648,917
Male	10 CC	78	78.00	221	502,050	6.34	989	4,137,729	3,876,642
Male	10 CC	85	85.00	274	621,650	6.20	927	4,802,246	4,504,149
Male	10 CC	92	92.00	4	10,136	6.20	927	78,301	73,440
Subtotal				595	1,351,413			11,215,239	10,505,027

TABLE C3 — Continued

Sex	Plan	Age True	Age Calc.	Number of Contracts	Annual Income	Load Percent	Factor with Load	Premium With Load	Premium No Load
				For Issues of 1977; with Interest of 7.5 Percent for the First 14 Years and 5.25 Percent Thereafter					
Female	Life	45	44.85	1	2,290	7.50	1,726	32,938	30,472
Female	Life	55	54.85	2	3,206	7.20	1,553	41,491	38,503
Female	Life	67	66.83	45	77,870	6.56	1,232	799,465	746,898
Female	Life	78	77.52	101	174,063	6.34	867	1,257,605	1,178,250
Female	Life	85	84.10	113	193,760	6.20	631	1,018,855	955,851
Female	Life	92	84.10	4	6,872	6.20	631	36,135	33,901
Subtotal				266	458,061			3,186,489	2,983,875
Female	10 CC	45	45.00	2	4,054	7.50	1,734	58,580	54,191
Female	10 CC	55	55.00	5	10,811	7.20	1,568	141,264	131,107
Female	10 CC	68	68.00	51	100,004	6.54	1,260	1,050,042	981,351
Female	10 CC	78	78.00	315	623,001	6.34	1,032	5,357,809	5,020,175
Female	10 CC	85	85.00	307	608,135	6.20	935	4,738,385	4,446,111
Female	10 CC	92	92.00	3	5,407	6.20	935	42,130	39,531
Subtotal				683	1,351,412			11,388,210	10,672,466
Subtotal life				507	999,675			6,826,742	6,389,815
Subtotal 10 CC				1,278	2,702,825			22,603,449	21,177,493
Subtotal male				836	1,893,027			14,855,492	13,910,967
Subtotal female				949	1,809,473			14,574,699	13,656,341
Total all issues				1,785	3,702,500			29,430,191	27,567,308

TABLE C3 — *Continued*

Sex	Plan	Age True	Age Calc.	Number of Contracts	Annual Income	Load Percent	Factor with Load	Premium With Load	Premium No Load
				For Issues of 1978; with Interest of 7.5 Percent for the First 14 Years and 5.25 Percent Thereafter					
Male	Life	35	34.85	0	0	7.50%	1,764	0	0
Male	Life	46	45.85	1	410	7.50	1,586	5,419	5,012
Male	Life	56	55.85	8	20,480	7.14	1,372	234,155	217,475
Male	Life	67	66.77	32	81,920	6.56	1,077	735,232	686,866
Male	Life	78	76.98	76	193,413	6.34	764	1,231,396	1,153,448
Male	Life	85	83.00	44	113,377	6.20	582	549,878	515,450
Subtotal				161	409,600			2,756,080	2,578,251
Male	10 CC	45	45.00	1	903	7.50	1,622	12,206	11,290
Male	10 CC	57	57.00	18	36,116	7.08	1,396	420,149	390,373
Male	10 CC	67	67.00	93	189,609	6.56	1,181	1,866,069	1,743,641
Male	10 CC	78	78.00	210	426,620	6.34	989	3,516,060	3,294,200
Male	10 CC	85	85.00	123	249,652	6.20	927	1,928,562	1,808,847
Male	10 CC	92	92.00	0	0	6.20	927	0	0
Subtotal				445	902,900			7,743,046	7,248,351

TABLE C3 — *Continued*

Sex	Plan	Age		Number of Contracts	Annual Income	Load Percent	Factor with Load	Premium	
		True	Calc.					With Load	No Load
				For Issues of 1978; with Interest of 7.5 Percent for the First 14 Years and 5.25 Percent Thereafter					
Female	Life	45	44.85	2	4,761	7.50	1,726	68,479	63,352
Female	Life	57	56.85	4	9,155	7.08	1,509	115,124	106,959
Female	Life	66	65.84	37	75,071	6.58	1,263	790,122	737,889
Female	Life	78	77.52	88	179,804	6.34	867	1,299,084	1,217,112
Female	Life	85	84.10	47	95,212	6.20	631	500,656	469,697
Female	Life	92	84.10	1	2,197	6.20	631	11,553	10,838
Subtotal				179	366,200			2,785,018	2,605,847
Female	10 CC	47	47.00	5	8,967	7.50	1,706	127,481	117,953
Female	10 CC	56	56.00	7	11,657	7.14	1,548	150,375	139,598
Female	10 CC	67	67.00	100	170,373	6.56	1,285	1,824,411	1,704,653
Female	10 CC	78	78.00	272	465,387	6.34	1,032	4,002,328	3,750,113
Female	10 CC	85	85.00	137	233,142	6.20	935	1,816,565	1,704,515
Female	10 CC	92	92.00	4	7,174	6.20	935	55,897	52,450
Subtotal				525	896,700			7,977,057	7,469,282
Subtotal life				340	775,800			5,541,098	5,184,098
Subtotal 10 CC				970	1,799,600			15,720,103	14,717,633
Subtotal male				606	1,312,500			10,499,126	9,826,602
Subtotal female				704	1,262,900			10,762,075	10,075,129
Total all issues				1,310	2,575,400			21,261,201	19,901,731

TABLE C3 — *Continued*

Sex	Plan	Age True	Age Calc.	Number of Contracts	Annual Income	Load Percent	Factor with Load	Premium With Load	Premium No Load
				For Issues of 1979; with Interest of 7.5 Percent for the First 14 Years and 5.25 Percent Thereafter					
Male	Life	46	45.85	1	1,454	7.50%	1,586	19,217	17,774
Male	Life	56	55.85	4	6,805	7.14	1,372	77,804	72,262
Male	Life	67	66.77	15	26,899	6.56	1,077	241,419	225,537
Male	Life	78	76.98	29	52,810	6.34	764	336,224	314,940
Male	Life	85	83.00	27	49,437	6.20	582	239,769	224,757
Male	Life	92	93.00	3	7,997	6.20	582	38,785	36,357
Subtotal				79	145,402			953,218	891,627
Male	10 CC	45	45.00	1	2,836	7.50	1,622	38,333	35,459
Male	10 CC	56	56.00	8	15,799	7.14	1,417	186,560	173,226
Male	10 CC	67	67.00	22	46,181	6.56	1,181	454,498	424,680
Male	10 CC	78	78.00	84	175,001	6.34	989	1,442,300	1,351,292
Male	10 CC	85	85.00	74	153,531	6.20	927	1,186,027	1,112,405
Male	10 CC	92	92.00	5	11,748	6.20	927	90,753	85,120
Subtotal				194	405,096			3,398,471	3,182,182

TABLE C3 — *Continued*

Sex	Plan	Age True	Age Calc.	Number of Contracts	Annual Income	Load Percent	Factor with Load	Premium With Load	Premium No Load
			For Issues of 1979; with Interest of 7.5 Percent for the First 14 Years and 5.25 Percent Thereafter						
Female	Life	45	44.85	1	528	7.50	1,726	7,594	7,026
Female	Life	57	56.85	4	4,965	7.08	1,509	62,435	58,007
Female	Life	67	66.83	27	14,451	6.56	1,232	148,364	138,608
Female	Life	78	77.52	47	44,495	6.34	867	321,476	301,191
Female	Life	85	84.10	21	36,762	6.20	631	193,307	181,353
Female	Life	92	84.10	1	4,438	6.20	631	23,336	21,893
Subtotal				101	105,639			756,512	708,078
Female	10 CC	45	45.00	1	1,306	7.50	1,734	18,872	17,458
Female	10 CC	55	55.00	6	10,448	7.20	1,568	136,521	126,705
Female	10 CC	67	67.00	26	46,147	6.56	1,285	494,157	461,720
Female	10 CC	78	78.00	116	202,873	6.34	1,032	1,744,708	1,634,761
Female	10 CC	85	85.00	97	169,786	6.20	935	1,322,916	1,241,316
Female	10 CC	92	92.00	3	4,789	6.20	935	37,314	35,013
Subtotal				249	435,349			3,754,488	3,516,973
Subtotal life				180	251,041			1,709,730	1,599,705
Subtotal 10 CC				443	840,445			7,152,959	6,699,155
Subtotal male				273	550,498			4,351,689	4,073,809
Subtotal female				350	540,988			4,511,000	4,225,051
Total all issues				623	1,091,486			8,862,689	8,298,860

TABLE C4

Gross Single Premiums
Assuming 1979 Company Mortality Table

Sex	Plan	Age True	Age Calc.	Number of Contracts	Annual Income	Load Percent	Factor with Load	Premium With Load	Premium No Load
				For Issues of 1980; with Interest of 9.22 Percent for the First 14 Years and 6.97 Percent Thereafter					
Male	Life	45	45.00	2	4,395	6.50%	1,375	50,359	47,072
Male	Life	55	55.00	2	4,884	6.50	1,242	50,549	47,273
Male	Life	67	67.00	7	17,092	6.32	1,013	144,285	135,137
Male	Life	78	78.00	17	38,909	6.16	724	234,751	220,313
Male	Life	85	85.00	22	50,703	6.05	526	222,248	208,995
Male	Life	92	92.00	3	6,105	6.05	526	26,760	25,164
Subtotal				53	122,088			728,952	683,954
Male	10 CC	45	45.00	1	3,125	6.50	1,387	36,120	33,766
Male	10 CC	57	57.00	3	5,134	6.47	1,247	53,351	49,885
Male	10 CC	68	68.00	11	29,016	6.31	1,076	260,177	243,698
Male	10 CC	78	78.00	59	154,098	6.16	926	1,189,123	1,115,606
Male	10 CC	85	85.00	93	243,290	6.05	864	1,751,688	1,645,324
Male	10 CC	92	92.00	4	11,740	6.05	864	84,528	79,395
Subtotal				171	446,403			3,374,987	3,167,674

TABLE C4 — *Continued*

Sex	Plan	Age True	Age Calc.	Number of Contracts	Annual Income	Load Percent	Factor with Load	Premium With Load	Premium No Load
				For Issues of 1980; with Interest of 9.22 Percent for the First 14 Years and 6.97 Percent Thereafter					
Female	Life	45	45.00	1	1,919	6.50	1,451	23,204	21,700
Female	Life	56	56.00	3	4,796	6.48	1,334	53,316	49,873
Female	Life	67	67.00	10	12,470	6.32	1,144	118,881	111,324
Female	Life	78	78.00	22	29,977	6.16	841	210,089	197,170
Female	Life	85	85.00	29	41,008	6.05	618	211,191	198,387
Female	Life	92	92.00	4	5,756	6.05	618	29,643	27,846
Subtotal				69	95,926			646,324	606,300
Female	10 CC	45	45.00	2	3,628	6.50	1,455	43,990	41,125
Female	10 CC	57	57.00	2	3,629	6.47	1,335	40,373	37,769
Female	10 CC	67	67.00	14	29,031	6.32	1,181	285,713	267,597
Female	10 CC	78	78.00	84	172,370	6.16	975	1,400,506	1,314,330
Female	10 CC	85	85.00	114	235,874	6.05	891	1,751,364	1,645,390
Female	10 CC	92	92.00	4	9,072	6.05	891	67,360	63,284
Subtotal				220	453,604			3,589,306	3,369,495
Subtotal life				122	218,014			1,375,276	1,290,254
Subtotal 10 CC				391	900,007			6,964,293	6,537,169
Subtotal male				224	568,491			4,103,939	3,851,628
Subtotal female				289	549,530			4,235,630	3,975,795
Total all issues				513	1,118,021			8,339,569	7,827,423

TABLE C4 — *Continued*

Sex	Plan	Age		Number of Contracts	Annual Income	Load Percent	Factor with Load	Premium	
		True	Calc.					With Load	No Load
				For Issues of 1981; with Interest of 9.22 Percent for the First 14 Years and 6.97 Percent Thereafter					
Male	Life	45	45.00	1	2,407	6.50%	1,375	27,580	25,780
Male	Life	55	55.00	1	5,379	6.50	1,242	55,673	52,065
Male	Life	66	66.00	3	13,449	6.34	1,036	116,110	108,714
Male	Life	77	77.00	12	47,000	6.17	752	294,533	276,459
Male	Life	85	85.00	13	50,680	6.05	526	222,147	208,900
Male	Life	92	92.00	5	22,650	6.05	526	99,283	93,362
Subtotal				35	141,565			815,326	765,280
Male	10 CC	45	45.00	1	1,537	6.50	1,387	17,765	16,607
Male	10 CC	55	55.00	3	7,683	6.50	1,274	81,568	76,246
Male	10 CC	67	67.00	6	17,607	6.32	1,092	160,224	150,127
Male	10 CC	78	78.00	31	92,263	6.16	926	711,963	667,946
Male	10 CC	85	85.00	62	185,039	6.05	864	1,332,281	1,251,384
Male	10 CC	92	92.00	5	16,007	6.05	864	115,250	108,252
Subtotal				108	320,136			2,419,051	2,270,562

TABLE C4 — *Continued*

Sex	Plan	Age		Number of Contracts	Annual Income	Load Percent	Factor with Load	Premium	
		True	Calc.					With Load	No Load
		For Issues of 1981; with Interest of 9.22 Percent for the First 14 Years and 6.97 Percent Thereafter							
Female	Life	45	45.00	1	1,337	6.50	1,451	16,167	15,119
Female	Life	55	55.00	1	3,085	6.50	1,348	34,655	32,405
Female	Life	67	67.00	3	6,171	6.32	1,144	58,830	55,090
Female	Life	77	77.00	16	35,688	6.17	873	259,630	243,486
Female	Life	85	85.00	21	47,310	6.05	618	243,647	228,875
Female	Life	92	92.00	4	9,257	6.05	618	47,674	44,783
Subtotal				46	102,848			660,603	619,758
Female	10 CC	45	45.00	2	4,505	6.50	1,455	54,623	51,066
Female	10 CC	55	55.00	6	13,861	6.50	1,360	157,091	146,887
Female	10 CC	67	67.00	13	31,188	6.32	1,181	306,942	287,480
Female	10 CC	78	78.00	40	100,495	6.16	975	816,522	766,279
Female	10 CC	85	85.00	74	185,397	6.05	891	1,376,573	1,293,277
Female	10 CC	92	92.00	4	11,090	6.05	891	82,343	77,361
Subtotal				139	346,536			2,794,094	2,622,350
Subtotal life				81	244,413			1,475,929	1,385,038
Subtotal 10 CC				247	666,672			5,213,145	4,892,912
Subtotal male				143	461,701			3,234,377	3,035,842
Subtotal female				185	449,384			3,454,697	3,242,108
Total all issues				328	911,085			6,689,074	6,277,950

TABLE C5

GROSS SINGLE PREMIUMS

ASSUMING 1981 COMPANY MORTALITY TABLE

Sex	Plan	Age True	Age Calc.	Number of Contracts	Annual Income	Load Percent	Factor with Load	Premium With Load	Premium No Load
				For Issues of 1982; with Interest of 11.45 Percent for the First 14 Years and 9.2 Percent Thereafter					
Male	Life	15	15.00	0	0	6.90%	1,231	0	0
Male	Life	25	25.00	0	0	6.90	1,219	0	0
Male	Life	35	35.00	0	0	6.90	1,193	0	0
Male	Life	45	45.00	0	0	6.90	1,142	0	0
Male	Life	50	50.00	2	2,533	6.90	1,104	23,304	21,698
Male	Life	65	65.00	25	63,256	6.70	932	491,288	458,372
Male	Life	76	76.00	37	179,014	6.49	731	1,090,494	1,019,826
Male	Life	85	85.00	17	126,325	6.40	535	563,199	527,572
Male	Life	92	92.00	0	0	6.40	535	0	0
Subtotal				81	371,128			2,168,285	2,027,468
Male	10 CC	17	17.00	1	1,200	6.90	1,230	12,300	11,452
Male	10 CC	26	26.00	1	2,500	6.90	1,218	25,375	23,633
Male	10 CC	36	36.00	2	19,837	6.90	1,193	197,213	183,606
Male	10 CC	45	45.00	2	12,075	6.90	1,152	115,920	107,953
Male	10 CC	56	56.00	9	28,147	6.88	1,078	252,854	235,377
Male	10 CC	66	66.00	77	315,743	6.68	980	2,578,568	2,407,423
Male	10 CC	76	76.00	72	295,504	6.49	874	2,152,254	2,012,819
Male	10 CC	85	85.00	41	169,881	6.40	801	1,133,956	1,061,974
Male	10 CC	92	92.00	1	2,359	6.40	801	15,746	14,747
Subtotal				206	847,246			6,484,186	6,058,984

TABLE C5 — Continued

Sex	Plan	Age True	Age Calc.	Number of Contracts	Annual Income	Load Percent	Factor with Load	Premium With Load	Premium No Load
				For Issues of 1982; with Interest of 11.45 Percent for the First 14 Years and 9.2 Percent Thereafter					
Female	Life	15	15.00	0	0	6.90	1,238	0	0
Female	Life	25	25.00	0	0	6.90	1,232	0	0
Female	Life	35	35.00	1	1,067	6.90	1,218	10,830	10,080
Female	Life	45	45.00	0	0	6.90	1,188	0	0
Female	Life	55	55.00	1	1,131	6.90	1,128	10,631	9,900
Female	Life	66	66.00	24	46,499	6.68	1,007	390,204	364,130
Female	Life	76	76.00	45	86,424	6.49	810	583,362	545,427
Female	Life	85	85.00	21	42,689	6.40	573	203,840	190,628
Female	Life	92	92.00	0	0	6.40	573	0	0
Subtotal				92	177,810			1,198,867	1,120,165
Female	10 CC	17	17.00	1	2,995	6.90	1,237	30,873	28,749
Female	10 CC	26	26.00	1	5,707	6.90	1,231	58,544	54,499
Female	10 CC	36	36.00	3	11,475	6.90	1,217	116,376	108,309
Female	10 CC	45	45.00	7	29,669	6.90	1,191	294,465	274,170
Female	10 CC	56	56.00	18	72,370	6.88	1,131	682,087	635,306
Female	10 CC	66	66.00	55	221,866	6.68	1,036	1,915,443	1,788,186
Female	10 CC	78	78.00	87	352,916	6.47	877	2,579,228	2,413,715
Female	10 CC	85	85.00	68	275,881	6.40	814	1,871,393	1,752,265
Female	10 CC	92	92.00	10	39,008	6.40	814	264,604	247,760
Subtotal				250	1,011,887			7,813,013	7,302,959
Subtotal life				173	548,938			3,367,152	3,147,633
Subtotal 10 CC				456	1,859,133			14,297,199	13,361,943
Subtotal male				287	1,218,374			8,652,471	8,086,452
Subtotal female				342	1,189,697			9,011,880	8,423,124
Total all issues				629	2,408,071			17,664,351	16,509,576

TABLE C5 — *Continued*

Sex	Plan	Age True	Age Calc.	Number of Contracts	Annual Income	Load Percent	Factor with Load	Premium With Load	Premium No Load
					For Issues of 1983; with Interest of 11.45 Percent for the First 14 Years and 9.2 Percent Thereafter				
Male	Life	10	10.00	1	10,851	6.90%	1,235	111,675	103,936
Male	Life	45	45.00	0	0	6.90	1,142	0	0
Male	Life	56	56.00	4	5,058	6.90	1,048	44,173	41,131
Male	Life	64	64.00	18	42,839	6.68	947	338,071	315,404
Male	Life	74	74.00	26	79,817	6.52	771	512,824	479,167
Male	Life	82	82.00	18	81,107	6.43	605	408,914	382,459
Male	Life	92	92.00	18	0	6.40	535	0	0
Subtotal				67	219,672			1,415,657	1,322,097
Male	10 CC	17	17.00	6	86,844	6.90	1,230	890,151	828,764
Male	10 CC	25	25.00	0	0	6.90	1,220	0	0
Male	10 CC	35	35.00	0	0	6.90	1,196	0	0
Male	10 CC	45	45.00	3	15,911	6.90	1,152	152,746	142,248
Male	10 CC	55	55.00	8	43,283	6.90	1,086	391,711	364,643
Male	10 CC	62	62.00	126	640,945	6.76	1,022	5,458,715	5,091,147
Male	10 CC	77	77.00	63	288,353	6.48	864	2,076,142	1,942,431
Male	10 CC	85	85.00	39	123,372	6.40	801	823,508	771,233
Male	10 CC	92	92.00	1	14,032	6.40	801	93,664	87,718
Subtotal				246	1,212,740			9,886,637	9,228,184

TABLE C5 — *Continued*

Sex	Plan	Age True	Age Calc.	Number of Contracts	Annual Income	Load Percent	Factor with Load	Premium With Load	Premium No Load
			For Issues of 1983; with Interest of 11.45 Percent for the First 14 Years and 9.2 Percent Thereafter						
Female	Life	35	35.00	0	0	6.90	1,218	0	0
Female	Life	45	45.00	0	0	6.90	1,188	0	0
Female	Life	52	52.00	4	8,179	6.90	1,151	78,450	73,018
Female	Life	63	63.00	22	42,077	6.74	1,047	367,122	342,396
Female	Life	73	73.00	28	92,026	6.49	879	674,090	630,128
Female	Life	85	85.00	33	84,803	6.40	573	404,934	378,688
Female	Life	92	92.00	0	0	6.40	573	0	0
Subtotal				87	227,085			1,524,596	1,424,230
Female	10 CC	18	18.00	1	2,153	6.90	1,237	22,194	20,658
Female	10 CC	28	28.00	2	11,807	6.90	1,229	120,923	112,561
Female	10 CC	36	36.00	4	41,565	6.90	1,217	421,538	392,318
Female	10 CC	43	43.00	1	4,126	6.90	1,198	41,191	38,356
Female	10 CC	56	56.00	18	75,910	6.88	1,131	715,452	666,383
Female	10 CC	65	65.00	89	338,731	6.70	1,048	2,958,251	2,760,137
Female	10 CC	73	73.00	132	480,004	6.54	944	3,776,031	3,528,240
Female	10 CC	83	83.00	62	254,766	6.42	828	1,757,885	1,644,412
Female	10 CC	92	92.00	3	9,174	6.40	814	62,230	58,269
Subtotal				312	1,218,236			9,875,695	9,221,334
Subtotal life				154	446,757			2,940,253	2,746,327
Subtotal 10 CC				558	2,430,976			19,762,332	18,449,518
Subtotal male				313	1,432,412			11,302,294	10,550,281
Subtotal female				399	1,445,321			11,400,291	10,645,564
Total all issues				712	2,877,733			22,702,585	21,195,845

TABLE C5 — *Continued*

Sex	Plan	Age		Number of Contracts	Annual Income	Load Percent	Factor with Load	Premium	
		True	Calc.					With Load	No Load
				For Issues of 1984; with Interest of 11.45 Percent for the First 14 Years and 9.2 Percent Thereafter					
Male	Life	35	35.00	0	0	6.90%	1,193	0	0
Male	Life	45	45.00	0	0	6.90	1,142	0	0
Male	Life	56	56.00	3	5,903	6.88	1,048	51,553	48,003
Male	Life	63	63.00	10	51,654	6.74	962	414,093	386,055
Male	Life	75	75.00	25	124,455	6.50	751	778,881	728,106
Male	Life	83	83.00	21	103,322	6.42	582	501,112	469,210
Male	Life	92	92.00	1	49	6.40	535	218	205
Subtotal				60	285,383			1,745,857	1,631,579
Male	10 CC	18	18.00	2	18,446	6.90	1,229	188,918	175,898
Male	10 CC	33	33.00	5	49,371	6.90	1,203	494,944	460,616
Male	10 CC	44	44.00	1	77,447	6.90	1,158	747,364	695,652
Male	10 CC	53	53.00	6	196,793	6.90	1,101	1,805,576	1,681,125
Male	10 CC	63	63.00	90	287,839	6.74	1,012	2,427,442	2,264,121
Male	10 CC	72	72.00	86	297,032	6.56	915	2,264,869	2,117,049
Male	10 CC	83	83.00	29	86,527	6.42	814	586,941	549,033
Male	10 CC	92	92.00	3	4,510	6.40	801	30,104	28,193
Subtotal				222	1,017,965			8,546,158	7,971,687

TABLE C5 — Continued

Sex	Plan	Age True	Age Calc.	Number of Contracts	Annual Income	Load Percent	Factor with Load	Premium With Load	Premium No Load
				For Issues of 1984; with Interest of 11.45 Percent for the First 14 Years and 9.2 Percent Thereafter					
Female	Life	35	35.00	0	0	6.90	1,218	0	0
Female	Life	45	45.00	0	0	6.90	1,188	0	0
Female	Life	56	56.00	2	7,905	6.88	1,120	73,780	68,682
Female	Life	62	62.00	19	50,268	6.76	1,059	443,615	413,596
Female	Life	75	75.00	28	97,735	6.50	834	679,258	634,992
Female	Life	82	82.00	31	69,963	6.43	653	380,715	356,296
Female	Life	92	92.00	8	5,878	6.40	573	28,067	26,248
Subtotal				88	231,749			1,605,435	1,499,814
Female	10 CC	15	15.00	0	0	6.90	1,238	0	0
Female	10 CC	25	25.00	1	2,596	6.90	1,232	26,652	24,809
Female	10 CC	47	47.00	7	56,219	6.90	1,183	554,226	515,959
Female	10 CC	56	56.00	15	61,349	6.88	1,131	578,214	538,558
Female	10 CC	63	63.00	107	320,459	6.74	1,070	2,857,426	2,664,226
Female	10 CC	75	75.00	111	392,549	6.50	916	2,996,457	2,802,169
Female	10 CC	85	85.00	59	263,276	6.40	814	1,785,889	1,672,204
Female	10 CC	92	92.00	3	5,352	6.40	814	36,304	33,993
Subtotal				303	1,101,800			8,835,168	8,251,918
Subtotal life				148	517,132			3,351,292	3,131,393
Subtotal 10 CC				525	2,199,765			17,381,326	16,223,605
Subtotal male				282	1,303,348			10,292,015	9,603,266
Subtotal female				391	1,333,549			10,440,603	9,751,732
Total all issues				673	2,636,897			20,732,618	19,354,998

TABLE C5 — *Continued*

Sex	Plan	Age		Number of Contracts	Annual Income	Load Percent	Factor with Load	Premium	
		True	Calc.					With Load	No Load
		For Issues of 1985; with Interest of 11.45 Percent for the First 14 Years and 9.2 Percent Thereafter							
Male	Life	15	15.00	0	0	6.90%	1,231	0	0
Male	Life	25	25.00	0	0	6.90	1,219	0	0
Male	Life	35	35.00	1	3,070	6.90	1,193	30,521	28,423
Male	Life	46	46.00	4	6,741	6.90	1,135	63,759	59,358
Male	Life	55	55.00	3	5,980	6.66	1,058	52,724	49,105
Male	Life	67	67.00	18	51,329	6.48	900	384,968	359,253
Male	Life	77	77.00	37	314,947	6.40	711	1,866,061	1,744,881
Male	Life	85	85.00	18	76,842	6.40	535	342,587	320,916
Male	Life	92	92.00	0	0	6.40	535	0	0
Subtotal				81	458,909			2,740,620	2,561,936
Male	10 CC	5	5.00	0	0	6.90	1,237	0	0
Male	10 CC	16	16.00	5	50,941	6.90	1,231	522,570	486,482
Male	10 CC	26	26.00	3	92,856	6.90	1,218	942,488	877,789
Male	10 CC	36	36.00	3	93,147	6.90	1,193	926,036	862,146
Male	10 CC	46	46.00	5	95,291	6.90	1,147	910,823	847,754
Male	10 CC	57	57.00	13	93,676	6.86	1,069	834,497	777,330
Male	10 CC	67	67.00	95	107,864	6.66	970	871,901	813,518
Male	10 CC	78	78.00	89	400,352	6.47	855	2,852,508	2,667,566
Male	10 CC	85	85.00	31	365,533	6.40	801	2,439,933	2,285,048
Male	10 CC	92	92.00	2	23,823	6.40	801	159,019	148,924
Subtotal				246	1,323,483			10,459,775	9,766,557

TABLE C5 — Continued

Sex	Plan	Age True	Age Calc.	Number of Contracts	Annual Income	Load Percent	Factor with Load	Premium With Load	Premium No Load
					For Issues of 1985; with Interest of 11.45 Percent for the First 14 Years and 9.2 Percent Thereafter				
Female	Life	15	15.00	0	0	6.90	1,238	0	0
Female	Life	25	25.00	0	0	6.90	1,232	0	0
Female	Life	35	35.00	0	0	6.90	1,218	0	0
Female	Life	45	45.00	0	0	6.90	1,188	0	0
Female	Life	56	56.00	12	11,364	6.88	1,120	106,064	98,735
Female	Life	66	66.00	47	92,239	6.68	1,007	774,039	722,316
Female	Life	76	76.00	39	128,358	6.49	810	866,417	810,075
Female	Life	85	85.00	23	101,947	6.40	573	486,797	455,245
Female	Life	92	92.00	0	0	6.40	573	0	0
Subtotal				121	333,908			2,233,317	2,086,371
Female	10 CC	5	5.00	1	5,785	6.90	1,241	59,827	55,706
Female	10 CC	15	15.00	3	29,986	6.90	1,238	309,356	288,047
Female	10 CC	25	25.00	4	21,484	6.90	1,232	220,569	205,318
Female	10 CC	35	35.00	3	36,119	6.90	1,219	366,909	341,460
Female	10 CC	45	45.00	10	46,610	6.90	1,191	462,604	430,721
Female	10 CC	57	57.00	12	51,271	6.86	1,124	480,238	447,162
Female	10 CC	67	67.00	117	170,902	6.66	1,024	1,458,364	1,361,573
Female	10 CC	78	78.00	117	612,777	6.47	877	4,478,379	4,190,995
Female	10 CC	84	84.00	76	560,077	6.41	821	3,831,860	3,584,222
Female	10 CC	92	92.00	2	18,644	6.40	814	126,468	118,418
Subtotal				345	1,553,655			11,794,574	11,023,622
Subtotal life				202	792,817			4,973,937	4,648,307
Subtotal 10 CC				591	2,877,138			22,254,349	20,790,179
Subtotal male				327	1,782,392			13,200,395	12,328,493
Subtotal female				466	1,887,563			14,027,891	13,109,993
Total all issues				793	3,669,955			27,228,286	25,438,486

TABLE C5 — *Continued*

For Issues of 1986; with Interest of 11.45 Percent for the First 14 Years and 9.2 Percent Thereafter

| Sex | Plan | Age | | Number of Contracts | Annual Income | Load Percent | Factor with Load | Premium | |
		True	Calc.					With Load	No Load
Male	Life	5	5.00	0	0	6.90%	1,237	0	0
Male	Life	19	19.00	1	3,995	6.90	1,227	40,849	38,042
Male	Life	25	25.00	0	0	6.90	1,219	0	0
Male	Life	35	35.00	0	0	6.90	1,193	0	0
Male	Life	45	45.00	0	0	6.90	1,142	0	0
Male	Life	57	57.00	4	11,764	6.86	1,037	101,661	94,690
Male	Life	66	66.00	30	61,522	6.68	916	469,618	438,350
Male	Life	75	75.00	37	124,300	6.50	751	777,911	727,200
Male	Life	84	84.00	21	69,741	6.41	559	324,877	304,203
Male	Life	92	92.00	0	0	6.40	535	0	0
Subtotal				93	271,322			1,714,916	1,602,485
Male	10 CC	5	5.00	5	36,460	6.90	1,237	375,842	349,938
Male	10 CC	16	16.00	8	48,632	6.90	1,231	498,883	464,431
Male	10 CC	26	26.00	7	25,149	6.90	1,218	255,262	237,739
Male	10 CC	36	36.00	5	13,279	6.90	1,193	132,015	122,907
Male	10 CC	48	48.00	11	70,024	6.90	1,135	662,310	616,493
Male	10 CC	57	57.00	5	31,071	6.86	1,069	276,791	257,829
Male	10 CC	68	68.00	69	235,399	6.64	959	1,881,230	1,755,830
Male	10 CC	77	77.00	75	301,241	6.48	864	2,168,935	2,029,248
Male	10 CC	85	85.00	44	175,581	6.40	801	1,172,003	1,097,606
Male	10 CC	92	92.00	3	4,720	6.40	801	31,506	29,506
Subtotal				232	941,556			7,454,777	6,961,527

TABLE C5 — *Continued*

| | | Age | | Number of | Annual | Load | Factor with | Premium | |
Sex	Plan	True	Calc.	Contracts	Income	Percent	Load	With Load	No Load
		For Issues of 1986; with Interest of 11.45 Percent for the First 14 Years and 9.2 Percent Thereafter							
Female	Life	5	5.00	0	0	6.90	1,242	0	0
Female	Life	15	15.00	0	0	6.90	1,238	0	0
Female	Life	26	26.00	0	0	6.90	1,231	0	0
Female	Life	35	35.00	0	0	6.90	1,218	0	0
Female	Life	45	45.00	0	0	6.90	1,188	0	0
Female	Life	51	51.00	3	1,771	6.90	1,157	17,075	15,901
Female	Life	64	64.00	27	81,644	6.72	1,035	704,180	656,542
Female	Life	75	75.00	48	96,563	6.50	834	671,113	627,378
Female	Life	84	84.00	15	72,212	6.41	599	360,458	337,362
Female	Life	92	92.00	1	1,884	6.40	573	8,996	8,413
Subtotal				94	254,074			1,761,822	1,645,596
Female	10 CC	5	5.00	6	15,621	6.90	1,241	161,547	150,421
Female	10 CC	15	15.00	7	30,320	6.90	1,238	312,801	291,255
Female	10 CC	25	25.00	7	24,089	6.90	1,232	247,314	230,214
Female	10 CC	35	35.00	8	34,943	6.90	1,219	354,963	330,342
Female	10 CC	45	45.00	4	14,448	6.90	1,191	143,396	133,513
Female	10 CC	57	57.00	12	30,101	6.86	1,124	281,946	262,527
Female	10 CC	67	67.00	84	458,949	6.66	1,024	3,916,365	3,656,437
Female	10 CC	78	78.00	112	431,386	6.47	877	3,152,713	2,950,399
Female	10 CC	85	85.00	96	515,714	6.40	814	3,498,260	3,275,570
Female	10 CC	92	92.00	2	6,488	6.40	814	44,010	41,209
Subtotal				338	1,562,059			12,113,315	11,321,887
Subtotal life				187	525,396			3,476,738	3,248,081
Subtotal 10 CC				570	2,503,615			19,568,092	18,283,414
Subtotal male				325	1,212,878			9,169,693	8,564,012
Subtotal female				432	1,816,133			13,875,137	12,967,483
Total all issues				757	3,029,011			23,044,830	21,531,495

TABLE D1

MORTALITY GROSS SINGLE PREMIUMS (NO LOADING)
ASSUMING 1965 COMPANY MORTALITY TABLE
WITH MORTALITY IMPROVEMENT BASED ON EXPERIENCE TABLES AND PROJECTION SCALES I AND J

Sex	Plan	Age		Number of Contracts	Annual Income	Factor		Premium	
		True	Calc.			Projection I	Projection J	Projection I	Projection J
		For Issues of 1966; with Interest of 4.75 Percent for the First 15 Years and 3.5 Percent Thereafter							
Male	Life	45	45.00	4	5,209	2,054	2,056	89,161	89,248
Male	Life	55	55.00	11	14,707	1,715	1,717	210,188	210,433
Male	Life	65	65.00	76	104,176	1,305	1,306	1,132,914	1,133,782
Male	Life	75	75.00	92	126,543	891	892	939,582	940,636
Male	Life	85	85.00	39	53,927	540	540	242,672	242,672
Male	Life	92	92.00	1	1,838	354	354	5,422	5,422
Subtotal				223	306,400			2,619,939	2,622,193
Male	10 CC	45	45.00	9	10,722	2,075	2,077	185,401	185,580
Male	10 CC	55	55.00	24	30,274	1,763	1,765	444,776	445,280
Male	10 CC	65	65.00	172	214,438	1,413	1,413	2,525,007	2,525,007
Male	10 CC	75	75.00	208	260,479	1,129	1,129	2,450,673	2,450,673
Male	10 CC	85	85.00	89	111,003	990	990	915,775	915,775
Male	10 CC	92	92.00	3	3,784	963	963	30,367	30,367
Subtotal				505	630,700			6,551,999	6,552,682

TABLE D1 — *Continued*

Sex	Plan	Age		Number of Contracts	Annual Income	Factor		Premium	
		True	Calc.			Projection I	Projection J	Projection I	Projection J
			For Issues of 1966; with Interest of 4.75 Percent for the First 15 Years and 3.5 Percent Thereafter						
Female	Life	45	45.00	4	4,945	2,223	2,229	91,606	91,853
Female	Life	55	55.00	12	15,216	1,917	1,922	243,076	243,710
Female	Life	65	65.00	79	101,567	1,518	1,520	1,284,823	1,286,515
Female	Life	75	75.00	137	176,125	1,049	1,049	1,539,626	1,539,626
Female	Life	85	85.00	60	77,602	619	619	400,297	400,297
Female	Life	92	92.00	4	4,945	381	381	15,700	15,700
Subtotal				296	380,400			3,575,128	3,577,701
Female	10 CC	45	45.00	8	9,068	2,233	2,239	168,740	169,194
Female	10 CC	55	55.00	24	27,900	1,940	1,946	451,050	452,445
Female	10 CC	65	65.00	162	186,232	1,578	1,580	2,448,951	2,452,055
Female	10 CC	75	75.00	280	322,942	1,215	1,215	3,269,788	3,269,788
Female	10 CC	85	85.00	124	142,290	1,006	1,006	1,192,865	1,192,865
Female	10 CC	92	92.00	8	9,068	966	966	72,997	72,865
Subtotal				606	697,500			7,604,391	7,609,344
Subtotal life				519	686,800			6,195,067	6,199,894
Subtotal 10 CC				1,111	1,328,200			14,156,390	14,162,026
Subtotal male				728	937,100			9,171,938	9,174,875
Subtotal female				902	1,077,900			11,179,519	11,187,045
Total all issues				1,630	2,015,000			20,351,457	20,361,920

TABLE D1 — *Continued*

Sex	Plan	Age		Number of Contracts	Annual Income	Factor		Premium	
		True	Calc.			Projection I	Projection J	Projection I	Projection J
				For Issues of 1967; with Interest of 5 Percent for the First 12 Years and 3.75 Percent Thereafter					
Male	Life	45	45.00	4	5,323	2,021	2,023	89,648	89,737
Male	Life	55	55.00	10	15,029	1,696	1,697	212,410	212,535
Male	Life	65	65.00	69	106,454	1,295	1,296	1,148,816	1,149,703
Male	Life	75	75.00	84	129,310	885	885	953,661	953,661
Male	Life	85	85.00	36	55,105	537	537	246,595	246,595
Male	Life	92	92.00	1	1,879	354	354	5,543	5,543
Subtotal				204	313,100			2,656,673	2,657,774
Male	10 CC	45	45.00	8	11,718	2,041	2,043	199,304	199,499
Male	10 CC	55	55.00	23	33,086	1,742	1,744	480,298	480,850
Male	10 CC	65	65.00	162	234,362	1,400	1,401	2,734,223	2,736,176
Male	10 CC	75	75.00	197	284,681	1,118	1,118	2,652,278	2,652,278
Male	10 CC	85	85.00	84	121,317	980	980	990,756	990,756
Male	10 CC	92	92.00	3	4,136	952	952	32,812	32,812
Subtotal				477	689,300			7,089,671	7,092,371

TABLE D1 — Continued

Sex	Plan	Age True	Age Calc.	Number of Contracts	Annual Income	Factor Projection I	Factor Projection J	Premium Projection I	Premium Projection J
				For Issues of 1967, with Interest of 5 Percent for the First 12 Years and 3.75 Percent Thereafter					
Female	Life	45	45.00	5	5,742	2,182	2,187	104,409	104,648
Female	Life	55	55.00	14	17,668	1,890	1,896	278,271	279,154
Female	Life	65	65.00	96	117,934	1,503	1,506	1,477,123	1,480,072
Female	Life	75	75.00	167	204,507	1,042	1,042	1,775,802	1,775,802
Female	Life	85	85.00	73	90,107	616	616	462,549	462,549
Female	Life	92	92.00	5	5,742	381	381	18,231	18,231
Subtotal				360	441,700			4,116,385	4,120,456
Female	10 CC	45	45.00	12	13,727	2,192	2,197	250,747	251,318
Female	10 CC	55	55.00	38	42,236	1,913	1,919	673,312	675,424
Female	10 CC	65	65.00	255	281,925	1,562	1,565	3,669,724	3,676,772
Female	10 CC	75	75.00	441	488,882	1,204	1,205	4,905,116	4,909,190
Female	10 CC	85	85.00	195	215,403	996	996	1,787,845	1,787,845
Female	10 CC	92	92.00	12	13,727	955	955	109,244	109,244
Subtotal				953	1,055,900			11,395,988	11,409,793
Subtotal life				564	754,800			6,773,058	6,778,230
Subtotal 10 CC				1,430	1,745,200			18,485,659	18,502,164
Subtotal male				681	1,002,400			9,746,344	9,750,145
Subtotal female				1,313	1,497,600			15,512,373	15,530,249
Total all issues				1,994	2,500,000			25,258,717	25,280,394

TABLE D1 — *Continued*

Sex	Plan	Age		Number of Contracts	Annual Income	Factor		Premium	
		True	Calc.			Projection I	Projection J	Projection I	Projection J
		For Issues of 1968; with Interest of 5.5 Percent for the First 13 Years and 3.75 Percent Thereafter							
Male	Life	45	45.00	4	5,834	1,930	1,931	93,830	93,879
Male	Life	55	55.00	10	16,474	1,628	1,630	223,497	223,772
Male	Life	65	65.00	75	116,688	1,254	1,255	1,219,390	1,220,362
Male	Life	75	75.00	91	141,742	865	865	1,021,724	1,021,724
Male	Life	85	85.00	39	60,403	530	530	266,780	266,780
Male	Life	92	92.00	1	2,059	352	352	6,040	6,040
Subtotal				220	343,200			2,831,261	2,832,557
Male	10 CC	45	45.00	8	10,775	1,949	1,951	175,004	175,184
Male	10 CC	55	55.00	23	30,422	1,673	1,674	424,133	424,387
Male	10 CC	65	65.00	161	215,492	1,355	1,355	2,433,264	2,433,264
Male	10 CC	75	75.00	195	261,759	1,090	1,090	2,377,644	2,377,644
Male	10 CC	85	85.00	83	111,549	958	958	890,533	890,533
Male	10 CC	92	92.00	3	3,803	932	932	29,537	29,537
Subtotal				473	633,800			6,330,115	6,330,549

TABLE D1 — *Continued*

Sex	Plan	Age True	Age Calc.	Number of Contracts	Annual Income	Factor Projection I	Factor Projection J	Premium Projection I	Premium Projection J
				For Issues of 1968; with Interest of 5.5 Percent for the First 13 Years and 3.75 Percent Thereafter					
Female	Life	45	45.00	5	5,893	2,079	2,084	102,096	102,342
Female	Life	55	55.00	16	18,132	1,808	1,814	273,189	274,095
Female	Life	65	65.00	107	121,031	1,449	1,452	1,461,449	1,464,475
Female	Life	75	75.00	185	209,878	1,015	1,016	1,775,218	1,776,967
Female	Life	85	85.00	81	92,473	607	607	467,759	467,759
Female	Life	92	92.00	5	5,893	380	380	18,661	18,661
Subtotal				399	453,300			4,098,372	4,104,299
Female	10 CC	45	45.00	13	14,639	2,088	2,093	254,719	255,329
Female	10 CC	55	55.00	40	45,044	1,830	1,836	686,921	689,173
Female	10 CC	65	65.00	267	300,669	1,506	1,509	3,773,396	3,780,913
Female	10 CC	75	75.00	464	521,385	1,171	1,172	5,087,849	5,092,194
Female	10 CC	85	85.00	204	229,724	974	974	1,854,593	1,864,593
Female	10 CC	92	92.00	13	14,639	935	935	114,062	114,062
Subtotal				1,001	1,126,100			11,781,540	11,796,264
Subtotal life				619	796,500			6,929,633	6,936,856
Subtotal 10 CC				1,474	1,759,900			18,111,655	18,126,813
Subtotal male				693	977,000			9,161,376	9,163,106
Subtotal female				1,400	1,579,400			15,879,912	15,900,563
Total all issues				2,023	2,556,400			25,041,288	25,063,669

TABLE D1 — *Continued*

Sex	Plan	Age		Number of Contracts	Annual Income	Factor		Premium	
		True	Calc.			Projection I	Projection J	Projection I	Projection J
			For Issues of 1969; with Interest of 5.7 Percent for the First 13 Years and 3.75 Percent Thereafter						
Male	Life	45	45.00	3	3,397	1,901	1,902	53,814	53,842
Male	Life	55	55.00	7	9,590	1,608	1,610	128,506	128,666
Male	Life	65	65.00	51	67,932	1,243	1,244	703,662	704,228
Male	Life	75	75.00	62	82,517	860	860	591,372	591,372
Male	Life	85	85.00	27	35,165	529	529	155,019	155,019
Male	Life	92	92.00	1	1,199	353	353	3,527	3,527
Subtotal				151	199,800			1,635,900	1,636,654
Male	10 CC	45	45.00	7	9,246	1,920	1,922	147,936	148,090
Male	10 CC	55	55.00	21	26,107	1,652	1,653	359,406	359,624
Male	10 CC	65	65.00	146	184,926	1,342	1,343	2,068,089	2,069,630
Male	10 CC	75	75.00	178	224,631	1,081	1,081	2,023,551	2,023,551
Male	10 CC	85	85.00	76	95,727	951	951	758,636	758,636
Male	10 CC	92	92.00	3	3,263	924	924	25,125	25,125
Subtotal				431	543,900			5,382,743	5,384,656

TABLE D1 — *Continued*

Sex	Plan	Age True	Age Calc.	Number of Contracts	Annual Income	Factor Projection I	Factor Projection J	Premium Projection I	Premium Projection J
				For Issues of 1969; with Interest of 5.7 Percent for the First 13 Years and 3.75 Percent Thereafter					
Female	Life	45	45.00	4	5,178	2,045	2,050	88,242	88,458
Female	Life	55	55.00	12	15,932	1,782	1,788	236,590	237,387
Female	Life	65	65.00	81	106,346	1,434	1,437	1,270,835	1,273,493
Female	Life	75	75.00	140	184,413	1,010	1,010	1,552,143	1,552,143
Female	Life	85	85.00	61	81,253	606	606	410,328	410,328
Female	Life	92	92.00	4	5,178	382	382	16,483	16,483
Subtotal				302	398,300			3,574,621	3,578,292
Female	10 CC	45	45.00	13	13,861	2,054	2,059	237,254	237,832
Female	10 CC	55	55.00	39	42,648	1,804	1,810	641,142	643,274
Female	10 CC	65	65.00	259	284,675	1,489	1,492	3,532,342	3,539,459
Female	10 CC	75	75.00	449	493,650	1,162	1,162	4,780,178	4,780,178
Female	10 CC	85	85.00	198	217,505	967	967	1,752,728	1,752,728
Female	10 CC	92	92.00	13	13,861	927	927	107,076	107,076
Subtotal				971	1,066,200			11,050,720	11,060,547
Subtotal life				453	598,100			5,210,521	5,214,946
Subtotal 10 CC				1,402	1,610,100			16,433,463	16,445,203
Subtotal male				582	743,700			7,018,643	7,021,310
Subtotal female				1,273	1,464,500			14,625,341	14,638,839
Total all issues				1,855	2,208,200			21,643,984	21,660,149

TABLE D2

MORTALITY GROSS SINGLE PREMIUMS (NO LOADING)
ASSUMING 1969 COMPANY MORTALITY TABLE
WITH MORTALITY IMPROVEMENT BASED ON EXPERIENCE TABLES AND PROJECTION SCALES I AND J

Sex	Plan	Age		Number of Contracts	Annual Income	Factor		Premium	
		True	Calc.			Projection I	Projection J	Projection I	Projection J
For Issues of 1970; with Interest of 7 Percent for the First 16 Years and 3.25 Percent Thereafter									
Male	Life	45	45.00	2	4,457	1,682	1,684	62,472	62,547
Male	Life	55	55.00	7	12,586	1,438	1,439	150,822	150,927
Male	Life	65	65.00	49	89,148	1,135	1,136	843,192	843,934
Male	Life	75	75.00	60	108,289	807	807	728,244	728,244
Male	Life	85	85.00	25	46,147	511	511	196,509	196,509
Male	Life	92	92.00	1	1,573	350	350	4,588	4,588
Subtotal				144	262,200			1,985,827	1,986,749
Male	10 CC	45	45.00	6	10,142	1,700	1,701	143,678	143,763
Male	10 CC	55	55.00	18	28,637	1,476	1,478	352,235	352,712
Male	10 CC	65	65.00	128	202,844	1,223	1,224	2,067,318	2,069,009
Male	10 CC	75	75.00	155	246,396	1,008	1,008	2,069,726	2,069,726
Male	10 CC	85	85.00	66	105,001	898	898	785,757	785,757
Male	10 CC	92	92.00	2	3,580	874	874	26,074	26,074
Subtotal				375	596,600			5,444,788	5,447,041

TABLE D2 — *Continued*

Sex	Plan	Age		Number of Contracts	Annual Income	Factor		Premium	
		True	Calc.			Projection I	Projection J	Projection I	Projection J
For Issues of 1970; with Interest of 7 Percent for the First 16 Years and 3.25 Percent Thereafter									
Female	Life	45	45.00	3	4,568	1,805	1,809	68,710	68,863
Female	Life	55	55.00	10	14,056	1,582	1,587	185,305	185,891
Female	Life	65	65.00	67	93,824	1,294	1,297	1,011,735	1,014,081
Female	Life	75	75.00	117	162,698	940	941	1,274,468	1,275,823
Female	Life	85	85.00	51	71,686	534	584	348,872	348,872
Female	Life	92	92.00	3	4,568	376	376	14,313	14,313
Subtotal				251	351,400			2,903,403	2,907,843
Female	10 CC	45	45.00	9	10,865	1,813	1,817	164,152	164,514
Female	10 CC	55	55.00	27	33,432	1,601	1,607	446,039	447,710
Female	10 CC	65	65.00	181	223,159	1,343	1,346	2,497,521	2,503,100
Female	10 CC	75	75.00	314	386,976	1,076	1,076	3,469,885	3,469,885
Female	10 CC	85	85.00	139	170,503	912	912	1,295,823	1,295,823
Female	10 CC	92	92.00	9	10,865	877	877	79,405	79,405
Subtotal				679	835,800			7,952,825	7,960,437
Subtotal life				395	613,600			4,889,230	4,894,592
Subtotal 10 CC				1,054	1,432,400			13,397,613	13,407,478
Subtotal male				519	858,800			7,430,615	7,433,790
Subtotal female				930	1,187,200			10,856,228	10,868,280
Total all issues				1,449	2,046,000			18,286,843	18,302,070

TABLE D2 — *Continued*

Sex	Plan	Age True	Age Calc.	Number of Contracts	Annual Income	Factor Projection I	Factor Projection J	Premium Projection I	Premium Projection J
				For Issues of 1971 with Interest of 7 Percent for the First 16 Years and 3.25 Percent Thereafter					
Male	Life	46	46.00	3	5,768	1,662	1,664	79,887	79,983
Male	Life	54	54.00	9	16,286	1,468	1,469	199,232	199,368
Male	Life	65	65.00	61	115,362	1,141	1,142	1,096,900	1,097,862
Male	Life	74	74.00	73	140,131	844	844	985,588	985,588
Male	Life	80	80.00	31	59,717	655	655	325,955	325,955
Male	Life	92	92.00	1	2,036	353	353	5,989	5,989
Subtotal				178	339,300			2,693,551	2,694,745
Male	10 CC	49	49.00	10	18,994	1,616	1,618	255,786	256,102
Male	10 CC	54	54.00	27	53,630	1,503	1,505	671,716	672,610
Male	10 CC	67	67.00	189	379,882	1,178	1,179	3,729,175	3,732,341
Male	10 CC	70	70.00	230	461,445	1,109	1,109	4,264,521	4,264,521
Male	10 CC	80	80.00	98	196,645	940	940	1,540,386	1,540,386
Male	10 CC	92	92.00	3	6,704	874	874	48,827	48,827
Subtotal				557	1,117,300			10,510,411	10,514,787

TABLE D2 — *Continued*

Sex	Plan	Age True	Age Calc.	Number of Contracts	Annual Income	Factor Projection I	Factor Projection J	Premium Projection I	Premium Projection J
				For Issues of 1971; with Interest of 7 Percent for the First 16 Years and 3.25 Percent Thereafter					
Female	Life	46	46.00	4	5,897	1,787	1,791	87,816	88,013
Female	Life	58	58.00	12	18,144	1,507	1,512	227,858	228,614
Female	Life	66	66.00	81	121,111	1,266	1,269	1,277,721	1,280,749
Female	Life	79	79.00	140	210,017	798	799	1,396,613	1,398,363
Female	Life	80	80.00	62	92,534	762	762	587,591	587,591
Female	Life	92	92.00	4	5,897	381	381	18,723	18,723
Subtotal				303	453,600			3,596,322	3,602,053
Female	10 CC	46	46.00	11	15,969	1,795	1,800	238,870	239,535
Female	10 CC	58	58.00	35	49,136	1,531	1,536	626,893	628,941
Female	10 CC	68	68.00	232	327,983	1,264	1,267	3,454,754	3,462,954
Female	10 CC	79	79.00	403	568,749	995	995	4,715,877	4,715,877
Female	10 CC	85	85.00	178	250,594	913	913	1,906,603	1,906,603
Female	10 CC	92	92.00	11	15,969	878	878	116,840	116,840
Subtotal				870	1,228,400			11,059,837	11,070,750
Subtotal life				481	792,900			6,289,873	6,296,798
Subtotal 10 CC				1,427	2,345,700			21,570,248	21,585,537
Subtotal male				735	1,456,600			13,203,962	13,209,532
Subtotal female				1,173	1,682,000			14,656,159	14,672,803
Total all issues				1,908	3,138,600			27,860,121	27,882,335

TABLE D2 — *Continued*

Sex	Plan	Age		Number of Contracts	Annual Income	Factor		Premium	
		True	Calc.			Projection I	Projection J	Projection I	Projection J
	For Issues of 1972; with Interest of 6.75 Percent for the First 16 Years and 3.25 Percent Thereafter

Sex	Plan	True	Calc.	Number of Contracts	Annual Income	Projection I	Projection J	Projection I	Projection J
Male	Life	47	47.00	3	5,350	1,679	1,681	74,855	74,945
Male	Life	56	56.00	8	15,106	1,448	1,450	182,279	182,531
Male	Life	68	68.00	59	106,998	1,064	1,065	948,716	949,607
Male	Life	74	74.00	72	129,971	860	861	931,459	932,542
Male	Life	82	82.00	30	55,387	606	606	279,704	279,704
Male	Life	92	92.00	1	1,888	359	359	5,648	5,648
Subtotal				173	314,700			2,422,661	2,424,977
Male	10 CC	46	46.00	8	13,263	1,721	1,723	190,214	190,435
Male	10 CC	56	56.00	23	37,450	1,489	1,490	464,692	465,004
Male	10 CC	65	65.00	160	265,268	1,253	1,254	2,769,840	2,772,051
Male	10 CC	75	75.00	195	322,223	1,027	1,027	2,757,692	2,757,692
Male	10 CC	85	85.00	83	137,315	910	910	1,041,305	1,041,305
Male	10 CC	92	92.00	3	4,681	884	884	34,483	34,483
Subtotal				472	780,200			7,258,226	7,260,970

TABLE D2 — *Continued*

Sex	Plan	Age		Number of Contracts	Annual Income	Factor		Premium	
		True	Calc.			Projection I	Projection J	Projection I	Projection J
				For Issues of 1972; with Interest of 6.75 Percent for the First 16 Years and 3.25 Percent Thereafter					
Female	Life	49	49.00	3	3,696	1,766	1,771	54,393	54,547
Female	Life	52	52.00	9	11,372	1,697	1,702	160,819	161,293
Female	Life	67	67.00	61	75,908	1,260	1,264	797,034	799,564
Female	Life	79	79.00	106	131,631	814	814	892,897	892,897
Female	Life	85	85.00	46	57,997	599	599	289,502	289,502
Female	Life	92	92.00	3	3,696	389	389	11,981	11,981
Subtotal				228	284,300			2,206,626	2,209,784
Female	10 CC	47	47.00	11	15,369	1,819	1,824	232,968	233,609
Female	10 CC	56	56.00	10	14,188	1,617	1,622	191,183	191,774
Female	10 CC	67	67.00	189	260,106	1,319	1,323	2,858,998	2,867,669
Female	10 CC	78	78.00	438	602,973	1,030	1,031	5,175,518	5,180,543
Female	10 CC	85	85.00	206	283,752	925	925	2,187,255	2,187,255
Female	10 CC	92	92.00	4	5,912	887	887	43,700	43,700
Subtotal				858	1,182,300			10,689,622	10,704,550
Subtotal life				401	599,000			4,629,287	4,634,761
Subtotal 10 CC				1,330	1,962,500			17,947,848	17,965,520
Subtotal male				645	1,094,900			9,680,887	9,685,947
Subtotal female				1,086	1,466,600			12,896,248	12,914,334
Total all issues				1,731	2,561,500			22,577,135	22,600,281

TABLE D2 — Continued

Sex	Plan	Age True	Age Calc.	Number of Contracts	Annual Income	Factor Projection I	Factor Projection J	Premium Projection I	Premium Projection J
				For Issues of 1973; with Interest of 7 Percent for the First 16 Years and 3.25 Percent Thereafter					
Male	Life	44	44.00	3	6,362	1,709	1,711	90,605	90,712
Male	Life	55	55.00	8	17,961	1,441	1,443	215,682	215,981
Male	Life	65	65.00	56	127,228	1,145	1,146	1,213,967	1,215,027
Male	Life	73	73.00	69	154,545	885	886	1,139,769	1,141,057
Male	Life	85	85.00	29	65,859	517	517	283,743	283,743
Male	Life	92	92.00	1	2,245	346	346	6,473	6,473
Subtotal				166	374,200			2,950,239	2,952,993
Male	10 CC	44	44.00	8	15,722	1,724	1,726	225,873	226,135
Male	10 CC	54	54.00	24	44,390	1,505	1,506	556,725	557,095
Male	10 CC	68	68.00	168	314,432	1,160	1,161	3,039,509	3,042,130
Male	10 CC	75	75.00	204	381,942	1,015	1,016	3,230,593	3,233,776
Male	10 CC	85	85.00	87	162,765	900	900	1,220,738	1,220,738
Male	10 CC	92	92.00	3	5,549	874	874	40,415	40,415
Subtotal				494	924,800			8,313,853	8,320,289

TABLE D2 — *Continued*

Sex	Plan	Age True	Age Calc.	Number of Contracts	Annual Income	Factor Projection I	Factor Projection J	Premium Projection I	Premium Projection J
				For Issues of 1973; with Interest of 7 Percent for the First 16 Years and 3.25 Percent Thereafter					
Female	Life	46	46.00	3	5,894	1,787	1,791	87,771	87,968
Female	Life	54	54.00	9	18,136	1,614	1,619	243,929	244,685
Female	Life	66	66.00	60	121,058	1,272	1,276	1,283,215	1,287,250
Female	Life	78	78.00	103	209,924	835	836	1,460,721	1,462,471
Female	Life	85	85.00	45	92,494	585	585	450,908	450,908
Female	Life	92	92.00	3	5,894	366	366	17,977	17,977
Subtotal				223	453,400			3,544,521	3,551,259
Female	10 CC	46	46.00	8	10,762	1,796	1,800	161,071	161,430
Female	10 CC	56	56.00	8	10,762	1,585	1,590	142,148	142,597
Female	10 CC	67	67.00	130	179,047	1,296	1,300	1,933,708	1,939,676
Female	10 CC	78	78.00	390	538,120	1,016	1,017	4,556,083	4,560,567
Female	10 CC	85	85.00	170	234,816	913	913	1,786,558	1,786,558
Female	10 CC	92	92.00	3	4,893	876	876	35,719	35,719
Subtotal				709	978,400			8,615,287	8,626,547
Subtotal life				389	827,600			6,494,760	6,504,252
Subtotal 10 CC				1,203	1,903,200			16,929,140	16,946,836
Subtotal male				660	1,299,000			11,264,092	11,273,282
Subtotal female				932	1,431,800			12,159,808	12,177,806
Total all issues				1,592	2,730,800			23,423,900	23,451,088

TABLE D3

MORTALITY GROSS SINGLE PREMIUMS (NO LOADING)
ASSUMING 1974 COMPANY MORTALITY TABLE
WITH MORTALITY IMPROVEMENT BASED ON EXPERIENCE TABLES AND PROJECTION SCALES I AND J

Sex	Plan	Age		Number of Contracts	Annual Income	Factor		Premium	
		True	Calc.			Projection I	Projection J	Projection I	Projection J
				For Issues of 1974 with Interest of 7.5 Percent for the First 14 Years and 5.25 Percent Thereafter					
Male	Life	45	45.00	2	4,435	1,543	1,544	57,027	57,064
Male	Life	55	55.00	7	12,523	1,358	1,359	141,719	141,823
Male	Life	65	65.00	48	88,706	1,106	1,107	817,574	818,313
Male	Life	75	75.00	58	107,752	807	807	724,632	724,632
Male	Life	85	85.00	25	45,919	516	516	197,452	197,452
Male	Life	92	92.00	1	1,565	343	343	4,473	4,473
Subtotal				141	260,900			1,942,877	1,943,757
Male	10 CC	45	45.00	7	10,834	1,559	1,561	140,752	140,932
Male	10 CC	55	55.00	19	30,590	1,394	1,396	355,354	355,864
Male	10 CC	65	65.00	131	216,682	1,188	1,189	2,145,152	2,146,957
Male	10 CC	75	75.00	159	263,205	992	993	2,175,828	2,178,021
Male	10 CC	85	85.00	68	112,165	881	881	823,478	823,478
Male	10 CC	92	92.00	2	3,824	856	856	27,278	27,278
Subtotal				386	637,300			5,667,842	5,672,530

TABLE D3 — *Continued*

Sex	Plan	Age		Number of Contracts	Annual Income	Factor		Premium	
		True	Calc.			Projection I	Projection J	Projection I	Projection J
				For Issues of 1974 with Interest of 5.5 Percent for the First 14 Years and 5.25 Percent Thereafter					
Female	Life	45	45.00	2	3,574	1,630	1,633	48,547	48,636
Female	Life	55	55.00	7	10,996	1,480	1,484	135,617	135,984
Female	Life	65	65.00	49	73,398	1,254	1,258	757,009	769,456
Female	Life	75	75.00	84	127,278	935	937	991,708	993,829
Female	Life	85	85.00	37	56,080	592	592	276,661	276,661
Female	Life	92	92.00	2	3,574	368	368	10,960	10,960
Subtotal				181	274,900			2,230,502	2,235,526
Female	10 CC	45	45.00	8	12,505	1,639	1,641	170,797	171,006
Female	10 CC	55	55.00	24	38,476	1,496	1,500	479,667	480,950
Female	10 CC	65	65.00	159	256,827	1,295	1,300	2,771,591	2,782,293
Female	10 CC	75	75.00	276	445,359	1,057	1,059	3,922,871	3,930,293
Female	10 CC	85	85.00	121	196,228	896	896	1,465,169	1,465,169
Female	10 CC	92	92.00	8	12,505	859	859	89,515	89,515
Subtotal				596	961,900			8,899,610	8,919,226
Subtotal life				322	535,800			4,173,379	4,179,283
Subtotal 10 CC				982	1,599,200			14,567,452	14,591,756
Subtotal male				527	898,200			7,610,719	7,616,287
Subtotal female				777	1,236,800			11,130,112	11,154,752
Total all issues				1,304	2,135,000			18,740,831	18,771,039

TABLE D3 — *Continued*

Sex	Plan	Age True	Age Calc.	Number of Contracts	Annual Income	Factor Projection I	Factor Projection J	Premium Projection I	Premium Projection J
				For Issues of 1975; with Interest of 7.5 Percent for the First 14 Years and 5.25 Percent Thereafter					
Male	Life	46	46.00	1	3,858	1,528	1,529	49,125	49,157
Male	Life	57	57.00	8	18,500	1,315	1,317	202,729	203,038
Male	Life	68	68.00	51	124,399	1,022	1,023	1,059,465	1,060,501
Male	Life	76	76.00	57	141,452	779	780	918,259	919,438
Male	Life	85	85.00	21	51,813	518	518	223,659	223,659
Male	Life	92	92.00	2	4,478	345	345	12,874	12,874
Subtotal				140	344,500			2,466,111	2,468,667
Male	10 CC	42	42.00	34	60,079	1,602	1,604	802,055	803,056
Male	10 CC	53	53.00	78	139,910	1,433	1,435	1,670,759	1,673,090
Male	10 CC	63	63.00	197	353,890	1,233	1,234	3,636,220	3,639,169
Male	10 CC	73	73.00	121	218,095	1,029	1,029	1,870,165	1,870,165
Male	10 CC	81	81.00	27	49,380	915	915	376,523	376,523
Male	10 CC	92	92.00	1	1,646	856	856	11,741	11,741
Subtotal				458	823,000			8,367,463	8,373,744

TABLE D3 — *Continued*

Sex	Plan	Age True	Age Calc.	Number of Contracts	Annual Income	Factor Projection I	Factor Projection J	Premium Projection I	Premium Projection J
				For Issues of 1975; with Interest of 7.5 Percent for the First 14 Years and 5.25 Percent Thereafter					
Female	Life	47	47.00	3	3,467	1,605	1,608	46,371	46,458
Female	Life	58	58.00	6	10,434	1,424	1,428	123,817	124,165
Female	Life	69	69.00	45	74,304	1,139	1,143	705,269	707,746
Female	Life	78	78.00	82	133,902	835	836	931,735	932,851
Female	Life	85	85.00	49	80,682	594	595	399,376	400,048
Female	Life	92	92.00	4	6,811	371	371	21,057	21,057
Subtotal				189	309,600			2,227,625	2,232,325
Female	10 CC	48	48.00	4	5,523	1,601	1,604	73,686	73,824
Female	10 CC	57	57.00	23	35,632	1,463	1,467	434,413	435,601
Female	10 CC	68	68.00	98	152,505	1,226	1,230	1,558,093	1,563,176
Female	10 CC	78	78.00	304	472,124	998	999	3,926,498	3,930,432
Female	10 CC	85	85.00	141	218,335	897	897	1,632,054	1,632,054
Female	10 CC	92	92.00	4	6,681	859	859	47,825	47,825
Subtotal				574	890,800			7,672,569	7,682,912
Subtotal life				329	654,100			4,693,736	4,700,992
Subtotal 10 CC				1,032	1,713,800			16,040,032	16,056,656
Subtotal male				598	1,167,500			10,833,574	10,842,411
Subtotal female				763	1,200,400			9,900,194	9,915,237
Total all issues				1,361	2,367,900			20,733,768	20,757,648

TABLE D3 — *Continued*

Sex	Plan	Age		Number of Contracts	Annual Income	Factor		Premium	
		True	Calc.			Projection I	Projection J	Projection I	Projection J
				For Issues of 1976; with Interest of 7.5 Percent for the First 14 Years and 5.25 Percent Thereafter					
Male	Life	48	48.00	8	18,179	1,495	1,497	226,480	226,783
Male	Life	58	58.00	9	20,946	1,295	1,297	226,042	226,391
Male	Life	64	64.00	62	136,739	1,140	1,142	1,299,021	1,301,299
Male	Life	76	76.00	66	147,014	782	783	958,041	959,266
Male	Life	85	85.00	31	68,765	520	521	297,982	298,555
Male	Life	92	92.00	2	3,557	348	348	10,315	10,315
Subtotal				178	395,200			3,017,881	3,022,609
Male	10 CC	47	47.00	21	51,115	1,532	1,534	652,568	653,420
Male	10 CC	54	54.00	25	58,894	1,417	1,419	695,440	696,422
Male	10 CC	63	63.00	160	384,475	1,236	1,237	3,960,093	3,963,296
Male	10 CC	75	75.00	172	413,366	996	997	3,430,938	3,434,383
Male	10 CC	85	85.00	81	193,349	883	883	1,422,726	1,422,726
Male	10 CC	92	92.00	4	10,001	857	857	71,424	71,424
Subtotal				463	1,111,200			10,233,189	10,241,671

TABLE D3 — *Continued*

Sex	Plan	Age True	Age Calc.	Number of Contracts	Annual Income	Factor Projection I	Factor Projection J	Premium Projection I	Premium Projection J
				For Issues of 1976; with Interest of 7.5 Percent for the First 14 Years and 5.25 Percent Thereafter					
Female	Life	49	49.00	3	4,303	1,578	1,581	56,584	56,692
Female	Life	52	52.00	10	16,854	1,532	1,536	215,169	215,731
Female	Life	68	68.00	53	88,574	1,173	1,177	865,811	868,763
Female	Life	77	77.00	105	174,997	873	875	1,273,103	1,276,020
Female	Life	85	85.00	40	66,700	597	597	331,833	331,833
Female	Life	92	92.00	4	7,172	374	374	22,353	22,353
Subtotal				215	358,600			2,764,853	2,771,392
Female	10 CC	45	45.00	2	889	1,640	1,643	12,150	12,172
Female	10 CC	57	57.00	36	65,608	1,464	1,468	800,418	802,605
Female	10 CC	67	67.00	135	245,530	1,253	1,258	2,563,742	2,573,973
Female	10 CC	78	78.00	289	525,309	1,000	1,002	4,377,575	4,386,330
Female	10 CC	85	85.00	147	266,880	898	899	1,997,152	1,999,376
Female	10 CC	92	92.00	3	7,784	860	860	55,785	55,785
Subtotal				612	1,112,000			9,806,822	9,830,241
Subtotal life				393	753,800			5,782,734	5,794,001
Subtotal 10 CC				1,075	2,223,200			20,040,011	20,071,912
Subtotal male				641	1,506,400			13,251,070	13,264,280
Subtotal female				827	1,470,600			12,571,675	12,601,633
Total all issues				1,468	2,977,000			25,822,745	25,865,913

TABLE D3 — *Continued*

For Issues of 1977; with Interest of 7.5 Percent for the First 14 Years and 5.25 Percent Thereafter

Sex	Plan	Age		Number of Contracts	Annual Income	Factor		Premium	
		True	Calc.			Projection I	Projection J	Projection I	Projection J
Male	Life	45	45.00	2	4,333	1,548	1,549	55,896	55,932
Male	Life	57	57.00	6	12,999	1,322	1,323	143,206	143,314
Male	Life	65	65.00	52	116,447	1,116	1,118	1,082,957	1,084,898
Male	Life	78	78.00	106	237,227	725	725	1,433,246	1,433,246
Male	Life	85	85.00	74	165,192	523	524	719,962	721,338
Male	Life	92	92.00	1	5,416	351	351	15,842	15,842
Subtotal				241	541,614			3,451,109	3,454,570
Male	10 CC	45	45.00	5	10,811	1,563	1,565	140,813	140,993
Male	10 CC	56	56.00	11	24,325	1,382	1,383	280,143	280,346
Male	10 CC	68	68.00	80	182,441	1,132	1,133	1,721,027	1,722,547
Male	10 CC	78	78.00	221	502,050	953	954	3,987,114	3,991,298
Male	10 CC	85	85.00	274	621,650	884	884	4,579,488	4,579,488
Male	10 CC	92	92.00	4	10,136	857	857	72,388	72,388
Subtotal				595	1,351,413			10,780,973	10,787,060

TABLE D3 — *Continued*

Sex	Plan	Age True	Age Calc.	Number of Contracts	Annual Income	Factor Projection I	Factor Projection J	Premium Projection I	Premium Projection J
			For Issues of 1977; with Interest of 7.5 Percent for the First 14 Years and 5.25 Percent Thereafter						
Female	Life	45	45.00	1	2,290	1,633	1,636	31,163	31,220
Female	Life	55	55.00	2	3,206	1,483	1,487	39,621	39,728
Female	Life	67	67.00	45	77,870	1,205	1,211	781,945	785,838
Female	Life	78	78.00	101	174,063	842	844	1,221,342	1,224,243
Female	Life	85	85.00	113	193,760	600	601	968,800	970,415
Female	Life	92	92.00	4	6,872	379	379	21,704	21,704
Subtotal				266	458,061			3,064,575	3,073,148
Female	10 CC	45	45.00	2	4,054	1,641	1,643	55,438	55,506
Female	10 CC	55	55.00	5	10,811	1,499	1,503	135,047	135,408
Female	10 CC	68	68.00	51	100,004	1,231	1,236	1,025,874	1,030,041
Female	10 CC	78	78.00	315	623,001	1,002	1,004	5,202,058	5,212,442
Female	10 CC	85	85.00	307	608,135	900	900	4,561,013	4,561,013
Female	10 CC	92	92.00	3	5,407	860	860	38,750	38,750
Subtotal				683	1,351,412			11,018,180	11,033,160
Subtotal life				507	999,675			6,515,684	6,527,718
Subtotal 10 CC				1,278	2,702,825			21,799,153	21,820,220
Subtotal male				836	1,893,027			14,232,082	14,241,630
Subtotal female				949	1,809,473			14,082,755	14,106,308
Total all issues				1,785	3,702,500			28,314,837	28,347,938

TABLE D3 — *Continued*

Sex	Plan	Age		Number of Contracts	Annual Income	Factor		Premium	
		True	Calc.			Projection I	Projection J	Projection I	Projection J
				For Issues of 1978; with Interest of 7.5 Percent for the First 14 Years and 5.25 Percent Thereafter					
Male	Life	35	35.00	0	0	1,681	1,683	0	0
Male	Life	46	46.00	1	410	1,533	1,535	5,238	5,245
Male	Life	56	56.00	8	20,480	1,347	1,349	229,888	230,229
Male	Life	67	67.00	32	81,920	1,063	1,064	725,675	726,357
Male	Life	78	78.00	76	193,413	729	730	1,174,984	1,176,596
Male	Life	85	85.00	44	113,377	527	527	497,914	497,914
Subtotal				161	409,600			2,633,699	2,636,341
Male	10 CC	45	45.00	1	903	1,565	1,566	11,777	11,784
Male	10 CC	57	57.00	18	36,116	1,365	1,366	410,820	411,120
Male	10 CC	67	67.00	93	189,609	1,155	1,157	1,824,987	1,828,147
Male	10 CC	78	78.00	210	426,620	955	956	3,395,184	3,398,739
Male	10 CC	85	85.00	123	249,652	885	885	1,841,184	1,841,184
Male	10 CC	92	92.00	0	0	857	857	0	0
Subtotal				445	902,900			7,483,952	7,490,974

TABLE D3 — *Continued*

Sex	Plan	Age		Number of Contracts	Annual Income	Factor		Premium	
		True	Calc.			Projection I	Projection J	Projection I	Projection J
				For Issues of 1978; with Interest of 7.5 Percent for the First 14 Years and 5.25 Percent Thereafter					
Female	Life	45	45.00	2	4,761	1,634	1,637	64,829	64,948
Female	Life	57	57.00	4	9,155	1,447	1,452	110,394	110,776
Female	Life	66	66.00	37	75,071	1,236	1,242	773,231	776,985
Female	Life	78	78.00	88	179,804	846	849	1,267,618	1,272,113
Female	Life	85	85.00	47	95,212	604	605	479,234	480,027
Female	Life	92	92.00	1	2,197	383	383	7,012	7,012
Subtotal				179	366,200			2,702,318	2,711,861
Female	10 CC	47	47.00	5	8,967	1,617	1,620	120,830	121,055
Female	10 CC	56	56.00	7	11,657	1,483	1,487	144,061	144,450
Female	10 CC	67	67.00	100	170,373	1,257	1,263	1,784,657	1,793,176
Female	10 CC	78	78.00	272	465,387	1,005	1,007	3,897,616	3,905,373
Female	10 CC	85	85.00	137	233,142	901	902	1,750,508	1,752,451
Female	10 CC	92	92.00	4	7,174	860	860	51,414	51,414
Subtotal				525	896,700			7,749,086	7,767,919
Subtotal life				340	775,800			5,336,017	5,348,202
Subtotal 10 CC				970	1,799,600			15,233,038	15,258,893
Subtotal male				606	1,312,500			10,117,651	10,127,315
Subtotal female				704	1,262,900			10,451,404	10,479,780
Total all issues				1,310	2,575,400			20,569,055	20,607,095

TABLE D3 — *Continued*

Sex	Plan	Age		Number of Contracts	Annual Income	Factor		Premium	
		True	Calc.			Projection I	Projection J	Projection I	Projection J
					For Issues of 1979; with Interest of 7.5 Percent for the First 14 Years and 5.25 Percent Thereafter				
Male	Life	46	46.00	1	1,454	1,535	1,537	18,599	18,623
Male	Life	56	56.00	4	6,805	1,350	1,352	76,556	76,670
Male	Life	67	67.00	15	26,899	1,067	1,069	239,177	239,625
Male	Life	78	78.00	29	52,810	733	734	322,581	323,021
Male	Life	85	85.00	27	49,437	531	531	218,759	218,759
Male	Life	92	92.00	3	7,997	359	359	23,924	23,924
Subtotal				79	145,402			899,596	900,622
Male	10 CC	45	45.00	1	2,836	1,566	1,568	37,010	37,057
Male	10 CC	56	56.00	8	15,799	1,386	1,388	182,478	182,742
Male	10 CC	67	67.00	22	46,181	1,158	1,160	445,647	446,416
Male	10 CC	78	78.00	84	175,001	957	958	1,395,633	1,397,091
Male	10 CC	85	85.00	74	153,531	886	887	1,133,571	1,134,850
Male	10 CC	92	92.00	5	11,748	857	857	83,900	83,900
Subtotal				194	405,096			3,278,239	3,282,056

TABLE D3 — Continued

Sex	Plan	Age True	Age Calc.	Number of Contracts	Annual Income	Factor Projection I	Factor Projection J	Premium Projection I	Premium Projection J
			For Issues of 1979; with Interest of 7.5 Percent for the First 14 Years and 5.25 Percent Thereafter						
Female	Life	45	45.00	1	528	1,635	1,638	7,194	7,207
Female	Life	57	57.00	4	4,965	1,448	1,453	59,911	60,118
Female	Life	67	67.00	27	14,451	1,211	1,217	145,835	146,557
Female	Life	78	78.00	47	44,495	850	854	315,173	316,656
Female	Life	85	85.00	21	36,762	608	609	186,261	186,567
Female	Life	92	92.00	1	4,438	389	389	14,387	14,387
Subtotal				101	105,639			728,761	731,492
Female	10 CC	45	45.00	1	1,306	1,643	1,645	17,881	17,903
Female	10 CC	55	55.00	6	10,448	1,501	1,505	130,687	131,035
Female	10 CC	67	67.00	26	46,147	1,259	1,265	484,159	486,466
Female	10 CC	78	78.00	116	202,873	1,007	1,010	1,702,443	1,707,514
Female	10 CC	85	85.00	97	169,786	902	903	1,276,225	1,277,640
Female	10 CC	92	92.00	3	4,789	861	861	34,361	34,361
Subtotal				249	435,349			3,645,756	3,654,919
Subtotal life				180	251,041			1,628,357	1,632,114
Subtotal 10 CC				443	840,445			6,923,995	6,936,975
Subtotal male				273	550,498			4,177,835	4,182,678
Subtotal female				350	540,988			4,374,517	4,386,411
Total all issues				623	1,091,486			8,552,352	8,569,089

TABLE D4

MORTALITY GROSS SINGLE PREMIUMS (NO LOADING)
ASSUMING 1979 COMPANY MORTALITY TABLE
WITH MORTALITY IMPROVEMENT BASED ON EXPERIENCE TABLES AND PROJECTION SCALES I AND J

Sex	Plan	Age True	Age Calc.	Number of Contracts	Annual Income	Factor Projection I	Factor Projection J	Premium Projection I	Premium Projection J
				For Issues of 1980; with Interest of 9.22 Percent for the First 14 Years and 6.97 Percent Thereafter					
Male	Life	45	45.00	2	4,395	1,302	1,303	47,686	47,722
Male	Life	55	55.00	2	4,884	1,184	1,185	48,189	48,230
Male	Life	67	67.00	7	17,092	963	965	137,163	137,448
Male	Life	78	78.00	17	38,909	694	695	225,024	225,348
Male	Life	85	85.00	22	50,703	518	519	218,868	219,290
Male	Life	92	92.00	3	6,105	352	352	17,908	17,908
Subtotal				53	122,088			694,838	695,946
Male	10 CC	45	45.00	1	3,125	1,313	1,314	34,193	34,219
Male	10 CC	57	57.00	3	5,134	1,186	1,187	50,741	50,784
Male	10 CC	68	68.00	11	29,016	1,022	1,023	247,120	247,361
Male	10 CC	78	78.00	59	154,098	883	884	1,133,904	1,135,189
Male	10 CC	85	85.00	93	243,290	825	825	1,672,619	1,672,619
Male	10 CC	92	92.00	4	11,740	799	799	78,169	78,169
Subtotal				171	446,403			3,216,746	3,218,341

TABLE D4 — *Continued*

Sex	Plan	Age True	Age Calc.	Number of Contracts	Annual Income	Factor Projection I	Factor Projection J	Premium Projection I	Premium Projection J
			For Issues of 1980; with Interest of 9.22 Percent for the First 14 Years and 6.97 Percent Thereafter						
Female	Life	45	45.00	1	1,919	1,356	1,358	21,685	21,717
Female	Life	56	56.00	3	4,796	1,251	1,253	49,998	50,078
Female	Life	67	67.00	10	12,470	1,073	1,078	111,503	112,022
Female	Life	78	78.00	22	29,977	796	799	198,847	199,597
Female	Life	85	85.00	29	41,008	584	585	199,572	199,914
Female	Life	92	92.00	4	5,756	406	406	19,474	19,474
Subtotal				69	95,926			601,079	602,802
Female	10 CC	45	45.00	2	3,628	1,361	1,362	41,148	41,178
Female	10 CC	57	57.00	2	3,629	1,253	1,255	37,893	37,953
Female	10 CC	67	67.00	14	29,031	1,112	1,117	269,021	270,230
Female	10 CC	78	78.00	84	172,370	924	927	1,327,249	1,331,558
Female	10 CC	85	85.00	114	235,874	838	839	1,647,187	1,649,152
Female	10 CC	92	92.00	4	9,072	803	803	60,707	60,707
Subtotal				220	453,604			3,383,205	3,390,778
Subtotal life				122	218,014			1,295,917	1,298,748
Subtotal 10 CC				391	900,007			6,599,951	6,609,119
Subtotal male				224	568,491			3,911,584	3,914,287
Subtotal female				289	549,530			3,984,284	3,993,580
Total all issues				513	1,118,021			7,895,868	7,907,867

TABLE D4 — Continued

Sex	Plan	Age True	Age Calc.	Number of Contracts	Annual Income	Factor Projection I	Factor Projection J	Premium Projection I	Premium Projection J
				For Issues of 1981; with Interest of 9.22 Percent for the First 14 Years and 6.97 Percent Thereafter					
Male	Life	45	45.00	1	2,407	1,302	1,304	26,116	26,156
Male	Life	55	55.00	1	5,379	1,186	1,187	53,162	53,207
Male	Life	66	66.00	3	13,449	987	989	110,618	110,842
Male	Life	77	77.00	12	47,000	722	723	282,783	283,175
Male	Life	85	85.00	13	50,680	520	521	219,613	220,036
Male	Life	92	92.00	5	22,650	358	358	67,573	67,573
Subtotal				35	141,565			759,865	760,989
Male	10 CC	45	45.00	1	1,537	1,314	1,315	16,830	16,843
Male	10 CC	55	55.00	3	7,683	1,212	1,213	77,598	77,662
Male	10 CC	67	67.00	6	17,607	1,039	1,040	152,447	152,594
Male	10 CC	78	78.00	31	92,263	884	885	679,671	680,440
Male	10 CC	85	85.00	62	185,039	825	826	1,272,143	1,273,685
Male	10 CC	92	92.00	5	16,007	800	800	106,713	106,713
Subtotal				108	320,136			2,305,402	2,307,937

TABLE D4 — *Continued*

Sex	Plan	Age		Number of Contracts	Annual Income	Factor		Premium	
		True	Calc.			Projection I	Projection J	Projection I	Projection J
			For Issues of 1981; with Interest of 9.22 Percent for the First 14 Years and 6.97 Percent Thereafter						
Female	Life	45	45.00	1	1,337	1,356	1,358	15,108	15,130
Female	Life	55	55.00	1	3,085	1,263	1,266	32,470	32,547
Female	Life	67	67.00	3	6,171	1,074	1,079	55,230	55,488
Female	Life	77	77.00	16	35,688	826	830	245,652	246,842
Female	Life	85	85.00	21	47,310	586	588	231,031	231,819
Female	Life	92	92.00	4	9,257	406	406	31,320	31,320
Subtotal				46	102,848			610,811	613,146
Female	10 CC	45	45.00	2	4,505	1,361	1,362	51,094	51,132
Female	10 CC	55	55.00	6	13,861	1,275	1,278	147,273	147,620
Female	10 CC	67	67.00	13	31,188	1,113	1,117	289,269	290,308
Female	10 CC	78	78.00	40	100,495	925	928	774,649	777,161
Female	10 CC	85	85.00	74	185,397	839	840	1,296,234	1,297,779
Female	10 CC	92	92.00	4	11,090	803	803	74,211	74,211
Subtotal				139	346,536			2,632,730	2,638,211
Subtotal life				81	244,413			1,370,676	1,374,135
Subtotal 10 CC				247	666,672			4,938,132	4,946,148
Subtotal male				143	461,701			3,065,267	3,068,926
Subtotal female				185	449,384			3,243,541	3,251,357
Total all issues				328	911,085			6,308,808	6,320,283

TABLE D5

MORTALITY GROSS SINGLE PREMIUMS (NO LOADING)
ASSUMING 1981 COMPANY MORTALITY TABLE
WITH MORTALITY IMPROVEMENT BASED ON EXPERIENCE TABLES AND PROJECTION SCALES I AND J

Sex	Plan	Age True	Age Calc.	Number of Contracts	Annual Income	Factor Projection I	Factor Projection J	Premium Projection I	Premium Projection J
					For Issues of 1982; with Interest of 11.45 Percent for the First 14 Years and 9.2 Percent Thereafter				
Male	Life	15	15.00	0	0	1,146	1,146	0	0
Male	Life	25	25.00	0	0	1,137	1,137	0	0
Male	Life	35	35.00	0	0	1,116	1,117	0	0
Male	Life	45	45.00	0	0	1,073	1,073	0	0
Male	Life	50	50.00	2	2,533	1,040	1,041	21,953	21,974
Male	Life	65	65.00	25	63,256	878	879	462,823	463,350
Male	Life	76	76.00	37	179,014	676	677	1,008,446	1,009,937
Male	Life	85	85.00	17	126,325	492	493	517,933	518,985
Male	Life	92	92.00	0	0	357	357	0	0
Subtotal				81	371,128			2,011,155	2,014,246
Male	10 CC	17	17.00	1	1,200	1,146	1,146	11,460	11,460
Male	10 CC	26	26.00	1	2,500	1,137	1,137	23,688	23,688
Male	10 CC	36	36.00	2	19,837	1,116	1,117	184,484	184,649
Male	10 CC	45	45.00	2	12,075	1,082	1,083	108,876	108,977
Male	10 CC	56	56.00	9	28,147	1,015	1,016	238,077	238,311
Male	10 CC	66	66.00	77	315,743	920	921	2,420,696	2,423,328
Male	10 CC	76	76.00	72	295,504	816	817	2,009,427	2,011,890
Male	10 CC	85	85.00	41	169,881	754	755	1,067,419	1,068,835
Male	10 CC	92	92.00	1	2,359	734	734	14,429	14,429
Subtotal				206	847,246			6,078,556	6,085,567

TABLE D5 — Continued

Sex	Plan	Age True	Age Calc.	Number of Contracts	Annual Income	Factor Projection I	Factor Projection J	Premium Projection I	Premium Projection J
				For Issues of 1982; with Interest of 11.45 Percent for the First 14 Years and 9.2 Percent Thereafter					
Female	Life	15	15.00	0	0	1,152	1,152	0	0
Female	Life	25	25.00	0	0	1,146	1,146	0	0
Female	Life	35	35.00	1	1,067	1,133	1,133	10,074	10,074
Female	Life	45	45.00	0	0	1,105	1,106	0	0
Female	Life	55	55.00	1	1,131	1,051	1,053	9,906	9,925
Female	Life	66	66.00	24	46,499	940	943	364,242	365,405
Female	Life	76	76.00	45	86,424	762	766	548,792	551,673
Female	Life	85	85.00	21	42,689	543	545	193,168	193,879
Female	Life	92	92.00	0	0	384	384	0	0
Subtotal				92	177,810			1,126,182	1,130,956
Female	10 CC	17	17.00	1	2,995	1,151	1,151	28,727	28,727
Female	10 CC	26	26.00	1	5,707	1,145	1,145	54,454	54,454
Female	10 CC	36	36.00	3	11,475	1,132	1,132	108,248	108,248
Female	10 CC	45	45.00	7	29,669	1,109	1,109	274,191	274,191
Female	10 CC	56	56.00	18	72,370	1,055	1,057	636,253	637,459
Female	10 CC	66	66.00	55	221,866	971	974	1,795,266	1,800,812
Female	10 CC	78	78.00	87	352,916	829	832	2,438,061	2,446,884
Female	10 CC	85	85.00	68	275,881	765	766	1,758,741	1,761,040
Female	10 CC	92	92.00	10	39,008	736	736	239,249	239,249
Subtotal				250	1,011,887			7,333,190	7,351,064
Subtotal life				173	548,938			3,137,337	3,145,202
Subtotal 10 CC				456	1,859,133			13,411,746	13,436,631
Subtotal male				287	1,218,374			8,089,711	8,099,813
Subtotal female				342	1,189,697			8,459,372	8,482,020
Total all issues				629	2,408,071			16,549,083	16,581,833

TABLE D5 — *Continued*

Sex	Plan	Age True	Age Calc.	Number of Contracts	Annual Income	Factor Projection I	Factor Projection J	Premium Projection I	Premium Projection J
			For Issues of 1983; with Interest of 11.45 Percent for the First 14 Years and 9.2 Percent Thereafter						
Male	Life	10	10.00	1	10,851	1,149	1,150	103,898	103,989
Male	Life	45	45.00	0	0	1,073	1,074	0	0
Male	Life	56	56.00	4	5,058	989	990	41,686	41,729
Male	Life	64	64.00	18	42,839	893	894	318,794	319,151
Male	Life	74	74.00	26	79,817	724	725	481,563	482,228
Male	Life	82	82.00	18	81,107	571	573	385,934	387,286
Male	Life	92	92.00	0	0	349	350	0	0
Subtotal				67	219,672			1,331,875	1,334,383
Male	10 CC	17	17.00	6	86,844	1,146	1,146	829,360	829,360
Male	10 CC	25	25.00	0	0	1,138	1,139	0	0
Male	10 CC	35	35.00	0	0	1,119	1,120	0	0
Male	10 CC	45	45.00	3	15,911	1,082	1,083	143,464	143,597
Male	10 CC	55	55.00	8	43,283	1,022	1,023	368,627	368,988
Male	10 CC	62	62.00	126	640,945	961	962	5,132,901	5,138,242
Male	10 CC	77	77.00	63	288,353	811	812	1,948,786	1,951,189
Male	10 CC	85	85.00	39	123,372	756	757	777,244	778,272
Male	10 CC	92	92.00	1	14,032	733	733	85,712	85,712
Subtotal				246	1,212,740			9,286,094	9,295,360

TABLE D5 — *Continued*

Sex	Plan	Age True	Age Calc.	Number of Contracts	Annual Income	Factor Projection I	Factor Projection J	Premium Projection I	Premium Projection J
				For Issues of 1983; with Interest of 11.45 Percent for the First 14 Years and 9.2 Percent Thereafter					
Female	Life	35	35.00	0	0	1,133	1,134	0	0
Female	Life	45	45.00	0	0	1,107	1,108	0	0
Female	Life	52	52.00	4	8,179	1,074	1,075	73,202	73,270
Female	Life	63	63.00	22	42,077	982	984	344,330	345,031
Female	Life	73	73.00	28	92,026	834	838	639,581	642,648
Female	Life	85	85.00	33	84,803	546	549	385,854	387,974
Female	Life	92	92.00	0	0	392	393	0	0
Subtotal				87	227,085			1,442,967	1,448,923
Female	10 CC	18	18.00	1	2,153	1,151	1,151	20,651	20,651
Female	10 CC	28	28.00	2	11,807	1,144	1,144	112,560	112,560
Female	10 CC	36	36.00	4	41,565	1,133	1,133	392,443	392,443
Female	10 CC	43	43.00	1	4,126	1,116	1,117	38,372	38,406
Female	10 CC	56	56.00	18	75,910	1,057	1,058	668,641	669,273
Female	10 CC	65	65.00	89	338,731	984	987	2,777,594	2,786,062
Female	10 CC	73	73.00	132	480,004	893	897	3,572,030	3,588,030
Female	10 CC	83	83.00	62	254,766	780	782	1,655,979	1,660,225
Female	10 CC	92	92.00	3	9,174	737	737	56,344	56,344
Subtotal				312	1,218,236			9,294,614	9,323,994
Subtotal life				154	446,757			2,774,842	2,783,306
Subtotal 10 CC				558	2,430,976			18,580,708	18,619,354
Subtotal male				313	1,432,412			10,617,969	10,629,743
Subtotal female				399	1,445,321			10,737,581	10,772,917
Total all issues				712	2,877,733			21,355,550	21,402,660

TABLE D5 — Continued

Sex	Plan	Age		Number of Contracts	Annual Income	Factor		Premium	
		True	Calc.			Projection I	Projection J	Projection I	Projection J
		For Issues of 1984; with Interest of 11.45 Percent for the First 14 Years and 9.2 Percent Thereafter							
Male	Life	35	35.00	0	0	1,117	1,117	0	0
Male	Life	45	45.00	0	0	1,074	1,074	0	0
Male	Life	56	56.00	3	5,903	989	990	48,651	48,700
Male	Life	63	63.00	10	51,654	907	908	390,418	390,849
Male	Life	75	75.00	25	124,455	705	707	731,173	733,247
Male	Life	83	83.00	21	103,322	552	553	475,281	476,142
Male	Life	92	92.00	1	49	350	351	143	143
Subtotal				60	285,383			1,645,666	1,649,081
Male	10 CC	18	18.00	2	18,446	1,145	1,145	176,006	176,006
Male	10 CC	33	33.00	5	49,371	1,124	1,125	462,442	462,853
Male	10 CC	44	44.00	1	77,447	1,087	1,088	701,541	702,186
Male	10 CC	53	53.00	6	196,793	1,037	1,038	1,700,620	1,702,259
Male	10 CC	63	63.00	90	287,839	951	952	2,281,124	2,283,523
Male	10 CC	72	72.00	86	297,032	858	859	2,123,779	2,126,254
Male	10 CC	83	83.00	29	86,527	768	769	553,773	554,494
Male	10 CC	92	92.00	3	4,510	733	733	27,549	27,549
Subtotal				222	1,017,965			8,026,834	8,035,124

TABLE D5 — *Continued*

Sex	Plan	Age		Number of Contracts	Annual Income	Factor		Premium	
		True	Calc.			Projection 1	Projection J	Projection 1	Projection J
				For Issues of 1984; with Interest of 11.45 Percent for the First 14 Years and 9.2 Percent Thereafter					
Female	Life	35	35.00	0	0	1,133	1,134	0	0
Female	Life	45	45.00	0	0	1,107	1,108	0	0
Female	Life	56	56.00	2	7,905	1,046	1,048	68,905	69,037
Female	Life	62	62.00	19	50,268	992	995	415,549	416,806
Female	Life	75	75.00	28	97,735	794	798	646,680	649,938
Female	Life	82	82.00	31	69,963	626	630	364,974	367,306
Female	Life	92	92.00	8	5,878	392	393	19,201	19,250
Subtotal				88	231,749			1,515,309	1,522,337
Female	10 CC	15	15.00	0	0	1,152	1,152	0	0
Female	10 CC	25	25.00	1	2,596	1,146	1,147	24,792	24,813
Female	10 CC	47	47.00	7	56,219	1,103	1,103	516,746	516,746
Female	10 CC	56	56.00	15	61,349	1,057	1,058	540,382	540,894
Female	10 CC	63	63.00	107	320,459	1,003	1,006	2,678,503	2,686,515
Female	10 CC	75	75.00	111	392,549	868	872	2,839,438	2,852,523
Female	10 CC	85	85.00	59	263,276	766	767	1,680,578	1,682,772
Female	10 CC	92	92.00	3	5,352	737	737	32,870	32,870
Subtotal				303	1,101,800			8,313,309	8,337,133
Subtotal life				148	517,132			3,160,975	3,171,418
Subtotal 10 CC				525	2,119,765			16,340,143	16,372,257
Subtotal male				282	1,303,348			9,672,500	9,684,205
Subtotal female				391	1,333,549			9,828,618	9,859,470
Total all issues				673	2,636,897			19,501,118	19,543,675

TABLE D5 — *Continued*

Sex	Plan	Age True	Age Calc.	Number of Contracts	Annual Income	Factor Projection I	Factor Projection J	Premium Projection I	Premium Projection J
		For Issues of 1985; with Interest of 11.45 Percent for the First 14 Years and 9.2 Percent Thereafter							
Male	Life	15	15.00	0	0	1,147	1,147	0	0
Male	Life	25	25.00	0	0	1,137	1,138	0	0
Male	Life	35	35.00	1	3,070	1,117	1,117	28,577	28,577
Male	Life	46	46.00	4	6,741	1,068	1,069	59,995	60,051
Male	Life	55	55.00	3	5,980	1,000	1,001	49,833	49,883
Male	Life	67	67.00	18	51,329	848	850	362,725	363,580
Male	Life	77	77.00	37	314,947	668	669	1,753,205	1,755,830
Male	Life	85	85.00	18	76,842	511	513	327,219	328,500
Male	Life	92	92.00	0	0	352	353	0	0
Subtotal				81	458,909			2,581,554	2,586,421
Male	10 CC	5	5.00	0	0	1,152	1,152	0	0
Male	10 CC	16	16.00	5	50,941	1,147	1,147	486,911	486,911
Male	10 CC	26	26.00	3	92,856	1,137	1,137	879,811	879,811
Male	10 CC	36	36.00	3	93,147	1,117	1,117	867,043	867,043
Male	10 CC	46	46.00	5	95,291	1,078	1,079	856,031	856,825
Male	10 CC	57	57.00	13	93,676	1,007	1,008	786,098	786,878
Male	10 CC	67	67.00	95	107,864	911	912	818,868	819,766
Male	10 CC	78	78.00	89	400,352	803	804	2,679,022	2,682,358
Male	10 CC	85	85.00	31	365,533	757	758	2,305,904	2,308,950
Male	10 CC	92	92.00	2	23,823	733	733	145,519	145,519
Subtotal				246	1,323,483			9,825,207	9,834,061

TABLE D5 — *Continued*

Sex	Plan	Age True	Age Calc.	Number of Contracts	Annual Income	Factor Projection I	Factor Projection J	Premium Projection I	Premium Projection J
				For Issues of 1985; with Interest of 11.45 Percent for the First 14 Years and 9.2 Percent Thereafter					
Female	Life	15	15.00	0	0	1,152	1,152	0	0
Female	Life	25	25.00	0	0	1,146	1,146	0	0
Female	Life	35	35.00	0	0	1,133	1,134	0	0
Female	Life	45	45.00	0	0	1,107	1,107	0	0
Female	Life	56	56.00	12	11,364	1,046	1,048	99,056	99,246
Female	Life	66	66.00	47	92,239	947	950	727,919	730,225
Female	Life	76	76.00	39	128,358	772	777	825,770	831,118
Female	Life	85	85.00	23	101,947	549	552	466,408	468,956
Female	Life	92	92.00	0	0	392	393	0	0
Subtotal				121	333,908			2,119,153	2,129,545
Female	10 CC	5	5.00	1	5,785	1,155	1,155	55,681	55,681
Female	10 CC	15	15.00	3	29,986	1,152	1,152	287,866	287,866
Female	10 CC	25	25.00	4	21,484	1,146	1,147	205,172	205,351
Female	10 CC	35	35.00	3	36,119	1,134	1,135	341,325	341,626
Female	10 CC	45	45.00	10	46,610	1,110	1,110	431,143	431,143
Female	10 CC	57	57.00	12	51,271	1,050	1,052	448,621	449,476
Female	10 CC	67	67.00	117	170,902	964	967	1,372,913	1,377,185
Female	10 CC	78	78.00	117	612,777	832	836	4,248,587	4,269,013
Female	10 CC	84	84.00	76	560,077	773	775	3,607,829	3,617,164
Female	10 CC	92	92.00	2	18,644	737	737	114,505	114,505
Subtotal				345	1,553,655			11,113,642	11,149,010
Subtotal life				202	792,817			4,700,707	4,715,966
Subtotal 10 CC				591	2,877,138			20,938,849	20,983,071
Subtotal male				327	1,782,392			12,406,761	12,420,482
Subtotal female				466	1,887,563			13,232,795	13,278,555
Total all issues				793	3,669,955			25,639,556	25,699,037

TABLE D5 — *Continued*

Sex	Plan	Age		Number of Contracts	Annual Income	Factor		Premium	
		True	Calc.			Projection I	Projection J	Projection I	Projection J
				For Issues of 1986; with Interest of 11.45 Percent for the First 14 Years and 9.2 Percent Thereafter					
Male	Life	5	5.00	0	0	1,151	1,151	0	0
Male	Life	19	19.00	1	3,995	1,144	1,144	38,086	38,086
Male	Life	25	25.00	0	0	1,137	1,137	0	0
Male	Life	35	35.00	0	0	1,117	1,117	0	0
Male	Life	45	45.00	0	0	1,074	1,075	0	0
Male	Life	57	57.00	4	11,764	981	982	96,171	96,269
Male	Life	66	66.00	30	61,522	865	866	443,471	443,984
Male	Life	75	75.00	37	124,300	706	707	731,298	732,334
Male	Life	84	84.00	21	69,741	532	534	309,185	310,347
Male	Life	92	92.00	0	0	354	354	0	0
Subtotal				93	271,322			1,618,211	1,621,020
Male	10 CC	5	5.00	5	36,460	1,152	1,152	350,016	350,016
Male	10 CC	16	16.00	8	48,632	1,147	1,147	464,841	464,841
Male	10 CC	26	26.00	7	25,149	1,137	1,137	238,287	238,287
Male	10 CC	36	36.00	5	13,279	1,117	1,117	123,605	123,605
Male	10 CC	48	48.00	11	70,024	1,068	1,069	623,214	623,797
Male	10 CC	57	57.00	5	31,071	1,007	1,008	260,737	260,996
Male	10 CC	68	68.00	69	235,399	901	902	1,767,454	1,769,416
Male	10 CC	77	77.00	75	301,241	811	812	2,035,887	2,038,397
Male	10 CC	85	85.00	44	175,581	757	758	1,107,623	1,109,087
Male	10 CC	92	92.00	3	4,720	734	734	28,871	28,871
Subtotal				232	941,556			7,000,535	7,007,313

TABLE D5 — Continued

Sex	Plan	Age True	Age Calc.	Number of Contracts	Annual Income	Factor Projection I	Factor Projection J	Premium Projection I	Premium Projection J
					For Issues of 1986; with Interest of 11.45 Percent for the First 14 Years and 9.2 Percent Thereafter				
Female	Life	5	5.00	0	0	1,155	1,155	0	0
Female	Life	15	15.00	0	0	1,152	1,152	0	0
Female	Life	26	26.00	0	0	1,145	1,146	0	0
Female	Life	35	35.00	0	0	1,133	1,134	0	0
Female	Life	45	45.00	0	0	1,107	1,107	0	0
Female	Life	51	51.00	3	1,771	1,080	1,081	15,939	15,954
Female	Life	64	64.00	27	81,644	971	974	660,636	662,677
Female	Life	75	75.00	48	96,563	794	800	638,925	643,753
Female	Life	84	84.00	15	72,212	576	580	346,618	349,025
Female	Life	92	92.00	1	1,884	392	394	6,154	6,186
Subtotal				94	254,074			1,668,272	1,677,595
Female	10 CC	5	5.00	6	15,621	1,155	1,155	150,352	150,352
Female	10 CC	15	15.00	7	30,320	1,152	1,152	291,072	291,072
Female	10 CC	25	25.00	7	24,089	1,146	1,147	230,050	230,251
Female	10 CC	35	35.00	8	34,943	1,134	1,135	330,211	330,503
Female	10 CC	45	45.00	4	14,448	1,110	1,110	133,644	133,644
Female	10 CC	57	57.00	12	30,101	1,050	1,052	263,384	263,885
Female	10 CC	67	67.00	84	458,949	964	967	3,686,890	3,698,364
Female	10 CC	78	78.00	112	431,386	833	836	2,994,538	3,005,322
Female	10 CC	85	85.00	96	515,714	767	768	3,296,272	3,300,570
Female	10 CC	92	92.00	2	6,488	737	737	39,847	39,847
Subtotal				338	1,562,059			11,416,260	11,443,810
Subtotal life				187	525,396			3,286,483	3,298,615
Subtotal 10 CC				570	2,503,615			18,416,795	18,451,123
Subtotal male				325	1,212,878			8,618,746	8,628,333
Subtotal female				432	1,816,133			13,084,532	13,121,405
Total all issues				757	3,029,011			21,703,278	21,749,738

APPENDIX II
SUMMARY OF QUESTIONNAIRE RESPONSES

Companies have been coded with the letters A to O. They retain their assigned code throughout all the responses shown.

1. Do you issue Joint Life Structured Settlement Annuities?

Out of 15 responses, 13 companies indicated they issue Joint Life annuities. Companies A and C indicated they do not issue such annuities.

2. What is the sex distribution of Structured Settlement Annuities you issue?

Company	No. of Lives Proportion				Amount of Premium Proportion Excluding Not Involving Life Premiums			Amount of Premium Proportion Including Not Involving Life Premiums			
	Male	Female	Joint	Unknown	Male	Female	Joint	Male	Female	Joint	Unknown
A	61.5%	38.5%	0	—	62.9%	37.1%	0	66.9%	33.1%	0	—
B	63.0	35.0	2.0%	—	N.R.	N.R.	N.R.	N.R.	N.R.	N.R.	—
C	56.0	44.0	0	—	68.0	32.0	0	66.0	34.0	0	—
D	N.R.	N.R.	N.R.		N.R.	N.R.	N.R.	N.R.	N.R.	N.R.	—
E	43.6	55.6	0.8	—	55.6	42.6	1.8%	50.5	48.3	1.2%	—
F	59.1	39.8	1.1	—	57.9	39.7	2.4	59.9	38.5	1.6	—
G	54.4	42.6	1.1	1.9	51.2	45.1	3.7	53.7	41.7	2.5	2.1%
H	57.9	41.7	0.4	—	56.4	42.9	0.7	59.6	40.0	0.4	—
I	62.0	37.0	1.0	—	55.0	43.0	2.0	61.0	37.0	2.0	—
J	62.2	37.4	0.4	—	58.7	39.6	1.7	70.0	29.8	0.2	—
K	N.R.	N.R.	N.R.	—	N.R.	N.R.	N.R.	N.R.	N.R.	N.R.	—
L	55.4	43.5	1.1	—	55.3	41.6	3.1	59.3	38.5	2.2	—
M	60.0	39.0	1.0	—	64.0	35.0	1.0	63.0	36.0	1.0	—
N	N.R.	N.R.	N.R.	—	N.R.	N.R.	N.R.	65.0	35.0	0	—
O	55.0	44.0	1.0	—	N.R.	N.R.	N.R.	53.0	44.0	3.0	—

N.R. = No response to the question.

3. What portion of the Structured Settlement Annuities involving life contingencies that you issue contains an annuity certain period of:

Company				Number of Years in Annuity Certain Period					
	0	1–9	10	11–19	20	21–29	30	31–39	40 or more
				Number of Lives Proportion					
A	5.1%	15.4%	12.8%	5.1%	38.5%	2.6%	17.9%	0	2.6%
B	28.1	5.3	26.2	7.0	24.6	1.8	7.0	0	0
C	22.0	0	27.0	0	31.0	0	15.0	2.0%	3.0
D	N.R.	N.R.	N.R.	N.R.	N.R.	N.R.	N.R.	N.R.	N.R.
E	7.7	1.7	9.7	5.6	36.9	4.7	25.8	1.3	6.6
F	5.4	1.6	9.0	6.1	33.6	5.4	27.8	1.6	9.5
G	12.6	2.8	21.7	5.6	30.7	3.5	21.0	0	2.1
H	0	2.5	18.8	7.3	49.0	9.8	9.2	1.8	1.6
I	5.2	2.6	11.2	8.6	18.8	9.8	17.2	8.4	18.2
J	5.6	7.0	14.1	7.0	56.4	0	9.9	0	0
L	7.5	2.0	9.5	8.2	28.6	8.2	27.2	2.0	6.8
M	2.0	0	16.0	5.0	36.0	3.0	23.0	0	15.0
N	N.R.	N.R.	N.R.	N.R.	N.R.	N.R.	N.R.	N.R.	N.R.
O	7.0	7.0	7.0	0	7.0	14.0	30.0	14.0	14.0

	0	1–10	11–20	21 or more					
K	6.8%	10.7%	43.8%	38.7%					

				Amount of Premium Proportion					
A	4.0%	16.9%	14.9%	1.4%	32.0%	0.5%	29.8%	0	0.5%
B	31.0	2.0	29.5	8.7	24.0	0.4	4.4	0	0
C	15.0	0	12.0	0	36.0	0	27.0	4.0%	6.0
D	N.R.	N.R.	N.R.	N.R.	N.R.	N.R.	N.R.	N.R.	N.R.
E	6.5	1.7	6.5	4.6	37.0	5.8	27.9	1.8	8.2
F	4.3	1.3	6.4	5.2	30.4	6.0	34.4	1.6	10.4
G	8.5	0.8	12.5	6.9	34.5	17.0	19.1	0	0.7
H	0	1.4	10.1	7.1	46.7	14.5	14.5	2.0	3.7
I	2.1	1.3	7.1	5.4	18.8	8.0	19.9	7.8	29.6
J	N.R.	N.R.	N.R.	N.R.	N.R.	N.R.	N.R.	N.R.	N.R.
L	9.7	1.0	7.9	7.5	27.0	6.0	32.1	1.0	7.8
M	1.0	0	18.0	1.0	30.0	6.0	19.0	0	25.0
N	0	0	50.0	0	50.0	0	0	0	0
O	4.0	3.0	1.0	0	2.0	9.0	47.0	22.0	12.0

	0	1–10	11–20	21 or more					
K	4.6%	6.0%	37.5%	51.9%					

4. What portion of all issues is on substandard lives?

| | Number of Lives | | | | Amount of Premium | | | | |
| | Including Annuities Certain and Lump Sums | | Excluding Annuities Certain and Lump Sums | | Including Annuities Certain and Lump Sums | | Excluding Annuities Certain and Lump Sums | | |
Company	Standard Lives	Sub-standard Lives	Standard Lives	Sub-standard Lives	Standard Lives	Sub-standard Lives	Standard Lives	Sub-standard Lives	This Information Is for the Period
A	70.7%	29.3%	41.2%	58.8%	58.9%	41.1%	15.5%	84.5%	Feb. '82 to present
B	75.0	25.0	N.R.	N.R.	56.0	44.0	N.R.	N.R.	Jan. '86 to 3/31/87
C	100.0	0	100.0	0	100.0	0	100.0	0	Not given
D	87.0	13.0	70.0	30.0	55.0	45.0	44.0	56.0	1984–1986
E	N.R.	N.R.	N.R.	N.R.	N.R.	N.R.	N.R.	N.R.	N.R.
F	N.R.	N.R.	N.R.	N.R.	N.R.	N.R.	N.R.	N.R.	N.R.
G	85.1	14.9	70.8	29.2	60.8	39.2	49.2	50.8	1981–1986
H	100.0	0	100.0	0	100.0	0	100.0	0	Not given
I	90.0	10.0	N.R.	N.R.	82.0	18.0	N.R.	N.R.	Aug. '85 to 12/31/86
J	98.0	2.0	99.0	1.0	96.0	4.0	96.0	4.0	Jan. '86 to 12/31/86
K	91.5	8.5	N.R.	N.R.	80.6	19.4	N.R.	N.R.	Jan. '86 to 12/31/86
L	96.6	3.4	91.2	8.8	95.3	4.7	93.0	7.0	Nov. '82 to 4/30/87
M	76.0	24.0	54.0	46.0	62.0	38.0	46.0	54.0	Jan. '86 to 12/31/86
N	N.R.	N.R.	N.R.	N.R.	N.R.	N.R.	N.R.	N.R.	N.R.
O	N.R.	N.R.	N.R.	N.R.	N.R.	N.R.	N.R.	N.R.	N.R

N.R. = No response to the question.

5. What portion of substandard quotes you made during that period were actually sold?

Company	If Annuities Certain and Lump Sums Were Included with Standard Lives	If Annuities Certain and Lump Sums Were Excluded from Standard Lives
A	3.0%	N.R.
B	3.0%	N.R.
C	Not applicable	Not applicable
D	N.R.	N.R.
E	N.R.	N.R.
F	N.R.	N.R.
G	N.R.	3.3%
H	Not applicable	Not applicable
I	N.R.	4.0
J	15.0	15.0
K	1.5	N.R.
L	4.0	6.0
M	3.0	N.R.
N	N.R.	N.R.
O	N.R.	N.R.

N.R. = No response to the question.

6. *What is the true age distribution of Structured Settlement Annuities you issued during this period (i.e., either use true age for age-rated lives or leave them out)?*

Company	Age										Unknown
	0–9	10–19	20–29	30–39	40–49	50–59	60–69	70–79	80–89	90–99	
	Number of Lives Proportion Based on Annuities with Life Contingencies Only										
A	10.7%	14.3%	28.6%	7.1%	14.3%	10.7%	7.1%	3.6%	3.6%	0%	
B	N.R.	N.R.	N.R.	N.R.	N.R.	N.R.	N.R.	N.R.	N.R.	N.R.	
C	8.0	19.0	18.0	22.0	11.0	15.0	6.0	1.0	0	0	
D	N.R.	N.R.	N.R.	N.R.	N.R.	N.R.	N.R.	N.R.	N.R.	N.R.	
E	N.R.	N.R.	N.R.	N.R.	N.R.	N.R.	N.R.	N.R.	N.R.	N.R.	
F	N.R.	N.R.	N.R.	N.R.	N.R.	N.R.	N.R.	N.R.	N.R.	N.R.	
G	13.4	12.2	18.6	16.5	13.6	12.7	9.1	2.1	1.3	0.5	
H	5.5	7.3	14.5	10.9	18.2	9.1	23.6	7.3	3.6	0	
I	3.3	0	3.3	0	23.3	16.8	33.3	20.0	0	0	
J	5.6	11.3	22.5	15.5	16.9	11.3	14.1	1.4	1.4	0	
L	12.9	16.3	20.4	17.0	15.0	13.6	4.8	0	0	0	
M	22.0	15.0	22.0	12.0	20.0	8.0	1.0	0	0	0	
N	N.R.	N.R.	N.R.	N.R.	N.R.	N.R.	N.R.	N.R.	N.R.	N.R.	
O	7.0	21.5	36.0	7.0	21.5	7.0	0	0	0	0	

	0–20		21–35		36–50		51–65		66 or older		
K	58.7%		20.1%		13.2%		6.7%		1.3%		

	Number of Lives Proportion Based on All Structured Settlement Annuities Including Annuity Certain and Lump Sum Only Annuities										
A	31.3%	21.8%	18.7%	4.7%	9.4%	7.8%	3.1%	1.6%	1.6%	0%	0%
B	N.R.	N.R.	N.R.	N.R.	N.R.	N.R.	N.R.	N.R.	N.R.	N.R.	N.R.
C	7.0	20.0	15.0	21.0	8.0	18.0	7.0	4.0	0	0	0
D	N.R.	N.R.	N.R.	N.R.	N.R.	N.R.	N.R.	N.R.	N.R.	N.R.	N.R.
E	30.2	22.5	16.3	12.5	8.9	6.3	2.2	0.5	0.5	0.1	0
F	25.3	23.5	14.1	15.3	11.4	6.9	2.6	0.4	0.4	0.1	0
G	19.5	20.4	14.5	13.2	10.7	8.9	5.4	1.3	0.6	0.2	5.3
H	15.6	15.9	15.3	15.3	15.5	11.4	6.6	3.9	0.5	0	0
I	15.0	22.6	10.7	14.2	12.0	7.5	5.8	11.4	0.8	0	0
J	8.2	28.0	16.8	20.0	12.3	7.5	6.6	0.4	0.2	0	0
L	19.1	23.6	15.1	13.8	12.7	9.6	4.8	0.8	0.5	0	0
M	25.0	23.0	25.0	9.0	12.0	5.0	1.0	0	0	0	0
N	N.R.	N.R.	N.R.	N.R.	N.R.	N.R.	N.R.	N.R.	N.R.	N.R.	N.R.
O	19.4	12.0	19.4	18.1	18.1	12.0	1.0	0	0	0	0

	0–20		21–35		36–50		51–65		66 or older		
K	67.2%		15.8%		10.4%		5.5%		1.1%		

N.R. = No response to the question.

6. — *Continued*

Company	Age										Unknown
	0–9	10–19	20–29	30–39	40–49	50–59	60–69	70–79	80–89	90–99	
Amount of Premium Proportion Based on Annuities with Life Contingencies Only											
A	12.9%	9.2%	40.6%	11.4%	13.6%	8.8%	2.7%	0.2%	0.6%	0%	
B	N.R.	N.R.	N.R.	N.R.	N.R.	N.R.	N.R.	N.R.	N.R.	N.R.	
C	8.0	19.0	18.0	22.0	11.0	16.0	5.0	1.0	0	0	
D	N.R.	N.R.	N.R.	N.R.	N.R.	N.R.	N.R.	N.R.	N.R.	N.R.	
E	22.9	12.2	23.2	18.9	11.9	7.2	2.9	0.6	0.2	0	
F	14.2	17.4	22.0	22.8	14.6	6.5	1.9	0.5	0.1	0	
G	21.9	15.7	22.4	15.8	11.3	8.1	3.5	0.5	0.4	0.4	
H	4.3	4.8	21.5	9.0	20.4	9.8	22.7	4.5	3.0	0	
I	3.4	0	19.1	0	38.1	17.6	13.0	8.8	0	0	
J	N.R.	N.R.	N.R.	N.R.	N.R.	N.R.	N.R.	N.R.	N.R.	N.R.	
L	13.9	16.0	22.8	15.4	16.6	9.5	5.8	0	0	0	
M	22.0	12.0	24.0	15.0	21.0	5.0	1.0	0	0	0	
N	N.R.	N.R.	N.R.	N.R.	N.R.	N.R.	N.R.	N.R.	N.R.	N.R.	
O	3.0	15.0	15.0	38.0	23.0	6.0	0	0	0	0	

	0–20		21–35		36–50		51–65		66 or older		
K	32.7%		34.2%		21.9%		10.0%		1.2%		

Company	Age										Unknown
	0–9	10–19	20–29	30–39	40–49	50–59	60–69	70–79	80–89	90–99	
Amount of Premium Proportion Based on All Structured Settlement Annuities Including Annuity Certain and Lump Sum Only Annuities											
A	18.0%	11.0%	28.0%	8.3%	9.8%	22.6%	1.8%	0.1%	0.4%	0%	0%
B	N.R.	N.R.	N.R.	N.R.	N.R.	N.R.	N.R.	N.R.	N.R.	N.R.	N.R.
C	7.0	20.0	15.0	21.0	8.0	18.0	7.0	4.0	0	0	0
D	N.R.	N.R.	N.R.	N.R.	N.R.	N.R.	N.R.	N.R.	N.R.	N.R.	N.R.
E	25.8	15.4	20.5	16.7	10.9	6.9	2.9	0.5	0.4	0	0
F	16.6	18.2	18.8	20.6	14.4	7.8	2.6	0.7	0.2	0.1	0
G	20.1	15.7	20.3	15.2	10.7	9.2	3.7	0.9	0.3	0.1	3.8
H	11.2	12.5	18.8	17.1	15.8	11.1	4.5	8.5	0.5	0	0
I	10.8	13.2	15.6	19.8	19.4	7.3	5.1	7.4	1.4	0	0
J	N.R.	N.R.	N.R.	N.R.	N.R.	N.R.	N.R.	N.R.	N.R.	N.R.	N.R.
L	13.9	17.2	17.7	17.5	15.1	8.2	6.9	3.4	0.1	0	0
M	18.0	11.0	29.0	13.0	24.0	4.0	1.0	0	0	0	0
N	N.R.	N.R.	N.R.	N.R.	N.R.	N.R.	N.R.	N.R.	N.R.	N.R.	N.R.
O	6.0	9.0	22.0	24.0	27.0	9.0	3.0	0	0	0	0

	0–20		21–35		36–50		51–65		66 or older		
K	46.4%		26.7%		18.1%		7.8%		1.0%		

N.R. = No response to the question.

7. What underlying mortality table is used in pricing standard annuities?

Company	1979–81 U.S. Pop.	1983 Table a	1971 GAM	1983 GAM	1971 IAM	1980 U.S. Pop.	Other	Modified	Comment	Information for the Year
A	X	X						X	Blended	1987
B	X							X		1987
C	X									1986–87
D	X							X	With mortality improvement	1987
E			X	X					Blended	1987
F			X	X					Blended	1987
G					X				Set forward n years	1981–86
H	N.R.									N.R.
I							X			1985–87
J					X					1986
K	N.R.									N.R.
L		X						X		
M	X									1986
N	X				X				Blended	1987
O									Company 1981 Annuity with mortality improvement, 10-year S & U	1982–86

N.R. = No response to the question.

8. How are your substandard annuities currently priced?

Company	Rated Age Using Life Expectancies	True Age Using Multiple Annuity Tables	Rated Age Using Multiple Annuity Tables	Rated Age Using Additional Deaths Added at Each Age
A	X			
B	X			
C	Not applicable			
D	X			
E	X			
F	X			
G	X			
H	Not applicable			
I	X			
J		X		
K	N.R.			
L	X			
M			X	X
N	X		X	
O	X			

N.R. = No response to the question.

9. Is a different table used to price substandard annuities (other than by the multiple table or additional death method)?

All companies writing substandard responded that the same table is used to price substandard annuities.

10. How do you value substandard annuities?

Company	Standard Reserve at True Age	Standard Reserve at Pricing Age	Multiple Mortality Annuity Table at True Age	Mortality Graded over a Given Period from Pricing Mortality to Standard Mortality
A	X			
B		X		
C	Not applicable			
D			X	
E		X		
F		X		
G		X		
H	Not applicable			
I		X		
J				X - years vary
K		X		
L			X	
M	X			
N		X		
O	X			

11. How are lump sums and certain annuities valued?

Answers combined with those from question 12; see below.

12. How are annuities with increasing benefit payments valued?

Company	Value Lump Sums and Certain Annuities		Value Increasing Benefit Annuities Same as Life Benefit Plans
	Same As Life Annuities	As Separate Contracts	
A	X		X
B	X		X
C	X		X
D	X		X
E	X		X
F	X		X
G	X		X
H	X		X
I	X		X
J		X	X
K		X	X
L	X		Interest rate varies with COLA %
M	X		X
N	X		X
O		X	X

N.R. = No response to the question.

13. Will you be in a position to contribute data to a mortality study of structured settlement annuities?

Company	Never	Yes	in X Years	X Equals	Other
A			X	?	
B			X	2	
C	X				
D			X	2	
E			X	3	
F			X	3	
G		X			
H		X			
I			X	8	
J			X	?	
K			X	3–5	
L		X			
M		X			
N			X	1–3	
O					X, i.e., if cost-justified

14. List the 10 most prevalent types of substandard cases for which you are asked to provide quotes and show the proportion each type bears to all the types you receive for quotes (e.g., brain damage, burns, etc.).

This information is for the period_____

Company	Birth Trauma	Brain Injury-Closed Head-Encepalopathy	Burns	Cancer-Sarcoma	Cerebral Palsy	Comatose	Diabetes	Drug Overdose	Heart-Cardiac
A		30.0%	10.0%						
B	20.0%								
C	Not applicable								
D	N.R.								
E		14.0	1.0						
F		15.0	5.0						
G	17.0	23.0	5.0						4.0%
H	Not applicable								
I		20.0	4.0	2.0%	11.0%		2.0%		
J		33.0		3.0				3.0%	3.0
K		70.0							
L	10.8	18.5	1.0						3.1
M		7.0	5.0		6.0	4.0%			8.0
N		50.0			5.0				
O		28.5							

Company	Mental Retardation	Miscell-aneous	Neurological	Psychiatric	Pulmonary	Renal Failure	Seizures	Spinal Cord-Quadriplegia-Paraplegia-Back
A	15.0%	5.0%						40.0%
B		80.0						
C	Not applicable							
D								
E	17.0	41.0						25.0
F	10.0	50.0						15.0
G		16.0		6.0%	2.0%			27.0
H	Not applicable							
I		28.0		3.0	2.0			17.0
J		1.0				7.0%		43.0
K		10.0						20.0
L		18.4	31.3%					16.9
M	19.0	10.0					5.0%	36.0
N		30.0						15.0
O		5.0						28.5

14. — Continued

Company	Stroke	Systemic	Vascular	Vegetative State
A				
B				
C	Not applicable			
D				
E				2.0%
F				5.0
G				
H	Not applicable			
I		3.0%	8.0%	
J	7.0%			
K				
L				
M				
N				
O			38.0	

N.R. = No response to the question.

15. What criteria do you evaluate in underwriting the prevalent types of substandard cases you mentioned in question 14?

Three companies submitted a response to this question — in a form too limited in nature to be of value here. See Section V for a discussion of the underwriting criteria applicable to the most prevalent injury types.

16. To the extent you are able to share this information, please furnish statistical sources used in evaluating the prevalent types of substandard cases you mentioned in question 14 (and a copy of the paper, if possible).

As an example, for Spinal Cord Injury one could mention *Spinal Cord Injury Statistics* by J.S. Young, P.E. Burns, A.M. Bowen and R. McCutchen, Good Samaritan Medical Center, Phoenix, Arizona, August 1982.

Company B:

Guides to the Evaluation of Permanent Impairment, American Medical Association, 1977

Cerebral Palsy... , Robert Grever, et al., Neurology 1985; 35: 900–903

Mortality of Workers Certified by Pneumoconiosis Panels as Having Asbestosis, G. Berry Bart, J. Ind Med 1981; 38: 130–137

Company I:

Statistical sources are not used.

Company L:

No specific studies or sources are used at this time. The review is usually conducted by an underwriter who will depend upon General Underwriting manuals and work experience in order to arrive at an evaluation. The company Medical Director is consulted when deemed appropriate.

17. *Are there any specific aspects of the underwriting, pricing and valuation of structured settlement annuities that you would like to see included in the paper? If yes, please elaborate.*

Company B:

1. Any known software available for asset/liability matching use.
2. Anyone using purchased software for administration processing.
3. How are profits recognized in the valuation process?
4. Investment yield assumptions used in the pricing formula.
5. Any differences in mortality and interest rate assumptions between pricing and valuation.
6. Total Structured Premiums in 1986; percent increase over 1985.
7. Maximum additions to age for substandard, if any.

Company C:

1. What do other companies use for age rate-ups on substandard lives? Who performs this function?
2. How is an annuity contract with a series of lump sum amounts valued?
3. How is a life annuity with first payment deferred more than one year valued?

Company H:

1. Investment assumptions.
2. Mortality assumptions.

Company L:

1. General overview of underwriting criteria for substandard evaluation.
2. Pricing for lump sums when they represent the major portion of the cost.
3. Pricing differentials for Deferred-Immediates:

> From a valuation viewpoint
> From an investment viewpoint.

Company N:

1. How should structured settlements be valued?
   - each benefit segment separately
   - by contract
   - by case
   - by issue year (i.e., group).
2. Should certain annuities be valued on a different basis than benefits involving life contingencies (see section 807c of the Stark-Moore Tax Act)?

DISCUSSION OF PRECEDING PAPER

VICTOR MODUGNO:

Mr. Teitelbaum is to be congratulated on this outstanding addition to actuarial literature. Although his paper is concerned with the effect of mortality on individual annuities, in most cases variations in investment earnings are more important than mortality experience. The annuity cash flows are fixed and generally of longer duration than the investment cash flow, which may be shortened even more as interest rates decrease. Thus there is a reinvestment risk for the net cash flow under these annuities.

To illustrate the relative sensitivity of investment earnings versus mortality variation, the following table compares a 1 percent decrease in future investment earnings to a 1 percent per year improvement in mortality for each year in the future at all ages using the 1983 GAM at 10 percent.

CHANGE IN COST RESULTING FROM

Age	1%/Year Mortality Improvement	1% Decrease in Investment Earnings
40	+0.8%	+9.2%
65	+2.0	+6.4
80	+2.5	+3.3

Those insurers who wrote immediate annuity business in the 1960s and 1970s made money regardless of how inadequate their mortality assumptions turned out to be, while those who wrote this business in the 1980s are likely to lose money no matter how conservative their mortality assumptions are. This is due to a secular upward trend in interest rates during the postwar period that peaked in the early 1980s. The long bond (the 30-year Treasury) yield rose from less than 3 percent in the early 1950s to more than 14 percent in the early 1980s. Since then, rates have come down significantly, and some economists are predicting that the rate on the long bond will average 6 percent or less during the 1990s.

Thus the unanticipated improvement in mortality in the 1970s and 1980s was more than offset by the unanticipated increase in interest rates. To illustrate this, I did an asset liability projection using a 1966 issue (1965 Company Mortality at 4.75 percent for 15 years, 3.5 percent) and a 1986 issue (1981 Company Table at 11.45 percent for 14 years, 9.2 percent thereafter) from Table B in Appendix I. Male age 55 life annuity was used for the liability with a 20-year bond yielding 2.5 percent over the pricing rate

835

(callable at par in five years if interest rates fall) as the asset. The rate for reinvestment in the 1990s was assumed to be 8 percent. The actual mortality experience was assumed to be the 1983 GAM, which would make the 1965 table inadequate and the 1981 table conservative. The 1986 issue had a loss equal to 1 percent of premium, while the 1966 issue had a profit equal to 16 percent of premium on a present value basis. This is due to the reinvestment at maturity of the bond for the 1966 issue at a higher rate and the early call and reinvestment of the bond at a lower rate for the 1986 issue.

Indeed, some regulators have become uncomfortable with the high interest rates underlying immediate annuity reserves under the dynamic valuation law for issues in the early to mid-1980s and are demanding asset/liability studies to demonstrate solvency of this block of business. I was surprised to see that the mortality assumption for valuation could be determined using the age rating used in pricing. Reserve strain could be avoided by using an age rating system off the 1983 IAM in pricing and setting up reserves for this block of business.

Except for extremely old age immediate annuity or substandard structured settlement annuity, it is the investment performance and not the underwriting experience that is the prime determinant of the profitability of annuity business.

(AUTHOR'S REVIEW OF DISCUSSION)

NAFTALI TEITELBAUM:

Victor Modugno, in his response, illustrates another principle already familiar to actuaries, which complements the sage advice with which I commenced this paper, "In order to know where you are going, examine from whence you come." He shows that the actuary must be aware of and state all salient assumptions in his or her product.

When I began work on the paper, it was in an environment in which interest rates were high and fluctuating, thereby causing frequent publication of new annuity gross premium scales—with seemingly no necessity to modify mortality assumptions. Therefore, this paper focused solely on the effects of mortality, albeit its relatively smaller effect on pricing when compared to the effects of interest rate variations. Mr. Modugno's comments are a welcome balance to the paper because he describes the effects of the prime determinant of annuity profitability. For this I am grateful to him. Starting from this point, however, my paper exhorts actuaries not to forget the effects of mortality in the pricing of annuities.

Mr. Modugno mentions his surprise at the reference I made to using the pricing age-rating of an annuity when valuing that annuity. That method has now been curtailed by New York State, which requires that substandard annuity reserves now grade to standard reserves by the end of the twentieth year, for 1987 and 1988 issues by year-end 1988 and for all other issue years by year-end 1990.

This could have the effect in New York State, depending upon issue age and the pricing age-rating, of increasing yearly costs by 3–4 percent of the single premium to provide for the needed increase in reserves. Such cost will exceed the cost of a 1 percent drop in interest yield. New issues should, of course, be priced to reflect this added cost of doing business.

The NAIC has not proposed such a requirement, but is instead expected to adopt a method that would produce lower substandard issue reserves than those required by New York State. Under the expected NAIC method, substandard annuity reserves for each duration would be calculated at true issue age assuming constant extra deaths added to standard valuation mortality rates. The present value of benefits at issue on that basis would be the same as that assuming pricing rated age at issue and only standard valuation mortality.

Clearly, mortality is not dead!

THE IMPACT OF AIDS ON LIFE AND HEALTH INSURANCE COMPANIES: A GUIDE FOR PRACTICING ACTUARIES

SOCIETY OF ACTUARIES AIDS TASK FORCE*

PREFACE

A. *The Task Force Report*

In April 1987, the Society of Actuaries established a Task Force on AIDS with the charge to examine the impact of AIDS on the solvency of life and health insurance companies. This report has been assembled by the Task Force as a comprehensive guide to practicing actuaries in evaluating the impact of AIDS on insurance companies. Following is a brief description of the various chapters of the report:

1. "The Impact of AIDS on Life and Health Insurance Companies" is a general overview of the Task Force report.

2. "A Practical Primer: AIDS and Life and Health Insurance" provides a comprehensive background on AIDS and the AIDS epidemic; this Primer was prepared by Tillinghast.

3. "AIDS, HIV Mortality and Life Insurance" is a report prepared by Michael J. Cowell and Walter H. Hoskins. This report combines techniques of actuarial science with modern epidemiology and biostatistics to develop a model for the spread of HIV infection and the associated financial impact on insurance companies.

4. "Modeling the Impact of AIDS-Related Life Insurance Claims" provides practical guidance to the actuary in developing a company model for the impact of AIDS.

5. "Projecting Extra AIDS Mortality for Individual Ordinary Life Insurance In Force" is a research report prepared by Milliman & Robertson, Inc. and has been included for its insights in modeling the impact of AIDS on individual companies as well as providing an alternative approach to developing models.

*David M. Holland, *Chairperson*, Philip J. Barackman, Robert W. Beal, Daniel F. Case, David J. Christianson, Michael J. Cowell, William C. Koenig, Barbara J. Lautzenheiser, David Llewellyn, Donald C. MacTavish, Daniel J. McCarthy, Carl F. Ricciardelli, John E. Tiller, Harry A. Woodman, and Michael L. Zurcher.

6. "A Model of the Impact of AIDS on Group LTD" is an example of an elementary model for group disability products constructed along the lines of the Cowell-Hoskins approach.

7. "Modeling the Impact of HIV on Group, Medical, Disability and Life Insurance Plans" provides a comprehensive stochastic model for tracing the progression from HIV infection to AIDS and finally death. Health insurance costs are assigned at each stage, and the model has been constructed so that the cost impact of various types of treatment can be included. As a simulation model, information is provided on the distribution of costs as well as expected values.

8. "AIDS in Canada" reviews the spread of the AIDS epidemic in Canada and provides information on the impact of AIDS on Canadian insurance companies.

9. "Management Strategies and the Role of the Valuation Actuary" discusses points for consideration for management in responding to the AIDS-HIV epidemic and reviews the responsibility of the U.S. valuation actuary with respect to recognizing additional claims from AIDS and HIV.

10. "What Is a Company To Do?" concludes this report with practical guidance for insurance company management in responding to the AIDS epidemic.

B. Individual Contributions

The work of the Task Force, including this report, is the product of many individual contributions. A number of contributions are from individuals who are not specifically members of the Task Force, but who have joined together with us to develop as comprehensive a view of the impact of this dread disease as possible. To everyone who contributed, the Task Force would like to express its sincere thanks and appreciation.

Given the goal of a comprehensive report on AIDS, the various chapters of this report represent individual assignments rather than the work of the Task Force as a whole. Accordingly, it seems appropriate to describe the contributors to each chapter as well as express appreciation for the assistance given by other colleagues.

Chapter 1 was drafted primarily by the chairperson as an expanded summary of the Task Force report. Special appreciation is expressed to Daniel F. Case, who made numerous improvements to this section and who served as liaison with the American Council of Life Insurance and as secretary of the Task Force, and to Carl Ricciardelli for bringing alternative models to our attention.

Chapter 2, "A Practical Primer," was prepared by Tillinghast, a division of Towers Perrin, and the Task Force very much appreciates being able to include this as part of the report. The Primer was prepared mainly by Tom Reese, who participated in a number of our meetings and made many other contributions. Other Tillinghast contributors to the Primer were Bob Beal, Jay Boekhoff and John Tiller. In addition to his many contributions as a Task Force member, we especially appreciate John Tiller bringing the Primer to our attention.

Chapter 3 is the already well-known Cowell-Hoskins paper "AIDS, HIV Mortality and Life Insurance." In addition to presenting this landmark paper, both Mike Cowell and Walt Hoskins contributed greatly to the work of the Task Force. The Task Force encouraged the release of this paper as soon as possible and, accordingly, expresses appreciation to the leadership of The Individual Life & Annuity Product Development Section, The Life Insurance Company Financial Reporting Section and The Reinsurance Section of the Society for publishing this paper as a Joint Special Report.

Chapter 4 on life insurance modeling guidance and considerations was prepared by a working group headed by Harry Woodman. The other members of the group were Task Force members Phil Barackman, David Christianson and Bill Koenig.

Chapter 5 is a research report prepared by Milliman & Robertson; we appreciate M&R allowing us to include it in our report. This report was written by Richard L. Bergstrom, Gary E. Dahlman, and Richard W. Mathes, who brought this report to our attention as well as making other contributions. Dan McCarthy also helped coordinate the inclusion of this in the Task Force report as well as participated on the Task Force.

Chapter 6 was authored by Bob Beal. The disability model used in this chapter was originally developed by Arthur L. Baldwin, who graciously provided it to the Task Force. Also, the Task Force would like to express appreciation to Paul Cooney for his participation and contributions to our work and to Dave Llewellyn, who served as liaison with the Health Insurance Association of America.

Chapter 7, including the concept and development of the Monte Carlo simulation model, is the work product of Mike Zurcher. The Appendix, "Dealing with the Impact of HIV on Group Insurance Plans," was prepared by Ron Colby and Mike Zurcher and is made available courtesy of Lincoln National Corporation.

"AIDS in Canada," Chapter 8, was prepared by Donald MacTavish, who also served as our liaison with the Canadian Institute of Actuaries.

"Management Strategies and the Role of the Valuation Actuary" was authored primarily by David Holland. Many Task Force members contributed comments, but special thanks go to Paul E. Sarnoff for his participation throughout the Task Force process but especially for his contributions regarding the role of the valuation actuary, to Donald D. Cody for his contributions regarding the role of the valuation actuary, and to Robin Michaelson for his invaluable input as liaison with the AIDS Working Party of the Institute of Actuaries in Great Britain.

The concluding chapter was prepared by Barbara Lautzenheiser, who also made many other contributions to the Task Force.

The Task Force would like to express its appreciation to the many actuaries who shared models, who gave advice and counsel, and who generally helped the development of our understanding of the process. At the risk of overlooking some who helped, we would like to specifically thank Donald R. Anderson, Mark D. Biglow, John K. Booth, William Carroll, John B. Dinius, Eli N. Donkar, Stephen Goss, James Hickman, Walter N. Miller, Harry H. Panjer, Peter W. Plumley, Jerome M. Stein, G. Todd Swim, and Jon K. Wilbur. We also would like to give special thanks to Dr. Ron Brookmeyer of Johns Hopkins University for his guidance and to Patricia L. Scahill and Chester T. Lewandowski, who served as liaison to the American Academy of Actuaries Committee on Risk Classification. Also, we appreciate the cooperation of the Joint ACLI/HIAA Ad Hoc AIDS Data Group, Joseph F. Crowe, chairman.

A critical component to the success of this Task Force has been the strong support and guidance of the leadership of the Society. Gary Corbett, President of the Society, and Allan Affleck, Vice President, have been instrumental in the formation and development of the Task Force. Also, Harold Ingraham, Immediate Past President, and Stephen Radcliffe, Vice President, have been of great support to the Task Force. Finally, Mark Doherty, Director of Research for the Society, has been of invaluable assistance throughout the work of the Task Force.

C. *Expressions of Opinion*

Expressions of opinion stated in this report are those of the authors of the individual chapters and are not the opinion or the position of the Society of Actuaries, its Sections or Committees. The Society assumes no responsibility for statements made or opinions expressed in this report.

CHAPTER 1

THE IMPACT OF AIDS ON LIFE AND HEALTH INSURANCE COMPANIES

1. OVERVIEW

"By the time America paid attention to the disease, it was too late to do anything about it. The virus was already pandemic in the nation having spread to every corner of the North American continent. The tide of death that would later sweep America could, perhaps, be slowed, but it could not be stopped.

"The AIDS epidemic, of course, did not arise full grown from the biological landscape; the problems had been festering throughout the decade. The death tolls of the late 1980s are not startling new developments but an unfolding of events predicted for many years."

– Randy Shilts, *And The Band Played On*

AIDS is devastating. Weekly reports by the Centers for Disease Control of AIDS cases and fatalities are like reports of dead and wounded in a war; in fact, it will not be long before the number of U.S. AIDS deaths surpasses the number of U.S. citizens killed in Vietnam. Yet AIDS is only the end stage of infection with Human Immunodeficiency Virus (HIV) that may have occurred years earlier.

The unfolding of the AIDS epidemic will have a significant impact on life and health insurance companies. Estimates of AIDS claims for business in force as of the end of 1986 measured through the year 2000 are of the order of magnitude of $50 billion just for ordinary life and group life coverages. Future ordinary life issues alone could add another $20 billion without considering the implications of group, health and disability coverages.

The impact to date is not being borne evenly by all companies. Based on reported claims for 1986, a large number of companies had AIDS claims of less than 0.5 percent of total ordinary claims, while a similarly large number had claims in excess of 1 percent of total ordinary claims. For some companies, AIDS accounted for more than 4 percent of ordinary claims. Because of the substantial variation by company, the Task Force report has focused on providing actuaries with tools that can be used in individual situations.

Actuaries in the U.S. are asked to render an opinion in conjunction with life insurance statutory statements that the reserves and other actuarial items make good and sufficient provision for unmatured obligations. The HIV-AIDS epidemic is becoming a measurable phenomenon and current signs are that there is very little reason for optimism in the near future regarding AIDS mortality and morbidity. As the impact of AIDS becomes more measurable, actuaries should recognize this in valuing the liabilities of an insurance company.

2. A KILLER IN OUR MIDST

As of the end of 1987, approximately 50,000 cases of AIDS had been reported to the U.S. Centers for Disease Control; of these, nearly 28,000 have died already. The expectation of life once AIDS develops is only about 2 years.

The killer in our midst is HIV, which destroys the immune system and leads to AIDS. HIV has been described by Dr. Robert C. Gallo, one of its codiscoverers, as "the most complicated and catastrophic human virus in recorded history." At the 1987 annual meeting of the American Council of Life Insurance (ACLI), there was a presentation by Dr. James O. Mason, the Director of the Centers for Disease Control. Dr. Mason indicated that based on cohorts studied for 9 years following infection with HIV, 45 percent of the infected individuals had developed AIDS. Dr. Mason said,

"if we observe these infected individuals long enough, a figure approaching 100 percent of those infected will develop symptoms of this disease that is invariably fatal. . . ."

Although much work is being done on the development of a vaccine for HIV infection, most people feel that the earliest a vaccine will be available is the middle of the next decade. A number of physicians and AIDS researchers feel that there will not be a vaccine in our lifetime.

The treatments that currently exist, such as the drug Zidovudine (AZT), tend to suppress the progression of the disease rather than reverse the infection. The treatment must be continued indefinitely, because once treatment ceases, the infection would again progress. Also, there are toxic side effects from treatment with AZT. From an insurance point of view, such treatments do not extend life sufficiently to reduce significantly the extra mortality cost, but on the other hand may increase the cost of health care by requiring longer and more expensive treatment.

The outlook for the development of a treatment that will reverse the infection is not very promising either. As a virus, HIV comprises a core of ribonucleic acid (RNA) and enzymes surrounded by a shell or envelope of proteins. The T-cell, which is an integral part of the human immune system, provides a specific receptor that is a perfect match for the HIV. After attaching itself to the T-cell, the virus passes through the cell's membrane, stripping its shell and introducing the RNA and enzymes into the cell. There the RNA is converted into DNA, which takes over the cell, causing more HIV to be produced. Once infected at the level of the DNA molecule, there is no known way to kill the infection without destroying the cell; once infected, an individual may be considered infected for life.

HIV can be transmitted by sexual contact with an infected individual, by contact with blood (or blood products) such as might occur with IV drug abusers sharing contaminated needles and with transfusions, and before or at childbirth from an infected mother to her newborn. Right now the major weapon in the fight against AIDS is education.

Given the long latency period from infection with HIV until the development of AIDS, a large number of cases that will develop AIDS in the next few years are already infected. Although a tremendous amount of research is going on with respect to both vaccines and treatments, there is very little reason for optimism regarding a major shift in the course of the epidemic in the next few years.

Additional information on AIDS in general is given in "A Practical Primer: AIDS and Life and Health Insurance" prepared by Tillinghast, which is Chapter 2 of this report. The situation in Canada is fortunately not as advanced as it is in the U.S.; a description of the impact of AIDS in Canada is given as Chapter 8 of this report.

3. THE IMPACT OF AIDS ON LIFE AND HEALTH INSURANCE IN GENERAL

3.1 *AIDS-Related Claims in 1986*

During 1986, life and health insurance companies in the U.S. paid over $290 million in AIDS-related claims according to estimates published by the American Council of Life Insurance (ACLI) and the Health Insurance Association of American (HIAA). (See "AIDS-Related Claims Survey—Claims Paid in 1986," prepared by William Carroll, *Actuary*, ACLI, December 31, 1987.) This survey was based on responses by 275 companies representing 46 percent of the total industry claims. The estimated AIDS-related claims paid by the industry in 1986 by line of business were estimated as follows:

Ordinary Life	$93.3
Group Life	79.4
Individual A & H	34.7
Group A & H	84.8
Total	$292.2

The survey strongly cautions that

"For a number of reasons, the survey results may significantly understate the number and amount of AIDS-related life and health insurance claims paid in 1986 by the responding companies."

In adjusting the survey responses to the level of the total industry, adjustments were not made for this understatement, which results from problems in identifying AIDS-related claims. In their joint cover letter to the survey, the Presidents of the ACLI and HIAA said:

"Since the Centers for Disease Control forecast a dramatic increase in the number of AIDS cases during the next five years, we expect industry AIDS-related claims to increase many-fold during that period."

3.2   The Cowell-Hoskins Model

In measuring the impact of AIDS on the insurance industry, models of the progression from HIV infection through AIDS to ultimate death were reviewed by the Task Force. The primary model used by the Task Force was the model by Michael Cowell and Walter Hoskins, as set out in "AIDS, HIV Mortality and Life Insurance" (see Chapter 3 of this Task Force report). Using what appears to be the best data available, Cowell and Hoskins constructed a model describing the progression of the epidemic and its impact on life insurance companies in general.

Cowell and Hoskins project that for business currently in force, life claims will amount to $50 billion over the remainder of this century. Assuming HIV infection decreases to zero by 1997 and assuming no AIDS claims from issues after 1986, AIDS claims on individual business currently in force will rise to around 18 percent of total claims in 1997. If HIV testing is not permitted and sales increase at a 5 percent annual rate, an additional $20 billion of individual AIDS claims is projected cumulatively by year-end 2000. These projections do not include AIDS-related claims for disability and health insurance, which would also be substantial. (Techniques for modeling the impact of AIDS on disability and health products are discussed in subsequent chapters of this report.)

Expected mortality levels are significantly increased for someone infected with HIV. To match the expectation of life for someone who is HIV+, standard mortality (based on the 1980 CSO Basic Male Nonsmoker Table) would have to be increased over 5000 percent. Most companies do not issue business where the expected mortality exceeds 500 percent of standard. The underlying patterns of mortality for someone who is HIV+ are so different from those of someone who is standard that it is questionable whether expressing such mortality as ratios of standard is meaningful. However, it is clear that the level of mortality for someone infected with HIV is extremely high compared to standard.

Another expression of the impact of the high level of mortality to be expected for someone who is HIV+ is to look at the present value of future claims. Cowell-Hoskins determined:

"Progression to AIDS and death under the slower SFCC/CDC assumptions produces death claims that, discounted at 6 percent interest, would require a net single premium of $515 per $1,000 issued to an HIV-infected individual."

3.3   Developing Models for Alternative Scenarios

Although Cowell and Hoskins used CDC data and projections, as well as industry data from the ACLI/HIAA, to fit their model, other scenarios could readily be developed. For example, alternative scenarios could be constructed using the Cowell-Hoskins techniques but varying items such as:

- the size of the at-risk group
- the factors for progression from at risk to infected (for example, level of progression, no progression after specified date, etc.)
- level of progression from infection to AIDS (for example, maximum percentage progressing, etc.)
- characteristics of risk group such as number of different sexual partners per annum (high, medium, low, monogamous) combined with various factors measuring progression from at risk to infected.

Health and disability lines also can be projected by using techniques in accordance with the methods used by Cowell and Hoskins. A sample disability model based on Cowell-Hoskins is set out in Chapter 6 of this report.

Projection techniques other than the Cowell-Hoskins are certainly appropriate for actuaries to use in measuring the impact of AIDS. An alternative approach for projecting the spread of the epidemic, designed to facilitate application to the circumstances of individual companies, is included as Chapter 5; this model was provided by Milliman & Robertson, Inc. A model to measure the impact of AIDS on group medical, disability and life plans is included as Chapter 7 of this report.

3.4   Cautions Regarding Extrapolations

Care should be taken in the interpretation of any models that involve significant extrapolation into the future—the further the distance from the present time, the greater the likelihood of significant deviation. The Cowell-Hoskins model presents one scenario based on a number of assumptions.

There are problems with the data currently available on AIDS and HIV infection, and these problems will affect the reliability of any estimate. The results can be much worse than projected by Cowell-Hoskins for various reasons, such as a widespread infection by HIV in the heterosexual community. Even if the spread into the heterosexual population is much slower than the spread into high-risk groups to date, the ultimate impact may be more serious because of the much larger number of people in the heterosexual population. Problems with data and points for consideration regarding the Cowell-Hoskins model are covered in Section 8 of this chapter and Appendix 1, respectively.

More optimistic mathematical projections of the spread of the epidemic are also possible. For example, a three-parameter logistic curve can be fitted via the least-squares method to actual AIDS cases reported to the CDC. Although the actual fit for 1981 through 1987 is quite good, this model produces numbers that are much lower than the Cowell-Hoskins projections; these projections also are much lower than the CDC projections, which the Task Force feels must be given significant weight.

In summary, *although the Cowell-Hoskins model has been used extensively in this report, there should be a realization that the ultimate results may diverge considerably from this model and may diverge in either direction.* Time will ultimately tell the course of this epidemic, and in the meantime, provision should be made for revision of projections as experience emerges.

4. THE IMPACT OF AIDS ON LIFE AND HEALTH INSURANCE COMPANIES

Especially at the early stages of this epidemic, the burden of AIDS is not falling uniformly on all companies. Based on information from the ACLI/HIAA report "AIDS-Related Claims Survey—Claims Paid in 1986," AIDS claims on ordinary life business amounted to 0.9 percent of total claims overall in 1986. Yet when viewed on an individual company basis, the results were quite varied. Companies representing over 40 percent of the overall claims reported had AIDS claims of less than 0.5 percent of total claims in 1986. On the other hand, companies representing over 35 percent of the overall claims reported had AIDS claims at the level of 1 percent or more of total 1986 claims. Some companies reported AIDS claims in excess of 4 percent of their total 1986 individual life claims. Wide dispersion of results also was evident for other lines of business studied too. Given this wide variation by company, the Task Force concentrated on developing tools that can be used by actuaries to project the impact of AIDS based on various individual situations.

There are a number of factors that can account for a significant variation in the effect of AIDS by individual company.

- One of the key factors initially will be the geographic mix of business written. There have been high concentrations of AIDS cases in certain cities and states. Companies that operate in limited geographic areas may have experienced excessively high claims or extremely favorable claims depending on how their geographic market corresponds to the geographic distribution of AIDS cases. This factor can be expected to diminish as AIDS becomes more widespread. Other key factors include the distributions by age and sex of insureds.

- The impact of AIDS will probably vary significantly by line of business. For instance, the process of risk selection should lead to different results for individual life, group life, and credit life. Different results can be expected from individual and group disability lines. Other lines also will be affected to varying degrees by AIDS.

- Even within a product line, the impact will be different by product and within product. For example, there will be a different impact between permanent and term based on the level of reserves accumulated. Even within a product such as universal life, there may be a wide variation at different underwriting levels (nonmedical, paramedical and medical).

- Assuming there has been antiselection in recent years, companies that have grown rapidly during this period are likely to have more AIDS claims than companies that have written a correspondingly lower percentage of their business recently.

- Marketing and underwriting philosophies also will affect the level of AIDS claims. Companies engaged in direct marketing programs may find that they have been subject to antiselection. Companies that were late in adjusting underwriting limits to reflect the need for testing for HIV also may have been selected against.

These variations by company increase the importance of a careful analysis of individual company AIDS experience by an actuary familiar with the detailed operations of the company. Guidance in modeling the impact of AIDS on an insurance company is given in Chapter 4 of this report.

5. STRATEGIES FOR MANAGEMENT IN RESPONDING TO THE AIDS EPIDEMIC

Through the end of 1986, the cumulative number of AIDS cases reported to the CDC was around 29,000, and for 1986, the ACLI estimates that total AIDS-related claims amounted to over $290 million. By the end of 1987, the cumulative number of AIDS cases had risen to nearly 50,000, and the total cost is not yet known. Currently the CDC estimates the number of people infected with HIV to be within the range of 420,000 to 1,649,000. Unfortunately, a large number of those currently infected with HIV can be expected to progress to AIDS, and this is compounded by the possibility of further spread of infection. The net result is a problem where millions of dollars of benefits can be expected to grow into billions of dollars of benefits and where the effects will last over many years.

Although the *current* level of claims does not represent a threat to industry solvency, the burden of claims is not falling equally on all companies and the burden can be expected to increase as infection spreads and as more infected people develop AIDS. Because of the very long-term nature of this epidemic, there is time for insurance company management to plan how to control exposure and how to finance the claims that will emerge.

The problems of what management should do must be considered for both in-force business and new business. For in-force business, there are opportunities to prefund the claims via reserve strengthening, reduce dividends on participating business, increase premiums and other nonguaranteed elements where permitted, or decline to renew certain products where renewal is at the option of the company. For new business, management tools include risk selection and classification, repricing, product redesign, reinsurance, or even product discontinuance. Based on a survey by Coopers & Lybrand, many companies are already considering such actions. Various options for management are discussed more fully in Chapter 9 of this report.

6. AIDS AND THE RESPONSIBILITY OF THE U.S. VALUATION ACTUARY

The U.S. valuation actuary is asked to provide an opinion that the reserves and other actuarial items make good and sufficient provision for the unmatured obligations guaranteed by the policies of the company. If the actuary has doubts as to whether the statutory reserves make good and sufficient provision, then professional practice standards of the American Academy of Actuaries require further testing such as a gross premium valuation using assumptions based on actual and anticipated experience.

AIDS is becoming a leading cause of death especially at certain ages, and because of the number of people already infected, its significance can be expected to increase. Given the complex nature of HIV, there is very little reason for optimism that the course of the epidemic will be reversed in the near future by vaccine or cure.

In terms of materiality, the impact of AIDS appears to be such that it should be considered by the valuation actuary as part of the determination of whether the reserves make good and sufficient provisions for future unmatured obligations. Accordingly, the impact of AIDS should be considered in establishing anticipated experience for purposes of a gross premium valuation. Various chapters of this report were designed to give practical guidance in measuring the impact of AIDS.

One of the advantages of the gross premium valuation method is that it provides for use of actual and anticipated experience of the company. Given situations such as AIDS where there is considerable variation by company, a company's own experience can be recognized in a gross premium valuation. Another advantage is that strategies adopted by management such as those with respect to dividends or nonguaranteed elements can be directly reflected.

In the event that there is concern about the level of security provided by current statutory valuation mortality tables, consideration should be given to the development of new valuation tables. New tables also could recognize improvements in mortality recognized at certain ages since the last tables were developed. Should it be felt that current statutory valuation tables are not adequate for in-force business, then reserve strengthening for in-force business also should be considered; this may be a by-product of the gross premium valuation, or some alternative approach could be adopted.

Key factors that must be kept in mind are that there are still very many unknowns about the ultimate course in this epidemic and that there is wide variation in results by company. Accordingly, considerations for dealing with the impact of AIDS should be pragmatic and provide for flexibility for adjustment as the true scope of the epidemic becomes known. The role of the valuation actuary with respect to recognizing the impact of AIDS is discussed in more detail in Chapter 9 of this report.

7. PROBLEMS WITH DATA ON HIV INFECTION AND AIDS

There are numerous problems with data relating to the scope of the AIDS epidemic. Some examples of problems or disparities in the information available are:

- Generally, the number of HIV-infected individuals in the U.S. has been assumed to be in the range of 1 million to 1.5 million. This is the number developed by the Public Health Service meeting at the Coolfont Conference Center in June 1986. This estimate has been recently reevaluated by the Public Health Service and the "Reevaluated Estimate of HIV Prevalence" for 1987 is now 945,000 to 1,400,000 infected (note that the Cowell-Hoskins estimate for 1987 was 920,000). However, using mathematical models, the number of persons infected with HIV at the end of 1987 ranges from

276,000 to 1,750,000 with their best estimate being from 420,000 to 1,649,000. In giving these estimates, the CDC observed:

"Procedures which produce such a wide range of results from the same data indicate that there are either insufficient dáta or insufficient models or both. Hence, there is need for improved data and model development to assist in monitoring HIV infection in this country."

- The above information on HIV prevalence is given in "Human Immunodeficiency Virus Infections in the United States: A Review of Current Knowledge and Plans for Expansion of HIV Surveillance Activities" prepared by the CDC, *et al*, for the Domestic Policy Council (November 30, 1987). An excerpt of this report is given as Appendix 3 of this chapter.
- Even actual cases reported by the CDC are subject to underreporting and delays in reporting. Dr. Mason of the CDC indicated in his address to the ACLI that reported AIDS cases are probably understated by 20% and reported AIDS deaths are understated by 10%. He also indicated that the Coolfont projections of AIDS cases are still within 5% of actual.
- As of September 1, 1987, the CDC revised the definition of AIDS; data are not yet available reflecting this new definition.
- Insurance company data also are subject to underreporting and misreporting. For many lines of business, companies may not have sufficient information or even attempt to record the cause of the claim, but only verify that it is a legitimate claim.

With problems such as those sketched above, extreme care should be taken in evaluating projections and data relating to AIDS. Further, care should be taken because projections can be prepared to fit almost any scenario (for example, match CDC data and then either increase rapidly, increase moderately, remain level, or decline).

One goal in mentioning this is to reemphasize the need for reliable data on AIDS and the prevalence of HIV infection. The CDC is implementing programs to develop more reliable information on the prevalence of HIV infection. The ACLI and HIAA have plans to collect information from insurance companies periodically. Such programs are of great importance as efforts are made to refine the measurements on the scope of the impact of HIV and AIDS. Insurance companies should make special efforts to track claims to determine the impact of AIDS; because of problems of misreporting of cause of claim, attention should be paid to all claims and not just AIDS-diagnosed claims.

Another goal is to emphasize that we are in the very early stages of modeling this epidemic. Although the results of the Cowell-Hoskins model appear to be the most reasonable projections currently available for our purposes, the ultimate course of the disease could be quite different. Should there be a widespread movement of HIV infection into the general hetero-sexual community, the results could be much worse than currently projected. On the other hand, development of a successful vaccine or treatment would be most beneficial. Rather than conclude that these estimates have been prepared once and for all with micrometric precision, these estimates must be continually updated and refined.

Finally, the further one projects into the future, the more likely it is that there will be significant deviations from current estimates. In setting reserves, long-term estimates that are too conservative can be just as devastating as estimates that are too liberal. The initial course should be a moderate one with provision for correction as more data become available.

8. RECOMMENDATIONS

The grim face of the AIDS epidemic is becoming recognizable. As those infected with HIV progress to AIDS and as more people become infected, the specter of this epidemic will become more ominous. At present, we are still at the early stages of comprehending the impact of AIDS and HIV infection on life and health insurance companies; however, we feel certain the impact of AIDS and HIV infection will be felt for years to come.

As a Task Force, our charge was the short-term assignment of analyzing and reporting on the impact of AIDS and HIV on the solvency of life and health insurance companies. It is hoped that our report will be made available to the membership of the Society and that they will find it helpful in recognizing and responding to the impact of AIDS.

The Task Force recommends that the Society assign standing committees the responsibility for continuing to monitor the spread of the AIDS and HIV epidemic and the responsibility for further analyzing the impact of AIDS on the role of the valuation actuary. The committee monitoring the spread of the epidemic should monitor and report data regarding the prevalence of HIV and AIDS, both from a population standpoint and that of the insurance industry, and should be involved with developing models for the spread of the epidemic. The committee responsible for considering the role of the valuation actuary in light of AIDS should consider and communicate to the membership valuation approaches to the recognition of the impact of AIDS via modeling for gross premium valuation, the development of alternative techniques for the recognition of AIDS, and the consideration of the development of new valuation mortality tables that would also recognize AIDS.

Although the Task Force has endeavored to produce a report that would be a useful guide for practicing actuaries, there are a number of insurance-related areas that were not addressed by the Task Force. For example, the Task Force did not specifically address the impact of AIDS on products such as annuities, supplementary benefits and options, etc. or on financial issues such as GAAP reporting and federal income tax. There also are a number of areas of interest to actuaries that were beyond the scope of an investigation of the impact of AIDS on life and health insurance companies. For example, AIDS may have a significant impact on social insurance programs such as Social Security, Medicare and Medicaid in the U.S. and on comparable programs in Canada. AIDS also may have an impact on retirement and employee benefit programs, whether funded by insurance or not. The fact that such items were not addressed should be considered a function of time and resources rather than significance. It is recommended that subsequent Task Forces address additional insurance areas to the extent further research is needed, and particularly in modeling and monitoring the epidemic, it is recommended that the scope of the Task Force be expanded beyond insurance.

APPENDIX 1

POINTS FOR CONSIDERATION REGARDING THE COWELL-HOSKINS MODEL

A key challenge in measuring the impact of AIDS has been to develop a model to estimate the number of people infected with HIV and to measure the progression from infection through development of AIDS to ultimate death. The Cowell-Hoskins model used for financial projections shows 900,000 people infected cumulative in 1987, rising to 2.5 million by the year 2000. By 2000, the cumulative number of AIDS cases is projected to be 1.6 million, of which 1.3 million would have died.

The Cowell-Hoskins paper represents a tremendous advance in modeling the impact of AIDS on the life insurance industry. Nevertheless, certain factors should be kept in mind when considering their results:

a.   The model is based on an assumed population at risk of AIDS of 3 million male homosexuals and bisexuals plus 750,000 IV drug abusers. These groups represent approximately 90 percent of the adult AIDS cases reported to date in the U.S. It should be noted that the assumed populations are based on broad estimates because exact data are unavailable.

b.   Additional information is needed on the spread of AIDS in the heterosexual population. Reported cases of heterosexual transmission account for approximately 4 percent of the AIDS victims overall, but 30 percent of the female cases. Because the heterosexual population is so large, a spread at even a much reduced rate could still result in a large infected population.

c. The model for estimating the number of people infected has been fitted to CDC data of AIDS cases and deaths. Although this is thought to be the most reliable information available, there are problems with underreporting and with delays in reporting to the CDC. A 20 percent increase in cases has been cited as a possible adjustment for underreporting. With respect to reporting delays, the December 29, 1986 CDC report showed 29,003 cases had been reported through that date, but in the December 28, 1987 report, 34,984 cases are shown as having been incurred by the end of 1986.

d. As of September 1, 1987, the CDC revised the definition of AIDS to include dementia and emaciation. These cases were previously considered AIDS Related Complex (ARC) rather than AIDS and were not in the AIDS tabulations. The revised data from the CDC should be carefully studied when available.

e. Although the Cowell-Hoskins model is consistent with other models such as the one by Jeffrey Harris at M.I.T., there are other models that produce significantly different results. A report prepared by the RAND Corporation states that the CDC ". . .figure is now thought by many to be too low, particularly because it employs a very conservative estimate of HIV (Human Immunodeficiency Virus) incubation or latency, which determines how many seropositives convert to symptomatic AIDS over a period of time. Others think that underreporting of AIDS cases is even more egregious than the official corrections would suggest and that the extent of heterosexual transmission has been underestimated. Thus, although 220,000 cases might serve as a low-range estimate, case load numbers of 400,000 and 750,000 in 1986-1991 are more credible mid- and high-range estimates."

There appear to be little hard data supporting the RAND report; until more data become available, the CDC estimate must be considered more reliable.

f. The Cowell-Hoskins financial models were fitted to AIDS preliminary reports of experience collected by the ACLI/HIAA for 1986. Data subsequently received indicate 1986 actual experience was higher than previously thought. Further, there are serious concerns that the most recent estimate of 1986 AIDS-related claims may be understated because of problems in identifying and reporting AIDS claims.

g. The financial numbers are based on a model that assumes that the rate of infection will decline to zero by 1997. This reduces the ultimate risk group by approximately one-third. The model is further based on the assumption that the insured population that is HIV+ will ultimately grow to only 58 percent of the total risk group.

*h. The emergence of AIDS-related claims will be affected by the extent to which insurance companies are able to test applicants for HIV infection. Legislative and regulatory restrictions on risk classification could result in substantial increases in claims.

i. In addition to claims from AIDS itself, increased claims can be expected for insureds who have the HIV infection and who will incur claims for sickness and death from complications of this infection without necessarily having reached full clinical AIDS.

j.   Further developments in treatment may affect the course of the disease. Although this may be somewhat advantageous from a life insurance point of view, such treatments may increase claims for health and disability insurance.

From the point of view of human compassion as well as concern over financial impact, it is hoped that events will be more favorable than the projection indicates. However, Cowell and Hoskins were striving for as fair a presentation as possible and these projections should be considered as a likely scenario.

APPENDIX 2

BIBLIOGRAPHY

A. ACTUARIAL AND INSURANCE-RELATED ARTICLES

1. "Risk Classification and AIDS," Committee on Risk Classification of the American Academy of Actuaries, May 1987.
2. "Preliminary Memorandum on AIDS," David Wilkie, R. Watson & Sons, July 1987.
3. "AIDS Dodelighed og Livsforsikring," Jakob Kolbye, July 1987.
4. "HIV Infection: Its Impact on Mortality and Underwriting," Jess L. Mast, *Reinsurance Reporter*, pp. 2–6.
5. "Thorns in Our Side: Some Problems in Underwriting for AIDS," Donald C. Chambers M.D., *Reinsurance Reporter*, pp. 6–11.
6. "AIDS: Survival Analysis of Persons Testing HIV +," Harry J. Panjer, Ph.D., Working Paper Series in Actuarial Science, August 24, 1987.
7. "AIDS and Life Insurance Company Solvency," American Academy of Actuaries Committee on Life Insurance, September 22, 1987.
8. "AIDS Bulletin No. 1," Report from Institute of Actuaries AIDS Working Party, September 1987.
9. "AIDS and Life Insurance," L. R. Mann, P. R. Muir, R. A. Collins, 1987 Convention of the Institute of Actuaries of Australia.
10. "AIDS Bulletin No. 2," Report from Institute of Actuaries AIDS Working Party, December 1987.

B. GENERAL ARTICLES

11. "Heterosexually Acquired HTLV-III/LAV Disease (AIDS-Related Complex and AIDS)," Robert R. Redfield, M.D., et al, *JAMA*, October 18, 1985, pp. 2094–2095.
12. *Confronting AIDS*, Institute of Medicine, National Academy of Sciences, National Academy Press, Washington D.C., 1986.

13. "The Economic Impact of the First 10,000 Cases of Acquired Immunodeficiency Syndrome in the United States," Ann M. Hardy, DPH, et al, *JAMA*, January 10, 1986, pp. 209–211.

14. "Association of Human T. Lymphotropic Virus Type III Antibodies with Sexual and Other Behaviors in a Cohort of Homosexual Men from Boston with and without Generalized Lymphadenopathy," Kenneth H. Mayer et al, *The American Journal of Medicine*, March 1986, pp. 357–363.

15. "A Quantitative Analysis of AIDS in California," George Deukmejian, Department of Health Services, March 1986.

16. "A Transmission Model for AIDS," E. G. Knox, *European Journal of Epidemiology*, September 1986, pp. 165–177.

17. "Minimum Size of the Acquired Immunodeficiency Syndrome (AIDS) Epidemic in the United States," Ron Brookmeyer, Mitchell H. Gail, *The Lancet*, December 6, 1986, pp. 1320–1322.

18. "Estimates of the Direct and Indirect Costs of Acquired Immunodeficiency Syndrome in the United States, 1985, 1986, and 1991," Anne A. Scitovsky, Dorothy P. Rice, *Public Health Reports*, January-February 1987, pp. 5–17.

19. "Risk Factors for Seroconversion to Human Immunodeficiency Virus among Male Homosexuals," *The Lancet*, February 14, 1987, pp. 345–348.

20. "The AIDS Virus," Robert C. Gallo, *Scientific American*, Volume 256, January 1987, pp. 46–56.

21. "Transmission Dynamics of HIV Infection," Robert M. May, Roy M. Anderson, *Nature*, March 12, 1987, pp. 137–142.

22. "Prevalence of Antibodies to Human Immunodeficiency Virus, Gonorrhea Rates, and Changed Sexual Behaviour in Homosexual Men in London," *The Lancet*, March 21, 1987, pp. 656–658.

23. "Plotting the Spread of AIDS," Roy Anderson, Robert May, *New Scientist*, March 26, 1987, pp. 50–59.

24. "The Sombre View of AIDS," Malcolm Rees, *Nature*, March 26, 1987, pp. 343–345.

25. "AIDS Surveillance in Europe: Report No. 13," World Health Organization Collaborating Centre on AIDS, March, 31, 1987.

26. "An Updated Quantitative Analysis of AIDS in California," George Deukmejian, Department of Health Services, April 1987.

27. "From Persistent Generalised Lymphadenopathy to AIDS: Who Will Progress?", C. A. Carne et al, *British Medical Journal*, April 4, 1987, pp. 868, 869.

28. "A Forgotten Factor in Pelvic Inflammatory Disease: Infection in the Male Partner," Martha Jacob et al, *British Medical Journal*, April 4, 1987, p. 869.

29. "Epidemiology of AIDS in Women in the United States," Mary E. Guinan, Ann Hardy, *JAMA*, April 17, 1987, pp. 2039–2042.

30. "The Costs of AIDS and Other HIV Infections: Review of the Estimates," Staff Paper, U.S. Congress, May 1987.

31. "The Costs of Treating AIDS under Medicaid," Anthony Pascal, A Rand Note, May 1987.
32. "Selection and Estimation of Growth Models with Application to Forecasting AIDS," Quang P. Duong, Bell Canada, Ian B. MacNeill, University of Western Ontario.
33. "The AIDS Epidemic: Looking into the 1990's," Jeffrey E. Harris, *Technology Review*, July 1987, pp. 59–65.
34. "Human Immunodeficiency Virus Infections among Civilian Applicants for United States Military Service, October 1985 to March 1986: Demographic Factors Associated with Seropositivity," Donald S. Burke et al, *The New England Journal of Medicine*, July 16, 1987, pp. 131–136.
35. "Financing the Struggle against AIDS," John K. Iglehart, *The New England Journal of Medicine*, July 16, 1987, pp. 180–184.
36. "Long Latency Precedes Overt Seroconversion in Sexually Transmitted Human-Immunodeficiency-Virus Infection," Annamari Ranki et al, *The Lancet*, September 12, 1987, pp. 589–592.
37. "Computer Models of AIDS Epidemiology," Peter J. Denning, *American Scientist*, July-August 1987, pp. 347, 348.
38. "Blood Transfusion and AIDS," Harvey G. Klein, M.D., Harvey J. Alter, M.D., American Medical Association Information on AIDS, July-August 1987, Volume 2, pp. 7–10.
39. "Serologic Tests for Human Immunodeficiency Virus (HIV)," Alfred J. Saah, M.D., "AIDS: Information for Practicing Physicians," *American Medical News*, July-August 1987, Volume 2, pp. 11–15.
40. "Epidemiology of Acquired Immunodeficiency Syndrome: A Brief Overview," John P. Phair, M.D., James P. Steinberg, M.D., "AIDS: Information for Practicing Physicians," *American Medical News*, July-August 1987, Volume 3, pp. 9,10.
41. "Clinical Trials of Drugs for the Treatment of AIDS," John R. LaMontagne, Ph.D., Maureen W. Myers, Ph.D., "AIDS: Information for Practicing Physicians," *American Medical News*, July-August 1987, Volume 3, pp. 5–8.
42. "Male-to-Female Transmission of Human Immunodeficiency Virus," Nancy Padian, Ph.D., et al, *JAMA*, August 14, 1987, pp. 788–790.
43. "Acquired Immunodeficiency Syndrome in Low-Incidence Areas," David W. Fleming, M.D., et al, *JAMA*, August 14, 1987, pp. 785–787.
44. "Revision of the CDC Surveillance Case Definition for Acquired Immunodeficiency Syndrome," *JAMA*, September 4, 1987, pp. 1143–1154.
45. "Acquired Immunodeficiency Syndrome (AIDS): An Update for the Clinician," Jonas A. Shulman, M.D., et al, *Emory University Journal of Medicine*, July/September 1987, pp. 157–190.
46. "Spontanverlauf der HIV-Infektion: Eine Bilanz 5 Jahre nach den ersten AIDS-Erkrankungen in Frankfurt/Main (Long Term Monitoring of HIV Infection: An Update 5 Years after the First AIDS Cases in Frankfurt on Main," Prof. Dr. E. B. Helm et al, *AIDS-Forschung (AIFO)*, October 1987, pp. 567–572.

47. "Human Immunodeficiency Virus Infections in the United States: A Review of Current Knowledge and Plans for Expansion of HIV Surveillance Activities," Department of Health and Human Services, Public Health Service, Centers for Disease Control, November 30, 1987.

C. PERIODICALS RELATING SPECIFICALLY TO AIDS

48. *AIDS Alert*, American Health Consultants, Inc., published monthly.
49. *AIDS Insurance Reports*, American Eagle Insurance Agency, Inc., published biweekly.
50. *AIDS Policy and Law*, Buraff Publications, published biweekly.
51. *AIDS Weekly Surveillance Reports*, Centers for Disease Control, published weekly.

APPENDIX 3
CDC ESTIMATES OF HIV PREVALENCE

The following is a copy of pages 15–24 of "Human Immunodeficiency Virus Infection in the United States—A Review of Current Knowledge and Plans for Expansion of HIV Surveillance Activities" prepared by the Department of Health and Human Services, Public Health Service, Centers for Disease Control, November 30, 1987.

VII. IMPLICATIONS FOR NATIONAL ESTIMATE OF HIV PREVALENCE

A. *The Public Health Service Estimate Approach Reconsidered*

In May 1986, during the Public Health Service (PHS) AIDS Planning Conference at Coolfont, West Virginia, a group of public health experts estimated the number of HIV infected persons in the United States to be 1 to 1.5 million. At the time, scientific speculation had focused on HIV levels several fold greater than this and no consensus had been attempted. The assembled group of nearly 100 individuals from within and outside Government who were experienced in the scientific and public health aspects of AIDS developed their working estimate based on the estimated size of populations at increased risk multiplied by the corresponding estimates of HIV prevalence from the limited data then available (Table 13). The group particularly expressed concern about the uncertainty of the size of groups at risk. The figure 1,000,000 to 1,500,000 was consistent with what was then known about the progression of HIV infection to AIDS (20% to 30% in 5 years) and the projected cumulative incidence of AIDS (270,000 diagnosed by the end of 1991). The Institute of Medicine, National Academy of Sciences subsequently reviewed the PHS working estimate and considered it reasonable for planning purposes (Institute of Medicine, 1986).

TABLE 13

PUBLIC HEALTH SERVICE ESTIMATE OF HIV PREVALENCE
IN THE UNITED STATES BY POPULATION GROUP, 1986

TOTAL POPULATION INFECTED	ESTIMATED SIZE	APPROXIMATE SEROPREVALENCE	
Exclusively homosexual throughout life[1]	2,500,000	15%–20%	375,000–500,000
Other homosexual contact[1]	2,500,000–7,500,000	10%	250,000–750,000
Regular (at least weekly) intravenous drug abuse[2]	750,000	30%	225,000
Less frequent IV drug use[2]	750,000	10%	75,000
Persons with hemophilia[3]	14,000	70%	10,000
Other groups (transfusion recipients, other hetero- sexuals, infants)	?	?	?
Total			1,000,000–1,500,000

[1]Kinsey, et al: *Sexual Behavior in the Human Male*, Philadelphia, Saunders Publishing Co., 1948; and U.S. Census data, 1980.
[2]National Institute on Drug Abuse (personal communication), 1986.
[3]National Hemophilia Foundation (personal communication), 1986.

Since 1986, additional data have become available on seroprevalence in risk groups and in other populations, and estimates of the size of two of the risk groups have been modified. Based on the 1986 and 1987 seroprevalence observations, the average estimated prevalence can be adjusted from a range of 15–20% to the range of 20–25% for exclusively homosexual men; from 10% to 5% for bisexuals and men with infrequent past homosexual exposures; from 30% to 25% for heavy users of IV drugs; and the rate of 35% can be used for hemophilia B patients. NIDA currently estimates there are 900,000 heavy users of IV drugs, and 200,000 occasional or intermittent users (NIDA, personal communication). The current estimated number of hemophilia A patients is 12,400, and hemophilia B patients, 3,100 (Host Factors Division, CDC, and National Hemophilia Foundation, personal communication). For heterosexual adults 15–59 years of age without specific identifiable HIV risk factors, the population figure 142,000,000 was used based on the 1985 U.S. Census estimate of 148,000,000 less the totals for persons at higher risk in the table. The HIV prevalence in this population is difficult to estimate with the limited data available, but in blood donors and military applicants persons without identifiable risk have accounted for less than about 15% of total infections when seropositives have been interviewed. Therefore, 15% of the age-, race-, and sex-adjusted rate for military applicants, or 0.021%, was selected as the HIV prevalence for this group. For the other groups (heterosexual partners of persons at high risk, heterosexuals born in Haiti and Central Africa, transfusion recipients, etc.) no population size or seroprevalence estimates are available. However, the data available from AIDS case surveillance suggest that this miscellaneous group may account for as many as 5% to 10% of total infections.

The estimate obtained by incorporating these revisions into the 1986 calculation (Table 14)—945,000 to 1,408,000—differs little from the earlier figure. The major limitation of both the original and the reevaluated estimate is the unknown size of the population of homosexual and bisexual men and the distribution within this population of the level of risk activity. In view of the limited impact of the new data and population size estimates, modifying the overall PHS working estimate for HIV infection in the United States does not appear warranted at this time based on this approach.

B. *Extrapolation from Observed Rates*

What if the prevalence or a multiple thereof from the only large currently observed groups, blood donors and military applicants, is used to estimate a national number of infected persons? The prevalence for first-time-tested donors, 0.043%, multiplied by the size of the population 13–59 years of age, 148,000,000, gives a national figure of 64,000. This is clearly an underestimate since persons at recognized high risk are largely excluded from the blood donor pool. (There also have been 45,000 AIDS cases reported as of early November 1987.) The military applicant adjusted prevalence of 0.14% multiplied by the size of the population 15–59 years of age gives an estimate of 207,000, also undoubtedly an underestimate because of the under-representation of persons at risk of HIV in the military applicant pool. Preliminary data from other populations including Massachusetts child-bearing women and sentinel hospitals provide prevalence estimates 2 to 3 times as high as those in geographically corresponding military applicants. However, even a 3-fold multiple of the applicant prevalence-based extrapolation, 621,000, is well below the PHS estimate. More representative prevalence information will be needed to add precision to an estimate made by this approach.

C. *Mathematical Model Approach*

Several researchers, including Dr. Ron Brookmeyer of the Department of Biostatistics at the Johns Hopkins School of Public Health, Drs. Victor De Gruttola and Stephen Lagakos of the Department of Biostatistics at the Harvard School of Public Health, Dr. Jeffrey Harris of the National Bureau of

TABLE 14

REEVALUATED PUBLIC HEALTH SERVICE ESTIMATE OF HIV PREVALENCE
IN THE UNITED STATES BY POPULATION GROUP, 1987

POPULATION	ESTIMATED SIZE	APPROXIMATE SEROPREVALENCE	TOTAL INFECTED
Exclusively homosexual throughout life[1]	2,500,000	20–25%	500,000–625,000
Other homosexual contact including highly infrequent[1]	2,500,000–7,500,000	5%	125,000–375,000
Regular (at least weekly) intravenous drug abuse[2]	900,000	25%	225,000
Occasional IV drug use[2]	200,000	5%	10,000
Persons with Hemophilia A[3]	12,400	70%	8,700
Persons with Hemophilia B[3]	3,100	35%	1,100
Heterosexuals without specific identified risks	142,000,000	0.021%[4]	30,000
Subtotal			900,000–1,270,000
Other groups (heterosexual partners of persons at high risk, heterosexuals born in Haiti and Central Africa, transfusion recipients, other)	additional 5–10% of total number of infections[4]		45,000–127,000
Total			945,000–1,400,000

[1]Kinsey, et al: *Sexual Behavior in the Human Male*, Philadelphia, Saunders Publishing Co., 1948; and U.S. Census data, 1980.
[2]National Institute on Drug Abuse (personal communication), 1987; excludes persons who have used drugs only once or twice.
[3]Host Factors Div., CDC, and National Hemophilia Foundation (personal communication), 1987.
[4]See Text (VIII. A.)

Economic Research in Cambridge, Massachusetts, as well as Mr. James Warner of the White House staff and AIDS coordinator for the Health Policy Group, have suggested that the number of persons infected with HIV can be estimated from data on reported AIDS cases in combination with data on the rate at which infected individuals progress on to AIDS. These approaches were considered in some detail at the October 15–17 workshop on mathematical modelling of AIDS and HIV infection sponsored by the Institute of Medicine, National Academy of Sciences. A variation of this technique is discussed below.

In all of the methods, the number of AIDS cases diagnosed each year can be calculated as the convolution of the number of persons infected in each preceding year and the number of those expected to be diagnosed with AIDS. For this particular approach, let $a(t)$ be the number of AIDS cases diagnosed in year t ($t = 1978, 1979, \ldots, 1987$), let $i(t)$ be the number newly infected in year t, and $d(x)$ be the proportion of infected persons expected to develop AIDS after x years ($x = 0,1,2. \ . \ .$) then:

$$a(t) = \sum_{z=1978}^{t} i(z) \cdot d(t-z) \qquad \text{(eq. 1)}$$

The number of cases of AIDS per year $a(t)$ is known from surveillance data and the disease progression rates $d(x)$ with accompanying 95% confidence bounds may be estimated from a prospective study of HIV-infected homosexual men in San Francisco. It is possible to estimate the number of persons infected, provided specific assumptions are made about the shape of $i(t)$. Three different sets of progression data were considered: one representing the best estimates from the cohort data, one representing the lower 95% confidence bounds (slowest rate of disease progression) and one representing the upper 95% confidence bounds (fastest rate of disease progression). Three different distributions for the infection curve were considered as follows:

logistic $I(t) = 1/(1 + k \, \exp(-rt))$;
log-logistic $I(t) = 1/(1 + (rt)^k)$; and
damped exponential $I(t) = k \, \exp(rt^x)$.

AIDS cases reported to the CDC through November 2, 1987, were used in the analysis. The totals were adjusted for reporting delays to give the number of diagnosed AIDS cases each year through 1987. The parameters in the different infection curves and the total infections through 1987 were estimated from equation (1) using weighted non-linear least squares methods. The final estimates were adjusted for under-recognition and under-reporting of AIDS cases. Validation studies done in five major U.S. cities in 1985 suggested that 20% or more of AIDS cases were either not reported to health departments, or were not diagnosed by a method which would allow them to be counted under the AIDS surveillance definition used prior to September 1987. Variations over time in the completeness of reporting (such as a large number of early AIDS cases being missed) would also influence the projected number of cases, but were not considered in these analyses.

The resulting estimates for the cumulative number infected by the end of 1987 are shown in Table 15. The range of estimated values is large, from 276,000 to 1,750,000 persons infected, reflecting both uncertainty in the progression rate for AIDS and the varied assumptions about the shape of the underlying infection curve. Using only the best estimate of the progression rate data from the San Francisco prospective study, the range of estimates is smaller, from 420,000 to 1,649,000.

TABLE 15

PERSONS INFECTED WITH HIV AT THE END OF 1987,
UNITED STATES, ESTIMATED[1] FROM REPORTED AIDS CASES,
BY RATE OF DISEASE PROGRESSION AND ASSUMED INFECTION CURVE

(with 95% confidence bounds in parentheses)

ASSUMED INFECTION CURVE[2]	Rate of Disease Progression[3]		
	SLOWEST PROGRESSION	MOST LIKELY PROGRESSION RATE	FASTEST PROGRESSION
Logistic	420,000*	420,000*	420,000*
	(403,000–438,000)	(312,000–528,000)	(268,000–572,000)
Log-logistic	1,363,000*	853,000*	276,000*
	(918,000–1,809,000)	(186,000–1,519,000)	(66,000–511,000)
Damped-	1,750,000	1,649,000*	1,468,000*
Exponential	(576,000–2,936,000)	(566,000–2,732,000)	(556,000–2,380,500)

*chi-square goodness-of-fit $p > .50$

Notes:
[1]Each of the estimates for the number infected has been increased by 20% to account for unreported or unrecognized AIDS cases.
[2]See text (VIII.C.) for discussion of limitations of each curve.
[3]Data for disease progression are taken from a study of infected homosexual men in San Francisco. The lower 95% confidence estimate (slowest progression rate) for the cumulative number of men developing AIDS after each of 1–11 years was taken as 0%, 0%, 0%, 2%, 5%, 9%, 17%, 21%, 26%, 31%, 36%; the best estimate (most likely progression rate) was taken as 0%, 0%, 2%, 5%, 10%, 15%, 24%, 30%, 36%, 42%; and the upper estimate (fastest progression rate) was taken as 0%, 0%, 4%, 8%, 15%, 21%, 31%, 39%, 46%, 52%, 58%. The rates for years 8–11 were not taken directly from the San Francisco data but were extrapolated from prior years.

These estimates must be evaluated in light of the assumptions made in the models about the shape of the curve and, hence, the spread of the infection. The logistic curve assumes that the spread of infection is limited to a closed group and that all persons in that group have an identical, constant risk for infection. The model does not take into account the addition of individuals who are newly at-risk, for example persons who only recently became sexually active or started using IV drugs. The logistic model also assumes that likelihood of transmission is the same for all those at-risk, whether they are homosexuals, IV drug users, hemophiliacs, transfusion recipients, or heterosexual partners of infected persons and that this risk is constant over time. As a consequence of these highly implausible assumptions, the fitted model indicates that virtually all those who will ever become infected with HIV were already infected by 1984. Current data show that substantial numbers of new infections continue to occur in all population groups except hemophiliacs and transfusion recipients. For all of these reasons, the logistic model is inappropriate and will severely underestimate the total number of persons now infected.

Although the log-logistic model also assumes a closed group at-risk, it allows for a relative slowing in the rate at which the virus is spreading. Such a slowing would be expected for two reasons. First, persons are not homogeneous but have considerably varied risk. Risks will vary by type of exposure (homosexual, IV drug use, heterosexual, etc.) and by the frequency of exposure. Particularly in a closed or relatively closed group, those at highest risk would have become infected earliest in the epidemic while the virus might later spread more slowly among those with lower risk. Second, prevention and education efforts would slow the rate of infection. Countering this, however, is the argument that since the major groups at risk are not really "closed," the increasing prevalence of HIV infection could lead to increased spread simply because more infected persons are available to transmit the infection. The log-logistic model is much more appropriate than the logistic, but will likely still underestimate the eventual number of persons who will become infected with HIV.

The third model, the damped-exponential, also allows for a relative slowing in the rate at which the infection is spread, but does not assume that the population at-risk is closed. On the contrary, it assumes that the number of HIV infections is limitless. While such an assumption may be unreasonable over the long-term, it may accurately represent the short-term spread of HIV in populations where prevalence is low and/or the number of persons entering the risk groups exceeds or equals number becoming infected.

Both the log-logistic and the damped-exponential models fit the AIDS surveillance data well, and their curves have similar shapes in the early stages of the epidemic, but diverge rapidly beyond 1984 due to the different assumptions underlying them. Since very few persons infected with HIV progress to AIDS during the first 2–3 years, AIDS case data alone cannot determine which of these models is more appropriate and, hence, what is currently happening with regard to HIV infection. Rather the AIDS cases seen today reflect primarily trends in infection through and including 1984, before current prevention activities, including screening of blood donations, testing and counseling efforts, and information and education activities be-gan. For example, application of the damped-exponential model to surveil-lance data for transfusion-associated cases would lead to the erroneous conclusion that HIV has spread rapidly in the blood supply since 1984, while application of the log-logistic model to the same data in 1985 would have been falsely reassuring at that time before blood donations were screened for HIV.

It is unlikely that any one of these models accurately describes the trans-mission of HIV in the population. Many different models are consistent with currently available AIDS surveillance data, and these data alone are not sufficient to determine the extent of HIV infection. Procedures that produce such a wide range of results from the same data indicated that there are either insufficient data or insufficient models or both. Carefully obtained HIV incidence and prevalence data will be essential.

Implications. The estimation of a total number of persons infected remains complex and inexact. The approaches described for computing or recom-puting a national HIV prevalence cannot be considered definitive. The re-sults, however, are consistent with the previous PHS working estimate of 1 to 1.5 million. None of the approaches suggest that that estimate is currently too low or too high, and the available data and mathematical models do not at present warrant a change in the estimate. Since some HIV transmission clearly has occurred in the past 17 months, this implies that the 1.5 million upper limit of the original estimate may have been high at that time. There is no substitute for carefully obtained HIV incidence and prevalence data. Additional surveys and studies are needed to determine the extent to which HIV is spreading through the population.

IX. OBSERVATIONS AND COMMENT

This review of the extent and trends of infection with the human immu-nodeficiency virus in the United States is necessarily descriptive and quali-tative. The marked variability in study design, sampling, and biases among the available serologic surveys and studies makes quantitative comparisons only approximate. Nevertheless, the picture emerges of extensive HIV in-fection in the recognized risk groups of homosexual and bisexual men, in-travenous drug users, and hemophiliacs, and their heterosexual partners. Exclusively heterosexual persons who do not abuse drugs and who are not knowingly the partners of persons with or at risk of HIV infection are at present much less likely to be infected. However, no infection trend infor-mation is yet available to evaluate whether the risk is rising for this latter group.

With few exceptions, HIV prevalence in observed groups from the general population, which includes high-risk as well as low-risk persons, are a fraction of 1%. At this time, IV infection, like AIDS, occurs primarily in young to early middle-aged adults, although insufficient information is currently available on young children. In general, males are currently much more likely than females to be infected, blacks and Hispanics more likely than whites. Geographic differences in infection prevalence remain consistent with the distribution of AIDS cases. While new infections continue to occur, the rate of new infection in many groups of homosexual men appears to have declined, which may have major implications for the overall incidence of new infection, since this group has previously accounted for the largest number of AIDS cases. However, information is not currently sufficient to evaluate infection trends in IV drug users, heterosexually active persons, or in specific geographic areas.

Many gaps in our knowledge remain. More precise and more consistently collected data on this prevalence of HIV infection must be collected for currently recognized risk groups, heterosexually active persons, and accessible segments of the general population. Better and more extensive information is essential for targeting and evaluating control and prevention efforts at local and State level, for predicting future health care needs, and for understanding where the HIV and AIDS epidemic is headed. Better models which make use of the specific data will also aid in our understanding of the spread of this virus. Surveillance of the prevalence and incidence of HIV infection by continually monitoring sentinel populations and expanding focused seroprevalence surveys and studies, as well as developing models to help interpret the data remain a critical element of the Nation's response to this major public health crisis.

Acknowledgements

This report was prepared by T.J. Dondero*, M. Pappaioanou*, I. Onorato*, T.S. Jones*, R. Cannon*, C. Shapiro*, R. Hahn*, J. Dougherty**, B. Miller*, C. White*, M. Morgan* J.W. Curran* and the HIV Data Analysis Team.†

The authors acknowledge the full support of the State and Territory Epidemiologists, and investigators at medical centers, at State and local health

*Centers for Disease Control
**National Institute on Drug Abuse/ADAMHA
***Multicenter AIDS Cohort Study (MACS), National Institutes of Health
†A. Bloch*, S. Bowen*, R. Byers*, K. Castro*, T. Chorba*, R. Fox***, H. Gayle*, A. Hardy*, C. Hayden*, S. Holmberg*, R. Horsburgh*, F. Ingram*, L. Jacobson***, H. Jaffe*, J. Stehr-Green*, J. Jason*, N. Lee*, S. Mannof*, B. Miller*, P. Moore*, L. Nelson**, A. Pershing*, L. Petersen*, K. Rauch*, D. Rodrigue*, G. Schmid*, R. Selik*, S. Schulz*

departments, and at many federal agencies, whose willingness to share their data made this report possible. The authors also acknowledge the skillful graphics work of Jean Smith, the statistical and data management support of Gloria Gavin and Tim Bush, and the fine clerical support of Linda Gimmestad and Earla Schwarz. Finally the authors are thankful for the critical reviews of the manuscript by Gary Noble, Walter R. Dowdle, and James O. Mason.

REFERENCES

BAKER JL, KELEN GD, SILVERTSON KT, QUINN TC. Unsuspected human immunodeficiency virus in critically ill emergency patients. *JAMA*. 1987;257:2609–11.

BLANCHE S, ROUZIOUX C, VEBER F, ET AL. Prospective study on newborns of HIV seropositive women [Abstract]. In: *Abstracts from the III International Conference on AIDS. 1–5 June 1987, Washington D.C.*; 1987:TH7.4.

BURKE DS, BRUNDAGE JF, HERBOLD JR, ET AL. Human immunodeficiency virus (HIV) infection among civilian applicants for United States military service, October 1985 to March 1986. Demographic factors associated with seropositivity. *N Eng J Med*. 1987;317:131–6.

CDC. Antibody to human immunodeficiency virus in female prostitutes. *MMWR*. 1987;36:157–61.

CDC. Diagnosis and management of mycobacterial infection and disease in persons with Human T-Lymphotropic Virus Type III/Lymphadenopathy-Associated Virus infection. *MMWR*. 1986;35:448–52.

CHAMBERLAND ME, DONDERO TJ. Heterosexually acquired infection with human immunodeficiency virus (HIV) [Editorial]. *Ann Int Med*. 1987;107:763–6.

DODD RY, NATH N, BASTIAANS MJ, BARKER LF. Hepatitis-associated markers in the American Red Cross donor population: ten years' experience. In: Viral Hepatitis 1981 International Symposium. *eds*. Szmuness W, Alter HJ, Maynard JE. Philadelphia: Franklin Institute Press. 1982; chap. 13:145–55.

GOEDERT JJ, EYSTER ME, BIGGAR RJ. Heterosexual transmission of human immunodeficiency virus (HIV): association with severe T4-cell depletion in male hemophiliacs [Abstract]. In: *Abstracts from the III International Conference on AIDS. 1–5 June 1987. Washington D.C.*; 1987:W.2.6.

HARDY AM, STARCHER ET, MORGAN WM, ET AL. Review of death certificates to assess completeness of AIDS case reporting. *Pub Hlth Reps*. 1987;102:386–391.

INSTITUTE OF MEDICINE/NATIONAL ACADEMY OF SCIENCES. Confronting AIDS. Directions for Public Health, Health Care, and Research. Washington: National Academy Press. 1986; pp 69–70.

MARWICK C. HIV antibody prevalence data derived from study of Massachusetts infants. *JAMA*. 1987;258:171–2.

Mok JQ, Giaquinto C, De Rossi A, et al. Infants born to mothers seropositive for human immunodeficiency virus. Preliminary findings from a multicenter European study *Lancet*. 1987;1:1164–8.

Nzilambi N, Ryder RW, Behets F, et al. Perinatal HIV transmission in two African hospitals [Abstract]. In: *Abstracts from the III International Conference on AIDS. 1–5 June 1987. Washington D.C.*; 1987:TH.7.6.

Peterman TA, Stoneburner RL, Allen JR, Jaffe HW, Curran JW. Risk of HIV transmission from heterosexual adults with transfusion-associated infections. *JAMA*. In press.

Potterat JJ, Phillips L, Muth JB. Lying to military physicians about risk factors for HIV infections [Letter]. *JAMA*. 1987;257:1727.

Scott GB, Mastrucci MT, Hutto SC, Parks WP. Mothers of infants with HIV infection: outcome of subsequent pregnancies [Abstract]. In: *Abstracts from the III International Conference on AIDS. 1–5 June 1987. Washington, D.C.*; 1987:THP.91.

Semprini EA, Vucetich A, Pardi G, Cossu MM. HIV infection and AIDS in newborn babies of mothers positive for HIV antibody. *Brit Med J*. 1987;294:610.

Shoenbaum EE, Selwyn PA, Klein RS, et al. Prevention of and risk factors associated with HTLV-III/LAV antibodies among IVDAs in methadone program in New York City [Abstract]. In: *Abstracts from the II International Conference on AIDS. 1986. Paris*. 1986:198.

Starcher ET, Biel JK, Rivera Castano R, et al. The impact of presumptively diagnosed opportunistic infections and cancers on national reporting of AIDS [Abstract]. In: *Abstracts from the III International Conference on AIDS. 1–5 June 1987. Washington, D.C.* 1987:WP.88.

Stoneburner RL, Chiasson MA, Solomon K, Rosenthal S. Risk factors in military recruits positive for HIV antibody [Letter]. *N Eng J Med*. 1986;315:1355.

Weiss SH, Ginzburg HM, Altman R, et al. Risk factors for HTLV-III/LAV infections and development of AIDS [Abstract]. In: *Abstracts from the II International Conference on AIDS. 1986. Paris*. 1986:204.

CHAPTER 2

A PRACTICAL PRIMER: AIDS AND LIFE
AND HEALTH INSURANCE

This primer gives an overview that can be a basis for further study about the effect of AIDS on a particular life or health insurer. This primer provides preliminary background information only—this is by no means a thorough study of the AIDS epidemic.

Information was collected from materials gathered during Tillinghast's AIDS research. Since this summary is intended only to establish an initial understanding of AIDS, reference notations have been excluded. For an explanation of material presented here, contact Tom Reese at (714) 553-1277.

These notes are condensed from the original studies and papers. For a full understanding, it is recommended that the original material be read. This overview is not a substitute for the papers listed as major references in the final section.

This paper was written by Tom Reese (Tillinghast-Irvine), with contributions by Bob Beal (Hartford), Jay Boekhoff (Minneapolis), and John Tiller (Irvine).

DEFINITIONS

AIDS	Acquired Immune Deficiency Syndrome
HIV	Human Immunodeficiency Virus, the causative agent for AIDS; previously used names were:
	LAV, lymphadenopathy-associated virus
	HTLV-III, human T-cell lymphotropic virus type III
	ARV, AIDS-associated retrovirus
HIV+	HIV positive (seropositive), an indication of being infected with HIV, whether symptomatic or not
HIV−	HIV negative (seronegative), not infected
Seroconversion	The appearance of antibodies directed against HIV in the serum of an exposed person
LAS	Lymphadenopathy Syndrome, the prolonged presence of greatly enlarged lymph nodes together with moderate cellular immune deficiency

871

ARC AIDS-Related Complex, LAS plus severe cellular immune deficiency, but without the presence of an opportunistic infection that would meet the CDC definition of AIDS

CDC Public Health Service's Centers for Disease Control in Atlanta

ELISA ⎫
Western Blot ⎬ HIV antibody blood tests, described in the section on Underwriting
T-Cell Ratio ⎭

CDC Criteria

To facilitate accurate reporting, the CDC has established strict criteria for the diagnosis of AIDS ("CDC AIDS"):

I. Without Laboratory Evidence of HIV Infection
If HIV tests were not performed or were inconclusive, a case qualifies as "AIDS" if the patient both:
A. Does not have a cause of immunodeficiency that disqualifies diseases as indicators of AIDS; a list of three types of causes is specified, and
B. Is definitively diagnosed for an AIDS indicator disease; a list of 12 indicator disease categories is specified.

II. With Laboratory Evidence of HIV Infection
Regardless of the presence of other causes of immunodeficiency, a case qualifies as "AIDS" if the patient:
A. Has a definitively diagnosed indicator disease from the list in I.B. or from another list of 12 specified disease categories, or
B. Has a presumptively diagnosed indicator disease from a list of seven specified disease categories.

III. With Laboratory Evidence Against HIV Infection
A diagnosis of AIDS is ruled out unless both:
A. All other causes of immunodeficiency (listed in I.A.) are ruled out, and
B. The patient has had either
1. Pneumocystis carinii pneumonia definitively diagnosed, or
2. Both:
a. A definitively diagnosed indicator disease from Section I.B., and
b. A T-helper/inducer (CD4) lymphocyte count below a specified level.

Note: Before September 1987, the CDC definition of AIDS was basically the test described in rule section I above. Laboratory evidence of HIV infection was not part of the definition. The first weekly surveillance report that used the new definition was the 10/12/87 report. The definition change added 265 AIDS cases to that report that met the new definition but not the old.

There have been concerns that these criteria are too strict. The CDC definition is designed to be very specific in order to achieve accurate and uniform tracking of disease. The symptoms of ARC, however, can sometimes be as debilitating as those of AIDS. Many have died without reaching the confines of the CDC surveillance definition.

Cowell-Hoskins Paper

Citations of this paper refer to the paper distributed to members of three special interest sections of the Society of Actuaries in August 1987. This significant early study provides some valuable estimates about AIDS epidemic parameters. A summary of this paper, along with a complete reference, is contained in the section: "Cowell-Hoskins Paper Summary." The entire paper is reproduced as Chapter 3 of this Task Force report.

DESCRIPTION

Acquired Immune Deficiency Syndrome

"Acquired" because the disease arises by an infection.

"Immune deficiency" because the condition results in the failure of the body's immune system.

"Syndrome" because a number of rare but devastating diseases (opportunistic infections) can take advantage of the body's weakened defenses.

Discovery

AIDS was first described in 1981. The first sign of a new disease was the appearance of a rare cancer (Kaposi's sarcoma) among the "wrong" patients and an increase in pneumonia caused by a normally harmless protozoan (Pneumocystis carinii pneumonia, or PCP). It became evident that an infectious form of immune deficiency had appeared. The name "AIDS" was coined. The disease was apparently associated with lifestyle, since it was quickly spreading among homosexuals, intravenous drug users, recipients of frequent blood transfusions, and Haitians.

Although only identified in 1981, AIDS cases have been diagnosed as early as 1977. The diagnosis was declared retroactively after the identification of the disease. The earliest signs of the virus have been found in serum samples taken in a small region of Central Africa in the 1950s.

Spread

The HIV virus is present in most body fluids. The amount of viral particles present in tears, saliva, and urine are so small that it is apparently very difficult to contract the disease by exposure to those fluids. However, we don't know if exposure to extremely low concentrations means that infection will not occur or if the incubation period is just extremely long.

Transmission of the virus is through blood, semen, and vaginal fluids. Transmission is through sexual activity, not by casual contact. The chance of infection is highly correlated with other sexually transmitted diseases.

The HIV Virus

Only three years after the disease was described, its cause was conclusively shown to be the HIV virus. HIV is the third human retrovirus discovered.

The first human retrovirus was discovered in 1978. HTLV-I (Human T-lymphotropic Virus I) causes leukemia. The second human retrovirus was isolated in 1982.

A retrovirus has RNA as its genetic material. When the virus enters a host cell, a viral enzyme called reverse transcriptase uses the viral RNA as a type of template to assemble a corresponding molecule of DNA. The DNA travels to the cell nucleus and inserts itself among the host's chromosomes. Then, as the cell multiplies, these altered chromosomes are copied into the new cells produced.

The host cell for HIV is often a T4 lymphocyte, a white blood cell that has a central role in regulating the immune system. Once it is inside a T4 cell, the virus may remain latent until the lymphocyte is immunologically stimulated by a secondary infection. Then the virus reproduces itself at a very rapid rate, and the lymphocyte dies. The resulting depletion of T4 cells leaves the patient vulnerable to "opportunistic" infections by agents that would not harm a healthy person.

When a person is first infected, the immune system responds by making antibodies. That response is clearly not adequate, however, and the virus takes hold. In many cases, lymphocytes multiply abnormally in the lymph nodes. The nodes' structure collapses, and the number of lymphocytes in the blood decreases, leaving the patient open to opportunistic infections.

CDC STATISTICS

United States AIDS cases reported as of October 12, 1987:

Transmission Categories

	Males	Females	Total
Adults/adolescents:			
Homosexual/bisexual males	27,986 (71%)		27,986 (66%)
IV drug abusers	5,516 (14%)	1,460 (49%)	6,976 (16%)
Homosexual male and IV drugs	3,196 (8%)		3,196 (8%)
Hemophiliacs/coagulation disorders	407 (1%)	16 (1%)	423 (1%)
Blood transfusions	569 (1%)	317 (11%)	886 (2%)
Heterosexual contact	220 (1%)	710 (24%)	930 (2%)
Heterosexual, other countries*	544 (1%)	140 (5%)	684 (2%)
Undetermined	977 (3%)	312 (10%)	1,289 (3%)
Subtotal	39,415 (93%)	2,955 (7%)	42,370 (100%)
Children (under age 13)	318	277	595
Total	39,733	3,232	42,965

*"Persons without other identified risks who were born in countries in which heterosexual transmission is believed to play a major role although precise means of transmission have not yet been fully developed."

Age of Diagnosis

Age Group	Number of AIDS Cases	Percentage
0–5	518	1%
5–12	77	0
13–19	174	0
20–29	8,996	21
30–39	19,998	47
40–49	8,936	21
50+	4,266	10
Total	42,965	100%

State of Residence

Every state has recorded at least five AIDS cases.

States with More Than 1,000 Cases	Number	Percentage of U.S. AIDS Cases	Population* (million)	Cases per Thousand Population
New York	12,012	28.0%	17.77	0.7
California	9.747	22.7	26.98	0.4
Florida	2,946	6.9	11.68	0.3
Texas	2,894	6.7	16.68	0.2
New Jersey	2,552	5.9	7.62	0.3
Illinois	1,186	2.8	11.55	0.1
Pennsylvania	1,094	2.5	11.89	0.1

*Preliminary 1986 year-end figures from the Census Bureau.

Standard Metropolitan Statistical Area of Residence

SMSA's with More Than 1,000 Cases	Number	Percentage of U.S. AIDS Cases	Population* (million)	Cases per Thousand Population
New York	10,924	25.4%	9.12	1.2
San Francisco	4,096	9.5	3.25	1.3
Los Angeles	3,627	8.4	7.48	0.5
Houston	1,440	3.4	2.91	0.5
Washington, D.C.	1,278	3.0	3.06	0.4
Miami	1,183	2.8	1.63	0.7
Chicago	1,069	2.5	7.10	0.2

*Populations reported in the 1980 census.

Underreporting

The CDC has estimated that its statistics may be low by 20 percent, 10 percent for cases not reported and 10 percent for cases not diagnosed.

Even though California physicians are required by law to report AIDS cases to the California Department of Health Service, follow-up checking estimated undercounting at 17–25 percent in a study published April 1987.

Reporting Delays

The following table shows how the CDC AIDS case reporting figures change over time:

Year of Diagnosis	Reported End of Year					
	1983	1984	1985	1986	1987†	Ultimate*
Before 1979				11	11	11
1979	8	10	12	13	13	13
1980	45	46	47	51	52	52
1981	236	251	260	261	267	267
1982	932	976	992	999	1,013	1,013
1983	1,829	2,628	2,717	2,764	2,806	2,806
1984		3,780	5,341	5,531	5,641	5,705
1985			6,571	9,475	9,810	10,147
1986				9,897	13,954	15,210
1987					8,787	18,764

*Projected by Roland Mandat (Tillinghast-Denver) using techniques for estimating unpaid claim liabilities.
†Reported through the end of the third quarter, that is, before the change in the CDC's definition of AIDS.

EXPERIENCE OUTSIDE THE U.S.

Africa

The World Health Organization reported in June 1986 that there were estimated to be at least 50,000 AIDS cases in Central Africa, with 1 to 2 million people infected by HIV.

Among adults in Zaire, Uganda, and other African countries, the proportion of HIV-infected adults is 6 to 10 percent of the total population. African men and women are infected in roughly equal numbers, suggesting heterosexual transmission of the disease.

Australia

Through July 30, 1987, there have been 562 AIDS cases reported in Australia, of which 254 are still living. The distribution of cases by transmission category is: homosexual/bisexual male, 86 percent; blood transfusions, 7 percent; heterosexual transmission, 2 percent; and IV drug abusers, 0.5 percent.

By some estimates, about 30 percent of Australia's homosexual population is HIV +. It has been estimated that there are about 50,000 HIV carriers in Australia, approximately 0.3 percent of the total population.

Canada

Reported September 8, 1987 by the Laboratory Centre for Disease Control (LCDC):

Year of Diagnosis	New AIDS Cases in Canada
1979	1
1980	3
1981	6
1982	22
1983	53
1984	141
1985	314
1986	448
1987	245
Total	1,233

Of adult cases, 84 percent are homosexual/bisexual males, 0.4 percent are IV drug users, 5 percent were transmitted through blood transfusions, 2 percent are heterosexual partners of high-risk individuals, and 5 percent are persons from an endemic area.

U.K.

As reported in the October 5, 1987, report of the Department of Health and Social Security:

"There have been 1,067 AIDS cases reported in the U.K. through the end of September 1987. Further, microbiologists have reported 7,557 HIV+ cases to the Communicable Disease Surveillance Centre (CDSC) in England and the Communicable Disease (Scotland) unit. The cases are reported by category:"

Category	AIDS Cases		HIV+ Cases	
	Number	Percentage	Number	Percentage
Homosexual/bisexual male	901	84%	3,381	45%
IV drug abuser (IVDA)	15	1	1,184	16
Homosexual and IVDA	17	2	45	1
Hemophilia	60	6	1,061	14
Blood recipient	23	2	70	1
Heterosexual:		4		4
Contact of above groups	8		56	
Contact of other groups*	29		155	
No information			111	
Child of HIV+ mother	12	1	74	1
Other†	2	0	1,420	19
Total	1,067	100%	7,557	100%

*"Includes persons without other identified risk from countries where heterosexual transmission is believed to play an important role."
†Includes 1,255 "no information" HIV+ cases from England and 157 "other risks/not known" HIV+ cases from Scotland.

"(The HIV +) data must be interpreted with care as not all those people who have been infected with HIV presented for testing. It is currently estimated that about 40,000 people in the U.K. have been infected."

(Note: a January 10, 1987 article in the *Times* reported that leading specialists believe that between 40,000 and 100,000 people in Britain are now carriers.)

The HIV + statistics come from stations set up in the U.K. to provide free HIV tests for whomever wants to be tested. Individuals' test results are strictly confidential and cannot be accessed by, for example, insurers or employers. Counseling is given before conducting the test, and post-test counseling is provided to HIV + persons.

The progression of the AIDS epidemic in the U.K. is indicated by the growth in reported cases:

Year of Reporting	Cumulative AIDS Cases	Cumulative Deaths	Cumulative HIV + Cases
1983	31	11	
1984	108	46	
1985	275	127	1,763
1986	610	280	3,877
1987*	1,067	605	7,557

*Through the end of September.

ESTIMATES OF THE INFECTION

1 to 1.5 Million—The Famous Figure

An estimate of the extent of the infection in the U.S. as of late 1986— Where did it come from?

Known as the "Coolfont estimates," they are part of the Public Health Service's official prediction. A group of about 10 scientists assembled in June 1986 at the Coolfont Conference Center in Berkeley Springs, W. Va.

The estimate:

Homosexual Men: estimated to be 4 percent of white men between ages 16 and 55 (1948 Kinsey data), assumed to be 18 percent infected.

Bisexual Men: estimated to be another 4 percent homosexual for three years or less plus another 10 percent bisexual (1948 Kinsey data), assumed to be 10 percent infected.

IV Drug Users: about 750,000 Americans use intravenous drugs at least weekly (National Institute on Drug Abuse data), assumed to be 30 percent infected. Another 750,000 use IV drugs less than weekly, assumed to be 10 percent infected.

Hemophiliacs: about 20,000, assumed to be 70 percent infected.

Other Groups: accounting for less than 10 percent of AIDS cases at the time, assumed to have a negligible rate of infection.

Summing these estimates produced a total of between 1 million and 1.5 million Americans infected with the AIDS virus in 1986.

The Coolfont projections assume that 20–30 percent of those infected in 1986 will develop AIDS by the end of 1991.

General Population Infection Rate

The U.S. population was 238.740 million in 1985. Assuming 1 to 1.5 million HIV infected results in a general population infection rate of about 0.5 percent. If those infections are generally among the 63.467 million males· age 20 through 59 in 1985, the U.S. infection rate would be about 2 percent.

Lincoln National has published an estimate of prevalence of HIV + cases under "probable scenario" assumptions. The mid-1987 HIV infection rate is estimated at 1.4 percent for males age 20–29, 3.4 percent for males age 30–39, and 2.3 percent for males age 40–49. These rates are based on 2 million persons infected in the U.S., eliminating certain classifications, such as IV drug users, not expected to be in the insurance market population.

At the Society of Actuaries annual meeting in Montreal on October 19, 1987, Howard Minuk (Chief Medical Officer of Mercantile & General Reinsurance in Toronto) gave these estimates of HIV + prevalence among males age 20–59: 1.0 percent in Canada, 1.8 percent in the U.S., 4.0 percent in California, and 5.7 percent in Los Angeles.

U.S. Military Blood Tests

From October 1985 through March 1986, blood samples from 306,061 civilian applicants for military service from the U.S. were tested for HIV; 460 subjects were HIV + (1.50 per thousand). Statistical breakdowns included:

Age: Prevalences increased directly and linearly with age from 18 years (0.25 per thousand) to 27 years (4.94). "These data suggest that teenagers and young adults have an appreciable risk of infection, and that the risk may be relatively constant and cumulative throughout this age group."

Sex: Sex-specific prevalences were 1.65 for males (263,572 tests) and 0.61 for females (42,489 tests).

Population Density: Low-density counties (less than 500 population per square mile) had a prevalence rate of 0.79 per thousand, while high-density counties had a rate of 5.70.

AIDS Endemicity: The prevalence rate among applicants from counties that were in metropolitan areas in which AIDS is considered endemic was 3.25. The rate for others was 1.25.

Insurance Test Results

The Home Office Reference Laboratory (HORL) in Shawnee Mission, Kans., reports these statistics for standard protocol HIV antibody tests performed in 1986 on specimens submitted to HORL by insurance companies:

Age	Percentage HIV+
1–19	0.25%
20–29	1.02
30–39	0.49
40–49	0.19
50–59	0.15
60+	0.04
All ages	0.30

The average HIV+ age was age 36.

Homosexuals

The homosexual population has been estimated to be over 50 percent HIV infected in San Francisco. It is thought that the homosexual infection rate is as low as 20 percent in other communities.

In a study of 799 homosexual/bisexual single men age 25–54 in San Francisco during the last half of 1984, seropositivity was 48 percent. The extent of the infection varied from 18 percent of those with no male sexual partners during the two years before entry to the study to 71 percent of those reporting 50 or more partners. Of the 65 men who gave a history of needle sharing within the past five years, 83 percent were HIV+.

The homosexual population, especially in areas of high concentration, has clearly changed practices to slow the spread of the disease. In San Francisco, the increase in new infections has slowed to a rate of about 1 percent per year, down about 12–14 percent annually during the peak years of the spread from 1980 through 1982.

IV Drug Users

In New York state, which has the greatest concentration of heroin addicts in the U.S., 60 percent are believed to be infected with the HIV virus.

Hemophiliacs

These are an estimated 20,000 individuals with hemophilia in the U.S. About half of these require infusion of clotting factor concentrates once a week. Commercial clotting factor concentrates are prepared from pools of plasma from as many as 20,000 donors and have long been associated with transmittable infections such as hepatitis. About 50–75 percent of hemophilia patients are HIV + .

No evidence of exposure has been found prior to 1978. The majority of seroconversions occurred during 1981–1983. The chance of further infection is small now that clotting factor concentrates are routinely treated by heating.

HETEROSEXUALS

The Greatest Uncertainty

The "first wave" of the AIDS epidemic is occurring among the initial "at risk" groups—primarily homosexuals and IV drug users. The "second wave" of the AIDS epidemic, if there is one at all, will be among heterosexuals.

The size of this second wave will determine whether the AIDS epidemic will be only an enormous expense for the insurance industry or whether it will prove to be catastrophic for many companies. Even relatively low rates of infection will produce considerably more AIDS deaths than those that will result from the populations currently considered "at risk."

Projections like those of the CDC and the August 1987 Cowell-Hoskins paper are based on the assumption that the epidemic will remain within the first "at risk" groups. The basis for such an assumption would be the theory that heterosexual transmission will be limited primarily to the sexual partners of IV drug users and the female sexual partners of bisexual males.

If there is a second wave, why haven't we seen it yet? Three factors could explain why a second wave may be coming but years delayed from the first wave. First, the risk of infection per exposure appears to be lower for heterosexual practices than for homosexual practices. Second, the progression from infection to disease may be slower for heterosexual transmission. Third, the circulation of exposure is slower in the heterosexual population than it was in the first wave "at risk" groups.

Further, it must be remembered that current AIDS case statistics are a result of infections from perhaps 10 years ago. The infections occurring now won't become AIDS cases for several years. The current 13-to-1 ratio of male to female AIDS cases may be quite different than current infection statistics. The military recruits HIV test results (see the "Estimates of the Infection" section) show a male to female HIV+ prevalence ratio of less than three to one.

Reported Cases

As of the October 12, 1987, CDC statistics:

	Males	Females	Total
Heterosexual contact	220	710	930
Heterosexual, other countries*	544	140	684
Total	764	850	1,614

*"Persons without other identified risks who were born in countries in which heterosexual transmission is believed to play a major role although precise means of transmission have not yet been fully developed."

Unreliability of Classifications

In a study by health department officials in Colorado, 20 military men were identified as infected by HIV. When they were interviewed by other enlisted personnel, 12 claimed heterosexual contact as their source of infection; but when they were reinterviewed by civilians, they described homosexual and bisexual practices.

Probability of Infection

A study published in August 1987 found 23 percent of 97 female partners of infected men were HIV +. All the women in the study had sexual contact within the last year with a man known to be seropositive for HIV or diagnosed as having AIDS or ARC. Women who used IV drugs or women with recent blood transfusions were eliminated from the analyses.

The number of sexual contacts was significantly associated with infection—seropositive women were 4.6 times more likely than seronegative women to have had more than 100 sexual exposures with their infected partner.

"The most likely interpretation of this funding is that each exposure is associated with a small probability of infection and that multiple contacts increase the probability of transmission."

In a 1987 survey of U.S. hemophilia treatment centers and physicians, 10 percent (77) of 772 spouses/sexual partners of HIV+ hemophiliac patients tested for HIV were seropositive.

Slower Progression Rate?

A section below discusses the rate of progression from HIV infection to AIDS. Studies available to date have been within the "first wave" risk groups. It is possible that the progression rate is slower for heterosexual transmission, just as the probability of infection per exposure seems to be less than for other risk groups.

Slower Circulation of Exposures

From a probability sampling of 1,034 single men age 25 to 54 in San Francisco:

No. of Sexual Partners in First Half of 1984	Homosexual Men	Bisexual Men		Heterosexual Men
		Male Partners	Female Partners	
0–1	29%	35%	83%	52%
2–9	44%	44%	15%	45%
10+	27%	21%	2%	3%

Over 20 percent of homosexual and bisexual men had more than ten partners in this half-year, compared with only 3 percent of heterosexual men.

Household Study

A study was undertaken to study the 45 spouses, 109 children, and 29 household contacts of 45 adult AIDS patients at the University of Miami School of Medicine. Enrollment in the study occurred at the time of AIDS diagnosis, with follow-up testing every 4 to 6 months for 1 to 3 years.

Of the 45 spouses, 13 were seropositive at the time of enrollment. The initial seropositive rate was 53 percent (9 of 17) for males and 14 percent (4 of 28) for females.

"The higher prevalence rate (for males) may be attributable to other factors, such as frequent other heterosexual contacts. Multiple other heterosexual partners were not noted among female spouses. When the seven male spouses with a history of other heterosexual partners were eliminated..., there was no significant difference... (20 percent for males, 14 percent for females)."

Of the 32 spouses who were seronegative at the time of enrollment, 13 seroconverted during the study.

"The length of sexual contact, number of contacts per week, and other types of sexual activity did not correlate with (HIV) antibody."

Experience varied greatly by category:

- Of the eight spouses no longer having sexual contact after enrollment, none became HIV+.
- Of the ten spouses who used barrier contraceptives after enrollment, one became HIV+.
- Of the other 14 spouses, 12 became HIV+.

Three of the eight HIV− male spouses converted to HIV+ during the study.

"In each instance, the female index patient acquired HIV infection from either blood transfusions or previous intravenous drug use. There was no identifiable risk factor for (HIV) infection in the three male spouses, nor did they have other sexual partners."

Ten of the 24 HIV− female spouses seroconverted during the study.

"We found that the seroconversion rate for male spouses (38%) was similar to that for female spouses (42%)."

Of the 109 children (age 3 months to 24 years), three had AIDS, ten had ARC, and two had LAS at the time of enrollment. All of these 15 children were less than four years old and had been born to HIV+ mothers.

"Two infants who were clinically and immunologically normal had (HIV) antibody when first tested at 3 and 6 months of age. Both became seronegative for (HIV) after 12 to 18 months of follow-up, suggesting passive transfer of maternal antibodies."

Two older children who were both sexually active young adults of Haitian ancestry who had spent about 13 years in Zaire before entering the U.S. were seropositive.

At entry to the study, 90 children were HIV−. None converted to HIV+.

Of the 29 adult household members, 20 were directly involved in the care of the AIDS patients in the household. All were HIV− at entry, and none converted to HIV+.

Link to Other Diseases

Heterosexual transmission is considered to be widespread in Africa, where there are often roughly equal numbers of males and females infected. Transmission may be higher in Africa than in developed countries because gonorrhea, genital ulcers, syphilis, and other sexually transmitted diseases are widespread. These often cause spores or ulcers in the genital epithelia and thereby make it easier for HIV to pass from one person to another.

Dr. Jay Levy, one of the two American discoverers of the AIDS virus, has been quoted as believing that the AIDS virus not only gives rise to opportunistic infections but is itself an opportunistic infection, flourishing in a body whose immune system has already been compromised by other agents, such as drugs, parasites, viruses, and malnutrition. That underlying immunodeficiency may be what the groups that have been associated with AIDS—namely, drug addicts, transfusion recipients, malnourished Africans and Haitians, and homosexuals—have in common. (Homosexuals are "immuno-compromised" as a group, exposed through multiple sexual contact to all sorts of fungal and bacterial infections routinely treated with antibiotics.)

PROGRESSION FROM INFECTION TO AIDS

Ultimate Level

No one knows what percentage of infected individuals will progress to full-blown AIDS. Early estimates were that only 20 percent would progress from HIV infection to AIDS. With the passage of time, it is now obvious that this early estimate was incorrect. Common estimates today are that 60 percent to 80 percent will progress to AIDS. Some have theorized that eventually 100 percent may progress to AIDS; some may simply have very long incubation periods of perhaps 20 years or more.

A research team in London claims to have identified genes that greatly affect the likelihood that a person infected by the AIDS virus will progress to AIDS. This work may be a basis for predicting that the ultimate progression percentage will be less than 100 percent.

Progression Studies

Data are very scarce, because it is usually not known when the virus was transmitted and when infection occurred. Some studies are available, however, to give some insight into the rates of progression from infection to AIDS:

- 83 cases of transfusion-associated AIDS diagnoses by 12/31/84 and reported to the CDC by 4/1/85 yield important data because the transmission date can be determined accurately.
- 543 subjects from groups at high risk of AIDS were studied at the University of Frankfurt from 1982 through 1985. This study is particularly valuable because it analyzed the progression through various discrete stages of the disease.
- 725 subjects in four separate HIV-infected populations in the U.S. and one in Denmark were studied for three years beginning in late 1982.
- Frozen blood samples dating back to 1978 for 719 San Francisco male homosexuals and bisexuals were available from a research project of Hepatitis B.

Initial studies have been among the highest risk groups. It may well be that different categories of transmission produce different patterns, rates of progression, and even ultimate levels of progression, to AIDS.

Progression Rates

The most significant data to date come from the Frankfurt study listed above. Two studies of these data have produced estimated progression rates from seroconversion to AIDS. The Cowell-Hoskins paper describes the Markov Chain model used in both studies. The second study was described by

Harry Panjer of the University of Waterloo in his paper dated August 24, 1987. The resulting progression rates are:

Years Since HIV Infection	Cowell-Hoskins		Panjer Cumulative
	Annual	Cumulative	
1	0.2%	0.2%	1.6%
2	2.5	2.7	8.1
3	9.9	12.4	18.8
4	12.9	23.7	31.3
5	12.7	33.4	43.7
6	12.3	41.6	55.0
7	12.5	48.8	64.6
8	12.9	55.5	72.6
9	13.2	61.4	78.9
10	13.5	66.6	83.9
11	13.8	71.2	87.8
12	14.1	75.3	90.8
13	14.3	78.8	93.1
14	14.5	81.9	94.8
15	14.7	84.6	96.1
16	14.9	86.8	97.1
17	15.1	88.8	97.8
18	15.2	90.6	98.4
19	15.4	92.0	98.8
20	15.5	93.2	99.1
21	15.7	94.3	99.4
22	15.8	95.2	99.5
23	15.9	96.0	99.6
24	16.0	96.6	99.7
25	16.1	97.2	99.8

The Panjer rates of progression are uniformly higher than the Cowell-Hoskins rates. This is generally because the Cowell-Hoskins study used the maximum length of the observation periods as an offset to the unknown time between progression and the current stage. The Panjer study was based on the average length of the observation periods.

MORTALITY

CDC Fatality Rates

United States AIDS deaths reported October 12, 1987:

Half-Year of Diagnosis	Number of Cases	Number of Known Deaths	Case-Fatality Rate
1981 (1)	86	78	91%
1981 (2)	181	164	91
1982 (1)	364	316	87
1982 (2)	641	560	87
1983 (1)	1,211	1,075	89
1983 (2)	1,580	1,354	86
1984 (1)	2,438	1,983	81
1984 (2)	3,179	2,551	80
1985 (1)	4,338	3,318	76
1985 (2)	5,437	3,825	70
1986 (1)	6,558	3,872	59
1986 (2)	7,456	3,133	42
1987 (1)	7,768	2,146	28
1987 (2)	1,652	259	16
Total	42,965	24,698	57%

Mortality Rates

From such statistics, mortality rates can be developed. An estimate was developed by Mike Cowell and Walter Hoskins as part of their August 1987 paper:

Years Since AIDS Diagnosis	Mortality Rate
1	45%
2	45
3	35
4+	25

ARC Mortality

AIDS certainly has an effect on mortality before the point of being class-ified as "CDC AIDS." There are documented deaths from ARC, and there have certainly been suicides by persons after finding out they are infected. Since these deaths don't fall under the CDC's surveillance definitions, no data are available.

DRUGS/VACCINES

Although just recently discovered, AIDS has been studied with such intensity that we know a great deal about the virus that causes it. The problems involved in HIV are so great, however, that there is little expectation of the discovery of a vaccine or a cure for AIDS at least within the next 5 years.

Plan of Attack

The virus can, hypothetically, be attacked at any of three points:

1. Kill the virus while it is still in the bloodstream,
2. Inhibit the action of the enzyme reverse transcriptase, preventing the RNA from producing its DNA copy and thus becoming part of the cell, and
3. Kill infected cells.

Human HIV antibodies do not kill the virus. The goal of a vaccine will be to cause the body to produce neutralizing antibodies that are different than those produced normally. This is not unusual; vaccines for polio and smallpox faced this obstacle.

It is unlikely that researchers will try to make a killed-virus vaccine such as is used against measles. If every last virus is not killed or weakened, such a virus might infect someone rather than protecting against the virus.

Another approach is to find a closely related, but nontoxic virus as a vaccine. Early smallpox vaccines used the cowpox viruses in this way. The goal will be to find a synthetic virus that is close enough to protect but far enough away not to cause disease.

Changing Target for Vaccines

HIV is like the flu virus—it keeps mutating into different forms. Just as an all-purpose flu vaccine does not exist, an AIDS vaccine may not be achievable.

Unlike many viruses that only have a few strains, HIV has many variants that form a continuum of related strains. An infected individual may actually harbor several strains of the virus. Although some neutralizing antibodies have been produced, all have been type-specific, neutralizing many but not all HIV variants.

AZT

Axidothymidine was formulated about 20 years ago as an anti-cancer drug. It was a failure in that role, but began being tested against AIDS in 1984.

A newer name for the drug is Retrovir (Zidovudine). The U.S. FDA authorized AZT for use in seropositive persons beginning September 15, 1987.

AZT follows the second plan of attack in the above list. The drug is a close chemical likeness of the virus' structure that forms DNA. When this likeness is supplied to an infected cell, reverse transcriptase incorporates it into a growing DNA chain. The likeness is enough different from the virus, however, that the altered DNA cannot integrate itself into the chromosomes or provide the basis for viral replication. Thus, the spread of the virus is stopped.

The cost of administering AZT is expected to be about $10,000 per year, and there appear to be serious side effects, requiring additional lab testing and blood transfusions. One serious side effect is the gradual destruction of the bone marrow.

A study of 160 AIDS and 122 ARC patients for 24 weeks revealed:

	AIDS		ARC	
	AZT	Placebo	AZT	Placebo
Probability of survival for 24 weeks	96%	76%	100%	81%
Probability of opportunistic infection in 24 weeks	36%	54%	9%	30%
Probability of death after 36 weeks (follow-up study)	6%	39%		

"The finding that AZT delayed progression to AIDS and resulted in sustained increase in level of CD4 cells in many patients with ARC suggests that AZT may be particularly beneficial to patients with less severe HIV infection."

It appears that AZT slows the progression of the disease but cannot reverse it. The impact on life insurance claims is apparently minor (simply pay the claim a little later). The impact on health and disability coverage should be major ($10,000 per year for the drug, plus a longer period of illness before death).

Ampligen

Described as "an experimental nontoxic drug," Ampligen "behaves like an artificial virus and causes the body to produce its own interferon." Announcing it in June 1987, the research team claimed the drug "showed ability both to strengthen the body's natural immune system and to suppress the

AIDS virus in patients with ARC and LAS." The U.S. FDA has approved a 6-month study of the drug.

Peptide T

The federal government has authorized tests on humans of a synthetic substance that appears to have a powerful inhibiting effect on the AIDS virus in laboratory experiments. Peptide T is a synthetic copy of a naturally oc-curring messenger chemical that permits communications between the brain and nerve cells. It appears to be able to block the virus from penetrating the cell membrane because it contains a pattern of amino acids similar to that of a piece of the AIDS virus. The hope is that Peptide T could prove effective as a vaccine against the AIDS virus.

Castanospermine

The National Cancer Institute has selected this "natural substance" drug for tests in animals. The drug is extracted from the seeds of an Australian chestnut tree. It appears to halt reproduction of the AIDS virus in the test tube.

MODELS

Micro vs. Macro

The first choice in designing a mathematical model to project AIDS claims is the level of detail to be modeled.

A "micro" model attempts to make projections from the finest level of detail, that is, the spread of the infection is modeled from assumptions about individual behavior. Example assumptions would be the frequency of dif-ferent types of exposure, the frequency and number of different partners, and probability of infection per exposure by type of exposure.

The greatest difficulty with micro models at present is that the assumptions made are largely guesswork because there is so little known about individual exposure statistics. Further, there is no way to verify modeled results, be-cause AIDS cases data generally are not available on a number and type-of-exposure basis.

Some AIDS micro models have been developed, however, and they are useful in understanding the spread of the virus. They also can be useful in helping to determine the reasonableness of assumptions for macro models.

Macro models begin by identifying a certain "at risk" population. They then assume a certain spread of the infection within that population. No specific assumptions are made about details such as the underlying number of exposures per individual and the probability of infection per exposure.

Key Assumptions

The major macro model assumptions are:

"At risk" Population: All AIDS cases are assumed to occur within this subgroup of the general population. An example group would be a percentage of males age 20–60. In determining what percentage of the general population in this category is "at risk," choices range from using a smaller percentage (the "most" at risk) with higher rates of infection to using a higher percentage with a lower infected proportion. Another consideration is whether the group should be subdivided into different at-risk populations with different assumptions. For example, males in their 20s will have a different level and pattern of infection spread than males in their 50s.

Infection Spread: The progress of the infection through the at-risk population, from the beginning of the spread through the end of the modeling period.

Progression from Infection to AIDS: The rates of conversion to AIDS (or perhaps ARC, if modeling medical or disability claims) after HIV infection. Different progression rates may be assumed for different at-risk populations, for example, heterosexual vs. homosexual groups.

AIDS Mortality: The rates of death from AIDS diagnosis.

Verification

While it can't be determined whether any model is "right," it is important to compare modeled AIDS cases and AIDS deaths with actual past experience to determine the reasonableness of results. It is important, in this process, to take account of the effects of reporting delays and underreporting.

Further "verification" of the reasonableness of modeled results can be made by comparing model projections to other commonly used projections such as the CDC projections. It must be remembered, however, that common acceptance of a particular projection doesn't make it valid—no one knows the course this epidemic will take in the future.

Insurance Models

Once a general epidemic model has been constructed, adjustments are made to fit the model to a specific insured population. Factors to consider include geographic distribution, distribution system, market, product, and underwriting standards. Because of changing forces in antiselection and underwriting, different assumptions might be used for business issued in different eras. A large part of fitting the model to an insured population is verification based on experienced AIDS claims.

Further assumptions required for insurance modes include claim size and, for medical and disability coverages, claim frequency and duration.

Trend Projection

Even model results that seem to be "verified" by reproducing historical AIDS statistics must be viewed in consideration of future changes in the course of the epidemic. Factors to consider include changes in the behavior of at-risk individuals, the possible spread of the epidemic beyond the "first wave" at-risk population, and the effects of vaccines and treatments.

LIFE COVERAGE

Net Single Premium Comparison

The following net single premium values give a rough indication of the impact of AIDS mortality on life insurance claims:

	Net Single Premium per Thousand Using	
	5.5% Interest	7.0% Interest
Newly HIV+ cohort, considering AIDS death rates* only	$573	$502
Newly diagnosed AIDS cohort, considering AIDS death rates* only	876	849
Male age 35 alb, 1980 CSO mortality	163	111
Male age 35 alb, 500% of 1980 CSO mortality	346	274
Male age 35 alb, 1975–80 Basic Table select mortality	134	86
Male age 35 alb, 500% of 1975–80 Basic Table select mortality	277	208

*These calculations use assumptions to show relative magnitudes only. Deaths and progression to AIDS are assumed to occur at the end of the year. Assumptions are:

Years Since Infection/Diagnosis	Rate of Progression from Infection to AIDS	Rate of Death from AIDS Diagnosis
1	0.2%	45%
2	3	45
3	10	35
4+	15	25

Insurance Company Experience

A 1987 survey by Mel Young (Tillinghast-Darien) of 28 U.S. reinsurers produced these results:

	AIDS Claims As a Percent of Total			
	By Number		By Amount	
	1985	1986	1985	1986
Reinsurance Accepted	0.5%	0.9%	0.9%	1.7%
Direct Issues	0.1	0.2	0.6	1.1
Total	0.3	0.4	0.8	1.5

Death Claim Projections

Models such as the one described in the Cowell-Hoskins paper generally project AIDS death claims in the mid-1990s around 15% of projected individual life claims, assuming no appreciable amount of heterosexual transmission.

Results are highly dependent on the assumptions used in the projection. Results are vastly different by age group. Further, there will be tremendous variation by company. Each company needs to model its own situation to measure the impact of AIDS on its business. For further explanation, see the "Models" section.

HEALTH COVERAGE

Cost Estimates

Data on the costs of treating AIDS patients are hard to come by. The following are some examples of estimates that have been published:

- The CDC estimated lifetime hospital costs of $147,000 per AIDS patient in a report released January 1987. The estimate was based on a lifetime use of 168 hospital days, an average survival time of about 13 months, and an $878 average charge per hospital day (including inpatient professional charges). AIDS patients average 3.2 hospitalizations per patient per 12-month period. The length of each hospital stay was generally in the 15- to 25-day range.
- A State of California study released in April 1987 estimated average billed lifetime medical costs of $70,000 per AIDS patient. This was based on an average life expectancy of 18 months after the onset of AIDS. The averages ranged from only $61,000 in San Francisco to $88,000 in Los Angeles to $102,000 in San Diego. The average

hospital inpatient length of stay was 13.6 days, ranging from only 11.4 days in San Francisco to 15.8 days in Los Angeles to 17.9 days in San Diego.
- ARC medical costs were estimated at $752 per month in the above California study. No lifetime estimate was made because they had no estimate of ARC life expectancy.

Treatment Variations

AIDS care in San Francisco is apparently about the best available, and it is achieved at about the lowest cost. A substantial support network has been developed in the homosexual community there. Nonprofit organizations provide counseling and coordination of outpatient help and care.

Hoping that the low costs in San Francisco can be repeated, the U.S. Public Health Service announced in October 1986 a $15-million program to fund AIDS home care hospice, case-management, and counseling. The program is targeted at the four areas hardest hit by the epidemic—New York, Los Angeles, San Francisco, and Miami.

AIDS patients are typically hospitalized about three times before death. In San Francisco, the average length of hospital stay has been 21 days, compared to 17 days in Los Angeles and more than 25 days in New York (1986 data).

Those treatment variations strongly support the need for managed care among AIDS patients. Prompt identification of AIDS patients for large case management can provide the most cost-efficient and -effective treatment practices.

Changing Costs

AIDS medical costs have apparently decreased over time, because of better understanding of the disease (especially its terminal nature) and because of better organization of treatment options.

AIDS drugs, however, are likely to increase costs dramatically. This is due to the costs of the drugs, the prolonged life expectancy of patients that may be achieved, and the treatment of side effects of the drugs.

Underwriting Implications

For individual and small-group policies, the underwriting implication and required actions are similar to those necessary for life insurance. Because of the time that may exist between HIV infection or even initial AIDS symptoms and substantial medical expenses, normal preexisting exclusion clauses may not be as effective in determining antiselection against health carriers.

This puts a greater burden upon medical underwriting selection in order to avoid an adverse distribution of risk. In response, companies are raising the minimum number of lives required for nonmedical issue, strengthening medical questionnaires, and requiring more attending physicians' statements. These standards may apply in large groups to COBRA extenders.

Other group underwriting standards, including excluded industries, minimum group sizes written, and prior number of carriers, should be reviewed.

DISABILITY COVERAGE

Disability AIDS Risk vs. Life AIDS Risk

A first impression is that disability insurance is relatively insulated from the AIDS risk because of the high mortality rate of AIDS patients. However, the expected number of monthly payments on a regular disability claim is not as long as one might expect:

	Average Monthly Payments for "To Age 65" Contract	
Age at Disability	30-Day Elimination Period	90-Day Elimination Period
50	11	29
40	14	36
50	15	38

With a life expectancy of about 2 years from the diagnosis of AIDS, the expected length of claim is not dissimilar between AIDS claimants and other claimants with a "To Age 65" benefit period. The primary disability insurance risk, as with life insurance, is the impact of AIDS on incidence of claims. In addition, drugs like AZT may lengthen the life expectancy of an AIDS patient, but not improve health sufficiently to allow return to work.

Group Disability Insurance

Group disability insurance has a significantly smaller AIDS risk than individual disability insurance.

- A group insurer may increase the rates of a case experiencing AIDS claims. On the other hand, the owner may choose to move the coverage to another insurer, leaving the first insurer with the AIDS claims.

- Group underwriting essentially eliminates the individual antiselection potential associated with individual insurance.
- It is easier for a group insurer to vary rates by state.
- Most group disability products integrate with Social Security, and most AIDS patients qualify for Social Security disability payments.

Individual Disability Insurance

The large majority of individual disability business involves noncancelable contracts (that is, rates and renewability guaranteed). Furthermore, noncancelable rates for most plans do not anticipate AIDS experience.

Guaranteed renewable contracts (that is, guaranteed renewability only) may increase rates, but such action can lead to high lapses of healthy insureds.

Additional risk exists from those HIV+ insureds not having progressed to AIDS to go on disability either as a result of involuntary termination of employment or voluntary termination because of fear of passing the virus to other people through normal duties of occupation. This latter situation might occur with doctors or dentists.

In states that restrict or prohibit HIV blood testing, companies should consider eliminating shorter benefit periods and requiring Social Insurance Supplement riders.

Market Trends in Individual Disability

There is a trend to writing more individual disability insurance on small group cases with a minimum of three lives. This market can reduce the antiselection risk, but some of the more liberal underwriting requirements introduced to this market during the last several years should be reviewed with respect to the increased exposure to the AIDS risk. Premiums for this market are typically discounted by 10–25 percent. This practice should be reviewed in light of the overall adequacy of the guaranteed rates.

Some companies have aggressively sought the endorsement of their products by professional associations. This has been accomplished with premium discounts and some underwriting guarantees. There is more opportunity for antiselection in the association market.

Individual Underwriting

Companies are introducing blood testing—generally for amounts ranging from $2,500 to $4,000. One company uses a $3,000 testing limit in most states but $2,000 in states with higher concentrations of AIDS victims.

Claims Experience

Companies are seeing an average number of payments on closed AIDS claims ranging from 7 to 13 months. This average reflects a high proportion of early deaths and should increase with time.

Many companies have not observed a significant percentage of AIDS claims in the first two policy years. However, the potential antiselection from HIV+ applicants extends far beyond the first two policy years.

Claim Reserves

Tabular claim reserves should be based on a different continuance table for AIDS claims. For non-AIDS claims, the recovery pattern causes increases in claim reserves with duration of claim, which is inappropriate for AIDS claims. Even though some AIDS claimants have returned to work, it may not be appropriate to release the claim reserve because the claimants will most likely go back on claim.

If the Incurred But Not Reported formula were developed by using past experience, they may not anticipate an appropriate level of AIDS claims.

Policy Reserves

Policy reserves based upon the 1964 CDT may be conservative enough to absorb the AIDS risk on business written prior to 1983 or 1984. However, the antiselection from new business, particularly in states that restrict or prohibit blood testing and its impact on reserve adequacy should be examined separately. If companies adopt the Commissioners Individual Disability "Table A" valuation basis, policy reserves on new business will decrease significantly, leaving less cushion to absorb the AIDS claims.

COWELL-HOSKINS PAPER SUMMARY

Epidemiological Model

A "macro" model is used to model the spread of the infection through an assumed "at risk" population of 750,000 IV drug users and 3 million homosexuals. An underlying theory is taken from patterns of past epidemics.

At a rate of transmission, "a," from infected to noninfected persons the spread of the infection is modeled from 0 percent of the population (before 1975) to 100 percent of the population (assumed in the year 2000). An alternative assumption stops the spread by 1997 at about two-thirds of the at-risk population being infected. The assumption in all scenarios is that 27 percent of the risk group is infected as of early 1987.

The rate of the spread of the infection is slowest at the beginning (when there are few infected persons to infect others) and at the end (when there are few noninfected persons to be infected). This produces the classical S-shaped curve that has been seen in historical epidemics.

Progression from Infection to AIDS

A Markov Chain model is used to study the progression of the disease through five stages, that is, At Risk But HIV −, HIV + But Asymptomatic, LAS, ARC, and CDC AIDS. The results of the study are shown in the "Progression from Infection to AIDS" section of this chapter.

AIDS Mortality Rates

CDC statistics are analyzed to obtain the mortality rates shown earlier in the "Mortality" section of this chapter.

Verification of the Model

Applying the assumed new infections each year to the assumed progression rates and the assumed AIDS mortality rates produced modeled AIDS deaths in each year that are similar to the CDC's past reports and projections through 1991. Indeed, the assumed infections were obtained by experimentation until this approximate reproduction of CDC AIDS deaths was achieved.

Projection Results

Three scenarios are modeled:

Year	Cumulative Infections	Cumulative Cases	Cumulative Deaths
"Infection continues to 100% of at-risk group"			
1987	919,566	46,864	30,018
1991	2,312,760	255,092	177,796
2000	3,687,388	1,937,640	1,602,979
"Infection declines to zero by 1997"			
1991	1,945,951	252,266	176,336
2000	2,485,433	1,554,819	1,316,711
"Infection stops in 1987"			
1991	919,566	236,244	167,827
2000	919,566	748,409	678,493

Implications for Life Insurance

Under simplified assumptions, projections of U.S. AIDS-related life claims through the end of this century are:

- More than $30 billion from individual business in force 12/31/86 with approximately $14 billion in claims from those already infected and another $18 billion from those that will become infected,
- $20 billion from group business in force 12/31/86, and
- $20 billion from new individual business if no testing is done.

By the mid-1990s, total individual life AIDS claims could exceed $2 billion annually or about 15 percent of projected individual life insurance claims for all U.S. companies.

TESTING

AIDS Antibody Tests

A blood test for the antibody produced in response to the HIV was implemented in March 1985 for all blood donations. The standard test protocol is so accurate that the U.S. blood supply has been considered safe since that time. Later in 1985, insurers began testing for HIV on large-risk applications. Tests available include:

ELISA (Enzyme Immunosorbent Assay): The ELISA test is designed to be sensitive because its primary purpose was to prevent contaminated blood from being used for transfusion. This test is inexpensive and is used to screen out most negative samples. The charge to an insurer for a standard protocol (see below) test is generally less than $10.

Western Blot: This test is specific for the AIDS antibody. It is expensive (about $90 per test) and is usually used to identify actual positive samples after two ELISA screens.

T-Cell Ratios: These tests look for abnormally low T-cell counts or an abnormally low ratio of T-helper cells (T4) to T-suppresser cells (T8). The cost to an insurer for this test is about $35. The test is not specific to AIDS. About 4 percent of the general population would fail a T-cell test. Worse, the test appears to miss approximately 15 percent of HIV+ cases.

Test Protocol

A negative ELISA result is interpreted as seronegative.

To be considered seropositive, the standard test protocol requires two positive (repeatedly reactive) ELISA tests followed by a positive Western

Blot test. This is one of the most accurate tests used in insurance under-writing. The number of false positives is considered to be less than one out of 100,000.

In states that prohibit the use of antibody tests (California and, temporar-ily, Wisconsin), the less sensitive and less specific tests of T-cell ratios are used to measure the immune competence of the individual.

Seroconversion Delay

Because the tests measure antibodies to HIV rather than the virus itself, they cannot detect infection until enough antibodies have been produced. Typical times between infection by the virus and seroconversion are between six to eight weeks, although reported cases have been documented as taking up to eight months. It is possible that this time delay could be longer for heterosexual transmission.

Virus Tests

Inexpensive tests may be available soon that detect the virus itself rather than antibodies to the virus. This development would eliminate the problems associated with "false negative" results because of seroconversion delay. Virus tests to date, however, are useful only before a large number of an-tibodies have been formed; thus these tests may be only a supplement to, rather than a replacement for, the antibody tests.

UNDERWRITING

Testing Limits

The largest need for AIDS exists at the issue ages that have the highest nonmedical issue limits. Most companies responded by establishing AIDS blood testing procedures at low levels in 1987.

In a May 1987 survey conducted by Denise Fagerberg (Tillinghast-Irvine), 1986 and 1987 HIV blood test limits were obtained for 21 of the 26 top producing life insurance companies in the U.S. Among the survey results were:

- Two companies had no established blood testing limit.
- Seven implemented or changed limits in 1986.
- Three had already changed limits in 1987.
- Eight were in the process of lowering the current limits within the next two months.

Although the survey showed a definite trend toward decreasing blood testing limits, there was no change in nonmedical limits from 1986 to 1987. In a few cases, the blood testing limits were lower than nonmedical limits.

The blood testing limits ranged from around $100,000 to more than $500,000, with a median of about $250,000. These results were measured in May 1987; it is important to remember that these limits are in the process of change during 1987.

Given the high cost of insuring an infected individual, it appears that testing limits could be justified at levels that apply to most new business applications.

Guidelines

AIDS testing and underwriting is an extremely sensitive issue. The "State Regulations" section that follows discusses state regulation of AIDS tests, underwriting rates, and application questions. Some basic underwriting guidelines are:

- Sexual orientation is not to be used in underwriting.
- Tests should be used on a nondiscriminating basis. Rules should apply equally to males and females and to marrieds and singles.
- There must be a valid reason for ordering the test. A routine "age and amount" basis is acceptable.
- The applicant should be notified in writing and should sign a permission slip for HIV tests.
- Strict confidentially must be maintained. The agent should not be given the test results. For employer-sponsored insurance, the employer must not be notified of the reason for the declination.
- An effort should be made to have the applicant discuss the test results with his or her physician. The applicant should be notified in writing that coverage was declined for an important reason and that you wish to correspond with the applicant's physician but need permission to release that information.

Medical Information Bureau

The MIB announced in mid-1987 that it will no longer keep records that show an applicant for insurance has tested positive for AIDS virus antibodies. Instead, information will be maintained only for nonspecific blood-test codes. MIB says that its decision is designed to assure confidentiality in AIDS testing of insurance applications.

ANTISELECTION

Transamerica Life Companies Experience

As reported by Lloyd Von Sprecken, Vice President, Underwriting:

- Business issued prior to 1980, when no one knew of AIDS risk—average AIDS death claim amount is less than one-half the average amount for claims for all causes.
- Business issued 1980 through 1983, when awareness of the disease was amongst the groups at highest risk—average AIDS death claims soared to more than five times the average size claim.
- Business issued 1984 and after, when medical directors and underwriters became aware of the mortality problems AIDS would create—average AIDS claims dropped to about three times the average.

Insurance Company Surveys

Denise Fagerberg (Tillinghast-Irvine) conducted informal surveys of life insurance company AIDS claims:

- *1985 Ordinary Life Claims*: 106 companies reported 438 AIDS claims. The average size AIDS claim was $53,600; the average size of the total claims was $7,000.
- *1986 Ordinary Life Claims:* 158 companies reported 1,913 AIDS claims. The average size AIDS claim was $44,500; the average size of the total claims was $8,400. The AIDS claims represented 0.05 percent of claims by volume and 0.2 percent by number.

STATE REGULATIONS

Examples of state AIDS regulations are given below.

NAIC Model

The NAIC released a proposed bulletin regarding "Medical/Lifestyle Questions and Underwriting Guidelines" in March 1987. Major provisions are summarized below:

- Sexual orientation may not be used in the underwriting process, and application questions may not be directed at this issue.
- Questions relating to the actual presence of AIDS or ARC are generally permissible.
- No adverse underwriting decision shall be made because the applicant has demonstrated AIDS-related concerns by seeking counseling from health care professionals.
- The use of AIDS tests must be revealed to the applicant, and written consent must be obtained. Established test protocol must be followed.
- An insurer may impose territorial rates for rating an applicant for health or life insurance if the rates are based on sound actuarial principles or are related to actual or reasonably anticipated experience.

District of Columbia

An act passed by the City Council in mid-1986 prohibits insurers from using any AIDS test in underwriting or rate-making. The act also prohibits the use of personal characteristics for the purpose of seeking to predict the risk of developing AIDS or ARC. The act does not prohibit refusing to insure or rating an applicant who has actually been diagnosed as having AIDS, providing compliance with certain procedures.

California

The use of AIDS antibody blood tests is prohibited, thus restricting testing in California to T-cell ratio tests.

Regulations prohibit refusing coverage because the applicant is homosexual or bisexual. This prohibition includes the use of special underwriting standards in certain geographical areas or occupations.

Wisconsin

An earlier prohibition against the use of HIV antibody testing was withdrawn after the state epidemiologist found that the standard test protocol "is highly predicative of a true infection with the HIV virus." The standard test protocol is still prohibited for individually underwritten group contracts, however.

Maine

Insurers must obtain written consent for AIDS testing on a approved form. All persons tested must be offered post-test counseling that provides test results, social and emotional consequences, preventive practices, and referrals for medical care and support services.

New York and Massachusetts

These insurance departments are attempting to adopt regulations prohibiting AIDS testing, at least for health insurance. Temporary court restraining orders have blocked the regulations at present.

Applications

AIDS-related questions on insurance applications must be specific. States vary widely in the questions and wording they will accept. Some states will no longer approve questions they once permitted.

Health Insurance Mandates

Some states have discussed requiring coverage of AIDS-related services, such as requiring coverage of AZT whether or not the contract has a prescription drug benefit.

AIDS Exclusions

A couple of states have regulations that would prohibit the exclusion of coverage for the treatment of AIDS or its complications. The prohibition also applies to the placing of dollar limits on the benefits payable for such illnesses (other than overall policy maximums).

MAJOR REFERENCES

1. "A Crisis in Public Health," *The Atlantic,* October 1985, pp. 18–41.
2. "AIDS = An Industry in Dire Straits," by David K. Nelson, *Best's Review,* May 1987, pp. 20–26, 130–131.
3. "AIDS: A Legislative Update," by Brice Oakley of the Blue Cross and Blue Shield Association, August 19, 1987.
4. "AIDS: Experts Predict Epidemic Will Place Heavy Burden on Society," *Los Angeles Times,* December 8, 1986.
5. "AIDS, HIV Mortality and Life Insurance," by Michael J. Cowell and Walter H. Hoskins, published by the Society of Actuaries, August 1987.
6. "AIDS: Just the Facts...From Specialists at Johns Hopkins," *Johns Hopkins Magazine,* December 1986, pp. 15–27.
7. "AIDS: Survival Analysis of Persons Testing HIV +," by Harry H. Panjer of the Department of Statistics and Actuarial Science of the University of Waterloo, August 24, 1987.
8. "AIDS Weekly Surveillance Report," from the Centers for Disease Control, October 12, 1987.
9. "An Updated Quantitative Analysis of AIDS in California," by Kenneth W. Kizer, John Rodriquez, and Gary F. McHolland, April 1987.
10. "Blood Transfusion and AIDS," by Harvey G. Klein and Harvey J. Alter, *AMA-Information of AIDS for the Practicing Physician,* Volume Two, pp. 7–10.
11. "Estimates of the Direct and Indirect Costs of Acquired Immunodeficiency Syndrome in the United States, 1985, 1986, and 1991," by Anne A. Scitovsky and Dorothy P. Rice, *Public Health Reports,* January-February 1987, Vol. 102, No. 1, pp. 5–17.
12. "Evaluation of Heterosexual Partners, Children, and Household Contacts of Adults with AIDS," *Journal of the American Medical Association,* February 6, 1987, Vol. 257, No. 5, pp. 640–644.

13. "HIV Infection: Its Impact on Mortality and Underwriting," by Jess L. Mast, *Lincoln National Reinsurance Reporter*, Issue No. 113, July 1987.

14. "Human Immunodeficiency Virus Infections among Civilian Applicants for United States Military Service, October 1985 to March 1986," *The New England Journal of Medicine*, July 16, 1987, Vol. 317, No. 3, pp. 131–136.

15. "Male-to-Female Transmission of Human Immunodeficiency Virus," *Journal of the American Medical Association*, August 14, 1987, Vol. 258, No. 6, pp. 788–790.

16. "Quarterly Figures on AIDS," a press release of the Department of Health and Social Security (U.K.), October 5, 1987.

17. "Revision of the CDC Surveillance Case Definition for Acquired Immunodeficiency Syndrome," *Morbidity and Mortality Weekly Report*, Supplement, August 14, 1987, Vol. 36, No. 1S.

18. Dr. Bill Roberts of the Home Office Reference Laboratory, phone conversations and letter.

19. "Selected Sexual Practices of San Francisco Heterosexual Men and Risk of Infection by the Human Immunodeficiency Virus (letter to the Editor)," by Warren Winkelstein, Jr., Michael Sammuel, Nancy Padian, and James Wiley of the University of California Berkeley, *Journal of the American Medical Association*, March 20, 1987, Vol. 257, No. 11, pp. 1470–1471.

20. "Sexual Practices and Risk of Infection by the Human Immunodeficiency Virus: The San Francisco Men's Health Study," *Journal of the American Medical Association*, January 16, 1987, Vol. 257, No. 3, pp. 321–325.

21. "Summary Report on AIDS in California: Quantitative Analysis," Department of Health Services, January 9, 1986.

22. The AIDS Epidemic: Looking into the 1990s," by Jeffrey E. Harris, *Technology Review*, July 1987, pp. 58–64.

23. "The AIDS Virus," by Robert C. Gallo, *Scientific American*, Volume 256, January 1987, pp. 47–56.

24. "The Efficacy of Azidothymidine (AZT) in the Treatment of Patients with AIDS and AIDS-Related Complex," *The New England Journal of Medicine*, July 23, 1987, Vol. 317, No. 4, pp. 185–191.

25. "The Projections: Guesses Based on Guesses," by Don Colburn, *The Washington Post*, June 2, 1987, p. 14.

26. "Update: 'AIDS' in Canada," The Federal Centre for AIDS, September 8, 1987.

CHAPTER 3

AIDS, HIV MORTALITY AND LIFE INSURANCE

FOREWORD

Acquired Immune Deficiency Syndrome was first identified clinically in 1981. However, it was some time before the epidemic became a serious issue for the general public.

Until about 1984, most accounts in the popular press identified the disease with its principal group of victims, young homosexual males. In the minds of most of the general public, AIDS was not a concern for them personally. This same general attitude prevailed in the life and health insurance community.

Few insurers thought in terms of the numbers of their policyholders, existing or prospective, who might be infected. Not until the Centers for Disease Control and the Surgeon General issued warnings of the epidemic spread of the disease did life and health companies begin to recognize its serious potential consequences for their operations. Most companies kept no records of AIDS-related deaths, disabilities or medical claims until 1985. It was 1986 before industry-wide attention was given to the actions that insurers needed to take in order to manage the impact that this epidemic could have on the financial soundness of their companies.

As of mid-1987, most writers of individual insurance that obtain medical evidence in their normal underwriting procedures are, within the requirements of laws and regulations in the jurisdictions in which they operate, testing applicants at specified ages and amount levels for HIV, the Human Immunodeficiency Virus. Few major life and health insurers believe that they have not paid at least one AIDS-related claim. For many, the numbers of claims so identified are amounting to several dozen and are growing monthly. The largest insurers in North America have already paid life, disability and medical claims numbering in the thousands. Estimates of the financial impact of the disease to date are still fragmentary and are a subject of this joint special report.

Estimates of AIDS-related life insurance claims based on company survey figures indicate that in 1986 alone they amounted to $100 million on individual policies and almost another $100 million under group insurance, or about 1 percent of total life claims paid. Taking into account claims prior to 1986 and AIDS-related disability income and medical insurance claims, the industry has already paid out several hundred million dollars on claims resulting from complications of HIV infection.

909

Concerned that the impact of this epidemic could overwhelm the life and health insurance industry both financially and in terms of lack of reliable data on which to act, the Society of Actuaries in April 1987 formed a Task Force on AIDS. One member of that Task Force has been heavily involved since early 1986 with regulatory proposals in his home state that would restrict insurers' prerogatives to test for HIV infection in new applicants. He felt that his research and that of his co-author might be of value to the Society in advance of the Task Force's report.

The information presented in this joint special report is the work of the two authors. The views expressed are theirs and do not necessarily reflect those of the three Sections.

It is also hoped that much of this research will be valuable to the Society's Task Force on the subject, but the data and the opinions in this joint special report should not be construed as representing the views of the Task Force or of the Society of Actuaries as a whole.

The two authors subjected their research to the review of actuaries, epidemiologists and life insurance medical directors in Canada, the U.S., Britain and other countries in Western Europe. We greatly appreciate the extensive and thorough analyses by our reviewers. We incorporated numerous changes in this final version of our report to reflect their comments and suggestions.

Like most researchers of the subject, we have amassed a vast quantity of literature in a short period. In assembling our information and in our attempts to present it in a cohesive fashion, we have been acutely aware of the need of our members for data they can put to work quickly and of the demands of our profession that our work be reliable. We recognize that we are researching on the fringes of epidemiology, where neither of us claims expertise, but we sensed that we had, nevertheless, reached a number of observations that could help ". . . substitute facts for appearances and demonstrations for impressions." Accordingly, we concluded that, on balance, our responsibilities could best be met by presenting our research at this time as an interim report of our findings.

In both gathering and analyzing our data, we relied on traditional approaches that may be loosely defined as falling within the subject matter of what were previously Parts 3, 4 and 5 of the Society's examination syllabus. In many situations, however, we resorted to approaches that are not referenced in the Society's literature. Our professional responsibility to rely on "facts" was tested in numerous instances where we needed information that existed only as fragmentary reports from items in the written or spoken news media. This was particularly problematic in the section of our report on the extent of the spread of HIV infection in the general population and in the insured population, and our estimates of its financial impact on insurance operations.

Our general approach was to validate as much of our information as possible with hard data from reliable sources. This was not always possible, and our projections must be interpreted in light of the paucity of data currently available.

Throughout this process, we were keenly aware that we would be presenting our findings long before all the "facts" became available. Indeed, we recognized that any report on this subject that waited for all the available facts would not be written in time for meaningful action to be taken. We incorporated some information in our report that did not become available until a few days before we went to press. This information was significant enough that we felt it should be included even though it could not all be fully validated.

Although the focus of this report is on life insurance, we believe that much of our research is also applicable to disability income and medical care coverages. Indeed, the part of our analysis that projects the progression of HIV infection through its various stages may be especially helpful to researchers attempting to project the financial impact of complications of HIV infection on disabilities and medical care costs.

Before proceeding into the body of our report, the reader might reflect on the efforts of an earlier researcher faced with the challenge of developing reliable information from fragmentary sources. In 1662, John Graunt constructed the first English life table from the crude records of births and deaths that he found in parish churches—the only data then available.

Reviewing that work at the tercentenary of its publication, a modern epidemiologist observed:

"Graunt did not wait for better statistics; he did what he could with what was available to him. And by so doing, he also produced a much stronger case for supplying better data."[*]

The authors will be satisfied if this joint special report is received in the spirit of the pragmatic ideals ascribed to John Graunt.

---

[*]Glass, David V., cited in Lilienfeld, Abraham M., *Foundations of Epidemiology*, New York, Oxford University Press, 1976, p. 23.

ACKNOWLEDGMENTS

The authors are indebted to Warren L. Kleinsasser, M.D. for bringing the Frankfurt Study to our attention and to his numerous ALIMDA colleagues for their helpful suggestions; to Daniel F. Case for his translation of the Frankfurt Study from the original German and his many draft reviews and suggestions including alternative models; to the Society of Actuaries and three sponsoring Sections for underwriting the cost of timely distribution; and to all the many other reviewers and contributors too numerous to mention.

We were especially encouraged by all those who told us that earlier drafts of this report had already helped them make further progress in unraveling the puzzle of AIDS and HIV infection. This puzzle can only be solved by many timely contributions, both in terms of independent original ideas and progressive cumulative refinements of existing ideas.

Finally, we wish to thank Carol J. Abraham, our untiring assistant, without whose help this report would not have been available on such a timely basis.

To all those who gave assistance and encouragement on this report, we express our appreciation.

I. AIDS AND LIFE INSURANCE

MICHAEL J. COWELL

1. ABSTRACT

Since its clinical identification in 1981, the presence of the Human Immunodeficiency Virus (HIV) [1] and its progression to Acquired Immune Deficiency Syndrome (AIDS) and resultant death have become a matter of worldwide concern. In addition to the 38,000 cases of AIDS reported in the U.S. through mid-July 1987, of which 22,000 have already resulted in death, the Centers for Disease Control (CDC) of the U.S. Public Health Service estimate that as many as 1.5 million Americans may be infected with HIV. AIDS cases in Canada have just passed the 1,000 mark, with half of the victims already dead. HIV infection appears to be at a considerably lower per-capita level in Canada than in the U.S.

The purposes of this report are to estimate the spread of HIV infection in the insured populations of the U.S. and Canada; to predict the mortality of those who test positive for HIV; to discuss the implications of immune deficiency disease for life insurance underwriting and pricing; and to project its long-term impact on insurance company solvency.

Estimates vary widely as to the percentages of HIV cases that will progress through stages of immune deficiency disease to AIDs-related complex (ARC) or fully developed AIDS. The longer a population of HIV-infected subjects is studied, the higher are the estimates of ultimate progression to AIDS. Increasingly, public health authorities are predicting that the vast majority of all HIV-infected subjects will progress to a serious immune impairment and eventually succumb to its complications.

Longevity prospects of HIV-infected populations studied to date are not encouraging. Mortality patterns of such populations bear no meaningful relationship to standard mortality in the general population nor to that of insured lives. From the time that fully developed AIDS is diagnosed, life expectancy is about 2.1 years. Mortality takes an extremely high toll, leaving fewer than one survivor in twenty after 8 years.

Life and health insurers in Canada and the U.S. are experiencing significant numbers of AIDS-related claims. Preliminary analysis of these claims suggests that the prevalence of HIV infection among the insured population is about half the rate in the general population, with infection among group insureds higher than among individual insureds. For those who are HIV-infected, the average amount of individual life insurance is substantially larger than the industry average. The disparity for group life insurance is less pronounced.

Under the assumption that those covered by life insurance include no "hard core" intravenous (IV) drug abusers at risk of AIDS, we estimate that at year-end 1986 approximately $20 billion of individual and $15 billion of group life insurance in the U.S. are on the lives of HIV-infected subjects. We project that by the year 2000, individually insured claims could amount to more than $30 billion, with about $14 billion coming from insurance on those already infected and another $18 billion from new infections on existing insureds.

Because there is less information currently available on AIDS claims under group than under individual life insurance, our estimates for the group line are not as detailed; the limited information we have suggests the overall mortality patterns will not differ significantly.

At the levels projected, AIDS-related deaths from existing business in force could alone exceed 10 percent of the life insurance industry's total claims for individual and group coverages by the mid-1990s. The cost of not screening new applicants for individual life insurance for HIV infection could amount to many additional billions in claims by the end of the century.

2. NATURE OF THE EPIDEMIC — SPREAD OF INFECTION

2.1. Introduction

Acquired immune deficiency disease is an epidemic different from any that has affected humans in recorded medical history. All previously reported epidemics were relatively short in duration — weeks or, at most, months — from infection to manifestation.

Epidemics within living memory or recent history — influenza, cholera, bubonic plague — spread rapidly, with a large percentage of the population either immune or dead within a relatively short period. The Black Death is believed to have killed as much as one-quarter of Europe's population in the 14th century. In that sense it was a much greater disaster than what we are now facing, yet in some respects it fitted the classic epidemiological mold more closely than does AIDS. In more recent memory, the influenza epidemic of 1918–1919 claimed almost 550,000 victims in the U.S and an estimated 20 million worldwide, but ran its entire course in less than a year.

Acquired immune deficiency disease has, in contrast, an unusually long latency period.

It is estimated that after 5 years from HIV infection, approximately 15 percent will reach full clinical AIDS. Data from the CDC and from other studies suggest that higher percentages of an HIV-infected population will progress to AIDS in the second five years following infection.

Prevailing medical thinking now is that the vast majority of those infected with HIV will eventually incur a serious impairment to their immune system and die prematurely from its complications. The emphasis is on *prevailing* medical thinking, because knowledge about HIV infection is so new, and constantly undergoing change, that researchers are not of one mind on this or on many other aspects of the disease.

Analysis of the progression of HIV infection and its ultimate mortality toll produces estimates of survival that we believe are reliable for insurance purposes. In other words, we believe that the mortality pattern for a given cohort of newly infected subjects can be predicted with reasonable certainty. This information is helpful in evaluating the financial consequences of not screening out cohorts of subjects who are HIV-infected at the time they apply for insurance, but who could have been detected if such screening had been part of the underwriting process.

What we do not know with any degree of certainty is the impact on financial operations of the disease in existing insureds who are already HIV-infected, including those who were HIV-infected at the time they applied for amounts of insurance below the company's testing level, in existing insureds who may still become infected, and in new insureds who become infected after testing negative at time of issue.

The impact of existing insureds who are already HIV-infected depends primarily on the percentage who are HIV-infected and when they became infected. Estimates from the Surgeon General and the CDC are that between one and one-and-a-half million Americans would test HIV-positive [2]. This translates to an overall population average of 8 per 1,000 in the population age 20 and above. Within the age group 20–59, the most important range for insurance purposes, the rate may be as high as 18 per 1,000 men, but is probably less than 1 per 1,000 women. Above age 60, however, infection rates are so low that they may be ignored for practical purposes.

The estimated level of HIV infection in Canada is believed to be still quite low, perhaps as few as 50,000 to 75,000 as of early 1987. With over 90 percent of all AIDS cases in Canada confined to males, this translates to an infection rate of 10 or fewer per 1,000 men aged 20–59. Among Canadian women, the infection rate is still so low as to be barely measurable in the overall population.

2.2. HIV Infection — An Epidemiological Puzzle

Because the epidemiology of acquired immune deficiency disease is so different from that of any other on record, it requires particularly careful analysis.

With a new strain of influenza, for example, symptoms are quickly manifested, and its overall effects soon become measurable. In contrast, HIV infection by itself gives its victims no warning signs. The long latency period before symptoms of the disease become apparent means that large numbers of the population can become infected before the impact of their disabilities and deaths is known.

Identifying the numbers of the population infected by such a "silent" disease is the most difficult phase of this epidemiological puzzle. Yet it is critical that we obtain as accurate a measure as possible of the course of HIV infection in order to make credible estimates of its financial impact. The frustration of researchers of this epidemic is that the most important part of the puzzle is the most unyielding to attempts to unravel it.

We are navigating through a thick fog with only the crudest of instruments to plot our current position, let alone our course.

Our approach to this problem was to start with the best estimates of the Surgeon General and the CDC and to fit these data to a mathematical model based on a plausible rationale. We then validated the results of the modeling process against reported numbers of AIDS cases and deaths. We constructed our model as a series of fairly simple processes, each one of which may be separately refined as more information becomes available.

We recognize that the ultimate goal is to obtain credible numbers from which to project the financial impact of the epidemic on the insurance industry. However, at this stage of our analysis, we place more importance on validating the reasonableness of the processes of our model than on the absolute numbers that it generates.

Also, it cannot be emphasized too strongly that we are attempting to use mathematical models developed by researchers on the experience of "traditional" epidemics. We are encouraged by the closeness of fit of our models to actual numbers of AIDS cases and deaths reported to the CDC. However, like most other projections in this report, results based on fitting a totally different kind of epidemic to classical models must be interpreted cautiously.

2.3. Epidemiological Models — "Micro" and "Macro"

Epidemiologists use a variety of mathematical models to simulate the spread of an infectious disease throughout a population. The models of the "micro" variety are based on detailed assumptions about such factors as frequency of activities that expose people to infection, probabilities of transmission from an infected to an uninfected person, and average duration of infectiousness. A "micro" model of HIV transmission based on numbers of partners in various kinds of sexual activity is described by Knox [3].

Models at the other end of the spectrum make broad "macro" assumptions as to population aggregates, without attempting to simulate transmission on a person-by-person basis. Between these two extremes, some approaches model the spread of the disease within stratified subgroups of the population and among such groups.

The principal focus of this report is the impact of the disease not on individuals but on the insured population in the aggregate and, as a consequence, on the solvency of the insurance industry. Thus, we chose a model of the "macro" form. We did review the work of researchers whose models track the epidemic by stratifying the population into groups according to degree of risk. We expect that further analysis of the spread of infection will depend on such models that address the process of transmission of the disease within and among significant subpopulations and also from subject to subject.

The underlying theory of the form of epidemiological model we used [4] is that the incidence of new infection at any time (t) is proportional to the product of the prevalence (p_t) of the infection in the population and the portion ($1 - p_t$) of the population uninfected, all reduced by the portion of the infected population that dies (q_t). The product of p_t and $1 - p_t$ is assumed to be related to the incidence of new infection by an infection factor that may be expressed as a constant (α) over time or in a more generalized form (α_t) as a function of time also. In the infinitesimal calculus mode, the incidence of new infection may thus be expressed as:

$$\frac{dp_t}{dt} = \alpha_t \cdot p_t \cdot (1 - p_t) - q_t \tag{1}$$

In its simpler form, where the infection factor is assumed to be a constant (α) over time and where the mortality term (q_t) is assumed to be sufficiently small to be treated separately, this formulation leads to the following expression for the prevalence of infection:

$$p_t = (1 + \alpha^{-\alpha't})^{-1} \qquad [2]$$

This formula produces the classical S-curve of the progress of an epidemic throughout a population, which is identified in Chart 1 as "theoretical" more for illustrative purposes than as necessarily representative of the likely future course of the disease. Estimates of the parameters for this equation, and its development in discrete form, more useful for period-by-period calculations where the infection factor (α_t) is assumed to vary over time, are contained in Appendix 1.

CHART 1

Epidemiological Model of HIV Spread

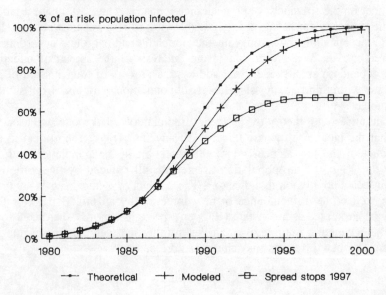

% of at risk population infected

Theoretical   Modeled   Spread stops 1997

2.4. How Large Are the Groups "At Risk"?

The next step was to fit what we know about the actual spread of infection to a "macro" model based on a classical S-curve as described above.

CDC data indicate that in the U.S., 17 percent of reported AIDS cases among adults are in the IV-drug-abusing population and 73 percent are in the male homosexual and bisexual populations. Canada, in contrast, has a minuscule IV drug abuse problem. The Canadian Laboratory Centre for Disease Control (LCDC) reports that almost 83 percent of its AIDS victims are male homosexuals and bisexuals.

The National Academy of Sciences (NAS) estimates that the U.S. has a "hard core" IV-drug-abusing population numbering about 750,000. Male homosexuals in the U.S. are estimated to number 3 percent of the adult population, or about 2.5 million. NAS also estimates that another 2.5 million U.S. men are bisexual during some part of their lives [5].

To date, we have no comparable estimates of such populations in Canada; the geographic distribution of Canada's 1,000 or so AIDS cases suggests that they are concentrated almost entirely among the male homosexual communities of Montreal, Toronto and Vancouver.

We took the NAS figure of 750,000 IV drug abusers and assumed that the highest at-risk group in the male homosexual and bisexual community in the U.S. numbers at least 3 million. This would mean that if the disease had progressed uniformly throughout these two highest at-risk populations — and CDC information suggests that it has — then approximately 30 percent of each group would be HIV-infected as of early 1987.

Estimates of the extent of infection in Canada are still sketchy, but if Canada has a similar representation of homosexuals in its male population as the U.S., then the corresponding figure for that group would be 350,000, with between 15 percent and 20 percent infected.

Recent studies of IV-drug-abusing populations in New York City and of male homosexual communities in New York and San Francisco show a prevalence of HIV infection ranging from a low of less than 20 percent to a high of 70% or more. Especially among homosexuals, infection rates are believed to be lower in communities further away from the principal concentrations of these populations. Data from the San Francisco studies show that infection rates among male homosexuals rise rapidly with increases in the numbers of reported partners [6].

We also know from the SFCC/CDC Study discussed in Section 3.4 that HIV infection was already established in San Francisco's male homosexual community by 1978, at which time it is estimated to have been 4 percent.

AIDS cases and deaths in the U.S. may be closely replicated under the assumption that HIV entered both the male homosexual and the IV-drug-abusing populations in 1975 and that it progressed along the modeled S-curve shown in Chart 1 to the point that by early 1987 it had infected approximately 27 percent of each population. The resulting numbers are an HIV-infected population of about 1 million. When taken together with independent estimates of fewer than 100,000 HIV-infected women — believed to be mostly partners of IV-drug-abusing men or of male bisexuals — and with a small but as yet unestimated number of infected heterosexuals, these numbers aggregate reasonably well to overall estimates by CDC and the Surgeon General of the extent of the infection in the U.S. population.

These population aggregates were used solely for purpose of validating the assumptions in the model. In reducing these numbers to the individually insured population, we excluded IV drug abusers and females.

3. MORTALITY OF AN HIV-INFECTED POPULATION

3.1. Introduction

The principal focus of this analysis, and a significant part of this entire report, is to determine the progression from HIV infection to AIDS.

Several reports have been published on the incidence of AIDS in HIV-infected populations. Three studies were identified that provide the most reliable data with respect to the progression to AIDS in persons who tested positive for HIV but were otherwise asymptomatic or who had progressed to more serious stages of the disease. The first of these studies also provides reliable data on the conversion to HIV of persons at high risk. The other two studies corroborate the patterns of progression observed from the first.

3.2. The Frankfurt Study

The major source of data for this report is the study by the Center for Internal Medicine of the University of Frankfurt, West Germany. It observed subjects in groups at high risk of AIDS through various stages in the progression from apparent good health to death primarily caused by AIDS [7].

The Frankfurt Study is the first published analysis of progression from HIV-infected status in otherwise asymptomatic subjects, through the more serious stages of immune system impairment, all the way to fully developed AIDS and resulting death.

The study uses five classifications, or stages, to identify progression from healthy status to AIDS. This approach closely follows what has been identified as the "Walter Reed Staging Method" [8]:

- Healthy persons at risk for HIV infection, but testing negative
- Otherwise asymptomatic persons testing HIV positive (HIV +)
- Patients with HIV infection and lymphadenopathy syndrome (LAS), together with moderate cellular immune deficiency
- Patients with HIV infection and LAS, together with severe cellular immune deficiency (AIDS-Related Complex, or ARC, as defined by CDC)
- Patients with AIDS as currently defined by CDC.

The sixth and final stage is death.

The Frankfurt Study yields information more valuable than that provided by other studies in one major respect. Rather than studying just the single rate of progression from HIV infection to AIDS, it analyzed the progression of impairment to the immune system through these various stages to AIDS and ultimate death in terms of a number of discrete steps. In this respect, it presents a particularly valuable link previously missing from the literature.

The Frankfurt Study observed 543 subjects from groups at high risk of AIDS from 1982 through 1985; 377 of the subjects were HIV-infected on entry into the study. A total of 307 subjects were observed from 3 months to as long as 3 years; 259 of these were HIV-infected on entry into the study.

A detailed analysis of the Frankfurt Study is presented in the Actuarial Note, *"HIV Mortality,"* which is part II of this chapter.

3.3. National Cancer Institute (NCI) Study*

The second report presented the results of a prospective study of the 3-year incidence of AIDS in four separate HIV-infected populations in the U.S. and of one in Denmark [9].

The NCI Study was based on clinical observation of 725 persons at high risk of AIDS who had enrolled before October 1982 in cohort studies of male homosexuals in Manhattan, NY, Washington, D.C., and Copenhagen, Denmark, of IV drug abusers in Queens, NY, and of hemophiliacs in Hershey, PA.

A total of 276 of the subjects were either HIV-infected at enrollment or developed the antibody during the course of the study. The 3-year incidence

*This study was not cited as having NCI sponsorship; it is identified here as the NCI study for convenient reference since its four principal authors are associated with that institution.

of AIDS ranged from a high of 34.2 percent in the cohort of Manhattan homosexuals, to a low of 8.0 percent in the Copenhagen homosexuals. These results gave rise to estimates during 1986 that perhaps 25 percent, or at most 35 percent of HIV-infected subjects would progress to AIDS.

The results from the NCI Study tend to corroborate those in the Frankfurt Study. However, it should be noted that the observed conversions in the NCI Study, all the way from HIV infection to AIDS without reference to intermediate stages of the disease, suggested faster progressions than those used in the model from the Frankfurt Study.

3.4. San Francisco City Clinic/CDC Study

A study by the CDC in cooperation with the San Francisco City Clinic (SFCC) was begun in 1978 as a research project on Hepatitis B [10]. Once AIDS was identified, the CDC and the SFCC recognized that the stored, frozen blood samples collected since 1978 on 6,700 male homosexuals and bisexuals could yield information about HIV infections and AIDS. Stored blood samples of two groups of volunteers showed that 4 percent were HIV positive as early as 1978. In one group, 19 percent had progressed to AIDS by 1985; in the other, 29 percent had progressed to AIDS and another 42 percent to ARC. Analysis of the SFCC/CDC data shows 14–15 percent of HIV subjects developing AIDS within 5 years after infection, 22–25 percent after 6 years, and 32–36 percent after 7 years.

The more rapid progression to AIDS after 5 years from infection has led the SFCC study director to observe that there is an increased risk of AIDS in the second 5 years.

More recently, both the CDC and the Surgeon General have supported what is coming to be viewed as a prevailing medical view, namely, that the vast majority of HIV-infected subjects will eventually progress to a more serious stage of the disease and succumb to its complications.

3.5. AIDS Cases and Deaths

Weekly reports from the CDC are the principal source of data on aggregate AIDS cases and deaths. Through June 29, 1987, the CDC reported a total of 37,867 cases of AIDS in the U.S., of which 21,776 had resulted in death [11].

The Laboratory Centre for Disease Control in Ottawa reported 1,001 cases of AIDS in Canada as of May 4, 1987, of which 503 had resulted in death [12].

CDC data are in the form of AIDS case fatality rates (ratio of known AIDS deaths to reported AIDS cases) by half-year of AIDS diagnosis. We derived annual AIDS mortality rates by assuming that CDC AIDS case fatality rates fully represent the underlying cumulative AIDS mortality. These annual AIDS mortality rates are 45 percent in the first and second years since progression to AIDS, 35 percent in the third year, and 25 percent thereafter. These rates produce a life expectancy of about 2.1 years from progression to AIDS and an 8-year AIDS survival rate of 4.7 percent.

Chart 2 compares CDC AIDS case fatality rates to modeled cumulative AIDS mortality for 8½ years. As nearly as can be determined from CDC AIDS Weekly Surveillance Reports, the case fatality rates for durations 7 years through 8½ or more years are based on only 16, 9, 2, and 6 deaths, respectively.

Canadian data are not yet presented by time since progression to AIDS. Although the incidence of HIV infection appears to be much lower in Canada, there is no reason to believe that AIDS mortality rates in the infected population are any different from those in the U.S.

A detailed analysis of the CDC data is presented in *"HIV Mortality,"* part II of this chapter.

3.6. HIV Mortality Model Based on Frankfurt and CDC Data

It might have been desirable to study the mortality of HIV-infected persons directly from the Frankfurt HIV progression rates and AIDS mortality rates based on CDC data. However, because of the multiple stages of the disease and the high periodic probabilities of progression from HIV to AIDS and resulting death, traditional actuarial approaches based on single decrement table formulae to study the mortality of an impaired group were of limited value in this analysis. A different approach was needed.

A Markov Chain model was used to study HIV mortality based on Frankfurt and CDC data. This model simulates the progression of a group of newly infected subjects through the stages of HIV disease to AIDS and death. The process is not unlike that of creating a life, or multiple decrement, table from a limited period of observation, by joining together the experience of successive cohorts, even though no one cohort was observed to progress through the entire range of ages or decrements represented in the table.

In the Frankfurt Study, a sufficient number progressed from HIV infection or from a more serious stage of the disease to one or more successively

CHART 2

Cumulative AIDS Mortality

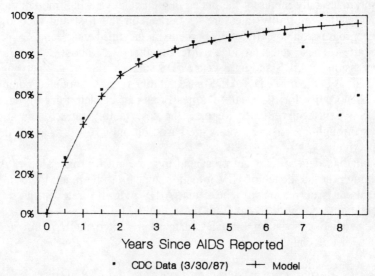

CDC Data (3/30/87)   —+— Model

Model Is 45%, 45%, 35%, 25% thereafter

worse stages, or to death, to enable the results from one stage progression to the next to be linked together.

A detailed description of development and results of this model is presented in *"HIV Mortality,"* part II of this chapter.

The results of this modeling process are illustrated in Chart 3, which shows the percentage of an HIV cohort by stage and duration since infection. For an explanation of the legend, see the description of the "The Walter Reed Staging method" in Section 3.2 (The Frankfurt Study).

For illustrative purposes only, we calculated the level equivalent multiple of 1980 CSO Basic Male Nonsmoker Table rates that produces the same life expectancy as that of a 35-year-old cohort of newly infected males. To match the same life expectancy as produced by projecting Frankfurt and CDC data, mortality would have to be elevated to over 5,100 percent of 1980 CSO Basic rates. In other words, the level of HIV mortality at this age is over

CHART 3

Progression of HIV Infection

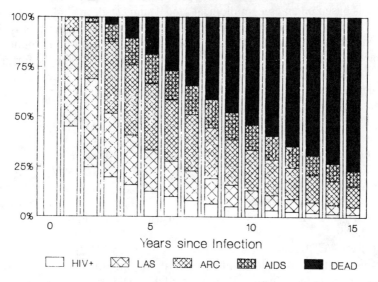

Years since Infection

☐ HIV+ ◫ LAS ▨ ARC ▦ AIDS ■ DEAD

10 times higher than the upper limit of what are considered by most insurers to be marginally acceptable substandard life insurance risks (500 percent).

As this analysis shows, the mortality patterns of an HIV-infected cohort are so different from those of insurable lives that comparisons to multiples of standard life mortality may result in misleading conclusions. This subject is addressed further in Sections 3.7 and 4.2.

Further discussion of comparisons to standard is presented in *"HIV Mortality,"* part II of this chapter.

3.7. Summary of All Studies

Progression from HIV infection to AIDS as described in the various studies and models is summarized in Chart 4. The Frankfurt and SFCC/CDC models are compared to the New York City, D.C., and Danish data from the NCI Study. While these patterns are not identical, the results are quite consistent in light of the different approaches used, the non-uniformity of identifying the time of infection, and the diversity of subjects studied.

Chart 4 also shows a fit of a Weibull function to the SFCC/CDC progression rates through the first seven years after infection. This progression pattern is based on an epidemiological model suggested, in slightly modified forms, by Brookmeyer and Gail [13], Elandt-Johnson and Johnson [14], Lui [15], and May and Anderson [16]. Referred to as a Weibull distribution, it assumes that the probability per unit time of progression to AIDS, for those HIV-infected subjects who ultimately reach that stage, increases with time (t) since infection. Under this assumption, the cumulative probability of progressing to AIDS by time t is expressed as:

$$F(t) = 1 - e^{-g \cdot t^2} \quad [3]$$

In its more general form, the Weibull function is expressed as:

$$F(t) = 1 - e^{-g \cdot t^C} \quad [4]$$

We found that the formula fitted SFCC/CDC progression rates quite closely for seven years with $c = 2$. The Weibull distribution in Chart 4 uses a value of $g = 0.009$.

The SFCC/CDC data measure progression from HIV infection to AIDS as a single-step progression without identifying intermediate stages of the disease. The application of a Weibull model to such rates results in a progression to AIDS that is initially slower than that from a model based on multiple step progressions from HIV infection to AIDS such as the Frankfurt Study.

The SFCC/CDC model was produced by projecting SFCC/CDC progression rates such that 82 percent of an infected cohort progresses to AIDS within 15 years of infection, as in the Frankfurt model. Beyond that stage, so few of an initial cohort of HIV-infected subjects are alive that the financial impact is quite insensitive to the minor differences among the various projections.

Even in the early years after infection, the differences between the faster progressions under the Frankfurt model and the slower progressions under the SFCC/CDC model are far less significant than they may appear from inspection of Chart 4.

Under the Frankfurt model, 77 percent of HIV-infected subjects will have progressed to a more serious stage of the disease or all the way to AIDS and will have died within 15 years of infection. Males who become HIV-infected at age 35, for example, can anticipate a life expectancy of almost

CHART 4

Progression from HIV Infection to AIDS

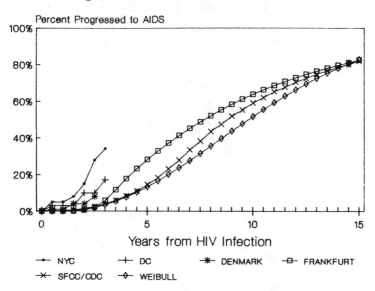

11 years from time of infection compared to almost 43 years for healthy uninfected men the same age. Looked at another way, infection with HIV has the same effect on a 35-year-old as advancing by almost 40 years along the mortality scale.

Under the SFCC/CDC model, 74 percent of HIV-infected subjects will have progressed to AIDS and died within 15 years of infection. Under these assumptions, males who become HIV-infected at age 35, for example, can anticipate a life expectancy of approximately 12 years from time of infection.

The progression rates from the Frankfurt and SFCC/CDC models may be thought of as the upper and lower bounds of a realistic set of progression rates developed from the most detailed and the longest duration of studies available. Notwithstanding the qualifications made earlier about modeling the progression of this epidemic, the available data clearly support prevailing medical opinion that longevity prospects of HIV-infected subjects are not encouraging.

As Chart 5 illustrates, the mortality of such populations rises steeply following infection. Because of the unusually high number of early deaths, mortality of an HIV-infected population cannot be expressed in multiples of standard that are meaningful in a life insurance underwriting context.

CHART 5

Annual Mortality Rates
HIV Infection at Age 35

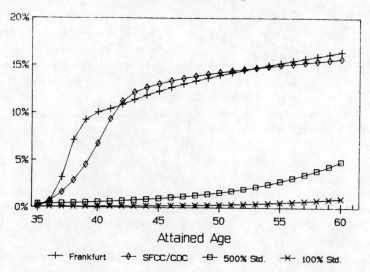

Both models assume that the mortality patterns observed in the studied populations persist, that is, that no major breakthroughs in medical technology will occur to arrest or control the progression of the disease in HIV-infected subjects or to extend the life of those who progress to AIDS. Recent experimentation with AZT and other "retroviral" drugs has offered hope for some limited progress in delaying death once the disease has progressed to full clinical AIDS. However, it will require documentation of significant success with such treatment before its impact can be translated into additional life expectancy.

Early estimates by CDC and others were that 10–20 percent of otherwise asymptomatic HIV-infected subjects would eventually progress to AIDS. Later, as the numbers of AIDS cases and related deaths grew, this estimate was revised upward closer to 50 percent. In a recent interview, the Surgeon General of the U.S. suggested that the ultimate progression rate might be closer to 100 percent. His view is consistent with the results suggested by projections based on the Frankfurt and SFCC/CDC data.

One final comment on these projections is that they reflect almost exclusively the progression of the disease and its ultimate death toll among the highest risk groups studied, namely, male homosexuals and IV drug abusers. There are some suggestions in the literature to the effect that the immune systems of these two groups were already seriously compromised before the introduction of the AIDS virus to Europe and North America. Increasingly, however, medical observers appear to be reaching the conclusion that the only factor of significance in the progress of the disease from HIV infection to AIDS is time.

Until much more is known about the spread of the disease in the healthy non-IV-drug-abusing heterosexual population, it remains somewhat conjectural whether this group will necessarily follow the same patterns of disease progression and mortality observed among the two highest-risk groups. In the absence of such data, we made no assumptions as to the extent of the spread of the disease beyond the existing groups considered to be at high risk of infection. To this extent, our estimates of AIDS deaths and claims costs are probably understated. However, a model developed by Harris [17] of HIV spread in the heterosexual population tends to confirm that it will be quite small relative to the high-risk groups for at least several years.

4. IMPLICATIONS FOR LIFE INSURANCE

4.1. Preliminary Observations

In a relatively free market environment, several conditions must exist for a risk to be insurable. Three of these conditions are fundamental to the actuarial soundness of an insurance plan. First, the risk must exist in sufficiently large numbers in the population to enable underwriters to establish a class in which each member has similar *a priori* likelihood of incurring a claim. Second, the likelihood of any one member incurring a claim must be random and relatively small within an initial time period, so that premium levels can be kept to a small fraction of the amount insured. Third, members of the insured class should have no influence over the occurrence of a claim.

Life insurance meets the first two conditions and sufficiently meets the third for practical purposes. Underwriters apply selection criteria to attempt to keep death claims among new entrants to the risk pool within a fairly narrow band around "standard" or "expected" mortality. Even up to the higher ages at which life insurance is sold, standard mortality is still in the range of 2 to 3 percent a year. For example, even as high as age 60, the 1980 CSO Basic Male Nonsmoker mortality is less than 1 percent a year.*

4.2. Underwriting and Pricing

Most major direct writers of life insurance that use a selection process are able to justify including a high percentage of all applicants in their "standard" class. For a combination of economic, marketing and other practical reasons, this may mean including some risks that are underwritten at 125–150 percent of standard. Most writers, however, will treat as "substandard" risks that they expect will incur claims two or more times standard. Even at three or four multiples of standard, mortality associated with certain coronary diseases, for example, rates may still be low enough to meet the insuring criteria. Even at 500 percent of standard, for example, the 1980 CSO Basic Nonsmoker mortality is less than 1 percent a year at age 45.†

In the vicinity of 400–500 percent of standard mortality, typified by more severe coronary cases, few direct writers issue enough cases to achieve an adequate spread of risk. Coverage at these levels of mortality is typically made available through reinsurance arrangements with specialty companies. Above these levels, the probability of claim becomes so high that the premiums required would attract few buyers and the potential for antiselection would be severe. While insurance arrangements are sometimes made even beyond these extremely high multiples of standard, they often take on characteristics more usually associated with catastrophe risks and frequently involve serious limitations on benefit levels during the early years of such coverage.

As stated in Sections 3.6 and 3.7, the mortality patterns of populations that test positive for HIV bear no meaningful relationship to multiples of standard mortality in the general population or of insured life mortality.

---

*1980 CSO Basic Male Nonsmoker Table: $1000 \times q_{60} = 9.76$.
†1980 CSO Basic Male Nonsmoker Table: $1000 \times q_{45} = 1.96$.

On the basis of these criteria and the likelihood that an extremely high percentage of HIV-infected subjects will progress to AIDS, we conclude that such subjects are not insurable for individually underwritten coverage in the normal context that such coverage is understood. We recognize that any conclusion leaving underwriters no alternative but outright declination will appear harsh. We are hopeful that others will, in due course, find more options. Our solution is the only course of action we can honestly recommend as being responsible in light of the information we have analyzed.

Readers interested in a more thorough treatment of theory of insurability in general, and of HIV-infected subjects in particular, may wish to refer to the technical paper by Hammond and Shapiro [18].

The issue of HIV infection as it affects pricing is similar in some respects to dealing with any other impairment. A company sets its underwriting guidelines in an attempt to screen for the impairment above a certain amount limit. These limits are established so that the cost of underwriting is more than offset by the mortality "saved" by not issuing at standard rates.

Depending on the severity of the impairment, the insurer may offer the applicant insurance at rates that reflect the expected higher mortality of the specific impairment. If the expected mortality is so high that the company cannot afford to bear the risk, it may decline the case outright or seek specialty reinsurance facilities.

The process is not dissimilar in underwriting for HIV infection, although the outcome will almost certainly be to decline known HIV-infected applicants. On the basis of the more optimistic life expectancy projections of the SFCC/CDC model described in Section 3.4, the discounted present value of AIDS-related claims in a cohort of newly infected individuals at 6 percent is $515 per $1,000 of potential insurance. On the basis of the faster progression to AIDS modeled from the Frankfurt Study described in Section 3.6, this value is $545. We believe that this clearly fits the situation described earlier, namely, that the required premium would attract few buyers and the potential for antiselection would be severe.

Given this information and on the basis of estimates of HIV infection at different ages, companies can calculate the mortality saved by screening for HIV infection at various amount thresholds. The costs of screening can be evaluated against the benefit of saving claims with a present value of more than $500 per $1,000 of insurance that would presumably be declined.

By way of a simplified example, if the HIV infection rate among all males age 20–59 applying for life insurance is 1 percent, then testing *all* such applicants could be justified at a cost of less than $5 per $1,000. At a cost of less than $50 for a three-test procedure of two ELISA tests followed by a Western Blot test, an insurer might justify HIV screening for amounts of insurance as low as $10,000. This three-test procedure has been reported to have only one false positive per 1,000 positive tests.

The decision as to testing level will, of course, depend on each insurer's specific situation, taking into account the additional underwriting complexity and delay involved in testing, the regulatory situation in each jurisdiction in which the company operates, and the marketing resistance to requiring tests for all but large amounts of insurance. Responsible underwriting management will include this kind of evaluation based on analysis of a company's known AIDS claims and its financial capacity to absorb claims below its screening threshold.

As with any testing procedure, a negative result does not always mean the individual is free of the disease. False negatives are, of course, much more difficult to identify than false positives. The latter can be detected from follow-up testing. The standard ELISA test has been reported to show negative results in a few cases per 1,000 individuals who subsequently are discovered to be HIV-infected. However, even for a company with well-developed testing procedures, it would be extremely difficult to estimate the impact of false negatives on mortality in a meaningful way that could be translated into pricing.

In addition to the cost of testing at the threshold the company establishes, some provision should be made for AIDS-related deaths among those who are HIV-infected when they apply, but who are applying for amounts of insurance below the company's testing threshold and are not discovered through other underwriting procedures. In the absence of specific knowledge about the makeup of a company's market, it is difficult to estimate this cost also. At the estimated population average infection rate exclusive of IV drug abusers, who are probably not purchasers of individual life insurance to any significant extent, we would again suggest an initial liability of $5 per $1,000 of insurance issued to males from 20 to 59. This estimate is based on $500 per $1,000 for each one newly insured assumed to be HIV-infected per 100 issues.

Finally, insurers should recognize that even with the most thorough testing procedures, some policyholders will become infected after issue. This is another potential source of AIDS-related claims that is difficult to quantify. While the potential spread of HIV infection among the non-IV-drug-abusing heterosexual population cannot be ignored, the most significant component of such claims for the next several years will be the further spread of HIV infection within the groups currently at high risk.

4.3. Life Company Solvency

As indicated in Section 3.7, estimates of the spread of the epidemic into the heterosexual population will for some time be even more speculative than for those groups at high risk. In the estimates that follow, we assumed no significant spread of HIV infection into the non-IV-drug-abusing hetero- sexual population and no AIDS-related claims on females. As discussed previously, we acknowledge that both assumptions understate the eventual magnitude of AIDS deaths. However, at this stage of the epidemic we have no reliable data on which to make such estimates. The model developed by Harris [17] suggests that 120,000 non-IV-drug-abusing heterosexuals will be HIV-infected by 1990; while not negligible, even at this number, our assumptions as to financial impact would not be seriously affected. Rather than adding estimates based on conjecture to our partially validated projec- tions, we elected to defer making estimates of the epidemic's spread beyond the existing groups at high risk.

This leaves the cost of the epidemic as it spreads further into the yet uninfected segments of the population considered to be at high risk. This cost has two major components: the financial impact of AIDS and related claims on in-force business, and the impact of taking on additional risks from new business. Both components depend for their analysis on the in- cidence of HIV infection in the insured and potentially insurable populations and on the prognosis for its further spread.

To estimate the first component, we assumed that new individual life business had been written on adult males since 1975 with the HIV infection levels developed in our model and that infection would begin to decline, peaking in 1997 as shown in Chart 1 at about 2 million, or just over 3 percent of all males age 20–59.

Information from the ACLI's Fact Book [19] and estimates for year-end 1986 put the amount of life insurance in force in the U.S. at $6.65 trillion. Of this total, $3.65 trillion was written individually, and the other $3 trillion was written on a group or credit basis.

From the ACLI's information on amounts of coverage by age and sex, we developed the following estimates of insurance coverage among U.S. males at the age groups most susceptible to HIV infection:

U.S. Males Attained Ages	Total Insurance In Force 1/1/87 (billions of dollars)		Estimated HIV-Infected 1/1/87 (billions of dollars)	
	Individual	Group	Individual	Group
20-29	$ 658	$ 209	$ 2.6	$ 0.9
30-39	675	504	9.9	6.3
40-49	505	436	6.6	4.7
50-59	277	301	1.5	1.1
20-59	$ 2,115	$ 1,450	$ 20.6	$ 13.0

Based on our estimates of the further growth of HIV infection and rates of progression to AIDS modeled from the SFCC/CDC data, we would expect individual life insurance in force in the U.S. as of year-end 1986 for these four 10-year male age groups to generate AIDS-related claims of over $30 billion through the end of the century. Approximately $14 billion of these claims will come from insurance on those already infected, and another $18 billion from new infections on existing insureds. In addition, we would expect approximately $20 billion of additional AIDS-related claims from group life insurance in force at year-end 1986. A projection of individual life claims under these assumptions is shown in Appendix 2. As more data become available on group life claims, we would expect to refine our estimates for this line.

Data on the extent of the epidemic in Canada are so sketchy at this time that our estimates of the financial impact on life operations in that country must be hedged.

Based on the lower incidence of AIDS cases and assumed HIV infection levels in Canada, it would appear that not much more than about $1 billion of the approximately $200 billion of individual, nor more than about $1.25 billion of the $200 billion or so group life coverage, as of year-end 1986 is on HIV-infected insureds. The apparently later entry of the infection into Canada suggests that the emergence of death claims may be somewhat slower than in the U.S. and that perhaps less than three-fourths of these HIV-infected amounts will show up as AIDS-related claims by the year 2000. The assumption of no significant spread of HIV infection beyond the male homosexual and bisexual community would, at this time, appear to represent less serious a problem of understatement of financial impact in Canada than in the U.S.

The second component of the financial impact is the additional risks the industry will assume by writing new business.

As discussed in Section 4.2, "Underwriting and Pricing," insurers will have to evaluate the risk not only of writing new business among the already HIV-infected population but also of insuring a population that will likely have even higher incidences of infection than today's levels. Although some limited testing may be undertaken for group insurance situations where individual evidence of insurability is routinely obtained, we assumed that new entrants into group plans would not normally be screened for HIV infection. Whatever impact AIDS deaths may have on group life claims will be reflected in rates for that business generally. However, if AIDS mortality were fully reflected in group life rates to such an extent that they were eventually to exceed individual life premium levels, it seems that a point could be reached at which employers might be unwilling to provide group life coverage.

For individual coverage, on the other hand, most insurers who obtain medical evidence are already screening new business applications, especially for high amounts of insurance. Although at the time of this report, each state allows some form of testing for individually underwritten life and disability income coverage, insurers' prerogatives to screen for HIV infection have already been challenged in some jurisdictions. In only one, however, the District of Columbia, has testing for HIV been entirely barred for insurance purposes. To date, there have been no such restrictions in Canada.

The ACLI estimates that approximately $1 trillion of new individual life insurance will be written in the U.S. in 1987. Of this total, over 60 percent will be written on males, and of that $600+ billion, approximately 85 percent will be written at the most critical ages for risk of AIDS, 20–59. We assumed $500 billion of new coverage distributed as follows:

U.S. Males Issue Ages	Estimated New Individual Life Insurance Written in 1987	
	Number of New Policies (millions)	Amount of New Insurance (billions of dollars)
20-29	2.400	$ 155
30-39	2.350	160
40-49	1.650	120
50-59	1.125	65
20-59	7.525	$ 500

With no testing, we estimate that approximately 55,000 of these 7.5 million policies would be issued on HIV-infected individuals, for a total insurance amount of more than $4 billion. The likelihood is that most, if not all, of this amount would result in premature death claims from complications of HIV infection. Progression to AIDS and death under the slower SFCC/ CDC assumptions produces death claims that, discounted at 6 percent interest, would require a net single premium of $515 per $1,000 issued to an HIV-infected individual. In other words, new individual life insurance written in the U.S. in 1987 could, if not screened for HIV infection, create an immediate additional liability for AIDS claims of over $2 billion.

With a 5 percent annual increase in new sales and the spread of new HIV infection declining to zero by 1997, then with no testing we could expect new business written from 1987 forward to generate $20 billion of AIDS claims by year-end 2000. With testing at successively lower dollar levels, an increasing proportion of this $20 billion would not have become insured.

We project that by the mid-1990s, annual claims from individual insurance in force at year-end 1986 and already HIV-infected will exceed $1 billion. Depending on the extent of the spread of infection among existing insureds, total AIDS claims could exceed $2 billion annually, or about 15 percent of projected individual life insurance claims for all U.S. companies. Even at this level, such extra claims would probably be within the ability of the industry to pay. Prudent financial management, in anticipation of additional claims at these levels, would probably call for reserves to be strengthened. At 10–15 percent of total claims, AIDS mortality would not likely lead to widespread insolvency.

However, without effective screening for HIV, the addition of several years of new business issued on infected applicants could double the level of projected AIDS claims by the mid- to late-1990s, at which point the industry would experience more serious problems, and some companies could face financial difficulties.

Preliminary analysis indicates that the cost of AIDS claims is not falling uniformly on all insurers. Companies that have grown faster in recent years during the very period that most HIV infections have occurred are bearing a disproportionate share of the added claims burden. Those marketing high-amount, low-premium-level products, especially at the most critical male ages 30–49 where infection levels are highest, will be harder hit than others. Companies with heavy concentrations of business in locations where the epidemic is more widespread will experience higher-than-average AIDS claims. Companies unfortunate enough to have combinations of two or more such sales patterns will obviously be the most seriously affected.

Further analysis will have to be performed on a company-by-company basis before conclusions can be drawn as to the magnitude of the problem in terms of AIDS claims that might exceed a company's ability to pay. Such analysis also will have to take account of the surplus strain that many insurers will incur from other fixed-premium, noncancelable lines of business and from the lag in pricing group life and health coverages to reflect the increasing levels of AIDS claims being experienced in those lines.

5. CONCLUSIONS

HIV is the most serious epidemic that society has faced in modern times. It will have a profound impact on the insurance industry. It appears that the HIV epidemic will not be as serious in Canada as in the U.S., but it will cost the life insurance industry in the two countries tens of billions of dollars in premature death claims from its complications before it runs its course.

Massive education efforts to change practices that spread the disease could bring the epidemic under control by early in the 21st century. Major breakthroughs in medical technology could significantly improve this prospect.

Insurance industry executives must take strong leadership positions in educating the public about the implications of this disease for the availability and affordability of insurance. The leaders of our industry must communicate these messages clearly to policyholders, home office employees, agents, the news media, and legislative and regulatory officials.

The impact of HIV infection and AIDS will be serious, but if the industry addresses quickly and responsibly the underwriting and financial management challenges presented, even an epidemic of this magnitude need not be catastrophic.

REFERENCES

1. *Public Health Service Plan for the Prevention and Control of AIDS and the AIDS Virus,* Report of the Coolfont Planning Conference, U.S. Public Health Service, Washington, 1986, p. 1.
2. Ibid., p. 4.
3. Knox, E.G., *A Transmission Model for AIDS*, European Journal of Epidemiology, September 1986, Vol. 2, Number 3, pp. 165–177.
4. Koch, Michael G., M.D., *AIDS: Our Future*, Stockholm, Swedish Carnegie Institute, 1985, excerpted by AIDS Insurance Reports, Vol. 2, No. 10, May 1986.
5. *Confronting AIDS*, Institute of Medicine, National Academy of Sciences, Washington, 1986, pp. 58–60.
6. Winkelstein, W., et al., *Sexual Practices and Risk of Infection by the Human Immunodeficiency Virus, The San Francisco Men's Health Study*; Journal of the American Medical Association, January 1987, Vol. 257, No. 3, pp. 321–325.

7. Brodt, H.R., Helm, E.B., Werner, A., Joetten, A., Bergmann, L., Kluver, A., and Stille, W., *Spontanverlauf der LAV/HTLV-III-Infektion; Verlaufsbeobachtungen bei Personen aus AIDS-Risikogruppen*; Deutsche Medizinische Wochenschrift, Stuttgart, Vol. 111 (1986), pp. 1175–1180.

8. *The Walter Reed staging classification for HTLV-III/LAV Infection*, New England Journal of Medicine, 1986, Vol. 314, No. 2, pp. 131–132.

9. Goedert, James J.; Biggar, Robert J.; Weiss, Stanley H.; Eyster, M. Elaine; Melbye, Mads; Wilson, Susan; et al., *Three-year Incidence of AIDS in Five Cohorts of HTLV-III-Infected Risk Group Members*; Science, Vol. 231 (1986), pp. 992–995.

10. *Study: Risk of AIDS progression rises each year after infection*, AIDS Alert, April 1987.

11. *AIDS Weekly Surveillance Report*, United States AIDS Program, Center for Infectious Diseases, Centers for Disease Control, Public Health Service, Department of Health and Human Services, Atlanta, GA, June 30, 1987.

12. Laboratory Centre for Disease Control, *AIDS in Canada*, Ottawa, May 4, 1987.

13. Brookmeyer, Ron, and Gail, Mitchell H., *Minimum Size of the Acquired Immunodeficiency Syndrome (AIDS) Epidemic in the United States*; The Lancet, December 1986.

14. Elandt-Johnson, R.C., and Johnson, N.L., *Survival Models and Data Analysis*, New York, John Wiley, 1980, p. 184.

15. Lui, Kung-Jong, et al., *A model-based approach for estimating the mean incubation period of transfusion-associated acquired immunodeficiency syndrome*; Proceedings of the National Academy of Sciences, Vol. 83, pp. 3051–3055, May 1986.

16. May, Robert M, and Anderson, Roy M., *Transmission Dynamics of HIV Infection*, Nature, Vol. 326, p. 139, March, 1987.

17. Harris, Jeffrey, *The AIDS Epidemic; Looking into the 1990s*; Technology Review, July 1987, pp. 59–65.

18. Hammond, J.D., and Shapiro, A.F., *AIDS and the Limits of Insurability*; The Milbank Quarterly, 1986, Vol. 64, Suppl. 1, pp. 143–167.

19. *1986 Life Insurance Fact Book and 1986 Estimate of Key Life Insurance Statistics*; American Council of Life Insurance; Washington, DC, (1986).

APPENDIX 1

Epidemiological Model of HIV Infection, AIDS Cases and Deaths, with CDC Data

	Infection Continues to 100% of At-Risk Group					CDC		Infection Declines to 0 by 1997					Infection Stops in 1987				
Year	a[t]	New HIV Infections	Total HIV Infections	Modeled Cumulative AIDS Cases	Modeled Cumulative AIDS Deaths	AIDS Cases	AIDS Deaths	a[t]	New HIV Infections	Total HIV Infections	Modeled Cumulative AIDS Cases	Modeled Cumulative AIDS Deaths	a[t]	New HIV Infections	Total HIV Infections	Modeled Cumulative AIDS Cases	Modeled Cumulative AIDS Deaths
1975		113	113						113	113				113	113		
1976	1.50	392	504					1.50	392	504			1.50	392	504		
1977	1.32	1,382	1,887	3	1			1.32	1,382	1,887	3	1	1.32	1,382	1,887	3	1
1978	1.16	4,125	6,011	15	8			1.16	4,125	6,011	15	8	1.16	4,125	6,011	15	8
1979	1.00	10,284	16,295	59	30			1.00	10,284	16,295	59	30	1.00	10,284	16,295	59	30
1980	0.85	21,609	37,904	199	106			0.85	21,609	37,904	199	106	0.85	21,609	37,904	199	106
1981	0.71	38,395	76,300	588	321	337	146	0.71	38,395	76,300	588	321	0.71	38,395	76,300	588	321
1982	0.59	59,129	135,429	1,538	862	1,337	528	0.59	59,129	135,429	1,538	862	0.59	59,129	135,429	1,538	862
1983	0.50	82,744	218,173	3,607	2,078	4,119	1,753	0.50	82,744	218,173	3,607	2,078	0.50	82,744	218,173	3,607	2,078
1984	0.44	110,032	328,205	7,677	4,548	9,697	4,582	0.44	110,032	328,205	7,677	4,548	0.44	110,032	328,205	7,677	4,548
1985	0.42	149,488	477,693	15,020	9,145	15,948	8,161	0.42	149,488	477,693	15,020	9,145	0.42	149,488	477,693	15,020	9,145
1986	0.40	192,926	670,619	27,354	17,095	29,003	16,301	0.40	192,926	670,619	27,354	17,095	0.40	192,926	670,619	27,354	17,095
1987	0.40	248,947	919,566	46,864	30,018	55,000	30,000	0.40	248,947	919,566	46,864	30,018	0.40	248,947	919,566	46,864	30,018
1988	0.40	304,623	1,224,189	76,182	49,942	88,000	51,000	0.36	271,873	1,191,439	76,182	49,942	0.00	0	919,566	76,182	49,942
1989	0.40	349,432	1,573,621	118,354	79,294	133,000	81,000	0.32	273,764	1,465,203	118,255	79,250	0.00	0	919,566	117,440	78,883
1990	0.40	372,330	1,945,951	176,780	120,877	191,000	122,000	0.28	256,127	1,721,330	176,062	120,529	0.00	0	919,566	171,162	118,123
1991	0.40	366,809	2,312,760	255,092	177,796	265,000	176,000	0.24	224,621	1,945,951	252,266	176,335	0.00	0	919,566	236,244	167,827
1992	0.40	334,492	2,647,252	356,776	253,259			0.20	185,909	2,131,859	348,753	248,868	0.00	0	919,566	310,175	226,984
1993	0.40	284,197	2,931,449	484,541	350,187			0.16	145,283	2,277,142	466,060	339,547	0.00	0	919,566	388,943	293,329
1994	0.40	227,313	3,158,762	639,622	470,692			0.12	105,836	2,382,978	602,741	448,504	0.00	0	919,566	465,748	362,695
1995	0.40	173,190	3,331,952	821,073	615,501			0.08	68,714	2,451,692	755,065	574,192	0.00	0	919,566	533,821	429,922
1996	0.40	127,130	3,459,082	1,025,399	783,492			0.04	33,740	2,485,433	917,678	713,476	0.00	0	919,566	591,682	491,746
1997	0.40	90,791	3,549,873	1,246,771	971,550			0.00	0	2,485,433	1,084,550	862,114	0.00	0	919,566	640,865	547,286
1998	0.40	63,575	3,613,449	1,477,774	1,174,839			0.00	0	2,485,433	1,249,705	1,015,318	0.00	0	919,566	682,670	596,654
1999	0.40	43,906	3,657,355	1,710,496	1,387,404			0.00	0	2,485,433	1,407,848	1,168,294	0.00	0	919,566	718,205	640,235
2000	0.40	30,033	3,687,388	1,937,640	1,602,979			0.00	0	2,485,433	1,554,819	1,316,711	0.00	0	919,566	748,409	678,493

As described in Section 2.3, the continuous form of the underlying epidemiological model, where the mortality term (q_t) is assumed to be sufficiently small to be treated separately, is:

$$\frac{dp_t}{dt} = \alpha_t \cdot p_t \cdot (1 - p_t) \qquad [1]$$

The solution of this equation is:

$$p_t = (1 + e^{-\alpha \cdot t})^{-1} \qquad [2]$$

The discrete form is developed as follows:

$$\Delta p_t = p_{t+1} - p_t \qquad [3]$$

$$= (1 + e^{-\alpha \cdot (t+1)})^{-1} - (1 + e^{-\alpha \cdot t})^{-1} \qquad [4]$$

$$= \frac{(e^{-\alpha \cdot t}) \cdot (1 - e^{-\alpha})}{(1 + e^{-\alpha \cdot (t+1)}) \cdot (1 + e^{-\alpha \cdot t})} \qquad [5]$$

$$= (1 - e^{-\alpha}) \cdot (1 - p_t) \cdot p_{t+1} \qquad [6]$$

$$= \frac{(1 - e^{-\alpha}) \cdot p_t \cdot (1 - p_t)}{1 - (1 - e^{-\alpha}) \cdot (1 - p_t)} \qquad [7]$$

The projections in this Appendix were developed from the discrete form with the value α varying over time. The values of α_t ("$a[t]$" in the projections) were chosen empirically to produce AIDS cases and deaths that most closely matched CDC reported numbers through 1986 and projections to 1991.

The theoretical expression of the S-curve in Chart 1 is based on a constant value of $\alpha = 0.485$, and the use of 1989 as t_m, the inflection year of the curve, in the formula:

$$p_t = (1 + e^{-\alpha (t - t_m)})^{-1} \qquad [8]$$

Note that:

$$p_{t_m} = 0.5 \qquad [9]$$

APPENDIX 2

ESTIMATE OF U.S. INDIVIDUAL LIFE AIDS CLAIMS 1976–2000
HIV INFECTION DECLINES TO 0 BY 1997

Year	Total HIV Infection	Insured HIV Infection	Insured HIV to Total Infection	CDC Deaths to 1991 Model to 2000 Cumulative	CDC Deaths Annual	Insured Deaths Annual	Insured as % of U.S. Deaths	Insurance Deaths Cumulative	U.S. Individual Insured Deaths Annually (mil.)	AIDS Claims to Total Ind. Claims	Average Claim	Annual Claims (000)	Cumulative (000)	Infection Stops 1987 (000)	Claims from Infections after 1987 (000)
1976	504	64	12.6%			0		0	$4,635	0.0%	$15,909	$0	$0	$0	
1977	1,887	312	16.5%			0		0	$4,879	0.0%	$16,421	$1	$1	$1	
1978	6,011	1,137	18.9%			1		1	$5,312	0.0%	$17,177	$12	$13	$13	
1979	16,295	3,442	21.1%			4		4	$5,548	0.0%		$62	$75	$75	
1980	37,904	8,908	23.5%			14		18	$6,094	0.0%	$18,168	$248	$323	$323	
1981	76,300	20,065	26.3%	146	146	43	30%	61	$6,640	0.0%	$19,367	$839	$1,162	$1,162	
1982	135,429	39,907	29.5%	528	382	120	31%	181	$6,993	0.0%	$20,798	$2,494	$3,655	$3,655	
1983	218,173	72,548	33.3%	1,753	1,225	295	24%	476	$7,306	0.1%	$22,472	$6,619	$10,275	$10,275	
1984	328,205	123,402	37.6%	4,582	2,829	653	23%	1,129	$7,959	0.2%	$24,414	$15,950	$26,225	$26,225	
1985	477,693	203,757	42.7%	8,161	3,579	1,330	37%	2,459	$8,789	0.4%	$26,625	$35,403	$61,628	$61,628	
1986	670,619	323,658	48.3%	16,301	8,140	2,524	31%	4,983	$9,600	0.8%	$29,118	$73,499	$135,127	$135,127	
1987	919,566	478,375	52.0%	30,000	13,699	4,527	33%	9,510	$10,368	1.4%	$31,903	$144,431	$279,558	$279,558	
1988	1,191,439	647,339	54.3%	51,000	21,000	7,713	37%	17,223	$11,197	2.4%	$34,782	$268,257	$547,815	$547,815	
1989	1,465,203	817,479	55.8%	81,000	30,000	12,468	42%	29,691	$12,093	3.9%	$37,461	$467,060	$1,014,875	$1,004,025	$10,850
1990	1,721,330	976,658	56.7%	122,000	41,000	19,088	47%	48,779	$13,061	5.8%	$39,766	$759,076	$1,773,951	$1,702,810	$71,140
1991	1,945,951	1,116,256	57.4%	176,000	54,000	27,687	51%	76,466	$14,106	8.2%	$41,667	$1,153,652	$2,927,603	$2,676,080	$251,523
1992	2,131,859	1,231,795	57.8%	249,000	73,000	38,108	52%	114,574	$15,234	10.8%	$43,202	$1,646,325	$4,573,928	$3,927,022	$646,906
1993	2,277,142	1,322,086	58.1%	340,000	91,000	49,795	55%	164,369	$16,453	13.4%	$44,385	$2,210,158	$6,784,086	$5,417,846	$1,366,240
1994	2,382,978	1,387,862	58.2%	449,000	109,000	61,757	57%	226,127	$17,769	15.7%	$45,224	$2,792,907	$9,576,993	$7,040,435	$2,536,558
1995	2,451,692	1,430,566	58.4%	574,000	125,000	72,792	58%	298,919	$19,190	17.4%	$45,786	$3,332,839	$12,909,833	$8,645,117	$4,264,716
1996	2,485,433	1,451,535	58.4%	713,000	139,000	81,851	59%	380,770	$20,726	18.2%	$46,161	$3,778,322	$16,688,155	$10,133,655	$6,554,500
1997	2,485,433	1,451,535	58.4%	862,000	149,000	88,229	59%	468,999	$22,384	18.3%	$46,417	$4,095,322	$20,783,477	$11,476,947	$9,306,531
1998	2,485,433	1,451,535	58.4%	1,015,000	153,000	91,583	60%	560,582	$24,174	17.7%	$46,595	$4,267,300	$25,050,778	$12,674,777	$12,376,001
1999	2,485,433	1,451,535	85.4%	1,168,000	153,000	91,906	60%	652,488	$26,108	16.4%	$46,721	$4,293,973	$29,344,751	$13,734,957	$15,609,794
2000	2,485,433	1,451,535	58.4%	1,317,000	149,000	89,488	60%	741,976	$28,197	14.9%	$46,811	$4,189,059	$33,533,810	$14,667,629	$18,866,181

Estimate of U.S. Individual Life AIDS Claims 1976–2000
HIV Infection Stops in 1987

Year	HIV Infection			CDC Deaths to 1991 Model to 2000		Insured Deaths Annual	Insured as % of U.S. Deaths	Insurance Deaths Cumulative	U.S. Individual Insured Deaths Annually (mil.)	AIDS Claims to Total Ind. Claims	AIDS Claims		
	Total HIV Infection	Insured HIV Infection	Insured HIV to Total Infection	Cumulative	Annual						Average Claim	Annual Claims (000)	Cumulative (000)
1976	504	64	12.6%			0		0	$4,635	0.0%	$15,909	$0	$0
1977	1,887	312	16.5%			0		0	$4,879	0.0%	$16,421	$1	$1
1978	6,011	1,137	18.9%			1		1	$5,312	0.0%	$17,177	$12	$13
1979	16,295	3,442	21.1%			4		4	$5,548	0.0%	$18,168	$62	$75
1980	37,904	8,908	23.5%			14		18	$6,094	0.0%		$248	$323
1981	76,300	20,065	26.3%	146	146	43	30%	61	$6,640	0.0%	$19,367	$839	$1,162
1982	135,429	39,907	29.5%	528	382	120	31%	181	$6,993	0.0%	$20,798	$2,494	$3,655
1983	218,173	72,548	33.3%	1,753	1,225	295	24%	476	$7,306	0.1%	$22,472	$6,619	$10,275
1984	328,205	123,402	37.6%	4,582	2,829	653	23%	1,129	$7,959	0.2%	$24,414	$15,950	$26,225
1985	477,693	205,757	42.7%	8,161	3,579	1,330	37%	2,459	$8,789	0.4%	$26,625	$35,403	$61,628
1986	670,619	325,658	48.3%	16,301	8,140	2,524	31%	4,983	$9,600	0.8%	$29,118	$73,499	$135,127
1987	919,566	478,375	52.0%	30,000	13,699	4,527	33%	9,510	$10,368	1.4%	$31,903	$144,431	$279,558
1988	919,566	478,375	52.0%	50,000	20,000	7,713	39%	17,223	$11,197	2.4%	$34,782	$268,257	$547,815
1989	919,566	478,375	52.0%	79,000	29,000	12,240	42%	29,462	$12,093	3.8%	$37,273	$456,210	$1,004,025
1990	919,566	478,375	52.0%	118,000	39,000	17,821	46%	47,283	$13,061	5.4%	$39,212	$698,785	$1,702,810
1991	919,566	478,375	52.0%	168,000	50,000	23,895	48%	71,178	$14,106	6.9%	$40,731	$973,270	$2,676,080
1992	919,566	478,375	52.0%	227,000	59,000	29,795	50%	100,973	$15,234	8.2%	$41,985	$1,250,942	$3,927,022
1993	919,566	478,375	52.0%	293,000	66,000	34,672	53%	135,645	$16,453	9.1%	$42,998	$1,490,824	$5,417,846
1994	919,566	478,375	52.0%	363,000	70,000	37,153	53%	172,798	$17,769	9.1%	$43,674	$1,622,589	$7,040,435
1995	919,566	478,375	52.0%	430,000	67,000	36,459	54%	209,257	$19,190	8.4%	$44,013	$1,604,682	$8,645,117
1996	919,566	478,375	52.0%	492,000	62,000	33,711	54%	242,968	$20,726	7.2%	$44,156	$1,488,538	$10,133,655
1997	919,566	478,375	52.0%	547,000	55,000	30,371	55%	273,338	$22,384	6.0%	$44,230	$1,343,292	$11,476,947
1998	919,566	478,375	52.0%	597,000	50,000	27,050	54%	300,389	$24,174	5.0%	$44,282	$1,197,831	$12,674,777
1999	919,566	478,375	52.0%	640,000	43,000	23,919	56%	324,307	$26,108	4.1%	$44,324	$1,060,180	$13,734,957
2000	919,566	478,375	52.0%	678,000	38,000	21,026	55%	345,333	$28,197	3.3%	$44,358	$932,672	$14,667,629

II. HIV MORTALITY

WALTER H. HOSKINS

1. ABSTRACT

In studying Acquired Immune Deficiency Syndrome (AIDS) and its causative agent Human Immunodeficiency Virus (HIV) to assess their impact on life insurance underwriting, pricing, and solvency, the authors were faced with a scarcity of data about the progression from HIV to AIDS. While the mortality of AIDS patients is well documented, the long latency period of HIV has not allowed long-term studies of HIV-infected patients.

Estimates vary widely as to the percentages of HIV-infected patients that will progress to fully developed AIDS. The longer a population of HIV-infected subjects is studied, the higher are the estimates of ultimate progression to AIDS. Early estimates by CDC and others were that 10–20 percent of otherwise asymptomatic HIV-infected subjects would eventually progress to AIDS. Later, as the numbers of AIDS cases and related deaths grew, this estimate was revised upward closer to 50 percent. In a recent interview, the Surgeon General of the U.S. suggested that the ultimate progression rate might be closer to 100 percent.

The purpose of this Actuarial Note is to estimate the mortality of a population that has just become infected with HIV. Data for studying progression from HIV infection to AIDS (Frankfurt) and AIDS mortality (CDC) were analyzed, and a model was built to use the data.

This note is a detailed discussion of the sources of data used in the model; the reasons for modeling; the assumptions, formulas, and methods used in the development of the model; the derivation of the modeled progression rates; and the results of the model.

2. SOURCES OF DATA

2.1. HIV Progression Rates — The Frankfurt Study

The major source of data for this note is a study by the Center for Internal Medicine of the University of Frankfurt, West Germany [1]. It observed subjects in groups at high risk of AIDS through various stages in the progression from apparent good health to death primarily caused by AIDS.

It appears to have been an extremely well-run prospective study, completely documented on a subject-by-subject basis. It is the first published study of its kind that analyzes the progression from an HIV-infected status

943

in otherwise asymptomatic patients, through more serious stages of immune system impairment, all the way to fully developed AIDS and resulting death.

The design of the Frankfurt Study yielded information of more value than that from other studies available in one major respect. Rather than studying the single rate of progression from HIV infection to AIDS, it analyzed the progression of the disease as a process involving a number of discrete steps.

The Frankfurt Study observed 543 subjects from groups at high risk of AIDS from 1982 through 1985; 377 of the subjects were HIV infected on initial examination. A total of 307 subjects were observed for 3 months or longer; 259 of these were HIV infected on initial examination.

The study uses five classifications, or stages, to identify progression from healthy status to AIDS. This approach closely follows what has been identified as the "Walter Reed Staging Method" [2]:

1a Healthy persons at risk for HIV infection, but testing negative for HIV (At-Risk) infection.

1b Patients testing positive for HIV infection but otherwise asymptomatic. (HIV+)

2a Patients with HIV infection and lymphadenopathy syndrome (LAS), (LAS) together with moderate cellular immune deficiency.

2b Patients with HIV infection and LAS, together with severe cellular (ARC) immune deficiency (AIDS-Related Complex, or ARC, as defined by CDC).

3 Patients with AIDS as currently defined by CDC. (AIDS)

The sixth and final stage was death.

The most significant data for the purposes of our analysis are summarized in Table 1. This table is essentially a restatement of Table 5 of the Frankfurt Study. It shows the results of a longitudinal study of all patients who were observed for at least three months.

Patients were grouped by:

1. the length of time they were observed in the study (Range of Observation Periods), and

2. their status at the start of their observation period (Stage 1a through Stage 3).

Each observation period/stage cell comprises a different, independent group of patients. For example, 120 patients were classified as stage 2a at the start of their observation period. Of these, 19 were observed for anywhere between 24 and 36 months. Of these patients, 14 progressed at least to stage

TABLE 1

FRANKFURT STUDY "TABLE 5" DATA

Range of Observation Periods	Stage 1a (At-Risk)	Stage 1b (HIV+)	Stage 2a (LAS)	Stage 2b (ARC)	Stage 3 (AIDS)	All Stages
(A) Number of Patients Observed by Stage and Observation Period						
3–6 months	10	9	21	8	6	54
6–12 months	14	18	51	29	9	121
12–24 months	21	20	29	20	7	97
24–36 months	3	5	9	7	1*	35
All Periods	48	52	120	64	23	307
(B) Number of Patients Whose Health Worsened by at Least One Stage or Who Died during the Observation Period						
3–6 months	1	1	3	0	4	9
6–12 months	6	10	20	3	6	45
12–24 months	9	15	14	10	5	53
24–36 months	2	4	14	4	0*	24
All Periods	18	30	51	17	15	131
(C) Percentage of Patients Observed Whose Health Worsened by at Least One Stage or Who Died During the Observation Period						
3–6 months	10%	11%	14%	0%	67%	17%
6–12 months	43	56	39	10	67	37
12–24 months	43	75	48	50	71	55
24–36 months	67	80	74	57	0*	69
All Periods	38%	58%	42%	27%	65%	43%

*One patient with AIDS was still alive 28 months after diagnosis of Kaposi's sarcoma; all others with AIDS had died before the end of 24 months.

2b while under observation. Progression to stage 2b could have occurred any time during the patient's observation period (between 0 and 36 months).

Table 1A shows the number of patients observed. Table 1B shows the number of patients whose health worsened while under observation. Table 1C shows cumulative HIV progression rates (cumulative HIV infection rates in the case of stage 1a, cumulative AIDS mortality in the case of stage 3) for the patients under study. These cumulative progression rates are *not* periodic progression rates.

Of the 20 observation period/stage cells, 19 had three or more patients under observation. The raw cumulative progression rates to the next stage of the disease increased with length of observation period for all of these 19 cells except for two cells, where they remained level. This is remarkable consistency considering that each cell was independent of all the others.

2.2. AIDS Mortality Rates — CDC Data

AIDS Weekly Surveillance Reports [3] from the U.S. Public Health Service's Centers for Disease Control (CDC) are the best available source of data on AIDS mortality. While the Frankfurt Study provided data on AIDS mortality, CDC data were used in our model because of the CDC data's high reliability resulting from the large numbers of patients studied. Through March 30, 1987, the CDC reported a total of 33,482 cases of AIDS in the U.S., of which 19,394 had resulted in death.

Table 2 is an excerpt from the March 30, 1987 CDC AIDS Weekly Surveillance Report. The deaths shown are those cases, reported by half-year of the date of AIDS diagnosis, that are known to have resulted in death. For example, of the 6,420 AIDS cases diagnosed between July 1, 1986 and December 31, 1986 *and* reported to CDC through March 30, 1987, a total of 1,817 AIDS deaths have been reported to CDC through March 30, 1987. It is probable that some AIDS deaths may go unreported even though their cases were reported.

TABLE 2

EXCERPT FROM SECTION G
AIDS WEEKLY SURVEILLANCE REPORT
UNITED STATES AIDS PROGRAM
CENTER FOR INFECTIOUS DISEASES
CENTERS FOR DISEASE CONTROL
MARCH 30, 1987
UNITED STATES CASES REPORTED TO CDC

Date of AIDS Diagnosis (by Half-Years)	Cases Reported to CDC through 3/30/87	Known Deaths Reported to CDC through 3/30/87	Case Fatality Rate through 3/30/87
1987 Jan. – March	1,460	229	16%
1986 July – Dec.	6,420	1,817	28
1986 Jan. – June	6,260	3,013	48
1985 July – Dec.	5,335	3,343	63
1985 Jan. - June	4,314	3,081	71
1984 July – Dec.	3,166	2,464	78
1984 Jan. – June	2,410	1,916	80
1983 July – Dec.	1,578	1,316	83
1983 Jan. – June	1,203	1,045	87
1982 July – Dec.	637	553	87
1982 Jan. - June	363	318	88
1981 July – Dec.	178	160	90
1981 Jan. – June	84	77	92
1980 and Earlier	74	62	84
Total	33,482	19,394	58

3. HIV MORTALITY MODEL BASED ON FRANKFURT AND CDC DATA

Analysis of Frankfurt HIV progression rates and CDC AIDS mortality rates yields valuable data needed for the development of HIV mortality rates. It would be desirable to be able to calculate HIV mortality rates directly from these data. However, traditional actuarial methods of analyzing mortality and other contingencies using single decrement formulae were of limited value in this situation. This is because of the multiple stages of the HIV disease and the high periodic probabilities of progression from one stage to the next. Multistage progression systems are not directly nor easily calculable. A different approach was needed.

A Markov Chain model was developed to study HIV mortality based on Frankfurt and CDC data. This model simulates the progression of a group of newly HIV-infected patients through the stages of the HIV disease to AIDS and death.

The process is not unlike that of creating a life, or multiple decrement, table from a limited period of observation, by joining together the experience of successive cohorts, even though no one cohort was observed to progress through the entire range of ages or decrements represented in the table. In the Frankfurt Study, a sufficient number progressed from one stage of the HIV disease to the next to enable the results from one stage progression to the next to be linked together.

The format of the data presented in the Frankfurt Study, showing progression from one stage of the disease to the next, is particularly useful for this method of modeling in that increasing the detail of the model decreases the impact that a specific graduation, projection, or other statistical technique has on the overall results of the model.

It is important to note that the assumptions of the model are determined by the format of the available data (in the case of the Frankfurt Study, rates of progression based on duration since progression to current stage). Different assumptions would almost certainly be used to build a model based on data available in a different format.

4. ASSUMPTIONS OF MODEL

4.1. Assumption 1 — Classification

At a particular time, everyone can be classified by stage and duration in stage (duration since progression to that stage). Note that duration for the stage "dead" is not applicable.

4.2. Assumption 2 — Progression or Nonprogression

In a particular time period, everyone either

1. progresses to the next stage, or
2. remains in current stage.

In other words, it is assumed that the disease is progressive and irreversible and that:

1. no one goes back a stage (The Frankfurt Study notes seven out of 307 [2.3 percent] going back one or more stages but suggests that this could be attributed to a misjudgment of initial condition as opposed to an actual improvement)
2. no one skips a stage (although rapid, almost instantaneous, successive progressions are allowed).

4.3. Assumption 3 — Probability of Progression

The probability of progression is:

1. dependent only on:
   a. stage, and
   b. duration in stage (duration since progression to that stage)
2. independent of:
   a. age, sex, and other usual underwriting factors,
   b. duration since HIV infection (This is different from duration since progression to current stage, factor 1.b. above. For example, the probability of progressing from ARC to AIDS depends on duration since progression to ARC, and not the time it took to progress from HIV infection to ARC.), and
   c. calendar year. (The model assumes persistence of current conditions and environment, i.e., no changes in attitudes especially with regard to sexual activity, no changes in available medical treatment, and no changes in the reportability of the HIV disease.)

By way of contrast to these assumptions, the number of HIV infections can be estimated by multiplying the "at-risk" population by the probability of HIV infection. The probability of HIV infection is almost certainly more dependent than successive progressions on:

a. age, sex, and other usual underwriting factors, because of the characteristics of observed "High-Risk" groups, and

b. calendar year because of changes in attitude especially with regard to sexual activity, changes in available medical treatments, and changes in the reportability of the HIV disease.

4.4. Assumption 4 — Uniform Force of Progression

A uniform force of progression is acceptable for time periods shorter than observation periods.

5. MODEL FORMULAS AND METHODS

5.1. Levels

Levels in this model are counts of patients by stage, duration in stage, and time since the start of the model. Levels are known as "states" in Markov Chain models and "nodes" in Operations Research models.

The count of patients in stage S, at duration D in stage, at time T since the start of the model, for a model using N time periods per year is:

$$L^{(N)}_{S,D,T} \tag{1}$$

where N is the number of time periods per year,
$\quad$ S is the stage,*
$\quad$ D is the duration in stage (in years), and
$\quad$ T is the time since the start of the model (in years).

Note that T is used only for recording the results of the model at a time since the start of the model and does not affect the probability of progression.

5.2. Flows

Since progression or nonprogression are the only two possible events, there are only two flows in the model:

1. Progression (from one stage to the next), and
2. Nonprogression.

Flows are known as "decisions" in Markov Chain and Operations Research models.

---

*0 = "1b" = "HIV+", 1 = "2a" = "LAS", 2 = "2b" = "ARC", 3 = "3" = "AIDS", and 4 = "Dead."

The probability of patients from stage S at duration D in stage, progressing to stage $S+1$ at duration 0 in stage, for a single time period, for a model using N time periods per year is:

$$Q_{S,D}^{(N)} \tag{2}$$

where N is the number of time periods per year,
      S is the stage, and
      D is the duration in stage (in years).

The probability of patients from stage S at duration D stage, remaining in stage S at duration $D+1$ in stage, for a single time period, for a model using N time periods per year is:

$$1 - Q_{S,D}^{(N)} \tag{3}$$

Where annual progression rates are defined, progression rates for an Nth of period are derived as follows:

$$Q_{S,D}^{(N)} = 1 - \left(1 - Q_{S,D}^{(1)}\right)^{1/N} \tag{4}$$

and

$$Q_{S,D+N/N}^{(N)} \, Q_{S,D}^{(N)}, \text{ for } H = 0 \text{ to } N - 1 \tag{5}$$

Where semiannual progression rates are defined, progression rates for an Nth of period are derived as follows:

$$Q_{S,D}^{(N)} = 1 - \left(1 - Q_{S,D}^{(2)}\right)^{2/N} \tag{6}$$

and

$$Q_{S,D+N/N}^{(N)} = Q_{S,D}^{(N)}, \text{ for } H = 0 \text{ to } \left(\frac{N}{2}\right) - 1 \tag{7}$$

5.3. Progression

The number of patients in a stage for duration of zero is equal to the number of patients in the previous stage at any duration who did progress during the previous time period.

$$L_{S,0,T}^{(N)} = \sum_{D=0}^{\infty} \left(L_{S-1,D,T-1/N}^{(N)} \times Q_{S-1,D}^{(N)} \right) \tag{8}$$

5.4. Nonprogression

The number of patients in a stage for a duration greater than zero is equal to the number of patients in that stage in the previous duration who did *not* progress during the previous time period.

$$L^{(N)}_{S,D,T} = L^{(N)}_{S,D-1/N,T-1/N} \times \left(1 - Q^{(N)}_{S,D-1/N}\right), \text{ for } D > 0 \qquad [9]$$

5.5. Time Periods — The Continuous Model

A significant issue in developing the model was the number of time periods per year to be used. Recall that "N" is the number of time periods per year. Since the first year of observation in the Frankfurt Study was in six-month intervals, the model should have at least two time periods per year ($N \geq 2$). Also, the number of time periods per year should be even.

However, the use of a six-month time period ($N=2$) would result in artificial restraint of a minimum time to progress four stages (from HIV infection to death) of two years. This would produce unacceptable distortions. Therefore a shorter time period (a larger N) had to be used. A continuous model ($N = \infty$, or an infinite number of infinitely short time periods per year) would eliminate the artificial minimum time to progress four stages.

Since a count was kept of all patients by stage and duration in that stage, doubling the number of time periods per year would double the number of cells modeled. In addition, the number of time periods in the duration of the model would also double. Therefore doubling the number of time periods per year would quadruple the time necessary to run the model. A continuous model therefore implies an infinitely long time to run a model.

However, it was discovered by experimentation that the counts of patients produced by a model based on a certain number (N) of time periods per year was nearly linearly related to the length ($1/N$) of the time period used. This near linearity was confirmed by testing up to $N=36$, a model of which took a prohibitively long time to run. The reason for this near linearity is unknown.

Using this discovery, we approximated a continuous model ($N = \infty$) from a one-month model ($N=12$) and a two-month model ($N=6$) by the following formula:

$$L^{(\infty)}_{S,D,T} = 2 \times L^{(12)}_{S,D,T} - L^{(6)}_{S,D,T} \qquad [10]$$

The derivation of this formula is in the Appendix.

5.6. Initial Values

The model starts with a single cohort group of 100,000 newly HIV infected patients. (Stage = 0 = "1b" = "HIV + ", duration = 0, and time = 0.)

$$L^{(N)}_{0,0,0} = 100,000 \qquad [11]$$

$$\text{else } L^{(N)}_{S,T,D} = 0 \qquad [12]$$

5.7. Reported Results

The model reported the number of patients by stage for successive six-month intervals. Duration within stage was not reported. Reporting results for intervals shorter than six months would not be helpful because the model assumptions are based on six-month data and the model produces rough linearity between six-month intervals.

6. MODELED PERIODIC PROGRESSION RATES

6.1. Date of HIV Infection

One issue in this and subsequent analysis is the difficulty in determining the precise time at which HIV infection occurs. HIV infection is defined as the initial progression from HIV negative status to HIV positive status. Even under clinically controlled conditions, it is difficult to precisely pinpoint such time.

Unless subjects at high risk of HIV infection, but actually HIV negative, are examined frequently enough to have a negative test closely followed by a positive test, the precise date of HIV infection cannot be determined. Because of the unknown time between HIV infection and initial observation of the infection, it is likely that progression appears to take place faster in studies than it does in reality. As the disease progresses, however, and more subjects come under medical observation, the measurements of progression to later stages are likely to be more precise.

6.2. HIV Progression Rates for the First Three Years

In building periodic HIV progression rates, it was assumed that each of the four ranges of observation periods fully represented the underlying cumulative HIV progression through the upper limit of the range. Specifically that the 3–6 month range represented the underlying cumulative HIV progression through the 6th month, the 6–12 month range represented the underlying cumulative HIV progression through the 12th month, and so on. Assumed periodic rates were derived from these assumed cumulative rates. Table 3 shows the development of the assumed periodic HIV progression rates. Section 6.6 discusses the choice of the upper limit of the range of length of the observation period as opposed to the average length.

TABLE 3

DEVELOPMENT OF ASSUMED PERIODIC HIV PROGRESSION RATES

Cumulative Period (months)	Assumed Cumulative Progression Rates	Period (months)	Not Yet Progressed at Start of Period	Progressed during Period	Assumed Periodic Progression Rates
(A) Progression from Stage 1b to Stage 2a					
0–6	11%	0–6	100%	11%	11%
0–12	56	6–12	89	44	50
0–24	75	12–24	44	19	44
0–36	80	24–36	25	5	20
(B) Progression from Stage 2a to Stage 2b					
0–6	14	0–6	100	14	14
0–12	39	6–12	86	25	29
0–24	48	12–24	61	9	15
0–36	74	24–36	52	25	49
(C) Progression from Stage 2b to Stage 3					
0–6	0	0–6	100	0	0
0–12	10	6–12	100	10	10
0–24	50	12–24	90	40	44
0–36	57	24–36	50	7	14

The raw assumed periodic progression rates were then graduated where necessary, with the objective of preserving as closely as possible the raw assumed cumulative progression rates. The amount of graduation was minimal because the high consistency of the raw progression rates implied little need for graduation. The impact of the minimal graduation was negligible and was tested by running the model with the raw progression rates.

The graduated periodic HIV progression rates for Stages 1b, 2a, and 2b for the first three years since progression to that stage are included in Table 4.

TABLE 4

PERIODIC PROGRESSION RATES USED IN THE MODEL

Period	Stage 1a (At-Risk)	Stage 1b (HIV+)	Stage 2a (LAS)	Stage 2b (ARC)	Stage 3 (AIDS)
First Six Months	N/A	10%	15%	[5%]	[26%]
Second Six Months	N/A	50	30	[5]	[26]
First Year	N/A	[55]	[40]	10	45
Second Year	N/A	45	35	45	45
Third Year	N/A	20	35	15	35
Fourth and Subsequent Years	N/A	20	20	20	25

Notes: Stage 1a progression rates (HIV Infection Rates) are not used in the Model.
Stage 1b, 2a, and 2b progression rates are derived from Frankfurt Study data. These rates are graduated for the first three years and projected for the fourth and subsequent years.
Stage 3 progression rates (AIDS Mortality Rates) are derived from CDC data. These rates are graduated for the first six years and projected for the seventh and subsequent years.
[ ] indicate effective rates calculated from either First and Second Six Month rates, or from First Year rates.

6.3. HIV Progression Rates for the Fourth Year and On

HIV progression rates for Stages 1b, 2a, and 2b for the fourth and subsequent years since progression to those stages were projected to be 20 percent. This is approximately the average of the third-year HIV progression rates for those stages. Results of models using this rate closely approximate the result of models using a continuation of the third-year rates. We consider this to be the most reasonable assumption.

The impact of projection is lessened because of the small number of survivors in a stage when the projected progression rates start being used. Since only 20 percent to 42 percent of the patients did not progress to the next stage of the disease before the start of the fourth year, the ultimate progression rates do not have as much impact on the model as do the rates for the first three years.

The projected periodic HIV progression rates for Stages 1b, 2a, and 2b for the fourth and subsequent years since progression to that stage are included in Table 4.

6.4. AIDS Mortality Rates

Table 5 shows the development of modeled AIDS mortality rates. These rates were developed from CDC data by assuming that CDC Case Fatality Rates for each half-year of AIDS diagnosis fully represented the underlying cumulative AIDS mortality from the midpoint of the half-year through the date of the report.

TABLE 5

MODELED AIDS MORTALITY RATES DERIVED FROM SECTION G
AIDS WEEKLY SURVEILLANCE REPORT
UNITED STATES AIDS PROGRAM
CENTER FOR INFECTIOUS DISEASES
CENTER FOR DISEASE CONTROL
MARCH 30, 1987

Date of AIDS Diagnosis (by Half-Years)	Assumed Average Years Since AIDS Diagnosis	Actual Cumulative AIDS Mortality	Modeled Annual AIDS Mortality Rate	Modeled Cumulative AIDS Mortality
1986 July – Dec.	0.5	28%	45%	26%
1986 Jan. – June	1	48	45	45
1985 July – Dec.	1.5	63	45	59
1985 Jan. – June	2	71	45	70
1984 July – Dec.	2.5	78	35	76
1984 Jan. – June	3	80	35	80
1983 July – Dec.	3.5	83	25	83
1983 Jan. – June	4	87	25	85
1982 July – Dec.	4.5	87	25	87
1982 Jan. – June	5	88	25	89
1981 July – Dec.	5.5	90	25	90
1981 Jan. – June	6	92	25	92

Modeled AIDS mortality rates are 45 percent annually in the first and second years since the progression to AIDS, 35 percent in the third year, and 25 percent thereafter. This produces a life expectancy of about 2.1 years from progression to AIDS and a 6-year AIDS survival rate of 8 percent.

Chart 1 compares modeled cumulative AIDS mortality to actual CDC Case Fatality Rates for the first six years since diagnosis of AIDS.

6.5. Summary of Modeled Periodic Progression Rates

Stage 1a progression rates (HIV Infection Rates) were not used in the model.

Stage 1b, 2a, and 2b progression rates were derived from graduated Frankfurt data for the first three years since progression to that stage and projected for the fourth and subsequent years.

CHART 1

Cumulative AIDS Mortality

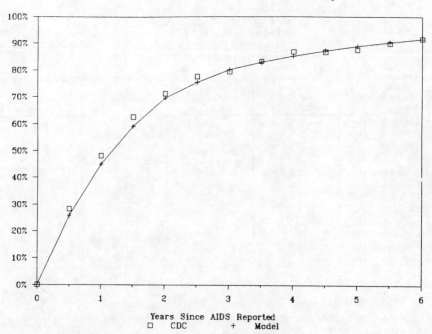

Years Since AIDS Reported
□   CDC   +   Model

Notes:

□   CDC Data are CDC AIDS Case Fatality Rates as of March 30, 1987.

+   Model Data are Cumulative AIDS Mortality based on Annual AIDS
    Mortality Rates of 45%, 45%, 35%, and 25% thereafter.

Stage 3 progression rates (AIDS Mortality Rates) were derived from graduated CDC data for the first six years since progression of AIDS and projected for the seventh and subsequent years.

Table 4 shows the progression rates used in the model. The rates are
periodic progression rates (i.e., second-year progression rates show the percent of patients who have been in the stage for one year who will progress
to the next stage in the second year).

Table 6 shows modeled cumulative progression rates resulting from the periodic progression rates in Table 4 for comparison to the raw cumulative progression rates in Tables 1–3 and 5. Not only are the modeled progression close to the assumed raw progression rates, but the results of models based on either set of rates are similar.

TABLE 6

MODELED CUMULATIVE PROGRESSION

Duration (months)	Duration (years)	Stage 1a (At-Risk)	Stage 1b (HIV +)	Stage 2a (LAS)	Stage 2b (ARC)	Stage 3 (AIDS)
6	0.5	N/A	10%	15%	5%	26%
12	1	N/A	55	41	10	45
24	2	N/A	75	61	51	70
36	3	N/A	80	75	58	80
48	4	N/A	84	80	66	85
60	5	N/A	87	84	73	89
72	6	N/A	90	87	78	92

Note: These cumulative progression rates were derived from the periodic progression rates in Table 4 for comparison with cumulative progression rates in Tables 1–3 and 5.

The expected number of years to progress from one stage of the disease to the next, based on Table 4 periodic progression rates, is:

2.25 years from Stage 1b (HIV +) to 2a (LAS),
2.74 years from Stage 2a (LAS) to 2b (ARC),
3.97 years from Stage 2b (ARC) to 3 (AIDS), and
2.10 years from Stage 3 (AIDS) to death.

This results in an expected number of years from HIV infection to death (HIV life expectancy) of 11.06 years.

6.6. "Low Assumptions" Versus "High Assumptions"

Where possible, "low assumptions" (i.e., lower progression rates) were used to offset any assumptions that might be construed as "high assumptions" (i.e., higher progression rates).

Periodic progression rates based on the duration since the start of the observation period would be considered "high assumptions" because this assumes the patients progressed to their stage at the start of their observation period, whereas they had probably been in the stage for some unknown time before the start of their observation period.

Periodic progression rates based on the maximum length of observation period (as opposed to the average length) would be considered "low assumptions" because this overstates the assumed duration of observed progressions.

It is likely that using the maximum length of observation periods offsets somewhat the unknown time between progression to current stage and the start of the observation period. This is why we used the maximum length of observation period, and not the average length, in deriving assumed progression rates.

Table 7 compares the maximum and average lengths of observation periods. This table shows that the use of the average length of observation period would result in progressions in approximately 80 percent (75–83 percent) of the time of progressions based on the maximum length.

TABLE 7

COMPARISON OF MAXIMUM AND AVERAGE LENGTHS OF OBSERVATION PERIODS

Range of Length of Observation Periods (months)	Maximum Length of Observation Periods (months)	Average Length of Observation Periods (months)	Ratio of Average Length to Maximum Length
3–6	6	4.5	75%
6–12	12	9	75
12–24	24	18	75
24–36	36	30	83

7. MODEL RESULTS AND COMPARISONS

The results of the model based on Frankfurt HIV progression rates and CDC AIDS mortality rates are shown in Tables 8 and 9 and in Chart 2. These results are compared to other mortality scenarios in Tables 10 and 11 and in Charts 3 and 4.

7.1. Frankfurt/CDC Model Results

The major results of the model, specifically the progression of the HIV disease in terms of the percent of a newly HIV infected cohort by stage of the disease and duration since HIV infection, are shown in Table 8 and illustrated in Chart 2. Half-year results not shown in Table 8 can be calculated by interpolation.

TABLE 8

RESULTS OF MODEL
BASED ON FRANKFURT STUDY HIV PROGRESSION RATES
AND CDC AIDS MORTALITY RATES

Years Since HIV Infection	Progression from HIV Infection to Death (Percent Distribution by Stage)				
	Stage 1b (HIV+)	Stage 2a (LAS)	Stage 2b (ARC)	Stage 3 (AIDS)	Dead
0	100.0%	0.0	0.0	0.0	0.0
0.5	90.0	9.2%	0.8%	0.0	0.0
1	45.0	48.2	6.6	0.2%	0.0
1.5	33.4	47.5	18.3	0.7	0.1%
2	24.8	44.2	28.3	2.2	0.5
2.5	22.1	37.3	33.9	5.1	1.5
3	19.8	31.8	36.0	8.8	3.6
3.5	17.7	27.5	36.5	11.6	6.7
4	15.8	24.6	35.9	13.3	10.4
4.5	14.2	22.5	34.6	14.3	14.4
5	12.7	20.7	33.2	14.8	18.6
6	10.1	17.7	30.6	14.9	26.7
7	8.1	15.0	28.0	14.6	34.2
8	6.5	12.7	25.3	14.2	41.3
9	5.2	10.8	22.7	13.5	47.9
10	4.2	9.1	20.2	12.6	54.0
11	3.3	7.6	17.9	11.7	59.5
12	2.7	6.4	15.7	10.7	64.6
13	2.1	5.3	13.7	9.7	69.1
14	1.7	4.5	12.0	8.7	73.2
15	1.4	3.7	10.4	7.8	76.8
16	1.1	3.1	9.0	6.9	79.9
17	0.9	2.6	7.7	6.1	82.7
18	0.7	2.1	6.6	5.4	85.2
19	0.6	1.8	5.7	4.7	87.3
20	0.4	1.5	4.9	4.1	89.1
21	0.4	1.2	4.1	3.6	90.7
22	0.3	1.0	3.5	3.1	92.1
23	0.2	0.8	3.0	2.7	93.3
24	0.2	0.7	2.5	2.3	94.3
25	0.1	0.6	2.1	2.0	95.2

CHART 2

Progression of HIV Infection

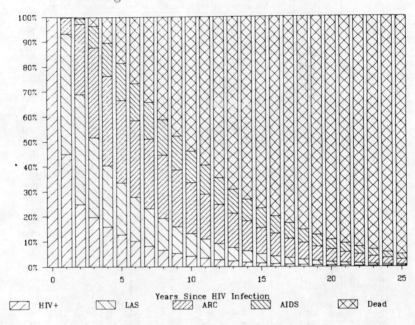

"Walter Reed Staging Method":

HIV+	1b	Patients testing positive for HIV infection but otherwise asymptomatic.
LAS	2a	Patients with HIV infection and lymphadenopathy syndrome (LAS), together with moderate cellular immune deficiency.
ARC	2b	Patients with HIV infection and LAS, together with severe cellular immune deficiency (AIDS-Related Complex, or ARC, as defined by CDC).
AIDS	3	Patients with AIDS as currently defined by CDC.

960

Table 9 shows annual rates of progression to AIDS, cumulative progression to AIDS, annual HIV mortality rates, and cumulative HIV mortality. Annual rates of progression to AIDS are defined as those progressing to AIDS during the year divided by those not yet progressed to AIDS as of the start of the year.

TABLE 9

RESULTS OF MODEL
BASED ON FRANKFURT STUDY HIV PROGRESSION RATES
AND CDC AIDS MORTALITY RATES

Years Since HIV Infection	(A) Progression from HIV Infection to AIDS		(B) HIV Mortality (HIV Infection to Death)	
	Annual Rate*	Cumulative Progression	Annual Rate†	Cumulative Mortality
0	0.2%	0.0	0.0	0.0
1	2.5	0.2%	0.5%	0.0
2	9.9	2.7	3.1	0.5%
3	12.9	12.4	7.0	3.6
4	12.7	23.7	9.2	10.4
5	12.3	33.4	10.0	18.6
6	12.5	41.6	10.3	26.7
7	12.9	48.9	10.7	34.2
8	13.2	55.5	11.2	41.3
9	13.5	61.4	11.7	47.9
10	13.8	66.6	12.1	54.0
11	14.1	71.2	12.5	59.5
12	14.3	75.3	12.8	64.6
13	14.5	78.8	13.1	69.1
14	14.7	81.9	13.4	73.2
15	14.9	84.6	13.7	76.8
16	15.1	86.9	13.9	79.9
17	15.2	88.8	14.1	82.7
18	15.4	90.5	14.3	85.2
19	15.5	92.0	14.5	87.3
20	15.7	93.2	14.7	89.1
21	15.8	94.3	14.9	90.7
22	15.9	95.2	15.0	92.1
23	16.0	96.0	15.2	93.3
24	16.1	96.6	15.3	94.3
25	16.2	97.2	15.4	95.2

*Of those HIV infected but not yet progressed to AIDS.
†Of those HIV infected but not yet dead.

7.2. Comparisons to Other Mortality Scenarios

Table 10 adds standard mortality to modeled HIV mortality and compares the results to standard mortality, marginally insurable substandard mortality, and two alternative HIV mortality scenarios. The standard mortality in this model is 1980 CSO Basic Male Nonsmoker. Marginally insurable substandard mortality is defined for this analysis as five times standard (500% of standard).

TABLE 10

EXPECTED MORTALITY UNDER VARIOUS SCENARIOS

Attained Age	Years	"FM-High"	"FM-Mid"	"FM-Low"	"500%"	"100%"
(A) Annual Mortality Rates						
35	0	0.2%	0.1%	0.1%	0.4%	0.1%
36	1	2.0	0.6	0.3	0.4	0.1
37	2	6.9	3.2	1.6	0.4	0.1
38	3	10.9	7.1	3.6	0.5	0.1
39	4	12.4	9.3	4.7	0.5	0.1
40	5	13.0	10.1	5.1	0.6	0.1
45	10	16.2	12.3	6.2	1.0	0.2
50	15	18.1	14.0	7.2	1.6	0.3
55	20	19.4	15.3	7.9	2.8	0.6
60	25	20.5	16.4	8.7	4.9	1.0
(B) Cumulative Morality						
36	1	0.2%	0.1%	0.1%	0.4%	0.1%
37	2	2.2	0.7	0.4	0.8	0.2
38	3	8.9	3.8	2.1	1.2	0.2
39	4	18.9	10.7	5.6	1.7	0.3
40	5	28.9	19.0	10.0	2.2	0.4
45	10	67.3	54.6	32.3	5.8	1.2
50	15	87.1	77.4	52.0	11.3	2.4
55	20	95.4	89.7	67.4	19.9	4.3
60	25	98.5	95.6	78.8	33.2	7.7

Scenario Descriptions: "FM-High"—HIV Mortality 20% faster than Model HIV Mortality plus 100% Standard Mortality.
"FM-Mid"—Model HIV Mortality plus 100% Standard Mortality.
"FM-Low"—One-Half of Model HIV Mortality plus 100% Standard Mortality.
"500%"—"Marginally Insurable Substandard Mortality" (500% Standard Mortality).
"100%"—"Standard Mortality" (1980 CSO Basic Male Nonsmoker Age 35).

The two alternative HIV mortality scenarios are introduced solely to provide a range of estimates around the best estimate. The original and two alternative HIV mortality scenarios are defined as follows.

FM-Mid is the original best-estimate model results discussed up to this point. FM-Mid is short for Frankfurt/CDC Model Midrange results.

FM-High approximates using the *average* observation period in determining the raw cumulative progression rates as opposed to using the *maximum* observation period. FM-High cumulative HIV mortality rates at *Y* years were set to FM-Mid cumulative HIV mortality rates at *Y*/0.80 years. In other words, FM-High takes only 80 percent of the time that FM-Mid takes to progress to a given cumulative HIV mortality. See Section 6.6 for the derivation of the 0.80 factor.

FM-Low arbitrarily uses one-half of the HIV mortality rates used in FM-Mid.

Annual mortality rates for each scenario is shown in Table 10A and illustrated in Chart 3. Cumulative mortality for each scenario are shown in Table 10B and illustrated in Chart 4.

Table 11A shows the complete expectation of life at HIV infection at age 35. HIV mortality rates under the three "FM" scenarios for the 26th and subsequent years were held at the 25th year rates for purposes of calculating the complete expectation of life.

For illustrative purposes only, the equivalent level multiples of 1980 CSO Basic Male Nonsmoker Table rates were calculated that would produce the same life expectancy of a 35-year-old cohort of males newly HIV infected. Table 11B shows the multiple of standard mortality that yields the same complete expectation of life as in Table 11A.

To match the same life expectancy as produced by projecting Frankfurt and CDC data, mortality would have to be elevated to over 51 times standard. In other words, this level of mortality is over 10 times higher than the upper limit of marginally acceptable substandard life insurance risks (5 times standard).

Table 11C shows the expected "half-life" of a group of patients HIV infected at age 35. "Half-life" is defined as the time in years at which cumulative mortality is expected to be 50 percent (i.e., half the patients are dead). Table 11D shows the multiple of standard mortality that yields the same expected "half-life" as in Table 11C.

Further analysis shows significant differences between the *patterns* of cumulative HIV mortality and cumulative mortality based on extreme multiples of standard mortality. As Chart 3 shows, HIV mortality rises steeply following infection. This produces an usually high number of early deaths even when compared to high multiples of standard. Such significant differences make comparisons of HIV mortality to multiples of standard mortality potentially misleading. This is demonstrated by the different "Equivalent Multiples of Standard Mortality" shown in Tables 11B and 11D.

CHART 3

Annual HIV Mortality Rates

HIV Infection at Age 35

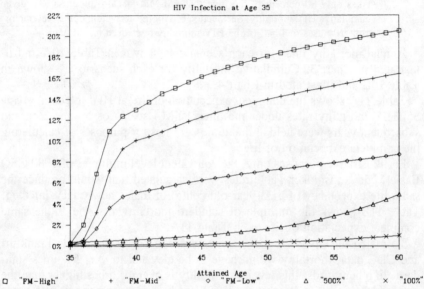

Scenario Descriptions:

□	"FM-High"	HIV Mortality 20% faster than Model HIV Mortality plus 100% Standard Mortality.
+	"FM-Mid"	Model HIV Mortality plus 100% Standard Mortality.
◇	"FM-Low"	One Half of Model HIV Mortality plus 100% Standard Mortality.
△	"500%"	"Marginally Insurable Substandard Mortality" (500% Standard Mortality).
×	"100%"	"Standard Mortality" (1980 CSO Basic Male Non Smoker Age 35).

CHART 4

Cumulative HIV Mortality

HIV Infection at Age 35

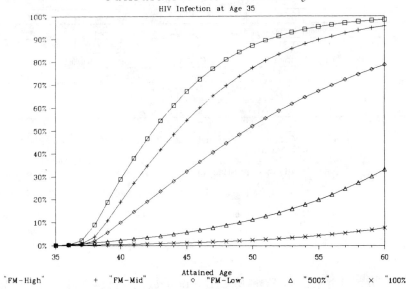

Attained Age

□ "FM-High"   + "FM-Mid"   ◇ "FM-Low"   △ "500%"   × "100%"

Scenario Descriptions:

□	"FM-High"	HIV Mortality 20% faster than Model HIV Mortality plus 100% Standard Mortality.
+	"FM-Mid"	Model HIV Mortality plus 100% Standard Mortality.
◇	"FM-Low"	One Half of Model HIV Mortality plus 100% Standard Mortality.
△	"500%"	"Marginally Insurable Substandard Mortality" (500% Standard Mortality).
×	"100%"	"Standard Mortality" (1980 CSO Basic Male Non Smoker Age 35).

965

TABLE 11

EXPECTATIONS OF LIFE UNDER VARIOUS SCENARIOS

"FM-High"	"FM-Mid"	"FM-Low"	"500%"	"100%"
(a) Complete Expectation of Life in Years at Age 35				
8.75	10.89	16.93	28.24	42.62
(B) Multiple of Standard Mortality for Same Complete Expectation of Life at Age 35				
74.6	51.3	20.8	5.0	1.0
(C) Expected "Half-Life" in Years at Age 35 (Years until 50% Cumulative Mortality)				
7.43	9.25	14.46	29.63	44.10
(D) Multiple of Standard Mortality for Same Expected "Half-Life" at Age 35 (Years until 50% Cumulative Mortality)				
87.0	63.6	30.2	5.0	1.0

Scenario Descriptions: "FM-High"—HIV Mortality 20% faster than Model HIV Mortality plus 100% Standard Mortality.
"FM-Mid"—Model HIV Mortality plus 100% Standard Mortality.
"FM-Low"—One-Half of Model HIV Mortality plus 100% Standard Mortality.
"500%"—"Marginally Insurable Substandard Mortality" (500% Standard Mortality).
"100%"—"Standard Mortality" (1980 CSO Basic Male Nonsmoker Age 35).

8. CONCLUSION

The model based on Frankfurt HIV progression rates and CDC AIDS mortality rates shows cumulative HIV mortality rates of approximately 19 percent for 5 years, 55 percent for 10 years, 77 percent for 15 years, 90 percent for 20 years, and 96 percent for 25 years. The results are consistent with the view of the U.S. Surgeon General that the progression from HIV infection to AIDS might ultimately reach close to 100 percent.

The magnitude of the results was corroborated by other studies discussed in *AIDS and Life Insurance,* part I of this chapter, and were useful in generating models of HIV infection and progression to AIDS and death.

Please read Section 3.7 of *AIDS and Life Insurance* for a discussion of the persistence of current HIV mortality and the appropriateness of deriving HIV progression rates from studies of high-risk groups and then applying them to other dissimilar groups.

Finally, a few closing observations on the usefulness of modeling:

• A mathematical model is a representation of an actual real-world system. Knowledge of the system is incorporated in the model and then the model can be used to predict the system. A model can confirm or refute an "intuitive feel" for the overall system.

A model has the ability to test the effect of changes in assumptions, including extrapolations.

- A model is especially useful in that a challenge to the overall results of a model must be supported by challenges to specific factors and/or assumptions. In other words, someone disagreeing with the results of a model must be able to dispute a specific assumption, relationship, or methodology.
- Forrester [4] has an excellent and highly recommended presentation on the construction and validation of mathematical models.

9. REFERENCES

1. BRODT, H.R., HELM, E.G., WERNER, A., JOETTEN, A., BERGMANN, L., KLUVER, A., AND STILLE, W., *Spontanverlauf der LAV/HTLV-III-Infektion; Verlaufsbeobachtungen bei Personen aus AIDS-Risikogruppen;* Deutsche Medizinische Wochenschrift, Stuttgart, Vol. 111 (1986), pp. 1175–1180.
2. *The Walter Reed staging classification for HTLV-III/LAV Infection,* New England Journal of Medicine, 1986, Vol. 314, No. 2, pp. 131–132.
3. *AIDS Weekly Surveillance Report,* United States AIDS Program, Center for Infectious Diseases, Centers for Disease Control, Public Health Service, Department of Health and Human Services, Atlanta, GA, March 30, 1987, p. 5.
4. FORRESTER, JAY W., *Industrial Dynamics,* Cambridge, MA, The M.I.T. Press, 1961, chapters 4 and 13.

10. APPENDIX

DERIVATION OF APPROXIMATION OF CONTINUOUS MARKOV CHAIN MODEL

Linearity between the counts ($L^{(N)}$) resulting from a model with N time periods per year and the length ($1/N$) of time period used gives:

$$\frac{\Delta(L^{(N)})}{\Delta(1/N)} = \text{a constant} \qquad [1]$$

and

$$\left(\frac{L^{(A)} - L^{(B)}}{1/A - 1/B}\right) = \left(\frac{L^{(B)} - L^{(C)}}{1/B - 1/C}\right) \qquad [2]$$

Solving for $L^{(A)}$ gives:

$$L^{(A)} = L^{(B)} + \left(\frac{1/A - 1/B}{1/B - 1/C}\right) \times (L^{(B)} - L^{(C)}) \qquad [3]$$

If $B = 2C$, then:

$$L^{(A)} = L^{(2C)} + \left(\frac{1/A - 1/2C}{1/2C - 1/C}\right) \times (L^{(2C)} - L^{(C)}) \qquad [4]$$

$$= L^{(2C)} + (1 - 2C/A) \times (L^{(2C)} - L^{(C)}) \qquad [5]$$

$$= 2 \times L^{(2C)} - L^{(C)} - (2C/A) \times (L^{(2C)} - L^{(C)}) \qquad [6]$$

If we define $L^{(\infty)} = \lim_{A \to \infty} L^{(A)}$, then:

$$L^{(\infty)} = \lim_{A \to \infty} [2 \times L^{(2C)} - L^{(C)} - (2C/A) \times (L^{(2C)} - L^{(C)})] \qquad [7]$$

$$= 2 \times L^{(2C)} - L^{(C)} - \lim_{A \to \infty} [2C/A] \times (L^{(2C)} - L^{(C)}) \qquad [8]$$

$$= 2 \times L^{(2C)} - L^{(C)} - 0 \times (L^{(2C)} - L^{(C)}) \qquad [9]$$

$$= 2 \times L^{(2C)} - L^{(C)} \qquad [10]$$

If $C = 6$ (and $B = 2C = 2 \times 6 = 12$), then:

$$L^{(\infty)} = 2 \times L^{(12)} - L^{(6)} \qquad [11]$$

Note: The model was designed to be capable of using any even number of time periods per year.

ADDENDUM #1

The following comments and tables should be of benefit to those working to reproduce Appendices 1 and 2 of part I of this chapter.

In developing the Appendices of part I, Mike Cowell used HIV progression rates from the SFCC/CDC Model instead of from the Frankfurt Model as might be expected. SFCC/CDC Model HIV progression rates are lower than Frankfurt Model HIV progression rates.

The SFCC/CDC Model

The SFCC/CDC Model is described in part I, Section 3.7. It is based on HIV progression rates from the San Francisco City Clinic/CDC Study (part I, Section 3.4), and AIDS mortality rates from CDC AIDS Cases and Deaths data (part I, Section 3.5).

The results of the SFCC/CDC Model are shown in the following tables. These tables are analogous to Tables 8 through 11 of part II, which show the results of the Frankfurt Model.

The results of the SFCC/CDC Model and the Frankfurt Model are illustrated in Charts 4 and 5 of part I.

The Frankfurt Model

The Frankfurt Model is described in part I, Section 3.6 and in part II.

TABLE 8

SFCC/CDC Model
RESULTS OF MODEL BASED ON
SAN FRANCISCO CITY CLINIC/CDC HIV PROGRESSION RATES
AND CDC AIDS MORTALITY RATES

Years Since HIV Infection	Stage 1b (HIV+))	Stage 2a (LAS)	Stage 2b (ARC)	Stage 3 (AIDSJ)	Dead
0	100.0	*	*	0.0	0.0
1	99.7	*	*	0.2	0.1
2	98.5	*	*	0.8	0.7
3	95.9	*	*	1.9	2.2
4	91.6	*	*	3.4	5.0
5	85.4	*	*	5.4	9.2
6	76.8	*	*	8.0	15.2
7	66.4	*	*	10.6	23.0
8	56.4	*	*	12.0	31.6
9	48.0	*	*	12.3	39.8
10	40.8	*	*	11.9	47.3
11	34.7	*	*	11.3	54.1
12	29.5	*	*	10.4	60.1
13	25.0	*	*	9.5	65.5
14	21.3	*	*	8.5	70.2
15	18.1	*	*	7.6	74.3
16	15.4	*	*	6.7	77.9
17	13.1	*	*	5.9	81.0
18	11.1	*	*	5.2	83.7
19	9.4	*	*	4.5	86.0
20	8.0	*	*	3.9	88.0
21	6.8	*	*	3.4	89.8
22	5.8	*	*	2.9	91.3
23	4.9	*	*	2.5	92.5
24	4.2	*	*	2.2	93.6
25	3.6	*	*	1.9	94.6

*Included in Stage 1b (HIV+).

TABLE 9

SFCC/CDC MODEL
RESULTS OF MODEL BASED ON
SAN FRANCISCO CITY CLINIC/CDC HIV PROGRESSION RATES
AND CDC AIDS MORTALITY RATES

Years Since HIV Infection	(A) Progression from HIV Infection to AIDS		(B) HIV Mortality (HIV Infection to Death)	
	Annual Rate	Cumulative Progression	Annual Rate	Cumulative Mortality
0	0.3%	0.0	0.1%	0.0
1	1.2	0.3%	0.6	0.1%
2	2.6	1.5	1.5	0.7
3	4.5	4.1	2.8	2.2
4	6.8	8.4	4.4	5.0
5	10.1	14.6	6.6	9.2
6	13.5	23.2	9.2	15.2
7	15.0	33.6	11.1	23.0
8	15.0	43.6	12.0	31.6
9	15.0	52.0	12.5	39.8
10	15.0	59.2	12.9	47.3
11	15.0	65.3	13.2	54.1
12	15.0	70.5	13.4	60.1
13	15.0	75.0	13.6	65.5
14	15.0	78.7	13.8	70.2
15	15.0	81.9	14.0	74.3
16	15.0	84.6	14.1	77.9
17	15.0	86.9	14.2	81.0
18	15.0	88.9	14.3	83.7
19	15.0	90.6	14.4	86.0
20	15.0	92.0	14.5	88.0
21	15.0	93.2	14.5	89.8
22	15.0	94.2	14.6	91.3
23	15.0	95.1	14.6	92.5
24	15.0	95.8	14.7	93.6
25	15.0	96.4	14.7	94.6

TABLE 10

SFCC/CDC MODEL
EXPECTED MORTALITY UNDER VARIOUS SCENARIOS

Attained Age	Years	SFCC/CDC Model
(A) Annual Mortality Rates		
35	0	0.1
36	1	0.6
37	2	1.5
38	3	2.8
39	4	4.4
40	5	6.6
45	10	12.9
50	15	14.0
55	20	14.5
60	25	14.7
(B) Cumulative Mortality		
36	1	0.1
37	2	0.7
38	3	2.2
39	4	5.0
40	5	9.2
45	10	47.3
50	15	74.3
55	20	88.0
60	25	94.6

TABLE 11

SFCC/CDC MODEL
EXPECTED MORTALITY UNDER VARIOUS SCENARIOS

	SFCC/CDC Model
(A) Complete Expectation of Life in Years at Age 35	11.85
(B) Multiple of Standard Mortality for Same Complete Expectation of Life at Age 35	43.9
(C) Expected "Half-Life" in Years at Age 35 (Years until 50% Cumulative Mortality)	11.30
(D) Multiple of Standard Mortality for Same Expected "Half-Life" at Age 35 (Years until 50% Cumulative Mortality)	54.0

972

CHAPTER 4

MODELING THE IMPACT OF AIDS-RELATED
LIFE INSURANCE CLAIMS

SOCIETY OF ACTUARIES
AIDS TASK FORCE SUBCOMMITTEE*

INTRODUCTION

The purpose of this paper is to provide the information, considerations and framework needed to formulate a model for estimating the effect of future AIDS-related life insurance claims. This paper is not meant to be an exhaustive treatment of the subject. It presents background information setting forth the main considerations in constructing a model and provides pertinent information about the nature and incidence of AIDS deaths, especially with respect to life insurance risks.

Alternative approaches for constructing a company model are then presented with some ways to explore implications on company mortality. Finally, sample models have been included. These are provided for demonstration only and are not meant to serve as actual projections of any company's experience. Each company must assess its own unique situation. The three models illustrate the range of detail that may be considered, from the simpler approach of example 1 to the more refined of example 3.

There are a variety of methods that can be used to construct an AIDS model. This paper will be successful if it provides some background and framework so that the reader can construct a model to fit his or her own unique needs. There is still much to be learned, and the actuary is encouraged to pursue alternative approaches.

I. GENERAL CRITERIA TO BE CONSIDERED IN MODEL CONSTRUCTION

A. Resources and Time Available

Resources available may dictate the type of model to be used. Data availability is another consideration. It makes little sense to use a very sophisticated model if detailed data on claims and in-force contracts are not available or are not credible. Creating models with PCs and speadsheet programs will

*Philip J. Barackman, David J. Christianson, William C. Koenig, and Harry A. Woodman; assisted by Steven D. Lash, Jeffrey S. Marks, and John K. Wilbur.

likely give good initial results as well as flexibility to make future modifications. Of course, mainframe applications might also be quite successful. If modeling is done manually, the model needs to be much simpler. One must consider what personnel are available to gather data, create models, run and update them. Finally, the time frame within which the results must be developed may have an impact.

B. Level of Detail

The level of detail needed depends in large part on the audience for which a report is being prepared, such as management, the board of directors, shareholders, or regulators, and the purpose for which the model is being run. More complex models should increase predictability as well as provide answers to a broader variety of questions and hypotheses regarding the potential impact of AIDS. On the other hand, complex models may be harder to understand than simpler models. They may also obscure the effect of weak assumptions in the model. It may be advantageous to run a simple model to check the results of a more complex model.

C. Frequency of Model Revisions

Any model must be occasionally revised to reflect evolving knowledge. If frequent revisions are expected, one must consider the flexibility of the model to accept improved or additional data and assumptions. In order to gain facility with assumptions of various types and degrees of refinement, it may be instructive to work with simple models prior to constructing a comprehensive one.

D. Intended Use of Model Results

The purpose for running the model should dictate the type of model constructed. There are a variety of reasons to run an AIDS model. The purpose may be to examine one or more of the following:

1. Viability of certain products or markets
2. Underwriting and blood-testing limits
3. Retention limits
4. Pricing changes
5. Policyholder dividend changes
6. Stockholder dividends
7. Company solvency and profitability
8. Setting aside extra reserves

9. Setting aside or earmarking surplus
10. Setting realistic GAAP benefit reserves
11. Tax effects of additional mortality
12. Effect on net worth of company.

In most cases, the actuary will be trying to estimate future claims from AIDS. However, projecting old and new business separately may be desirable to permit use of the data to set underwriting and blood-testing limits. If the issue is stockholder dividends, the model must produce current as well as future earnings or at least be able to tie into other models that will produce earnings. Reserves may be looked at in total in examining solvency issues for the company, but it may be necessary to look at them at selected ages for GAAP benefit reserves.

E. Willingness to Undertake Original Research

The actuary must decide whether to perform original research into the likely spread of AIDS or to accept someone else's projections. Advantages of the former include the possibility of a new model contributing to everyone's understanding of AIDS. The actuary doing the work will certainly gain a fuller understanding of the disease. Disadvantages include the difficult and specialized nature of the disciplines involved, which are likely to be unfamiliar to the actuary. Further, results will be questioned to the extent they differ from prevailing "expert" opinion.

The advantages of using previously published estimates of the disease's spread include:

1. Instant credibility, if CDC estimates are used;
2. Ease of interpretation, in that estimates can fairly easily be described as more or less severe than the CDC estimates, or be related to a specific environmental assumption; and,
3. Ease in effort, in that little or no original work is required.

II. CONSTRUCTING A POPULATION FRAMEWORK

A. Micro and Macro Projections

Macro projections are estimates of total AIDS deaths without subdivision into risk groups. Micro projections subdivide AIDS risk groups by extent of sexual activity or other exposure characteristics with different assumptions as to probabilities of infection for each group. Depending on the resources available and the purpose of the model, either a greater or lesser reliance on micro assumptions may be appropriate. At this point in time, the degree of certainty in any projection is so limited that any significant degree of refinement generally seems unwarranted. Further information is needed before micro projections will achieve any degree of reliability. However, work on micro projections should be encouraged in order to develop and refine methodology as data become available and also to determine what data will be useful and hence to focus efforts on obtaining such data. One micro consideration, the spread of the disease through the heterosexual population, becomes more and more important as the length of the projection period increases.

The actuary will choose whether to use a model incorporating macro population assumptions or a more sophisticated projection using micro assumptions. Should the actuary choose to segment a population AIDS projection into currently recognized at-risk groups, the effort will be most useful to:

1. Recognize that different at-risk groups have had different insurance needs and buying characteristics;
2. Separate the more certain parts of the analysis (the disease's spread through the male homosexual population) from the more speculative (the disease's spread into the heterosexual population); and
3. Recognize differences in transmission rates for the infection among different at-risk groups, to the extent these differences are shown to exist.

B. Characteristics of At-Risk Groups

1. *Homosexual AIDS Susceptibles.* The Cowell-Hoskins model makes reasonable assumptions as to the numbers of males infected because of homosexual activity. Their assumption is that only 60 percent of an estimated 2.5 million homosexuals and 2.5 million bisexuals are "AIDS susceptible," i.e., engage in high-risk activity that exposes them to infection.

2. *Heterosexual AIDS Susceptibles.* The Cowell-Hoskins model does not account for any significant extent of AIDS infection in the heterosexual population. Some experts feel that infection through heterosexual activity will become extensive. Others feel that it will not be a problem. Though a spread through heterosexual contact is not a principal problem currently (CDC data indicate that U.S. born heterosexuals account for only 2 percent of AIDS deaths), it should not be ignored. Factors to consider are:

a. AIDS Susceptibles. Those likely to be at significant risk are those who have promiscuous sexual activity or who have an infected partner (e.g., a partner who is an IV drug user or who received contaminated blood). The percent of heterosexuals who are AIDS susceptible is unknown.

b. Infection Incidence. Because transmission of the AIDS virus appears to be less likely through vaginal sex than anal sex, the prevalence of infection among AIDS-susceptible heterosexuals may be at a lower rate than among homosexuals.

c. Progression from Infection to AIDS. Some experts speculate that repeated exposure quickens the progression from infection to AIDS. Should this be shown to be the case, progression may be slower among heterosexuals than among homosexuals because of a lower frequency of exposure to infected persons after initial infection.

The combination of the above three factors may account for the present low number of heterosexuals who have AIDS.

3. *IV Drug Users*. As suggested in the Cowell-Hoskins paper, they are not likely to be a significant factor in estimating life insurance AIDS claims. They do represent, however, a significant proportion of current AIDS victims. It is possible that the spread of infection and/or progression from infection to AIDS may be faster among IV drug users than among homosexuals.

4. *Contaminated-Blood Victims*. These persons are a factor in estimating life insurance AIDS claims although, according to CDC figures, they represent only 4 percent of AIDS deaths. The spread of infection is currently well contained because of testing of blood donors. However, the progression from infection to AIDS may be slower than average, suggesting that the number of such persons getting AIDS may not decrease rapidly.

C. Course of the Disease

The ultimate spread of the disease through the population is as yet unknown. However, there is no shortage of estimates, and they vary widely. Factors that contribute to wide differences in estimates include assumptions as to:

a. The number of lives presently HIV+;
b. The progression rate from initial infection to full-blown AIDS;
c. The future rate of infection among high-risk groups given modified behavior;
d. The extent to which the disease crosses into the heterosexual population, and how easily it is transmitted once there; and,
e. The likelihood of discovering an effective vaccine.

A projection of AIDS claims will be relatively meaningless unless placed in the context of a particular set of assumptions as to the course of the disease through the total population. Once this environmental assumption is made, the impact of AIDS on a particular company operating in this environment can be projected with due recognition to the company's particular characteristics.

D. Elements of an AIDS Projection

The elements of an AIDS population projection will include:

1. The total HIV-infected lives in each year of the projection;
2. The number of AIDS cases in each year;
3. The number of AIDS deaths in each year; and,
4. An estimate of the population death rate due to AIDS.

In addition, a projection may include the number of lives at *each* AIDS classification by the "Walter Reed Staging Method." This will be more useful for lines other than life insurance. As more information becomes available, it will be useful to estimate the number of lives by age groupings.

E. Credibility of Projections

A satisfactory population AIDS projection will be one that either reproduces credible data or differs only in ways that can be explained and justified. The projection must be internally consistent with respect to:

1. Total lives infected each year;
2. The probability of HIV+ lives progressing to AIDS in any year;
3. AIDS mortality rates; and
4. Total AIDS deaths each year.

With the current state of knowledge, all long-term projections are extremely speculative.

III. INFORMATION NEEDED AT THE COMPANY LEVEL

A. Lapse Rates

At this time, the actuary will have little concrete basis for setting lapse assumptions of HIV+ and high-risk insureds. It is prudent to be conservative and to test the effect of variations in this assumption.

1. Lower lapse rates can be expected of persons who have a higher expectation of becoming a claimant or who believe that they would be prohibited from reestablishing coverage should their current coverage be lost. In modeling the future impact of AIDS on life insurance, ignoring this fact can lead to a serious understatement.
2. AIDS victims are unlikely to allow life insurance coverage to lapse, although some may be forced into lapsing by financial difficulty and/or the placement of a higher priority on maintaining health coverage.
3. Asymptomatic HIV+ insureds will no doubt exhibit much better persistency than average if they have knowledge of their HIV status or if they perceive themselves as

being at high risk. Increased testing and education will likely increase the portion of HIV + insureds exhibiting better persistency.

B. Nature of In-Force Business

To project the impact of AIDS for a particular company, the actuary will need to analyze the impact on both the in-force business and new business. For the in-force business, cells must be defined that are significantly relevant for the purpose at hand, but not more refined than is warranted by the tenuous nature of some of the required assumptions. However, it may pay to construct a somewhat more refined model than is warranted by current assumptions with the hope that in the future, assumptions can become more refined.

In representing the in-force business by cells, the following factors are especially relevant:

a. *Sex of Insureds*. Over the near term, AIDS will predominantly be a male disease. Females represent only about 7 percent of cases reported to date with about half of those being IV drug abusers, who are probably not in the insured population. Projections over longer terms should reflect an increase in HIV infection in females according to the results of epidemiological modeling of HIV spread beyond the current high-risk groups.

b. *Age of Insureds*. Since AIDS does not follow the typical mortality age pattern, it is important to consider age in analyzing its impact on life insurance business. By age at diagnosis, about 90 percent of AIDS cases fall into the 20 to 49 age range and 10 percent into the age 50+ range. Of the 90 percent, about half fall into the 30s and one quarter each fall into the 20s and 40s. It is not clear how this distribution will change over the long term.

C. Antiselection Scenario

Any estimate of future claims from "new sales" must recognize the likelihood that at-risk lives will select against companies in their own best interests. HIV testing, and underwriter awareness of the medical problems that are often associated with the early stages of immune deficiency disease, are the defenses available to combat antiselection. Below the testing limit, the actuary should expect both larger-size issues (bounded, of course, by the testing limit) and more issues to HIV + lives. Above the limit, known HIV +'s are excluded, but at-risk HIV −'s will buy more often and in larger amounts than they would have before. Testing limits should be assumed to be public knowledge.

D. Current Underwriting Standards

Underwriting needs to perform two critical functions with respect to AIDS:

a. The screening of AIDS victims. These are clearly uninsurable.
b. The screening of HIV+ applicants who do not yet have AIDS. These are also uninsurable. The Cowell-Hoskins Report (see Chapter 3) is required reading on this point.

Several factors need to be considered relating to underwriting.

a. Full use of the company's rights during the contestable period will be necessary for those AIDS or ARC deaths where it appears the insured misrepresented his medical condition.
b. Only testing for HIV or HIV antibodies can screen asymptomatic HIV+ applicants. In states where testing is not allowed or only the T-cell test allowed, assumptions will be required regarding how many HIV+ applicants are being accepted for insurance, recognizing the greater likelihood of antiselection. The T-cell test is a test of the immune system. It is not an AIDS-specific test. It will produce negative results for some individuals who would have given a positive HIV test. The actuary must recognize the limited effectiveness of the T-cell test.
c. Even HIV testing is not 100 percent effective for newly infected individuals nor for those with a ravaged immune system. An assumption reflecting lack of total effectiveness needs to be developed. (Of course, HIV testing does not prevent claims from those who become infected after testing negative.)
d. Many companies continue to write life insurance without required testing below a threshold amount of insurance. This presents an opportunity for HIV+ applicants to obtain coverage. Testing limits may not be low enough to discourage antiselection. The market is not ignorant of testing limits. The presence of HIV+ insureds in new business at subtesting threshold amounts should not be ignored in AIDS impact modeling.

E. Geographic Distribution

AIDS cases reported to date are not distributed geographically in proportion to the U.S. population nor probably to any company's insured population. It is also clear that the distribution is changing over time (see recent CDC AIDS Weekly Surveillance Reports showing cases by SMSA and date of diagnosis). It is reasonable to assume that the geographic distribution of current HIV+'s bears some semblance to the current reported AIDS case distribution (but, unfortunately, more like what the reported case distribution will look like several years from now).

Companies with concentrations of in-force in the high AIDS-per-capita states and cities will need to make appropriate adjustments to total population HIV+ estimates.

Companies with low concentrations in these areas should be cautious in fully adjusting total population HIV + estimates based on the geographic distribution of cases reported to date. The latter actually reflect the HIV + distribution several years ago.

F. Markets Served/Marketing Objectives

It will be important to consider how the current markets served and future marketing objectives are different than those which have generated the existing in-force business.

Representation of current and future new business by cells for the purpose of AIDS impact modeling will need to reflect any changes in relevant characteristics implied by changes in markets or marketing. Such characteristics would include sex, age, socioeconomic group, and geographic distributions, as well as target market selection of at-risk groupings and any underwriting changes.

The results of this analysis may be critical input to reshaping a company's marketing strategies and objectives in light of AIDS. Although the initial response to AIDS has been primarily one of underwriting, changes in marketing may also be required to provide safe passage through the AIDS era.

G. Company AIDS Experience/AIDS Claim Profile

AIDS impact modeling should be viewed not as a one-shot task, but as an iterative process in which actual company experience plays a key function. In order to validate an AIDS impact model and to provide a firmer and more refined basis for future assumptions, it is imperative that each company monitor and analyze its own AIDS experience. Results will vary significantly by company. Each model must be customized to reflect particular company characteristics. (Unfortunately, the fact that a model replicates past experience is no guarantee as to its predictive value. This is a necessary, not sufficient, requirement.)

It may become of increasing importance to determine what portion of AIDS claims are coming from insureds who tested negative at issue. As HIV spreads, assumptions regarding post-issue infection will need to be refined.

A basic problem is the identification of AIDS-related claims. Adjustments should be made for underreporting of AIDS claims, both in U.S. data and company statistics. Many claimants and attending physicians do not disclose the true cause of the claim. A working definition of a "suspected AIDS claim" needs to be developed to help offset the veiled or misstated cause problem. Following are some AIDS-related diseases that may be helpful in developing such a definition:

a. Kaposi's sarcoma
b. Pneumocystis carinii pneumonia
c. Toxoplasmosis
d. Cryptosporidiosis
e. Cytomegalovirus infection
f. Primary lymphoma of the brain
g. Candida esophagitis
h. Atypical mycobacterial infection
i. Cryptococcal infection
j. Chronic mucocutaneous herpes simplex infection
k. Chronic interstitial pneumonitis (pediatric).

The AIDS claim profile for a specific company is an invaluable source of information regarding the characteristics of HIV + insureds (as of several years ago) and the degree of antiselection by amount, etc. Studying individual claims will provide pointers for sharpening underwriting procedures and skills.

IV. ADJUSTING POPULATION ASSUMPTIONS TO REFLECT COMPANY CHARACTERISTICS

A. Company Characteristics

Once an environmental scenario has been constructed, the actuary must review the particular characteristics of a company to estimate the extent of its exposure to the assumed AIDS deaths. If the population AIDS projection were segmented by at-risk grouping, then each segment can be considered individually. The ultimate impact of the disease on any company is as yet unknown. Estimates can vary widely, based not only on differences in population AIDS projections, but also on differences in estimates as to:

1. The rate at which at-risk lives select against companies through larger purchases, more frequent purchases, or through purchases at amounts designed to avoid automatic testing;
2. The effectiveness of testing, especially the T-cell test;
3. The remedial effect of heightened underwriter awareness of AIDS symptoms;
4. The protective value of publicity about testing;
5. The unproven effectiveness of AIDS exclusion riders when used; and
6. The degree to which the company differs from the general population with respect to

the percentage of its insureds in high-risk groups (as indicated by geographical/age/sex distributions).

B. At-Risk Groupings

Although it is impossible to classify individual policies by sexual preference and activity or drug use, it will be quite important to make such a classification in defining representative cells based on population estimates and judgment. (Different groups may well have different insurance-buying habits.) AIDS claims over the near term will come mainly from the current high-risk groups (homosexuals, bisexuals, and IV drug abusers). Over the longer term, promiscuous heterosexuals may contribute more to claims. Some degree of cell definition by at-risk group allows the results of epidemiological modeling to be easily included in the impact model. This will be particularly important as the question regarding heterosexual spread becomes better quantified and projected.

1. *Homosexual and Bisexual AIDS Susceptibles.* The proportion of this group may be significantly lower among insureds than in the general population because such persons do not have a high level of personal need for insurance and, in some cases, lifestyle may not be consistent with an interest in insurance. The proportion among those insured (before antiselection became a factor) may only be 25–50 percent of that in the general population.

2. *Heterosexual AIDS Susceptibles.* The proportion of this group among insureds may also be lower than that in the general population. However, it is likely that the proportion will be higher than for homosexuals, perhaps 50–75 percent. There is some speculation that women in this group are more susceptible to AIDS infection than men. This may further reduce the proportion of AIDS susceptibles among insureds if the company insures a lower proportion of women than in the general population.

3. *IV Drug Users.* They are not a significant factor in an insurance population. Not only is the lifestyle inconsistent with an interest in insurance, but insurers routinely underwrite for drug abuse.

4. *Contaminated-Blood Victims.* The proportion of this group in the company population is likely to be somewhat lower than in the general population. Hemophiliacs are less likely to obtain insurance because of uninsurability or high extra premiums. Others that have received blood may also have insurability problems related to underlying disease.

V. UNDERWRITING ERA

The actuary will probably want to differentiate in his/her analysis between "in-force" business and "new sales." There are probably three distinct blocks of business for most companies:

A. The first era would include business written before the early 1980s, predating any underwriting response to AIDS, but also predating a level of knowledge regarding AIDS necessary for significant antiselection. This business presumably would reflect little antiselection, but would still be subject to post-issue HIV infection. The level of AIDS claims in this group would likely represent the underlying proportion of company exposure to AIDS out of the general population.
B. The second era would include business written between the early 1980s and the implementation of the company's underwriting response to AIDS. This business could reflect a significant degree of antiselection and contain more HIV + insureds at issue purchasing large policies.
C. The third era would reflect business written after implementation of the company's underwriting response to AIDS. The second and third eras may have an imprecise boundary, since underwriting for AIDS has and continues to evolve.

VI. CONSTRUCTING THE COMPANY MODEL

A. General Criteria

In setting up an AIDS model the general criteria to consider are:

1. The medium to be used, PCs or mainframes, spreadsheet or specifically written programs.
2. The level of detail of the model.
3. The flexibility to change data and assumptions.
4. The purpose of creating a model, will the desired results be produced?

B. Population Assumptions

A general AIDS population projection must be incorporated.

1. Select whether it will be based on original research or published data.
2. The data will be incorporated in either a macro or micro model.
3. No matter which is selected (macro or micro), estimates of the future course of the disease must be considered. In a macro projection, overall factors should be applied to estimate future changes. In a micro model each subgroup projection is tailored to the estimate.
4. The AIDS projection will include the following elements:
   a. The total HIV-infected lives in each year of the projection;
   b. The number of AIDS cases in each year;

c. The number of AIDS deaths in each year; and,

d. An estimate of the population death rate due to AIDS.

C. Profile of In-Force Contracts

Given that HIV+ lives are assumed to be a percentage of the population (by sex, age, and geographical cells, if available), a company can review its "in-force" to see what percentage of the population it insures and thus estimate the number of HIV+'s in its insured population. However, this simple estimate must be tempered by recognizing particular company characteristics:

1. Some IV drug users and victims of contaminated blood transfusions, to whatever extent they sought insurance, may have been screened out by pre-AIDS underwriting;
2. Unmarried and childless homosexual or bisexual males have had less traditional need for life insurance;
3. HIV+'s are heavily concentrated in a relatively few geographic areas. The actuary should consider whether the company's in-force has a higher or lower than expected concentration in those areas and to what extent the geographical distribution of AIDS claims is expected to change over time.

D. Comparison with Recent Death Claims

Once an estimate of the company's percentage of HIV+ lives among its in-force is made, it can be validated by a comparison with actual recent AIDS claims. Care must be taken to identify all company AIDS deaths, since underreporting could lead to a major understatement of the company's exposure among HIV+ lives. Even after careful checking, some estimate of further underreporting should probably be included.

E. In-Force Exposure

Future claims arising from in-force business can then be estimated. Either:

1. An average policy size is determined, perhaps increasing over time to recognize additions. This average size is applied to the number of company AIDS deaths expected from the in-force block, given:
   a. The population pattern of AIDS deaths;
   b. The company's share of the population;
   c. The company's estimated share of the HIV+ population.
2. Or, the estimated population death rates due to AIDS can be applied directly to the amount of business assumed to be in-force on AIDS susceptibles, if the actuary has segmented the population AIDS projection by at-risk group.

In either case, the implicit assumption is that current HIV− lives in the company's population will become infected and die of AIDS at the same rate as the general population, but in the same reduced proportion as indicated by the analysis in Section VI.B. If population estimates are segmented by risk group, the future claims from the in-force can be split as well, highlighting differences in company exposure and the estimated future course of the disease among the groups.

F. Persistency

One further refinement is suggested. It is to be expected that at-risk lives will exhibit excellent persistency. This may be reflected in a number of ways:

1. If the population AIDS projection has been segmented by at-risk groups, the company's block of business within each group may be assumed to experience a significantly reduced lapse rate;
2. A less satisfactory solution focuses on HIV+ lives rather than at-risk groups. The HIV+'s in the insured population are assumed to experience a significantly reduced (zero?) lapse rate; or,
3. At least, the actuary should estimate the effect on the company's mix of HIV+/ HIV− lives of a reduced HIV+ lapse rate and increase the assumption of the company's share of HIV+'s, over time, as a proxy for a more direct approach.

G. Antiselection and Remedial Action

Antiselection and remedial action can be recognized in two ways:

1. The business can be split into tested and nontested blocks. This permits specific recognition of the different characteristics of the blocks, both estimates of antiselection as to lives and amounts, the heavier mix of HIV+ lives expected in the nontested group, and the effectiveness of HIV testing; or
2. An overall "protective factor" may be estimated and applied to the company's percentage of participation in the epidemic. The factor would be made up of separate elements for fear of testing (publicity), underwriter awareness, and the proportion of business tested.

Under either approach the value of changing testing limits can be estimated.

H. Weakness of the T-Cell Test

The actuary must recognize the limited effectiveness of the T-cell test. Business written in jurisdictions where only the T-cell test is permitted may be recognized by:

1. Setting up a separate block for that business, with appropriate assumptions as to the percentage of HIV+ lives accepted; or
2. Adjusting the "protective factor."

I. New Sales

Future claims arising from new sales can then be estimated by:

1. If new sales are segmented by testing status:
   a. Average policy sizes are determined for each block;
   b. These are increased to reflect antiselection; and
   c. The results are applied to the anticipated deaths in each block given the assumed percentage of HIV+ new entrants in each (near zero for HIV-tested, company average for untested);
2. If new sales are not segmented by testing status:
   a. An average size policy is determined;
   b. It is adjusted to reflect antiselection and the remedial protective factor; and
   c. The results are applied to the anticipated deaths.
3. If the actuary has segmented his/her population projection by at-risk group, the estimated population death rates due to AIDS can be applied directly to the amount of business assumed to be in-force on AIDS susceptibles.

In any case, the implicit assumption is that HIV− lives among the company's new entrants will become infected and die of AIDS at the same rate as the general population, but in increased proportion due to antiselection and in decreased proportion due to protective factors.

If population estimates were split by at-risk group, the claims from new sales can be split as well, highlighting differences in company exposure among the groups and emphasizing the major impact of a spread into the heterosexual population.

VII. MORTALITY PROJECTIONS

The projected company AIDS deaths can be matched against a projection of total company in-force, year by year, to estimate AIDS extra mortality rates. Alternatively, they can be matched against a pre-AIDS projection of claims to estimate the increase expected due to AIDS. Also, they can be used to determine annual costs of AIDS claims and additional reserves needed to cover AIDS claims.

The distribution of AIDS claims by sex and age is most important. A 15 percent increase in overall mortality might indicate a 100 percent increase for males age 25–45. Distribution of claims by age can be recognized either by:

1. Including age-sex cells in all modeling; or
2. Distributing total estimated AIDS deaths, by age and sex, in proportion to the current population distribution.

VIII. SCENARIOS

Because so much is still unknown, the actuary should experiment with assumptions and become familiar with the impact on his/her company if events are more or less favorable than his "best guess" would indicate.

DESCRIPTION OF METHODOLOGY FOR A SIMPLIFIED AIDS PROJECTION

HYPOTHETICAL LIFE MODEL EXAMPLE 1

This model is put together to illustrate a method of modeling and is not meant to reflect the actual situation of any company. Each company should develop its own set of assumptions based on its own situation.

This company is a medium-sized company with $10 billion of participating business in force on 500,000 policyholders (with a $20,000 average size). The company is an older company operating in the family and middle-income markets. Sales have occurred at all ages, but particularly among young to middle-aged adults and their children. Persistency has been good. About 50 percent of the current policyholders are males aged 20–49, about 0.5 percent of the U.S. population at those ages.

General Criteria

It is decided to use a PC model, developed on a spreadsheet program. Since the actuarial staff is small and so many of the assumptions are subject to wide variability, a simple model is used. This model will allow changes to population data as well as adjustments to the data on a broad basis. The model is being constructed to consider company solvency and profitability, setting aside extra reserves, pricing changes and policyholder dividend changes.

Population Assumptions

This model relies on having available one or more credible scenarios of how AIDS is expected to spread through the general U.S. population and focuses on attempting to relate these to the company.

Taking as a given the general population AIDS scenario as found in the Cowell-Hoskins paper is easier than developing one. It saves time and the need to explain differences with ones already developed by the "experts."

Currently, there is a great deal of uncertainty in making any long-term projection of the number of AIDS infections and deaths in the U.S. This is due to the uncertainty over not only how many people are currently infected but also the future rate of spread among the various subpopulations (or at-risk groups). The rate of spread depends to a large degree on how much people are willing to modify their high-risk sexual behavior, something that these actuaries do not feel well-qualified to predict.

A macro model is built, starting with the number of general population AIDS deaths and estimating the company's expected share of these deaths.

Profile of In-Force Contracts

First, the number of policyholders in the predefined high-risk group of all males aged 20–49 is compared with the number of such persons in the general population. If the company's policyholders in this group were representative of the general population, then a direct proportion of AIDS deaths would be used. However, there are various reasons why this proportion is reduced. One that can be measured is the difference in geographical distribution among the at-risk population. Since a smaller proportion of the company's business is found in New York and California than in the general population distribution, the proportion of AIDS deaths is reduced. Differences are also assumed for presumed differences between the company's policyholders and the general population high-risk group in terms of drug use, sexual orientation and promiscuity. That is, the direct percentage needs adjusting for differences that largely can only be guessed at but that would explain any difference between the company's current AIDS experience from what would be expected by applying its "share" of the high-risk U.S. population to the number of AIDS deaths currently in the U.S.

There are three scenarios modeled. Each starts in 1987 with company AIDS deaths expected to be adjusted to only 40 percent of the 0.5 percent share of U.S. population AIDS deaths. However, this 40 percent adjustment factor is assumed to increase each year in scenarios 2 and 3 due to antiselection and a changing geographical distribution of AIDS deaths.

Comparison with Recent Death Claims

After a reasonable adjustment factor is arrived at, estimated deaths are compared with actual AIDS deaths among policyholders, adjusted for assumed underreporting of 10 percent. The adjustment factor appears to reasonably correlate estimated and actual deaths.

In-Force Exposure and Persistency

An average size policy of $25,000 was discovered by analysis of in-force contracts of the at-risk group, adjusted by correlation to actual AIDS claims. A 4 percent annual increase in size is assumed, due to dividend additions and assumed better persistency.

Antiselection, Remedial Action and New Business

The greater a company is selected against, the larger will be its share of U.S. AIDS deaths in the future. A weakness of this simplified model is that antiselection is not explicitly included because new business is not separately projected from in-force business. Rather, some assumptions are needed to factor in antiselection, specifically how a company's "share" of AIDS deaths and its average size AIDS claim will increase due to its issuing insurance to infected persons. These assumptions may be developed better by projecting new business separately from in-force, but in this particular model some simplifying rates of increase were used, increasing average size claims by an additional 2 percent and 4 percent per year in scenarios 2 and 3, respectively.

The company has AIDS blood-testing limits at $100,000 and plans to lower them as the industry reduces its limits. Due to its market and geographical location and examining recent claims, little antiselection is assumed.

T-cell Test

Since little business is written in California, no specific adjustment is made.

Shortcomings

The model is not a well-refined one. As more data become available or as different issues need to be researched, a new, more complex model will

TABLE 1

A HYPOTHETICAL AIDS PROJECTION*
(IMPACT ON DEATH CLAIMS, SURPLUS)

Calendar Year	Scenario 1 Infection Stops in 1987 (A) Expected U.S.A.	(B) Deaths Co.	(C) Death Claim Cost	Scenario 2 Infection Stops by 1997 (A) Expected U.S.A.	(B) Deaths Co.	(C) Death Claim Cost	Scenario 3 Infection Rate Continues (A) Expected U.S.A.	(B) Deaths Co.	(C) Death Claim Cost	(D) Projected Mortality w/o AIDS	Projected Surplus w/o AIDS
1987	12,923	26	$ 650	12,923	26	$ 650	12,923	26	$ 650	$ 25,000	$150,000
1988	19,924	40	1,040	19,924	41	1,086	19,924	41	1,107	28,000	168,000
1989	28,941	58	1,568	29,308	61	1,713	29,352	63	1,837	31,400	188,200
1990	39,240	78	2,194	41,279	88	2,620	41,583	94	2,960	35,100	210,800
1991	49,704	93	2,895	55,807	121	3,819	56,919	133	4,524	39,300	236,100
1992	59,157	118	3,589	72,532	160	5,353	75,463	184	6,759	44,100	264,400
1993	66,345	133	4,207	90,679	204	7,234	96,928	245	9,720	49,300	296,100
1994	69,366	139	4,573	108,957	250	9,398	120,505	317	13,582	55,300	331,600
1995	67,227	134	4,585	125,688	295	11,755	144,809	396	18,324	61,900	371,400
1996	61,824	124	4,412	139,284	333	14,065	167,991	478	23,888	69,300	416,000
1997	55,540	111	4,108	148,638	362	16,207	188,058	557	30,063	77,600	465,900
1998	49,368	99	3,810	153,704	382	18,129	203,289	626	36,490	87,000	521,800
1999	43,581	87	3,482	152,976	388	19,518	212,565	681	42,872	97,400	584,400
2000	38,258	77	3,205	148,417	384	20,476	215,575	718	48,818	109,100	654,500
P.V. of Claims (8%)			$25,371			$65,645			$113,975		

Scenario assumptions:

(1) Adjustment factor of 40% is increased annually due to antiselection at: 0% / 2% / 4%

(2) Average size claim increasing from a 1987 value of $25M at an annual rate of: 4% / 6% / 8%

*For a hypothetical company with 500,000 contracts for $10 billion in-force, 50% of which are in the high-risk group (male attained ages 20–49). When compared to the about 50 million males aged 20–49 in the U.S.A. population, this 250,000 is 0.5% of the U.S.A. high-risk group.

(A) Expected AIDS deaths (U.S.A.) = based on the three scenarios found in Appendix 1 of Michael Cowell's paper "AIDS and Life Insurance."

(B) Expected AIDS deaths (company) = expected AIDS deaths (U.S.A.) + 0.5% + adjustment factor (40%), increased for antiselection (see scenario assumption (1) as noted above).

(C) Death claim cost (company) = expected AIDS deaths (company) + average size AIDS claim ($25M), adjusted for normal increase and antiselection (see scenario assumption (2) as noted above).

(D) Projected mortality and surplus (without AIDS) are assumed to have increased at 12% per year, based on a separate projection of company financials.

likely be built. Since original research was not done, there is less understanding of the future course of AIDS and its effect on the company. As mentioned above, antiselection is not explicitly modeled.

HYPOTHETICAL LIFE MODEL EXAMPLE 2

A. General Criteria

The purpose of this example model is to project AIDS claims for a hypothetical company for 1988 through 2000. This model has a moderate level of detail with flexible assumptions. For example, the model could be changed to illustrate the impact of changing testing limits. Please note that all the factors are illustrative only and not guidelines. Each company should develop its own set of assumptions based on its own situation.

B. Population Assumptions

This example uses the Cowell general AIDS population projection that assumes that the HIV infection declines to 0 by 1997 (see Appendix 2). Here we will assume that all the HIV infecteds will be males 18–54. Table 2 gives the appropriate projections.

TABLE 2

AIDS PROJECTION FOR U.S. POPULATION
FROM COWELL PAPER (INCLUDING 9/17/87 ADDENDUM #1) AND SOA DISKETTE
ASSUMES HIV INFECTION DECLINES TO 0 IN 1997

Year	Total HIV Infection	Cumulative AIDS Cases	Annual AIDS Deaths	U.S. Population Males 18–54	General Population AIDS Mortality Rate
1988	1,191,439	76,181	19,925	63.2	0.00032
1989	1,465,203	118,255	29,309	63.8	0.00046
1990	1,721,330	176,062	41,280	64.4	0.00064
1991	1,945,951	252,266	55,807	65.1	0.00086
1992	2,131,859	348,753	72,534	65.7	0.00110
1993	2,277,142	466,060	90,679	66.4	0.00137
1994	2,382,978	602,740	108,958	67.0	0.00163
1995	2,451,692	755,065	125,690	67.7	0.00186
1996	2,485,433	917,677	139,286	68.4	0.00204
1997	2,485,433	1,084,549	148,640	69.1	0.00215
1998	2,485,433	1,249,704	153,206	69.8	0.00220
1999	2,485,433	1,407,847	152,978	70.5	0.00217
2000	2,485,433	1,554,819	148,418	71.2	0.00209

Actual numbers taken from SOA diskette and may differ slightly from paper. U.S. population data derived from census data; assumes population grows at 1% annually.

C. Profile of In-Force Contracts

In this example, we are assuming that the at-risk group is males 18–54. Therefore, the company's exposure will be measured by the number of males 18–54 insured. In this example, we will assume that this company's insured population will experience 40 percent of the general population AIDS mortality rate. This recognizes factors such as geographical distribution of business, lack of insurability of IV drug abusers, etc. This is a very important assumption and requires actuarial judgment in recognizing each company's unique characteristics.

D. Comparison with Recent Death Claims

In developing a model for an actual company, the next step would be to compare the model to the company's recent AIDS death claims. This step will be bypassed in this example of a hypothetical company.

E. In-Force Exposure

The projection model starts on 1/1/88. The business will be divided into three underwriting eras as described in Section V. For this example, era 1 will be all business sold prior to 1/1/84. This will represent business sold before measurable antiselection and testing. Era 2 will be business sold from 1/1/84 to 12/31/87. This will represent business sold with some antiselection but before testing. There are 100,000 male 18–54 lives in force as of 1/1/88 for era 1 and 30,000 for era 2. Era 3 is all sales (males 18–54) after 1/1/88 that are subject to current antiselection and testing. Era 2 business in this age group has a $50,000 average size on 1/1/88. Era 3 has a $60,000 average size. Both are assumed to grow by $2,500 annually (to represent additions).

F. Persistency

To simplify this example, one annual factor is used to incorporate lapses and deaths. The era 1 block will decrease by a constant 4 percent annually, era 2 at 5 percent, and era 3 by 7 percent. It would be relatively easy to vary this assumption by duration.

To account for the fact that those who are already HIV-infected or who believe they are strongly at risk to become HIV-infected will exhibit excellent persistency, the company's share of general population infected (40 percent) is increased each year. For example, the company is assumed to experience 40 percent in year 1, 42 percent in year 2, 50 percent in year 6, and 57 percent in year 13.

G. Antiselection and Remedial Action

Each era has its own antiselection factor. No measurable antiselection is assumed for era 1; therefore its factor is 1.00. Era 2 is assumed to have moderate antiselection (factor = 1.25). Era 3 is divided into tested and untested blocks. The tested block has an antiselection factor of 1.25 (those who are not yet infected but believe they are strongly at risk will buy more insurance). The untested block has an antiselection factor of 2.00.

H. Weakness of T-cell Test

This example assumes HIV testing nationwide and ignores the T-cell test. Therefore, the projections are understated depending on the amount of business in T-cell states.

I. New Sales

Sales are assumed to be 10,000 males 18–54 in 1988, growing 5 percent annually. It is assumed that 25 percent of the policies each year will be over $100,000 and therefore HIV-tested. The average size of the untested issue is $50,000 regardless of issue year. These policies will accumulate $2,500 of additions each year after issue. The average size of a tested issue in 1988 is $200,000. The average issue size will grow by $10,000 each year. These policies will accumulate $10,000 of additions each year after issue.

The projection method for the untested block of new sales is very similar to era 1 and era 2. All use the general population AIDS mortality rate (technically, the mortality rate for the untested block should be lower than the general population AIDS mortality rate to recognize that while asymptomatic HIV-infecteds will be accepted, the AIDS question should screen those with actual AIDS). The tested block of business will experience a much lower mortality rate, which will vary by year of issue. Table 3 will help explain this.

Table 3 is derived from the Cowell paper and the SOA diskette. It shows the number dying from AIDS annually by year of infection. This is important in calculating the mortality rate for the tested blocks. We assume that testing will identify all of those who are currently infected. So the tested block of 1988 issues only experiences the deaths from those who become infected from issue (1988 on). For example, there are 55,807 projected AIDS deaths in 1991, but only 6,103 (4,075 + 1,687 + 346) of those are from people infected from 1988 on. The mortality rate for era 1, era 2, and the untested block is 0.00086 (55,807/65.1 million). The mortality rate for the tested block of 1988 issues is 0.00009 (6,103/65.1 million). For 1989 tested issues it is 0.00003 (2,028/65.1 million).

J. Future Enhancements

Several assumptions could be developed further in future versions of the model. The lapse assumption could vary by duration, and a separate non-AIDS mortality rate could be used. A more direct way of accounting for the good persistency of the HIV-infected could be developed. The weakness of the T-cell test could be recognized.

The two assumptions with the most impact on the projections are the percentage of the general population AIDS mortality rate that the company experiences (e.g., 40 percent) and the antiselection factors. These two should be constantly reviewed and refined to reflect the current thinking.

TABLE 3

AIDS PROJECTION FOR U.S. POPULATION

FROM COWELL PAPER (INCLUDING 9/17/87 ADDENDUM # 1) AND SOA DISKETTE

ASSUMES HIV INFECTION DECLINES TO 0 IN 1997

Year of Infection	Number Dying Year by Year after Infection in Year Indicated																								
	1976	1977	1978	1979	1980	1981	1982	1983	1984	1985	1986	1987	1988	1989	1990	1991	1992	1993	1994	1995	1996	1997	1998	1999	2000
1976	0	1	3	8	14	21	30	39	43	41	38	34	30	27	24	21	18	16	14	12	10	9	7	6	4
1977	0	0	2	8	21	38	58	84	108	118	114	104	94	84	74	65	57	50	43	37	32	28	24	21	18
1978	0	0	0	6	25	62	112	173	249	322	352	339	311	280	249	221	194	170	148	129	111	96	83	71	61
1979	0	0	0	0	14	63	154	280	432	621	803	877	846	775	697	622	550	484	423	369	321	278	240	207	178
1980	0	0	0	0	0	29	133	324	588	907	1,305	1,688	1,844	1,777	1,628	1,465	1,306	1,156	1,016	890	775	674	583	504	434
1981	0	0	0	0	0	0	52	236	575	1,044	1,612	2,319	2,999	3,276	3,157	2,893	2,603	2,320	2,053	1,806	1,581	1,378	1,197	1,036	895
1982	0	0	0	0	0	0	0	80	363	886	1,608	2,483	3,571	4,619	5,044	4,862	4,455	4,008	3,573	3,162	2,781	2,434	2,122	1,843	1,596
1983	0	0	0	0	0	0	0	0	112	508	1,240	2,251	3,475	4,998	6,464	7,059	6,803	6,234	5,609	5,001	4,425	3,892	3,407	2,969	2,579
1984	0	0	0	0	0	0	0	0	0	149	676	1,649	2,993	4,621	6,646	8,595	9,387	9,047	8,290	7,459	6,650	5,884	5,176	4,530	3,948
1985	0	0	0	0	0	0	0	0	0	0	202	918	2,240	4,067	6,278	9,029	11,677	12,753	12,291	11,263	10,134	9,034	7,994	7,032	6,154
1986	0	0	0	0	0	0	0	0	0	0	0	260	1,185	2,892	5,248	8,102	11,653	15,071	16,459	15,863	14,535	13,079	11,659	10,317	9,075
1987	0	0	0	0	0	0	0	0	0	0	0	0	336	1,529	3,731	6,772	10,455	15,037	19,447	21,239	20,469	18,756	16,876	15,045	13,313
1988	0	0	0	0	0	0	0	0	0	0	0	0	0	367	1,670	4,075	7,396	11,418	16,422	21,238	23,194	22,354	20,483	18,430	16,431
1989	0	0	0	0	0	0	0	0	0	0	0	0	0	0	370	1,682	4,103	7,447	11,497	16,536	21,385	23,356	22,510	20,626	18,559
1990	0	0	0	0	0	0	0	0	0	0	0	0	0	0	0	346	1,573	3,839	6,967	10,756	15,470	20,008	21,851	21,060	19,297
1991	0	0	0	0	0	0	0	0	0	0	0	0	0	0	0	0	303	1,380	3,367	6,110	9,433	13,567	17,547	19,163	18,469
1992	0	0	0	0	0	0	0	0	0	0	0	0	0	0	0	0	0	251	1,142	2,786	5,057	7,807	11,229	14,522	15,860
1993	0	0	0	0	0	0	0	0	0	0	0	0	0	0	0	0	0	0	196	892	2,177	3,952	6,101	8,775	11,349
1994	0	0	0	0	0	0	0	0	0	0	0	0	0	0	0	0	0	0	0	143	650	1,586	2,879	4,445	6,393
1995	0	0	0	0	0	0	0	0	0	0	0	0	0	0	0	0	0	0	0	0	93	422	1,030	1,869	2,886
1996	0	0	0	0	0	0	0	0	0	0	0	0	0	0	0	0	0	0	0	0	0	46	207	506	918
1997	0	0	0	0	0	0	0	0	0	0	0	0	0	0	0	0	0	0	0	0	0	0	0	0	0
1998	0	0	0	0	0	0	0	0	0	0	0	0	0	0	0	0	0	0	0	0	0	0	0	0	0
1999	0	0	0	0	0	0	0	0	0	0	0	0	0	0	0	0	0	0	0	0	0	0	0	0	0
2000	0	0	0	0	0	0	0	0	0	0	0	0	0	0	0	0	0	0	0	0	0	0	0	0	0
Total	0	1	5	22	74	213	539	1,215	2,470	4,598	7,951	12,924	19,925	29,309	41,280	55,807	72,534	90,679	108,958	125,690	139,286	148,640	153,206	152,978	148,418

TABLE 3–*Continued*

$$\text{Deaths}_{ti} = \text{HIV}_i \left(\sum_{j=0}^{t-i} r_{j+1} \, q_{1+(t-i)-j} \right)$$

where

t = calendar year of AIDS death
i = calendar year of infection
HIV_i = total number of new infections in year i
r_j = percent contracting AIDS j years after infection
q_j = percent dying from AIDS j years after contracting AIDS.

Example

$\text{Deaths}_{91\ 88}$ = number of AIDS deaths in 1991 from those who were infected in 1988
= $\text{HIV}_{88} \, (r_1 \, q_4 + r_2 \, q_3 + r_3 \, q_2 + r_4 \, q_1)$
= $271{,}873 \, (0.000 \times 0.04916 + 0.003 \times 0.10588 + 0.012 \times 0.2475 + 0.026 \times 0.45)$
= $4{,}075$

J	1	2	3	4	5	6	7	8	9	10	11	12	13	14	15	16	17	18	19	20	21	22	23	24	25
r	.00000	.00300	.01200	.02600	.04300	.06200	.08600	.10400	.09960	.08466	.07196	.06117	.05199	.04419	.03756	.03193	.02714	.02307	.01961	.01667	.01417	.01204	.01024	.00870	.00000
q	.45000	.24750	.10588	.04916	.03687	.02765	.02074	.01555	.01167	.00875	.00656	.00492	.00369	.00277	.00208	.00156	.00117	.00088	.00066	.00049	.00037	.00028	.00021	.00000	.00000

I	1976	1977	1978	1979	1980	1981	1982	1983	1984	1985	1986	1987	1988	1989	1990	1991	1992	1993	1994	1995	1996	1997	1998	1999	2000
HIV	504	1,383	4,124	10,284	21,609	38,396	59,129	82,744	110,032	149,488	192,926	248,947	271,873	273,764	256,127	224,621	185,908	145,283	105,836	68,714	33,741	0	0	0	0

TABLE 4

COMPANY PROJECTIONS FOR ERA 1 AND ERA 2

Year	(1) Male 18–54 Lives	(2) Insured % of Gen. Pop.	(3) Antiselection	(4) Gen. Pop. AIDS Mort. Rate	(5) AIDS Deaths $1 \times 2 \times 3 \times 4$	(6) Av. Death Benefit	(7) AIDS Claims 5×6
			Era 1 — Business Sold Prior to 1/1/84				
1988	100,000	0.40%	1.00	0.00032	13	$50,000	$650,000
1989	96,000	0.42	1.00	0.00046	19	52,500	997,500
1990	92,160	0.44	1.00	0.00064	26	55,000	1,430,000
1991	88,474	0.46	1.00	0.00086	35	57,500	2,012,500
1992	84,935	0.48	1.00	0.00110	45	60,000	2,700,000
1993	81,537	0.50	1.00	0.00137	56	62,500	3,500,000
1994	78,276	0.51	1.00	0.00163	65	65,000	4,225,000
1995	75,145	0.52	1.00	0.00186	73	67,500	4,927,500
1996	72,139	0.53	1.00	0.00204	78	70,000	5,460,000
1997	69,253	0.54	1.00	0.00215	80	72,500	5,800,000
1998	66,483	0.55	1.00	0.00220	80	75,000	6,000,000
1999	63,824	0.56	1.00	0.00217	78	77,500	6,045,000
2000	61,271	0.57	1.00	0.00209	73	80,000	5,840,000
			Era 2 — Business Sold from 1/1/84 to 12/31/87				
1988	30,000	0.40%	1.25	0.00032	5	$60,000	$300,000
1989	28,500	0.42	1.25	0.00046	7	62,500	437,500
1990	27,075	0.44	1.25	0.00064	10	65,000	650,000
1991	25,721	0.46	1.25	0.00086	13	67,500	877,500
1992	24,435	0.48	1.25	0.00110	16	70,000	1,120,000
1993	23,213	0.50	1.25	0.00137	20	72,500	1,450,000
1994	22,053	0.51	1.25	0.00163	23	75,000	1,725,000
1995	20,950	0.52	1.25	0.00186	25	77,500	1,937,500
1996	19,903	0.53	1.25	0.00204	27	80,000	2,160,000
1997	18,907	0.54	1.25	0.00215	27	82,500	2,227,500
1998	17,962	0.55	1.25	0.00220	27	85,000	2,295,000
1999	17,064	0.56	1.25	0.00217	26	87,500	2,275,000
2000	16,211	0.57	1.25	0.00209	24	90,000	2,160,000

TABLE 5

COMPANY PROJECTIONS FOR ERA 3 UNTESTED
DETAILED EXAMPLE OF 1988 AND 1989 SALES

Year	(1) Male 18–54 Lives	(2) Insured % of Gen. Pop.	(3) Antiselection	(4) Gen. Pop. AIDS Mort. Rate	(5) AIDS Deaths $1 \times 2 \times 3 \times 4$	(6) Av. Death Benefit	(7) AIDS Claims 5×6
Era 3 — New Business Sold *Only in* 1988 — Untested								
1988	7,500	0.40%	2.00	0.00032	2	$50,000	$100,000
1989	6,975	0.42	2.00	0.00046	3	52,500	157,500
1990	6,487	0.44	2.00	0.00064	4	55,000	220,000
1991	6,033	0.46	2.00	0.00086	5	57,500	287,500
1992	5,610	0.48	2.00	0.00110	6	60,000	360,000
1993	5,218	0.50	2.00	0.00137	7	62,500	437,500
1994	4,852	0.51	2.00	0.00163	8	65,000	520,000
1995	4,513	0.52	2.00	0.00186	9	67,500	607,500
1996	4,197	0.53	2.00	0.00204	9	70,000	630,000
1997	3,903	0.54	2.00	0.00215	9	72,500	652,500
1998	3,630	0.55	2.00	0.00220	9	75,000	675,000
1999	3,376	0.56	2.00	0.00217	8	77,500	620,000
2000	3,139	0.57	2.00	0.00209	7	80,000	560,000
Era 3 — New Business Sold *Only in* 1989 — Untested								
1988	0	0	0	0.00032	0	0	0
1989	7,875	0.40	2.00	0.00046	3	$50,000	$150,000
1990	7,324	0.42	2.00	0.00064	4	52,500	210,000
1991	6,811	0.44	2.00	0.00086	5	55,000	275,000
1992	6,334	0.46	2.00	0.00110	6	57,500	345,000
1993	5,891	0.48	2.00	0.00137	8	60,000	480,000
1994	5,479	0.50	2.00	0.00163	9	62,500	562,500
1995	5,095	0.51	2.00	0.00186	10	65,000	650,000
1996	4,738	0.52	2.00	0.00204	10	67,500	675,000
1997	4,407	0.53	2.00	0.00215	10	70,000	700,000
1998	4,098	0.54	2.00	0.00220	10	72,500	725,000
1999	3,811	0.55	2.00	0.00217	9	75,000	675,000
2000	3,545	0.56	2.00	0.00209	8	77,500	620,000

Similar outputs for new business sold in 1990–2000.

TABLE 6

SUMMARY OF COMPANY PROJECTIONS FOR ERA 3 UNTESTED

Year	Male 18–54 Lives	AIDS Deaths	AIDS Claims
New Business Sold after 12/31/87			
1988	7,500	2	$ 100,000
1989	14,850	6	307,500
1990	22,079	12	630,000
1991	29,216	22	1,177,500
1992	36,287	34	1,857,500
1993	43,319	52	2,897,500
1994	50,337	73	4,142,500
1995	57,367	100	5,770,000
1996	64,432	120	7,027,500
1997	71,557	143	8,502,500
1998	78,765	164	9,895,000
1999	86,079	175	10,690,000
2000	93,522	185	11,427,500

TABLE 7

Company Projections for Era 3 Tested
Detailed Example of 1988 and 1989 Sales

Year	(1) Male 18–54 Lives	(2) Insured % of Gen. Pop.	(3) Antiselection	(4) Gen. Pop. AIDS Mort. Rate	(5) AIDS Deaths $1 \times 2 \times 3 \times 4$	(6) Av. Death Benefit	(7) AIDS Claims 5×6
Era 3 — New Business Sold *Only in* 1988 — Tested							
1988	2,500	0.40%	1.25	0.00000	0	$200,000	0
1989	2,325	0.42	1.25	0.00001	0	210,000	0
1990	2,162	0.44	1.25	0.00003	0	220,000	0
1991	2,011	0.46	1.25	0.00009	0	230,000	0
1992	1,870	0.48	1.25	0.00020	0	240,000	0
1993	1,739	0.50	1.25	0.00037	0	250,000	0
1994	1,617	0.51	1.25	0.00059	1	260,000	$260,000
1995	1,504	0.52	1.25	0.00086	1	270,000	270,000
1996	1,399	0.53	1.25	0.00113	1	280,000	280,000
1997	1,301	0.54	1.25	0.00135	1	290,000	290,000
1998	1,210	0.55	1.25	0.00149	1	300,000	300,000
1999	1,125	0.56	1.25	0.00155	1	310,000	310,000
2000	1,046	0.57	1.25	0.00155	1	320,000	320,000
Era 3 — New Business Sold *Only in* 1989 — Tested							
1988	0	0	0	0.00000	0	$200,000	0
1989	2,625	0.40%	1.25	0.00000	0	210,000	0
1990	2,441	0.42	1.25	0.00001	0	220,000	0
1991	2,270	0.44	1.25	0.00003	0	230,000	0
1992	2,111	0.46	1.25	0.00009	0	240,000	0
1993	1,964	0.48	1.25	0.00019	0	250,000	0
1994	1,826	0.50	1.25	0.00035	0	260,000	0
1995	1,698	0.51	1.25	0.00055	1	270,000	$270,000
1996	1,579	0.52	1.25	0.00079	1	280,000	280,000
1997	1,469	0.53	1.25	0.00102	1	290,000	290,000
1998	1,366	0.54	1.25	0.00119	1	300,000	300,000
1999	1,270	0.55	1.25	0.00129	1	310,000	310,000
2000	1,182	0.56	1.25	0.00132	1	320,000	320,000

Similar outputs for new business sold in 1990–2000.

TABLE 8

SUMMARY OF COMPANY PROJECTIONS FOR ERA 3 TESTED

Year	Male 18–54 Lives	AIDS Deaths	AIDS Claims
New Business Sold after 12-31-87			
1988	2,500	0	0
1989	4,950	0	0
1990	7,360	0	0
1991	9,739	0	0
1992	12,096	0	0
1993	14,440	0	0
1994	16,779	1	$ 260,000
1995	19,122	2	540,000
1996	21,477	3	840,000
1997	23,852	3	870,000
1998	26,255	4	1,200,000
1999	28,693	5	1,550,000
2000	31,174	5	1,600,000

TABLE 9

SUMMARY OF AIDS PROJECTION MODEL

Year	AIDS Deaths					AIDS Claims (Mils)				
			Era 3					Era 3		
	Era 1	Era 2	Untested	Tested	Total	Era 1	Era 2	Untested	Tested	Total
1988	13	5	2	0	20	$ 0.6	$ 0.3	$ 0.1	0	$ 1.0
1989	19	7	6	0	32	1.0	0.4	0.3	0	1.7
1990	26	10	12	0	48	1.4	0.6	0.6	0	2.7
1991	35	13	22	0	70	2.0	0.9	1.2	0	4.1
1992	45	16	34	0	95	2.7	1.1	1.9	0	5.7
1993	56	20	52	0	128	3.5	1.4	2.9	0	7.8
1994	65	23	73	1	162	4.2	1.7	4.1	$0.3	10.4
1995	73	25	100	2	200	4.9	1.9	5.8	0.5	13.2
1996	78	27	120	3	228	5.5	2.2	7.0	0.8	15.5
1997	80	27	143	3	253	5.8	2.2	8.5	0.9	17.4
1998	80	27	164	4	275	6.0	2.3	9.9	1.2	19.4
1999	78	26	175	5	284	6.0	2.3	10.7	1.5	20.6
2000	73	24	185	5	287	5.8	2.2	11.4	1.6	21.0
Total	721	250	1,088	23	2,082	$49.6	$19.6	$64.4	$6.9	$140.5

HYPOTHETICAL LIFE MODEL EXAMPLE 3

This model has been developed for the purpose of estimating future individual life insurance AIDS claims by using assumptions that reproduce known and projected population data from the CDC and other acknowledged experts. To the extent that the model tracks known and authoritative projected data, some degree of credibility can be assumed. However, there is much that is still unknown about AIDS, and there are many variables that can affect projected results.

The model can be used to test a variety of assumptions to determine the effect that different scenarios have on claims and at what point in the future the maximum effect may occur. This will permit planning to mitigate this effect.

The hypothetical examples attached give AIDS claims projections for two risk groups that are of primary concern to life insurance companies:

1. Homosexual and bisexual males, which constitute most of our exposure to AIDS currently, and
2. Heterosexual males and females, which present a future problem if there is a significant spread of the AIDS virus in the heterosexual population.

A description of these and other risk groups is given in Table 10. The assumptions used in making the homo-bisexual and heterosexual projections and the basis for those assumptions are given in Tables 11 and 12.

TABLE 10

The percentage distribution of AIDS victims according to November 16, 1987 CDC data is as follows (excludes undetermined):

	Males	Females	Children
IV drug user	21%	4%	—
Homosexual/bisexual	67	—	—
Heterosexual			
Infected Overseas	1.5	0.5	—
Infected in U.S.	0.5	1.5	—
Contaminated Blood	2	1	1
	92%	7%	1%

Two projections have been made to estimate future AIDS claims from the groups that are significant to individual life insurance experience: homo-bisexual males, which represents the current problem, and heterosexual males and females, which represent a possible future problem.

IV drug users, which constitute a significant proportion of AIDS victims, are not included in the insurance projections because we feel that only an insignificant proportion of such risks are insured. For the same reason, heterosexual males who were infected with the AIDS virus in Africa or Haiti are excluded.

Persons who become infected with contaminated blood (including children) are also not directly included in the projections, but expected claims from this group are added to the results to approximate such persons in the insurance population that will die from AIDS. This amount should not be large because very few additional persons should become infected now that blood donors are being checked for exposure to the AIDS virus. Nevertheless, we have added a constant 5 percent to the homo-bisexual projection.

TABLE 11

MODEL ASSUMPTIONS FOR PROJECTIONS OF HOMO-BISEXUAL AND
HETEROSEXUAL CLAIMS IN HYPOTHETICAL LIFE MODEL—EXAMPLE 3
(See Table 12 for Explanation of Assumptions)

	Homo-bisexual Males Ages 20–59	Heterosexual Males and Females Ages 20–59
Population		
1. % AIDS susceptible	6%	10%
2. % AIDS susceptible infected by 1996	59.5%	25%
2A. % AIDS susceptible who tested negative at issue infected by 1996	16.7%	4.8%
3. % Infected getting AIDS within 20 years	90.6%	90.6%
4. % With AIDS dying		
Within 1 year	45.0%	45.0%
Within 2 years	69.8%	69.8%
Within 3 years	80.3%	80.3%
Company — AIDS		
5. % AIDS susceptible assuming no antiselection	2.4%	2%
6. Annual termination rate among AIDS susceptible (excluding AIDS deaths)	0%	0%
7. Antiselection factor among AIDS susceptible	1.5X	1.5X
8. Testing factor		
1/1/87 to 7/1/87	30%	30%
7/1/87 and later	50%	50%
Company — General		
9. In force 1/1/87		
Total	$100 billion	$100 billion
Ages 20–59	$65 billion (M)	$85 billion (M&F)
10. New issues		
1987	$10 billion	$10 billion
Ages 20–59	$6.5 billion (M)	$8.5 billion (M&F)
Annual increase	5%	5%
11. Annual death rate		
1987–1990 IF	3.0%	3.0%
1991–1995 IF	2.9%	2.9%
1996–2000 IF	2.8%	2.8%
12. Annual termination rate		
In force	7.5%	7.5%
New issues	7.5%	7.5%

TABLE 12

BASIS FOR ASSUMPTIONS IN PROJECTION OF CLAIMS
FOR HYPOTHETICAL LIFE MODEL — EXAMPLE 3

Homo-Bisexual

1. *U.S. AIDS-Susceptible Population.* We have assumed that 6% of males, ages 20–59, are AIDS susceptible because of homosexual activity (80%) or IV drug use (20%).

2. *U.S. Population Infected.* Line 5 of Table 13 is from Cowell paper, Appendix 2. Assumes no new infections after 1996.

3. *% Getting AIDS after Infection.* Derived from Cowell data.

4. *% Dying after Getting AIDS.* From Cowell paper.

5. *AIDS-Susceptible Insurance Population.* It is reasonable to assume that there is a lower percentage of AIDS-susceptible risks among insureds than in the general population because of a lesser desire or need for insurance. We have assumed that IV drug users (20%) are not included in the insurance population and that the pre-AIDS proportion of homo-bisexuals is one-half of that in the general population (one-half of 80% = 40%).

6. *Antiselection Termination Factor.* It is reasonable to assume that AIDS-susceptible insureds will have a low lapse rate. Therefore, we have assumed no terminations other than AIDS deaths on the assumption that increases through paid-up additions and option exercises will offset terminations and non-AIDS deaths.

7. *Antiselection at Issue Factor.* It is expected that AIDS-susceptible risks will have a greater incentive to buy than heretofore. We have assumed that this incentive will increase by 50% the percentage of AIDS-susceptible applicants.

8. *Testing Factor.* This is the proportion by amount for which HIV testing is performed. This protective factor does not account for those jurisdictions where HIV testing is not permitted.

9. *In Force.* Assumes $100,000,000 in force 1/1/87 with 65% on males ages 20–59.

10. *New Issues.* Assumes $10,000,000 new issues in 1987, increasing 10% per year, with 65% on males ages 20–59.

11. *Annual Death Rate.* This is total death rate (excluding AIDS deaths) projected for some mortality improvement (can be obtained from annual statement data).

12. *Annual Termination Rate.* This is a total termination rate (excluding AIDS deaths) and is assumed to remain constant (can be obtained from annual statement data).

Heterosexual

1. AIDS-susceptible heterosexuals include (1) persons who have regular activity with a single infected partner and (2) persons who have heterosexual activity with a variety of partners, thus having a possiblity of exposure to one or more infected partners. We estimate that such persons (i.e., AIDS susceptible) may constitute 10% of the heterosexual population, ages 20–59.

2. Because the transmission of the AIDS virus is less likely in vaginal sex than anal sex, the spread of infection is assumed to be at a lower rate for heterosexuals than for homo-bisexuals, reaching 25% of AIDS susceptibles by 2000. Assumes that new infections continue after 1996.

5. The pre-AIDS proportion of AIDS-susceptible heterosexuals among insureds is estimated at only 20% of that in the general population (as compared to 40% for AIDS susceptible homo-bisexuals). The proportion is lower than for homo-bisexuals because a high proportion of AIDS-susceptible heterosexuals are partners of IV drug users and thus have a lifestyle inconsistent with the purchase of insurance.

9–10. New issues and in force are 85% of total for males and females ages 20–59, as compared to 65% for males ages 20–59 in the homo-bisexual projection.

Assumption 3–4, 6–8 and 11–12 are the same as those in the homo-bisexual projection.

1005

Although data are still limited and immature, the assumptions used in the homo-bisexual population projection are reasonable. However, for the heterosexual projection, data are virtually nonexistent, and the projection is extremely hypothetical. To the present, only 2 percent of AIDS victims have been heterosexual non-IV drug users infected within the U.S., and this percentage has not grown. Nevertheless, it is expected that this percentage will increase as the rate of AIDS infection among homo-bisexuals and IV drug users decreases. The progression in the heterosexual population is slow because very few heterosexuals are currently infected and a promiscuous heterosexual encounter has a low probability of AIDS infection. The assumptions used in the heterosexual projection illustrate a scenario in which the spread to the heterosexual population begins to have a major impact in the late 1990s.

This model has been developed on a PC using a Lotus 1-2-3 spreadsheet. The examples are not subdivided by age or by other risk characteristics, which would produce greater refinement. However, such subdivisions can be readily made. Of course, changes in both the population and company assumptions currently used can also be readily made.

The company assumptions are hypothetical and are not necessarily representative of any company's experience. Therefore, the results are illustrative and not predictive. In using this type of model, the company actuary should select assumptions that will produce results that reproduce actual claims experience. There are also refinements that could be made to improve the accuracy of the projections. However, given the questionable nature of many of the assumptions, the emphasis in this illustration has been on simplicity of presentation in lieu of refinement.

In Tables 13 and 14, the model projects the number of AIDS-susceptibles in the population that become infected. In this projection, the numbers infected have been set to equal those in the Cowell model. In Tables 15 and 16, rates of conversion (i.e., rate of getting AIDS after infection) are applied to obtain the number of AIDS cases in each calendar year.

TABLE 13

ESTIMATE OF AIDS-SUSCEPTIBLE HOMOSEXUAL-BISEXUAL AND IV DRUG USER MALES IN GENERAL POPULATION BECOMING INFECTED WITH THE AIDS VIRUS
(Numbers in Thousands)

	1981	1982	1983	1984	1985	1986	1987	1988	1989	1990	1991	1992	1993	1994	1995	1996	1997	1998	1999	2000
Assumption 1: AIDS-Susceptible = 6.0% of Males Ages 20–59																				
1. U.S. population (males 20–59)	60,731	61,339	61,918	62,484	63,047	63,614	64,187	64,765	65,348	65,936	66,529	67,128	67,732	68,342	68,957	69,577	70,203	70,835	71,473	72,116
2. AIDS-susceptible (0.06 × line 1)	3,644	3,680	3,715	3,749	3,783	3,817	3,851	3,886	3,921	3,956	3,992	4,028	4,064	4,100	4,137	4,175	4,212	4,250	4,288	4,327
Assumption 2: Infected Population Increases as Indicated to 59.5% in 1996 (no additional infections after 1996)																				
3. % of AIDS-susceptible population infected	2.1%	3.7%	5.9%	8.7%	12.6%	17.6%	23.9%	30.6%	37.4%	43.5%	48.8%	52.9%	56.0%	58.1%	59.3%	59.5%	59.0%	58.5%	57.9%	57.4%
4. % Infected in year	2.1%	1.6%	2.8%	2.8%	3.9%	5.0%	6.3%	6.7%	6.8%	6.1%	5.3%	4.1%	3.1%	2.1%	1.2%	0.3%	0.0%	0.0%	0.0%	0.0%
5. AIDS-susceptible population infected line 2 × line 3 (from Cowell paper)	76	135	218	328	478	671	920	1,191	1,465	1,721	1,946	2,132	2,277	2,383	2,452	2,485	2,485	2,485	2,485	2,485
6. Number becoming infected in year (1978 = 4, 1979 = 10, 1980 = 22)	40	59	83	110	150	193	249	271	274	256										

TABLE 14

Estimate of Aids-Susceptible Heterosexual Non-IV Drug User Males and Females Ages 20–59 in General Population Becoming Infected with the AIDS Virus (Numbers in Thousands)

	1981	1982	1983	1984	1985	1986	1987	1988	1989	1990	1991	1992	1993	1994	1995	1996	1997	1998	1999	2000
Assumption 1: AIDS-Susceptible = 10% of Males and Females, 20–59																				
1. U.S. population (males and females, 20–59)	123,533	124,769	125,947	127,098	128,244	129,398	130,563	131,738	132,923	134,120	135,327	136,545	137,774	139,014	140,265	141,527	142,801	144,086	145,383	146,691
2. AIDS-susceptible (.10 × line 1)	12,353	12,477	12,595	12,710	12,824	12,940	13,056	13,174	13,292	13,412	13,533	13,654	13,777	13,901	14,026	14,153	14,280	14,409	14,538	14,669
Assumption 2: Infected Population Increases to 59.5% in 1996 (no additional infections after 1996)																				
3. % of AIDS-susceptible population infected	0.035%	0.050%	0.070%	0.10%	0.14%	0.20%	0.28%	0.40%	0.56%	0.80%	1.10%	1.50%	2.20%	3.10%	4.40%	6.20%	8.80%	12.50%	17.60%	25.00%
4. % Infected in year	0.035%	0.015%	0.02%	0.03%	0.04%	0.06%	0.08%	0.12%	0.16%	0.24%	0.3%	0.4%	0.7%	0.9%	1.3%	1.8%	2.6%	3.7%	5.1%	7.4%
5. AIDS-susceptible population infected line 2 × line 3 (from Cowell paper)	4	6	9	13	18	26	37	53	74	107	149	205	303	431	617	877	1,257	1,801	2,559	3,667
6. Number becoming infected in year (1980 and prior = 0)	4	2	3	4	5	8	11	16	22	33	42	56	98	128	186	260	379	544	758	1,109

TABLE 15

NUMBER OF HOMOSEXUAL-BISEXUAL AND IV DRUG USER MALES IN GENERAL POPULATION GETTING AIDS YEAR BY YEAR AFTER INFECTION IN YEAR INDICATED (Numbers in Thousands)

Assumption 3 Year	% Getting AIDS after Infected	Infected in Year	1978	1979	1980	1981	1982	1983	1984	1985	1986	1987	1988	1989	1990	1991	1992	1993	1994	1995	1996	1997	1998	1999	2000
1	0.0%	1978	0	12	48	104	172	248	344	416	400	336	288	244	208	180	148	128	108	92	80	68	56	48	40
2	0.3%	1979		0	30	120	260	430	620	860	1,040	1,000	840	720	610	520	450	370	320	270	230	200	170	140	120
3	1.2%	1980			0	66	264	572	946	1,364	1,892	2,288	2,200	1,848	1,584	1,342	1,144	990	814	704	594	506	440	374	308
4	2.6%	1981				0	120	480	1,040	1,720	2,480	3,440	4,160	4,000	3,360	2,880	2,440	2,080	1,800	1,480	1,280	1,080	920	800	680
5	4.3%	1982					0	177	708	1,534	2,537	3,658	5,074	6,136	5,900	4,956	4,248	3,599	3,068	2,655	2,183	1,888	1,593	1,357	1,180
6	6.2%	1983						0	249	996	2,158	3,569	5,146	7,138	8,632	8,300	6,972	5,976	5,063	4,316	3,735	3,071	2,656	2,241	1,909
7	8.6%	1984							0	330	1,320	2,860	4,730	6,820	9,460	11,440	11,000	9,240	7,920	6,710	5,720	4,950	4,070	3,520	2,970
8	10.4%	1985								0	450	1,800	3,900	6,450	9,300	12,900	15,600	15,000	12,600	10,800	9,150	7,800	6,750	5,550	4,800
9	10.0%	1986									0	579	2,316	5,018	8,299	11,966	16,598	20,072	19,300	16,212	13,896	11,773	10,036	8,685	7,141
10	8.4%	1987										0	747	2,988	6,474	10,707	15,438	21,414	25,896	24,900	20,916	17,928	15,189	12,948	11,205
11	7.2%	1988											0	813	3,252	7,046	11,653	16,802	23,306	28,184	27,100	22,764	19,512	16,531	14,092
12	6.1%	1989												0	822	3,288	7,124	11,782	16,988	23,564	28,496	27,400	23,016	19,728	16,714
13	5.2%	1990													0	768	3,072	6,656	11,008	15,872	22,016	26,624	25,600	21,504	18,432
14	4.5%	1991														0	675	2,700	5,850	9,675	13,950	19,350	23,400	22,500	18,900
15	3.7%	1992															0	558	2,232	4,836	7,998	11,532	15,996	19,344	18,600
16	3.2%	1993																0	435	1,740	3,770	6,235	8,990	12,470	15,080
17	2.7%	1994																	0	318	1,272	2,756	4,558	6,572	9,116
18	2.3%	1995																		0	207	828	1,794	2,967	4,278
19	2.0%	1996																			0	99	396	858	1,419
20	1.7%	1997																				0	0	0	0
21	1.4%	1998																					0	0	0
22	1.2%	1999																						0	0
23	1.0%	2000																							0
	94.2%																								
1. Total			0	12	78	290	816	1,907	3,907	7,220	12,277	19,530	29,401	42,175	57,901	76,293	96,562	117,367	136,708	152,328	162,593	166,852	165,142	158,137	146,984
2. Cumulative			0	12	90	380	1,196	3,103	7,010	14,230	26,507	46,037	75,438	117,613	175,514	251,807	348,369	465,736	602,444	754,772	917,365	1,084,217	1,249,359	1,407,496	1,554,480
3. CDC Data			–	–	–	337	1,337	4,119	9,697	15,948	29,003	55,000	88,000	133,000	191,000	265,000									
4. Ratio of line 2 to line 3			–	–	–	113%	89%	75%	72%	89%	91%	84%	86%	88%	92%	95%									

TABLE 16

Number of Non-IV Drug User Males and Females Ages 20–59 in General Population
Getting AIDS Year by Year after Infection in Year Indicated (Numbers in Thousands)

Assumption 3

Year	% Getting AIDS after Infected	Infected in Year	1978	1979	1980	1981	1982	1983	1984	1985	1986	1987	1988	1989	1990	1991	1992	1993	1994	1995	1996	1997	1998	1999	2000
1	0.0%	1978	0	0	0	0	0	0	0	0	0	0	0	0	0	0	0	0	0	0	0	0	0	0	0
2	0.3%	1979		0	0	0	0	0	0	0	0	0	0	0	0	0	0	0	0	0	0	0	0	0	0
3	1.2%	1980			0	0	0	0	0	0	0	0	0	0	0	0	0	0	0	0	0	0	0	0	0
4	2.6%	1981				0	13	52	112	186	268	372	450	432	363	311	264	225	195	160	138	117	99	86	74
5	4.3%	1982					0	6	23	50	82	119	165	199	191	161	138	117	100	86	71	61	52	44	38
6	6.2%	1983						0	8	31	67	111	160	222	268	258	217	186	157	134	116	95	82	70	59
7	8.6%	1984							0	12	47	101	167	241	335	405	389	327	280	238	202	175	144	125	105
8	10.4%	1985								0	16	63	136	226	325	451	545	524	441	378	320	273	236	194	168
9	10.0%	1986									0	24	95	206	341	491	682	824	793	666	571	483	412	357	293
10	8.4%	1987										0	32	128	278	459	694	918	1,111	1,068	897	769	651	555	481
11	7.2%	1988											0	48	194	420	662	1,001	1,388	1,678	1,614	1,356	1,162	984	839
12	6.1%	1989												0	65	261	565	935	1,348	1,870	2,261	2,174	1,826	1,565	1,326
13	5.2%	1990													0	99	394	854	1,413	2,037	2,826	3,417	3,286	2,760	2,366
14	4.5%	1991														0	125	499	1,081	1,787	2,577	3,574	4,323	4,156	3,491
15	3.7%	1992															0	168	671	1,455	2,406	3,469	4,812	5,820	5,596
16	3.2%	1993																0	295	1,179	2,555	4,226	6,094	8,453	10,222
17	2.7%	1994																	0	384	1,534	3,324	5,497	7,926	10,994
18	2.3%	1995																		0	559	2,235	4,842	8,008	11,546
19	2.0%	1996																			0	781	3,124	6,768	11,193
20	1.7%	1997																				0	1,138	4,550	9,859
21	1.4%	1998																					0	1,633	6,533
22	1.2%	1999																						0	2,273
23	1.0%	2000																							0
1. Total	94.2%		0	0	0	0	13	58	143	278	480	789	1,205	1,703	2,360	3,315	4,675	6,578	9,271	13,119	18,647	26,530	37,780	54,054	77,456
2. Cumulative			0	0	0	0	13	71	214	492	972	1,761	2,966	4,669	7,029	10,345	15,019	21,597	30,868	43,987	62,635	89,165	126,945	180,999	258,454
3. 2% of CDC Data (Heterosexual U.S. born M & F)			—	—	—	7	27	82	194	319	580	1,100	1,760	2,660	3,820	5,300									
4. Ratio of line 2 to line 3			—	—	—	0%	49%	86%	110%	154%	168%	160%	169%	176%	184%	195%									

In Tables 17 and 18, the rates of death among those who have AIDS are applied to produce AIDS deaths; these deaths are compared to projected CDC deaths in the last line.

In Tables 19 and 20, population death rates for AIDS infected, ages 20–59, are calculated by taking the ratio of AIDS deaths to AIDS infected. These death rates are applied in Tables 21–24 to AIDS-infected insureds to determine company AIDS claims.

Also shown in Tables 19 and 20 (line 3A) are the cumulative death rates for persons who tested HIV − at time of issue but who became infected after issue. These are the same rates as in line 3 but starting in 1987 instead of 1979 (we assume 1979 = 0, 1980 = 1.0 and 1981 = 2.0). That is, they are the rates that applied at the start of the epidemic when virtually none of the AIDS-susceptibles was infected.

We assume those who are tested have the same proportions of infected-noninfected as those who are not tested. Hence, the death rates in line 3 are applicable to those not tested. Those who are tested but test negative will have a lesser rate of infection (as indicated in assumption 2A) and after infection will have a deferred death rate as indicated in line 3A.

The infection rates in assumption 2A are cumulative; that is, the rate of infection for 1987 applies, of course, only to 1987 issues. The rate for 1988 applies to 1987 and 1988 issues and has been taken, for simplicity, as the average for those two years of issue. The rate for 1989 is the average of the rate for 1987, 1988 and 1989 issues, and so on. The rate of infection in 1997–2000 decreases (but is greater than zero) because although there are no new infections after 1996, there are persons who become infected after issue but before 1996 who are included among those infected in 1997–2000.

TABLE 17

Number of Homosexual-Bisexual and IV Drug User Males in General Population Dying Year by Year after Getting AIDS in Year Indicated (Numbers in Thousands)

| Assumption 4 | | | | | | | | | | | | | | | | | | | | | | |
Year	% Dying after Getting AIDS	Getting AIDS in Year	1981	1982	1983	1984	1985	1986	1987	1988	1989	1990	1991	1992	1993	1994	1995	1996	1997	1998	1999	2000
1	45.000%	1981 & Prior	171	94	40	19	14	11	8	6	4	3	2	2	1	1	1	1	0	0	0	0
2	24.750%	1982		367	202	86	40	30	23	17	13	10	7	5	4	3	2	2	1	1	1	1
3	10.588%	1983			858	472	202	94	70	53	40	30	22	17	13	9	7	5	4	3	2	2
4	4.916%	1984				1,758	967	414	192	144	108	81	61	46	34	26	19	14	11	8	6	5
5	3.687%	1985					3,249	1,787	764	355	266	200	150	112	84	63	47	36	27	20	15	11
6	2.765%	1986						5,525	3,039	1,300	604	453	339	255	191	143	107	81	60	45	34	26
7	2.074%	1987							8,789	4,834	2,068	960	720	540	405	304	228	171	128	96	72	54
8	1.555%	1988								13,230	7,277	3,113	1,445	1,084	813	610	457	343	257	193	145	108
9	1.167%	1989									18,979	10,438	4,465	2,073	1,555	1,166	875	656	492	369	277	208
10	0.875%	1990										26,055	14,330	6,131	2,846	2,135	1,601	1,201	900	676	507	380
11	0.656%	1991											34,332	18,883	8,078	3,751	2,813	2,110	1,582	1,186	890	668
12	0.492%	1992												43,453	23,899	10,224	4,747	3,560	2,670	2,003	1,502	1,127
13	0.369%	1993													52,815	29,048	12,427	5,770	4,327	3,245	2,434	1,825
14	0.277%	1994														61,519	33,835	14,475	6,721	5,040	3,780	2,835
15	0.208%	1995															68,548	37,701	16,128	7,488	5,616	4,212
16	0.156%	1996																73,167	40,242	17,215	7,993	5,995
17	0.117%	1997																	75,083	41,296	17,666	8,202
18	0.088%	1998																		74,314	40,873	17,485
19	0.066%	1999																			71,162	39,139
20	0.049%	2000																				66,143
	99.855%																					
1. Total			171	461	1,100	2,335	4,472	7,860	12,884	19,939	29,358	41,343	55,875	72,600	90,739	109,001	125,714	139,291	148,635	153,200	152,974	148,425
2. Cumulative			171	632	1,733	4,068	8,540	16,399	29,284	49,222	78,580	119,923	175,798	248,398	339,136	448,138	573,852	713,143	861,778	1,014,978	1,167,952	1,316,377
3. CDC Data			146	528	1,753	4,582	8,161	16,301	30,000	51,000	81,000	122,000	176,000									
4. Ratio of line 2 to line 3			117%	120%	99%	89%	105%	101%	98%	97%	97%	98%	100%									

TABLE 18

Number of Non-IV Drug User Males and Females Ages 20–59 in General Population Dying Year by Year After Getting AIDS in Year Indicated (Numbers in Thousands)

Assumption 4

Year	% Dying after Getting AIDS	Getting AIDS in Year	1981	1982	1983	1984	1985	1986	1987	1988	1989	1990	1991	1992	1993	1994	1995	1996	1997	1998	1999	2000
1	45.000%	1981 & Prior	0	0	0	0	0	0	0	0	0	0	0	0	0	0	0	0	0	0	0	0
2	24.750%	1982		6	3	1	1	0	0	0	0	0	0	0	0	0	0	0	0	0	0	0
3	10.588%	1983			26	14	6	3	2	2	1	1	1	1	0	0	0	0	0	0	0	0
4	4.916%	1984				64	35	15	7	5	4	3	2	2	1	1	1	1	0	0	0	0
5	3.687%	1985					125	69	29	14	10	8	6	4	3	2	2	1	1	1	1	0
6	2.765%	1986						216	119	51	24	18	13	10	7	6	4	3	2	2	1	1
7	2.074%	1987							355	195	84	39	29	22	16	12	9	7	5	4	3	2
8	1.555%	1988								542	298	128	59	44	33	25	19	14	11	8	6	4
9	1.167%	1989									766	421	180	84	63	47	35	26	20	15	11	8
10	0.875%	1990										1,062	584	250	116	87	65	49	37	28	21	15
11	0.656%	1991											1,492	821	351	163	122	92	69	52	39	29
12	0.492%	1992												2,104	1,157	495	230	172	129	97	73	55
13	0.369%	1993													2,960	1,628	696	323	243	182	136	102
14	0.277%	1994														4,172	2,295	982	456	342	256	192
15	0.208%	1995															5,904	3,247	1,389	645	484	363
16	0.156%	1996																8,391	4,615	1,974	917	688
17	0.117%	1997																	11,939	6,566	2,809	1,304
18	0.088%	1998																		17,001	9,351	4,000
19	0.066%	1999																			24,324	13,378
20	0.049%	2000																				34,855
	99.855%																						
		1. Total	0	6	29	80	167	303	513	809	1,187	1,679	2,367	3,341	4,709	6,639	9,382	13,309	18,915	26,916	38,431	54,998
		2. Cumulative	0	6	35	115	282	586	1,099	1,908	3,095	4,774	7,141	10,482	15,191	21,829	31,212	44,520	63,436	90,352	128,783	183,781
		3. 2% of CDC Data (Heterosexual U.S. born M & F)	3	11	35	92	163	326	600	1,020	1,620	2,440	3,520									
		4. Ratio of line 2 to line 3	0%	55%	100%	126%	173%	180%	183%	187%	191%	196%	203%									

TABLE 19

Estimate of Infected Population Death Rate Due to AIDS for Males Ages 20–59 (Excluding Heterosexuals)

	1981	1982	1983	1984	1985	1986	1987	1988	1989	1990	1991	1992	1993	1994	1995	1996	1997	1998	1999	2000
1. AIDS deaths [line 1 from Table 17]	171	461	1,100	2,335	4,472	7,860	12,884	19,939	29,358	41,343	55,875	72,600	90,739	109,001	125,714	139,291	148,635	153,200	152,974	148,425
2. Live infected (000's) [line 1 from Table 17]	76	135	217	326	474	663	907	1,171	1,436	1,680	1,890	2,059	2,186	2,274	2,326	2,346	2,336	2,332	2,332	2,337
3. Death rate per 1,000 live infected line 1 × line 2	2.255	3.428	5.073	7.171	9.444	11.852	14.204	17.026	20.449	24.614	29.562	35.253	41.504	47.934	54.041	59.381	63.618	65.700	65.597	63.522
3A. Death rate per 1,000 live infected (for those testing negative at issue)	—	—	—	—	—	—	0.0000	1.000	2.000	3.428	5.073	7.171	9.444	11.852	14.204	17.026	20.449	24.614	29.562	35.253

TABLE 20

Estimate of Infected Population Death Rates Due to AIDS for Heterosexual Males and Females Ages 20–59

	1981	1982	1983	1984	1985	1986	1987	1988	1989	1990	1991	1992	1993	1994	1995	1996	1997	1998	1999	2000
1. AIDS deaths [line 1 from Table 18]	0	6	29	80	167	303	513	809	1,187	1,679	2,367	3,341	4,709	6,639	9,382	13,309	18,915	26,916	38,431	54,998
2. Live infected (000's) [line 5 from Table 18]	4	6	9	13	18	26	36	52	73	106	146	201	298	424	608	864	1,238	1,774	2,520	3,612
3. Death rate per 1,000 live infected line 1 ÷ line 2	0.000	0.937	3.317	6.338	9.412	11.858	14.231	15.597	16.208	15.899	16.156	16.581	15.781	15.646	15.437	15.401	15.282	15.171	15.249	15.225
3A. Death rate per 1,000 live infected (for those testing negative at issue)	—	—	—	—	—	—	0.000	0.000	0.000	0.937	3.317	6.338	9.412	11.858	14.231	15.597	16.208	15.899	16.156	16.581

In Tables 21 and 22, AIDS-susceptibles among the 1/1/87 in force are estimated. In the homo-bisexual projection, it is estimated that insurance on males ages 20–59 constitutes 65 percent of total insurance in force and that 2.4 percent of this amount is on AIDS-susceptibles (40 percent of the 6.0 percent in the U.S. population). This 2.4 percent figure is obtained by eliminating IV drug users (1.2 percent) and assuming that the pre-AIDS proportion of AIDS-susceptible homo-bisexuals is only one-half of that in the general population. Rates of infection from Tables 13 and 14 are then applied to the AIDS-susceptibles to determine the number infected. Then the death rates from line 3 of Tables 19 and 20 are applied. A similar approach is used in the heterosexual projection.

TABLE 21

ESTIMATE OF COMPANY DEATH CLAIMS CAUSED BY AIDS ON 1986 AND PRIOR ISSUES
FOR AIDS-SUSCEPTIBLE HOMO-BISEXUAL MALES AGES 20–59
(Dollar Amounts in Thousands)

Year	(1) AIDS-Susceptible (Beginning of Year) Prior Year (2) − (6)	(2) Terminations (Assumption 6)	(3) Percentage of AIDS-Susceptible Infected (line 3, Table 13)	(4) AIDS Infected (1) × (3)	(5) Death Rate per Thousand (line 3, Table 19)	(6) AIDS Death Claims (4) × (5)
1987	1,560,000	0	23.9%	372,661	14.204	$5,293
1988	1,554,707	0	30.6%	476,509	17.026	8,113
1989	1,546,594	0	37.4%	577,875	20.449	11,817
1990	1,534,777	0	43.5%	667,659	24.614	16,434
1991	1,518,343	0	48.8%	740,202	29.562	21,882
1992	1,496,462	0	52.9%	792,135	35.253	27,925
1993	1,468,537	0	56.0%	822,816	41.504	34,150
1994	1,434,386	0	58.1%	833,593	47.934	39,957
1995	1,394,429	0	59.3%	826,399	54.041	44,659
1996	1,349,770	0	59.5%	803,466	59.381	47,711
1997	1,302,059	0	59.0%	768,152	63.618	48,868
1998	1,253,191	0	58.5%	732,728	65.700	48,140
1999	1,205,050	0	57.9%	698,296	65.597	45,806
2000	1,159,244	0	57.4%	665,761	63.522	42,291
						$443,047

Assumptions 1 and 5

1. U.S. AIDS-susceptible 6.0%

5. Company AIDS-susceptible 2.4%

Assumption 6

Antiselection
termination factor 0.0

Assumption 9

In force for males ages 20–59 is 65% of total in force
1/1/87 Total in force $100,000,000
1/1/87 Infected males ages 20–59 $65,000,000
AIDS-susceptible (see assumption 5)
0.0240 × $65,000,000 = $1,560,000

TABLE 22

Estimate of Company Death Claims Caused by AIDS on 1986 and Prior Issues
for AIDS-Susceptible Heterosexual Males and Females Ages 20–59
(Dollar Amounts in Thousands)

Year	(1) AIDS-Susceptible (Beginning of Year) Prior Year (2)−(6)	(2) Terminations (Assumption 6) 0.0 × (1)	(3) Percentage of AIDS-Susceptible Infected (line 3, Table 14)	(4) AIDS Infected (1) × (3)	(5) Death Rate per Thousand (line 3, Table 20)	(6) AIDS Death Claims (4) × (5)
1987	1,700,000	0	0.3%	4,760	14.231	68
1988	1,699,932	0	0.4%	6,800	15.597	106
1989	1,699,826	0	0.6%	9,519	16.208	154
1990	1,699,672	0	0.8%	13,597	15.899	216
1991	1,699,456	0	1.1%	18,694	16.156	302
1992	1,699,154	0	1.5%	25,487	16.581	423
1993	1,698,731	0	2.2%	37,372	15.781	590
1994	1,698,141	0	3.1%	52,642	15.646	824
1995	1,697,318	0	4.4%	74,682	15.437	1,153
1996	1,696,165	0	6.2%	105,162	15.401	1,620
1997	1,694,545	0	8.8%	149,120	15.282	2,279
1998	1,692,266	0	12.5%	211,533	15.171	3,209
1999	1,689,057	0	17.6%	297,274	15.249	4,533
2000	1,684,524	0	25.0%	421,131	15.225	6,412
						$21,888

Assumptions 1 and 5

1. U.S. AIDS-susceptible   10.0%

5. Company AIDS-susceptible 2.0%

Assumption 6

Antiselection
termination factor   0.0%

Assumption 9

In force for males and females ages 20–59 is 85% of total in force

1/1/87 Total in force	$100,000,000
1/1/87 In force M and F, ages 20–59	$85,000,000
AIDS-susceptible (see assumption 5)	
$85,000 × 0.02	= $1,700,000

In Tables 23–26, AIDS-susceptibles among 1987 and later issues are estimated. In the homo-bisexual projection, the 2.4 percent estimate of AIDS-susceptibles is, in effect, increased by an antiselection factor of 1.5 (to reflect the greater incentive of AIDS-susceptibles to obtain insurance) and reduced by a testing factor that equals the proportion of new insurance being tested. Rates of infection from Tables 13 and 14 are then applied to the AIDS-susceptibles who were not tested. For those who were tested, the rates of infection from assumption 2A are applied to those who tested negative (those testing positive were declined for insurance) and then the death rates from line 3A of Tables 16 and 17 are applied.

In Table 27, company death claims excluding AIDS are obtained by applying estimated total company death rates to total in force. The ratios of total AIDS claims to total death claims including AIDS claims are then obtained as a measure of the incidence and cumulative effect of AIDS claims on total company experience.

TABLE 23

ESTIMATE OF COMPANY DEATH CLAIMS CAUSED BY AIDS ON 1987 AND LATER ISSUES FOR AIDS-SUSCEPTIBLE HOMO-BISEXUAL MALES AGES 20–59

Year	(1) Total New Issues during Year	(2) AIDS-Susceptible (1) × 0.65 × 0.024 × Assumption 7	(3) AIDS-Susceptible Not Tested (2) × (1-Z)	(4) AIDS-Susceptible Not Tested (Beginning of Year) Prior Year of (7)	(5) AIDS-Susceptible Exposure (4) + (3)/2	(6) Terminations 0.0 × (5)	(7) AIDS-Susceptible (End of Year) (4) + (3) − (6) − (10)	(8) AIDS-Susceptible Infected (5) × (line 3, Table 13)	(9) Death Rate per Thousand (line 3, Table 19)	(10) AIDS Death Claims (Not Tested) (8) × (9)	(11) AIDS Death Claims (Tested Negative at Issue) (from Table 25)	(12) Total AIDS Death Claims (10) + (11)
1987	10,000,000	234,000	140,000	0	70,200	0	140,162	16,770	14.204	238	0	238
1988	10,500,000	245,700	122,900	140,162	201,612	0	262,010	61,793	17.026	1,052	11	1,063
1989	11,025,000	258,000	129,000	262,010	326,510	0	388,515	121,998	20.449	2,495	53	2,548
1990	11,576,250	270,900	135,500	388,515	456,265	0	519,130	198,484	24.614	4,885	152	5,037
1991	12,155,063	284,400	142,200	519,130	590,230	0	652,823	287,741	29.562	8,506	323	8,829
1992	12,762,816	298,600	149,300	652,823	727,473	0	788,548	385,080	35.253	13,575	583	14,158
1993	13,400,956	313,600	156,800	788,548	866,948	0	925,188	485,748	41.504	20,161	907	21,068
1994	14,071,004	329,300	164,700	925,188	1,007,538	0	1,061,821	585,530	47.934	28,067	1,277	29,344
1995	14,774,554	345,700	172,900	1,061,821	1,148,271	0	1,197,945	680,515	54.041	36,776	1,629	38,404
1996	15,513,282	363,000	181,500	1,197,945	1,288,695	0	1,333,894	767,111	59.381	45,552	1,982	47,534
1997	16,288,946	381,200	190,600	1,333,894	1,429,194	0	1,470,854	843,156	63.618	53,640	2,396	56,036
1998	17,103,394	400,200	200,100	1,470,854	1,570,904	0	1,610,608	918,491	65.700	60,345	2,905	63,250
1999	17,958,563	420,200	210,100	1,610,608	1,715,658	0	1,755,493	994,180	65.597	65,215	3,526	68,741
2000	18,856,491	441,200	220,600	1,755,493	1,865,793	0	1,908,027	1,071,536	63.522	68,066	4,277	72,343
										408,573	20,019	428,593

Assumptions 1 and 5

1. U.S. AIDS-susceptible   6.0%
5. Company AIDS-susceptible   2.4%
    (pre-1/1/87)

Assumptions 6–8

6. Antiselection termination factor   0.0
7. Antiselection at issue factor   1.5
8. Testing factor   Z
    1/1/87–7/1/87   0.30
    after 7/1/87   0.50

Assumption 10

New issues are $10,000,000 in 1987 and increase by 5% per year. New issues for males 20–59 are 65% of total new issues.

TABLE 24

Estimate of Company Death Claims Caused by AIDS on 1987 and Later Issues for AIDS-Susceptible Heterosexual Males and Females Ages 20–59
(Dollar Amounts in Thousands)

Year	(1) Total New Issues during Year	(2) AIDS-Susceptible New Issues (1) × 0.85 × Assumption 7 × 0.024	(3) AIDS-Susceptible Not Tested (2) × (1 − Z)	(4) AIDS-Susceptible Not Tested (Beginning of Year) Prior Year of (7)	(5) AIDS-Susceptible Exposure (4) + [(3)/2]	(6) Terminations 0.0 × (5)	(7) AIDS-Susceptible End of Year (4) + (3) − (6) − (10)	(8) AIDS-Susceptible Infected (5) × (line 3, Table 14)	(9) Death Rate per Thousand (line 3, Table 20)	(10) AIDS Death Claims (Not Tested) (8) × (9)	(11) AIDS Death Claims (Tested Negative at Issue) from Table 26	(12) Total AIDS Death Claims (10) + (11)
1987	10,000,000	255,000	153,000	0	76,500	0	152,997	214	14.231	3	0	3
1988	10,500,000	267,800	133,900	152,997	219,947	0	286,883	880	15.597	14	0	14
1989	11,025,000	281,100	140,600	286,883	357,183	0	427,451	2,000	16.208	32	0	32
1990	11,576,250	295,200	147,600	427,451	501,251	0	574,987	4,010	15.899	64	2	66
1991	12,155,063	310,000	155,000	574,987	652,487	0	729,871	7,177	16.156	116	13	129
1992	12,762,816	325,500	162,800	729,871	811,271	0	892,469	12,169	16.581	202	45	247
1993	13,400,956	341,700	170,900	892,469	977,919	0	1,063,030	21,514	15.781	340	130	470
1994	14,071,004	358,800	179,400	1,063,030	1,152,730	0	1,241,871	35,735	15.646	559	287	846
1995	14,774,554	376,800	188,400	1,241,871	1,336,071	0	1,429,363	58,787	15.437	907	589	1,496
1996	15,513,282	395,600	197,800	1,429,363	1,528,263	0	1,625,704	94,752	15.401	1,459	1,072	2,532
1997	16,288,946	415,400	207,700	1,625,704	1,729,554	0	1,831,078	152,201	15.282	2,326	1,830	4,156
1998	17,103,394	436,100	218,100	1,831,078	1,940,128	0	2,045,499	242,516	15.171	3,679	2,909	6,588
1999	17,958,563	457,900	229,000	2,045,499	2,159,999	0	2,268,702	380,160	15.249	5,797	4,664	10,461
2000	18,856,491	480,800	240,400	2,268,702	2,388,902	0	2,500,009	597,225	15.225	9,093	7,512	16,605
										24,591	19,052	43,644

Assumptions 1 and 5

1. U.S. AIDS-susceptible   10%
5. Company AIDS-susceptible (pre-1/1/87)   20%

Assumptions 6–7

6. Antiselection termination factor   0.0
7. Antiselection at issue factor   1.5
8. Testing factor   Z
    1/1/87–7/1/87   0.30
    after 7/1/87   0.50

Assumption 10

New issues are $10,000,000 in 1987 and increase 5% per year.
New issues for males and females 20–59 are 85% of total new issues.

TABLE 25

AIDS CLAIMS ON THOSE WHO TESTED NEGATIVE AT ISSUE FOR AIDS-SUSCEPTIBLE HOMO-BISEXUAL MALES AGES 20–59

(Dollar Amounts in Thousands)

Year	(1) AIDS-Susceptible New Issues Tested from Table 23	(2) Those from (1) Infected (Declined) (1) × (line 3, Table 13	(3) Those from (1) Not Infected (1)−(2)	(4) AIDS-Susceptible Beginning of Year Prior Year of (7)	(5) AIDS-Susceptible Exposure (4)+(3)/2	(6) Terminations (Assumption 6) 0.0 × (5)	(7) AIDS-Susceptible End of Year (4)+(3)−(6)−(10)	(8) AIDS-Susceptible Infected during Year (5) × Assumption 2A	(9) Death Rate per Thousand line 3A, Table 19	(10) AIDS Death Claims (Tested Negative at Issue) (8)×(9)
1987	93,600	22,360	71,240	0	35,620	0	71,240	2,244	0.000	0
1988	122,800	37,638	85,162	71,240	113,822	0	156,392	11,268	1.000	11
1989	129,000	48,200	80,800	156,392	196,792	0	237,139	26,370	2.000	53
1990	135,400	58,902	76,498	237,139	275,388	0	313,485	44,337	3.428	152
1991	142,200	69,323	72,877	313,485	349,923	0	386,039	63,686	5.073	323
1992	149,300	79,030	70,270	386,039	421,173	0	455,726	81,286	7.171	583
1993	156,800	87,855	68,945	455,726	490,198	0	523,764	96,079	9.444	907
1994	164,600	95,657	68,943	523,764	558,235	0	591,429	107,739	11.852	1,277
1995	172,800	102,409	70,391	591,429	626,625	0	660,192	114,672	14.204	1,629
1996	181,500	108,040	73,460	660,192	696,922	0	731,670	116,386	17.026	1,982
1997	190,600	112,445	78,155	731,670	770,748	0	807,430	117,154	20.449	2,396
1998	200,100	116,996	83,104	807,430	848,982	0	887,629	118,008	24.614	2,905
1999	210,100	121,748	88,352	887,629	931,805	0	972,455	119,271	29.562	3,526
2000	220,600	126,692	93,908	972,455	1,019,409	0	1,062,087	121,310	35.253	4,277
										20,019

Assumption 2A

Infection Subsequent to Issue

1987	6.3%
1988	9.9%
1989	13.4%
1990	16.1%
1991	18.2%
1992	19.3%
1993	19.6%
1994	19.3%
1995	18.3%
1996	16.7%
1997	15.2%
1998	13.9%
1999	12.8%
2000	11.9%

Assumption 6
Antiselection termination factor   0.0

where 1987 = 6.3 [1987 issues]
1988 = (0.5 × 13.0) [1987 issues] + (0.5 × 6.7) [1988 issues]
etc.

TABLE 26

AIDS Claims on Those Who Tested Negative at Issue
(Dollar Amounts in Thousands)

Year	(1) AIDS-Susceptible New Issues Tested (2)−(3) from Table 24	(2) Those from (1) Infected (Declined) (1)×(line 3, Table 14)	(3) Those from (1) Not Infected (1)−(2)	(4) AIDS-Susceptible Beginning of Year Prior Year of (7)	(5) AIDS-Susceptible Exposure (4)+(3)/2	(6) Terminations 0.0 × (5)	(7) AIDS-Susceptible End of Year (4)+(3)−(6)−(10)	(8) AIDS-Susceptible Infected during Year (5) × Assumption 2A	(9) Death Rate per Thousand (line 3A, Table 20)	(10) AIDS Death Claims (Tested Negative at Issue) (8)×(9)
1987	102,000	286	101,714	0	50,857	0	101,714	41	0.000	0
1988	133,900	536	133,364	101,714	168,397	0	235,079	269	0.000	0
1989	140,500	787	139,713	235,079	304,935	0	374,792	823	0.000	0
1990	147,600	1,181	146,419	374,792	448,002	0	521,209	1,971	0.937	$ 2
1991	155,000	1,705	153,295	521,209	597,857	0	674,491	3,886	3.317	13
1992	162,700	2,441	160,260	674,491	754,621	0	834,706	7,093	6.338	45
1993	170,800	3,758	167,042	834,706	918,227	0	1,001,618	13,865	9.412	130
1994	179,400	5,561	173,839	1,001,618	1,088,537	0	1,175,170	24,166	11.858	287
1995	188,400	8,290	180,110	1,175,170	1,265,225	0	1,354,692	41,373	14.231	589
1996	197,800	12,264	185,536	1,354,692	1,447,460	0	1,539,156	68,754	15.597	1,072
1997	207,700	18,278	189,422	1,539,156	1,633,867	0	1,726,748	112,900	16.208	1,830
1998	218,000	27,250	190,750	1,726,748	1,822,123	0	1,914,589	182,941	15.899	2,909
1999	228,900	40,286	188,614	1,914,589	2,008,896	0	2,098,539	288,678	16.156	4,664
2000	240,400	60,100	180,300	2,098,539	2,188,689	0	2,271,327	453,059	16.581	7,512
										$19,052

Assumption 2A

Infection Subsequent to Issue	
1987	0.08%
1988	0.16%
1989	0.27%
1990	0.44%
1991	0.65%
1992	0.94%
1993	1.51%
1994	2.22%
1995	3.27%
1996	4.27%
1997	6.91%
1998	10.04%
1999	14.37%
2000	20.70%

Assumption 6

Antiselection termination factor   0.0

where 1987 = 0.08 [1987 issues]
1988 = (0.5 × 0.2) [1987 issues] + (0.5 × 0.12) [1988 issues]
etc.

TABLE 27

ESTIMATE OF TOTAL COMPANY DEATH CLAIMS AND RATIO OF AIDS TO TOTAL DEATH CLAIMS
(Dollar Amounts in Thousands)

Year	(1) In Force Beginning of Year	(2) Mid-Year In Force (Year i + year i +1)/2	(3) Total Death Claims Excluding AIDS $q \times$ (2)	(4) AIDS Death Claims on '86 and Prior Issues Col. (6) of Tables 21 and 22	(5) AIDS Death Claims on '87 and Later Issues Col. (12) of Tables 23 and 24	(6) Heterosexual AIDS Death Claims (4) + (5)	(7) Homo-Bisexual AIDS Death Claims (from Homo-Sexual Proj.)	(8) Contaminated-Blood AIDS Death Claims 0.05 × (7)	(9) Total AIDS Death Claims (6)+(7)+(8)	(10) Total Death Claims (3)+(9)	(11) Percentage of Heterosexual AIDS Death Claims to Total Death Claims (6)/(10)	(12) Percentage of Total AIDS Death Claims to Total Death Claims (9)/(10)
1987	$100,000,000	100,875,000	302,625	68	3	71	5,531	277	5,878	308,503	0.02%	1.9%
1988	101,750,000	102,790,625	308,372	106	14	120	9,176	459	9,755	318,126	0.04%	3.1%
1989	103,831,250	105,036,641	315,110	154	32	187	14,365	718	15,270	330,380	0.06%	4.6%
1990	106,242,031	107,611,971	322,836	216	66	282	21,471	1,074	22,826	345,662	0.08%	6.6%
1991	108,981,910	110,516,805	320,499	302	129	431	30,711	1,536	32,677	353,176	0.12%	9.3%
1992	112,051,700	113,752,563	329,882	423	247	669	42,083	2,104	44,856	374,739	0.2%	12.0%
1993	115,453,427	117,321,866	340,233	590	470	1,060	55,218	2,761	59,039	399,272	0.3%	14.8%
1994	119,190,304	121,228,507	351,563	824	846	1,669	69,301	3,465	74,435	425,998	0.4%	17.5%
1995	123,266,710	125,477,440	363,885	1,153	1,496	2,649	83,064	4,153	89,866	453,751	0.6%	19.8%
1996	127,688,170	130,074,757	364,209	1,620	2,532	4,151	95,244	4,762	104,157	468,367	0.9%	22.2%
1997	132,461,343	135,027,681	378,078	2,279	4,156	6,435	104,904	5,245	116,584	494,661	1.3%	23.6%
1998	137,594,018	140,344,562	392,965	3,209	6,588	9,797	111,390	5,570	126,757	519,721	1.9%	24.4%
1999	143,095,106	146,034,875	408,898	4,533	10,461	14,994	114,548	5,727	135,269	544,167	2.8%	24.9%
2000	148,974,644	152,109,222	425,906	6,412	16,605	23,017	114,634	5,732	143,383	569,288	4.0%	25.2%
	155,243,800											
Cumulative												
1991			1,569,441	846	244	1,090	81,254	4,063	86,407	1,655,848	0.1%	5.2%
1996			3,319,214	5,455	5,834	11,289	426,164	21,308	458,761	3,777,975	0.3%	12.1%
2000			4,925,060	21,888	43,644	65,531	871,640	43,582	980,753	5,905,813	1.1%	16.6%

Assumption 9

Total in force as of 1/1/87 = $100,000,000

Assumption 10

New issues are $10,000,000 in 1987
and increase 5% per year.

Assumption 11

q = Total company death rate per thousand	3.0 for 1987–1990
	2.9 for 1991–1995
	2.8 for 1996–2000

Assumption 12

Persistency rates	
In force	92.5%
New issues	92.5%

CHAPTER 5

PROJECTING AIDS MORTALITY FOR INDIVIDUAL ORDINARY LIFE INSURANCE IN FORCE

GARY E. DAHLMAN, RICHARD L. BERGSTROM, AND
RICHARD W. MATHES

I. INTRODUCTION

This research update presents the results of several projections using a model developed to estimate AIDS and AIDS-related mortality based on U.S. AIDS population statistics and current medical knowledge. The goal of the model is to present a simple, yet credible method that permits any company to project extra mortality due to AIDS claims. The model and assumptions used herein are presented so that the actuary may adjust any one or more of the basic input assumptions to arrive at his/her own projection of extra AIDS mortality.

For illustrative purposes and to show the sensitivity of results to selected assumptions, the model projects extra AIDS mortality under three scenarios (described more fully below). These are referred to as scenario I, scenario II, and scenario III.

The report includes a numerical example wherein specific adjustments are made to basic population data to better fine-tune results to reflect an insurance-oriented situation. From this example, the actuary should begin to appreciate the flexibility of the model and can further this appreciation and understanding by experimenting with the various input parameters. The Appendix contains a list of these parameters.

It should be noted at the outset that the use of the words "extra AIDS mortality" is more indicative of "premature" in the context of the model. For example, attempting to analyze true "extra" insured mortality requires an analysis that includes considering changes in anticipated persistency, term conversion rates, and application of guaranteed insurability features by insureds who select adversely against insurance companies. The model does not attempt to analyze such changes directly; it projects future AIDS and AIDS-related deaths and then suggests how companies might translate these population statistics into more useful and relevant insurance data based on their unique situations.

The discussion herein applies solely to the U.S. Further, we did not attempt to employ sophisticated modeling techniques because we felt that the available data have many interpretations, and hence, many models might fit.

The model uses data on AIDS diagnoses, deaths, and mortality rates gleaned from information published weekly by the Centers for Disease Control (CDC) of the Public Health Service in Atlanta, Georgia. Unfortunately, such data are not reported in a format that is readily usable by actuaries, and we (and others) have necessarily had to make certain assumptions in order to use the CDC data for actuarial purposes.

II. DEFINITIONS

"Human Immunodeficiency Virus (HIV)" is the AIDS virus that attacks T-4 lymphocytes in the body, rendering it unable to combat even routine infections. It was originally designated Human T-Lymphotropic Virus, Type III (HTLV-III) in the U.S. and Lymphadenopathy-Associated Virus (LAV) in France.

"AIDS"—Acquired Immune Deficiency Syndrome—is the condition resulting from T-4 lymphocyte destruction by the HIV. Most individuals with the HIV do not immediately develop AIDS; rather there can be a fairly lengthy latent period. Whether all individuals infected with the HIV ultimately develop AIDS is still unknown at this time, but medical thinking is leaning more and more in that direction. Note that AIDS is not a disease like measles that has well-defined symptoms. Rather, it is a *condition* that allows disease-causing organisms to infect the body.

"Exposed population" (or "exposures") means a group of individuals infected with the HIV (also called HIV+, meaning HIV positive). So far it appears that once infected, one remains infected.

"Conversion" is the *process* of the HIV (in an infected population) actively destroying the T-4 cells, leading to a full-blown AIDS condition. Any disease-causing organism increases T-4 cell production. Thus, any subsequent infection may cause HIV-reproduction as well, speeding up the conversion process.

"Conversion rate" is the annual percentage of HIV+ individuals who convert to an AIDS condition in the years following infection (see Section IV, no. 5). The rate is applied on a select basis to the HIV+ individuals still living who have not yet been diagnosed as having AIDS.

"AIDS-related complex" (ARC) is now called "persistent generalized lymphadenopathy" (PGL), a condition of generally nonfatal illnesses (fever, diarrhea, etc.), which seems to precede AIDS.

"AIDS-related causes" are conditions that can cause death, but have not necessarily been defined as AIDS by the CDC. The model assumes that *all* HIV + individuals who have not converted to AIDS are exposed to increased mortality risk, and the level of such increased risk varies by scenario. These conditions include brain disease and miscellaneous other conditions that were not initially recognized as AIDS-related because of a lack of knowledge about AIDS. Certain brain diseases have now been deemed diagnostic of AIDS by CDC; however, such conditions were not included in CDC AIDS statistics prior to 1987 unless an autopsy proved the presence of the HIV.

III. SUMMARY OF SCENARIOS

Table 1 summarizes the assumptions used in each of the three modeled scenarios.

Tables 2A, 2B, and 2C show the new annual HIV infections assumed to occur in each of the following three scenarios, respectively:

a. *Scenario I.* Annual historic and future infections are low because it is assumed that most infected persons eventually convert to AIDS. That is, observed AIDS deaths to date are not the tip of the iceberg, but rather a large portion of it. New annual HIV infections may have already peaked, and in the model these are further assumed to decline to zero over the next 20 years.

b. *Scenario II.* As with scenario I, the heterosexual component of HIV infections is assumed to not expand beyond current levels. In fact, because of widespread publicity and increasing safety precautions, new infections are also assumed to ultimately diminish to zero, although not as fast as in scenario I. Scenario II might also be representative of the future spread of AIDS if a means of inoculative prevention (*not* a cure) is found in the near future. Scenario II most closely reproduces CDC data to date.

c. *Scenario III.* The heterosexual component of HIV infections will continue to grow, but not at the exponential rate experienced by homosexual males in the last 10 years. Current (and future) educational efforts will slow the rate of HIV spread experienced to date, but not stop it. This scenario assumes a peak of 2,000,000 new annual infections from 1992 to 1996, with diminishing new annual infections after that, ultimately reaching zero by 2040.

IV. MODEL ASSUMPTIONS

1. Current HIV Infections

Unfortunately for statistical and medical purposes, there are no national registers of individuals with HIV infection. The model's estimates of infected individuals reflect those in the press, tempered by estimated incidence rate

TABLE 1

SUMMARY OF MODEL ASSUMPTIONS

Assumption*	Scenario		
	Scenario I	Scenario II	Scenario III
Heterosexuals will become infected	No	Not generally	Yes
Cumulative HIV infections			
1986	813,000	1,245,000	2,033,000
2006	1,848,000	3,653,000	33,883,000
Conversion pattern to AIDS of HIV-infected lives by year since infection†			
1	1.5 %	1.0%	0.6%
2	2.25	1.5	0.9
3	3.0	2.0	1.2
4	3.75	2.5	1.5
5	4.5	3.0	1.8
6	6.0	4.0	2.4
7	7.5	5.0	3.0
8	9.0	6.0	3.6
9	10.5	7.0	4.2
10	12.0	8.0	4.8
11	13.5	9.0	5.4
12	15.0	10.0	6.0
13	16.5	11.0	6.6
14	18.0	12.0	7.2
15	19.5	13.0	7.8
16	21.0	14.0	8.4
17+	22.5	15.0	9.0
Mortality in the model of HIV-infected individuals dying annually from other AIDS-related causes (percentage of standard population mortaltiy)‡	100%	300%	700%

Annual AIDS death rate by year since diagnosis of AIDS (all scenarios)	Year	Rate
	1	45%
	2	45
	3	29
	4+	21

Standard population mortality
  (all scenarios) 85% of 1965–80 Male, Ultimate Table, age last birthday

*See Model Assumptions and Summary of Scenarios sections for a more detailed explanation of this table.
†Medical studies initially indicated total conversion to AIDS within 9 years, with a median time of 5 years. This time frame is now expanding as studies of longer durations become available. The conversion rate also appears to be flatter than originally envisioned.
‡These multiples are illustrative only.

1026

TABLE 2A

New Annual HIV Infections According to Scenario I

Year	New Annual Exposures	Conversions to AIDS		AIDS Deaths		AIDS-Related Deaths		Other Deaths		HIV + Still Living and Not Yet Converted to AIDS
		Yearly	Cumulative	Yearly	Cumulative	Yearly	Cumulative	Yearly	Cumulative	
1976	200	0	0	0	0	0	0	0	0	200
1977	500	3	3	1	1	0	0	0	0	697
1978	667	12	15	4	4	1	1	1	1	1,350
1979	2,000	27	42	11	15	2	2	2	2	3,320
1980	10,000	66	108	26	42	4	6	4	6	13,247
1981	50,000	239	347	82	124	14	20	14	20	62,981
1982	100,000	1,082	1,429	340	464	65	85	65	85	161,768
1983	116,667	3,027	4,456	1,104	1,568	169	254	169	254	275,070
1984	150,000	5,905	10,361	2,585	4,154	293	546	293	546	418,581
1985	183,333	10,036	20,396	4,909	9,063	454	1,000	454	1,000	590,972
1986	200,000	15,628	36,025	8,261	17,324	654	1,653	654	1,653	774,037
1987	175,000	22,807	58,832	12,821	30,145	876	2,529	876	2,529	924,478
1988	150,000	31,185	90,017	18,625	48,770	1,079	3,608	1,079	3,608	1,041,134
1989	125,000	40,400	130,417	25,523	74,292	1,263	4,871	1,263	4,871	1,123,210
1990	100,000	50,154	180,571	33,297	107,589	1,423	6,294	1,423	6,294	1,170,210
1991	90,000	60,110	240,680	41,712	149,301	1,559	7,852	1,559	7,852	1,196,983
1992	80,000	70,023	310,703	50,531	199,832	1,682	9,534	1,682	9,534	1,203,596
1993	70,000	79,274	389,977	59,445	259,277	1,789	11,323	1,789	11,323	1,190,744
1994	60,000	87,320	477,297	68,035	327,312	1,877	13,200	1,877	13,200	1,159,670
1995	50,000	93,716	571,013	75,863	403,175	1,941	15,141	1,941	15,141	1,112,072
1996	40,000	98,140	669,154	82,538	485,713	1,979	17,120	1,979	17,120	1,049,973
1997	30,000	100,490	769,644	87,763	573,476	1,988	19,108	1,988	19,108	975,506
1998	20,000	100,762	870,406	91,357	664,832	1,967	21,075	1,967	21,075	890,811
1999	15,000	98,993	969,399	93,221	758,054	1,915	22,990	1,915	22,990	802,987
2000	10,000	95,401	1,064,800	93,346	851,400	1,840	24,830	1,840	24,830	713,906
2001	8,000	90,311	1,155,111	91,829	943,229	1,744	26,574	1,744	26,574	628,108
2002	6,000	84,064	1,239,175	88,856	1,032,085	1,634	28,207	1,634	28,207	546,778
2003	4,000	76,979	1,316,154	84,653	1,116,738	1,513	29,720	1,513	29,720	470,773
2004	2,000	69,300	1,385,544	79,466	1,196,204	1,387	31,107	1,387	31,107	400,609
2005	0	61,683	1,447,226	73,576	1,269,780	1,259	32,366	1,259	32,366	336,409
2006	0	54,125	1,501,352	67,266	1,337,045	1,132	33,498	1,132	33,498	280,020
Total	1,848,367									

Conversion Rates (in %): 1.5, 2.25, 3, 3.75, 4.5, 6, 7.5, 9, 10.5, 12, 13.5, 15, 16.5, 18, 19.5, 21, 22.5 thereafter.
Yearly AIDS-related deaths are 1 times the assumed population mortality.

TABLE 2B

New Annual HIV Infections According to Scenario II

Year	New Annual Exposures	Conversions to AIDS Yearly	Conversions to AIDS Cumulative	AIDS Deaths Yearly	AIDS Deaths Cumulative	AIDS-Related Deaths Yearly	AIDS-Related Deaths Cumulative	Other Deaths Yearly	Other Deaths Cumulative	HIV+ Still Living and Not Yet Converted to AIDS
1976	300	0	0	0	0	0	0	0	0	300
1977	750	3	3	1	1	1	1	0	0	1,046
1978	1,000	12	15	4	5	3	4	1	1	2,030
1979	3,000	27	42	11	16	7	11	2	4	4,994
1980	15,000	66	108	27	43	16	27	5	9	19,907
1981	75,000	240	348	82	125	62	89	21	30	94,586
1982	150,000	1,085	1,433	341	466	293	382	98	127	243,114
1983	175,000	3,037	4,470	1,108	1,574	761	1,143	254	381	414,075
1984	225,000	5,936	10,406	2,596	4,170	1,320	2,463	440	821	631,404
1985	275,000	10,119	20,525	4,941	9,111	2,053	4,516	684	1,505	893,592
1986	325,000	15,817	36,342	8,338	17,449	2,966	7,482	989	2,494	1,198,889
1987	300,000	23,447	59,789	13,047	30,496	4,067	11,549	1,356	3,850	1,470,125
1988	275,000	32,679	92,468	19,223	49,719	5,135	16,684	1,712	5,561	1,705,752
1989	250,000	43,275	135,743	26,815	76,534	6,171	22,855	2,057	7,618	1,904,456
1990	225,000	55,066	190,809	35,709	112,243	7,172	30,027	2,391	10,009	2,065,098
1991	200,000	67,837	258,646	45,779	158,022	8,137	38,164	2,712	12,721	2,186,758
1992	180,000	81,333	339,979	56,873	214,895	9,055	47,219	3,018	15,740	2,273,779
1993	160,000	94,984	434,963	68,731	283,626	9,932	57,151	3,311	19,050	2,326,066
1994	140,000	108,215	543,178	80,969	364,595	10,752	67,903	3,584	22,634	2,344,114
1995	120,000	120,493	663,671	93,143	457,738	11,498	79,401	3,833	26,467	2,328,973
1996	100,000	131,347	795,018	104,811	562,549	12,148	91,549	4,049	30,516	2,282,180
1997	90,000	140,378	935,396	115,554	678,103	12,682	104,231	4,227	34,744	2,215,698
1998	80,000	147,374	1,082,770	125,017	803,120	13,111	117,342	4,370	39,114	2,131,682
1999	70,000	152,065	1,234,835	132,905	936,025	13,419	130,761	4,473	43,587	2,032,573
2000	60,000	154,294	1,389,129	138,959	1,074,984	13,598	144,359	4,533	48,120	1,920,978
2001	50,000	154,167	1,543,296	143,016	1,218,000	13,643	158,002	4,548	52,667	1,799,406
2002	40,000	151,782	1,695,078	145,028	1,363,028	13,557	171,559	4,519	57,186	1,670,265
2003	30,000	147,359	1,842,437	145,025	1,508,053	13,348	184,907	4,449	61,636	1,535,738
2004	20,000	141,158	1,983,595	143,109	1,651,162	13,025	197,932	4,342	65,977	1,397,738
2005	10,000	133,635	2,117,230	139,479	1,790,641	12,605	210,537	4,202	70,179	1,257,708
2006	8,000	125,165	2,242,395	134,409	1,925,050	12,098	222,635	4,033	74,212	1,114,847
Total	3,653,050									

Conversion Rates (in %): 1, 1.5, 2, 2.5, 3, 4, 5, 6, 7, 8, 9, 10, 11, 12, 13, 14, 15 thereafter.
Yearly AIDS-related deaths are 3 times the assumed population mortality.

TABLE 2C

New Annual HIV Infections According to Scenario III

Year	New Annual Exposures	Conversions to AIDS Yearly	Conversions to AIDS Cumulative	AIDS Deaths Yearly	AIDS Deaths Cumulative	AIDS-Related Deaths Yearly	AIDS-Related Deaths Cumulative	Other Deaths Yearly	Other Deaths Cumulative	HIV + Still Living and Not Yet Converted to AIDS
1976	500	0	0	0	0	0	0	0	0	500
1977	1,250	3	3	1	1	4	4	1	1	1,743
1978	1,667	12	15	4	4	12	16	2	2	3,383
1979	5,000	27	42	11	15	25	40	4	6	8,328
1980	25,000	66	108	27	42	61	102	9	15	33,191
1981	125,000	240	348	83	124	242	344	35	49	157,675
1982	250,000	1,085	1,433	341	466	1,142	1,486	163	212	405,285
1983	291,667	3,038	4,472	1,108	1,574	2,961	4,447	423	635	690,529
1984	375,000	5,943	10,415	2,599	4,172	5,138	9,585	734	1,369	1,053,714
1985	458,333	10,143	20,558	4,949	9,121	7,997	17,581	1,142	2,512	1,492,766
1986	500,000	15,883	36,441	8,363	17,484	11,568	29,149	1,653	4,164	1,963,663
1987	750,000	23,351	59,793	13,053	30,538	15,587	44,736	2,227	6,391	2,672,498
1988	1,000,000	34,138	93,931	19,531	50,069	21,582	66,318	3,083	9,474	3,613,695
1989	1,250,000	48,902	142,832	28,579	78,648	29,626	95,944	4,232	13,706	4,780,936
1990	1,500,000	68,348	211,180	40,901	119,550	39,802	135,746	5,686	19,392	6,167,100
1991	1,750,000	93,100	304,279	57,135	176,684	52,217	187,963	7,460	26,852	7,764,323
1992	2,000,000	123,582	427,861	77,847	254,531	66,966	254,930	9,567	36,419	9,564,209
1993	2,000,000	160,698	588,559	103,641	358,172	84,141	339,070	12,020	48,439	11,307,349
1994	2,000,000	203,720	792,279	134,886	493,058	102,065	441,136	14,581	63,019	12,986,983
1995	2,000,000	252,553	1,044,832	171,598	664,657	120,777	561,913	17,254	80,273	14,596,399
1996	2,000,000	306,985	1,351,817	213,738	878,395	140,293	702,206	20,042	100,315	16,129,079
1997	1,920,000	366,681	1,718,498	261,210	1,139,605	160,605	862,811	22,944	123,259	17,498,848
1998	1,840,000	430,685	2,149,183	313,706	1,453,311	181,110	1,043,921	25,873	149,132	18,701,180
1999	1,760,000	497,368	2,646,551	370,501	1,823,812	201,734	1,245,655	28,819	177,951	19,733,258
2000	1,680,000	565,110	3,211,661	430,509	2,254,321	222,345	1,468,001	31,764	209,714	20,594,040
2001	1,600,000	632,554	3,844,215	492,532	2,746,853	242,786	1,710,787	34,684	244,398	21,284,016
2002	1,520,000	698,320	4,542,535	555,376	3,302,229	262,853	1,973,640	37,550	281,949	21,805,293
2003	1,440,000	760,924	5,303,459	617,800	3,920,029	282,308	2,255,948	40,330	322,278	22,161,731
2004	1,360,000	819,124	6,122,583	678,548	4,598,577	300,896	2,556,844	42,985	365,263	22,358,726
2005	1,280,000	871,408	6,993,991	736,343	5,334,920	318,350	2,875,193	45,479	410,742	22,403,490
2006	1,200,000	916,586	7,910,578	789,900	6,124,820	334,424	3,209,617	47,775	458,517	22,304,705
Total	33,883,417									

Conversion Rates (in %): 0.6, 0.9, 1.2, 1.5, 1.8, 2.4, 3, 3.6, 4.2, 4.8, 5.4, 6, 6.6, 7.2, 7.8, 8.4, 9 thereafter.
Yearly AIDS-related deaths are 7 times the assumed population mortality.

by group (homosexuals, etc.), and all assumptions produce results that closely match historical CDC AIDS diagnoses and deaths through July 1987. For example, the last column of Table 3 is the model's estimate of the current and future annual HIV infections for scenario II over the next 20 years. This scenario assumes that widespread AIDS publicity and the increasing saturation of certain high-risk groups have caused the number of new HIV infections to decline beginning in 1987, with the decline continuing in subsequent years, ultimately reaching zero new infections by the year 2012.

2. Current Infected Population Groups

The CDC inventory of diagnosed AIDS cases can provide an estimate of current infection if all infected population groups (i) follow the same conversion path to full-blown AIDS and (ii) are correctly labeled as such by CDC. That is, the already-*infected* group totals are assumed to be proportional to the CDC AIDS *diagnosed* totals through 1986. For example, since about 72 percent of diagnosed AIDS cases are homosexual or bisexual males, the model assumes 72 percent of HIV infections are homosexual or bisexual as well.

This assumption is certainly open to some debate since CDC experiences varying lag times in collecting and assimilating data from many parts of the country. Also, percentages can (and do) change as figures are updated because of the manner and format in which they are reported. Further, it can be argued that different risk categories might have varying conversion patterns due to duplicity of factors that make some groups more susceptible than others. These arguments are potentially valid. Nevertheless, this assumption eliminates the need to project conversion and diagnosis patterns by risk group.

Table 3 also shows estimated future annual infections for other various risk groupings.

3. Future Infected Population

Scenarios I and II assume the heterosexual population will generally not become infected. This follows from the assumption that "straight" sex between males and females is not a major method of transmission. The medical argument for this presumes that the HIV primarily enters the body through lesions in the skin (blood) or by penetrating thin membranes, such as in the rectum. IV drug abusers, transfusions, and hemophiliac CDC categories are blood-related transmission categories. Isolated examples of health-worker

TABLE 3

ESTIMATE OF ANNUAL NUMBER OF HIV INFECTIONS
SCENARIO II*

Year	(1) Homosexual/ Bisexual Males (72%)	(2) IV Drug Abusers (17%)	(3) Female Partners (3%)	(4) Blood Recipients/ Hemophiliacs (3%)	(5) Other (5%)	Total
1976						300
1977						750
1978						1,000
1979						3,000
1980						15,000
1981						75,000
1982						150,000
1976–1982†	176,450	41,650	7,350	7,350	12,250	245,050
1983	126,000	29,750	5,250	5,250	8,750	175,000
1984	162,000	38,250	6,750	6,750	11,250	225,000
1985	198,000	46,750	8,250	8,250	13,750	275,000
1986	234,000	55,250	9,750	9,750	16,250	325,000
1987	216,000	51,000	9,000	9,000	15,000	300,000
1988	198,000	46,750	8,250	8,250	13,750	275,000
1989	180,000	42,500	7,500	7,500	12,500	250,000
1990	162,000	38,250	6,750	6,750	11,250	225,000
1991	144,000	34,000	6,000	6,000	10,000	200,000
1992	130,000	30,600	5,400	5,400	9,000	180,000
1993	115,000	27,200	4,800	4,800	8,000	160,000
.	.	.	.	.	.	.
2006	6,000	5,760	240	240	400	8,000
Total infections through 2006	2,630,000	621,000	110,000	110,000	182,000	3,653,050
Assumed 1986 population	4,000,000	750,000				240,000,000
Percentage of assumed 1986 population infected by 2006	66%	83%				1.5%

(1) CDC categories "homosexual" and "homosexual/IV drug abuser."
(2) CDC category "IV drug abuser."
(3) CDC female category "heterosexual" and "undetermined."
(4) CDC "transfusion" and "hemophiliac"—includes children.
(5) All others (male heterosexual, male/children undetermined, children with parents at risk of AIDS).
*See Summary of Scenarios and Model Assumptions sections.
†Because the early numbers are so small, years 1976–1982 are not broken down by group. Since the disease may not necessarily follow parallel infection curves, credible extrapolation back to 1976 is difficult.

HIV infection through skin breaks (dermatitis, open sores) are also in this category. Homosexual males are undoubtedly susceptible to transmission through thin rectal membranes; medical studies seem to indicate that heterosexuals are much less efficient at transmitting the HIV.

4. Ultimate Level of AIDS Conversions

Again, medical science provides no single answer, and unfortunately, it may be many years before the correct answer is known with any certainty. In 1984, it was commonly estimated that 2–20 percent of HIV-infected individuals would ultimately develop AIDS. More recent estimates are much higher.

The model uses a higher conversion pattern for scenario I than for scenarios II or III, but applies it to a lower estimated HIV-infected pool. This was done to illustrate the fact that a low number of HIV infections combined with a high conversion rate can match the CDC AIDS statistics just as well as having more infections and a lower conversion rate.

5. Pattern of Conversion to AIDS

The model assumes the following patterns of AIDS conversion over the first 17 years following infection by the HIV:

CONVERSION TO AIDS
(by year since infection)

Year Following Infection by the HIV	Percentage of Infected Individuals Remaining Alive Who Subsequently Convert to AIDS Each Year		
	Scenario I	Scenario II	Scenario III
1	1.50%	1.0%	0.6%
2	2.25	1.5	0.9
3	3.00	2.0	1.2
4	3.75	2.5	1.5
5	4.50	3.0	1.8
6	6.00	4.0	2.4
7	7.50	5.0	3.0
8	9.00	6.0	3.6
9	10.50	7.0	4.2
10	12.00	8.0	4.8
11	13.50	9.0	5.4
12	15.00	10.0	6.0
13	16.50	11.0	6.6
14	18.00	12.0	7.2
15	19.50	13.0	7.8
16	21.00	14.0	8.4
17+	22.50	15.0	9.0

Early medical studies indicated a variety of conversion patterns over the first 10 years following infection. Current studies seem to suggest a lengthening of the conversion period and a flattening of the conversion rate. The above patterns are based on these studies. Since these are input parameters to the model, they can be varied as desired.

6. AIDS Annual Death Rate

CDC data to date indicate that 20–45 percent of AIDS-diagnosed cases die each year. A difficulty with determining a pattern of true death rates is that one must first know when conversion from initial infection to a full-blown AIDS condition occurs. This is seldom known with any great precision because it depends, in part, on when a person is diagnosed as having an AIDS condition, and there can be, and are, some significant time lags in seeking medical diagnosis. CDC registers an AIDS case as soon as it is reported (sometimes not until after death) and records the date of conversion to AIDS; however, CDC must oftentimes try to reconstruct when conversion to AIDS actually occurred. The death rate appears to start at 40–50 percent in the first year or two after conversion and declines somewhat thereafter. The model uses a mortality rate pattern of 45 percent in each of the first two years after conversion, 29 percent in year 3, and 21 percent thereafter (years 4+). This, too, is a variable input parameter.

7. Other Deaths

The HIV also infects the brain. Initially CDC did not include brain disease as conclusive evidence of AIDS (they now do). The model includes AIDS-related deaths to add conservatism, since other deaths currently not regarded as AIDS-related may in fact be due to AIDS. Some AIDS deaths have also been purposely misreported so as not to "hurt" family or friends.

Each scenario assumes that AIDS-related deaths are a certain multiple of standard population mortality. This is not a forecast. This parameter is included in the model for both illustrative purposes and conservatism. Nevertheless, such a parameter does improve the flexibility of the model.

The model assumes standard population mortality is equal to 85 percent of the 1975–80 Modified Basic Ultimate Mortality Table for males, age last birthday. This is another variable input parameter. (See Table 1 for the multiple of this table used in the various scenarios for AIDS-related deaths.)

V. LIMITATIONS OF THE ASSUMPTIONS

There is little long-term experience measuring AIDS mortality to date. Although assumptions used in the model reasonably reproduce current statistics, existing data are still rather scanty and subject to change, such as when different definitions are used, or when definitions change. Medical knowledge on AIDS is still at such an elementary level that projections of future deaths based on extrapolations of past experience cannot be made with a high degree of statistical confidence (at least not compared to traditional actuarial mortality projections). The following questions and comments illustrate some of the difficulties in projecting the HIV populations and subsequent death rates:

1. How many individuals are now HIV+ (often estimated between 1 and 2 million)? Techniques used to determine positive infection vary in degree of certainty, and obviously, not everyone in the U.S. has been tested.
2. What percentage of persons infected with the HIV will actually convert to AIDS? Early estimates of ultimate conversion to AIDS varied from 2 percent to 20 percent or more of the HIV infection pool. The Surgeon General, however, recently suggested that 100% of all HIV-infected individuals may eventually progress to more serious stages of the disease and die prematurely of AIDS or other opportunistic infections.
3. The "experts" can be completely wrong about the total infected pool, the ultimate AIDS conversion rate, and the pattern of conversion to AIDS, and yet their calculations can still match the observed AIDS cases to date. Credible projections of future deaths depend upon refining the accuracy of each of these variables. We are, in effect, trying to solve a single equation with at least three unknown variables.
4. What happens to infected persons who do not develop AIDS in the first few years following infection to the virus? Many could die or be handicapped by progressive brain disease. But how fast? And what proportion? Will other abnormalities manifest themselves later that we are not even aware of now?
5. Can "straight" sex transmit the virus among heterosexuals? Similar to hepatitis B, there is a medical question as to whether bleeding or skin breaks must occur to allow viral entry. This question is extremely important in projecting the ultimate spread of the HIV, especially into the heterosexual community. If one concludes that bleeding is necessary and that vaginal sex does not spread the disease (or at least not very efficiently), then HIV infection in the heterosexual population will not expand as rapidly as it has in the homosexual population.
6. When (if ever) will preventive vaccines be developed? This may not help the current HIV-infected groups, but it could limit or even eliminate future infections in all other groups.
7. The impact of widespread educational efforts and subsequent changes in sexual practices and IV-drug abuse could materially decelerate the spread of the HIV virus.

8. Can the HIV be aspirated like tuberculosis? If so, is it contagious? Current studies indicate the virus must penetrate the skin, so it would probably not be contagious. However, could it somehow be absorbed in the mouth or other soft tissues?

VI. VALIDATION OF RESULTS OF THE MODEL

The previous section listed some of the limitations in determining the true path of the spread of the HIV and AIDS. Table 4 shows how the scenario II projections compare to current CDC figures. It is important to note that diagnoses may be reported to CDC many months after real diagnosis, although reported deaths usually are only several weeks late. In fact, in many cases CDC first learns of an AIDS diagnosis *after* a death is reported.

TABLE 4

CUMULATIVE CONFIRMED AND PROJECTED AIDS CASES
AS OF JULY 27, 1987

Year	Diagnoses		Deaths		
				M&R Model	
	CDC*	M&R Model†	CDC*	AIDS Deaths‡	AIDS-Related Deaths§
1979	—	108	—	43	27
1980	75	108	63	43	27
1981	342	348	N/A	125	89 ·
1982	1,353	1,433	317	466	382
1983	4,159	4,470	1,292	1,574	1,143
1984	9,782	10,406	3,665	4,170	2,463
1985	19,557	20,525	8,161	9,111	4,516
1986	33,254	36,342	16,481	17,449	7,482
1987	39,263‖	59,789	22,548‖	30,496	11,549

*CDC-defined AIDS diagnoses as of July 27, 1987. Note that CDC retroactively increases previous years' diagnoses as new diagnoses are reported (which often is not until deaths are reported). For example, the 1982 diagnoses increased by 7 during 1986 and by 12 so far in 1987. The CDC *deaths* listed above, however, are taken from the CDC year-end reports and are not subsequently adjusted for deaths reported to the CDC in following years.
†Projection based on scenario II assumptions (complete years).
‡The model assumes mortality rates for AIDS victims are 45%, 45%, 29%, and 21% thereafter for select years after diagnosis of AIDS.
§Assumes mortality rates for other AIDS-related deaths are equal to three times standard population mortality rates.
‖Through 7/27/87.

Scenario II tracks historical CDC data fairly well, particularly if one assumes an underreporting of current diagnoses of about 20–25 percent because of time lag. It is also important to note that historical CDC figures can change as additional data are received. For example, published data on prior years' diagnoses can and do increase because diagnoses are reported by year of diagnosis, not year of reporting.

VII. PROJECTING AIDS MORTALITY

The model projects three scenarios of future annual incidence of HIV infection in the general population and subsequent annual deaths from AIDS and other AIDS-related causes (Tables 2A, 2B, and 2C). The resulting general population AIDS mortality rates per 100,000 U.S. lives as of year-end 1986, shown in Tables 5A, 5B, and 5C, can be further adjusted to be more representative of the AIDS risk inherent in a company's in-force file as of 1986.

TABLE 5A

AIDS AND AIDS-RELATED DEATHS FOR SCENARIO I

| Year | Initial Population | Yearly Deaths | | AIDS Only Deaths per 100,000 of Initial Population | AIDS and AIDS-Related Deaths per 100,000 of Inital Population |
		AIDS	AIDS-Related*		
1986	240,000,000				
1987		12,821	876	5.34	5.71
1988		18,625	1,079	7.76	8.21
1989		25,523	1,263	10.63	11.16
1990		33,297	1,423	13.87	14.47
1991		41,712	1,559	17.38	18.03
1992		50,531	1,682	21.05	21.76
1993		59,445	1,789	24.77	25.51
1994		68,035	1,877	28.35	29.13
1995		75,863	1,941	31.61	32.42
1996		82,538	1,979	34.39	35.22
1997		87,763	1,988	36.57	37.40
1998		91,357	1,967	38.07	38.89
1999		93,221	1,915	38.84	39.64
2000		93,346	1,840	38.89	39.66
2001		91,829	1,744	38.26	38.99
2002		88,856	1,634	37.02	37.70
2003		84,653	1,513	35.27	35.90
2004		79,466	1,387	33.11	33.69
2005		73,576	1,259	30.66	31.18
2006		67,266	1,132	28.03	28.50

*This column is illustrative only; for this scenario the assumed AIDS-related mortality is 1 times standard population mortality.

TABLE 5B

AIDS AND AIDS-RELATED DEATHS FOR SCENARIO II

Year	Initial Population	Yearly Deaths		AIDS Only Deaths per 100,000 of Initial Population	AIDS and AIDS-Related Deaths per 100,000 of Initial Population
		AIDS	AIDS-Related*		
1986	240,000,000				
1987		13,047	4,067	5.44	7.13
1988		19,223	5,135	8.01	10.15
1989		26,815	6,171	11.17	13.74
1990		35,709	7,172	14.88	17.87
1991		45,779	8,137	19.07	22.46
1992		56,873	9,055	23.70	27.47
1993		68,731	9,932	28.64	32.78
1994		80,969	10,752	33.74	38.22
1995		93,143	11,498	38.81	43.60
1996		104,811	12,148	43.67	48.73
1997		115,554	12,682	48.15	53.43
1998		125,017	13,111	52.09	57.55
1999		132,905	13,419	55.38	60.97
2000		138,959	13,598	57.90	63.57
2001		143,016	13,643	59.59	65.27
2002		145,028	13,557	60.43	66.08
2003		145,025	13,348	60.43	65.99
2004		143,109	13,025	59.63	65.06
2005		139,479	12,605	58.12	63.37
2006		134,409	12,098	56.00	61.04

*This column is illustrative only; for this scenario the assumed AIDS-related mortality is 3 times standard population mortality.

The following section highlights examples of such adjustments. Although we personally believe that scenario II is reasonable in light of current statistics and medical thinking, scenarios I and III are included to show the sensitivity of mortality to differences in underlying assumptions.

VIII. INDIVIDUAL COMPANY ADJUSTMENTS

Tables 5A, 5B, and 5C illustrate future AIDS death rates per 100,000 U.S. lives as of December 31, 1986 for each scenario. For example, the projected number of AIDS and AIDS-related deaths in 1987 using scenario II assumptions is estimated to be 13,047 and 4,067, respectively (Table 5B). As a ratio to a total population of 240 million, this is 7.13 deaths per 100,000 lives. However, the Table 5B death rates are probably not directly applicable to an insurance company's in force because that would presume the company insures a "uniform slice" of the U.S. population (i.e., the company in force has the same proportion of current and future infected individuals as observed or estimated in the entire country). Instead, there are a number of adjustments

TABLE 5C

AIDS AND AIDS-RELATED DEATHS FOR SCENARIO III

Year	Initial Population	Yearly Deaths		AIDS Only Deaths per 100,000 of Initial Population	AIDS and AIDS-Related Deaths per 100,000 of Initial Population
		AIDS	AIDS-Related*		
1986	240,000,000				
1987		13,053	15,587	5.44	11.93
1988		19,531	21,582	8.14	17.13
1989		28,579	29,626	11.91	24.25
1990		40,901	39,802	17.04	33.63
1991		57,135	52,217	23.81	45.56
1992		77,847	66,966	32.44	60.34
1993		103,641	84,141	43.18	78.24
1994		134,886	102,065	56.20	98.73
1995		171,598	120,777	71.50	121.82
1996		213,738	140,293	89.06	147.51
1997		261,210	160,605	108.84	175.76
1998		313,706	181,110	130.71	206.17
1999		370,501	201,734	154.38	238.43
2000		430,509	222,345	179.38	272.02
2001		492,532	242,786	205.22	306.38
2002		555,376	262,852	231.41	340.93
2003		617,800	282,308	257.42	375.05
2004		678,548	300,896	282.73	408.10
2005		736,343	318,350	306.81	439.46
2006		789,900	334,424	329.13	468.47

*This column is illustrative only; for this scenario the assumed AIDS-related mortality is 7 times standard population mortality.

that companies might consider making to transform this population-oriented mortality into insurance-oriented mortality.

Some of the possible adjustments are as follows:

1. Adjust Death Rates by Age

AIDS is primarily a disease of people aged 20–50 (see table below for actual age distribution). The heavily infected groups (such as IV drug abusers, active homosexuals, etc.) are, not coincidentally, also mostly aged 20–50. Because of resulting high mortality, most infected persons will not survive another 20 years. Thus, an attained-age breakdown of a company's in force is desirable so that a weighted average age factor can be developed and applied to this in force.

We suggest that the factors below be considered to adjust the AIDS population death rates if the in force can be grouped by attained age:

Ages	CDC AIDS Distribution*	U.S. Population Distribution (1984)	Factor†
0–19	1.8%	30%	0.060
20–29	20.9	18	1.161
30–39	46.6	15	3.107
40–49	20.7	11	1.882
50–59	9.9	9	1.100
60+	0.0 (assumed)	17	0.000
	100.0%	100.0%	

*Diagnosed as of 7/27/87.
†(CDC percentage) ÷ (U.S. population distribution).

The example in the next section illustrates this adjustment for a single age for each of the two plans highlighted in the example.

2. Adjust Death Rates by Sex

Females are only 7 percent of the current HIV-infected population. Making the simplistic assumption that the female age distribution is identical to that of males, the factors required to adjust the Table 5 death rates by sex are approximately:

$$\text{Male:} \quad 93\% \div 50\% = 1.86$$
$$\text{Female:} \quad 7\% \div 50\% = 0.14$$

Thus, to estimate death rates for an in-force file consisting of 80 percent males and 20 percent females, Table 5 rates would need to be multiplied by 1.52 (equals 0.8 × 1.86 plus 0.2 × 0.14).

3. Adjust Death Rates for Infected Populations Not Insured

Most companies have never intentionally marketed to chronic IV drug abusers, nor would significant numbers of IV drug abusers probably have applied for insurance in the past. Further, many companies market only in geographic areas where there appears to be a low HIV incidence (e.g., rural communities). These types of adjustments are admittedly subjective, but an attempt should be made to estimate the impact of such factors. The following should, therefore, only be considered as rough guidelines:

- Business issued prior to 1984. The general public did not really understand the AIDS threat before 1984, and willful adverse-selection by new applicants was probably minimal. Adjusting population experience by, say, 50 percent would appear to be reasonable for pre-1984 issues to reflect the reduced anticipated insurance risk versus the general population risk. Tables 5A–5C should be adjusted to reflect the potential number of AIDS victims that would actually be part of an in-force file (as opposed to the general population), and in the example below, a rate of 50 percent was used for pre-1984 business issued. The intention, of course, is to exclude IV drug abusers and other largely high-risk noninsured groups from the company's pre-1984 in force.

- Issues of 1984 and later. The following are some of the factors that companies are exploring to help reduce their potential exposure to the AIDS risk:
  - Required blood tests on medically underwritten policies.
  - Reduction in nonmedical limits.
  - The proportion of high net-amount-at-risk products being offered in the portfolio.
  - The proportion of direct-marketed products (especially guaranteed-issue products) being offered in the portfolio, and the age distribution of the target market.

  If a company feels it has minimized the recent-issue adverse-selection risks, the same adjustment factors used for pre-1984 issues might be used here also. If not, higher factors are called for. For example, a direct response or simplified issue product may need an adjustment of about 1.50 or more to reflect little or no underwriting on applications solicited via such distribution methods.

  Of course, if a company believes it is getting more than its proportionate share of HIV+ individuals (between 1–2 percent of recent applications are reported to be HIV+), then a more substantial adjustment factor should be used (e.g., 2.00 or higher).

- Geographic issues. Companies with heavy concentrations of in-force business in high-risk areas should use adjustment factors greater than 1.0 to assist them in projecting future AIDS claims. Areas identified by the CDC as high-risk areas are California, Texas, New York, New Jersey, and Florida. Companies with an in-force distribution that roughly mirrors the general population geographically should probably not make a specific adjustment for geographic risk. The example below assumes the adjustment factor for geographic risk is 1.0 (general population mirrors in force).

IX. EXAMPLE OF USE OF EXTRA AIDS CLAIMS RATES/ADJUSTMENTS

To illustrate how the adjustment factors can be applied to Table 5B, assume a company has the following business in force as of December 31, 1986:

Total In-force Face Amount	Average Attained Age
$100,000,000 Term (direct mail)	35 (70% male)
$100,000,000 Universal life (agent sold)	55 (85% male)

Assume further that the company has asked AIDS-related questions and requires blood tests on its recent UL policy applications and that, of its business currently in force, 25 percent was issued after 1983.

Illustrative Adjustment Factors	Term	UL
Age	3.107	1.100
Sex	1.344*	1.602†
Issues prior to 1984	0.500	0.500
1984 + issues	1.500‡	0.400§
Geographic issues	1.000	1.000

*(0.70 × 1.86) + (0.30 × 0.14) = 1.344.
†(0.85 × 1.86) + (0.15 × 0.14) = 1.602.
‡With no AIDS questions, adverse selection could have occurred. The 1.5 factor is illustrative only.
§The AIDS questions reduce potential adverse selection. The 0.4 factor is illustrative only.

Therefore, for issues prior to 1984 the adjustments are:

$$3.107 \times 1.344 \times 0.50 = 2.088 \text{ for the term policy}$$

and

$$1.100 \times 1.602 \times 0.50 = 0.881 \text{ for the UL policy.}$$

For issues of 1984–86, the adjustments are:

$$3.107 \times 1.344 \times 1.50 = 6.264 \text{ for the term policy}$$

and

$$1.100 \times 1.602 \times 0.4 = 0.705 \text{ for the UL policy.}$$

From Table 5B, the 1987 AIDS death rate per 100,000 lives as of December 31, 1986, is 7.13. Thus, the estimated 1987 extra AIDS and AIDS-related death claims are:

	Term	UL
1983 and prior issues	$11,166*	$4,711†
1984 + issues	11,166‡	1,257§
Subtotal	$22,332	$5,968
Grand total	$28,300, or $0.14 per $1000 in force as of 1986.	

*$1,000 × 0.75 × 2.088 × 7.13 = $11,166.
†$1,000 × 0.75 × 0.881 × 7.13 = $ 4,711.
‡$1,000 × 0.25 × 6.264 × 7.13 = $11,166.
§$1,000 × 0.25 × 0.705 × 7.13 = $ 1,257.

This same methodology is followed for all future years as well.

It is also possible to relate these expected values to anticipated benefit costs. For example, if standard mortality rates at ages 35 and 55 are 1.02 and 6.49 deaths per 1,000, respectively, then anticipated benefit costs for the two policies in 1987 are:

Term: $100,000,000 \times 0.00102 = \$102,000$
UL: $100,000,000 \times 0.00649 = \$649,000.$

Thus, as a percentage of expected claims, the AIDS claims are approximately an additional 22 percent for the term policy and only about 1 percent for the UL policy.

If an existing-business projection is available, Tables 5A–5C should be modified to produce factors readily usable in the projection. For example, since a projection considers both future lapsation and mortality, the current Table 5 factors need to be *divided by* the ratio of each future year's in-force business to the company's 1986 in-force business. This approach then yields AIDS death rates per 100,000 as a function of *future* in-force data, not 1986 in-force data. The example in the following section should help clarify this concept.

X. SAMPLE PROJECTION

To illustrate the concept of adjustments, the simplified term/UL distribution illustrated in the previous section was projected over the years 1987 through 1996. Tables 6A and 6B show the input assumptions and sample output for this projection using the assumptions of Scenario II. In addition, the following assumptions were made:

(i)   Age distribution:

Age Group	Adjustment Factor	Distribution	
		Term	UL
Under 20	0.060	0%	0%
20–29	1.161	20	10
30–39	3.107	50	25
40–49	1.882	25	30
50–59	1.100	5	30
60–69	0.000	0	5
Composite Factor:		2.3112	1.7875

(ii) Even though an age distribution was assumed to reflect increased exposure to the AIDS risk by age group, for simplicity the model assumes each plan experiences overall mortality identical to that of a single issue age. That is, standard mortality for the term plan is a function of age 35 mortality in 1987, age 36 mortality in 1988, etc. For the UL plan, the mortality pattern begins with age 55 in 1987. More refined calculations could use composite mortality based on actual age distributions.

(iii) The adjustment factors for the male/female splits are 1.34 (70 percent male) for the term plan and 1.602 (85 percent male) for the UL plan.

(iv) The adjustment factor for underwriting selection for issues prior to 1984 is 50 percent for both plans. The adjustment factors for 1984 and later issues are 150 percent for the term plan and 40 percent for the UL plan.

TABLE 6A

EXAMPLE OF PROJECTED AIDS DEATHS

Year	(1) Total Termination Rate	(2) Projected Insurance In Force (000)	(3) Standard Mortality (q_x) per 1,000	(4) AIDS and AIDS-Related Deaths per 100,000
		Term		
1987	0.30	100,000	1.0200	7.13
1988	0.20	70,000	1.0625	10.15
1989	0.15	56,000	1.1220	13.74
1990	0.15	47,600	1.1985	17.87
1991	0.15	40,460	1.2835	22.46
1992	0.15	34,391	1.3855	27.47
1993	0.15	29,232	1.5215	32.78
1994	0.15	24,847	1.6745	38.22
1995	0.15	21,120	1.8615	43.60
1996	0.15	17,952	2.0825	48.73
		UL		
1987	0.12	100,000	6.4940	7.13
1988	0.10	88,000	7.1570	10.15
1989	0.09	79,200	7.8880	13.74
1990	0.08	72,072	8.7040	17.87
1991	0.07	66,306	9.6220	22.46
1992	0.06	61,665	10.6505	27.47
1993	0.05	57,965	11.7895	32.78
1994	0.05	55,067	13.0220	38.22
1995	0.05	52,313	14.3565	43.60
1996	0.05	49,698	15.8185	48.73

(v)   75 percent of all in-force business was issued prior to 1984, and 25 percent was issued from 1984 to 1986.

(vi) The total termination rate column includes terminations for both lapses and standard mortality.

(vii) 100 percent persistency is assumed for in-force policyholders who have been or ever will be infected with the HIV.

Column 4 of Table 6B shows the percentage of AIDS and AIDS-related deaths as a function of standard deaths. The major reason for the huge difference between the term and the UL plan relates to the assumed differences in age distribution for each type of policy.

Column 5 of Table 6B illustrates the annual gross cost per $1000 of insurance in force for AIDS and AIDS-related deaths by plan. Note here that we are not referring to true claims costs, but rather to claim dollars as a ratio to remaining in-force amounts of insurance (i.e., reserves were ignored).

TABLE 6B

EXAMPLE OF PROJECTED AIDS DEATHS

Year	(1) Projected Insurance In Force (000)	(2) Projected Other Deaths (in Dollars)	(3) Projected AIDS and AIDS-Related Deaths (in Dollars)	(4) AIDS Deaths as Percentage of Other Deaths	(5) AIDS Deaths per $1,000 In Force (in Dollars)
			Term		
1987	$100,000	$102,000	$ 16,613	16.3%	$0.17
1988	70,000	74,375	23,644	31.8	0.34
1989	56,000	62,832	32,019	51.0	0.57
1990	47,600	57,049	41,625	73.0	0.87
1991	40,460	51,930	52,336	100.8	1.29
1992	34,391	47,649	63,996	134.3	1.86
1993	29,232	44,477	76,359	171.7	2.61
1994	24,847	41,607	89,034	214.0	3.58
1995	21,120	39,316	101,575	258.4	4.81
1996	17,952	37,386	113,532	303.7	6.32
			UL		
1987	$100,000	$649,400	$ 9,699	1.5%	$0.10
1988	88,000	629,816	13,805	2.2	0.16
1989	79,200	624,730	18,695	3.0	0.24
1990	72,072	627,315	24,303	3.9	0.34
1991	66,306	637,999	30,557	4.8	0.46
1992	61,665	656,761	37,364	5.7	0.61
1993	57,965	683,377	44,582	6.5	0.77
1994	55,067	717,078	51,983	7.2	0.94
1995	52,313	751,036	59,305	7.9	1.13
1996	49,698	786,143	66,286	8.4	1.33
			Combined		
1987	$200,000	$751,400	$ 26,312	3.5%	$0.13
1988	158,000	704,191	37,449	5.3	0.24
1989	135,200	687,562	50,714	7.4	0.38
1990	119,672	684,363	65,928	9.6	0.55
1991	106,766	689,929	82,893	12.0	0.78
1992	96,056	704,410	101,361	14.4	1.06
1993	87,197	727,854	120,941	16.6	1.39
1994	79,914	758,685	141,016	18.6	1.76
1995	73,434	790,352	160,880	20.4	2.19
1996	67,650	823,528	179,819	21.8	2.66

APPENDIX

INPUT PARAMETERS TO THE MODEL

1. Number of years to be projected (up to 100).
2. Initial population (report uses 240,000,000).
3. Yearly infections (1976 to end of projection period).
4. Mortality table for general population (report uses 85 percent of 1975–80 male, ultimate, age last birthday).
5. Percentages of standard population mortality for other AIDS-related deaths (report uses 100 percent, 300 percent, and 700 percent for scenarios I, II, and III, respectively).
6. Conversion pattern to AIDS from HIV infections.
7. AIDS mortality rates (report uses 0.45, 0.45, 0.29, and 0.21 thereafter).

Notes: Assumption 7 is based on years since conversion.
          Assumption 6 is based on years since infection.

CHAPTER 6

A GROUP LONG-TERM DISABILITY MODEL
OF THE IMPACT OF AIDS

ROBERT W. BEAL

This chapter illustrates a simple application of the Cowell-Hoskins paper to measure the impact of AIDS on group long-term disability (LTD) benefits in the U.S. The key components of the model are explained below. The projected costs for calendar years 1985 through 200 are then presented for three scenarios.

This particular model illustrates some of the main components of any model that projects the cost of AIDS on group LTD benefits, whether for the industry in total or for individual companies. Most of the assumptions described herein are in need of better data and often are set arbitrarily in order to illustrate the model's results. The reader should not conclude that the results of the three scenarios necessarily represent realistic projections of the impact of AIDS on the industry's group LTD business.

The Spread of AIDS throughout the Population

To project the spread of AIDS throughout the population, a model must first project the spread of HIV and then assume a pattern of progression from HIV infection to AIDS. For both of these items, the LTD model uses results developed by Michael J. Cowell and Walter H. Hoskins in their paper, "AIDS, HIV Mortality and Life Insurance" (see Chapter 3 of this Task Force report), which assume that the number of new infections declines to zero by 1997. Cowell and Hoskins limited these projections to infected persons in the insured population, which they concluded consists primarily of homosexuals and bisexuals. Table 1 shows the development of the estimate of new U.S. AIDS cases for years 1976 to 2000.

Total Number Qualifying for Disability in a Year

The model assumes that 50 percent of those getting AIDS in a year satisfy the definition of disability in the same year and the other 50 percent in the following year.

Percentage of AIDS Cases Covered for Group LTD

The model assumes that 20 percent of the AIDS cases are covered by LTD insurance. This is based upon the 1985 ratio of the number of LTD covered insureds to the working population in the U.S. This allows the model to assume the same progression rates as in the general population.

Effective Covered Wages

The effective covered wage per claimant is assumed to be $25,000 annually in 1986 and increases at a 5 percent annual rate.

Average Disability Benefit as Percentage of Covered Wages

The model also assumes that LTD benefits are equal to 60 percent of covered wages. Companies that offer a range of products should take the distribution of business by product into consideration.

Average Social Security Offset

The average Social Security offset for annual wages of $25,000 is assumed to be 50 percent.

Present Value of Disability Benefits

The present value of disability benefits depends upon when the first LTD benefits are received in relation to the time AIDS is diagnosed, the mortality rates during disability, and the interest rate for discounting benefits.

The first two scenarios assume mortality follows the Cowell-Hoskins AIDS death rates of 45 percent in each of the first two years following progression to AIDS, 35 percent in year 3, and 25 percent in each year thereafter. The third scenario assumes that a medical breakthrough occurs in the treatment of AIDS, reducing the annual death rate to 25 percent in each of the first five years following progression to AIDS and 10 percent each year thereafter for new AIDS cases in years 1993 and later.

The first and third scenarios assume benefits begin six months after the commencement of AIDS. The second scenario benefits begin at the same time AIDS is contracted, assuming the waiting period is satisfied while the claimant has ARC. The disability benefits in all three scenarios are discounted at 7 percent.

The resulting present values of the LTD benefits to the date of disablement for the three scenarios are as follows:

Scenario	Present Value LTD Benefits*
1	$17.02
2	21.71
3	17.02 (through year 1992)
	35.47 (for years 1993 and later)

*Per $1.00 of monthly benefit.

Tables 5, 6, and 7 illustrate the calculations of the present value of LTD benefits factors.

Cumulative LTD Benefits Due to AIDS

Tables 2, 3, and 4 provide the results of the three scenarios. The following table compares the projected cumulative disability benefits incurred in years 1986 through 2000 under the three scenarios.

CUMULATIVE LONG-TERM DISABILITY BENEFITS DUE TO AIDS
($ MILLIONS)

Year	Scenario 1	Scenario 2	Scenario 3
1986	$ 20.9	$ 26.7	$ 20.9
1987	56.5	72.1	56.5
1988	113.8	145.1	113.8
1989	201.7	257.3	201.7
1990	330.8	422.0	330.8
1991	512.8	654.1	512.8
1992	758.9	968.1	758.9
1993	1,078.9	1,376.3	1,425.8
1994	1,478.1	1,885.4	2,257.7
1995	1,995.0	2,493.8	3,251.6
1996	2,500.7	3,189.8	4,388.9
1997	3,100.2	3,954.5	5,638.2
1998	3,734.5	4,763.5	6,960.0
1999	4,382.9	5,590.7	8,311.5
2000	5,025.6	6,410.4	9,650.7

Many of the LTD model assumptions are set arbitrarily. Again, the reader is cautioned not to interpret the results in the above table as necessarily reasonable projections of the group LTD benefits due to AIDS. As more information is developed, these assumptions can be improved, leading to possibly more realistic projections. This model was originally developed by Arthur Baldwin of Paul Revere Life and has been somewhat enhanced by David Holland.

TABLE 1

DISABILITY MODEL BASED ON COWELL PAPER
INFECTED POPULATION: INFECTION DECLINES TO 0 BY 1997

	1976	1977	1978	1979	1980	1981	1982	1983	1984	1985	1986	1987
Number HIV Infected	0.504	1.887	6.011	16.295	37.904	76.300	135.429	218.173	328.205	477.693	670.619	919.566
Number Becoming Infected in Year	0.392	1.383	4.124	10.284	21.609	38.396	59.129	82.744	110.032	149.488	192.926	248.947

Number Getting AIDS Year by Year, After Infection in Year Indicated at Left

Years from Infection	Percentage with AIDS	Year of Infection	Pre-1978	1978	1979	980	1981	1982	1983	1984	1985	1986	1987
1	0.0000%	1975	1	3	5	7	10	12	11	10	8	7	6
2	0.3000	1976	1	5	10	17	24	34	41	39	33	28	24
3	1.2000	1977	0	4	17	36	59	86	119	144	138	117	100
4	2.6000	1978		0	12	49	107	177	256	355	429	411	349
5	4.3000	1979			0	31	123	267	442	638	884	1,070	1,024
6	6.2000	1980				0	65	259	562	929	1,340	1,858	2,247
7	8.6000	1981					0	115	461	998	1,651	2,381	3,302
8	10.4000	1982						0	177	710	1,537	2,543	3,666
9	9.9600	1983							0	248	993	2,151	3,558
10	8.4660	1984								0	330	1,320	2,861
11	7.1961	1985									0	448	1,794
12	6.1167	1986										0	579
13	5.1992	1987											0
14	4.4193	1988											
15	3.7564	1989											
16	3.1929	1990											
17	2.7140	1991											
18	2.3069	1992											
19	1.9609	1993											
20	1.6667	1994											
21	1.4167	1995											
22	1.2042	1996											
23	1.0236	1997											
24	0.8700	1998											
	—	1999											
	95.0697	2000											
Total			3	12	44	140	389	950	2,069	4,070	7,343	12,334	19,510
(1) Cumulative			3	14	58	198	587	1,538	3,606	7,676	15,020	27,354	46,863
(2) CDC Data			—	—	—	—	337	1,337	4,119	9,697	15,948	29,003	55,000
(3) Ratio (1) to (2)			—	—	—	—	174%	115%	88%	79%	94%	94%	85%

TABLE 1 — Continued

	1988	1989	1990	1991	1992	1993	1994	1995	1996	1997	1998	1999	2000
Number HIV Infected	1191.439	1465.203	1721.330	1945.951	2131.859	2277.142	2382.978	2451.692	2485.433	2485.433	2485.433	2485.433	2485.433
Number Becoming Infected in Year	271.873	273.764	256.127	224.621	185.908	145.283	105.836	68.714	33.741	0.000	0.000	0.000	0.000

Number Getting AIDS Year by Year, After Infection in Year Indicated at Left

Years from Infection	Percentage with AIDS	Year of Infection	1988	1989	1990	1991	1992	1993	1994	1995	1996	1997	1998	1999	2000
1	0.0000%	1975	5	4	4	3	3	2	2	2	1	1	1	1	1
2	0.3000	1976	20	17	15	13	11	9	8	7	6	5	4	3	3
3	1.2000	1977	85	72	61	52	44	38	32	27	23	20	17	14	12
4	2.6000	1978	297	252	214	182	155	132	112	95	81	69	58	50	42
5	4.3000	1979	871	740	629	535	454	386	328	279	237	202	171	146	124
6	6.2000	1980	2,152	1,829	1,555	1,322	1,123	955	812	690	586	498	424	360	306
7	8.6000	1981	3,993	3,824	3,251	2,763	2,349	1,996	1,697	1,442	1,226	1,042	886	753	640
8	10.4000	1982	5,085	6,149	5,889	5,006	4,255	3,617	3,074	2,613	2,221	1,888	1,605	1,364	1,159
9	9.9600	1983	5,130	7,116	8,605	8,241	7,005	5,954	5,061	4,302	3,657	3,108	2,642	2,246	1,909
10	8.4660	1984	4,731	6,822	9,463	11,443	10,959	9,315	7,918	6,730	5,721	4,863	4,133	3,513	2,986
11	7.1961	1985	3,887	6,428	9,268	12,856	15,547	14,889	12,656	10,757	9,144	7,772	6,606	5,615	4,773
12	6.1167	1986	2,315	5,016	8,296	11,961	16,592	20,064	19,215	16,333	13,883	11,801	10,031	8,526	7,247
13	5.1992	1987	747	2,987	6,473	10,705	15,435	21,409	25,890	24,795	21,076	17,914	15,227	12,943	11,002
14	4.4193	1988	0	816	3,262	7,069	11,691	16,856	23,381	28,275	27,079	23,017	19,564	16,630	14,133
15	3.7564	1989		0	821	3,285	7,118	11,772	16,973	23,544	28,471	27,267	23,177	19,700	16,745
16	3.1929	1990			0	768	3,074	6,659	11,013	15,880	22,027	26,637	25,510	21,684	18,431
17	2.7140	1991				0	674	2,695	5,840	9,659	13,927	19,317	23,361	22,372	19,016
18	2.3069	1992					0	558	2,231	4,834	7,994	11,526	15,988	19,334	18,516
19	1.9609	1993						0	436	1,743	3,777	6,247	9,008	12,494	15,109
20	1.6667	1994							0	318	1,270	2,752	4,551	6,562	9,102
21	1.4167	1995								0	206	825	1,787	2,955	4,260
22	1.2042	1996									0	101	405	877	1,451
23	1.0236	1997										0	0	0	0
24	0.8700	1998											0	0	0
	—	1999												0	0
	95.0697	2000													0
Total			29,318	42,074	57,806	76,204	96,487	117,308	136,680	152,324	162,613	166,872	165,155	158,143	146,972
(1) Cumulative			76,181	118,255	176,062	252,266	348,753	466,060	602,740	755,065	917,677	1,084,549	1,249,704	1,407,847	1,554,819
(2) CDC Data			88,000	133,000	191,000	265,000									
(3) Ratio (1) to (2)			87%	89%	92%	95%									

TABLE 2

Scenario 1*

Disability Model Based on Cowell Paper

Infected Population: Infection Declines to 0 by 1997

Year	AIDS Cases		Total Number Qualifying for Disability in Year†	Percentage of AIDS Cases Covered for Group LTD	Total Number of AIDS Cases That Are Insured	Projected Inflation Rate for Wages	Effective Monthly Covered Wages	Average Disability Benefit			Present Value of Disability Benefit	PV Benefit Times Number Disabled (Millions)	Cumulative Disability Benefits Incurred (Millions)
	Total No.	Cumulative						As Percentage of Covered Wages	Before Social Security Offset	After 50% Social Security Offset			
Pre-1978	3	3											
1978	12	14											
1979	44	58											
1980	140	198											
1981	389	587											
1982	950	1,538											
1983	2,069	3,606											
1984	4,070	7,676											
1985	7,343	15,020											
1986	12,334	27,354	9,839	20.00%	1,968	5.00%	$2,083	60.00%	$1,250	$625	$10,637	$20.9	$20.9
1987	19,510	46,863	15,922	20.00	3,184	5.00	2,188	60.00	1,313	656	11,169	35.6	56.5
1988	29,318	76,181	24,414	20.00	4,883	5.00	2,297	60.00	1,378	689	11,720	57.3	113.8
1989	42,074	118,255	35,696	20.00	7,139	5.00	2,412	60.00	1,447	724	12,314	87.9	201.7
1990	57,806	176,062	49,940	20.00	9,988	5.00	2,532	60.00	1,519	760	12,930	129.1	330.8
1991	76,204	252,266	67,005	20.00	13,401	5.00	2,659	60.00	1,595	798	13,576	181.9	512.8
1992	96,487	348,753	86,346	20.00	17,269	5.00	2,792	60.00	1,675	838	14,255	246.2	758.9
1993	117,308	466,060	106,897	20.00	21,379	5.00	2,931	60.00	1,759	879	14,968	320.0	1,078.9
1994	136,680	602,740	126,994	20.00	25,399	5.00	3,078	60.00	1,847	923	15,716	399.2	1,478.1
1995	152,324	755,065	144,502	20.00	28,900	5.00	3,232	60.00	1,939	970	16,502	476.9	1,955.0
1996	162,613	917,677	157,469	20.00	31,494	5.00	3,394	60.00	2,036	1,018	17,327	545.7	2,500.7
1997	166,872	1,084,549	164,742	20.00	32,948	5.00	3,563	60.00	2,138	1,069	18,194	599.5	3,100.2
1998	165,155	1,249,704	166,013	20.00	33,203	5.00	3,741	60.00	2,245	1,122	19,103	634.3	3,734.5
1999	158,143	1,407,847	161,649	20.00	32,330	5.00	3,928	60.00	2,357	1,179	20,058	648.5	4,382.9
2000	146,972	1,554,819	152,557	20.00	30,511	5.00	4,125	60.00	2,475	1,237	21,061	642.6	5,025.6

*Scenario 1: Cowell-Hoskins AIDS mortality; AIDS claimants must satisfy six-month waiting period.
†Average of AIDS cases in current and prior years.

TABLE 3

SCENARIO 2*

DISABILITY MODEL BASED ON COWELL PAPER

INFECTED POPULATION: INFECTION DECLINES TO 0 BY 1997

Year	AIDS Cases Total No.	AIDS Cases Cumulative	Total Number Qualifying for Disability in Year†	Percentage of AIDS Cases Covered for Group LTD	Total Number of AIDS Cases That Are Insured	Projected Inflation Rate for Wages	Effective Monthly Covered Wages	Average Disability Benefit As Percentage of Covered Wages	Average Disability Benefit Before Social Security Offset	Average Disability Benefit After 50% Social Security Offset	Present Value of Disability Benefit	PV Benefit Times Number Disabled (Millions)	Cumulative Disability Benefits Incurred (Millions)
Pre-1978	3	3											
1978	12	14											
1979	44	58											
1980	140	198											
1981	389	587											
1982	950	1,538											
1983	2,069	3,606											
1984	4,070	7,676											
1985	7,343	15,020											
1986	12,334	27,354	9,839	20.00%	1,968	5.00%	$2,083	60.00%	$1,250	$625	$13,569	$26.7	$26.7
1987	19,510	46,863	15,922	20.00	3,184	5.00	2,188	60.00	1,313	656	14,247	45.4	72.1
1988	29,318	76,181	24,414	20.00	4,883	5.00	2,297	60.00	1,378	689	14,960	73.0	145.1
1989	42,074	118,255	35,696	20.00	7,139	5.00	2,412	60.00	1,447	724	15,707	112.1	257.3
1990	57,806	176,062	49,940	20.00	9,988	5.00	2,532	60.00	1,519	760	16,493	164.7	422.0
1991	76,204	252,266	67,005	20.00	13,401	5.00	2,659	60.00	1,595	798	17,318	232.1	654.1
1992	96,487	348,753	86,346	20.00	17,269	5.00	2,792	60.00	1,675	838	18,183	314.0	968.1
1993	117,308	466,060	106,897	20.00	21,379	5.00	2,931	60.00	1,759	879	19,093	408.2	1,376.3
1994	136,680	602,740	126,994	20.00	25,399	5.00	3,078	60.00	1,847	923	20,047	509.2	1,885.4
1995	152,324	755,065	144,502	20.00	28,900	5.00	3,232	60.00	1,939	970	21,050	608.3	2,493.8
1996	162,613	917,677	157,469	20.00	31,494	5.00	3,394	60.00	2,036	1,018	22,102	696.1	3,189.8
1997	166,872	1,084,549	164,742	20.00	32,948	5.00	3,563	60.00	2,138	1,069	23,207	764.6	3,954.5
1998	165,155	1,249,704	166,013	20.00	33,203	5.00	3,741	60.00	2,245	1,122	24,367	809.1	4,763.5
1999	158,143	1,407,847	161,649	20.00	32,330	5.00	3,928	60.00	2,357	1,179	25,586	827.2	5,590.7
2000	146,972	1,554,819	152,557	20.00	30,511	5.00	4,125	60.00	2,475	1,237	26,865	819.7	6,410.4

*Scenario 2: Cowell-Hoskins AIDS mortality; AIDS claimants receive disability benefits at commencement of AIDS.
†Average of AIDS cases in current and prior years.

TABLE 4

SCENARIO 3*

DISABILITY MODEL BASED ON COWELL PAPER
INFECTED POPULATION: INFECTION DECLINES TO 0 BY 1997

Year	AIDS Cases Total No.	AIDS Cases Cumulative	Total Number Qualifying for Disability in Year†	Percentage of AIDS Cases Covered for Group LTD	Total Number of AIDS Cases That Are Insured	Projected Inflation Rate for Wages	Effective Monthly Covered Wages	Average Disability Benefit As Percentage of Covered Wages	Average Disability Benefit Before Social Security Offset	Average Disability Benefit After 50% Social Security Offset	Present Value of Disability Benefit	PV Benefit Times Number Disabled (Millions)	Cumulative Disability Benefits Incurred (Millions)
Pre-1978	3	3											
1978	12	14											
1979	44	58											
1980	140	198											
1981	389	587											
1982	950	1,538											
1983	2,069	3,606											
1984	4,070	7,676											
1985	7,343	15,020											
1986	12,334	27,354	9,839	20.00%	1,968	5.00%	$2,083	60.00%	$1,250	$625	$10,637	$20.9	$20.9
1987	19,510	46,863	15,922	20.00	3,184	5.00	2,188	60.00	1,313	656	11,169	35.6	56.5
1988	29,318	76,181	24,414	20.00	4,883	5.00	2,297	60.00	1,378	689	11,728	57.3	113.8
1989	42,074	118,255	35,696	20.00	7,139	5.00	2,412	60.00	1,447	724	12,314	87.9	201.7
1990	57,806	176,062	49,940	20.00	9,988	5.00	2,532	60.00	1,519	760	12,930	129.1	330.8
1991	76,204	252,266	67,005	20.00	13,401	5.00	2,659	60.00	1,595	798	13,576	181.9	512.8
1992	96,487	348,753	86,346	20.00	17,269	5.00	2,792	60.00	1,675	838	14,255	246.2	758.9
1993	117,308	466,060	106,897	20.00	21,379	5.00	2,931	60.00	1,759	879	31,194	666.9	1,425.8
1994	136,680	602,740	126,994	20.00	25,399	5.00	3,078	60.00	1,847	923	32,753	831.9	2,257.7
1995	152,324	755,065	144,502	20.00	28,900	5.00	3,232	60.00	1,939	970	34,091	993.9	3,254.6
1996	162,613	917,677	157,469	20.00	31,494	5.00	3,394	60.00	2,036	1,018	36,111	1,137.3	4,388.9
1997	166,872	1,084,549	164,742	20.00	32,948	5.00	3,563	60.00	2,138	1,069	37,916	1,249.3	5,638.2
1998	165,155	1,249,704	166,013	20.00	33,203	5.00	3,741	60.00	2,245	1,122	39,812	1,321.9	6,960.0
1999	158,143	1,407,847	161,649	20.00	32,330	5.00	3,928	60.00	2,357	1,179	41,802	1,351.5	8,311.5
2000	146,972	1,554,819	152,557	20.00	30,511	5.00	4,125	60.00	2,475	1,237	43,893	1,339.2	9,650.7

*Scenario 3: Cowell-Hoskins AIDS mortality; AIDS claimants must satisfy six-month waiting period.
†Average of AIDS cases in current and prior years.

TABLE 5

DISABILITY MODEL BASED ON COWELL PAPER

CALCULATION OF AN ANNUITY OF $1 PER MONTH VALUED AT BENEFIT COMMENCEMENT DATE

Year	Annual P [Death] q	Interest Rate	Effective Monthly q'	Monthly i	Equivalent j	Benefit Months	1-Year Annuity $1/mo.	Probability of Survival	PV of $1 at Benefit Start	PV of 1 Year Annuity	PV of t Year Annuity
1	0.45	0.07	0.05108	0.0056	0.0567	6	5.25	0.7416	1	3.89	3.89
2	0.45	0.07	0.05108	0.0056	0.0567	12	9.02	0.5500	0.96673	4.80	8.69
3	0.35	0.07	0.03655	0.0056	0.0422	12	9.66	0.3025	0.90349	2.64	11.33
4	0.25	0.07	0.02426	0.0056	0.0299	12	10.26	0.1966	0.84438	1.70	13.03
5	0.25	0.07	0.02426	0.0056	0.0299	12	10.26	0.1475	0.78914	1.19	14.23
6	0.25	0.07	0.02426	0.0056	0.0299	12	10.26	0.1106	0.73751	0.84	15.06
7	0.25	0.07	0.02426	0.0056	0.0299	12	10.26	0.0830	0.68926	0.59	15.65
8	0.25	0.07	0.02426	0.0056	0.0299	12	10.26	0.0622	0.64417	0.41	16.06
9	0.25	0.07	0.02426	0.0056	0.0299	12	10.26	0.0467	0.60203	0.29	16.35
10	0.25	0.07	0.02426	0.0056	0.0299	12	10.26	0.0350	0.56264	0.20	16.55
11	0.25	0.07	0.02426	0.0056	0.0299	12	10.26	0.0262	0.52584	0.14	16.69
12	0.25	0.07	0.02426	0.0056	0.0299	12	10.26	0.0197	0.49143	0.10	16.79
13	0.25	0.07	0.02426	0.0056	0.0299	12	10.26	0.0148	0.45928	0.07	16.86
14	0.25	0.07	0.02426	0.0056	0.0299	12	10.26	0.0111	0.42924	0.05	16.91
15	0.25	0.07	0.02426	0.0056	0.0299	12	10.26	0.0083	0.40116	0.03	16.94
16	0.25	0.07	0.02426	0.0056	0.0299	12	10.26	0.0062	0.37491	0.02	16.97
17	0.25	0.07	0.02426	0.0056	0.0299	12	10.26	0.0047	0.35038	0.02	16.98
18	0.25	0.07	0.02426	0.0056	0.0299	12	10.26	0.0035	0.32746	0.01	17.00
19	0.25	0.07	0.02426	0.0056	0.0299	12	10.26	0.0026	0.30604	0.01	17.00
20	0.25	0.07	0.02426	0.0056	0.0299	12	10.26	0.0020	0.28602	0.01	17.01
21	0.25	0.07	0.02426	0.0056	0.0299	12	10.26	0.0015	0.26731	0.00	17.01
22	0.25	0.07	0.02426	0.0056	0.0299	12	10.26	0.0011	0.24982	0.00	17.02
23	0.25	0.07	0.02426	0.0056	0.0299	12	10.26	0.0008	0.23347	0.00	17.02
24	0.25	0.07	0.02426	0.0056	0.0299	12	10.26	0.0006	0.21820	0.00	17.02

Present value of a disabled life annuity of $1 per month commencing 6 months after contracting AIDS = $17.02

Annuity calculation procedure:

1-year annuity = sum$[(v^\wedge t)^* tpx]$ for t = 0/12, 1/12, 2/12, . . . , 11/12
   calculate $i[12] = [(1+i)^\wedge(1/12)] - 1$

   assume constant force of mortality over the year such that
   $tpx = (1-qx)^\wedge t$ for $0 \leq t \leq 1$ and
   $p[12] = 1 - q[12] = (1-qx)(1/12)$

1-year annuity = sum$\{[(1+i[12])^\wedge(-t)]^* [(1-q[12])^\wedge t]\}$ for t = 0, 1, 2, . . . , 11
   and let $q'[12] = q[12]/(1+q[12]) = (1-qx)^\wedge(-1/12) - 1$ and it can be shown that

1-year annuity = sum$[(1+i[12]+q'[12])^\wedge(-t)]$ for t = 0, 1, 2, . . . , 11
   which is a simple annuity due at $j = i[12] + q'[12]$

1055

TABLE 6

Disability Model Based on Cowell Paper
Calculation of an Annuity of $1 per Month Valued at Benefit Commencement Date

Year	Annual P [Death] q	Interest Rate	Effective Monthly q'	Monthly i	Equivalent j	Benefit Months	1-Year Annuity $1/mo.	Probability of Survival	PV of $1 at Benefit Start	PV of 1 Year Annuity	PV of t Year Annuity
1	0.45	0.07	0.05108	0.0056	0.0567	12	9.02	1.0000	1	9.02	9.02
2	0.45	0.07	0.05108	0.0056	0.0567	12	9.02	0.5500	0.93457	4.64	13.66
3	0.35	0.07	0.03655	0.0056	0.0422	12	9.66	0.3025	0.87343	2.55	16.21
4	0.25	0.07	0.02426	0.0056	0.0299	12	10.26	0.1966	0.81629	1.65	17.85
5	0.25	0.07	0.02426	0.0056	0.0299	12	10.26	0.1475	0.76289	1.15	19.01
6	0.25	0.07	0.02426	0.0056	0.0299	12	10.26	0.1106	0.71298	0.81	19.82
7	0.25	0.07	0.02426	0.0056	0.0299	12	10.26	0.0830	0.66634	0.57	20.38
8	0.25	0.07	0.02426	0.0056	0.0299	12	10.26	0.0622	0.62274	0.40	20.78
9	0.25	0.07	0.02426	0.0056	0.0299	12	10.26	0.0467	0.58200	0.28	21.06
10	0.25	0.07	0.02426	0.0056	0.0299	12	10.26	0.0350	0.54393	0.20	21.26
11	0.25	0.07	0.02426	0.0056	0.0299	12	10.26	0.0262	0.50834	0.14	21.39
12	0.25	0.07	0.02426	0.0056	0.0299	12	10.26	0.0197	0.47509	0.10	21.49
13	0.25	0.07	0.02426	0.0056	0.0299	12	10.26	0.0148	0.44401	0.07	21.56
14	0.25	0.07	0.02426	0.0056	0.0299	12	10.26	0.0111	0.41496	0.05	21.60
15	0.25	0.07	0.02426	0.0056	0.0299	12	10.26	0.0083	0.38781	0.03	21.64
16	0.25	0.07	0.02426	0.0056	0.0299	12	10.26	0.0062	0.36244	0.02	21.66
17	0.25	0.07	0.02426	0.0056	0.0299	12	10.26	0.0047	0.33873	0.02	21.68
18	0.25	0.07	0.02426	0.0056	0.0299	12	10.26	0.0035	0.31657	0.01	21.69
19	0.25	0.07	0.02426	0.0056	0.0299	12	10.26	0.0026	0.29586	0.01	21.69
20	0.25	0.07	0.02426	0.0056	0.0299	12	10.26	0.0020	0.27650	0.01	21.70
21	0.25	0.07	0.02426	0.0056	0.0299	12	10.26	0.0015	0.25841	0.00	21.70
22	0.25	0.07	0.02426	0.0056	0.0299	12	10.26	0.0011	0.24151	0.00	21.71
23	0.25	0.07	0.02426	0.0056	0.0299	12	10.26	0.0008	0.22571	0.00	21.71
24	0.25	0.07	0.02426	0.0056	0.0299	12	10.26	0.0006	0.21094	0.00	21.71

Present value of a disabled life annuity of $1 per month commencing 0 months after contracting AIDS = $21.71

Annuity calculation procedure:

1-year annuity = sum[(v^t)*tpx] for t = 0/12, 1/12, 2/12, . . . , 11/12
  calculate $i[12]$ = [$(1+i)^{(1/12)}$] − 1

  assume constant force of mortality over the year such that
  tpx = $(1-qx)^t$ for $0 \leq t \leq 1$ and
  $p[12]$ = 1 − $q[12]$ = $(1-qx)^{(1/12)}$

1-year annuity = sum{[$(1+i[12])^{(-t)}$] * [$(1-q[12])^t$]} for t = 0, 1, 2, . . . , 11
  and let $q'[12]$ = $q[12]/(1+q[12])$ = $(1-qx)^{(-1/12)}$ − 1 and it can be shown that

1-year annuity = sum[$(1+i[12]+q'[12])^{(-t)}$] for t = 0, 1, 2, . . . , 11
  which is a simple annuity due at j = $i[12]$ + $q'[12]$

TABLE 7

SCENARIO 3
DISABILITY MODEL BASED ON COWELL PAPER
CALCULATION OF AN ANNUITY OF $1 PER MONTH VALUED AT BENEFIT COMMENCEMENT DATE

Year	Annual P [Death] q	Interest Rate	Effective Monthly q'	Monthly i	Equivalent j	Benefit Months	1-Year Annuity $1/mo.	Probability of Survival	PV of $1 at Benefit Start	PV of 1 Year Annuity	PV of t Year Annuity
1	0.45	0.07	0.05108	0.0056	0.0567	6	5.25	0.7416	1	3.89	3.89
2	0.45	0.07	0.05108	0.0056	0.0567	12	9.02	0.5500	0.96673	4.80	8.69
3	0.35	0.07	0.03655	0.0056	0.0422	12	9.66	0.3025	0.90349	2.64	11.33
4	0.25	0.07	0.02426	0.0056	0.0299	12	10.26	0.1966	0.84438	1.70	13.03
5	0.25	0.07	0.02426	0.0056	0.0299	12	10.26	0.1475	0.78914	1.19	14.23
6	0.25	0.07	0.02426	0.0056	0.0299	12	10.26	0.1106	0.73751	0.84	15.06
7	0.25	0.07	0.02426	0.0056	0.0299	12	10.26	0.0830	0.68926	0.59	15.65
8	0.25	0.07	0.02426	0.0056	0.0299	12	10.26	0.0622	0.64417	0.41	16.06
9	0.25	0.07	0.02426	0.0056	0.0299	12	10.26	0.0467	0.60203	0.29	16.35
10	0.25	0.07	0.02426	0.0056	0.0299	12	10.26	0.0350	0.56264	0.20	16.55
11	0.25	0.07	0.02426	0.0056	0.0299	12	10.26	0.0262	0.52584	0.14	16.69
12	0.25	0.07	0.02426	0.0056	0.0299	12	10.26	0.0197	0.49143	0.10	16.79
13	0.25	0.07	0.02426	0.0056	0.0299	12	10.26	0.0148	0.45928	0.07	16.86
14	0.25	0.07	0.02426	0.0056	0.0299	12	10.26	0.0111	0.42924	0.05	16.91
15	0.25	0.07	0.02426	0.0056	0.0299	12	10.26	0.0083	0.40116	0.03	16.94
16	0.25	0.07	0.02426	0.0056	0.0299	12	10.26	0.0062	0.37491	0.02	16.97
17	0.25	0.07	0.02426	0.0056	0.0299	12	10.26	0.0047	0.35038	0.02	16.98
18	0.25	0.07	0.02426	0.0056	0.0299	12	10.26	0.0035	0.32746	0.01	17.00
19	0.25	0.07	0.02426	0.0056	0.0299	12	10.26	0.0026	0.30604	0.01	17.00
20	0.25	0.07	0.02426	0.0056	0.0299	12	10.26	0.0020	0.28602	0.01	17.01
21	0.25	0.07	0.02426	0.0056	0.0299	12	10.26	0.0015	0.26731	0.00	17.01
22	0.25	0.07	0.02426	0.0056	0.0299	12	10.26	0.0011	0.24982	0.00	17.02
23	0.25	0.07	0.02426	0.0056	0.0299	12	10.26	0.0008	0.23347	0.00	17.02
24	0.25	0.07	0.02426	0.0056	0.0299	12	10.26	0.0006	0.21820	0.00	17.02

Present value of a disabled life annuity of $1 per month commencing 6 months after contracting AIDS = $17.02 use through 1992

Annuity calculation procedure:

1-year annuity = $\text{sum}[(v^{t})^{*}{}_{t}p_{x}]$ for $t = 0/12, 1/12, 2/12, \ldots, 11/12$
   calculate $i[12] = [(1+i)^{(1/12)}] - 1$

  assume constant force of mortality over the year such that
   ${}_{t}p_{x} = (1-q_{x})^{t}$ for $0 \le t \le 1$ and
   $p[12] = 1 - q[12] = (1-q_{x})^{(1/12)}$

1-year annuity = $\text{sum}\{[(1+i[12])^{(-t)}] * [(1-q[12])^{t}]\}$ for $t = 0, 1, 2, \ldots, 11$
  and let $q'[12] = q[12]/(1+q[12]) = (1-q_{x})^{(-1/12)} - 1$ and it can be shown that

1-year annuity = $\text{sum}[(1+i[12]+q'[12])^{(-t)}]$ for $t = 0, 1, 2, \ldots, 11$
  which is a simple annuity due at $j = i[12] + q'[12]$

1057

TABLE 7 — *Continued*

Year	Annual P [Death] q	Interest Rate	Effective Monthly q'	Monthly i	Equivalent j	Benefit Months	1-Year Annuity $1/mo.	Probability of Survival	PV of $1 at Benefit Start	PV of 1 Year Annuity	PV of t Year Annuity
1	0.25	0.07	0.024263	0.005654	0.029917	6	5.58	0.8660	1	4.83	4.83
2	0.25	0.07	0.024263	0.005654	0.029917	12	10.26	0.7500	0.9667364	7.44	12.27
3	0.25	0.07	0.024263	0.005654	0.029917	12	10.26	0.5625	0.9034920	5.21	17.48
4	0.25	0.07	0.024263	0.005654	0.029917	12	10.26	0.4219	0.8443850	3.65	21.14
5	0.25	0.07	0.024263	0.005654	0.029917	12	10.26	0.3164	0.7891449	2.56	23.70
6	0.1	0.07	0.008818	0.005654	0.014472	12	11.10	0.2373	0.7375186	1.94	25.64
7	0.1	0.07	0.008818	0.005654	0.014472	12	11.10	0.2136	0.6892697	1.63	27.27
8	0.1	0.07	0.008818	0.005654	0.014472	12	11.10	0.1922	0.6441773	1.37	28.65
9	0.1	0.07	0.008818	0.005654	0.014472	12	11.10	0.1730	0.6020348	1.16	29.81
10	0.1	0.07	0.008818	0.005654	0.014472	12	11.10	0.1557	0.5626494	0.97	30.78
11	0.1	0.07	0.008818	0.005654	0.014472	12	11.10	0.1401	0.5258405	0.82	31.60
12	0.1	0.07	0.008818	0.005654	0.014472	12	11.10	0.1261	0.4914398	0.69	32.28
13	0.1	0.07	0.008818	0.005654	0.014472	12	11.10	0.1135	0.4592895	0.58	32.86
14	0.1	0.07	0.008818	0.005654	0.014472	12	11.10	0.1022	0.4292425	0.49	33.35
15	0.1	0.07	0.008818	0.005654	0.014472	12	11.10	0.0919	0.4011612	0.41	33.76
16	0.1	0.07	0.008818	0.005654	0.014472	12	11.10	0.0827	0.3749170	0.34	34.10
17	0.1	0.07	0.008818	0.005654	0.014472	12	11.10	0.0745	0.3503897	0.29	34.39
18	0.1	0.07	0.008818	0.005654	0.014472	12	11.10	0.0670	0.3274670	0.24	34.64
19	0.1	0.07	0.008818	0.005654	0.014472	12	11.10	0.0603	0.3060440	0.20	34.84
20	0.1	0.07	0.008818	0.005654	0.014472	12	11.10	0.0543	0.2860224	0.17	35.01
21	0.1	0.07	0.008818	0.005654	0.014472	12	11.10	0.0489	0.2673106	0.14	35.16
22	0.1	0.07	0.008818	0.005654	0.014472	12	11.10	0.0440	0.2498230	0.12	35.28
23	0.1	0.07	0.008818	0.005654	0.014472	12	11.10	0.0396	0.2334795	0.10	35.38
24	0.1	0.07	0.008818	0.005654	0.014472	12	11.10	0.0356	0.2182051	0.09	35.47

Present value of a disabled life annuity of $1 per month commencing 6 months after contracting AIDS = $35.47 use for 1993 onward

CHAPTER 7

MODELING THE IMPACT OF HIV ON GROUP MEDICAL, DISABILITY, AND LIFE INSURANCE PLANS

MICHAEL L. ZURCHER

ABSTRACT

This paper describes the development of a model that projects group insurance plan costs attributable to HIV-related diseases. Following the explanation of the development of the model and its assumptions is a summary of its projected results, including costs by duration, a claim cost table, and five-year projections. The stochastic, as opposed to deterministic, nature of the model distinguishes it from the typical spread-sheet type of model. Many of the associated cost patterns as well as the progression through the various stages of HIV disease are simulated using Monte Carlo techniques. The application of stochastic simulation has the advantages of providing a means of measuring the expected variability of the modeled results for a given set of assumptions and allowing the integration of a multitude of cost and progression distributions into a single simulation.

INTRODUCTION

The impact of HIV on group insurance plans has not received as much attention as the impact on individual life insurance. This probably has occurred because of the ability of insurers to rerate group plans at least once a year. Insurers anticipate increasing rates each year as necessary so that premiums will adequately cover the expected HIV costs. However, the ability to rerate does not necessarily guarantee adequate premiums, as is illustrated by historical cycles. The rerating process will be successful only to the extent that historical cost levels are known and future trends can be predicted — neither of which is the case with HIV. Also, medical claims are incurred over the course of the disease, not at a single point in time as with life coverages.

A group HIV model will provide an estimation of the HIV costs under a given set of assumptions. This information will be valuable because the use of internal claims data as the basis for projecting future claims may not be reliable due to the inherent difficulties in identifying an HIV-related claim.

1059

Additionally, a model will provide the ability to test the impact of alternative assumptions and scenarios.

The model presented in this paper comprises two components. The first component is the prevalence module. This module develops the number of HIV-infected insured employees by current HIV-disease stage and duration within that stage given the geographic distribution of a block of in-force group insureds. It also projects the number of insureds that are modeled to become seropositive in future years. The output of the first module provides input to the second, the cost module. In this module, the future progression through the HIV stages and the associated costs are calculated for each HIV-infected life. Each infected life enters the model in the month, year, stage, and duration as determined in the prevalence module. The progression paths and costs are derived using monthly formulations and stochastic processes.

Following the detailed description of the components of the model, analysis of the modeled results is presented. The analysis includes the development of various costs by duration since infection, a five-year projection of group plan costs assuming an initial cohort of 1,000 infected lives, sensitivity testing to the five-year projection changing assumptions such as progression rates and cost patterns, and estimated medical claim costs by deductibles.

It is important to note while reviewing this paper that all "costs," except for life benefits, represent full charges to the claimant rather than insurance company benefit costs. There have been no assumptions made as to the plan design features of the group insurance coverage (that is, costs have not been adjusted for deductibles, coinsurance, plan eligibility, coordination of benefits, and so on). Also, the life benefits are those paid at time of death; they do not include any waiver-of-premium benefits. Finally, the medical coverage is assumed to continue until death, even if disability occurs. There is no differentiation as to whether coverage is extended due to the employer continuing to pay the premiums, COBRA, or other means.

The reader should keep in mind that the utility of this model, like any other model, is largely derived from the assumptions that drive the model and the data from which the assumptions are developed. In many instances, the assumptions were not generated from the analysis of hard data, but rather from the "guesstimates" of well-informed actuaries, medical doctors, and others with practical experience in HIV-related medical practice patterns. In other cases, the bases of the assumptions were recognized studies such as the Cowell-Hoskins report (see Chapter 3 of this Task Force report). The assumptions are generally validated with the per-life modeled costs, the only actual insurance data presently available to test results for reasonableness.

This certainly emphasizes the need for improved identification, collection, and analysis of group insurance HIV-claim data.

The results of the model are still valuable notwithstanding these validation limitations. In many instances, the relative comparisons of the projected cost data and the relative changes seen under alternative assumptions provide more value than the actual dollar amount variations. The greatest strengths of the model are in its structure and processes. As more research, studies, and data become available, the flexibility of the model will allow the incorporation of the new information, increasing the reliability of the modeled results.

MODEL DEVELOPMENT AND ASSUMPTIONS

I. *Prevalence Module*

The prevalence module develops the expected number of HIV-infected lives by geographic region for a given block of group insured employees. The HIV-related costs these lives will generate are subsequently modeled in the cost module. The prevalence module actually consists of three steps. First, a deterministic approach is used to derive the number of HIV-infected employees for each geographic region. Next, stochastic processes allocate those lives to an HIV stage and duration within that stage. Lastly, in-force lives currently seronegative that will become seropositive in future modeled years are "cloned" from in-force infected lives, again by a stochastic process.

A. *Number of HIV-Infected Lives by Region*

The number of HIV-infected lives by each geographic region is calculated using the following formula:

Insured Infected Lives = (Insured Males) * {Insured Regional Prevalence Rate}

= (Number of Insured Employees in Region * Percentage of Employees That Are Male) * {General Population Male Prevalence Rate * AIDS Normalized Factor * HIV+ Normalized Factor * Percentage of HIV-Infected Lives Insured and Employed}

The model develops infected lives based on male employees only (that is, no females, dependent males, or dependent children). Dependent males have been excluded because of their marital status. Females and dependent children were excluded because they currently represent a low percentage of total AIDS cases (probably even lower on an insured basis). These assumptions will have to be reviewed for appropriateness as conditions change. The other factors of the formula are discussed more fully below.

The seropositive prevalence rate for males in the general population was developed using the following technique, similar to that presented by Mast [1]. It assumes that the distribution of HIV-infected lives by age and sex follows that of reported AIDS cases. The prevalence rates by age categories are weighted by a group insurance male employee distribution to calculate the age-weighted rate (only insured lives between 20–59 were considered, comprising 95 percent of male employees). The seropositive prevalence rate is obviously driven by the estimated national number of cases. An example assuming 1,250,000 total U.S. seropositives of which 93 percent are male (1,162,500) will generate a 1.67 percent prevalence rate as follows:

| | Age in Years | | | | Males |
	20–29	30–39	40–49	50–59	20–59
AIDS male distribution	21.0%	46.6%	20.8%	8.0%	96.4%
Number of seropositive cases	244,000	542,000	242,000	93,000	1,121,000
Males in U.S. population (million-1986 estimate)	21.3	19.6	12.8	10.6	64.3
Prevalence of seropositive cases	1.15%	2.76%	1.89%	0.88%	1.74%
Group insured male employee distribution	31.5%	29.2%	19.5%	14.6%	95.0%
Employee age-weighted prevalence rate	0.36%	0.81%	0.37%	0.13%	1.67%

The AIDS normalized factor is simply the ratio of 1987 reported new cases of AIDS from the CDC Weekly Surveillance Report [2] to the 1986 estimated population for each geographic region (Table 1), normalized to the national average. The factor was calculated for each of the metropolitan areas in the CDC report. A value was estimated for all other metropolitan areas and several high-risk states. The balancing value was used for all the other states.

The HIV+ normalized factor is used to adjust the AIDS factor to account for the fact that the number of reported AIDS cases in a geographic region is somewhat a function of the age of the epidemic in that region. Using the iceberg analogy to illustrate (the tip of the iceberg representing AIDS cases and the portion underwater representing all non-AIDS seropositive cases), a region with an initial infection year of 1975 would expect to have a larger percentage of the iceberg exposed (and a smaller percentage underwater) than a region where the epidemic began in 1980. Projecting the region-specific prevalence rate based on the reported AIDS cases by applying the

TABLE 1

MODEL GEOGRAPHIC REGION FACTORS

Area	Cost Region	Area Factor	Alternative Care Group	Area	Cost Region	Area Factor	Alternative Care Group
New York City	1	1.43	2	Delaware	7	1.00	4
Los Angeles	2	1.33	3	Minn/St. Paul	7	1.00	4
Long Island	2	1.33	3	Virginia	7	1.00	4
Miami	2	1.33	3	Wisconsin	7	1.00	4
Ft. Lauderdale	2	1.33	3	Maine	7	1.00	4
Chicago	2	1.33	3	Denver	7	1.00	4
Philadelphia	2	1.33	3				
				Atlanta	8	0.88	4
San Fran/Oakl	3	1.20	1	Seattle	8	0.88	4
				Alabama	8	0.88	4
Newark/Jers C	4	1.16	2	Colorado-O	8	0.88	4
				Illinois-O	8	0.88	4
Boston	5	1.21	3	Indiana	8	0.88	4
Wash. D.C.	5	1.21	3	Kentucky	8	0.88	4
Detroit	5	1.21	3	Louisiana-O	8	0.88	4
Anaheim/Rivers	5	1.21	3	Arkansas	8	0.88	4
Houston	5	1.21	3	Arizona-O	8	0.88	4
				Maryland-O		0.88	4
Pittsburgh	6	1.09	3	Minnesota	8	0.88	4
Baltimore	6	1.09	3	Missouri-O	8	0.88	4
Cleveland	6	1.09	3	Nebraska	8	0.88	4
San Diego	6	1.09	3	N. Dakota	8	0.88	4
San Jose	6	1.09	3	Oklahoma	8	0.88	4
Nevada	6	1.09	3	Oregon	8	0.88	4
New Orleans	6	1.09	3	Tennessee	8	0.88	4
Alaska	6	1.09	3	Texas-O	8	0.88	4
Tampa/St. Pete	6	1.09	3	W. Virginia	8	0.88	4
Michigan-O	6	1.09	3	Kansas-O	8	0.88	4
Mass-O	6	1.09	3				
St. Louis	6	1.09	3	Georgia-O	9	0.77	4
Dallas/Ft. W	6	1.09	3	Idaho	9	0.77	4
California-O	6	1.09	3	Mississippi	9	0.77	4
				Montana	9	0.77	4
Kansas City	7	1.00	4	New Hampshire	9	0.77	4
New York-O	7	1.00	4	New Mexico	9	0.77	4
Ohio-O	7	1.00	4	N. Carolina	9	0.77	4
Phoenix	7	1.00	4	S. Carolina	9	0.77	4
Cincinnati	7	1.00	4	S. Dakota	9	0.77	4
Penns-O	7	1.00	4	Utah	9	0.77	4
Connecticut	7	1.00	4	Vermont	9	0.77	4
Rhode Island	7	1.00	4	Washington-O	9	0.77	4
Hawaii	7	1.00	4	Wyoming	9	0.77	4
New Jersey-O	7	1.00	4	Iowa	9	0.77	4
Florida-O	7	1.00	4				

*Inpatient hospital costs = {inpatient costs/month * geographic factor * diagnosis & duration factor * alternative care factor * life-extending drug adjustment factor * trend}

* Group	Areas	Probabilities Levels of Alternative Care				Expected Savings Levels of Alternative Care				Total Expected Savings
		None	Low	Med.	High	None	Low	Med.	High	
1	San Fran	0%	5%	15%	80%	0%	10%	20%	40%	35.5%
2	NYC/Newark	30	35	25	10	0	4	8	15	4.9
3	Other Met	15	20	45	20	0	4	8	15	7.4
4	Rural	40	40	15	5	0	3	6	10	2.1

AIDS normalized factor to the national prevalence rate would overstate the estimate of seropositives in the "1975" region and understate the estimate in the "1980" region. The HIV+ factor attempts to adjust the AIDS factor in each region to reflect the percentage of the iceberg underwater relative to its exposed tip. For example, a region might have a normalized AIDS factor of 3.0, but since the tip of the iceberg is greater than the national norm because of an earlier initial infection year, the HIV+ adjusted factor might be only 2.6.

These factors were developed using the progression rates presented in Table 8 of the Cowell-Hoskins paper [3] in combination with the number of new HIV infections by year from Appendix 1 [4]. The ratio of reported new AIDS cases in 1987 to total seropositives was determined for the initial infection years of 1975, 1977, 1978, and 1980. These ratios were the basis for the HIV+ factors for these years. The actual factors were derived after assigning an initial infection year to each geographic region.

The employed and insured percentage is also region-specific, adjusting the general population prevalence rate to reflect the likelihood of the infected individual being employed and having group insurance. The factors were based on a process developed by Todd Swim for the HIAA/ACLI AIDS Task Force, which reviewed regional AIDS claims by risk group and race using data obtained from the CDC Public Information Data Set. He then assigned probabilities of employment and insurance to each cell to develop regional probabilities. For example, California would exhibit a high relative probability because of the low incidence of IV drug user AIDS cases. Conversely, New York would have a low relative probability because of the higher incidence of IV drug users. The aggregate mean for the toal U.S. was that 64 percent of AIDS cases were expected to be covered by a group medical plan.

Assuming a block of insured group employees is 62.5 percent male, the aggregate expected prevalence rate for this block is 0.67 percent using the 1.67 percent male rate calculated above (0.67% = 1.67% * 62.5% * 64% employed and insured). The modeled geographic region prevalence rates will vary around this aggregate rate due to the region-specific assumptions.

B. HIV Stage and Duration within Stage

It is important in modeling the medical costs associated with HIV to also model the progression through the HIV stages as costs will vary by stage. In modeling an in-force block of group insurance lives, an assumption must be made as to the HIV stage at which the infected lives will enter the model.

Using the same methodology developed for the HIV+ normalized factor, the distribution by the four stages as presented in Cowell-Hoskins (HIV+, LAS, ARC, and AIDS) can be determined for each geographic region given an assumed initial infection year. In addition, estimates can be made for the distribution of duration within stage. Each HIV-infected life is assigned a stage and duration using random numbers, and this information is then passed to the cost module.

C. New Seropositives

The model implicitly assumes that there is no change in the total number of insured employees throughout the projection period. However, the model does provide for seronegative lives that will become seropositive (that is, seroconversion) in future years. These lives will enter the cost module in the seroconversion year beginning in the first stage and duration.

The methodology used was to develop ratios of new seropositive lives for each future year to the living 1987 seropositives using the Cowell-Hoskins report [5]. For example, the number of new seropositives in 1988 is 34 percent of the infected population alive at the end of 1987. The model generates a random number between zero and one for each 1987 in-force infected life, and if it is less than 0.34, a new seropositive is "cloned" to enter the model in 1988 (with the same geographic region as the in-force life). This same process is repeated for each infected in-force life for every projection year allowing for new seropositives to enter the model throughout the projection period. The month of the year the cloned life enters the model is determined randomly.

II. Cost Module

The cost module determines the infection path and rate of progression for each infected life passed from the prevalence module. The cost module also calculates monthly medical and disability charges and a death benefit if death occurs prior to the end of the projection period. These costs are summarized allowing various types of analysis. The characteristics of each modeled life, its path, and its rate of progression can be saved to permit deterministic sensitivity testing of alternative assumptions.

A. Progression through the HIV Stages

The progression through the HIV stages is modeled independently for each life using Monte Carlo techniques. Monthly progression rates were derived from the periodic rates as presented in Table 5 of the Cowell-Hoskins report [6]. The monthly rates will therefore vary by HIV stage and duration within stage and are constrained by the assumptions documented by Hoskins in Section 4 of his report [7]. The starting point in the model of an infected life can be any stage or duration, and the life is modeled until the end of the projection period or death.

Within each HIV stage, substages have been defined to allow cost variations resulting from the several manifestations of the virus in terms of diagnosis and/or symptoms (Table 2). The virus is assumed to manifest itself by affecting either the central nervous system or the immune system. The probability of progressing to the next HIV stage is assumed to not vary by substage (except in the AIDS stage as explained below), and the substage within a stage is determined randomly. The AIDS substage distribution is based on the CDC Weekly Surveillance Report, adjusted for the assumption that dementia is the primary diagnosis of 5 percent of the AIDS cases.

The progression rates from AIDS to death (Table 3) are adjusted to reflect the different expected lifetimes by AIDS diagnosis. The adjustment is made using relative factors applied to the aggregate AIDS-stage progression rates. These factors vary by duration and will result in significant variation by diagnosis, even though the expected aggregate rate remains unchanged. The adjustment factors for PCP, Kaposi's sarcoma, and "other" diseases were derived from the paper by Rothenberg et al. [8] and ignores the influence of other risk variables on the diagnosis. The dementia factors were calculated assuming a uniform rate of progression that produces an expected lifetime from AIDS until death equal to nine months.

There is also an adjustment made to the progression rates if the modeled life is being administered a life-extending drug (LED), such as AZT. The factors (Table 3) assume the effectiveness of the drug wears off over time. They were developed in part based on a paper by Fischl et al. [9]. The model assumes the drug is used only in the ARC and AIDS stages with differing utilization rates that vary by substage. Utilization is determined randomly for each life, and if used, the drug is assumed to be used until death. The initial utilization of the drug is assumed to be the first month of the ARC or AIDS stage.

B. Monthly HIV Costs

Each month, costs are determined for several types of group life, medical, and disability coverages. These costs will vary according to the HIV stage

TABLE 2

Model Treatment Stages

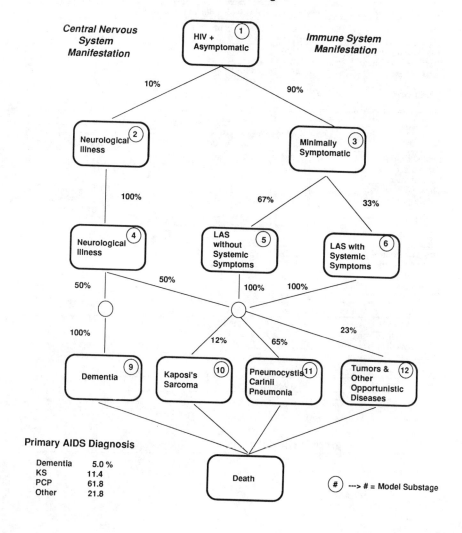

Central Nervous System Manifestation

Immune System Manifestation

1 — HIV + Asymptomatic

10% → 2 Neurological Illness
90% → 3 Minimally Symptomatic

2 Neurological Illness — 100% → 4 Neurological Illness

3 Minimally Symptomatic — 67% → 5 LAS without Systemic Symptoms
33% → 6 LAS with Systemic Symptoms

4 Neurological Illness — 50% / 50%

5 LAS without Systemic Symptoms — 100%
6 LAS with Systemic Symptoms — 100%

100% → 9 Dementia
12% → 10 Kaposi's Sarcoma
65% → 11 Pneumocystis Carinii Pneumonia
23% → 12 Tumors & Other Opportunistic Diseases

Death

Primary AIDS Diagnosis

Dementia	5.0 %
KS	11.4
PCP	61.8
Other	21.8

(#) ---> # = Model Substage

TABLE 3

MODEL PROGRESSION RATE FACTORS

					Progression Rates to Next Stage (Cowell-Hoskins) (A)

	Stage 1b (HIV+)	Stage 2a (LAS)	Stage 2b (ARC)	Stage 3 (AIDS)	Cumulative Mortality at End of Period since Onset of AIDS
First six months	10%	15%	5%	26%	26.0%
Second six months	50	30	5	26	45.2
Second year	45	35	45	45*	69.1
Third year	20	35	15	35	80.4
Fourth year +	20	20	20	25	85.3 (4th)
					89.0 (5th)

Progression Rate Reduction Factors If Life-Extending Drug Used (B)

	Stage 1b (HIV+)	Stage 2a (LAS)	Stage 2b (ARC)	Stage 3 (AIDS)	Cumulative Mortality at End of Period since Onset of AIDS
First six months	0%	0%	80%	80%	5.2%
Second six months	0	0	60	60	15.1
Second year	0	0	40	30*	41.8
Third year	0	0	20	10	60.1
Fourth year +	0	0	10	0	70.1 (4th)
					77.6 (5th)

Progression Adjustment Factors during AIDS by HIV-Related Disease (C)

	Dementia	Kaposi's	PCP	Other	
First six months	1.42	0.52	0.98	1.15	
Second six months	1.42	0.52	0.98	1.15	
Second year	2.27	0.77	1.10*	0.70	
Third year	5.54	1.07	0.94	0.85	
Fourth year +	6.89	0.92	0.81	1.43	

Expected Number of Months to Progress to Next Stage

HIV+ Cowell-Hoskins	27.0 months	
LAS Cowell-Hoskins	32.9	
ARC Cowell-Hoskins	47.6	
AIDS Cowell-Hoskins	25.2	HIV+ to Death = 11.1 years
AIDS C-H − LED	41.7	

Monthly Progression Rate Formula

$[1 - \{1 - [A * (1 - B)]\} ** 1/6 \text{ (or } 1/12)] * C$

"*" example $= [1 - \{1 - [0.45 * (1 - 0.3)]\} ** 1/12] * 1.10$

$= [1 - \{1 - [0.315]\} ** 1/12] * 1.10$

$= [1 - 0.969] * 1.10 = 0.0341$

the life is in and the diagnosis/symptom (substage) within the stage. Additionally, the costs will be adjusted for items such as geographic area, level of alternative care applied within that area, trend factors, duration within stage, life-extending drug usage, income, and antiselection. Some of the charges are calculated as a fixed cost per month; for others, whether or not the cost is incurred is determined on a random basis. The medical costs are assumed to be the additional costs that are caused by the HIV infection before the application of any plan design factors such as coinsurance and deductibles. A detailed discussion of each modeled cost type is provided below. The actual dollar assumptions are displayed in Table 4. Unless otherwise noted, the cost and probability estimates are based upon Lincoln National data and/or estimates.

Outpatient Drugs. These charges represent prescription drugs taken on an outpatient basis. They are a fixed monthly cost with an annual trend factor applied.

Psychological/Psychiatric Treatment. These charges represent the monthly cost of psychological or psychiatric counseling. The costs are assumed to be $50 per session. The utilization of counseling services is determined randomly each month for each life based on probabilities that increase as the life progresses through the HIV stages. Also, higher probabilities are assumed for patients with central nervous system symptoms. A trend factor is applied annually.

Hospital Inpatient. These charges represent all costs associated with inpatient hospital confinement. The model was originally designed to calculate costs based on probability of admission, average length of stay, and cost per day but was modified for simplicity to a monthly fixed cost that varies by substage. The monthly fixed costs are adjusted for the following factors: geographic area, AIDS diagnosis and duration, level of alternative care, adjustment for LED, and a trend factor. The formula is shown in Table 1.

The geographic area of the modeled life is determined in the prevalence module. The geographic areas have been reduced to nine "cost areas" to simplify the reflection of area cost differences. These cost areas are made up of geographic areas that have been grouped together based on similar area cost factors.

The AIDS diagnosis factor and the AIDS duration factor have been combined into one factor. It is used to adjust inpatient hospital costs for two variables in the AIDS stage. The first is to adjust the standard monthly cost assumption to reflect differing levels of costs, utilization, and treatment patterns by AIDS diagnosis. The second adjustment reflects the higher costs

TABLE 4

MODEL MONTHLY COST ASSUMPTIONS

Frankfurt Stage	Stage 1b (HIV+)	Stage 2a (LAS)		Stage 2b (ARC)			Stage 3 (AIDS)				Annual Trend
Model Substage	1 HIV+	2 CNS	3 Min. Sym	4 CNS	5 w/o Sym	6 w/Sym	9 Demen	10 KS	11 PCP	12 Other	Years 2-4/5-10
Outpatient drugs ($)	10	40	10	40	10	40	75	50	60	75	8%/5%
Psychl/psycho trmt ($)	50	50	50	75	50	50	150	150	50	100	4%/4%
Probability*	0.02	0.35	0.05	0.50	0.05	0.20	0.75	0.60	0.40	0.50	
Hospital inpatient ($)	0	300	0	600	0	300	1250	1250	1250	1250	8%/5%
Disease adj factors											
First 2 months	—	—	—	—	—	—	1.4	1.2	3.8	1.6	
Other months	—	—	—	—	—	—	0.6	0.3	1.0	0.4	
Last 4 months	—	—	—	—	—	—	2.5	2.0	3.2	2.3	
Outpatient/diagnostic	10	100	20	100	40	80	240	160	200	160	12%/5%
Disease adj factors											
First 2 months	—	—	—	—	—	—	1.0	0.6	0.5	0.6	
Other months	—	—	—	—	—	—	1.0	1.0	1.0	1.0	
Last 4 months	—	—	—	—	—	—	1.0	0.75	0.5	0.75	
Life-extending drug ($)	0	0	0	0	0	800	800	800	800	800	0%/0%
Probability†	0	0	0	0.05	0	0.20	0.05	0.30	0.60	0.30	
Hosp. in savings (%)	0	0	0	35	0	0	35	50	50	50	
STD probabilities*	0	0	0	0.08	0.02	0.04	0.25	0.08	0.12	0.10	
LTD probabilities†	0	0	0	0	0	0	0.80	0.20	0.40	0.30	

*Probabilities of utilization determined monthly.
†Probabilities of utilization determined only once per stage; once utilization begins, continues for remainder of life.

TABLE 4 — *Continued*

"Other" Benefit Assumptions:

LIFE — Death Benefit = $20,000 (1 × salary). Probability of AIDS claimant having life coverage = 100%. Annual Trend = 4%.

STD (Weekly Income) — Monthly Benefit = $750 (assumes 60% payout for 3/4 of month). If AIDS claimant has STD coverage but no LTD coverage, a random number is generated each month to determine whether STD benefits are paid that month. If the claimant has STD and LTD coverages and the LTD benefit will be paid (see below), then STD benefits are assumed to be paid for the six months prior to the LTD benefits beginning. If no LTD benefits will be paid, STD continues to be determined each month randomly. Annual Trend = 4%.

LTD — Monthly Benefit = $667 (assumes 40% payout). If AIDS claimant has LTD coverage, a random number is generated when the claimant reaches the AIDS stage and is compared to the probability of being disabled under the substage within the AIDS stage. If the claimant will be disabled, LTD benefits are assumed to begin seven months after the onset of AIDS and continue until death. Annual Trend = 4% (trend is not applied once benefits commence).

All three benefits are also adjusted to recognize that these benefits vary by the income of the claimant. The following income distribution is used to adjust the $20,000 average salary assumed in all the benefit above. It is determined randomly for each claimant. The expected income level using the distribution below is $26,850.

Factor	Income	Probability	Cumulative Probability
0.50	$10,000	5%	5%
0.65	13,000	10	15
0.85	17,000	15	30
1.00	20,000	35	65
1.50	30,000	15	80
2.00	40,000	10	90
3.00	60,000	5	95
4.00	80,000	5	100

The death benefit is additionally adjusted to reflect that there is the possibility of some antiselection resulting from choices group insureds can often make in terms of multiples of salary for their death benefit. This is reflected using the factors from the following selection distribution, once again determined randomly for each claimant.

Factor	Probability	Cumulative Probability	
1.0	80%	80%	
1.5	10	90	
2.0	5	95	(exp. factor = 1.2)
2.5	2	97	
3.0	2	99	
4.0	1	100	

that are usually incurred immediately after diagnosis and immediately preceding death. The model assumes such factors are applicable in the first two months after diagnosis and the four months prior to death. The factors were based on studies published by Kizer [10] and Scitovsky and Rice [11].

Each modeled life is randomly determined to utilize one of four levels of alternative care (Table 1). These levels — no care, low, medium, and high — vary by geographic region. Corresponding to the level of care for each region is the assumed savings in terms of the percentage reduction in hospital inpatient costs due to the use of alternative care facilities and alternative care treatment. The alternative care network in the San Francisco area is assumed to have the greatest utilization and savings, while alternative care in "rural" areas is assumed to be less utilized and developed. These factors would be significantly modified if a specific company was being modeled to reflect the company's ability to manage large claims.

A life-extending drug factor is applied to hospital inpatient costs if the life is using such a drug. The hospital costs are assumed to be reduced because of less frequent admissions and severity. The assumptions are a 35 percent reduction during the ARC stage and a 50 percent reduction during AIDS.

Hospital Outpatient/Diagnostic. These charges represent the costs incurred for hospital outpatient visits, physician visits, home health care, and laboratory/diagnostic testing costs. The geographic factor and a trend factor are applied. Additionally, a diagnosis and duration factor is applied during the AIDS stage. These factors are greatest during the months when the inpatient diagnosis and duration factors are the least severe. These factors were based on the Scitovsky and Rice study.

Life-Extending Drug. The costs of using a drug like AZT are assumed to be $650/month plus an additional $150/month for increased physician visits, tests, transfusions, and complications arising from side effects. These costs reflect the recently announced price reduction by the manufacturer of the drug. Utilization probabilities vary by substage, and usage is assumed to be only during the ARC and AIDS stages (Table 4). The utilization of the drug is determined randomly for each modeled life, and if the drug is used, it is assumed to be used until death. Using the assumed LED utilization probabilities, approximately 50 percent of the modeled infected lives will ultimately use the drug. This is probably a reasonable result currently, but most likely will understate utilization rates in the future. Offsetting this understatement, however, is some indication that many users will be forced to discontinue use of the drug due to the severity of the side effects.

Life and Disability. The model calculates monthly short-term and long-term disability benefits using a stochastic process, and a death benefit is calculated upon progression to death from the AIDS stage. All three benefits have an income factor applied, and the death benefit has a selection factor as well. The assumptions and processes for these benefits are documented in Table 4.

The model can vary the percentage of insureds eligible for the life and disability benefits vis-a-vis medical coverage (if used for company specific modeling), but for this paper it was assumed 100 percent of the modeled lives were eligible for all benefits.

ANALYSIS OF MODELED RESULTS

III.   *Analysis of Mean HIV Lifetime Costs and Costs by Duration*

This analysis of modeled results centers on the average progression rates and costs that are obtained when a large number of lives are run through the model from seroconversion until death. The review of these averages provides an idea of the implicit progression and cost assumptions the model will produce from the consolidation of all the explicit assumptions. The mean rates and costs should be viewed as the lifetime expected values in terms of year-end 1987 rates of progressions, treatment patterns and cost structure, drug usage, and so on. Therefore, these values will be different than averages based on 1986 knowledge and certainly will be different from estimates made in 1989 or later.

A cohort of 1,000 lives was run through the model with all lives entering the model as new seropositives (stage 1, duration 1) and continuing until death. There were no new seropositive lives entering the model in future years, and costs were kept in year-end 1987 terms by disengaging trend or inflation assumptions. The assumed geographical distribution of the cohort was the expected HIV+ distribution if a block of group insured lives had the same distribution as the U.S. general population. Each modeled life was assumed to be eligible for all life, disability, and medical benefits.

A. Mean HIV Lifetime Costs and Durations

Table 5 shows the mean lifetime costs (in year-end 1987 terms) for the 1,000 lives for medical, disability, and life coverages. The mean lifetime cost for all three coverages was $117,600. The mean lifetime medical cost

TABLE 5

Mean Lifetime Costs and Path Durations
1,000 Newly Infected HIV Lives — Year-end 1987 Assumptions

	Lifetime Costs ($000's)					
		Standard	Values from 1,000 Modeled Lives			
	Mean	Deviation	Min.	5%	95%	Max.
All Cases (1,000)						
Total life	$30.3	$23.1	$10.0	$10.0	$80.0	$320.0
Short-term disability	6.2*	7.3	0.4	0.6	19.5	87.0
Long-term disability	8.8*	33.3	0.4	1.3	109.4	696.3
Medical excluding LED	50.8	45.9	1.9	9.3	150.4	335.7
Life-extending drug	21.5	36.2	0.8	5.6	127.2	229.6
Total medical	72.3	74.5	1.9	9.3	210.0	468.6
Cases w/o LED (497)						
Medical excluding LED	39.7	38.3	1.9	226.1		
Life-extending drug	0.0	0.0	0.0	0.0		
Total medical	39.7	38.3	1.9	226.1		
Cases with LED (503)						
Medical excluding LED	61.8	50.0	4.0	335.7		
Life-extending drug	42.8	41.3	0.8	229.6		
Total medical	104.6	89.5	4.8	468.6		

	Path Durations (in Months)			
		Standard		
	Mean	Deviation	Minimum	Maximum
All Cases (1,000)				
HIV+	29.1	43.9	1.0	412.0
LAS	33.5	40.4	1.0	255.0
ARC	48.8	48.1	1.0	273.0
AIDS	35.7	42.6	1.0	286.0
Total	147.1	86.5	21.0	516.0
Cases w/o LED (497)†				
ARC	46.7	49.4	1.0	268.0
AIDS	24.7	34.2	1.0	243.0
Total	136.1	84.7	21.0	451.0
Cases with LED (503)†				
ARC	50.8	46.8	1.0	273.0
AIDS	46.6	47.2	1.0	286.0
Total	157.9	87.0	21.0	516.0

*For the 956 cases actually incurring a STD claim, the mean was $6,500. For the 295 cases actually incurring an LTD claim, the mean was $29,900.
†The life-extending drug is assumed to be used only in the ARC and AIDS stages, so no path durations are shown for the HIV+ and LAS stages.

totals $72,300, consisting of $50,800 for all medical benefits except the life-extending drug, and $21,500 for the drug. The $72,300 value must be interpreted with the following considerations. The costs are lifetime costs rather than annual and represent total charges before the application of coinsurance, deductibles, and so on. Also, over 20 percent of the costs were incurred prior to reaching the AIDS stage; a good percentage of these pre-AIDS costs historically have probably not been identified as HIV claims when collecting per life data. Finally, the costs include, for approximately 50 percent of the cohort, the full lifetime impact of taking a life-extending drug. The full lifetime cost of the drug would not yet be reflected in present average cost data collected by insurance companies. The mean cost for the lives that did not use the LED was $39,700. Those lives using the drug had costs averaging more than 2.5 times the costs of those who did not; the mean of $104,600 includes an average LED cost of $42,800.

The mean short-term disability (STD) benefits were $6,200 per life for the entire cohort (41 percent of disability costs), while the mean long-term benefits (LTD) were $8,800 per life (59 percent of disability costs). For the 956 lives actually incurring a STD claim, the mean benefit was $6,500. The model produced 295 lives incurring a LTD claim averaging $29,900 per life. The mean life benefit was $30,300 (all 1,000 lives remained in the model until death). Also shown in Table 5 is the mean duration in each HIV stage for all lives, lives using LED, and lives not using LED. For this trial of 1,000 lives, the duration in the AIDS stage is 22 months longer when using the LED.

Table 6 provides a percentage breakdown of the Table 5 lifetime medical costs by various categories. These categories are HIV stage, AIDS stage manifestation, medical benefit, and region. Of particular note is the 22.7 percent of medical costs incurred in the pre-AIDS stages of the disease. Also note the much higher mean costs for PCP are largely due to the greater utilization of the LED than the other diagnoses.

B. Lifetime HIV Costs by Duration

Table 7 shows the cumulative percentage of ultimate incurred costs by year since seroconversion for life, disability, and medical. Also shown is the breakdown of medical costs by HIV stage. The table indicates that 50 percent of ultimate costs are not incurred for the life, disability, and medical coverages until the eleventh year following seroconversion.

TABLE 6

BREAKDOWN OF TOTAL LIFETIME MEDICAL COSTS, INCLUDING LED
1,000 NEWLY INFECTED HIV LIVES

HIV Stage	HIV+	LAS	ARC		AIDS	Total
Distribution (%)	0.9	4.1	17.7		77.3	100.0
Mean ($)	650	2,950	12,800		55,900	72,300
AIDS Stage Diagnosis	Dementia	Kaposi's	PCP		Other	Total
Distribution (%)	4.0	8.0	73.7		14.3	100.0
Mean ($)	66,100	59,800	84,000		46,000	72,300

Medical Benefit	Outpatient Drugs	Psychiatric Treatment	Inpatient Hospital	Outpatient Diangosis	LED	Total
Distribution (%)	5.6	2.5	45.7	16.4	29.8	100.0
Mean ($)	4,000	1,800	33,100	11,900	21,500	72,300

Cost Region	Distribution (%)	Mean ($)*
New York City	14.4	86,600
Very high	17.1	80,300
S.F./Oakland	7.6	64,700
Newark/J.C.	2.3	75,200
High	12.8	75,500
Medium high	15.5	70,700
Medium low	11.1	68,800
Low	15.0	63,800
Very low	4.2	59,300
	100.0	72,300

*All regions include $21,500 for life-extending drug costs.

1076

TABLE 7

Year Since Seroconversion	Life	Total Disability	Total Medical	Total Medical by HIV Stage			
				HIV+	LAS	ARC	AIDS
1	0.0%	0.0	0.6%	33.8%	5.5%	0.3%	0.0%
2	0.5	0.7	2.2	48.2	21.3	3.7	0.4
3	1.9	3.0	5.5	57.8	34.6	10.6	2.2
4	6.1	7.4	11.0	65.8	45.4	18.7	6.7
5	12.3	13.0	17.3	72.4	55.0	26.7	12.5
6	19.1	19.1	23.8	77.8	63.8	33.9	18.8
7	27.0	25.3	30.4	82.1	71.2	40.8	25.3
8	32.7	31.4	36.5	85.7	77.3	47.3	31.3
9	40.5	38.3	42.7	88.6	82.2	53.3	37.6
10	46.6	44.3	48.4	90.6	85.8	59.2	43.5
11	51.8	50.7	53.9	92.2	88.6	65.0	49.1
12	56.0	56.7	59.0	93.4	90.8	70.3	54.4
13	62.0	61.9	63.9	94.5	92.6	74.9	59.6
14	65.8	66.6	68.6	95.3	94.1	78.4	64.7
15	71.4	70.8	72.8	96.1	95.2	81.2	69.5
16	75.2	74.9	76.6	96.7	96.1	83.6	73.7
17	78.2	78.3	79.7	97.2	97.0	85.8	77.2
18	80.9	81.5	82.7	97.5	97.9	87.6	80.5
19	83.5	84.1	85.2	97.9	98.4	89.5	83.3
20	86.7	86.3	87.4	98.2	98.8	91.2	85.7
21	88.0	88.0	89.3	98.4	99.1	92.9	87.9
22	90.0	89.5	91.0	98.7	99.4	94.3	89.8
23	91.4	90.9	92.4	98.9	99.7	95.4	91.2
24	92.5	92.1	93.5	99.1	99.8	96.4	92.5
25	93.2	93.1	94.5	99.3	99.8	97.3	93.5
Total	100.0%	100.0%	100.0%	100.0%	100.0%	100.0%	100.0%
Percentage after 25 Years	6.8%	6.9%	5.5%	0.7%	0.2%	2.7%	6.5%
Total Cost (000,000)	$30.3	$15.0	$72.3	$0.6	$3.0	$12.8	$55.9

C. Lifetime HIV Medical Cost Distribution

The frequency distribution by total (including LED) lifetime medical costs is shown in Table 8. The mean and median values were $72,300 and $46,100, respectively, with a mode of $24,000. The distribution exhibits properties of a log-normal distribution with parameters of 10.760 for the mean and 0.9528 for the standard deviation. The following graph illustrates the modeled lifetime claim frequency distribution plotted against the log-normal distribution.

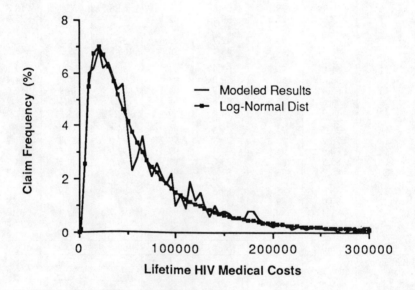

D. Lifetime HIV Duration Distribution

The stochastic progression processes used in the model add a degree of continuity to the possible progression paths infected lives can follow from seroconversion to death. Each life follows a unique progression path that varies by duration within the four stages, HIV manifestation, and LED utilization. Even though the model requires passage through all four HIV-disease stages prior to death, the stochastic progression model more effectively simulates the many possible paths and durations an actual HIV case could follow than a deterministic model.

TABLE 8

TOTAL LIFETIME HIV MEDICAL CLAIM DISTRIBUTION
1,000 NEWLY INFECTED HIV LIVES

Total Lifetime Medical Cost	Percentage	Cumulative Percentage	Total Lifetime Medical Cost	Percentage	Cumulative Percentage
$ 1,250	0.1%	0.1%	180,000	0.8%	93.0%
5,000	2.7	2.8	185,000	0.5	93.5
10,000	6.0	8.8	190,000	0.4	93.9
15,000	6.2	15.0	195,000	0.3	94.2
20,000	6.9	21.9	200,000	0.2	94.4
25,000	6.2	28.1	205,000	0.3	94.7
30,000	6.4	34.5	210,000	0.3	95.0
35,000	5.8	40.3	215,000	0.3	95.3
40,000	5.4	45.7	220,000	0.1	95.4
45,000	5.6	51.3	225,000	0.2	95.6
50,000	3.6	54.9	230,000	0.2	95.8
55,000	2.3	57.2	235,000	0.1	95.9
60,000	2.8	60.0	240,000	0.2	96.1
65,000	3.6	63.6	245,000	0.2	96.3
70,000	2.7	66.3	250,000	0.2	96.5
75,000	2.1	68.4	255,000	0.1	96.6
80,000	2.6	71.0	260,000	0.1	96.7
85.000	2.2	73.2	265,000	0.1	96.8
90,000	1.8	75.0	280,000	0.1	96.9
95,000	2.2	77.2	285,000	0.2	97.1
100,000	1.0	78.2	295,000	0.5	97.6
105,000	1.4	79.6	310,000	0.2	97.8
110,000	0.9	80.5	320,000	0.2	98.0
115,000	1.9	82.4	330,000	0.1	98.1
120,000	1.2	83.6	340,000	0.1	98.2
125,000	1.5	85.1	350,000	0.1	98.3
130,000	1.0	86.1	360,000	0.2	98.5
135,000	0.6	86.7	370,000	0.1	98.6
140,000	1.0	87.7	390,000	0.1	98.7
145,000	0.7	88.4	400,000	0.3	99.0
150,000	0.8	89.2	410,000	0.3	99.3
155,000	0.7	89.9	420,000	0.1	99.4
160,000	0.5	90.4	430,000	0.2	99.6
165,000	0.5	90.9	440,000	0.1	99.7
170,000	0.5	91.4	460,000	0.2	99.9
175,000	0.8	92.2	470,000	0.1	100.0

Table 9 presents the lifetime HIV duration distribution (seroconversion to death) for the 1,000 lives modeled. The durations range from 21 to 516 months with a mean of 147 months and a median of 125 months.

TABLE 9

TOTAL LIFETIME HIV DURATION DISTRIBUTION
(SEROCONVERSION TO DEATH)
1,000 NEWLY INFECTED HIV LIVES

Total Lifetime HIV Duration (Months)	Percentage	Cumulative Percentage	Total Lifetime HIV Duration (Months)	Percentage	Cumulative Percentage
1–10	0.0%	0.0%	261–270	1.7%	90.5%
11–20	0.0	0.0	271–280	1.0	91.5
21–30	0.8	0.8	281–290	1.2	92.7
31–40	2.0	2.8	291–300	0.5	93.2
41–50	5.0	7.8	301–310	0.3	93.5
51–60	5.5	13.3	311–320	0.3	93.8
61–70	6.1	19.4	321–330	1.0	94.8
71–80	5.6	25.0	331–340	0.7	95.5
81–90	6.7	31.7	341–350	0.9	96.4
91–100	4.7	36.3	351–360	0.8	97.2
101–110	5.0	41.3	361–370	1.0	98.2
111–120	5.3	46.7	371–380	0.4	98.6
121–130	4.7	51.4	381–390	0.3	98.9
131–140	4.2	55.6	391–400	0.1	99.0
141–150	3.5	59.1	401–410	0.3	99.3
151–160	4.2	63.3	411–420	0.0	99.3
161–170	3.6	66.9	421–430	0.0	99.3
171–180	4.7	71.6	431–440	0.1	99.4
181–190	3.2	74.8	441–450	0.2	99.6
191–200	2.9	77.7	451–460	0.2	99.8
201–210	2.5	80.2	461–470	0.0	99.8
211–220	2.7	82.9	471–480	0.0	99.8
221–230	1.9	84.8	481–490	0.0	99.8
231–240	1.5	86.3	491–500	0.0	99.8
241–250	1.1	87.4	501–510	0.1	99.9
251–260	1.4	88.8	511–520	0.1	100.0

IV. *Analysis of Five-Year, In-Force Block Projection*

The second analysis of modeled results looks at the expected charges incurred by an in-force block of group insurance over a five-year projection period of 1988 to 1992. This projection will provide an estimate of the total costs the block of HIV-infected lives will incur by calendar year of incurral.

This type of information is valuable for several reasons. First, these estimates can be useful in developing trend factors for the rerating process. Second, the projections can be used in both the financial and strategic planning functions. The additional claim costs can be incorporated into the financial planning process and can provide an "expected" measure to which actual HIV claim experience can be monitored. On the strategic side, the modeled results give an estimate as to the total costs of HIV on a block of business and alert management as to the full extent of their potential impact. With these projections, management can better plan its response to HIV in terms of rerating, underwriting, alternative care management, product design, and regulatory, legislative, and social implications. Finally, sensitivity testing of the results can provide some validation of the financial and strategic responses management might choose to implement.

The block of group business modeled for this analysis is assumed to be made up of 150,000 employees distributed geographically the same as the U.S. general population. With prevalence module assumptions (see Section IIA) of 1,250,000 total U.S. seropositives at year-end 1987 and a 62.5 percent male employee distribution, the module calculates the current number of in-force seropositives to be 1,000 (a prevalence rate of 0.67%). These lives are also assigned an HIV stage and a duration within the HIV stage. Although the size of the in-force block is assumed to remain the same over the projection period, lives becoming seropositive in future years are modeled. New seropositives entering the model in years 1988 through 1992 are approximately 350, 400, 425, 390, and 390, respectively. These lives enter the model in a random month during the year of seroconversion starting in the HIV+ stage with a duration of one. All the modeled lives were eligible for all coverages. Trend factors were applied to benefits in 1989 and beyond (Table 4).

Following are four types of analysis performed on the five-year projections. First, an HIV claim cost distribution is developed and compared to a major medical distribution. Second, the projected total costs are presented by year and coverage. Also shown is a breakdown of medical costs by several categories. Next, sensitivity analysis is performed to the base projection using alternative assumptions. Finally, the variability of the total costs of the cohort for 1988 is analyzed.

A. 1988 HIV Claim Cost Analysis

The annual claim costs for the 1,346 HIV infected lives (1,000 in-force and 346 new seropositives) were developed for the first year (1988) of the projection. Table 10 shows the medical cost distribution by frequency for the 1,346 HIV lives. The costs include the life-extending drug charges if utilized. By frequency, more than 50 percent of the annual costs were under $350 and 90 percent were under $5,000. This reflects the large percentage of pre-AIDS stage lives.

From this claim probability distribution (and the 99.1 percent of employees not incurring an HIV claim), a claim cost table by deductible was developed for the HIV lives. This is presented in Table 11. The HIV claim probability distribution was then convoluted with a projected 1988 adult, comprehensive major medical claim probability distribution. The last column in Table 11 represents the additional claim cost percentage by deductible of the convoluted HIV and major medical distribution claim costs relative to the major medical distribution claim costs. The additional HIV morbidity of 2.47 percent is greatest at the $5,000 deductible, declining to no additional morbidity at the $50,000 deductible. (The maximum annual claim in 1988 that could be generated with the model assumptions is around $55,000.) The additional annual morbidity is also shown for plans with various deductibles and stop-loss limits, all close to the 2.0 percent mark. Although no specific claim cost analysis was performed, the additional morbidity would be expected to increase at a rate in the neighborhood of 40 percent per year in the years beyond 1988 (see below).

B. Five-Year Projection of Costs

Table 12 shows the 1988–1992 projection of total HIV costs by coverage for the 150,000-insured-employee cohort (the projections are actually the means of five independent trials). Again the medical amounts are the total additional charges for the modeled lives before applying any plan design features. The annual rates of increase over the the projection period are 45 percent for life, 50 percent for disability, and 49 percent for medical. Taking out the impact of trend, the rates become 41 percent for life, 44 percent for disability, and 39 percent for medical.

For the five-year period, the additional HIV-related medical charges for the 150,000 insured lives were $32.5 million, or $217 per employee. Short-term and long-term disability costs for the five years were $5.5 million, or $37 per employee. The total life benefits were $11.0 million, or $73 per

TABLE 10

1988 ANNUAL HIV MEDICAL CLAIM PROBABILITY DISTRIBUTION
1,346 IN-FORCE HIV-INFECTED LIVES FROM 150,000 INSURED EMPLOYEES

Total Annual Medical Cost	Annual Percentage	Cumulative Annual Percentage
$25	4.23%	4.23%
75	4.83	9.06
125	4.98	14.04
175	3.86	17.90
225	9.81	27.71
275	15.16	42.87
325	10.48	53.34
375	6.84	60.18
425	5.27	65.45
475	4.83	70.28
550	4.75	75.04
650	3.27	78.31
750	2.75	81.05
850	1.86	82.91
950	0.15	83.06
1,125	0.45	83.51
1,375	0.30	83.80
1,625	0.22	84.03
1,875	0.30	84.32
2,250	0.59	84.92
2,750	0.89	85.81
3,500	2.23	88.04
4,500	2.01	90.04
5,500	1.11	91.16
6,500	1.19	92.35
7,500	0.89	93.24
8,500	0.89	94.13
9,500	0.30	94.43
10,500	0.52	94.95
11,500	0.37	95.32
12,500	0.45	95.77
13,500	0.45	96.21
14,500	0.67	96.88
15,500	0.15	97.03
16,500	0.07	97.10
17,500	0.37	97.47
18,500	0.15	97.62
19,500	0.15	97.77
21,000	0.45	98.22
23,000	0.30	98.52
25,000	0.37	98.89
27,000	0.15	99.03
29,000	0.30	99.33
31,250	0.07	99.41
33,750	0.15	99.55
36,250	0.22	99.78
38,750	0.07	99.85
41,250	0.07	99.93
46,250	0.07	100.00

TABLE 11

1988 HIV MEDICAL CLAIM COST AND ADDITIONAL MORBIDITY

Annual Deductible	Annual Claim Cost	Percentage of $0 Deductible Cost	Monthly Claim Cost	Percentage Additional HIV Morbidity
$ 0	$16.68	100.00%	$1.39	1.72%
250	14.70	88.16	1.23	1.91
500	13.68	82.02	1.14	1.94
1,000	12.74	76.37	1.06	2.01
1,500	12.00	71.97	1.00	2.12
2,000	11.30	67.73	0.94	2.22
2,500	10.61	63.64	0.88	2.30
3,000	9.97	59.76	0.83	2.35
5,000	7.85	47.02	0.65	2.47
7,500	5.96	35.72	0.50	2.37
10,000	4.62	27.67	0.38	2.24
15,000	2.70	16.21	0.23	1.95
20,000	1.55	9.32	0.13	1.51
25,000	0.82	4.90	0.07	1.07
30,000	0.42	2.50	0.03	0.73
35,000	0.17	1.00	0.01	0.42
40,000	0.05	0.30	0.00	0.20
45,000	0.01	0.05	0.00	0.10
50,000	0.00	0.00	0.00	0.00

ADDITIONAL HIV MEDICAL CLAIM COST FOR SEVERAL PLAN TYPES

Deductible	80/20 Up To	Percentage Additional HIV Morbidity
$ 100	$ 2,500	1.89%
250	2,500	1.96
500	5,000	2.00
1,000	5,000	2.06

employee. The additional mortality per $1000 of benefit for each of the five years 1988 to 1992 was 18.9 cents, 23.1 cents, 34.8 cents, 52.5 cents, and 71.0 cents, respectively.

Also shown in Table 12 are the medical cost distributions by year for the HIV stage, medical benefits, and cost region. The HIV stage breakdown shows the AIDS costs relative to all HIV medical costs, increasing from 51.3 percent to 64.8 percent over the projection period as the HIV-infected population begins to mature. Another way to look at this is to recognize that between 40 percent and 50 percent of medical costs are incurred in the pre-AIDS stages for an in-force block. However, the actual percentage of benefits paid for pre-AIDS claimants would be lower after the application of deductibles and coinsurance. The LED costs hover around the 20 percent

TABLE 12

FIVE-YEAR PROJECTION OF HIV COSTS AND BREAKDOWN OF MEDICAL COSTS
150,000 IN-FORCE GROUP INSURED EMPLOYEES

	1988	1989	1990	1991	1992
	Total Projected Costs ($000)				
Total Life	$ 931	$1,182	$1,853	$2,907	$ 4,087
Long-term dis.	134	240	449	645	863
Short-term dis.	255	419	598	771	1,103
Total Disability	$ 389	$ 659	$1,047	$1,416	$ 1,966
Total Medical	$2,464	$3,955	$5,744	$8,316	$12,051
	Medical Cost Breakdown (includes LED)				
HIV Stage					
HIV+	5.8%	4.4%	3.8%	3.1%	2.4%
LAS	13.5	12.5	11.0	10.2	8.2
ARC	29.4	28.7	29.2	28.5	24.6
AIDS	51.3	54.4	56.0	58.2	64.8
	100.0	100.0	100.0	100.0	100.0
Medical Benefit					
Outpatient drugs	9.3%	8.7%	8.1%	7.9%	6.8%
Psych. treatment	3.2	3.1	3.0	2.8	2.4
Inpatient hospital	47.5	46.5	45.2	47.0	53.5
Outpatient/diagnostic	21.9	22.0	23.1	22.7	19.3
Life-extending drug	18.1	19.7	20.6	19.6	18.0
	100.0	100.0	100.0	100.0	100.0
Cost Region					
New York City	16.9%	15.9%	14.7%	14.7%	15.0%
Very high	18.7	17.4	16.7	17.7	17.4
S.F./Oakland	7.9	7.7	7.2	6.8	6.9
Newark/J.C.	4.0	3.0	3.0	3.1	3.5
High	12.3	13.2	12.1	10.6	10.8
Medium high	15.0	16.7	16.6	15.7	15.4
Medium low	10.1	11.4	12.4	13.5	12.8
Low	11.8	11.5	13.2	13.7	13.6
Very low	3.3	3.2	4.1	4.2	4.6
	100.0	100.0	100.0	100.0	100.0

range for the projection period. The benefit breakdown shows consistent percentages by benefit throughout the five years. The cost region distribution shows a small relative decrease in costs in the currently high-HIV-incidence regions.

C. Five-Year Projections under Alternative Assumptions

Table 13 shows the relative cost comparisons of the five-year projections using alternative assumptions to the "standard" projection. The standard projection results were presented in Tables 10, 11, and 12. Table 13 provides the ratio of life, disability, and medical costs by year to the corresponding costs presented in Table 12. It should be noted that the alternative assumption

TABLE 13

FIVE-YEAR PROJECTION — ALTERNATIVE ASSUMPTIONS
RELATIVE COMPARISON TO STANDARD PROJECTION*

	1988	1989	1990	1991	1992
Panjer Progression Rates					
Total life	182%	209%	201%	161%	161%
Total disability	115	110	121	118	107
Medical excluding LED	104	106	113	112	104
Life-extending drug	84	92	103	112	105
Total medical	100%	103%	111%	112%	104%
LED Alternative Assumption					
Total life	50%	74%	86%	90%	74%
Total disability	91	100	104	105	105
Medical excluding LED	65	66	69	71	71
Life-extending drug	200	203	200	224	226
Total medical	89%	93%	96%	101%	99%
Alternative Care Alternative Assumption					
Inpatient hospital	87%	92%	97%	90%	87%

*Ratio of annual projected costs of the alternative assumption trials to the mean costs of the trials presented in Table 12, which were based on "standard assumptions."

projections were based on only one run due to time constraints. Because of the variability built into the model (see Section IVD), multiple runs would provide a better estimate as to the expected differences between assumptions. However, these results provide an idea as to the relative differences in costs using alternative assumptions. In many instances the results will be difficult to interpret as many factors offset one another.

This is only a small sample of the many types of alternative scenarios that could be tested; other progression rates could be modeled, cost and utilization factors updated, and geographic distributions modified. Of course, making a different assumption as to the total seropositive population in the U.S. would impact the number of modeled insured seropositives and their attendant costs proportionately.

The first alternative scenario is the prospective impact of using progression rates from the paper by Panjer [12], instead of the Cowell-Hoskins rates. The Panjer model of the Frankfurt data uses a continuous time Markov process with a constant intensity for each HIV stage. Consequently, it requires no assumption about the duration in a stage before entering the study. Cowell-Hoskins used the maximum length of the observation period in making their assumption as to the duration before entering the study. The Panjer progression rates result in a life expectancy of 7.3 years from seropositivity until death. This is substantially less than the life expectancy of 11.1 years using the Cowell-Hoskins rates. Additionally, the Panjer AIDS stage life expectancy is 0.93 years, compared to Cowell-Hoskins' 2.10 years.

For the alternative scenario run, the Panjer data were converted to monthly progression rates, constant across all durations within a stage. Comparing the projected costs using the Panjer progression rates to the standard Cowell-Hoskins costs, Table 13 indicates the life costs are significantly greater for the Panjer rates. This would be expected with the shorter life expectancies, especially in the final AIDS stage. Disability and medical costs are slightly higher as well. This results from the infected lives progressing to the ARC and AIDS stages at a faster pace and shifting the incurral of the more severe medical costs assumed to occur near death to earlier projection years when compared to the standard projection. This is offset somewhat by the shorter duration in the AIDS stage.

A second alternative scenario involves changing the assumptions related to the life-extending drug. The cost was increased from $800 per month to $1500, and the inpatient hospital cost reduction factor was increased to 75 percent from 50 percent. The utilization was increased to 10 percent, 25 percent, 35 percent, and 75 percent for the HIV+, LAS, ARC, and AIDS stages, respectively. Also, the effectiveness of the drug in prohibiting progression to the next stage was increased to 10 percent, 25 percent, 50 percent, and 75 percent for the four HIV stages, respectively. In general, the effectiveness, utilization, and cost were significantly increased over the standard assumptions, while the cost savings for reduced hospital care were also increased.

As expected, life costs were much lower under this scenario as the progression to death slowed. Somewhat surprisingly, total medical costs were slightly lower compared to the standard projection even though the LED costs were over two times greater. The higher LED costs were offset by the hospital savings and by the slower progression into the higher cost ARC and AIDS stages. Total ultimate costs would be expected to be higher under this alternative scenario, but the higher costs seem to have been pushed back beyond the five-year projection period. Under this scenario then, total five-year costs (life, disability, and medical) are less than the standard costs.

The final scenario shows the impact on inpatient hospital costs by increasing the utilization and effectiveness of alternative care management. The utilization factors were changed for all regions to be the same as the San Francisco area assumptions. The effectiveness factors (inpatient cost savings) were modified to be 50 percent as effective as the San Francisco area. The resulting inpatient savings averaged 9 percent for the five-year period, which would translate to total medical savings in the 5 percent range.

One analysis that was not performed due to time constraints was a five-year projection using progression rates based on information provided from a San Francisco City Clinic study [13]. The expected time of progression from seroconversion to AIDS is 18–24 months longer using the SFCC data than using Cowell-Hoskins progression rates. This would impact modeled results in two ways. First, the percentage of infected lives in the AIDS stage (the tip of the iceberg) would be relatively lower than the Cowell-Hoskins percentage due to the longer progression period. Therefore, fewer modeled lives in the in-force projection would have AIDS as the beginning HIV stage, producing a decrease in projected costs over the five-year projection period. Second, the progression to the ARC and AIDS stages would be slower, resulting in the delay of the higher costs in these stages to later years. The progression rate assumption is an important consideration when making the total U.S. seropositives assumption as the two are directly related.

D. Variability in 1988 Modeled Results

To develop a sense of the variability in the total costs modeled for an in-force cohort of lives, forty trials of the model were run using the standard assumptions for the first projection year. The variability can come from several sources. In the prevalence module, the major source is the HIV-disease stage at which lives will enter the model. Although the distribution by stage would be expected to remain relatively constant from trial to trial if modeling a large block of lives, the distribution by region will change with each trial, which will impact medical costs.

In the cost module, the medical cost variability sources include progression durations, HIV disease manifestation, LED utilization, alternative care utilization and effectiveness, and counseling treatment. The life, short-term disability, and long-term disability benefits are all affected by progression duration. In addition, these three benefits are impacted by the modeled income of the claimant ($20,000 adjusted by the income and selection distributions).

For the 1988 projection year, following are several statistics for total costs from the forty trials modeling the in-force block. Shown for each of the major coverages are the forty-trial mean, standard deviation, minimum value, ten and ninety percentile values, and the maximum value. For each of the coverages, the costs appear to be normally distributed. These statistics are for a beginning cohort of 1,000 infected in-force lives. A smaller or larger number of infected lives would be expected to have more or less variability accordingly. Tables 10 and 11 were based on a trial that generated total medical costs of $2,557,000. This value should be kept in mind when reviewing the two tables.

TOTAL 1988 COSTS BY COVERAGE — FORTY TRIALS OF IN-FORCE BLOCK (000'S)

Coverage	Mean	Standard Deviation	Minimum	10%	90%	Maximum
Life	$ 713.3	$201.8	$ 333.0	$ 457.3	$ 960.5	$1,131.5
STD	260.1	28.7	194.7	223.2	301.1	320.9
LTD	147.4	42.5	57.9	96.0	205.6	254.4
Medical	2,411.2	156.2	2,076.0	2,227.3	2,629.3	2,720.4
LED	451.8	69.9	328.0	367.2	543.6	669.6
Total Med.	2,863.0	202.3	2,459.6	2,559.4	3,165.3	3,219.4

OTHER CONSIDERATIONS

An attempt was made in the development of this model to account for the major factors that impact group insurance HIV-related claims. However, there are other alternative methods, enhancements, and related considerations that were not incorporated into the model because of time limitations. Some of the more important of these factors are:

HIV Regional Prevalence Factors. The factors developed for use in deriving regional prevalence factors assumed that all regions followed the same curve in modeling the spread of the epidemic, with regional variation (the iceberg effect) accounted for by the degree of progression along the curve (initial year of infection). In reality a regional curve is a composite of several underlying curves, representing multiple subepidemics, that vary significantly by risk class and size of risk class. Use of such curves developed at a regional level could provide a more accurate regional estimate of infected lives. Additionally, the future seroconversions were based on the slope of a national curve; thus, use of slopes recognizing regional curves would generate better estimates of future seroconversions by region.

Model HIV Stages. The progression stages used in the model were those defined in the Frankfurt Study [14]. The costs assumed in the second stage of the model did not totally follow the clinical definition of "LAS" from the Frankfurt staging, but more represented the types of costs incurred between asymptomatic infection and ARC. A model may be more widely accepted if the progression rates by HIV stage are consistent with an official staging convention (clinical or immunologic).

Life-Extending Drug. What is the impact on the pattern of disability incidence if a life-extending drug is being utilized? Some users of a life-extending drug cannot continue long-term administration of the drug due to side effects. How should this be reflected?

Annual Medical Costs. The maximum 1988 annual cost of $55,000 does not adequately provide for the very severe utilization of medical services that occur during the AIDS stage for a small percentage of insured lives. On the other hand, others will incur less intense care than is assumed in the model. A random factor/distribution could be built into the model permitting infrequent higher (and lower) annual costs than the assumed monthly averages, reflecting differing intensity or frequency of utilization. The overall mean costs would not have to change.

Plan Design. The ability to incorporate and modify plan design features, such as deductibles and coinsurance, directly into the structure of the model would add value to its projection capabilities.

Other. How large is the impact of HIV-related costs from insured (employee or dependent) women and children and what is the best way to account for these costs? What is a realistic pattern of coverage continuation, taking into consideration disability, COBRA, conversions, and so on? What effect will cost-shifting due to government programs such as Medicaid and Medicare have on group insurance HIV costs?

CONCLUSION

There are basically only three questions in making a projection as to the impact of HIV on insurance plans. How many lives are infected? How fast are they progressing? What is the size of their claims? All three questions are of equal importance, although most of the emphasis in group insurance has been on the amount of the HIV-related claims. This model provides some new approaches to answering all three questions. Also, the ability to measure the variability around the mean values and the creation of probability distributions are two added dimensions provided by the use of stochastic processes throughout the model.

The results of the model presented in this paper provide useful insight to the patterns, distributions, and amounts of HIV-related group insurance claim costs. The results appear to be a realistic prediction of the real-world HIV-related costs that the model is attempting to simulate. However, these results represent the projections under a set of assumptions based on current knowledge, which is deficient in many areas. The predictive value and reliability of the model will increase as more is learned regarding the assumptions and relationships that are built into the structure of the model.

REFERENCES

1. MAST, JESS L., "HIV Infection: Its Impact on Mortality and Underwriting," *Reinsurance Reporter*, Fort Wayne, IN, July 1987, No. 113, p. 6.
2. "AIDS Weekly Surveillance Report," United States AIDS Program, Center for Infectious Diseases, Centers for Disease Control, Atlanta, GA, November 23, 1987, pp. 1–5.
3. HOSKINS, WALTER H., "HIV Mortality," *AIDS, HIV Mortality and Life Insurance*, Itasca, IL, August 1987, p. 26.

4. COWELL, MICHAEL J., "AIDS and Life Insurance," *AIDS, HIV Mortality, and Life Insurance*, Itasca, IL, August 1987, p. 28.

5. Ibid., p. 28.

6. Hoskins, p. 24.

7. Ibid., pp. 4–6.

8. ROTHENBERG, RICHARD, et al., "Survival with the Acquired Immunodeficiency Syndrome: Experience with 5833 Cases in New York City," *The New England Journal of Medicine,* November 19, 1987, Vol. 317, No. 21, pp. 1297–1302.

9. FISCHL, MARGARET A., et al., "The Efficacy of Azidothymidine (AZT) in the Treatment of Patients with AIDS and AIDS-Related Complex: A Double-Blind, Placebo-Controlled Trial," *The New England Journal of Medicine*, July 23, 1987, Vol. 317, No. 4, pp. 185–191.

10. KIZER, KENNETH W., et al. (State of California Department of Health Services), *A Quantitative Analysis of AIDS in California*, March 1986, pp. 19–25.

11. SCITOVSKY, ANNE A. AND DOROTHY P. RICE, "Estimates of the Direct and Indirect Costs of Acquired Immunodeficiency Syndrome in the United States, 1985, 1986, and 1991," *Public Health Reports*, January-February 1987, Vol. 102, No. 1, pp. 5–17.

12. PANJER, HARRY H., "AIDS: Survival Analysis of Persons Testing HIV +," *Working Paper Series in Actuarial Science*, ACTSC 87-14, Waterloo, Ontario, August 24, 1987, pp. 1–14.

13. HESSOL, NANCY A., et al., "The Natural History of Human Immunodeficiency Virus Infection in a Cohort of Homosexual and Bisexual Men: A 7-Year Prospective Study," Third International Conference on AIDS, Washington, D.C., June 1, 1987 (speech).

14. COWELL, pp. 8–9.

ACKNOWLEDGMENTS

The author wishes to thank Ronald Colby, Richard Girard, Arthur DeTore, and Merit Smith for their contributions to the assumptions, relationships, and processes used in the model; Karen DeVoy and Kent Somers for their development of the model systems; and the many others who provided assistance and support in the development of this project.

APPENDIX
DEALING WITH THE IMPACT OF HIV
ON GROUP INSURANCE PLANS

RONALD B. COLBY AND MICHAEL L. ZURCHER

ABSTRACT

What is commonly called the Acquired Immune Deficiency Syndrome (AIDS) epidemic may be appropriately identified as the Human Immunodeficiency Virus (HIV) epidemic, for it is the presence of the HIV that leads to AIDS and ultimately death. It is important while reviewing this report to keep in mind that the epidemic is caused by the HIV and that fully developed AIDS is but the final stage of the HIV infection. This is especially important for group medical insurance where a significant portion of the costs result from HIV-related conditions other than AIDS.

Beginning around 1985, the impact that AIDS has had and will continue to have on the individual life insurance industry has been a topic of numerous internal memorandums and external reports. An increasing amount of meaningful published material can be found on a multitude of subjects concerning individual life products. These subjects include financial and solvency impacts, mortality and pricing studies, seropositive and death projections, testing and nonmedical limit discussions, underwriting responses, product and marketing considerations, state regulatory and legislative environments, confidentiality and counseling issues, and application questions. In spite of all the individual life studies and research completed to date, there is still a vast amount of work to be done and knowledge to be gained.

On the other hand, there has been only a minimal amount of written discussion on the impact of HIV on group insurance products. The impact has usually been rather lightly dismissed because "you can increase your rates for the AIDS risk in group insurance." This is true in the sense that group products are typically written on a renewable-term basis and each year a group insurer has the opportunity to rerate products for the anticipated HIV costs. Additionally, because traditional group underwriting philosophies largely omit individual risk underwriting, most of the individual life underwriting issues are not relevant to group writers. Thus, the HIV impact on group insurance has been largely ignored because of the annual rerating ability and the seeming lack of underwriting issues.

The current decline in the group medical underwriting cycle illustrates that the ability to rerate does not necessarily guarantee an adequate premium.

Also, the rerating process relies heavily on the ability to project future trends based on historical data. The historical data available for HIV claims will be underreported because of the difficulty in identifying actual HIV and AIDS claims and will probably not include claims arising from HIV-related conditions other than AIDS (for example, AIDS-Related Complex). The rerating process will only be successful if past costs are known and future trends are predictable — neither of which is the case with HIV.

There are two other reasons the impact of HIV on group insurance should not be ignored. Although there are fewer underwriting issues in group insurance than in individual life and health, group underwriting issues do exist, and effectively addressing these issues can have a significant positive impact. Second, the HIV exposure group insurance exists while the claimant is still alive. Things such as more costly and effective drugs, more widespread and earlier utilization of drugs, and new technologies and treatments will likely result in higher medical costs.

The ability of a group insurer to successfully deal with the impact of HIV will largely depend on its ability to communicate the issues and responses throughout the organization. HIV issues will affect all functions of the group operation from underwriting to marketing to claims administration.

INTRODUCTION

This appendix represents a compilation of issues related to the impact of HIV on a group insurance operation. The appendix does not address the impact in terms of costs, trends, and projections. Instead, it will hopefully provide group insurance actuaries and management a resource in their efforts to better manage the risks presented by HIV.

The appendix is composed of five sections. The first section provides an overview of basic group underwriting and pricing methods and strategies, in order to assure that all readers will have sufficient context with which to frame subsequent issues. Those readers already familiar with group procedures may wish to proceed to the second section.

The remaining sections identify specific issues related to the impact of HIV and, for most issues, a possible response for effectively dealing with the issue. The second section identifies HIV-related data collection issues. The third and fourth sections deal with issues related to the pricing and underwriting of group products. Finally, the fifth section identifies several other issues outside the sphere of pricing and underwriting, including case management of large HIV claims.

In general, the primary approach to dealing with HIV in group insurance lines will be through pricing and underwriting, although pricing mechanisms will probably be used to a much greater degree than selection mechanisms. Each group contract may be repriced each year (or more frequently, if necessary), thus providing an opportunity to cover near-term expectations of increasing HIV costs. At the same time, individual screening of employees and dependents within a group for asymptomatic conditions (such as HIV infection) is impractical.

As mentioned in the abstract, communication will also be a key ingredient if group insurers wish to successfully manage the HIV risk. One approach to better managing HIV would be to establish a Group HIV Task Force, with representatives from functional areas such as pricing, product development, underwriting, claims, and planning. The primary objectives of the Task Force would be to provide a comprehensive analysis of the current and future impact of HIV on the group operation, to develop plans for dealing with these impacts, and to ensure implementation of these plans. An additional objective would be to promote a broadly based understanding of the HIV issues throughout the organization, not forgetting field employees. This includes serving as a focal point for the identification of issues relating to HIV and as a clearing-house for the collection and dissemination of HIV information within the group operation.

HIV is an epidemic that will have unparalleled economic and social impact in the coming years. The execution of an action plan will not guarantee a successful response to the risks presented by HIV. The consideration of HIV impacts must become a standard part of all strategic and operational decision-making processes, and the implications of such HIV-related decisions to the group insurance operation must be understood by everyone making them. These are the challenges to be met.

Overview of Costs

Direct medical expenses incurred during the lifetime of an AIDS patient are variously estimated at $60,000 to $150,000. There are many uncertainties relating to cost patterns in the future. Treatment patterns emphasizing less inpatient care that are evolving are helping to reduce costs, but technology (for example, AZT) may continue to develop that will provide more expensive treatment and also prolong the life of the HIV patient, consequently increasing the total cost of care. Most estimates of the direct medical costs in the year 1991 for AIDS patients range from $8 to $16 billion. Costs for ARC patients and asymptomatic HIV carriers may double those estimates.

It is unclear how much of the direct costs for HIV patients will be funded by private group insurance plans. Estimates of the amount funded by Medicaid range from 15 percent to 42 percent, with another 1–3 percent coming from Medicare. Costs paid by the individuals and unfunded costs may account for 25 percent. This would leave private insurers and Blue Cross/Blue Shield plans with 30–60 percent of the bill for HIV-related direct medical costs.

There may be indirect costs as well. HIV patients will place increasing burden on the capacity of hospitals and health care providers to deliver care, particularly in areas of high HIV concentration (for example, New York). Additional capacity may need to be funded in these areas. Both the pressure of HIV on Medicaid funding and the substantial unfunded medical cost of HIV patients will increase the magnitude of cost shifting to private payors.

I. OVERVIEW OF GROUP UNDERWRITING AND PRICING

This section discusses general background relating to pricing and underwriting of traditional group insurance products. The remaining sections deal with specific pricing, underwriting, and other issues related to HIV. Each section also identifies a potential response a group insurer could have to each issue. Some readers may wish to skip directly to Section II.

The overall philosophy underlying group pricing and underwriting rests on the principle that "groups" of people tend toward average mortality and morbidity characteristics. The larger the group, the more predictable that group's life and health insurance experience will be.

Case Selection

Case selection depends upon certain characteristics of the group, such as the age distribution within the group or the industry and/or the occupation of the people within the group. Some industries, for example, are not acceptable group risks, either because the people in the group are exposed to a high-risk work environment (for example, explosive manufacturers) or because the nature of their employed population is expected to be more transitory and/or unstable (for example, restaurants, which have high turnover and many part-time employees). In addition, if it can be determined that the group being considered for insurance has had morbidity claim experience significantly higher than average, the group would not be written. As a general rule, information about the health characteristics of the individuals within a group are not part of the group underwriting process, except for the smallest groups (usually less than 10 employees) where short-form health questionnaires accompany the application for insurance.

Pricing

Virtually all group products are written on a guaranteed-renewable-term basis. Rates are typically guaranteed for the first year of the contract and can be raised anytime thereafter with 31 days notice. The insurer typically cannot cancel the policy except for nonpayment of premium. By convention, nearly all groups are rerated each year on the anniversary date of their policy.

At the time of rerating for a given group, the claim experience for that group over the past 12 months is examined. It is "projected" into the subsequent 12 months by making assumptions relative to changing conditions (for example, plan changes, census changes, and for medical insurance, expected changes in the average cost of medical services). Expected expenses and required risk and profit margins are added to the projected claims to determine the rate level that would be needed to profitably cover these projected costs. At the same time, "standard" rates (referred to as "manual rates") for the case in question are reviewed. On a small case, manual rates are used, with some consideration given to the rate suggested by the projected experience of the case. For a larger case, the rate suggested by the case's own projected experience is used with some consideration given to manual rates.

Manual rates are set by reviewing the claims experience of an entire class of business and projecting it forward to a future time period for which the rates will be effective. This process is completed two to four times per year for medical — less frequently for life pricing.

Entry and Exit from a Group

New hires typically become eligible for the group plan shortly after hire. If they join the plan within 31 days of becoming eligible, no underwriting is done. The medical plan typically limits payment for pre-existing conditions on such new hires to $1,000 or $2,500 within the first twelve months of coverage. (There is usually no pre-existing conditions limitation on original members of the group.) Someone entering the plan after the 31-day window is subject to short-form health insurance questions and may be refused coverage if there are significant health impairments. A similar process applies to dependents seeking coverage under the plan. Any entrant to the group plan during the year is charged the same rate as others in the group.

For employers offering one or more HMOs in addition to traditional group medical plans, once each year an "open enrollment" period is held, during which time employees may move back and forth between the HMO plan and the traditional plan without being subjected to underwriting or pre-existing conditions limitations.

Recent legislation (dubbed COBRA) has mandated that medical coverage be offered to employees or dependents losing group coverage for any reason other than termination of the entire group plan or termination of employment for gross misconduct. Such coverage lasts for 18–36 months, depending upon the circumstances under which coverage was lost. Such coverage must provide the same benefits enjoyed by continuing members of the group and must be offered at a price no higher than 102 percent of the premiums being charged for continuing members. In lieu of or subsequent to COBRA continuation, a disabled employee typically may extend medical coverage for a period of 3–12 months. The extended coverage would apply to the disabling condition only. In addition, an employee may convert life and/or medical coverage to individual policies upon the cessation of group coverage or COBRA continuation. They may convert their term life coverage to any individual permanent plan, without being subjected to underwriting. The medical conversion plans usually have lower benefits than were available under the group plan, and premiums charged for medical conversions are significantly higher than group premiums. Medical conversion plans are subject to periodic rate increases, but are typically not cancelable by the insurer except for nonpayment of premium.

Underwriting for Benefit Selection

Traditional group plans offer little or no opportunity for employees to select benefit levels. Flexible benefit plans are an exception to this rule, however. Employees can often select from among several levels of medical coverage and several levels of term life coverage. Coverage options may be changed by the employee annually. Underwriting guidelines limit the amount of benefit upgrade that can be made by the employee without being subjected to individual underwriting and/or pre-existing conditions limitations.

Supplemental life insurance plans are sometimes sold. These allow individuals to elect life insurance amounts in addition to the amounts provided under the group term life program. Such elections are subject to individual underwriting.

Many term life insurance plans provide coverage at one, two, or three times the amount of annual salary for the employee. Highly compensated individuals may be eligible for very high amounts of life insurance under the group plan in these cases. Guidelines limit the amount of group term life that can be issued under these schedules without the benefit of individual underwriting.

II. GROUP HIV CLAIM DATA COLLECTION — ISSUES AND RESPONSES

Pricing for the overall impact of HIV will require complete, accurate and timely data upon which to base assumptions. Because the identification and collection of internal HIV claims are still somewhat infrequent, the use of internal data is typically not credible for purposes of making pricing distinctions such as factors for geographic regions. For this reason, internal data must be supplemented with data available from external sources (for example, CDC, HIAA/ACLI). At a minimum, internal sources need to identify calendar year AIDS experience by major product line (for example, life, health, and disability), geographic area and even individual case data (for example, age, sex, and employment/dependent status). Additionally, other internal information that will prove useful includes diagnosis, duration since diagnosis, costs by type of provider, costs by type of treatment, degree of alternative care provided, number of admissions, length of hospital stay, and whether the claimant is being treated with a life-extending drug like AZT. These latter data are usually more difficult to collect. An HIV data base can be constructed and procedures put in place to gather and store HIV claim data in detail. Periodic reports should be produced and distributed to key managers needing access to this information to make pricing and underwriting decisions. In addition, ad hoc reports may be designed and produced to gain more specialized information.

Issue: Obtaining complete data on HIV claims is difficult, due both to the difficulty in identifying any given claim as being directly attributable to HIV or AIDS and to the difficulty in maintaining consistently high attention to screening criteria on the part of claim examiners. In fact, it has been estimated that as many as 40–50 percent of group medical AIDS claims actually incurred will not be identified for inclusion in an HIV data base.

Response: Both the importance of identifying HIV claims and the guidelines for spotting HIV claims must be periodically reemphasized to claim examiners. Specific diagnoses strongly indicative of HIV should be distributed to the examiners, and the examiners should have procedures for following up on questionable claims. Where possible, HIV claim "templates" should be incorporated into the claim system to assist claim examiners in spotting potential HIV claims. Life claims can be cross-referenced to medical claims. Periodically, extracts can be taken from the overall claim file identifying claims that may be suggestive of HIV. Each is tracked back to the source for determination of whether it is an HIV claim. Benefits of this process are to be found both in terms of completing the data base and in providing direct feedback to examiners regarding HIV claims they failed to identify.

In addition, pricing assumptions must recognize that HIV data will remain incomplete. External data can be funneled through the HIV Task Force to pricing and underwriting staff to supplement internal data on HIV incidence. Pricing assumptions must include "completion factors" to account for the incomplete data.

Issue: ARC claims are particularly difficult to track. In addition, there are medical services being utilized by seropositive individuals, specifically arising from the knowledge or fear that they are seropositive, and these too are difficult to identify separately.

Response: Although it is possible to define certain typical treatment patterns (including the use of AZT) that may give some indication of the magnitude of these costs and the rate at which such costs are rising, it will not be possible to comprehensively identify claims for ARC patients and other seropositives in the internal data. It will be necessary to rely on modeled results and external data to make estimates of the magnitude of these costs.

III. GROUP PRICING — ISSUES AND RESPONSES

A group insurer can include explicit factors to reflect the anticipated cost of HIV-related conditions in the regular repricing of each group insurance product line. These can be established after an analysis of internal and external claims data, adjustment for "completion" (assumed unidentified AIDS, ARC and related claims), and projections of assumed trends in both frequency and average costs for HIV claims. Major lines for which such factors are developed include term life, major medical, short- and long-term disability, prescription drug coverages, and specific stop loss coverages.

Issue: Several geographic areas have had a much higher incidence of AIDS claims than others. At the same time, AIDS and HIV-related diseases are spreading to previously "low-risk" areas. CDC data by geographic area identify AIDS claims with the location in which the patient was diagnosed. However, many patients subsequently migrate to other locations. Internal data will not provide statistically credible samples when broken into small cells such as geographic locale. The treatment costs for HIV claimants vary significantly by geographic location and are changing at differing rates and sometimes even in opposite directions. The availability and utilization of alternative treatment facilities will vary both by location and over time for a given location. The underwriting standards permitted by each state will impact the expected HIV experience differently.

Response: For term life insurance rates, geographic differences in anticipated HIV experience can be reflected by raising life rates in the higher incidence areas. For medical manual rates, some type of "area factors" have always been a part of the rating process. Ideally, it would be possible to directly reflect location-specific HIV projections in the area factors and trend assumptions of the manual rates, but this approach would be difficult to implement and would require more credible data than are currently available.

An alternative approach would be to provide for adequate premium to cover the expected HIV claims in aggregate for the entire insured block and also allow some degree of equity among geographic regions. Because manual rate area factors are updated in response to observed rates of change in total medical claims in a given area, any increase in HIV claims experience in a particular locale will be indirectly reflected in the revised area factors. Additionally, an explicit loading for the anticipated aggregate cost of HIV claims can be included in the overall trend assumption for manual rates rather than varying trend assumptions by area.

If region-specific factors are developed (assuming use of zip code areas), a "geographic area" most likely would not be defined to be as small as a zip code within a major metropolitan area. Within New York City, for example, one or two zip codes for higher area factors would not be singled out. The whole of New York City proper might have a higher rate basis than the surrounding counties, however, owing to a higher incidence of HIV.

Issue: Manual rates usually provide for different rate levels by industry. Should industry factors specifically consider the HIV risk?

Response: Historically, specific claim diagnosis has not been a part of the industry rating process; instead, actual emerging total claims experience has been relied upon to adjust industry rating factors. As in area factors, poor

HIV claims experience in a specific industry will present itself in the review of total claims loss experience by industry. In this way, higher HIV claims in a specific industry would become part of the rating structure over time. In addition, industries that experience loss ratios outside of acceptable norms may be assigned to an underwriting "decline" list, implying insurance would not be offered in the future to groups within that industry.

Issue: The incidence of HIV claims has been much higher in the younger male population than in other populations. Should manual rates for younger males be adjusted to reflect this fact?

Response: Most likely both life and health rates for group insurance products are age- and sex-specific. They reflect the different mortality and morbidity expected for individuals in each age category and of each sex. This allows the rates of each category to as closely as possible reflect the expected claim costs of that category. Accordingly, a group insurer should plan to adjust both life and health rate structures to reflect the projected changes in mortality and morbidity by age and sex that are attributable to HIV.

Issue: Incidence of HIV claims has been much higher in the male homosexual population than in the population at large. Is it appropriate to develop rating classes for sexual orientation when it can be determined, or use sexual orientation in the case selection or individual underwriting process?

Response: It would not be appropriate to use sexual orientation or any surrogate for sexual orientation in the underwriting or rating process. Surrogates for sexual orientation include such things as marital status and beneficiary designation. It is clear that membership in a so-called "high-risk group," such as homosexual males, is not the determinant of the risk of HIV infection. Rather, it is engaging in high-risk behaviors that is at issue. A history of sexually transmitted disease is indicative of high-risk behavior. As such, a factually determined history of sexually transmitted disease is an example of a factor appropriate for use in the underwriting process. To distinguish further, the presence of HIV antitbodies is not a surrogate for either high-risk behavior or membership in a "high-risk group." The presence of HIV antibodies is indicative of the fact of HIV infection, an organic medical condition associated with extremely high mortality and morbidity. The presence of HIV antibodies is an appropriate underwriting factor.

Issue: Projecting HIV costs into the future is particularly difficult. Wide ranges of estimates exist as to the number of seropositives, the rate of progression from seroconversion to AIDS and then to death, and the percentage of seropositives ultimately developing AIDS. The cost of caring for an HIV patient is not definitively known and is likely to change rapidly in response to new drugs, technologies, and the availability of alternative treatment facilities. There is little known about the progression of HIV disease beyond 5–7 years, and much uncertainty surrounds the prognosis for prevention or cure. The legislative environment remains uncertain. The ability to retain pricing and underwriting tools necessary to deal effectively with HIV is problematic. The extent to which COBRA continuation requirements will alter the insurance industry's share of the overall funding of HIV claims has not yet become clear.

Response: It is important to develop a comprehensive model of the impact of HIV on group medical costs for two reasons. First, a model will provide some indication as to what an insurer's HIV claims could be under the assumptions used in the model. Because of the problems discussed earlier with respect to a company's ability to collect data internally, utilizing internal data as a basis for projecting future claims is not reliable. A model can provide estimates of what a company's true HIV costs have been instead of relying on those claims that have been identified as HIV. This will further develop the company's ability to adequately price for future HIV claims. Second, a model will provide rapid analysis of the pricing impact of changes in assumptions relative to HIV, such as changes in HIV prevalence and progression rates. In addition, this provides the ability to test many alternative scenarios such as more effective and costly drugs in terms of life extension, new technology and treatment patterns, movement to increased treatment through alternative care facilities, and the impact of geographic mix. This sensitivity testing will enhance contingency planning capabilities. A model can also facilitate the development of more direct, area-specific analysis of potential future costs of HIV claims.

A company should also evaluate the advisability of establishing contingency reserves in light of the uncertainties stemming from the HIV epidemic. Pricing methodologies that recognize these inherent uncertainties may need to be tied to reserving changes to fully provide for these contingencies.

Issue: The cost of AZT on a direct basis (expected to average $8,000 annually per patient) and indirect basis (additional medical expenses as a direct result of complications from the drug, as well as costs associated with prolonged survival) may be very large. Initial policy restricts the usage of AZT, but pressure is likely to increase for earlier and wider distribution of the drug, perhaps to the limit of undermining patent protection to increase production capacity. New drugs are likely to be developed that alone or in combination with AZT will further increase longevity and add cost.

Response: A company should regularly reevaluate expected prescription drug costs for both major medical products and stand-alone prescription drug benefits. The indirect costs associated with AZT must be considered in all assumptions when projecting changing medical costs associated with HIV. It is advisable that the HIV Task Force serve as a clearing-house for HIV information and advise pricing and underwriting areas of developments relating to AZT (and other new drug therapies) availability and usage.

Issue: The impact of the HIV epidemic on funding mechanisms for health care (for example, Medicaid) and directly on providers (due to increases in unfunded care) will translate into considerably higher pressure to shift costs to the private payors. These impacts will be regional.

Response: HIV is but one of the factors adding to increased cost shifting and destabilized local pricing patterns on the part of providers. It is important to develop and maintain, if not already in place, a strong medical cost trend analysis process. This includes both techniques for comprehensively gathering and analyzing trend data from internal claims as well as utilizing external data sources and expertise. Once again, the HIV Task Force can be a clearing-house for relevant information relating to both national trends and specific local developments that may impact costs to private payors.

Issue: The degree of antiselection among COBRA continuees having conditions such as HIV has yet to be quantified.

Response: Specific pricing factors for assumed antiselection should be included in COBRA pricing. Data collection methods should be reviewed to ensure the availability of data on COBRA experience as it develops. The impact on conversion pricing should also be studied, and consideration might be given to limiting the Extension of Benefits provision where it is possible to do so.

IV. GROUP UNDERWRITING — ISSUES AND RESPONSES

Issue: The expected financial performance of a potential group case can be greatly impacted by the number of HIV patients in the group population. These can be active employees, dependents, or continuees. The number of seropositives is a predictor of future AIDS exposure, but the availability of information to the underwriter concerning seropositives in a particular group is problematic due to both the uncertain regulatory climate and the practical problems of obtaining such information in a group setting.

Response: Case selection for very small groups often relies on short-form individual medical information. In such cases, health questionnaires request information from the applicant regarding any history of immune disorder and any known positive results of HIV antibody tests. (These questionnaires must, of course, be modified in several jurisdictions where one or both of those lines of inquiry is prohibited.) Guidelines for reviewing these applications now include attention to clinical parameters of HIV (for example, hemophilia or sexually transmitted disease).

On larger groups, case selection procedures can be strengthened by requiring more detailed information at the time of application regarding the claim history of the group and details of any active or continued disabled employees or dependents. Claims experience should be scrutinized wherever available for indications of HIV-related diseases. These techniques will provide an adequate screen for AIDS, but do not quantify exposure to seropositives within the group. The determination of the latter is probably not practical at this time in the group setting.

Issue: Exposure to the HIV risk may come from additions to the group coverage, particularly late applicants.

Response: Late applicant underwriting is typically addressed through short-form individual health questionnaires. These were discussed in the previous response as they relate to small group cases. In addition, the ability to identify pre-existing claims during the adjudication process should be reviewed and programs developed to strengthen any deficiencies. It must be recognized that identification of HIV claims during an investigation of pre-existing conditions is particularly difficult due to the sensitivities of both the claimant and many physicians relating to HIV.

Issue: During renewal underwriting, it will be critical to identify how rating actions should be modified on a particular case to reflect group-specific HIV risks.

Response: Like numerous other medical conditions, there is a need to identify HIV claims for the underwriter on a group-by-group basis. Consideration should be given to developing formulas for adjusting underwriting reserves and reserves established for end-of-policy-year refund calculations in the presence of identified large claim risks (such as HIV). Also, methods to avoid selection by policyholders opting for nonstandard medical pooling limits should be considered.

Issue: Group-specific information regarding HIV claims (and other catastrophic claims) is crucial to the underwriting process. In addition to HIV claim identification weaknesses that exist in traditional indemnity claim processes, insurers that offer multi-option plans are likely to have an even more difficult time identifying HIV claims that occur through the PPO or

HMO options. Business that is administered through third-party administrators may also lack the necessary procedures to identify and capture HIV claim information. Usually there is more than one claim "system" involved when plans are offered through multiple delivery systems or administrators.

Response: The identification of HIV claims in a traditional indemnity environment was addressed earlier in the section on data collection. Similarly rigorous collection and analysis techniques should be required when claim administration has been relegated by the insurer to an outside party such as a PPO, HMO, or TPA.

Issue: Some products allow benefit choices to be made by employees, potentially allowing antiselection. A few term life plans provide for high amounts of group term life insurance on a few individuals (usually the highly compensated members of the group).

Response: Because the significant upgrade of term life insurance amounts is usually the key area of concern, underwriting guidelines should be reviewed to assure antiselection within the flexible benefit plan for group term life amounts is precluded by pre-existing condition limitations. A review of the underwriting guidelines for supplemental and excess life may also be necessary. Consideration should be given in each of these reviews to the advisability of developing separate benefit restrictions or underwriting guidelines for some major metropolitan areas (high risk for HIV) than for other areas. A guiding principle of the review can be to preclude any availability of life insurance in amounts in excess of prudent nonmedical issue limits (as for individual products) without strict individual underwriting requirements.

Issue: There may be instances where clients ask for benefit limitations or exclusions for HIV risks.

Response: A company offering insured products that include either a benefit limitation for AIDS or any form of AIDS exclusions runs the risk of sending an inconsistent message to both regulators and the general public. This is especially so if the company has been espousing the necessity for individual products to underwrite HIV risks like any other medical impairments (that is, testing, questions, and MIB medical history). The exclusion of HIV benefit limitations or exclusions from plans is more consistent with a policy that approaches the underwriting of HIV like any other major illness or injury, making no special deviation from standard underwriting practices. An exception to this posture might be considered in jurisdictions where standard underwriting or pricing techniques are not available to prevent antiselection losses. A related question, that of whether to agree to administer a self-insured plan that had been defined by an employer to include such a benefit limitation or exclusion, must be carefully reviewed. It may not be practical to distinguish between insured and self-insured plans in this regard, however. Regulators, media, and the public may view the issue of exclusions and limitations more broadly, without distinction between insured and self-insured approaches.

The Role of Blood Testing in Group Insurance Underwriting

There is much controversy surrounding the appropriate use of HIV antibody testing (that is, ELISA and Western blot). A good deal of this controversy surrounds the use of such tests by insurers in the underwriting process. Part of the argument centers on the issue of confidentiality, but the larger part of the argument concerns an insurer's right to use the presence of HIV antibodies as a basis to refuse to issue insurance.

Some jurisdictions have ruled on insurer's rights to use testing. California, for example, has ruled that antibody testing cannot be used. In California, insurers substitute a T-cell subset test that indicates ratios of certain types of white blood cells. This test does not detect HIV antibodies, but does detect abnormalities in the blood that are predictive of HIV infection. This test is a poor substitute for the HIV antibody tests. The District of Columbia has prohibited insurers from using any test results to determine the presence of HIV. This has caused most individual life insurers to exit the D.C. market.

The consideration of blood testing by an insurer must include not only the cost and procedures needed to accomplish the testing itself, but must also consider the notification process. Transmission of information in the nature of positive HIV test results must be done both confidentially and compassionately. The role of counseling should be considered.

Insurers writing individual products must use HIV antibody testing in their underwriting process. Level premiums and the potential for antiselection make it economically unfeasible to insure HIV-infected individuals. For most, this is a matter of "folding in" HIV blood tests and procedures to existing test regimens and lowering the limit for nonmedical issue.

The economics of group insurance are different, as are the traditional underwriting practices. The group underwriting process provides no opportunity to examine the health characteristics of individuals in the group. Medical exams or even blood tests of all the employees and dependents to be insured under an employer's group plan are not a feasible undertaking. Fortunately, the group pricing mechanism allows opportunity to cover costs associated with changing claim costs. If the group insurer can predict the costs associated with HIV, it can cover those costs with prudent pricing.

Though not in the traditional group underwriting process, there are selected situations in which group underwriters do rely upon information relative to individual health characteristics. Some of these situations were outlined previously in this section. In a few of these situations, such as underwriting excess amounts of group term life coverage, the economics are quite similar to those of individual lines of insurance, with the exception that potential antiselection on the part of the insured is much less of a consideration. It is likely that in these types of situations, group insurers will have to use blood testing, wherever amounts at risk so warrant, to protect against unreasonably high HIV claims.

V. OTHER ISSUES

Managing Large HIV Claims

Issue: Treatment patterns and costs still vary widely for HIV claims, particularly by geographic area. Such patterns often provide opportunity for reducing claim outlays by intervening at the point of claim and attempting to influence treatment pattern, provide for alternative treatment facilities, and/or obtain lower cost prescriptions, services or supplies. For such a program of claim management to be effective, both early identification of intervention opportunities and access to lower cost alternatives are required, as well as skill in effectively intervening with patients, families, and physicians.

Response: A company (or its vendor) can strengthen its large claim management capabilities in a number of ways. Case management nurses can be added to increase capacity, and procedures for the referral of HIV cases from field claim offices can be improved. The identification of HIV cases through the utilization review process can promote quicker and more effective case management. In addition, improved processes to obtain discounted services from providers can be developed, and systems to organize information on such discounts for effective use within the claim management function can also improve case management effectiveness.

Additional Considerations and Issues

The identification and response to issues relating to the impact of HIV on group insurers must be met with an ongoing commitment to communication, study, and action. Each day brings new research, new regulation and legislation, new technology and treatments, and new public perceptions and policies. Each day brings new issues. These issues must be identified before appropriate responses can be developed and implemented. Following are several potential issues that after further research and development may require some future response.

Issue: The regulatory environment is uncertain and rapidly changing. The recent developments in Texas provude an excellent case study in which apparently both the insurance lobby and the state insurance department were caught unaware by the broad implications of a legislative initiative dealing with HIV testing and discrimination. The HIV Task Force needs to work closely with the governmental relations department or the legal department to quickly identify the implications of HIV legislation (proposed or enacted) and quickly disseminate clear information to affected line areas. The Task Force may also play a role in distilling relevant issues pertaining to HIV and the group insurance business into position papers for lobbying efforts by a governmental relations area or other areas. The Task Force can also serve to clarify positions that can be advocated with industry counterparts.

Issue: The strategic implications of HIV must be considered, including key strategic questions such as:

1. What does the HIV epidemic imply about market entry or exit? What about product entry or exit?
2. Medical insurance is being equated in many HIV debates with access to care. What are the implications to policymakers? What is the impact on the likelihood of government health care initiatives?
3. How can/should the HIV epidemic be funded? What is the appropriate public policy? What is the role of pools for uninsurables, and who should fund them?
4. What structural changes may occur in the medical delivery industry in the next 5–10 years due to the burden of providing care to so many HIV victims?

HIV IN A LARGER CONTEXT

As difficult and complex as the HIV issue is for the group insurer, it must be considered within the even larger context in which the question is currently framed. Society at large is facing significant and fundamental questions concerning the cost and availability of health care in general in this country. The issue of HIV is intertwined with these fundamental societal issues, and all come to bear on the question of the shape of the continuing role to be played by group insurers in the financing of health care.

Total spending for health care in the U.S. exceeded $500 billion in 1987. This represents an increase of roughly 7 percent over the previous year, a rate of increase much higher than the general level of inflation in the economy. This, of course, is not new. For most or all of this decade, the increase in health care spending has outstripped the rate of inflation. Health care spending currently makes up in excess of 11 percent of total GNP, up by more than two percentage points over the ratio in 1980. Funding such cost increases is stressing all the primary underwriters of these costs—the Medicare system, the Medicaid system, and private payors (employers, either directly or through their group insurers).

At the same time, there remain perhaps as many as 35 million persons in this country who are uninsured or underinsured with respect to health insurance. And increasingly, access to adequate health insurance equates to access to the health care system itself. These uninsured and underinsured persons find it increasingly difficult to access high-tech, high-cost medical services, yet society does not appear ready to accept the idea of two-tiered health care (one level of care for those who can pay and a lesser level of care of those who cannot).

HIV impacts both aspects of the problem. By most accounts, HIV will add $8 to $16 billion annually to the total cost of health care by 1991, as well as putting much additional pressure on the medical delivery system. In addition, many HIV patients are uninsured or may lose employment-related insurance coverage after prolonged disability.

In many respects, the group insurer finds itself in the middle. On one hand, employers (who ultimately fund the cost of most health care) are largely looking to insurers to build solutions to the problem of escalating health care costs. At the same time, policymakers are wrestling not only with problems of the total cost of health care but also with questions of access to health care and of funding mechanisms, that is, the role of public funding versus private funding of health care costs.

In comparison to these fundamental questions of access and funding, the issues surrounding the funding of HIV medical costs and the related impacts on group insurance plans provide a more definable and immediate focus. However, such issues should be viewed as part of these larger questions as the questions are considered by employers, insurance companies, and policymakers.

CHAPTER 8

AIDS IN CANADA

DONALD C. MACTAVISH

AIDS IN THE GENERAL POPULATION

The Laboratory Centre for Disease Control (LCDC) publishes reports updating the spread of the disease in Canada, similar to those distributed by the Centers for Disease Control in the U.S. The most recent statistics are shown at the end of this chapter and reflect reporting to December 7, 1987. While the incidence of the disease in Canada is less than one-third of that in the U.S., it is still a cause for grave concern as it ranks in the top 10 percent among the nations that report to the World Health Organization. While the ratio of deaths/cases reported is slightly less than that in the U.S., it is still 53 percent. Only Great Britain and Australia, in addition to the U.S. and Canada, show a ratio of deaths to reported cases over 50 percent. This is probably indicative of a much more sophisticated reporting system.

About 89 percent of the AIDS cases in Canada have arisen in British Columbia, Ontario and Quebec. If the incidence was spread uniformly over all provinces, the expected results would be 73 percent. British Columbia has by far the highest incidence at 97 per million of population, followed by Quebec at 63 and Ontario at 61. The national average is 55. Reported cases are concentrated in the major metropolitan areas of Toronto, Montreal and Vancouver.

Table 1 compares the spread of the disease between the two countries. Canadian statistics are not available prior to the second quarter of 1986, so a comparison over the entire time frame is not possible.

The Canadian absolute numbers seem to be running fairly consistently at about 1/30th of the U.S. numbers, while, if population were the only consideration, the relationship would be expected to be about 1/10th. Whether this means that Canada is entering the AIDS cycle at a later time than U.S. or that the experience of the Canadian population will not mirror that of the U.S. is conjectural—likely a bit of both.

There are two important reasons why it is unlikely that Canadian experience will approach that in the U.S. In the U.S., the prevalence of AIDS among the black and hispanic populations is relatively high and AIDS cases involving IV drug abusers account for about 25 percent of the adult experience. These are not significant factors in Canada. Table 2 shows the distributions of reported

TABLE 1

	United States			Canada		
	No. of Reported Cases	Quarterly Increase	Rate of Increase	No. of Reported Cases	Quarterly Increase	Rate of Increase
1985						
End of 1st quarter	8,945		16.2%			
End of 2nd quarter	11,271	2,326	26.0			
End of 3rd quarter	13,611	2,340	20.8			
End of 4th quarter	15,948	2,337	17.2			
1986						
End of 1st quarter	18,883	2,935	18.4			
End of 2nd quarter	22,173	3,290	17.4	614		
End of 3rd quarter	25,650	3,477	15.7	743	129	21.0%
End of 4th quarter	29,003	3,453	13.1	830	87	11.7
1987						
End of 1st quarter	33,482	4,479	15.4	966	136	16.4
End of 2nd quarter	37,867	4,385	13.1	1,124	158	16.4
End of 3rd quarter	42,354	4,487	11.8	1,303	179	15.9

TABLE 2

	U.S. (28/9/87)			Canada (7/12/87)	
Category	Number	% (a)	% (b)	Number	%
Adults					
Homosexual/bisexual male	27,579	65.1	77.8	1,122	79.8
IV drug abuser	6,885	16.2		9	0.6
Homosexual male and IV drug abuser	3,138	7.4	8.8	42	3.0
Heterosexual cases	916	2.2	2.6	35	2.5
Recipient of blood or blood products	1,272	3.0	3.6	56	4.0
Person from an endemic area	744	1.8	2.1	73	5.2
Other	1,236	2.9	3.8	42	3.0
	41,770	98.6	98.4	1,379	98.1
*****Children**					
Parent at risk	458	1.1	1.3	22	1.6
Recipient of blood or blood products	102	0.2	0.2	4	0.3
Other	24	0.1	0.1	0	0.0
	584	1.4	1.6	26	1.9
Total	42,354	100.0	100.0	1,405	100.0

*U.S.—14 and under, Canada 12 and under.

cases in the two countries among various categories. Column % (b) in the U.S. statistics removes IV drug abusers from that country's statistics. With this adjustment, the Canadian statistics are relatively consistent with those in the U.S.

AIDS IN LIFE INSURANCE

Life insurance in Canada is provided by federally licensed companies, by provincially licensed companies and by fraternal benefit societies. Estimates of in force at the end of years 1986 and 1987 follow (in billions):

End of Year	1986	1987
Individual Insurance		
Federally licensed	$340	$375
Other	35	40
Total	$375	$415
Group Insurance		
Federally licensed	$425	$460
Other	25	30
Total	$450	$490

Amounts are in Canadian dollars.

The Canadian Life and Health Insurance Association conducted a survey of its members to determine the extent of AIDS on claims among Canadian lives insured. Responses were received from about 70 companies, and of the federal companies that responded, the percentages of individual and group insurance represented by those companies of the total Canadian market were 87 percent and 75 percent, respectively.

Individual Insurance

Claims for 1986 reported in the survey among the federally licensed companies were 58 policies for $3,768,000. Grossing those amounts up to approximate the total Canadian experience would result in about 75 policies for $4.8 million. The total Canadian death claims for the reporting companies amounted to about $540 million, so in 1986 AIDS claims represented about 0.7 percent of Canadian life insurance claims for those companies.

When experience is so scanty, wide fluctuations in results can occur. In particular, claims on two policyholders in which there was considerable evidence of antiselection accounted for over 55 percent of the total claims. If current blood testing limits had been in place at the time of these applications, there is a strong likelihood that the policies would never have been issued. Removing these two claimants from the overall statistics would reduce the ratio of AIDS claims to total claims to 0.3 percent. This amount is probably a better indicator of the experience of companies who did not participate in the survey.

The number of AIDS deaths reported to LCDC during 1986 was approximately 225. Relating this to the estimate of policies terminating by death, indicates that about one-third of deaths resulting from AIDS involve individual life insurance.

Companies also contributed their claim statistics for the first six months of 1987. Projecting for the balance of 1987 on a linear basis using the same assumptions as for 1986 would result in 1987 claims of about 100 policies for $8.5 million. This would translate into about 1.1 percent of claims. Once again, two very large claims are distorting the experience. Removing the effect of these would reduce the ratio of AIDS to total to about 0.5 percent. Total reported AIDS deaths for 1987 are expected to be about 340, so the one-third ratio is still maintaining.

Many companies have not experienced any AIDS claims as yet. The following table indicates the distribution of ratios of AIDS claims to total claims:

No. of companies	56
AIDS claims	$3,768,000
Total claims	$540,000,000
Ratio	0.70%
Minimum ratio	nil
Maximum ratio	7.87%

Distribution of company responses by ratio

nil	30
less than 0.25%	9
0.25% but less than 0.50%	8
0.50% but less than 0.75%	2
0.75% but less than 1.00%	1
1.00% and over	6
	56

Group Insurance

1986 claims reported by the contributing companies totaled 42 certificates for $1,322,000. Using similar gross-up methods to those used for individual insurance results in estimated 1986 claims of 60 certificates for about $1.9

million. The ratio of AIDS to total claims in the group line is 0.2 percent of claims. Antiselection does not have the same impact on group experience as it has on individual. Again, the number of insured claims relative to the total AIDS deaths is in the 30 percent range.

As in the case of individual insurance, 1987 experience is proving to be worse than 1986. Estimates of 1987 experience are 100 certificates for $4.9 million. This would represent 0.5 percent of total claims.

The following table gives similar information for 1986 ratios of AIDS to total as was shown for individual insurance. Some companies were not able to provide group information, while others are not active in this line of business.

No. of companies	46
AIDS claims	$1,322,000
Total claims	$675,000,000
Ratio	0.20%
Minimum ratio	nil
Maximum ratio	3.22%

Distribution of company by ratio

nil	30
less than 0.25%	10
0.25% but less than 0.50%	2
0.50% but less than 0.75%	1
0.75% but less than 1.00%	1
1.00% and over	2
	46

VALUATION IMPLICATIONS

Valuation actuaries in Canada are required to comply with the valuation legislation in the Canadian and British Insurance Companies Act and to follow the financial reporting recommendations developed by the Canadian Institute of Actuaries. The pertinent requirements are outlined briefly in the following.

The Legislation

1. Assumptions must be appropriate to the circumstances of the company and the policies in force and must be acceptable to the Superintendent of Insurance.
2. Reserves are equal to present value of unmatured obligations less the present value of valuation premiums.

3. Gross premium less valuation premium must be greater than value of future expenses and also dividends on present scale, in the case of par insurance.

4. Reserves must make good and sufficient provision for unmatured obligations guaranteed under the terms of the policies.

5. Actuary must disclose in the report to the Superintendent any prospective changes in dividend scale assumed in the valuation.

6. Reserves published in any statement to the public must be the same as those used in any statement to the regulatory authority.

The Professional Recommendations:

Assumptions

1. Each assumption should be appropriate and is required for each contingency which materially affects the company's net income.

2. The effect of a change in valuation assumption should not be spread over more than one valuation date.

3. Each assumption is a combination of expected experience and provision for adverse deviations with a larger provision for adverse deviations where there is less confidence in the expected experience.

4. A statement of the valuation actuary to the effect that the amount of the reserves is proper and a proper charge with respect to the reserves has been reflected in the income statement is required in the company's report to shareholders and/or policyholders.

The Impact of AIDS on Valuation

The principal impact of AIDS will be felt on existing business. For new issues, it is likely that the effects of the disease will be reflected in the pricing, dividend scales and valuation, although it is doubtful if many Canadian companies are on this course as yet. The spread and incidence of the disease in Canada has not approached the magnitude it has in the U.S.

The liability under fixed-premium policies is the most far-reaching. Where premiums (costs) are adjustable, a company can reduce the effect of AIDS by increasing premiums, reducing the mortality component of the dividend scale or both. In group life and health operations, a part of the increased costs arising from AIDS can be passed on to the employer through the experience-rating mechanism. Also, rate guarantees are generally for not more than one year in the group lines so there is the opportunity to re-price the business as the knowledge about the disease increases. The cost of hospital and medical care does not have quite the same impact in Canada as in the U.S. because of provincial medicare plans. However, should the disease spread as predicted, increased costs will surely result and existing treatment facilities will be severely strained.

Because of the valuation requirement that assumptions be appropriate, recognition of the AIDS threat in the reserving process will likely become essential to the key male ages of 20 through 50. The increase in the assumption may be postponed for a while because of the present relatively low effect of AIDS on the total claims picture. As experience unfolds, companies will be better able to respond to the problem. Until such time, however, the additional claims resulting from AIDS will be an indirect charge against surplus as the existing valuation assumptions do not anticipate an epidemic of these proportions.

Many uncertainties still exist that will impact upon the ultimate valuation assumptions. Will AIDS expand through a "select" insurance-buying population at the same rate as it does through the general population? From the limited experience available in Canada, it appears that fewer than 50 percent of AIDS deaths are insured. How effective will education be in changing the sexual habits of individuals? There is some indication that concentrated programs help. What effect will blood testing have on AIDS experience? Two years ago, virtually no Canadian company had blood profiles as a part of its normal underwriting requirements. Now most are in the $250,000 range for all policies, and many expect to be at $100,000 by the end of 1988. It does appear that a very few number of claimants are responsible for a significant part of the overall AIDS experience.

The Proposed Reserving Process in Canada

The whole matter of reserves in Canada has been under review for several years, and the recognition of AIDS does add some complications to the process. The Canadian Institute of Chartered Accountants has proposed that the policy premium method (gross premium) be GAAP for Canadian life companies. Conservatism in valuation margins is significantly reduced but coupled with the reduction are very substantial requirements for appropriated surplus. It is recognized that experience will fluctuate around that contemplated by the assumption and the margin in the assumption is intended to cover mis-estimation of the mean and possible deterioration of the mean. The greater the uncertainty of the expected experience, the greater the valuation margin. However, in material prepared to date, it is likely that the maximum mortality margin proposed will be inadequate should AIDS proceed unchecked.

In a similar vein, the surplus appropriation required for mortality risks involves the application of parameters to amounts at risk. Here again, the proposed formulas recognize some contagion but not to the extent of an AIDS epidemic. Some rethinking will likely be required in this area as well.

There are many actuaries in Canada who are uncomfortable with the ramifications of the proposed method. In particular, the required changes in the legislation to accommodate this method have not been made. AIDS adds another dimension to the concerns and will likely require changes in the thinking that has taken place to date.

Federal Centre for AIDS
OTTAWA, Ontario
K1A 0L2
tel. (613) 957-1772

December 7, 1987

SURVEILLANCE UPDATE: AIDS IN CANADA

The Federal Centre for AIDS has received reports of 1405 cases which meet the surveillance case definition for AIDS (revised September 1, 1987). These include 1379 adults and 26 pediatric cases (< 15 years of age). A total of 730 deaths (52.0%) have been reported.

In this report, cases accepted for surveillance purposes which meet the revised definition but would not have been included under the previous case definition are indicated in Section VII to allow assessment of the effect of the expanded definition on the surveillance statistics.

I. All Cases

		Alive	Dead	Total
Adults	Males	638	672	1310
	Females	30	39	69
	Subtotal	668	711	1379
Children	Males	3	10	13
	Females	4	9	13
	Subtotal	7	19	26
Total		675	730	1405

Adult Cases

	Cases (%)	Deaths (% of cases)
1. Risk Factors*		
Homosexual/bisexual activity	1122 (81.4)	556 (49.6)
IV drug abuse	9 (0.7)	7 (77.8)
Both of the above	42 (3.0)	22 (52.4)
Recipient of blood/blood products	56 (4.1)	36 (64.3)
Heterosexual activity†:		
(a) origin in endemic area	73 (5.3)	52 (71.2)
(b) sexual contact with person at risk	35 (2.5)	16 (45.7)
No identified risk factors	42 (3.0)	22 (52.4)
Total	1379 (100.0)	711 (51.6)
2. Age Group (yrs)		
15–19	4 (0.3)	2 (50.0)
20–29	289 (21.0)	135 (46.7)
30–39	629 (45.6)	319 (50.7)
40–49	318 (23.1)	172 (54.1)
50 and over	137 (9.9)	83 (60.6)
Unknown	2 (0.1)	0 (0.0)
Total	1379 (100.0)	711 (51.6)
3. Primary Diagnosis		
KS without PCP	288 (20.9)	140 (48.6)
PCP without KS	763 (55.3)	378 (49.7)
Both KS and PCP	41 (3.0)	25 (61.0)
Other OI	241 (17.5)	146 (60.6)
Other malignancies	37 (2.7)	20 (54.1)
HIV wasting syndrome	6 (0.4)	2 (3.3)
HIV encephalopathy	3 (0.2)	0 (0.0)
Total	1379 (100.0)	711 (51.6)

*Risk factors listed in hierarchial order.
†Heterosexual activity includes (a) persons originating in or residing in countries with a high prevalence of HIV and where heterosexual transmission of HIV is common; and (b) persons reporting heterosexual activity with person(s) at risk of HIV infection.
Note: This applies to all risk factor breakdowns in this report.

III. Adult Males

	Cases (%)	Deaths (% of cases)
1. Risk Factors		
Homosexual/bisexual activity	1122 (85.6)	556 (49.6)
IV drug abuse	8 (0.6)	6 (75.0)
Both of the above	42 (3.2)	22 (52.4)
Recipient of blood/blood products	43 (3.3)	28 (65.1)
Heterosexual activity:		
(a) origin in endemic area	51 (3.9)	38 (74.5)
(b) sexual contact with person at risk	9 (0.7)	4 (44.4)
No identified risk factors	35 (2.7)	18 (51.4)
Total	1310 (95.0)	672 (51.3)
2. Age Group (yrs)		
15–19	4 (0.3)	2 (50.0)
20–29	264 (20.2)	122 (46.2)
30–39	606 (46.3)	305 (50.3)
40–49	311 (23.7)	167 (53.7)
50 and over	123 (9.4)	76 (61.8)
Unknown	2 (0.2)	0 (0.0)
Total	1310 (95.0)	672 (51.3)
3. Primary Diagnosis		
KS without PCP	286 (21.8)	139 (48.6)
PCP without KS	727 (55.5)	357 (49.1)
Both KS and PCP	41 (3.1)	25 (61.0)
Other OI	212 (16.2)	130 (61.3)
Other malignancies	35 (2.7)	19 (54.3)
HIV wasting syndrome	6 (0.5)	2 (3.3)
HIV encephalopathy	3 (0.2)	0 (0.0)
Total	1310 (95.0)	672 (51.3)

1120

IV. Adult Females

	Cases (%)	Deaths (% of cases)
1. Risk Factors		
IV drug abuse	1 (1.4)	1 (100.0)
Recipient of blood/blood products	13 (18.8)	8 (61.5)
Heterosexual activity:		
(a) origin in endemic area	22 (31.9)	14 (63.6)
(b) sexual contact with person at risk	26 (37.7)	12 (46.2)
No identified risk factors	7 (10.1)	4 (57.1)
Total	69 (5.0)	39 (56.5)
2. Age Group (yrs)		
15–19	0 (0.0)	0 (0.0)
20–29	25 (36.2)	13 (52.0)
30–39	23 (33.3)	14 (60.9)
40–49	7 (10.1)	5 (71.4)
50 and over	14 (20.3)	7 (50.0)
Unknown	0 (0.0)	0 (0.0)
Total	69 (5.0)	39 (56.5)
3. Primary Diagnosis		
KS without PCP	2 (2.9)	1 (50.0)
PCP without KS	36 (52.2)	21 (58.3)
Both KS and PCP	0 (0.0)	0 (0.0)
Other OI	29 (42.0)	16 (55.2)
Other malignancies	2 (2.9)	1 (50.0)
HIV wasting syndrome	0 (0.0)	0 (0.0)
HIV encephalopathy	0 (0.0)	0 (0.0)
Total	69 (5.0)	39 (56.5)

V. Pediatric Cases

	Male	Female	Total (%)
1. Risk Factors			
Perinatal transmission	11	11	22 (84.6)
Recipient of blood/blood products	2	2	4 (15.4)
Total	13	13	26 (100.0)

	Male	Female	Total (%)
2. Age Group (yrs)			
<1	4	7	11 (42.3)
1–4	6	5	11 (42.3)
5–9	3	1	4 (15.4)
10–14	0	0	0 (0.0)
Total	13	13	26 (100.0)

	Cases (%)	Deaths (%)
3. Primary Diagnosis		
PCP	9 (34.6)	7 (77.8)
LIP	5 (19.2)	3 (60.0)
CMV	5 (19.2)	5 (100.0)
Other OI	7 (26.9)	4 (80.0)
Total	26 (100.0)	19 (73.1)

VI. Geographic Distribution

Province*	Male	Female	Total (%)	Deaths	Rate/Mill.† Population (cumulative)
British Columbia	275	7	282 (20.1)	158	97.4
Alberta	77	5	82 (5.8)	43	34.9
Saskatchewan	17	0	17 (1.2)	12	16.7
Manitoba	24	0	24 (1.7)	12	22.4
Ontario	537	14	551 (39.2)	256	60.7
Quebec	360	54	414 (29.5)	233	62.9
New Brunswick	6	1	7 (0.5)	5	9.7
Nova Scotia	20	1	21 (1.5)	8	23.8
P.E.I.	1	0	1 (0.1)	1	7.9
Newfoundland	5	0	5 (0.4)	2	8.6
N.W.T.	1	0	1 (0.1)	0	19.2
Yukon	0	0	0 (0.0)	0	0.0
Total	1,323	82	1,405 (100.0)	730	55.4

*Cases are attributed to the province where onset of the illness occurred.
†Population estimates from Statistics Canada (July 1, 1985).

VII. Cases Reported by Date of Diagnosis

Year	Number of Cases	* (revised case def'n)	Number of Deaths	Case-Fatality (%)
1979	1		1	100.0
1980	3		3	100.0
1981	6		6	100.0
1982	22		22	100.0
1983 01–03	14		12	85.7
04–06	15		15	100.0
07–09	11		9	81.8
10–12	14		14	100.0
Total	54		50	92.6
1984 01–03	28		21	75.0
04–06	33		28	84.8
07–09	40		29	72.5
10–12	41		36	87.8
Total	142		114	80.3
1985 01–03	60		44	73.3
04–06	74		56	75.7
07–09	90		64	71.1
10–12	94		60	63.8
Total	318		224	70.4
1986 01–03	89		52	58.4
04–06	118		59	50.0
07–09	117		64	54.7
10–12	134		51	38.1
Total	458		226	49.3
1987 01–03	123		31	25.2
04–06	147	(1)	29	19.7
07–09	110	(7)	24	21.8
10–12	21	(1)	—	0.0
Total	401		84	20.9
Total	1405		730	52.0

*Numbers in parentheses refer to those cases that have been accepted as AIDS under the revised case definition and would not have been included previously. They are included in the total frequencies presented for cases and deaths.

1123

VIII. Frequencies over Time by Sex and Risk Factors

	Year of Diagnosis					
	pre-1983	1983	1984	1985	1986	1987
Adults						
Males	23	44	133	292	438	380
Females	6	6	5	15	18	18
Children						
Males	1	1	3	7	1	0
Females	2	3	1	4	1	2
Adult Risk Factors						
Homosexual/bisexual activity	11	31	109	255	382	334
IV drug abuse	2	0	0	0	2	5
Both of the above	1	3	4	9	9	16
Recipient of blood/blood products	1	1	1	13	23	17
Heterosexual activity:						
(a) origin in endemic area	11	11	17	16	12	6
(b) sexual contact with person at risk	3	2	4	7	11	8
No identified risk factors	0	2	3	7	17	13
Pediatric Risk Factors						
Perinatal transmission	2	4	4	9	1	2
Blood transfusion recipient	1	0	0	2	1	0

IX. Projected Cases of AIDS in Canada

Estimates of the number of new cases of AIDS that will occur in 1987–1991 have been derived using modeling techniques. Two empirical models, the logistic model and the polynomial model, have been applied to these data and estimates of new cases per year and cumulative totals are displayed below. Data used for these projections include AIDS cases reported to the FCA by September 14, 1987 and diagnosed to the end of 1986.

Year	Logistic Model		Polynomial Model	
	Cases	Cumulative	Cases	Cumulative
1987	552	1542	653	1643
1988	590	2132	890	2533
1989	604	2736	1161	3694
1990	608	3344	1469	5163
1991	609	3953	1811	6974

The number of reported cases is doubling every 13 months.

X. International Statistics

Country	Total Cases	Dead	Rate per 1,000,000†	
Canada	1,405	730	55.3	12/87
United States	47,298	26848	189.2	11/87
Total North America	48,703			
Brazil	2,013	—	14.9	09/87
Dominican Rep.	200	—	32.3	03/87
Haiti	912	88	140.3	09/87
Mexico	534	—	6.8	06/87
Remaining South and Central Americas	1,283	392	8.7	06/87
Total South and Central Americas	4,942			
Austria	93	—	12.4	06/87
Belgium	255	—	25.8	06/87
Czechoslovakia	7	—	0.4	03/87
Denmark	176	—	34.5	06/87
Finland	19	—	3.9	06/87
France	1,980	30	36.3	06/87
German Dem. Rep.	4	—	0.2	06/87
Germany	1,400	316	23.0	09/87
Greece	49	12	4.9	06/87
Hungary	5	—	0.5	06/87
Iceland	4	—	20.0	06/87
Ireland	19	—	5.3	06/87
Italy	1,025	—	17.9	08/87
Luxembourg	7	—	17.5	03/87
Malta	6	—	20.0	06/87
Netherlands	308	—	21.2	06/87
Norway	49	—	12.0	06/87
Poland	2	—	0.1	06/87
Portugal	67	—	6.6	06/87
Romania	2	—	0.1	03/87
Spain	508	—	13.2	06/87
Sweden	141	—	17.0	10/87
Switzerland	299	68	47.5	09/87
United Kingdom	1,123	624	20.0	10/87
U.S.S.R.	58	—	0.2	06/87
Yugoslavia	11	—	0.5	06/87
Total Europe	7,617			
China	2	—	0.0	04/87
China (Taiwan)	1	—	—	01/86
Cyprus	3	—	5.0	06/87
Eastern Med. Region	36	—	0.5	09/87
Hong Kong	4	—	0.7	12/86
India	9	—	0.0	05/87
Indonesia	1	—	0.0	04/87
Israel	42	—	10.0	09/87
Japan	50	13	0.4	10/87
Lebanon	3	—	1.2	06/87
Malaysia	1	—	0.1	09/87
Qatar	9	—	30.0	05/87
Rep. of Korea	1	—	0.0	04/87
Singapore	2	—	0.8	06/87
Sri Lanka	2	—	0.1	04/87
Thailand	11	—	0.2	06/87
Turkey	21	—	0.4	06/87
Total Asia	198			

X. *International Statistics — Continued*

Country	Total Cases	Dead	Rate per 1,000,000†	
Australia	648	347	41.3	11/87
New Zealand	54	—	16.4	09/87
Total Oceania	702			
Algeria	5	—	0.2	06/87
Angola	6	—	0.7	09/86
Benin	3	—	0.8	05/87
Botswana	13	—	11.8	06/87
Burundi	128	—	27.2	03/87
Cameroon	25	—	2.6	03/87
Central Africa	254	—	4.3	10/86
Chad	1	—	0.2	11/86
Congo	250	—	147.1	11/86
Cote D'Ivoire	118	—	12.0	11/86
Ethiopia	5	—	0.1	06/87
Gabon	13	—	11.8	07/87
Gambia	14	—	23.3	03/87
Ghana	145	—	10.7	05/87
Kenya	625	—	30.3	07/87
Lesotho	1	—	0.7	11/86
Liberia	2	—	1.0	06/87
Malawi	13	—	1.9	11/86
Mozambique	1	—	0.1	06/87
Nigeria	5	—	0.1	05/87
Rwanda	705	—	117.5	02/87
South Africa	81	—	2.2	09/87
Swaziland	7	—	11.7	07/87
Tanzania	1,130	—	50.4	04/87
Tunisia	2	—	0.3	05/86
Uganda	1,138	—	73.9	02/87
Zaire	335	—	11.2	06/87
Zambia	395	—	59.8	06/87
Zimbabwe	380	—	43.7	08/87
Total Africa	5,800			
Total Cases	67,962			

*Total cases reported based on currently available data.
†1985 population estimates provided by the population division of the Dept. of International Economic and Social Affairs of the United Nations Secretariat.
Source: W.H.O Surveillance Program
        CDC Weekly Surveillance Report — U.S.
        CDR — AIDS: United Kingdom
        University of New South Wales — Australia

CHAPTER 9

MANAGEMENT STRATEGIES AND THE ROLE OF THE VALUATION ACTUARY

DAVID M. HOLLAND

1. STRATEGIES FOR MANAGEMENT IN RESPONDING TO THE AIDS EPIDEMIC

The AIDS epidemic will result in billions of dollars in claims for the life and health insurance industry. Prudent management requires planning to meet the AIDS claims on in-force business and to minimize the adverse impact of AIDS on new business issued. The actuary should recognize expected losses from this epidemic in valuing the business and should discuss with management strategies for dealing with these claims. In order to assess the impact of AIDS on a particular company, it is also important for the actuary to establish procedures for accurately tracking AIDS claims. Various strategies for management are described below.

1.1 Strategies for In-Force Business

Regardless of actions taken with respect to future issues, AIDS claims will emerge on in-force business. Based on an analysis of resources and projections of the timing and level of claims, management must decide on a strategy to meet these obligations.

1.1.1 Pay As You Go

Pay as you go is the default strategy; if management takes no specific actions, the claims will be charged against earnings as they emerge. Reduced earnings will also reduce the amount available for dividends to shareholders of stock companies or for the company to keep as retained earnings. Depending on the level of claims, there may be operating losses in statutory (and GAAP) statements. Any losses will be charged against surplus. Substantial losses could result in insolvency. If the pay-as-you-go strategy is adopted, it is especially important for the actuary to keep management appraised of the possible effects of this strategy.

1.1.2 Reduce Dividends to Policyholders

Participating policies share in the results of the operations of the company. To the extent gains are reduced as a result of adverse mortality from AIDS, the amount available for distribution to policyholders will also be reduced. Experience factors such as mortality rates and claims factors are accepted elements of dividend determination (see also "Dividend Recommendations and Interpretations" of the American Academy of Actuaries). Traditionally, policyholder dividends have been reduced to reflect adverse mortality experience; consider the following from *Life Insurance* by Joseph B. MacLean (ninth edition, pp. 598–599):

> *"Epidemic*. The influenza epidemic which commenced in the fall of 1918 had a much more serious effect on the companies' mortality experience than either of the two wars. The epidemic, which was world-wide, probably accounted for more than 10 million deaths. In the United States the number of deaths directly attributable to the epidemic was estimated at more than 450,000, that is, more than 3 per 1,000 of the population. The financial effect on the life-insurance companies was greatly increased by the fact that death claims from the epidemic were mostly among the younger policyholders whose policies had been only a short time in force. The epidemic, however, affected all ages and all classes of the population and caused an increase in the companies' mortality cost of 50 to over 100 per cent. . . . The smaller and more recently organized companies, whose policyholders were mostly persons at the lower ages, were most severely affected, many of them experiencing an increase in mortality cost of considerably over 100 percent. The severity and cost of this epidemic were unprecedented in the history of life insurance and provided a striking demonstration of the necessity for adequate contingency funds. Nearly all companies found it necessary to reduce (and in some cases to eliminate) dividends on participating policies for a year or more. . . ."
>
> *"Depression*. . . The rate of interest had commenced the sustained fall which was to continue for about 15 years (until 1947). The mortality rate increased during the depression years. A feature of this increase was the large number of suicides, which rose to 30 percent above normal during the early 1930s. Much of this excess mortality was on policies of large amount. In addition, disability claims and losses had increased to such an extent that practically all companies had either abandoned the disability-income coverage or radically altered its terms. These unfavorable elements led to many reductions in dividends, which in most cases were the first reductions in 10 years or more. Premium rates for nonparticipating policies were also generally increased to reflect the lower interest rates obtainable."

When dividend decreases are considered, a number of questions relating to equity amongst classes of policyholders must be considered. One consideration is whether to charge additional mortality to the affected groups only or to spread the effects over all ages and both sexes. Another issue is whether only past experience will be reflected or if anticipated sharp future increases in mortality should be anticipated. Also, there is the question of adjusting only the mortality component of the dividend formula versus an overall lowering of dividends.

1.1.3 Increase Premiums or Other Nonguaranteed Charges Where Permitted

For products for which the current premium is not guaranteed, it may be possible to increase the premium actually being charged to reflect additional mortality from AIDS. Premiums may be increased for certain ordinary life products, group life products, guaranteed renewable health products, and collectively renewable health products. For products such as Universal Life, charges for the cost of insurance and interest loads may be revised to the extent permitted. Although this strategy sounds straightforward, it may be difficult to implement. Increasing premiums to anticipate losses may result in lapses by those individuals who are in better health and can get a cheaper rate from another company. Thus, this option should not be considered lightly, but in the event the impact of AIDS on mortality becomes severe, many products do provide this most important tool for responding to adverse mortality results.

1.1.4 Renewal Actions

Products that are periodically renewable on nonguaranteed terms present opportunities for action to reflect increased experience costs such as AIDS mortality. For example, group insurance is often written on a one-year term basis with the company having the option to reprice or terminate coverage each year. Although credit insurance rates are generally regulated, this is often a short-term coverage, and the company could decide to get out of this market or file for a rate deviation if experience is adverse. Many health insurance products also present opportunities for renewal actions in which the insurance company could adjust for its exposure to extra AIDS costs.

1.1.5 Prefund Additional Claims via Extra Reserves

When faced with future contingent payouts that can be estimated, traditional actuarial methodology has been to establish reserves to provide for those payouts. It is possible to project the present value of future AIDS claims and to include this amount in reserves. However, because of the uncertain future of the long-term course of the AIDS epidemic, it would be desirable to have the flexibility to strengthen reserves over time as experience emerges. It is expected that the impact of AIDS will be realized over many years, and thus there is time to spread out the cost.

1.2 Strategies for New Business

1.2.1 Risk Selection and Classification

Risk classification is an integral part of the life and health insurance process. Companies must be able to select risks if they are going to be able to price adequately and equitably. The expected mortality for someone who is infected with Human Immunodeficiency Virus (HIV) is extremely high. Companies must be able to test for infection with HIV or else they will be faced with the ultimate risk classification question of whether or not they can continue to accept any new business. There is no reason to consider AIDS and HIV infection differently from other high-risk conditions. With respect to specific risk classification issues, refer to the American Academy of Actuaries statement on "Risk Classification and AIDS."

1.2.2 Repricing

To the extent AIDS claims are anticipated on future new business, the acutary should consider this extra mortality in product pricing. Some jurisdictions do not permit the use of AIDS antibody tests, such as ELISA with confirmation by a Western Blot test; in some of those jurisdictions alternative tests that are not as effective (for example, T-cell ratio tests) are permitted. Pricing may need to vary by the efficacy of testing in such instances. Even with testing for HIV infection as part of the risk selection process, some new insureds will become infected after issue, and this extra mortality should be provided for. In cases in which the policy provides for both guaranteed maximum premiums and current premiums, an increase in the guaranteed premium would provide room for further revision in the event of adverse experience.

1.2.3 Product Evolution

Product evolution is a natural process particularly when facing adverse experience. Companies will have to decide if basic changes to policy terms and conditions can improve results in light of AIDS. For example, to dampen the effect of mortality fluctuation, there may be more emphasis on longer term plans with higher premiums than on competitive term products. There may also be more interest in policies that are issued for short periods of time and for which there is no guarantee of renewal or conversion; such products could be completely reunderwritten if continuation of coverage is desired. There has been discussion of policy provisions such as an AIDS exclusion if evidence of HIV-free status is not provided at the time of underwriting; however, serious concerns have been expressed about the efficacy and desirability of an AIDS exclusion provision. In light of the long-term uncertainty regarding the impact of AIDS, products that charge a competitive current premium but that have the right to increase the premium at the option of the company should be attractive to the consumer but yet provide the company with the flexibility to increase premiums in the event mortality experience warrants such an action.

1.2.4 Reserving Procedures

Additonal reserves may be required to reflect the impact of AIDS. These reserves should be considered in pricing and profitability tests of new products. Possible approaches for developing reserves are discussed in subsequent portions of this chapter.

1.2.5 Reinsurance

When companies are uncertain of the ultimate level of mortality of a product, they often will seek a reinsurer to share the mortality risk. By reducing the amount retained on any one life, the direct company is also reducing the potential impact of excess claims. Such reinsurance may be used to transfer the risk of excess mortality from AIDS for in-force business as well as new business. It must be recognized that reinsurers are also susceptible to adverse experience from AIDS, possibly even more so than direct companies. Financial stability should be a key criterion in selecting a reinsurer. In addition, reinsurers cannot be the permanent loss absorbers for the insurance industry, but must be able to follow the fortunes of ceding companies, particularly in areas such as premium increases on in-force business as a response to adverse mortality experience.

In addition to traditional risk reinsurance, certain reinsurers are also developing special reinsurance programs that would cover risks such as catastrophic mortality including AIDS; advance funding via reinsurance may also result in financial advantages to the ceding company. Care should be taken by ceding companies that long-term commitments on the direct side are not supported by short-term reinsurance coverage such as a stop loss cover that is cancelable at the option of the reinsurer and can thus be withdrawn when it is needed most.

1.2.6 Discontinuance of a Product Line

It may be that for some products, even changes in risk classification, pricing, and product design will not be sufficient to ensure that the product line can be written on a self-supporting basis. In this case, there should be serious consideration of whether or not to continue marketing of the product.

2. AIDS AND THE RESPONSIBILITY OF THE U.S. VALUATION ACTUARY

2.1   The Responsibility of the Valuation Actuary

In accordance with current requirements, the annual statement of a U.S. life insurance company must contain the opinion of a qualified actuary relating to the policy reserves and other actuarial items. The annual statement instructions state:

> "The Opinion paragraph should indicate that, in the actuary's opinion, the reserves and other actuarial items. . . make a good and sufficient provision for all unmatured obligations of the company guaranteed under the terms of its policies. . . ."

The Valuation Actuary in the U.S. must consider "Recommendation 7: Statement of Actuarial Opinion for Life Insurance Company Statutory Annual Statements" of the American Academy of Actuaries. This recommendation states:

> "In those instances wherein. . . the statutory reserves might not make good and sufficient provision for unmatured obligations, then the actuary should make further tests (possibly by a gross premium valuation as described in general terms below) before expressing an opinion as to such policy reserves and other actuarial items.
> "A gross Premium valuation may be made for an entire line of business or a major block of business. The results of such a gross premium valuation for a line or block of business are considered satisfactory for this purpose if the current reserve on the reserve basis being tested provides an appropriate margin over the excess of:
> (a) the then present value of future benefits and anticipated expenses, [over]
> (b) the then present value of future guaranteed gross premiums using interest, mortality, morbidity, lapse, expense and any other appropriate assumptions selected as of the valuation date reflecting actual and anticipated experience. . . ."

2.2   *Recognizing the Impact of AIDS in Valuations*

AIDS presents the Valuation Actuary with problems:

- Pricing and reserve standards at the time of issue of in-force business probably did not anticipate the AIDS risk.
- Margins that may have been included were included for a variety of adverse scenarios and cannot be fully allocated to AIDS without creating potential for failure to cover adverse deviation from these other scenarios.
- Since there is a long latency period with HIV infection, adverse AIDS claims are expected to emerge over time with increasing significance.
- Knowledge about the true impact of AIDS is still emerging.

Nevertheless, AIDS is a grim reality, and there is very little reason for optimism regarding a short-term eradication of the epidemic. The impact of the disease in the short run is becoming measurable, especially given that a large number of people are already infected with HIV. Accordingly, the Valuation Actuary should consider the impact of AIDS in determining whether or not the reserves make good and sufficient provision for guarantees provided.

The gross premium valuation process can be used to test the impact of AIDS. A gross premium valuation using traditional methods and assumptions could be performed without special consideration of AIDS. Additional AIDS claims could then be projected using methods as described elsewhere in this report. These additional AIDS claims could be used to adjust the results of the traditional gross premium valuation. The results of a gross premium valuation may range from the conclusion that the funds currently held are adequate to the conclusion that substantial losses can be anticipated already and should be provided for.

Gross-premium-type tests of certain plans performed by the Task Force produced somewhat problematic results. In some cases, gross premium valuations showed profits in the early years that dwindle down to break-even results for a few years and are ultimately followed by significant losses in the later years. For these cases, it is the responsibility of the actuary to describe this situation to management and to develop a strategy for making adequate provision for later years when significant losses are expected to emerge. This may result in the need for additional reserves or the development of targeted surplus.

Various questions arise regarding the selection of appropriate assumptions for a gross premium valuation and the recognition of the impact of strategies selected by management in responding to the AIDS epidemic (for example, the use of "guaranteed" premiums as provided by the Academy Recommendation or the use of "current" premiums if there is no intention of increasing current premiums to the guaranteed level). Further work is needed on reserve techniques for valuing the impact of AIDS. Some possible reserve techniques are discussed subsequently, but until other methods are developed the gross premium valuation is an accepted standard.

2.3 AIDS Reserves vs. Targeted Surplus

A natural question is whether the impact of AIDS should be provided for as a reserve or as targeted surplus. The opinion of the actuary in the U.S. relates to "reserves and other actuarial items" or "policy reserves and related actuarial items." In addition to reserves, the items in the actuarial opinion usually include net deferred and uncollected premiums and policy and contract claims. Surplus is not explicitly specified as an item covered by the actuarial opinion.

A number of people would argue that the actuarial opinion does not and should not relate to surplus. Excerpts from the "Report of the Task Force on the Valuation Actuary to the ACLI Board of Directors, August 1986" were included in *The Valuation Actuary Handbook* published by the Society of Actuaries in June 1987. In discussing the evolution of the Valuation Actuary concept in the U.S., this ACLI Task Force recommended:

". . . the ACLI oppose any regulatory requirements that the valuation actuary report on the adequacy of surplus. . . ."

A further condition on the ACLI's overall support of the Valuation Actuary concept was:

"The regulatory authorities would be no more involved in the oversight of company surplus levels than they are at the present time. . . ."

An interesting topic for debate might be "if the actuary is not supposed to report on the adequacy of surplus overall, is it proper for the actuary to render an opinion regarding surplus targeted for special contingencies such as AIDS?" This raises many questions regarding the nature of surplus and the actuary's opinion that are beyond the scope of this report on AIDS. However, the current requirement is that if "reserves and other actuarial items" are inadequate, the actuary's opinion should be qualified; a consistent interpretation would then require the provision for AIDS to be included in "reserves and other actuarial items."

2.4   *The Evolving Role of the Valuation Actuary*

The concept of the Valuation Actuary is undergoing evolution in the U.S. The responsibility is already much broader than the rote application of statutory reserve standards to a block of business and is becoming broader than the gross premium standard defined above. In recent discussions regarding the Valuation Actuary, various classes of risk have been enumerated as C-1 (asset default), C-2 (pricing inadequacy), C-3 (interest fluctuations), and C-4 (accounting risks not otherwise reflected). Writing in "A Potential Approach to Valuation of Reserves and Surplus in Statutory Financial Statements" (*The Valuation Actuary Handbook*), Donald D. Cody defines the C-2 risk as follows:

> "*C-2 Risk*: Losses from increases in claims and expenses and from pricing deficiencies, other than those from C-1 and C-3 risks. This is a large and varied category of classic concern by actuaries: Increases in aggregate death claims, disability claims, medical claims; decreases in annuitant deaths; epidemics and earthquakes; accidental catastrophes; inflated expenses; irrecoverable expenditures on products and systems; increased expense rates from inefficiency. Provision for smaller ('reasonable') deviations from expected should be made in reserves. But large ('plausible') deviations are matters for surplus provision; and losses from earthquakes, epidemics and magnitude increases in annuitant life expectancies are exclusively matters for surplus."

In discussing deviations in death claims other than stochastic deviations in total claims, Mr. Cody states:

> "Epidemics (e.g., influenza, AIDS), earthquakes, and quantum changes in life expectancy affecting life annuity losses are matters solely for surplus provision and not for reserve provision. They should be handled by appropriate scenarios of plausible deviations corresponding to ruin probability p_2, with offsets for tolerable reductions in policyholder dividends and credits, stockholder dividends, and retained earnings" (ibid, p. VI–25).

At the time the preceding quotes were originally written, there was very little information on the ultimate impact and long-term nature of the AIDS epidemic. Based on discussions within the Task Force and with a number of Valuation Actuaries, including Mr. Cody, the consensus is that surplus is to provide for *future* catastrophic events of an unknown nature. But once the event occurs and the impact of it becomes reasonably measurable, then it is appropriate to provide for this extra risk via reserves rather than surplus. For example, a sharp downturn in investment return is a risk that is covered by surplus; however, once such an event occurs, then reserve strengthening is an appropriate response. This interest downturn scenario actually occurred in the late 1930s, and the response was to strengthen reserves (see "The Strengthening of Reserves" in *Transactions of the Actuarial Society of America,* Volume XLV, pp. 297–342).

3. RESPONDING TO CHANGE UNDER THE TRADITIONAL VALUATION ENVIRONMENT

In the current U.S. environment for statutory valuation, standards are specified that are generally expected to be adequate for a large number of situations; in the event that there is concern about adequacy, the question of developing new standards should be considered. However, new standards do not generally apply to in-force business, and for in-force, reserve strengthening may need to be considered. Both of these concepts are discussed further in this section.

3.1   New Valuation Tables and Mortality Projection Scales

Valuation mortality tables include an element of conservatism and are presumed to be a safe valuation basis across a wide spectrum of companies. Accordingly, valuations using statutory tables have typically made good and sufficient provision for unmatured obligations, at least from the expected mortality perspective. The general trend over most of the twentieth century has been for mortality improvement, and for life insurance, this means that the need for revisions in valuation mortality tables has not been driven by mortality deterioration.

However, it now appears that with AIDS there will be a deterioration at least at certain ages. As an alternative to developing the necessary increase in reserves for AIDS via gross premium valuation, consideration should be given to the development of a new valuation table. There have been a number of developments following the 1970–75 experience period underlying the development of the 1980 CSO Table including substantial improvements in mortality at certain ages.

Developing a new valuation table is a major undertaking in general and is beyond the scope of this Task Force. There will be a number of additional challenges in determining how to recognize the impact of AIDS in a new valuation table. Because the impact of AIDS is expected to be of increasing significance year by year, the tables may need to be in select and ultimate form to reflect this degradation by year. Also, because of the change over time, it may be necessary to develop new valuation tables more frequently than in the past; for example, it may be necessary to develop new tables every five years or so. The net result practically becomes a series of generation tables.

As an alternative to the development of series of new tables, it may be possible to develop mortality projection scales that can be used to update an initial table. Mortality projection scales have been an accepted technique for annuities for some time. Also, projection scales have been used to provide flexibility to reflect individual company characteristics as well as future trends in mortality. Also, projection scales by their nature can define "generation" mortality tables as are needed to reflect the impact of AIDS over time.

As an historical example of use of mortality projection scales, consider the 1971 Individual Annuity Mortality (IAM) Table whose development is described in *The Transactions of the Society of Actuaries (TSA)*, Volume XXIII. The 1971 IAM was considered to be a "safe" table for the valuation of all types of annuities based on 1971 levels of mortality and was proposed as a valuation standard without projection. However, its developers observed:

> "We feel that the minimum valuation standard should continue to allow flexibility with regard to provision for future decreases in mortality, since there are wide differences of opinion as to how future mortality levels will change over a long period of years. . . . The judgment of different companies with respect to provision for future mortality improvements will vary not only because of differences of opinion with regard to the average long-term trends but also because of differences in the nature and composition of annuity business sold by specific companies and differences in their actual past experience." (*TSA, XXIII,* pp. 518–519)

The sections of the Standard Valuation Law in the U.S. dealing with annuities specify certain valuation mortality tables and go on to say "or any modification of these tables approved by the Commissioner...." Presumably, the modification could be the application of a mortality projection scale.

For ordinary insurance, there is no specific reference to a "modification" of a valuation table; however, a new table could also be determined as a modification or projection of an existing table. The 1980 amendments to the Standard Valuation Law provide an option (for business issued after the effective date of Section five-c of the Standard Nonforfeiture Law) of

> "any ordinary mortality table, adopted after 1980 by the National Association of Insurance Commissioners, that is approved by regulation promulgated by the commissioner for use in determining the minimum standard of valuation for such policies."

The Task Force recommends that the possibility of developing new ordinary life valuation tables, possibly including mortality projection scales, be addressed by an appropriate committee of the Society. Because new valuation tables generally apply only to new issues after an effective date, some other approach may be needed to strengthen reserves for in-force business.

3.2   *Strengthening of Reserves*

Additional reserves that are required because of gross premium valuations that indicate that the statutory tabular reserves do not make good and sufficient provision for future unmatured obligations, result in a *de facto* strengthening of reserves. Reserve strengthening for in-force business was a major actuarial topic at the time Guertin wrote his *TASA* XLV paper on "The Strengthening of Reserves"; this paper is well worth consideration even though it deals with the need for strengthening due to a decline in interest yields. Guertin indicates that there does not have to be a quantum jump in reserve from one level to another; he indicates that

"Ordinarily, the change would be made in steps of 1/4 percent or 1/2 percent, so that over a period of several years the required rate will have been dropped by the full fraction contemplated."

He even indicates that reserves at irregular interest rates could also be used in this grading process.

Guertin points out that although reserve-strengthening programs are typically thought of in terms of adopting a new valuation basis as if it had been the valuation basis at issue, other approaches are possible. For example, given an actual reserve as of a specified date, a new net premium could be calculated on the basis of the new valuation assumptions to fund the present value of future benefits net of the existing reserve over the remaining duration of the policy.

The regulatory reaction to allow reserve strengthening to occur over a period of years appears to be a very pragmatic approach. There are elements of the current situation with respect to AIDS that also call for pragmatic consideration. By the nature of the data available, it is not possible to have an extremely high level of confidence in long-term mortality projections regarding AIDS. Thus, for this situation, consideration should be given to programs that allow for reserve strengthening to occur over time as the nature of the extra mortality emerges.

In the appendixes to this chapter, two approaches are set out for general information. Neither approach is being proposed for adoption. Until there is some change in accepted practice, the responsibility of the Valuation Actuary in rendering an opinion about the reserves and other actuarial liabilities will continue to have the gross premium valuation as set out by the Academy as the ultimate test.

APPENDIX 1 – AN AIDS MORTALITY RESERVE

In order to test current reserves, a gross premium valuation reflecting AIDS may be prepared. One approach would be to prepare the gross premium valuation using mortality that has been modified to take the impact of AIDS into account. Another approach may be to prepare a gross premium valuation without regard to AIDS and to adjust the results of that valuation by adjusting for additional mortality as a result of AIDS.

In lieu of performing special tests, some actuaries may want to consider the establishment of an AIDS Mortality Reserve as generally set out below. Note that this is not being recommended as a standard of practice but is included as a possible approach that should be investigated further.

Let AMR_t = AIDS Mortality Reserve at time t

then

$$AMR_{t+1} = (AMR_t + LC_t)*(1 + j_t) - AM_t$$

where

LC_t = Level (annual) cost for AIDS mortality
j_t = Net interest earned during year t
AM_t = Actual AIDS mortality during year t that is, actual AIDS claims).

LC_t should be calculated as follows:

$$LC_t = (PVAM_t - AMR_t)/\ddot{a}_{\overline{n}|i}$$

where
$PVAM_t$ = The present value of AIDS mortality calculated at time t.

An annuity due at interest rate i, payable for n years certain is given by

$$\ddot{a}_{\overline{n}|i}$$

The value for n should be large enough so that there is a reasonable period to accumulate the necessary reserve but not so large that the accumulation is deferred indefinitely. Initially, a value of n of from 15 to 20 is suggested.

AIDS claims could be determined in accordance with models set out in other parts of this report and discounted at either interest or interest and survivorship. Because the present value of AIDS claims ($PVAM$) would be redetermined each year, the reserve would be automatically updated for revisions regarding the impact of the AIDS epidemic.

By subtracting actual mortality (AM) for AIDS, in determining the reserve, the reserve would be written down as actual AIDS claims emerge and thus would match the reserve release with the time the excess mortality is incurred. The minimum value of the catastrophic mortality reserve could be set at zero.

Similarly, the level cost (LC) could go negative if AIDS experience improves so much that the present value of future claims is less than the reserve on hand. This would be the natural mechanism for gradually running off the reserve if experience improves.

In developing the AIDS mortality reserve, due consideration should be given to strategies adopted by management in providing funds to meet future AIDS claims. For example, if the gross premium valuation did not reflect management's decision to take actions such as revising dividends because of AIDS, this could be brought into consideration in calculating the AIDS mortality reserve.

A number of refinements could be applied to this approach such as the use of net amount at risk rather than face amount. Another refinement would be to provide only for the AIDS mortality in excess of otherwise expected mortality. Again, this approach is not being proposed as recommended for anything other than further consideration as a pragmatic approach to dealing with expected AIDS mortality.

APPENDIX 2 — THE APPROACH USED BY THE INSTITUTE OF ACTUARIES

The Institute of Actuaries' AIDS Working Party published "AIDS Bulletins" in September and December 1987. "Bulletin No. 1" included various projections of the possible impact of AIDS on insurance mortality; Projection A had the highest extra mortality and Projection F the lowest. Yet Projection A should not be considered highly pessimistic especially should there be a widespread expansion into the heterosexual community. "Bulletin No. 1" concluded that extra mortality from AIDS can be expected to be related to both age and calendar year; this greatly complicates modifying existing valuation mortality tables in that a separate generation table would be required for each year of birth.

"Bulletin No. 2" included, among other topics, recommendations regarding reserving for AIDS. This Bulletin indicated:

"Nevertheless, we are satisfied that the assumptions underlying Projection F are sufficiently moderate for it to be essential for insurance companies to have regard to the possibility of an incidence of HIV infection at least at this level. On the basis of information already available, there [is] no reason to delay making changes to reserves and to pricing structures to take this into account. At this level, there should not be any reliance placed on the presence of a solvency margin, which is needed to provide some protection against more adverse scenarios.

"We do not envisage, on the other hand, that companies need establish technical reserves at this stage to enable them to cope with a situation such as that described by Projection A, neither would it be sensible, nor commercially viable, to establish non-profit premium rates now on such pessimistic assumptions. Companies should, however, examine the possible implications of such a pessimistic scenario, particularly with regard to finding out whether the total resources available to the company, including margins in valuation bases, surplus carried forward, reserves and shareholders' funds, would be adequate to enable the company to survive, allowing for new business written on guaranteed premium terms over the next few years."

A net premium approach was used to determine the reserves needed to cover AIDS exposure. "Old" basis reserves and net premiums were calculated based on the mortality assumptions excluding loading for AIDS and other assumptions regarding interest, dividends, etc. "New" basis reserves were calculated using the additional mortality loading for AIDS but using the "old" basis net premiums. The excess of the "new" basis reserves over the "old" basis reserves was taken as the extra reserve required for AIDS.

Even though companies start out using Projection F (low), they recommend that companies develop a strategy for further strengthening reserves over the next year or two to a more moderate projection they call "BC."

The additional reserves using these bases appear to be quite substantial. Consider the following per thousand extra reserves at issue for policies issued in 1988 to an individual age 30:

Projection	F	BC	A
20-Year Term	7.32	13.06	22.21
Whole Life	8.69	15.38	25.90

This net premium approach and underlying U.K. valuation assumptions should be studied for information purposes. However, the purpose of this appendix is *not* to recommend this approach for adoption in the U.S. environment, but rather to make people aware of what is being done in other countries.

CHAPTER 10

WHAT IS A COMPANY TO DO?

BARBARA J. LAUTZENHEISER

The purpose of this paper is to provide the actuary with a summary of the prior chapters of the Society of Actuaries' AIDS Task Force report to enable him or her to alert company management to the fact that AIDS will have an impact on all life and health insurance companies, to better estimate the extent of that impact, and to provide a prescription for possible future actions that could lessen that impact.

By its very nature, this chapter deals with matters that are more practical than theoretical, in the hope that some of the directions will help management focus on an appropriate response to the impact of HIV infection and AIDS.

1.0 HIV INFECTION AND AIDS IMPACT ON ALL LIFE AND HEALTH INSURANCE COMPANIES

Information about HIV infection and AIDS has grown rapidly over the last few years. The more that is learned, the more there is concern about the initially slow and then rapid progression from infection to AIDS, the mortality and morbidity of the disease, its level of entrance into the heterosexual population, and its financial impact on life and health insurance companies.

Claims levels of many insurance companies are currently low. This, however, is not surprising because of the slowness of the progression of the disease. According to the San Francisco City Clinic (SFCC) Study, three years after infection with HIV, only 4 percent of those infected have AIDS. By year 5, 14 percent to 15 percent have AIDS, and by year 9, 45 percent have AIDS. Each year after infection, percentages have continued to climb. Thus, in spite of the fact that AIDS claims are not large and may even seem small, it is only because what is seen today is the result of HIV infections from years ago. What is seen today is only the beginning of the slowly increasing curve of progression from infection to AIDS. Insurance companies cannot wait until claims are large and use only those claims to quantify their impact, because by then it is too late to do something. Companies must take action today to minimize the impact tomorrow. Those insurance companies that do nothing will experience a growing financial impact with little or no control over their ability to moderate that impact.

1143

Just as there is certainty that a company will be financially impacted, there is also certainty that that impact will differ from that of other companies. Each company must determine, therefore, its financial impact, review possible strategies for actions, and implement those determined as most appropriate.

1.1   *Knowledge about the Disease and Its Impact*

Much has been learned about HIV infection and AIDS since the first known cases were reported in the U.S. in 1981. Unfortunately, as more information has been recorded, analyzed, and reported, the effects of the disease have shown it to have even greater impact and a longer duration of impact than originally thought. For example, as time has passed, studies of the progression from infection to AIDS continue to show the percentages going up. In January of 1986, the Centers for Disease Control (CDC) stated that 5 percent to 19 percent of those infected had been observed to progress to AIDS in 2 to 5 years. In June 1986, the Public Health Service published an estimate of 20 percent to 30 percent in 5½ years; in July 1986, the National Institutes of Health estimated the figure to be 35 percent in 6 to 8 years; the National Academy of Sciences, in October 1986, estimated 25 percent to 50 percent within 5 to 10 years; and the SFCC study, in mid-1987, estimated 14 percent to 15 percent in 5 years, 22 percent to 25 percent in 6 years, and 33 percent to 36 percent in 7 years. The latest data from the SFCC study show 45 percent progressing to AIDS within 9 years of infection.

As a result of this latter study, the following observations were reported:

Paul O'Malley, director of the research project at the SFCC, was quoted in the *Orange County Register*, February 29, 1987, as saying: "What we're seeing now is that the risk of actually developing AIDS increases in the second five years compared to the first five years."

The New York Times of March 3, 1987, quoted Dr. George Rutherford, also of the SFCC, as saying: "The longer one is infected, the higher are the chances of developing AIDS."

In the same *Times* article, Dr. Harold S. Jaffe, an AIDS epidemiologist at the CDC, working on the study with the San Francisco Health Department, said they were unable to identify any factor other than time that triggers the onset of the disease.

Major Robert Redfield of the Walter Reed Army Institute of Research, in his presentation to the Society of Actuaries 1987 annual meeting, stated that 90 percent of those in their study progressed to AIDS over time.

Dr. James Mason, director of the CDC, indicated in his presentation to the 1987 annual meeting of the American Council of Life Insurance that "a figure approaching

100 percent of those infected will develop symptoms of this disease that is invariably fatal. . ."

The mortality rate for the known cases has also been studied and documented in the 1987 paper by Michael J. Cowell and Walter H. Hoskins, "AIDS, HIV Mortality and Life Insurance" (Chapter 3 of this report). From the time AIDS is diagnosed, mortality rates of 45 percent in the first year, 45 percent in the second year, 35 percent in the third year, and 25 percent in each year thereafter were determined. The average life expectancy of someone with AIDS is only 2.1 years. Combining progression rates projected from the study by the Center for Internal Medicine of the University of Frankfurt in West Germany and these mortality rates, Cowell and Hoskins produced mortality rates for persons newly infected with HIV of 19 percent for 5 years, 55 percent for 10 years, 77 percent for 15 years, 90 percent for 20 years, and 96 percent for 25 years. Using these combined rates produces an average life expectancy of 11 years for a 35-year-old newly infected male compared to an almost 43-year life expectancy for a healthy male age 35. The mortality of this 35-year-old male who newly tests positive for HIV is in excess of 5000 percent of standard, based on the 1980 CSO male non-smoker table, if it were a level equivalent multiple of that table. As such, this level of mortality is ten times higher than the highest substandard rate generally considered insurable by companies today. The mortality, however, is not a level multiple of standard, because of the slow progression and then sharp increase from HIV infection to AIDS, making its impact even more severe.

Also known is the fact that the disease has a very long latency period. That, too, extends longer as time and knowledge of the disease increase. In 1986, the Public Health Service stated that there was an average 4-year latency period. In November 1987, Dr. Mason stated:

". . .after 9 years of observation, only about 45 percent of those individuals (cohorts infected and studied) have developed symptoms which would enable us to classify their disease as AIDS."

Thus, the average latency period may be even longer than 9 years.

What also is known is that the disease is most prominent at the sexually active ages. AIDS has been thought of as a young person's disease; however, a more accurate description is that it is a disease that is prominent at the sexually active ages. Consistently, 21 percent of the cases have been between the ages of 20 and 29, and 46 percent are between 30 and 39. However, almost one-third are 40 or over (21 percent are between 40 and 49, and 10 percent are over 49). The remaining 1 percent are children under the age of 5. Although through the end of 1987 there were some 300 cases diagnosed in children between the ages of 5 and 19, they did not even constitute 1 percent of the cases. Major Redfield has stated that "the most important variable is age for a sexually transmitted disease."

1.2   Knowledge Not Yet Known, But of Concern, about the Disease

Preliminary information is also available that, although not yet fully developed, is sufficiently credible and of such concern as to warrant consideration. The vast majority of our data comes from observation of males (93 percent of adult cases—that is, those 13 and above—are males). The limited data we have on women with AIDS indicate they are dying more quickly than men with AIDS. Males also have different mortality depending on the opportunistic disease they acquire. Estimates of entrance of the infection into the heterosexual population range from minimal to substantial.

Occupational data are not available from the CDC, but individual disability income data from 16 companies, representing 60 percent of the new individual disability premium issued in 1986 and 60 percent of the individual disability premium in force at the end of 1986, showed insured data may not be indicative of population data. In terms of monthly indemnity, the highest percentages of AIDS claims were in four occupations: doctors (31.9 percent), dentists (12.1 percent), executives (7.8 percent), and attorneys (4.6 percent).

Unfortunately, these data have the potential of aggravating rather than alleviating the impact of the disease on the insured population. As such, they increase a company's need not only to initially determine the financial impact of the disease, but also to continue to do so.

1.3   Knowledge about the Disease That Must Be Estimated

In addition, there is other information that is not known and that may never be known; it can be estimated, however. Two such numbers are the level of infection in the general population and in the insured population. Estimates for the general population are as low as 300,000 and as high as 3,000,000, with even greater divergence of projections into 1991 and 2000. The most current numbers available are the latest Public Health Service estimates of 945,000 to 1,400,000.

Although the exact prevalence of the infection is not known, the spread of AIDS is. As of year-end 1987 no state had fewer than fives cases, only five states added less than a dozen cases in 1987, and only 12 states had no cases on children. Analysis of detailed data on all cases reported to the CDC by the end of the third quarter of 1987 also indicated that the rate of spread is significantly higher than the national average in areas where current prevalence is lower than the national average, that is, in the Central SMSA, the Mid-Atlantic SMSA, and among people living in the SMSA of one million or less inhabitants.

1.4   Legislative and Regulatory Effect on Impact

In addition, legislative and/or regulatory activity banning AIDS testing, or prohibiting asking questions regarding prior AIDS testing, limiting the amount levels at which AIDS testing can be done, requiring added costs of specialized informed consent forms or pre- or postcounseling for all who are tested, as well as the cost of AIDS testing itself, will all have an impact on the mortality, morbidity, and expense factors that enter all new business issued currently and in the future. This, too, must be addressed and its potential impact quantified.

1.5   Need To Quantify the Financial Impact of the Disease

All these data indicate that life and health companies have been and will continue to be impacted by HIV infection and AIDS. Also, because of the nature of this disease—that is, its long latency period causing its "invisible" spread—there will be no company whose impact from HIV infection will not have the potential of a significant increase in the future. The slow progression from infection to AIDS means companies cannot estimate the future by looking only at the past or even at today. Like looking at a star, by the time its light reaches our eyes, its impact has long since been established and is unchangeable. Looking only at a company's current or past claims is not an adequate determination of the future impact of HIV infection and AIDS.

The impact on each company has been differing and will continue to differ because of the company's marketing and underwriting actions. The impact is also affected by the ages at which business was and is written, the geographic areas in which the company markets and the extent of the business written in each area, the lines of business (for example, individual, group, or credit for life, health, or disability income), the products written within each line (for example, whole life, universal life, term, major medical, hospital indemnity, or long-term disability), the underwriting limits at which

AIDS testing has been and is being done, and how soon the limits were introduced and reduced. Indicative of this is that the impact of AIDS in 1986 on some companies has been less than 0.5 percent of total ordinary life claims in some companies, but over 4 percent of ordinary life claims in others.

Therefore, a detailed analysis of these factors—past, present, and expected in the future, as well as current claims experience and the reasons it is at the level that it is—is necessary to obtain an objective, quantitative measurement of the impact on a company.

2.0 NEED TO ADDRESS THE IMPACT FROM A COMPANY-WIDE PERSPECTIVE

Because those elements that impact the cost of HIV infection and AIDS to a life and health insurance company and the actions to minimize that cost cross so many lines, it is important to address the impact from a company-wide perspective. One of the ways to accomplish this is to establish a task force, comprised of all the specialties, to address the concerns in a total cohesive manner. These specialties include actuarial, underwriting, claims administration, sales, legal, medical, public relations, and government relations. If a task force is not formed, the person(s) responsible for the analysis should nonetheless address all these areas.

2.1   Responsibilities of the Task Force of Person(s) Charged with the Analysis

This task force of person(s) should be charged with:

- The quantification and determination of the impact on the company.
- The review and determination of the appropriate management strategies and actions that should be taken.
- The communication of the impact and recommended strategies and actions to top management.
- The pressing for approval from top management of the action steps necessary to reduce and minimize the impact.
- The implementation of the approved actions.
- The ongoing redetermination of the impact following the company's actions and as changes in knowledge about the disease become known.

2.2   Benefits of a Task Force Approach

With all specialties represented, several benefits arise:

- Quantification of the impact will be better because of utilization of the knowledge and perspectives of all the specialties involved to establish the assumptions to be used, because quantifications will require determinations to be made about the underwriting standards, product mix, age, geographic mix, etc. of the business, as well as a determination of probable legislative actions on testing availability. A detailed analysis of past claims experience will also be necessary.

- Coordination of the project through the task force will facilitate the expediency and efficiency of the quantification of the impact, the determination of strategies to minimize the impact, and the implementation of actions arising from these strategies.
- Determination of the management strategies through the task force, especially in coordination with sales, also produces more balanced results. There are risks of over-conservatism as well as under-conservatism. Actions may be necessary on new business underwriting to maintain pricing competitiveness and on new business pricing to maintain adequacy. Such changes should be communicated to the field force and consumers in such a way as to explain their necessity because of fairness and in such a way as not to create undue concern.

  Abrupt, substantial pricing increases may also cause even more severe antiselection. When prices increase quickly and dramatically, it is more difficult to attract the better risks and to sell more and larger policies. This causes not only an increase in mortality and morbidity costs but also an increase in fixed expenses per policy, because fewer policies will be sold over which these expenses can be spread. What then results is the need for yet another price increase. If this continues over time, prices continue to rise, leading to the traditional assessment spiral.

  Overly conservative actions taken by companies selling participating and non-guaranteed premium policies can create an in-force problem as well from excess lapses. All the pricing competitiveness considerations identified above can affect the nonguaranteed premium and/or the dividends on in-force policies. If these premiums increase sharply and substantially or the dividends decrease dramatically, a larger number of policies could lapse. As with new business, better mortality and morbidity risks may not persist, fixed expense unit costs may rise, and sales costs may be impacted. In addition, unrecovered acquisition expenses will no longer be recoverable. Once again, an assessment spiral could occur.

- Recognition of any needed action and implementation of that action are facilitated because of the awareness of the issues involved and their impact on the company by all the areas of the company through their representatives on the task force.

3.0 DETERMINATION OF THE FINANCIAL IMPACT

The financial impact should be determined for both the in-force business and the new business. At a minimum, in the U.S., determinations need to be made for fulfillment of the U.S. Life Insurance Company Annual Statement requirements. Current requirements are that the annual statement must contain the opinion of a qualified actuary that the reserves and other actuarial items "make a good and sufficient provision for all unmatured obligations of the company." In addition, the Valuation Actuary must consider *Recommendation 7* of the American Academy of Actuaries. This recommendation states:

> In those instances wherein. . .the statutory reserves might not make good and sufficient provision for unmatured obligations, then the actuary should make further tests (possibly by gross premium valuation. . .) before expressing an opinion as to such policy reserves and other actuarial items. (See Chapter 9 for further information.)

Pricing adequacy of all currently issued lines and products should also be determined. This is particularly important for products more sensitive to the HIV infection and AIDS impact, such as term insurance and for coverage at younger ages where prevalence of the disease is greatest.

3.1 *Determination of Claims Experience*

Initially, a determination should be made of the current impact on the company's business. This must be much more detailed than is normally undertaken because of:

- The long latency period of the virus.
- The fact that persons do not die of AIDS but rather from opportunistic diseases. These opportunistic diseases can be diseases other than the more frequently identified diseases such as Kaposi's sarcoma or pneumocystis carinii pneumonia (for example, meningitis or tuberculosis).
- Antiselection resulting from the applicant obtaining information about the company's AIDS testing limits and subsequently purchasing lower amounts just to avoid testing.
- Avoidance of notations of AIDS as a cause of death to "protect" family and friends.
- Restriction in jurisdictions, such as New York, that permit only three causes of death to be noted, that is, homicide, suicide, and natural causes.
- The number of health and disability income claims that are not attributed to AIDS until well into the disease; this is a more severe problem in cases of AIDS in women and heterosexuals, because the frequency of the infection to date is lower in these populations.

This detailed claims analysis should therefore involve a review of claims with:

- Any cause of death or disability that could have been contributed to by AIDS or HIV infections.
- All amounts including those below the AIDS testing limit and especially those just below the testing limit, and those at usual amounts (that is, multiples of 5,000, 10,000 or 25,000 for life, or of 1,000 or 2,5000 for disability).
- Death, disability, or claim beyond the contestable period as well as those within it.

The review should also include the normal analysis for both number of policies and volume of claims by geographic areas and sales areas, age, sex, policy duration, etc.

Some adjustment for underreporting may also be necessary in spite of the thoroughness of the claims review. The CDC has estimated that as many as 20 percent of deaths from HIV infection may be going unreported.

If AIDS testing limits were changed during the period(s) reviewed, separate analyses should be done for issues in each period.

3.2 Determination of Antiselection in New Business

Current antiselection should also be analyzed from the standpoint of any changes in new business. If more term, more large amounts, more policies just below the AIDS testing limit, or more policies or larger amounts at young male ages, or in more volume in areas of high AIDS concentration have been written with no intentional change in marketing to account for them, they may be indicators of antiselection.

Even more frequent use of the waiver-of-premium provision could be an indication of the need for doing further review. In disability income, changes toward shorter waiting periods could be an additional indicator. In medical expense policies, trends toward lower deductibles or sudden sales increases in a geographical area, a sales area or in general, could be additional indicators.

3.3 Estimation of the Level of Infection in the Insured Population

Once the claims review and new business review are done, the data therefrom should be used to estimate the level of infection in the company's insured population and the expected level of infection in the prospective insured population from new sales. In doing so, it must be remembered that the claims experience reflects infection levels of several years back, as well as current infection levels. Thus, low claims levels may indicate low levels of longer duration infections or larger levels of early infection, or both, since the progression to AIDS is very slow in early years.

The claims experience can reflect antiselection from as early as 1981, when the disease was first identified in the U.S. However, because widespread knowledge about the disease did not occur until 1984–1985, it is possible that little antiselection occurred before that time. Key in the assumptions of antiselection are the dates and levels at which a company began testing and the dates and levels at which it changed its testing. These actions not only affected the levels at which HIV infection was actually determined by testing, but also influenced the frequency with which those who knew or suspected they were infected sought to buy insurance from the company.

This translation of claims experience to infection level in the company's insured population should also be made for different groups of risks. The two most significant are sex and age. Currently, 93 percent of adults with AIDS are males and the percentage of that male population that has AIDS varies dramatically by age. The CDC's "AIDS Weekly Surveillance Reports" have consistently shown 21 percent are ages 20 to 29, 46 percent are 30 to 39, 21 percent are 40 to 49, and 10 percent are 50 or over.

The male general population data further comprise cases caused by IV drug abuse and sexually transmitted AIDS. IV drug abusers are not likely to be in the insured population, not only because of their general disinterest in insurance but also because of companies' usual routines of underwriting for drug abuse.

The population data also contain a small proportion of AIDS cases contracted through contaminated blood or blood products, but this proportion is likely to be even smaller in the insured population because of uninsurability of some of the underlying diseases requiring the blood transfusion or blood products.

The insured population generally comprises, therefore, HIV infection contracted sexually. It is this prevalency of HIV infection due to sexually transmitted disease among heterosexuals and homosexuals that makes the age distribution so significant in estimates of HIV infection in the insured population.

The third factor of significance in the translation of the claims experience to the estimated level of infection in the insured population is the geographic distribution of the disease. This is particularly critical in the case of new issues and recent years' issues.

3.4   Modeling the Financial Impact of the Disease

This estimated level of infection in the insured population should then be combined with the progression rates of the infection and merged with the other data about the company—for example, age distribution, gender distribution, product line and product-type distribution, geographic distribution, average size policy above and below the AIDS testing limits, year of issue, persistency, etc.—to model the financial impact of the infection on the company.

The refinement used to determine the level of infection among those insured, as well as the level of detail as to the number of characteristics and cells utilized in the model for determining the financial impact, will depend on how critical each of these characteristics is in the company. The current level of knowledge about the disease, the extent of the changes possible in those areas where the knowledge is lacking, and the impact of those changes on overall results will also affect the level of refinement.

The model should be developed to allow adequate flexibility as new information is determined. This flexibility is especially critical in the areas that could most affect the company, that is, the infection level in the insured population, progression rates of the disease, the infection rate, mortality and morbidity among females and heterosexual males, treatment for the disease, and persistency, which could change because of antiselection and actions taken by the company in response to the impact of the disease. Because the data we have available are very new, long-term projections should be interpreted with caution.

The model used can be one developed in-house, one already developed by others (see Chapters 4–7), or a combination of both. The model used will be affected by the equipment it is to be run on, the level of detail desired, and the output format required. The ultimate use of the study may also affect the model selected.

4.0 DETERMINATION OF THE APPROPRIATE MANAGEMENT STRATEGIES AND ACTIONS THAT SHOULD BE TAKEN

Once the financial impact has been measured, the management strategies necessary to moderate and minimize the HIV infection and AIDS impact can then be addressed. These should include a review of the strategies available, followed by the identification, recommendation, approval, and implementation of one or more of them. Which strategies are more appropriate will, of course, depend on the level of the impact of HIV infection and AIDS without moderating action as determined in the financial impact analysis, as well as the potential impact of changes in the disease, its treatment, changes of the level of infection in the general and insured population, and changes in the legislative or regulatory environment. Each of these strategies has its own advantages and disadvantages and includes considerations such as:

- Equity among and within lines, products, ages, generations of policyholders, geographic areas, etc.
- Current and future net worth.
- Impact on sales force.

- Impact on competitiveness.
- Ability to obtain regulatory approval of actions if approval is necessary (for example, health insurance premium increases).
- Legislative or regulatory restrictions.

4.1 Strategies for In-Force Business

Options available for in-force business include the following:

- Pay as you go.
- Reduce dividends on participating policies.
- Increase premiums or other nonguaranteed charges and/or reduce nonguaranteed credits, where permitted.
- Strengthen reserves.
- Establish extra reserves.
- Earmark surplus.
- Set aside surplus.
- Purchase catastrophic reinsurance.

4.2 Strategies for New Business

Options available for new business include the following:

- Reprice products or lines.
- Modify underwriting.
- Reduce AIDS testing limits.
- Address viability of certain products or markets.
- Reduce retention limits.
- Purchase catastrophic reinsurance.
- Modify policy terms and conditions.
- Strengthen reserves.

4.3 Legislative and Regulatory Strategies

Risk classification is an integral part of the life and health insurance voluntary insurance mechanism. Companies must be able to select risks if they are going to be able to price adequately and equitably. The expected mortality of a 35-year-old male, newly infected with HIV, is more than ten times the level that is generally considered acceptable at even the highest substandard rating. If companies are not allowed to test for HIV infection, they will be faced with the ultimate risk classification question of whether or not they can continue to accept any new business.

Several states are challenging the right of insurance companies to do HIV testing. Additional regulatory activity is beginning to challenge the industry's right to test for other diseases as well. Insurance (health, life and disability) is increasingly perceived by some as an entitlement. Although entitlement insurance may be appropriate in a social system (such as health, life and disability insurance contained in Social Security), it is not appropriate in a voluntary insurance system because it ultimately leads to inequitable premiums, market dislocations, and, in the case of imminently life-threatening diseases, possible insolvencies.

Some of the legislative and regulatory actions are reflecting this entitlement by disallowing testing for all or some fixed amounts of life, disability, and health insurance. To minimize the impact of HIV infection and AIDS on a company, proposed legislation and regulations restricting AIDS and other testing should be addressed not only in a company's domiciliary state but also in other jurisdictions as well.

4.4   Educational Strategies

4.4a Education on Insurance, Risk Classification, and Pricing

One of the main reasons entitlement and testing ban regulations and legislation are occurring is that regulators, legislators, and the general public do not understand how insurance, risk classification, and insurance pricing work. Education should be initiated to build that understanding. It should start with company personnel, including top management, many of whom are not familiar with risk classification principles. Education of the field force should also occur at sales meetings and through written materials. This can reap multiple rewards, because the field force is in constant contact not only with policyholders, but also with the general public as well. When well informed on the issue, field representatives also serve as excellent speakers at service organizations. Communication to policyholders should also be done by the home office. Stockholders, too, should receive communication on the issues. Directors not only need to understand risk classification issues, but they can become strong centers of influence in the legislative process if well informed on the issues.

4.4b Education on HIV Infection and AIDS

There is currently no known cure for HIV infection or AIDS and at present no vaccine. AZT prolongs short-term survival in some and reduces symptoms in others, but is not a cure. It will probably not extend life long enough to help life insurance costs, and it will likely increase healthcare costs. AZT can also cause its own side effects, such as anemia and suppression of bone marrow production.

AIDS vaccines have just begun to be tested in humans, but even if successful the vaccines are not expected to be available for general use before the mid-1990s.

On the heels of the announcement of human tests of vaccines, however, comes research from Los Alamos National Laboratory in New Mexico, showing the AIDS virus is mutating its genetic code as much as five times faster than the flu virus. Gerald Myers, a molecular geneticist who measured the rate of change at the laboratory, said the Los Alamos finding "casts bewildering shadows" on prospects for reliable diagnosis, effective treatment, and a vaccine to block all forms of the virus. Therefore, were an AIDS vaccine developed, it is likely that new vaccines would have to be continually developed to keep up with the virus' behavior change.

As Dr. Jay Levy of the University of California has noted:

"The virus that causes mononucleosis was discovered 20 years ago, and we still haven't got a vaccine for it."

With no known cure and no vaccine likely to be available in the next five years, education about the disease and how it is not transmitted is currently the only control of expansion of the disease in the general population and consequently in the insured population. Education, therefore, is a major element in controlling the impact of the disease on a life and health insurance company.

Because HIV infection and AIDS is a sexually transmitted or blood-to-blood transmitted disease, it can be contained if education is disseminated effectively enough to influence attitudes and behavior. As with education on insurance and risk classification, education on HIV infection and AIDS should be distributed to home office personnel, the field force, policyholders, stockholders, directors, and the general public.

5.0 NECESSITY FOR ONGOING DETERMINATION OF FINANCIAL IMPACT

Because much is yet unknown about the disease, because much is being continuously learned about the disease and its treatment, and especially because the level of infection in the general population, the insured population, and in a company is unknown, it is imperative that ongoing studies be conducted.

This is particularly appropriate because of the lack of data on females and on the level of entrance of the disease into the heterosexual population, and the possible differences in mortality and morbidity between the heterosexual and homosexual infected populations.

As previously noted, the vast majority of our data comes from observation of male homosexuals and IV drug abusers. The limited data on females indicate that studies done on women with AIDS in New York, Miami, and California show women are sicker and are dying more quickly than men who have the disease. In New York, women diagnosed as having AIDS survived less than two years after diagnosis, while the average for the men diagnosed with AIDS was two and one-half years. Dr. Margaret Fischl's University of Miami study showed women survived an average of 6.6 months after diagnosis, while men survived 12 to 14 months. In Miami, the women not only died sooner but were sicker. Nearly one-third had several infections where men often had just one. In a California study, women with AIDS lived an average of 40 days after being diagnosed, while the men lived more than a year. Analysis of third-quarter 1987 data from the CDC showed substantially higher early mortality among adult females. The mortality was twice as high as among males in the first half-year after diagnosis, nearly 50 percent higher in the second half-year, nearly 33 percent higher in the third half-year, and nearly 10 percent higher in the fourth half-year. There could be nonbiological reasons for the difference, such as later identification and reporting of the disease, but some of these reasons have already been studied and rejected.

Also, as previously noted, the two leading opportunistic diseases (Kaposi's sarcoma and pneumocystic carinii pneumonia) have different mortality rates. *The New York Times* of January 5, 1988, reported:

"Those who have Kaposi's sarcoma but no other AIDS-related infections 'tend to have a better prognosis' than those with other manifestations of AIDS, according to Dr. Jaffe of the CDC. But, he added, this cancer 'occurs almost entirely in gay men.' In addition, homosexual men as a group tend to live longer than other groups after they are diagnosed as having AIDS. Experts say they are not sure whether this is because the disease is different in homosexual men or because these men tend to seek medical care earlier than drug users or women."

Estimates of the entrance of the infection into the heterosexual population range from minimal to substantial. Most of those studying the disease agree that it can be transmitted heterosexually. As Nancy Padian, an epidemiologist at the University of California at Berkeley, has said,

"Heterosexual transmission is not only plausible, it's well established."

At a Congressional hearing on February 19, 1988, Surgeon General C. Everett Koop stated:

> "It is just not true that there is no danger from normal vaginal intercourse. What is unknown is the level of that danger. But there is always a danger whenever people engage in casual sex. Even if their promiscuity is heterosexual."

Affecting the level of this entrance is whether or not the disease can be spread as easily from woman to man as from man to woman. Many feel, as Dr. Mason stated at the American Council of Life Insurance 1987 annual meeting, that

> "although men readily spread the disease to women, it is less readily spread back the other way, although it does occur."

Other studies, however, have shown the disease is equally efficiently transmitted between the sexes. For example, Major Redfield's studies at the Walter Reed Army Institute of Research showed that 44 percent of the wives of men with AIDS were infected. Forty-three percent of the husbands of women with AIDS were infected. He stated:

> "In a prospective study, the ability of a woman [who has AIDS] to give this virus to a man is equivalent to the ability of a man [who has AIDS] to give this to a woman."

In Dr. Fischl's study of 58 couples at the University of Miami, 16 AIDS patients continued to have unprotected intercourse, despite doctors' warnings, over periods ranging from one to three years. Thirteen of the partners (80 percent) became infected. The February 6, 1987, *JAMA* article, "Evaluation of Heterosexual Partners, Children, and Household Contact of Adults with AIDS," reporting Dr. Fischl's data, stated:

> "These data, along with those of Redfield et al. and others further document that HTLV-III/LAV is a bidirectionally transmitted virus. . . . Further we found that the seroconversion rate for male spouses (42 percent) was similar to that for female spouses (38 percent). These findings suggest that HTLV-III/LAV may be transmitted heterosexually in either direction with a similar efficiency."

Major Redfield has further stated:

> "The fact is that the sexual transmission is the major mode of transmission in society today. Heterosexual transmission actually is the major mode of transmission in the world today. . .in the absence of scientific solution, it will be the major mode of transmission in North America also."

Dr. Jaffe, who said in June 1987, "For most people the risk of AIDS is essentially zero," was quoted in November 1987 *Money* magazine as saying:

"Clearly AIDS can be transmitted through heterosexual contact, and over time the risk to everyone is going to increase. Heterosexual contact could become the major means of transmission in this country. But we have an opportunity now to slow its spread, and we should take advantage of that."

All these data emphasize the need to continue to monitor the effect of the disease on different segments of the population, the effect of treatment and possible vaccines on the impact of the disease, and the changes in the spread of the disease within the general population, insured population, and a company's insured and new applicant population. Additionally, estimates of the level of infection in the company's insured and new applicant population could have initially been set too high or too low, so claims experience, too, must be monitored and reanalyzed. As new data become available, a new impact analysis should be determined, and if the impact on the company changes, strategies, too, must change. With a disease of such long-term significant impact, it will require continuous long-term analyses and solutions.

ABOUT THE AUTHORS

E. Paul Barnhart, F.S.A. 1960, has spent all but the first three months of an actuarial career spanning more than 30 years in the field of health insurance, beginning as an actuarial student with Transamerica Occidental Life in 1954. In 1964 he opened a consulting practice in St. Louis, specializing in health insurance. St. Louis has served as his "home office" location ever since. Mr. Barnhart has served on the Board of Governors of the Society and on the Board of Directors of the American Academy of Actuaries. He served as President of the Society of Actuaries for the 1978–79 year and as original chairperson of the new Health Insurance Section of the Society in 1982 and 1983. He has served as chairperson of the American Academy of Actuaries' Committee on Health and is currently a member of the Actuarial Standards Board. His paper "The Benefit Ratio Reserve Method," appearing in this volume of the *Transactions*, is his tenth paper to be so published.

David N. Becker, F.S.A. 1979, is second vice president and individual life product actuary at Lincoln National Life Insurance Company, a company he joined in 1975 as an actuarial student. He received a bachelor's degree in mathematics from St. Louis University in 1967, a master's degree in mathematics from Washington University in 1969, and a Ph.D. in mathematics from St. Louis University in 1973. Mr. Becker has served on the Society's Part 5 Examination Committee and the Professional Development Committee and is currently a member of the Society's Product Development Section Council and Research Policy Committee and of the Academy's Life Committee and Universal Life Task Force. His papers have appeared not only in *Transactions* but also in *Best's Review* and *Reinsurance Reporter*.

James D. Broffitt, A.S.A. 1980, received a B.A. in mathematics from DePauw University in 1963, an M.S. in statistics from Colorado State University in 1965, and a Ph.D. in statistics from Colorado State University in 1969. He is currently a professor in the department of statistics and actuarial science at the University of Iowa, where he has been on the faculty since 1970. From 1970 until 1980 he taught statistics, but in 1980 switched to the field of actuarial science. He was also a visiting professor at the University of Western Ontario during the 1985–86 academic year. He has published about two dozen papers in statistical and actuarial journals. His most recent publications in the field of actuarial science concern the estimation and graduation of mortality rates. He was awarded the 1984 Halmstad Memorial Prize for his paper "Maximum Likelihood Alternatives to Actuarial Estimators of Mortality Rates," *TSA*, Vol. XXVI, 1984, pp. 77–142.

Donald D. Cody, F.S.A. 1939, received an A.B. degree, summa cum laude in mathematics, from Harvard in 1934. From 1934 to 1950, he was with Equitable Life, where he became associate actuary. During World War II, he was a member of the famous Navy Anti-Submarine Warfare Operations Research Group and later developed Navy airborne fire control systems. From 1951 to 1967, he was with the New York Life, where he had the title of vice president and group actuary. In 1967 he joined New England Life as senior vice president of ordinary operations and later of long-range corporate planning. Retiring in 1978, he has since been a consulting actuary and has been very active in the development of the valuation actuary concept. From 1984 to 1987, he was a member of the Society's Board of Governors. A member of the Committee on Valuation and Related Areas, he was its chairperson from 1981 to 1985. He also is a charter member of the Joint Committee on the Valuation Actuary and of the NAIC Standing Technical Advisory Committee and its Subcommittee on Surplus and Solvency. His two papers in this volume of the *Transactions* were written to fill perceived voids in the valuation actuary literature. He is the author of numerous papers in the *Transactions* and *Record*, some of which are cited in the bibliographies of the two papers. He also wrote a chapter in the *Valuation Actuary Handbook*.

Christian J. DesRochers, F.S.A. 1976, received a bachelor's degree from the University of Connecticut in 1970. He joined the Hartford Life Insurance Co., being an actuary there until 1982. He has been a consulting actuary since 1982 and is employed by Chalke, Incorporated in Washington, D.C. He specializes in life insurance company matters, including product development, statutory and GAAP financial reporting, the appraisal of life insurance companies, and the federal income taxation of life insurance companies and policyholders. For the Society, he is chairperson of the Fall Core Examination Committee and a member of the Product Development Section program committee. He is a member of the Academy's Committee on Continuing Care Retirement Communities. A frequent speaker and author, he has published papers in the *Transactions* as well as in *Insurance Tax Review, the New England Insurance Times*, and the Product Development Section newsletter.

Mark D. J. Evans, F.S.A., received a B.S. with high distinction from the University of Nebraska–Lincoln in 1977. He has been assistant vice-president and actuary at Capital Holding Corporation since 1980. Previously, he was assistant actuary at American National Insurance Company (1977–80). For the Society he has served on Examination Committees since 1982. He is also a member of the American Academy of Actuaries, Phi Beta Kappa, and Mensa, and a Fellow of the Life Management Institute. In addition to the paper in this volume of the *Transactions*, he has published "Increasing Insurances under the Uniform Distribution of Deaths Assumption" (with Calvin D. Cherry, *ARCH* 1979.2), "Exponential Decay Model for Withdrawal Rates" (*The Actuary*, February 1987), and "FAS No. 97 Brings Sweeping Changes" (*The Actuary*, July/August 1988).

Edward W. Frees, F.S.A. 1986, is an associate professor of business and statistics at the University of Wisconsin–Madison. Professor Frees received a Ph.D. in mathematical statistics in 1983 from the University of North Carolina at Chapel Hill. Prior to being at Chapel Hill, he was employed by M & R Services, John Eriksen's and Partners (a New Zealand actuarial consulting firm), and the United Kingdom's Government Actuaries Department. Research interests include stochastic models of insurance and finance and statistical inference. His articles have appeared in *Insurance: Mathematics and Economics, Journal of Finance, Journal of Business and Economic Statistics, Annals of Statistics, Journal of the American Statistical Association, Stochastic Processes and Their Applications, Sequential Analysis, Naval Research Logistics Quarterly, ASTIN Bulletin, Management Science*, and *Scandinavian Journal of Statistics*.

Charles Fuhrer, F.S.A. 1977, received a B.A. in mathematics from the University of Chicago in 1971. He joined Benefit Trust Life in 1973, being involved mostly in group insurance actuarial work until 1985; then he left to join Blue Cross/Blue Shield of Illinois, where he is involved with group health actuarial work. He is the chairperson of the Society's Committee on Research on Theory and Applications, coeditor of *ARCH*, and a member of the Research Policy Committee, the Committee on Papers, and the Publications Committee. In 1988, he won the AERF Practitioners Award for work entitled "A Method for the Calculation of Aggregate Stop-Loss Premiums." He presented some AIDS projections at the Society's AIDS Symposium in Chicago in May 1988, at the Society's Annual Research Conference in Connecticut in August 1988, and at an open forum at the Society's Annual Meeting in Boston in October 1988.

Thomas N. Herzog, A.S.A. 1977, is currently the chief actuary of the Federal Housing Administration, where he is primarily involved with the FHA mortgage guarantee insurance programs. He previously worked as a mathematical statistician for both the Social Security Administration and the National Highway Traffic Safety Administration. He has an Sc.B. in applied mathematics from Brown University and a Ph.D. in mathematical statistics from the University of Maryland. Dr. Herzog is the author of numerous technical articles, including the Society's Part 3 study note on credibility. He has also taught various science courses at a number of universities and companies in the Washington, D.C. area.

Merlin F. Jetton, F.S.A. 1980, received a bachelor of science in mathematics from the University of Illinois in 1973. He is an actuary with Allstate Life Insurance Co. He has extensive experience in the development and pricing of interest-sensitive products. He is currently responsible for asset liability management for Allstate's business sold through Dean Witter.

Rama Kocherlakota, not a member of the Society, is a graduate student in mathematics at Harvard University. He holds a bachelor's degree from Princeton and a master's from Harvard. He worked for several summers at the Great-West Life Assurance Company, supplementing his education with stimuli from the real world of business. Beginning in September 1989, he will be a National Science Foundation Post-Doctoral Fellow at the Mathematical Sciences Research Institute in Berkeley, Calif.

Louis J. Lombardi, F.S.A. 1982, is chief pricing actuary at Connecticut Mutual in Hartford. Mr. Lombardi's responsibilities include not only actuarial product development for participating and interest-sensitive products but also Connecticut Mutual's Group Universal Life product line. He has extensive experience in financial analysis, experience studies, reserve valuation and the development of large-scale information systems.

Robert J. Myers, F.S.A. 1940, served in various actuarial positions with the U.S. Social Security Administration from 1934 until 1970, including chief actuary (1947–70). Since then he has been a member of the National Commission on Social Security (1978–81), executive director of the National Commission on Social Security Reform (1982–1983), chairman of the Railroad Unemployment Compensation Committee (1983–85), and Deputy Commissioner of Social Security (1981–82). He is currently chairman of the Commission on Railroad Retirement Reform. He also has been an actuarial consultant to various Congressional Committees and the Federal Judiciary, and a member of missions of technical assistance in connection with Social Security or pension programs in many foreign countries. He was President of the Society of Actuaries in 1971–72 and President of the American Academy of Actuaries, also in 1971–72. He is a Fellow of the Casualty Actuarial Society, the Conference of Actuaries in Public Practice, the American Statistical Association, the American Association for the Advancement of Science, and the Royal Statistical Society. His numerous awards include the Triennial Prize from the Actuarial Society of America and the Distinguished Service Award from the U.S. Department of Health, Education, and Welfare. Mr. Myers is the author of several books, including *Social Insurance and Allied Government Programs* (Richard D. Irwin, Inc., 1965), *Medicare* (Irwin, 1970), *Society Security* (Irwin, 1st ed., 1975; 2nd ed., 1981; 3rd ed., 1985), and *Indexation of Pension and Other Benefits* (Irwin, 1978). He has published 737 papers in technical and scientific journals, of which 31 have appeared in the *Transactions*, the *Transactions of the Actuarial Society of America*, and the *Record of the American*

Institute of Actuaries; about 567 discussions, book reviews, and letters to the editor; and 110 testimonies before Congressional Committees and advisory groups.

Harry H. Panjer, F.S.A. 1976 and F.C.I.A. 1977, is professor of actuarial science at the University of Waterloo, Ontario, and Director of the Institute of Insurance and Pension Research at the university. He received a B.A. in 1969, an M.A. in 1971, and a Ph.D. in 1975, all from the University of Western Ontario. He is currently serving on the Board of Governors of the Society and has served on numerous committees of the Society and the Canadian Institute of Actuaries. He chaired the CIA's Task Force on AIDS subcommittee on modelling, which together with the valuation subcommittee proposed guidelines for valuation of the AIDS risk in life insurance. He is the author of more than 30 papers that have appeared in *Transactions, Journal of Risk and Insurance, Insurance: Mathematics and Economics, Transactions of International Congress of Actuaries, ASTIN Bulletin,* and *Journal of Econometrics*.

E. S. Rosenbloom, not a member of the Society, is an associate professor in the department of actuarial and management sciences at the University of Manitoba. He obtained a B.Sc. (Hons) degree in mathematics and a M.Sc. degree in mathematics from the University of Manitoba, in 1970 and 1971, respectively. He obtained a Ph.D. in operational research from the University of Waterloo in 1976. Before joining the University of Manitoba, Dr. Rosenbloom taught at the University of Lethbridge and at the University of Alberta. His research interests include manpower scheduling and operational research models in finance. Dr. Rosenbloom has published in *Mathematics of Computation* and *European Journal of Operational Research*.

Richard G. Schreitmueller, F.S.A. 1960, received a B.S. in electrical engineering from the University of Notre Dame. His employment history includes positions as group actuary and later director of group pension planning at Aetna Life & Casualty; consulting actuary, The Wyatt Company; vice president and actuary, William M. Mercer, Inc.; actuary, Social Security Administration; actuary, U.S. Senate Committee on Governmental Affairs; and acting chief actuary, Federal Retirement Thrift Investment Board. He is currently pension research actuary for A. Foster Higgins & Co., Inc. Mr. Schreitmueller is a member of the Society's Pension Section Council and Pension Research Committee. He has been chairperson of the Society's Committee on Review of Literature, associate editor of the *Enrolled Actuaries Report* of the American Academy of Actuaries, and president and executive board member of the Middle Atlantic Actuarial Club. He has written and spoken on a wide range of employee benefit subjects.

Elias S. W. Shiu, A.S.A. 1977, is a professor in the department of actuarial and management sciences at the University of Manitoba. He obtained a B.Sc. (Hons) degree and M.Sc. degree from the University of Manitoba in 1971 and a Ph.D. degree from the California Institute of Technology in 1975. He is vice-chairperson of the Committee on Research on Theory and Applications and serves on one of the Examination Committees of the Society. Since 1976 he has been a consultant for the Great-West Life Assurance Company. His current research interests are asset/liability management, graduation, and risk theory.

Robert W. Stein, F.S.A. 1974, received a B.S. and a B.A. in accounting and actuarial science from Drake University. He is national director of actuarial services for Ernst & Whinney and managing partner of Huggins Financial Services. He provides senior consulting services to the life and health insurance industry in the areas of mergers and acquisitions, financial planning and forecasting, performance measurement and line of business reporting, asset/liability management, financial reporting, and other insurance company and managerial issues. Mr. Stein is chairperson of the Society's Committee on Valuation and Related Areas, a member of the American Academy of Actuaries' Committee on Relations with Accountants, and past chairperson of the Society's Financial Reporting Section.

 **Joseph H. Tan**, F.S.A. 1984, is a senior consultant in the New York office of the actuarial, benefits, and compensation consulting division of Coopers & Lybrand. Prior to joining Coopers & Lybrand, he was the financial planning and control director of the individual insurance products division of CIGNA. Before that, he was associated with Penn Mutual Life Insurance Co. He graduated magna cum laude with a bachelor of science degree in statistics from the University of the Philippines. He also received his master of science degree in mathematics (actuarial science) from the same university. He received his doctorate degree in business administration from Temple University; he also received the Conwell Russell Fellowship from Temple University. He is a Fellow of the Life Management Institute and a member of the American Academy of Actuaries. Mr. Tan spoke at the 1988 and 1989 Society spring meetings on sources of profit analysis. As a member of the Financial Reporting Section, he has published papers on GAAP accounting and return on equity in the Financial Reporting Section newsletter. His paper "Source of Earnings Analysis under FAS 97 Universal Life Accounting" will appear in Volume XLI of the *Transactions*.

 **Naftali Teitelbaum**, F.S.A. 1973, received a bachelor's degree in mathematics from Yeshiva University. He has held actuarial positions with Consulting Actuaries International, Inc., Bankers Security Life Insurance Society, Actuarial Analysts, Inc., Executive Life Insurance Company, and The Equitable Life Assurance Society of the United States, and is currently vice president and actuary at The North Atlantic Life Insurance Company of America. His principal areas of work are pension and insurance company valuation and managing actuarial department, life and annuity product development. A major accomplishment was the implementation from scratch of the structured settlement annuities line of business in a large company. He is a member of the American Academy of Actuaries and an Enrolled Actuary.

FINANCIAL REPORT

BALANCE SHEETS

ASSETS

	YEAR ENDED JULY 31	
	1988	1987
Current Assets:		
Cash and short-term investments........................	$2,671,661	$1,998,648
Accounts receivable, less allowances		
of $18,000	198,728	144,986
Inventories—at cost	182,184	99,273
Other..	263,977	317,246
Total current assets	$3,316,550	$2,560,153
Long-Term Investments—Note B..........................	1,277,479	1,184,592
Furniture, Equipment and Leasehold		
Improvements—at cost, less allowances		
for depreciation and amortization		
(1988—$148,444; 1987—$154,143)	144,746	160,154
Custodian Funds—primarily short-term		
investments, at cost which approximates		
market—Note E	368,170	368,852
	$5,106,945	$4,273,751

LIABILITIES AND MEMBERSHIP EQUITY

Current Liabilities:		
Accounts payable and accrued liabilities	$1,415,671	$1,164,276
Unearned revenues.....................................	932,529	874,485
Due to International Actuarial Association..................	54,052	28,608
Advances (principally on publications)....................	45,131	32,785
Total current liabilities...............................	$2,447,383	$2,100,154
Custodian Funds—accounts payable—Note E	21,892	18,118
Custodian Funds—Note E...............................	346,278	350,734
Membership Equity	2,291,392	1,804,745
	$5,106,945	$4,273,751

See notes to financial statements.

1171

STATEMENTS OF REVENUES AND EXPENSES
AND CHANGES IN MEMBERSHIP EQUITY

	YEAR ENDED JULY 31	
	1988	1987
Revenues:		
Membership dues	$1,680,293	$1,517,509
Meeting registration fees	841,387	884,445
Seminar fees	779,035	527,009
Examination fees, calculator sales and educational material sales	3,333,500	2,437,320
Sale of publications	129,141	82,333
Income from allied organizations	157,382	153,413
Investment income	218,375	188,487
Other	19,328	41,032
Total Revenues	$7,158,441	$5,831,568
Expenses:		
Salaries and related expenses	2,009,317	1,766,886
Printing	1,250,329	1,028,603
Travel and honoraria	1,368,730	1,158,736
Postage and mailing	643,431	533,801
Grading services and item writers	389,298	338,773
Cost of calculators sold	34,977	39,004
Rent	313,093	209,448
Office	232,584	197,213
Computer	87,004	82,297
Miscellaneous	79,265	86,937
Telephone	38,213	32,272
Professional fees	84,509	86,561
Depreciation—books	39,171	19,280
Depreciation—office	28,267	26,206
Insurance	24,867	21,815
Research development	25,000	16,559
Math contest	7,500	7,500
Professional association	6,000	6,000
Conference Board of the Mathematical Sciences	1,500	1,400
Library	8,739	7,695
Total Expenses	$6,671,794	$5,666,986
Excess of revenues over expense	486,647	164,582
Membership equity at beginning of year	$1,804,745	$1,640,163
Membership equity at end of year	$2,291,392	$1,804,745

See notes to financial statements.

STATEMENTS OF CASH FLOWS

	YEAR ENDED JULY 31	
	1988	1987
Operating Activities:		
Excess of revenues over expenses.............	$486,647	$164,582
Add (deduct) items not affecting cash:		
Depreciation and amortization.............	52,821	46,832
Decrease (increase) in accounts		
receivable..........................	(53,742)	206,178
Increase in other current assets............	(29,642)	(130,880)
Increase in unearned revenues		
and advances........................	95,834	139,748
Increase in accounts payable and		
accrued liabilities.....................	251,395	138,611
Net cash provided by		
operating activities.......................	$ 803,313	$ 565,071
Investing Activities:		
Purchase of long-term investments............	(193,079)	(718,013)
Proceeds of long-term investments sold		
or matured...........................	100,192	303,821
Additions to furniture, equipment and		
leasehold improvements..................	(37,413)	(33,890)
Net cash used by		
investing activities.......................	$ (130,300)	$ (448,082)
Net increase in cash and		
short-term investments....................	673,013	116,989
Cash and short-term investments		
at beginning of year......................	1,998,648	1,881,659
Cash and short-term		
investments at end of year.................	$2,671,661	$1,998,648

See notes to financial statements.

NOTES TO FINANCIAL STATEMENTS
TWO YEARS ENDED
July 31, 1988 and 1987

NOTE A—SUMMARY OF SIGNIFICANT ACCOUNTING POLICIES

Short-term investments consist of highly liquid securities, principally United States Government obligations. These investments are carried at cost which approximates market.

Long-term investments are carried at amortized cost since it is the Society's intent to hold such investments until maturity.

Membership dues are deferred and recognized as income on a pro rata basis over the Society's membership period.

Provisions for depreciation and amortization of furniture, equipment and leasehold improvements are computed on the straight-line method based on the estimated useful lives of the assets or the terms of the leases.

Certain amounts in the 1987 financial statements have been reclassified to conform with the 1988 presentation.

NOTE B—LONG-TERM INVESTMENTS

Long-term investments consist of the following:

| | AMORTIZED COST | | MARKET VALUE | |
	1988	1987	1988	1987
United States				
Treasury bonds	$1,215,579	$1,122,699	$1,210,033	$1,118,110
Corporate bonds......	61,900	61,893	52,980	54,333
	$1,277,479	$1,184,592	$1,263,013	$1,172,443

NOTE C—TAX-EXEMPT STATUS

The Society is qualified as a tax-exempt organization under section 501(c)(3) of the Internal Revenue Code. Therefore, its current activities do not result in liabilities for income taxes.

NOTE D—RETIREMENT PLAN

All employees of the Society, subject to minimum eligibility requirements, are covered by a retirement plan. The Society contributes 15% of the employees' basic salaries and the employees may contribute amounts up to the limitation as defined in the Internal Revenue Code. These contributions are applied to purchase deferred annuity contracts from insurance companies. The Society's policy is to fund retirement costs accrued. Pension expense for the years ended July 31, 1988 and 1987 was $207,318 and $232,048, respectively.

NOTE E—CUSTODIAN FUNDS

The Society is custodian for funds contributed by members for a minority recruitment program, a scholarship fund, an educational award fund, a research and development fund, and special interest sections. Disbursements to support these programs are made upon the authorization of the program directors. Revenues and expenses of the custodian funds are excluded from the results of operations of the Society. The fund balances of the various custodian funds are as follows:

	YEAR ENDED JULY 31	
	1988	1987
Minority recruitment program	$116,624	$163,447
Smith Scholarship	–	141
Educational award fund	13,993	13,773
Research and development fund	26,590	–
Special interest sections:		
Individual life insurance and annuity product development.............	71,124	57,758
Life insurance company financial reporting	25,810	22,550
Pension	41,554	39,837
Health insurance	15,438	10,082
Futurism	3,824	11,263
Reinsurance (deficit)	(483)	12,736
Nontraditional marketing....................	18,377	14,811
Investment.................................	13,427	4,336
Total	$346,278	$350,734

NOTE F—LEASE COMMITMENTS

The Society occupies office space under an operating lease agreement through 2001 which includes escalation clauses to cover future increases in operating costs above base year costs. The lease provides for a period of free rent through 1992, the effects of which are being recognized over the lease term on a straight-line basis. Total rent expense amounted to $313,093 and $209,448 in 1988 and 1987, respectively.

As of July 31, 1988, future minimum rental commitments for the noncancelable lease are $30,000 in 1992, $366,000 in 1993, and $2,925,000 for all years thereafter through 2001.

We have audited the accompanying statements of financial condition of the Society of Actuaries as of July 31, 1988 and 1987, and the related statements of revenues and expenses and changes in membership equity, and cash flows for the years then ended. These financial statements are the responsibility of the Society's management. Our responsibility is to express an opinion on these financial statements based on our audits.

We conducted our audits in accordance with generally accepted auditing standards. Those standards require that we plan and perform the audit to obtain reasonable assurance about whether the financial statements are free of material misstatement. An audit includes examining, on a test basis, evidence supporting the amounts and disclosures in the financial statements. An audit also includes assessing the accounting principles used and significant estimates made by management, as well as evaluating the overall financial statement presentation. We believe that our audits provide a reasonable basis for our opinion.

In our opinion, the financial statements referred to above present fairly, in all material respects, the financial position of the Society of Actuaries as of July 31, 1988 and 1987, and the results of its operations and its cash flows for the years then ended, in conformity with generally accepted accounting principles.

[*Signed*] ERNST & WHINNEY

BOOK REVIEWS

E. J. Moorhead, *Our Yesterdays: the History of the Actuarial Profession in North America, 1809-1979*, pp. 437, published by Society of Actuaries, Schaumburg, Ill. 60173, 1989; $60.

Every actuary should read this fascinating history, so long overdue. As far back as 1982, Dwight Bartlett, a past Society President, first began voicing his concern about the crying need for a history of our profession on this continent. His efforts finally bore fruit with the Council of Presidents in 1983, and the Society was indeed fortunate that a man as well qualified and dedicated as Jack Moorhead was persuaded to tackle this mammoth job. It is extremely difficult to comprehend the enormity of the task that faced the author, the mass of material that had to be dug out of the archives, the voluminous amount of reading required to uncover long-forgotten facts, and the struggles of so many of our predecessors in the days when there was no Institute of Actuaries, no Society or Faculty, no Journals or *Transactions* to record our storehouse of knowledge about things actuarial here and abroad.

The following extract from a letter from Jack Moorhead to the reviewer not only reveals his frustrations in bringing together the mass of material that is the basis of this book, but also includes some suggestions that deserve consideration by some of us who are retired but can still serve our profession.

"1. It is extraordinary, and distressing, that much of this writing was not done years ago. It's baffling to try to understand why this gap was allowed to widen and widen while eyewitnesses were lost by death and valuable records were lost or destroyed.

"2. By no means do I consider that the job is done. My hope is that the book's division of the subject into fourteen parts may encourage others to explore one or more of those parts more thoroughly than I have managed to do even with all the help I received. (I shall even mention some sources that I know have been inadequately tapped.)

"3. Maybe the fact that a retired member in his upper 70s has done this much may remind the powers-that-be that the ranks of the retired include some people who might be put to work on projects to which they can give time that actuaries still on the active list seem less and less able to spare."

If just a handful of retired actuaries would respond to this appeal, that would be the best way to repay the great debt we owe the author.

Chapter I begins in 1809, reciting the struggles of our predecessors over a fifty-year period. The author's criticism of Fackler's unjustified comment in 1909 is well founded. The section headed "Premiums Charged in Early Days" would have been improved if a brief description of the various mortality tables then in use had been included.

Chapter II covers the next thirty years (1859–1888) before the founding of the Actuarial Society of America, which would probably have been established many years sooner had it not been for the intense and unbridled competition that developed between the larger companies and involved many unsound practices that eventually resulted in the Armstrong Investigation in 1905. This chapter is a fascinating, and most illuminating, account of the highlights of those rather hectic days in the life insurance business in the United States. Canada, as usual, showed greater moderation and control.

Chapter III covers the thirty years from 1889 to 1918, perhaps the most eventful period in the early history and formative years of the profession. Table III.1, listing charter members of the Actuarial Society, shows an overwhelming concentration geographically, as follows:

East	28
Middle West	4
South	1
Far West	1
Canada	4
Total	38

No wonder the American Institute of Actuaries was formed in 1909, with the following distribution of charter members:

East	1
Middle West	35
South	3
Far West	3
Canada	0
Total	42

The section on "Preliminary Term Valuation" reminds this reviewer that J.B. Maclean, in his Presidential Address in October 1943 (*T.A.S.A.* Vol. 44, p. 223), referred in a positive way to the use of this type of reserve, but in practice he never recommended it to his own company. The attitude of the old established companies was undoubtedly a somewhat snobbish one, the argument being that by changing to that weaker basis, the company's surplus got a one-time shot in the arm and thereafter it made little difference to earnings. Of course, this is true only if the volume and type of new business remain constant, which they never do. Eventually the accounting profession quite justifiably insisted on a more realistic basis for measuring current earnings.

The section "Scottish Influence in Pre-Merger Days" impels this reviewer to make some rather personal comments. Henry Moir, one of the leaders in the early days of the Actuarial Society, left the "Scottish Life Assurance Company" in Edinburgh when he emigrated to the United States in 1901. This reviewer left the Scottish Life in 1931 to emigrate to Canada and had been honored by a visit from Henry Moir in 1930, when Moir came to Edinburgh to play golf with some of his former colleagues. While at his old company, Moir remarked that this reviewer was seated at the same old rolltop desk that Moir used thirty years before in 1901. Moir tried to recruit me for a job in the United States, which I refused, but this visit resulted a year later in my being the last actuarial student to emigrate to North America from the Scottish Life after 1931. In that year I was also the first candidate to take an examination of the Actuarial Society in Scotland by special arrangement at Edinburgh University and doubt that this has happened since. I had the great privilege of meeting most of the Scottish actuaries referred to in this book and found that, even in the 1930s, this small group of men still had considerable influence in the profession on this continent.

The section headed "World War I" mentions briefly the existence of business in foreign countries, and there are also two references on this subject in the Appendix to Chapter III, viz., papers by the eminent Dr. Arthur Hunter to the Fourth and Seventh International Congresses. The three largest U.S. companies, Mutual Life, New York Life and Equitable, had large foreign operations in Europe early in this century, which they closed down after World War I. A small group of Canadian companies later became an important factor in Great Britain and much of the British Empire, Latin America and even some countries in the Far East. Some of these operations of Canadian companies exist even to the present day.

Chapter V is headed "1949-1964: Expansion and Fresh Directions." It could just as well have been titled "The Relentless Speed of Change," although one must admit that the years 1965–1979, covered in Chapter VI, could equally well qualify for such a title. Indeed there is no sign to this day of any slowing down in the speed of change as we approach the end of this century. This relentless pressure and ever-increasing mechanization are beginning to be a frightening aspect of modern civilization. We do not seem to have enough time to assimilate what we have just completed before we are called upon to tackle something new.

In many ways the multitude of subjects covered in such a masterful way in Chapters V and VI may be regarded as the heart of this book. At the same time, so many other things that occurred at a slower pace before and after this most eventful thirty-year period are most certainly important in the history of our profession.

The section in Chapter V headed "Pensions" deserves special comment. The landmark paper "Fundamentals of Pension Funding" was a most important supplement to the classic British papers. The later Trowbridge paper on funding methods (*TSA*, Vol. XV, p. 151) is another important work. The earlier paper in *TSA*, Vol. XI, p. 920, by Warters and Rae and the author's comments thereon are worthy of special emphasis as they lament the decline of such formal papers and the overemphasis on informal discussions, which cannot possibly have the depth of thought that is so important.

The American Society of Pension Actuaries is referred to in Chapter V, page 187, and in Chapter VI, pages 222 and 268. One of the motivations involved in the formation of this organization was the use of "split-funded" pension plants financed by a combination of individual whole life policies with a "side fund" designed to convert these policies to life annuities at retirement date, using the settlement options. This involved an actuarial calculation of the level premium pure endowment payment required into these trust funds each year, a rather simple calculation. It also required actuarial assumptions for interest and mortality, and the total cost of the plan depended on the amount of these payments plus the net cost under the policies.

These plans involved high commissions to the agent and excessive costs to the employer, especially in businesses with high rates of turnover and large numbers of employees. Many of the companies active in these operations were not in the group pension business, and those that were had to establish limits defining the size of case that required use of the group product with consequent lower cost. Perhaps the actuaries should have taken a stronger stand in defining these limits than seemed practical at the time.

The section in Chapter VI on "Policy Cost Comparisons" gives a frank and competent discussion of a particularly thorny subject. In the opinion of this reviewer, this is an example of a failure of our profession to face up to a serious problem. As was inevitable, the void was filled by others less competent than our profession to deal with a matter so complicated and important to the public relations of our industry. We have not yet seen the end of this story.

The section about elections in the Society of Actuaries mentions the desirability of adequate representation geographically and by type of employment. In the twenty-year period 1967–86, there were twelve Presidents from life companies, seven from consulting firms, and one from government. However, in this period only two Presidents were Canadians, and more attention is needed to remedy this important problem.

The major changes in life insurance reserves, statutory minimum nonforfeiture benefits, and finally changes in statutory valuation requirements with substantial broadening in the responsibility of the actuary certifying the reserves are all very well described in several sections of Chapter VI.

The last section of Chapter VII, "Our Profession in 1979," summarizes the disquieting changes that were happening so rapidly, accompanied by the masses of paper generated by computers, which made it more and more difficult to decide what the answers should be.

Chapter VIII describes the sad story of income disability benefits attached to life insurance policies, surely a long series of disastrous decisions that actuaries would prefer to forget. The account given is much kinder than some of us would have expected.

Chapter IX is a fascinating account of the evolution from simple desk calculators to the modern electronic computer in so short a time. The meeting at Staple Inn Hall in London in 1936, at which Phillips presented his paper "Binary Calculations," was one that this reviewer was privileged to attend and that he will never forget.

It is to be hoped that our members will study and profit from this most excellent work. It should make us proud of our heritage and inspire us to do our part in shaping the future of our profession.

CHARLES F. B. RICHARDSON

Newton L. Bowers, Jr., Hans U. Gerber, James C. Hickman, Donald A. Jones, and Cecil J. Nesbitt, *Actuarial Mathematics*, pp. 624, published by Society of Actuaries, Itasca, Ill. 60143, 1986; $65.

From a pedagogical point of view, the presentation of the book is impeccable; interesting examples illustrate each new concept. An interpretation is provided for the most important formulas. Each chapter concludes with a lengthy series of exercises. (The solution of most exercises, without derivation, is to be found in an appendix. A worthwhile addition to the textbook is the study manual published annually by ACTEX and distributed by The Actuarial Bookstore, P.O. Box 318, Abington, Connecticut 06230. It contains detailed solutions to all the textbook exercises, a lot of supplementary problems and multiple choice questions, and the solution to recent Society of Actuaries examination questions. Study manual #150, $42.00, #151, $18.00.) Among the seven appendixes to this book, Appendix 4 is especially noteworthy, because it presents a comprehensive survey of the international actuarial notation.

The major innovation introduced by this book is the totally probabilistic approach in the treatment of the mathematics of life contingencies. This breakthrough is definitely not going to facilitate the work of actuarial students, but it is long overdue. It is best illustrated by the very first examples from the life insurance chapter. Example 4.1 reads: The density function of the time-until-death random variable is assumed to be uniform over the range $(0, 80)$. At a given force of interest δ, calculate the net single premium, the variance and the 90th percentile of the claim random variable for a whole life insurance of unit amount issued to (x). Example 4.2 is: Assume that each of 100 independent lives is age x, is subject to a constant force of mortality of 0.04, and is insured for a death benefit amount of 10 units, payable at the moment of death. The benefit payments are to be withdrawn from an investment fund earning 6%. Calculate the minimum amount at time $t = 0$ so that the probability is approximately 0.95 that sufficient funds will be on hand to withdraw the benefit payment at the death of each individual.

A knowledge of basic aspects of financial mathematics is assumed at all times, as well as a solid background in undergraduate calculus and probability theory. A three-page appendix reminds the reader of the most common probability distributions and of some formulas from the calculus of finite differences, but, otherwise, many theorems from calculus and probability theory are routinely used without restatement. The reader should be prepared for a constant use of conditional expectations, moment-generating functions, integration-by-parts, and so on. Quite often only the key steps of a mathematical derivation are provided, and some computation is required to "move from one line to the next."

Before reviewing the work chapter by chapter, it might be useful to mention what the book does not cover:

a. Stochastic interest rates. The interest rates used to convert future payments to a present value are considered deterministic at all times and are usually taken as constants.

b. Estimation of parameters. The construction of mortality tables, for instance, is not discussed.

c. Computing methods. Issues like the optimal organization of input data, simulation, and computation in actuarial models are not discussed.

The study of Chapters 3–10, 14 and 15 is required from all students of the Society of Actuaries as preparation for their most important examination on life contingencies. Chapters 2 and 11–13 cover the material of the examination on risk theory. Students of the Casualty Actuarial Society have to study Chapters 3–7 and 9 for their Part 4 examination. Very little of the material is specific to the United States or Canada, so the book could be adopted by other associations of actuaries and by non-American universities.

Chapter 1 provides an introduction to the economics of insurance, using utility theory. It serves as a background for the remainder of the book, but it is not essential, because utility theory is not used in the sequel. Chapter 2 is best read as a preparation to the risk theory material that forms Chapters 11–13. It will be reviewed later on.

Chapter 3, "Survival Distributions and Life Tables," introduces the basic random variables that are used throughout the text: the survival function, the (continuous) time-until-death for a person aged x, the (discrete) curtate-future-lifetime, and the force of mortality. An illustrative mortality table is presented and discussed. It is used in many exercises in the sequel. Assumptions for fractional ages are briefly discussed, as well as the most classical analytical laws of mortality, and the use of select-and-ultimate tables.

Chapter 4, "Life Insurance," develops models for the most common insurance payable at the moment of death: term, whole life, endowment. Classical variants are presented: deferred insurances, varying benefits, insurances payable at the end of the year of death. An important theorem allows, for unit-amount policies, the computation of the j-th moment around the origin of the claim random variable Z: $E[Z^j]$ calculated at force of interest δ equals $E[Z]$ calculated at the force of interest $j\delta$. This result allows among others the computation of the variance of the claim amount for all classical policies. Recursion equations and commutation functions are only briefly introduced at the end of the chapter. Chapter 5, "Life Annuities," presents similar developments for annuities. Some practitioners may regret the rather theoretical presentation of these and other chapters. The continuous approach, based on integrals, is always presented before the discrete approach. Readers need to study several chapters thoroughly before getting some acquaintance with insurance practice.

Chapter 6 deals with net premiums. Its presentation focuses on the financial loss random variable. This probabilistic approach allows the computation of not only net annual premiums, but also variances for the major contracts. It also allows a glimpse at premium calculation principles other than the expected value principle. Several examples illustrate the ruin probability principle, applied directly to the random loss variable, or to a portfolio of independent policies by normal approximation.

Net premium reserves are discussed in Chapter 7. The random variable "prospective future loss on a contract already in force" is investigated, in both the continuous and the discrete case. The reserve is defined as the expected value of this variable and obtained for all usual policies. The probabilistic approach allows the computation of the variance of the loss in most cases. Important sections deal with classical recursive formulas, reserves as fractional durations, differential equations, allocation of the loss to the policy years (including Hattendorff's theorem and applications).

Chapter 8 is an introduction to multiple life functions. The (two-life) joint-life status (failure upon the first death) and the last-survivor status (failure upon the last death) are defined, and their distributions are obtained, assuming independence. Formulas for net single premiums for annuity and insurance contracts involving two lives are established. Those premiums are then evaluated under specific mortality laws (Gompertz, Makeham), and assumptions (uniform distribution of deaths).

In Chapter 9, "Multiple Decrement Models," a single life is considered but with multiple contingencies like withdrawal, retirement, death, disability. Two random variables, the continuous time-until-termination from a status and the discrete cause of decrement need to be defined, and their distributions characterized. This allows the construction of multiple decrement tables and the associated single decrement tables. This model is applied to calculating actuarial present values of benefits and contributions for a participant in a pension plan in Chapter 10, "Valuation Theory for Pension Plans." All usual cases for the benefit rate function are considered, and numerous examples (step-rate plan, offset plan, add-on plan, . . .) familiarize the reader with the practice of employee benefits plans. Withdrawal and disability benefits are also studied and illustrated by interesting examples.

Expenses are—at last—introduced in Chapter 14, "Insurance Models Including Expenses." The individual model is extended to incorporate acquisition and administrative expenses and accounting requirements. The different loading techniques and modified reserve methods are discussed, mainly through examples.

Nonforfeiture benefits and dividends form the subjects of Chapter 15. A model derived from multiple decrement theory is applied to the determination of the nonforfeiture benefits, the benefits that will not be lost because of the premature cessation of premium payments. The use of multiple decrement theory is motivated by considerations of fairness between the two classes of policyholders, those who terminate before their contractual obligations are fulfilled and those who do not. The different options in case of cessation of payments (paid-up insurance, extended term, . . .) are described. The same principles are then used to obtain formulas for asset shares and experience adjustments such as dividends. Some parts of Chapters 14 and 15 (valuation laws, regulations for nonforfeiture benefits) are specific to the United States and Canada, hence of lesser value to actuaries that do not practice in North America.

The sequence of Chapters 2–11–12–13 provides an excellent and modern introduction to risk theory, despite the fact that some important recent developments had to be bypassed, being outside the scope of the book. Chapter 2, "Individual Risk Models for a Short Term," provides a welcome survey of important probabilistic concepts, presented in an insurance framework. The computation of the sum of independent random variables and its approximation by means of the central limit theorem are reviewed through several examples.

Chapter 11, "Collective Risk Models for a Single Period," focuses on the computation of the aggregate claims distribution. The compound Poisson and compound negative binomial models are introduced. For the former, three different methods that allow the computation of the distribution are presented and abundantly illustrated (two methods compute convolutions; the third is the recursive method). Approximations by the normal and the translated gamma distributions conclude the chapter.

The surplus process is analyzed in Chapter 12, "Collective Risk Models over an Extended Period." The adjustment coefficient is defined in the continuous and discrete cases, and the theorems that enable the computation of the (infinite horizon) ruin probability in both cases are stated. The maximal aggregate loss random variable is characterized, as well as the distribution of the first surplus below the initial level.

Some interesting applications of risk theory are outlined in Chapter 13. It is for instance shown how to compute net stop loss premium using the recursive formula of Chapter 12, and how stop loss reinsurance is linked to a dividend formula in group insurance. The effect of reinsurance on the probability of ruin is illustrated by means of examples, both for proportional and nonproportional reinsurance. Those examples naturally lead to a theorem that states the superiority of nonproportional over proportional reinsurance, if the (unrealistic) assumption is made that the reinsurance loadings are the same.

Chapter 16 to 19 develop special topics and are not included as examination material. They are nevertheless of extreme importance for practitioners. Chapter 16, "Special Annuities and Insurance," computes actuarial present values, net and gross premiums, and net premium reserves, for a wide variety of policies providing special annuity and insurance benefits: installment refund and cash refund annuities, family income and mortgage protection policies, and disability benefits. Of special importance is section 16.5; it deals with variable products, in which benefit levels and reserves depend on the performance of an investment fund. Also important is section 16.6, which addresses another recent major trend in U.S. life products: flexibility. Options for changing benefit amounts, premium, and plan of insurance (such as the possibility of increasing the death benefit of a term insurance, or of switching from a pure term to a policy with a savings component) are briefly discussed and illustrated.

In Chapter 17, "Advanced Muliple Life Theory," the elementary models for plans involving two lives, analyzed in Chapter 8, are extended to incorporate contingencies based on a larger number of lives and more complicated benefits, such as reversionary annuities. More general statuses than the two-life, joint-life, and last-survivor are defined, and a fundamental theorem is used to express the survival functions of these statuses in terms of only joint-life survival functions, under the usual assumptions of independent lifetimes.

Chapter 18 provides a most welcome introduction to population theory. The Lexis diagram is the main tool for the presentation of general population models, which are then applied to tracing the progress of life insurance benefits provided on a group, or population, basis. In Chapter 19, "Theory of Pension Funding," similar aggregate models are applied to the evolution of retirement income benefits provided on a group basis. The major actuarial cost or funding methods for defined benefit plans are presented and analyzed.

The length of this review is indicative of the thoughts of the reviewer concerning the book. The Society of Actuaries and the five authors have to be commended for producing a superb textbook that will be used throughout the world by actuarial students for many years.

JEAN LEMAIRE

George H. Andrews and John A. Beekman, *Actuarial Projections for the Old-Age, Survivors, and Disability Insurance Program of Social Security in the United States of America*, pp. 193, published by Actuarial Education and Research Fund, Itasca, Ill. 60143, 1987; $25.

George Andrews and John Beekman have written a long-needed, monumental monograph describing in detail (and also auditing) the assumptions and methodology underlying the actuarial estimates for the Old-Age, Survivors, and Disability Insurance system (OASDI) that are made by the Social Security Administration (SSA). The only such information available previously was in publications of the Federal Government (such as in the annual reports of the Board of Trustees of the OASDI Trust Funds or the Actuarial Studies issued by the SSA) or in writings of those who had been closely associated with the system (such as this reviewer's book, *Social Security*, 3rd edition, Richard D. Irwin, Inc., Homewood, Ill., 1985). So, an independent overview of the actuarial estimates for this extremely important government program by two distinguished academic actuaries is more than welcome.

The monograph contains seven chapters, an Addendum (which briefly points out possible future studies of a similar nature that might be made—such as for the Medicare program), and an Appendix. The first chapter briefly describes the provisions of OASDI (a more detailed description is given in the Appendix).

The second chapter deals with the demographic assumptions (fertility, mortality, immigration, and family composition) and the resulting projection of the total population of the United States. Then, the next chapter relates the economic assumptions underlying the actuarial estimates—such as labor-force participation, trends of wages and prices, and projections of the Gross National Product (GNP).

The fourth chapter carries forward the contents of the previous two chapters by describing the methodology underlying the long-range (75-year) projections of such elements as (1) number of covered workers, insured persons, retired workes and their benefit amounts, and (2) taxable payroll and GNP. This reviewer believes that the GNP estimates are much more susceptible to question than are the estimates of benefits and contributions (taxes). This is especially so because the latter are best used when considered relative to each other (that is, cost as a percentage of taxable payroll), whereas the former involve many elements that are not interrelated (for example, proportion of compensation paid in other than cash, and not taxable under OASDI). This chapter also discusses the past experience and future assumptions as to disability incidence and termination rates.

The fifth chapter describes the special features of the short-range (five-year) estimates, while the following chapter deals with the long-range (75-year) estimates. The latter goes into detail as to how the auxiliary (spouse and child) and survivor beneficiaries and benefit disbursements are derived. Dealt with are such complexities as dual entitlement adjustments (in which persons are eligible for more than one type of benefit—for example, as a worker and a surviving spouse—but, in essence, receive only the largest). Finally, the concept of "actuarial balance" is defined and illustrated.

The final chapter gives an overview of the short-range and long-range actuarial estimates, explaining why they are needed and describing the several measures of actuarial soundness. Selected projection items, such as the fund balances at the end of the following year and the fifth year, and the long-range actuarial balances (and their components), are presented for OASI and DI separately for the annual Trustees Reports in 1978–1985. The results of sensitivity tests (changing one cost element at a time) for the long-range estimates are given. The chapter concludes with a strong endorsement of the work of the SSA actuarial staff over the years, both as to its quality and as to the "absolute wealth of excellent material" that is made publicly available to interested parties. As is stated, "one of the purposes of this monograph has been to help condense the enormous amounts of material into a smaller study." May the monograph serve as the "key" to unlock this store of riches to many people!

It is "standard operating procedure" for reviewers of books to make at least a few adverse comments and point out some factual errors; otherwise, it will appear that a thorough perusal was not done! As to factual accuracy, this reviewer had the opportunity to review in detail the final manuscript and would be most embarrassed to find any factual errors now. The monograph is truly excellent and should be made "required reading" for any actuary or non-actuary who is interested in the OASDI system, especially if writing a paper or book in the field of OASDI financing. In fact, editors of scholarly journals should require prospective authors in that field to certify that they have diligently and thoroughly studied the Andrews-Beekman monogaph!

ROBERT J. MYERS

J. J. McCutcheon and W. F. Scott, *An Introduction to the Mathematics of Finance*, pp. x + 463, published for the Institute of Actuaries and the Faculty of Actuaries by Heinemann, London, 1986.

The description on the back cover of this comprehensive, well-written book places it in context: "In today's money markets interest rates are all-important. This book, which is intended as a successor to D.W.A. Donald's *Compound Interest and Annuities-Certain*, develops the classical theory of compound interest (in which the force of interest is constant) as a special case of a more general model.

"There is a concise but thorough treatment of the basic compound interest functions, nominal rate of interest, and the yield (or internal rate of return) and there are many examples on discounted cash flow. Also discussed are applications of the theory to capital redemption policies (including a discussion of reinvestment rates), the valuation of stock market securities (with allowance for income tax, capital gains tax and index-linking), and consumer credit calculations. The final chapter provides a simple introduction to stoachastic interest rate models."

The book, primarily written for the actuarial student in the United Kingdom, like its predecessors by Donald (1953, 1970) and Todhunter [1], sets a high standard of expectation—as to theory and especially the solving of involved, practical problems. The McCutcheon and Scott text is noteworthy for containing clear solutions, not only to its 100⁺ well-chosen examples, helpfully distributed throughout most sections of the various chapters, but also (in 130 pages near the end of the book) to all the 176 exercises, stated at the end of the chapters. The near-quadrupling of the number of exercises overcomes a previous criticism of Donald. In this reviewer's opinion, the instructive solutions enhance the value of the book to qualified, serious readers.

Professors McCutcheon and Scott are both Fellows of the Faculty of Actuaries and teach at Heriot-Watt University in Edinburgh, in the Department of Actuarial Mathematics and Statistics. John McCutcheon has prior actuarial experience in life insurance and consulting and on the University of Manitoba faculty. William Scott has taught at the Universities of Glasgow and Michigan. That both have U.K. and North American experience brings a valuable extra dimension to their broad interpretation of the mathematics of finance. U.S. and Canadian works are well-represented in their list of 58 references, which includes books on capital investment and managerial finance.

In the light of recent developments in computation and of interdisciplinary endeavors, *Mathematics of Finance* is timely and up-to-date, particularly as to U.K. practice. The books by Donald, by S.G. Kellison, and by M.V. Butcher and C.J. Nesbitt [2], all of which go back to the early 1970s, are slightly dated and, in some important respects, less complete. Although likewise presupposing primarily a calculus background, the new book is, in general, more intensive and more difficult than the American books, especially in many (but not all) of its realistic applied problems. While purposely greatly influenced by Donald, Professors McCutcheon and Scott have contributed significantly to their subject through their selection of topics (exclusions as well as inclusions), articulate mathematical development, and choice of problems; they have collaborated very effectively.

The introductory chapter justifies accumulation at *compound* interest. Chapter 2 covers valuing (1) single sums at *variable* discrete and continuous rates of interest, with emphasis on varying forces of interest, and (2) cash flows, whether discrete or continuous. Thus, this chapter with its general model of interest rates anticipates Chapters 3 and 4, in which the key rates are constant (δ and $i^{(p)}$, respectively), and Chapter 5, devoted to discounted cash flow.

The third and fourth chapters develop the classical model for compound interest. Chapter 3 discusses the basic compound interest functions and ideas, such as effective rates of interest and discount, equations of value, the yield of a transaction (including criteria for its existence), simple annuities of most standard types, and loan (that is, amortization) schedules. Correspondingly, Chapter 4 deals with nominal rates and more general annuities. There are some adroit verbal interpretations, which become mnemonic devices. The technique of replacing actual with equivalent annuity payments is stressed. The selection of topics for inclusion, their arrangement, and the concise articulation in these chapters seem particularly felicitous.

For illustrative numerical work, the book has brief interest tables (at 1, 2, . . . , 15, 20, 25 percent), with ($Ia_{\overline{n}|}$ usefully replacing $l/s_{\overline{n}|}$ (or $1/a_{\overline{n}|}$). The emphasis throughout this text is on basic understanding of ideas, not details of calculations (except for an Appendix on iterative methods).

Chapter 5, "Discounted Cash Flow," is practical and modern. Involving terminology and measures familiar to some economists, business managers, accountants and actuaries, the "chapter is largely concerned with some applications of compound interest theory to the financial assessment of investments and business ventures" (p. 86). Among topics considered are *net* cash flows and their *present values (NPV)*, yield and profitability of a single investment project or competing ones, the effects of inflation, and various measures of rate of return on investments, including on unitized funds.

The capital redemption policy, though now rare even in the U.K., is ably presented in Chapter 6 as an introduction to life insurance mathematics. The chapter ends with an elegant theoretical development of the accumulated amount under varying *reinvestment* rates of (1) a sequence of unit sums and (2) a single unit sum.

The subject of Chapter 7 is prices and yields of fixed-interest securities, with interest income possibly liable to income tax. Chapter 8 studies the effect of capital gains tax on these securities, according to current U.K. practice. Because terminology and sometimes practice may differ from North American [3], the reader should note the authors' descriptions and definitions. Like their predecessors, McCutcheon and Scott focus on net (after tax) yield and Makeham's formula. Typically the formula also applies (if necessary, adjusted by additive terms) to a security redeemable in installments [4]. In solving numerous complicated problems for price or yield, the authors show how ingenious, possibly repeated, use of Makeham's formula may be efficient. There is a nice discussion of the effect of the term to redemption on the yield, applicable in the case of optional redemption dates. Chapter 7 ends with a section on *real* (that is, inflation-adjusted) yields and index-linked investments, illustrated by U.K. practice.

Many of the concepts and applications of Chapters 7–10 are of interest to the institutional investor, such as an insurance company or pension fund. Chapter 9 is about a particular kind of fixed-interest security once common in the U.K., namely, a loan repayable by a cumulative sinking fund. The American reader finds this equivalent to amortization, with complications (for example, taxes and payments on principal at premium prices such as 110 percent).

Chapters 5 and 10–12 supplement the traditional material of compound interest books and were outside the scope of Donald's book. Some of the topics of Chapter 10 relate to fixed-interest securities: yield curves; discounted mean term, $T(\delta)$, of a project; and the volatility (when interest rates change slightly) of a project. From the definition of volatility (at force δ) as $-NPV'(\delta)/NPV(\delta)$, it follows easily that volatility $= T(\delta)$; the greater its magnitude for a fixed small change in interest rates, the greater the relative profit or loss on an investment. Other topics of Chapter 10 relate to assets and liabilities: matching and immunization, to protect an investor against changes in interest rates. The text presents Redington's theory (1952) of immunization, which protects against *small* rate changes; one consequence is that (at the current force δ_o) the discounted mean terms of total assets and total liabilities are equal. The Butcher and Nesbitt book also discusses the Redington theory, but McCutcheon and Scott's book goes further in presenting a theory of "full" immunization, in which the investor profits from *any* immediate rate changes. A requirement of this theory—the linking with *each* item of liability-outgo of *two* items of total assets, one due before and the other after the liability—may in reality be difficult to attain [5].

Chapter 11 on consumer credit is mainly concerned with recent U.K. legislation and regulations respecting (1) disclosure of the total charge for credit and the annual percentage rate of charge and (2) the minimum interest rebate on early repayment. For some comparison with the U.S., one might refer to Kellison and to Butcher and Nesbitt.

The final chapter, an introduction to stochastic interest rate models, will be appealing to readers of the Society's *Actuarial Mathematics* (1986). To allow for uncertainty in the future, one uses probability theory to provide variations in interest rates and relies on computers and simulation techniques. The authors state (p. 270): "Stochastic interest rate models offer a powerful tool for the analysis of financial problems. . .fundamentally different from the deterministic approach" of their previous eleven chapters. Assuming that annual yields, i_t, are *independent* random variables, they consider the random variables S_n and A_n, which denote the accumulation of a unit sum and of an annuity-due of n unit payments, respectively, and they derive the mean and variance of each. Then, based on assumptions about the distribution of the i_t, probabilities concerning S_{15} and A_{15} are calculated. For example, if the $1 + i_t$ are assumed to have identical, specific log-normal distributions, then $\log(1 + i_t)$ and $\log S_n$ have specific normal distributions, so exact probability statements about S_{15} can be made; since the distribution of A_{15} is not apparent, the authors carried out 10,000 simulations to approximate it and estimate probabilities. Next, they briefly discuss simple forms of *dependent* interest rates and illustrate A_{15}. The chapter ends with an application of Brownian motion to a single premium investment.

This attractive book proceeds smoothly and carries the reader along, but—if one is not careful—the reader who completes it may find the extent of the coverage and the amount of detail somewhat overwhelming. Nevertheless, the main ideas, because of the lucid presentation and repetition, should be very clear. All in all, this new *Mathematics of Finance* should be valuable and interesting to North American actuarial students, educators, and Society members.

MARJORIE V. BUTCHER

END NOTES

1. TODHUNTER, RALPH. *Interest Including Annuities-Certain. Part 1 of Institute of Actuaries Text-Book of the Principles of Interest, Life Annuities, and Assurances, and Their Practical Application.* London: Charles and Edwin Layton, 1901; 3d ed. rev. and enl. by R.C. Simmonds and T.P. Thompson. Cambridge: Ulrich, Institute of Actuaries, 1931.
2. Reviewed in *TSA*: VI, 617 and XXIII, 629; XXI, 627; and XXIII, 628, respectively.
3. For example, bonds in U.S. nomenclature are often called stocks in the U.K.
4. This might be a whole bond issue or a loan being amortized.
5. The text is substantially error-free, but has two errors here in its first printing, corrected in later printings. In equations (10.8.3) and (10.8.4), the first factor should read $\exp(-\delta t_1)$, and on p. 248 for $x<0$, $f'(x)<0$. An errata sheet is available from the authors.

Annie N. and Lloyd K. Friedman: *On the Trail of Actuaries in Texas, 1844–1964*, pp. 216, published by Watercress Press, San Antonio, Texas, 1988.

In the fall of 1983, the Actuaries' Club of the Southwest set an example that other clubs and writers would do well to follow when its president, Edwin E. Hightower, proposed as one of its projects a "history of the Club and actuarial practices in the Southwest." The hour produced not just the man but the married couple—Lloyd K. Friedman, F.S.A. 1937, and his wife, Annie. Would that other laborers in the historical vineyard could be half as fortunate! These authors, with the acknowledged aid of other enthusiasts, required less than five years to produce a thoroughly entertaining, informative, and even inspiring volume.

The book is in three chronological parts of four chapters each, ending with an epilogue and three appendixes descriptive of the 1949 foundation of the sponsoring club. The volume's frontispiece portrays the two actuaries whose impacts upon the profession's maturing in the Southwest were exceptional—Lawrence M. Cathles (1877–1958), an immigrant from Scotland, and Texas-born Paul V. Montgomery (1886–1980).

Annie and Lloyd made extensive use of taped interviews, some of them giving the words of widows of the actuaries concerned, and also dug deeply into documentary accounts for the biographies. Readers are thus favored with an appreciation of the activities, mind-sets, and eccentricities of more actuaries than most outsiders would have guessed contributed to the significance and reputation of our profession in Texas. More than sixty men and women received greater-than-passing mention.

Readers should feel even further indebted to the Friedmans for devoting ten pages to a charming O. Henry story about the chivalry of Luke Coonrod Standifer, Texas Commissioner of Insurance, Statistics, and History in the 1880s. This is icing on the cake.

The North American actuarial profession, although rightly considering itself one of the learned societies, has a sadly spotty record when it comes to putting on paper the story of its own heritage. The founders of the Actuarial Society of America in 1889 behaved almost as though no profession existed before their time; a few personal reminiscences and trade paper news items are all that we have today about eighty years of struggle and experimentation. And the Actuarial Society placed a low valuation upon its library; sporadic appropriation to buy books were voted, but in general the quantity now on the shelves is far less than it should be, especially considering the vigor for many years of the book review sections of actuarial journals.

Curiously, the Friedman's book is not for sale. The largest supply of copies sits at the *Yearbook* address of Jack A. Rollier. Requests accompanied by a check for $15 per copy payable to the Actuaries' Club of the Southwest to help cover publication costs will be cheerfully received. If a desire for good reading about the profession prevails among today's actuaries, Mr. Rollier's supply surely will be quickly exhausted.

E. J. MOORHEAD

Obituary

SAMUEL N. AIN
MORGAN HANLON ALVORD
ALBERT WILLIAM ANDERSON
EDWARD CHARLES BENHAM
EDMUND CALLIS BERKELEY
JOHN ALLEN BRADFORD
ALEXANDER THOMSON BROOKS
JOSEPH A. BUDINGER
ALDEN THOMSON BUNYAN
JOSEPH ANDREW CHRISTMAN
BARRETT N. COATES, JR.
HARVEY H. CONKLIN, JR.
THOMAS KILBURN DODD
FRANCIS THOMAS DRISCOLL
ROBERT DONALD DRISKO
MAURICE HOWARD FARRANT
CARL HAHN FISCHER
GEORGE R. FRASER
JOSEPH B. GLENN
GEORGE WILLIAM KEITH GRANGE
HENRY STRONG HUNTINGTON, III
ROBERT JAMES KIRTON
MYRON HENRY MARGOLIN
WILLIAM CRAIG McCARTER
JOSEPH TREVOR McNEELY
JOHN HAYNES MILLER
HARRY D. MORGAN
BENNET BRONSON MURDOCK
THOMAS JOHN NORRIS
MELVIN C. PRYCE
ANTHONY J. SAVASTA
MICHAEL C. SCHLUSSEL
EDWARD JAMES SELIGMAN
PHILLIP JOHN SHORE
CHARLES W. SOUTHERN
MARGARET WALKER
HAROLD GRAHAM WALTON
MAX S. WEINSTEIN
CHARLIE THOMAS WHITLEY
WILLIAM SHELLY YORK

1913   Samuel N. Ain   1988

Samuel N. Ain, an Associate of the Society and of the Casualty Actuarial Society, a Fellow of the Conference of Actuaries in Public Practice, a member of the American Academy of Actuaries, and an Enrolled Actuary, died on February 1, 1988. He was seventy-five years old.

Mr. Ain graduated from Brooklyn College with a B.S. in chemistry and received a master's degree in actuarial mathematics from the University of Michigan in 1936.

Shortly thereafter, Mr. Ain began his actuarial career at the firm of George B. Buck, where he worked until being called to active duty in the U.S. Navy in 1941 just before the attack on Pearl Harbor. He had previously applied to and already been accepted by the U.S. Naval Reserve in 1938. After being called to active duty, he served in the Navy for four years, first as an officer on a destroyer and later as a cryptoanalyst in Washington, D.C. with the rank of Lieutenant Commander.

After leaving the Navy, Mr. Ain worked as an actuary for four years with the Pension Trust Division of the Internal Revenue Service in Washington, D.C. In 1950, he established his own consulting firm in New York, which he operated until 1976, when he merged his firm with The Wyatt Company, from which he retired on June 30, 1978.

His activities, however, were not limited solely to the actuarial sphere. He was a long-time, devoted member of Congregation Shearith Israel, the oldest congregation in North America. He served as trustee, honorary trustee, and chairman of its Synagogue Insurance Committee.

He is survived by his wife, Dorothy, a daughter, a son, one granddaughter, and five sisters and one brother.

1902   Morgan Hanlon Alvord   1988

Morgan H. Alvord, a Fellow of the Society, died in Bloomfield, Connecticut, on March 20, 1988. He was in his eighty-sixth year.

Born in Hartford on March 31, 1902, Mr. Alvord graduated from Yale University with academic and athletic honors in 1924. He then joined the actuarial staff of Connecticut General Life Insurance Company, qualifying as a Fellow of the Actuarial Society of America in 1942.

Mr. Alvord's career was entirely with Connecticut General until his retirement in 1967 from the rank of vice president. His leadership in the company's group pension department was credited with establishing its high competitive standing in that line. He was a founder of the American Pension Conference.

His numerous contributions to actuarial literature included a paper at the 1957 International Congress of Actuaries; otherwise, they were mainly through pension journals. Among his community activities was chairmanship of the West Hartford Pension Board.

An actuarial colleague describes him thus: "Always a gentleman, Morgan was at the same time adventurous, courageous, demanding and generous. He was stimulating to be with at work, at the poker table, on a ski slope or a golf course.... Morgan was a kind man, a great competitor and a good friend."

He is survived by his second wife, Dorothy, a daughter, two grandchildren, and two great-grandsons.

1905   Albert William Anderson   1989

Albert W. Anderson, a Fellow of the Society and of the Canadian Institute of Actuaries, died on January 13, 1989, in his eighty-fourth year.

Born in London, Ontario, on June 12, 1905, Mr. Anderson attended Bowmanville High School and obtained his senior matriculation from the London Collegiate Institute. He became a Fellow of the Actuarial Society of America in 1936, being one of the few who achieved this without the benefit of university mathematical training. He was also a Fellow of the Chartered Institute of Secretaries.

Mr. Anderson joined London Life Insurance Company in 1923 and for several years was a member of the actuarial department. He was promoted to the position of executive assistant in the secretary's office in 1937 and subsequent appointments were: assistant secretary, 1946; comptroller, 1951; secretary, 1958; vice-president and secretary, 1960; then vice-president and executive secretary in 1966. He was named executive vice-president and a shareholders' representative on London Life's board of directors in 1967. He represented his company on industry matters for more than 23 years.

Mr. Anderson was a member of the Board of Directors of the Life Office Management Association and served on the standing committee concerned with taxation and public health in the Canadian Life Insurance Association.

Mr. Anderson was a member of the committee of stewards at Metropolitan United Church.

He and his wife were enthusiastic fishers.

He is survived by his wife, Mary, a daughter, a son, and six grandchildren.

1912　　　Edward Charles Benham　　　1986

Edward C. Benham, an Associate of this Society, died on November 7, 1986. He was seventy-four years old.

Born in Harrow, England, on September 16, 1912, Mr. Benham qualified as a Fellow of the Institute of Actuaries in 1946. In 1955 he came to Canada as Resident Actuary of the Canadian Life Branch of his company, the Pearl Assurance Company of London. He was admitted as an Associate of the Society of Actuaries in 1956.

In 1959, Mr. Benham joined the Quebec Mutual Life Assurance Company of Montreal, serving as its actuary until his retirement in 1979. He continued living in Montreal until his death.

Mr. Benham is remembered as a faithful attender at actuarial gatherings in Canada for a quarter of a century.

1909　　　Edmund Callis Berkeley　　　1988

Edmund C. Berkeley, a Fellow of the Society, died in Boston on March 7, 1988. Although his final illness was by no means brief, he had been active until the last few months of his life. He was just short of his seventy-ninth birthday.

Mr. Berkeley was born in New York City on March 20, 1909. After graduation from Harvard College in 1930, he was employed briefly at Prudential and then from October 1930 until June 1934 in the actuarial department of Mutual Life of New York. In October 1934 he rejoined the actuarial staff of the Prudential, qualifying in 1941 as a Fellow of the predecessor bodies of the Society.

From 1942 to 1946 Mr. Berkeley served in the U.S. Naval Reserve. During part of that time he was stationed at the Harvard Computation Laboratory, where he assisted Professor Howard Aiken in designing "Mark I," the first information-processing digital computer.

The actuarial profession's debt to Mr. Berkeley arises from his initiative, soon after his return to the Prudential in 1946, in spurring actuaries to appreciate the potential of the computer. The minutes of the Actuarial Society's Council meeting of February 28, 1947, make this abundantly clear:

> The President [E.W. Marshall] referred to correspondence and conversations which he and the Secretary [Walter Klem] had had with Mr. E.C. Berkeley of the Prudential Insurance Company regarding projects for the development and construction of sequence controlled calculators for use in life insurance company problems. Following discussion, the Council authorized the President to appoint a special committee to explore the possibilities for Society participation in such projects.

Within the next three months two major steps had been taken. Malvin E. Davis, chairman of the Committee on Society Participation in Development of Calculators, had submitted his report recommending appointment of the landmark Committee on Recording Means and Computing Devices, and Mr. Berkeley had presented a paper (*TASA*, Vol. 48, pp. 36–52), "Electronic Machinery for Handling Information, and Its Uses in Insurance."

During the following two years Mr. Berkeley founded the Association for Computing Machinery, published a popular book, *Giant Brains or Machines That Think*, and started the business that was to occupy all the rest of his life, Berkeley Enterprises, Inc. of Newtonville, Massachusetts.

Mr. Berkeley, having quickly become a world-renowned lecturer and prolific writer on computer-related subjects, was rarely seen in actuarial circles, but the *Transactions* for 1964 (*TSA*, Vol. 16, p. 182) contains a short discussion in which he urged actuaries to broaden their fields of endeavor. In 1980 (*The Actuary*, November issue) he responded delightfully to an invitation to compare thirty years of computer development with the prophecies made in his *Giant Brains* book and to make a fresh set of forecasts.

Mr. Berkeley was a genius whose eccentricities had become proverbial even before his talents were widely recognized. He was as friendly and obliging as he was understandable in his analyses and his ideas for the future. He is survived by his wife, Suzanne, two sons, a daughter, and a granddaughter.

1926 John Allen Bradford 1987

John A. Bradford, an Associate of the Society since 1969, died in Yorkville, Illinois, on September 8, 1987, at age sixty.

Mr. Bradford was born in Benton, Illinois, on October 29, 1926. After graduation from the University of Chicago in 1948 and brief employment at Metropolitan Life, he joined Continental Casualty Company in 1952. He was appointed associate actuary in 1958 and later became actuarial supervisor in the company's accident and health division. In 1975 he became a health and special risks actuary with the American International Group in New York City, continuing there until his death.

Although handicapped for many years by a debilitating ailment, Mr. Bradford was active in wilderness hiking and nature conservancy. He kept himself informed on computers from their earliest days and on advances in the actuarial fields of his specialization.

He is survived by his parents.

1924   Alexander Thomson Brooks   1988

Alexander (Alec) T. Brooks, a 1951 Fellow of the Faculty of Actuaries who was admitted as an Associate of the Society in 1954, died on March 27, 1988, while holidaying in Antigua. He was sixty-three years old.

Born in India on October 3, 1924, Mr. Brooks graduated in 1942 from George Watson's Boys' College, Edinburgh. His actuarial studies, interrupted by World War II, were completed while he was employed in Edinburgh insurance companies.

In 1954 Mr. Brooks entered the American International Group as actuary of the Philippine American Life Insurance Company. He served in Manila until 1981, when he transferred to London for the past seven years.

A capable actuary with a sunny disposition, he was well known to a number of actuaries in the United States who saw him mainly at International Congresses.

His wife, Chris, died in 1987; three children survive.

1896   Joseph A. Budinger   1982

Word has belatedly arrived of the death of Joseph A. Budinger, a Fellow of the Society, on August 13, 1982, in Phoenix, Arizona. He was eighty-six years of age.

He was born in Chicago and lived in the Kansas City area until moving to Phoenix when he retired in 1970.

Mr. Budinger's career at Kansas City Life began in 1930 and spanned 40 years. He became a vice president in 1939, was elected to the board of directors in 1940, and became executive vice president of the company in

1958. Beginning in 1964, he served two years as vice chairman of the board and was an active member of the board until 1970.

He also served as a consulting actuary to the Kansas City Police Department and as an honorary director of Rockhurst College.

He was a Knight of the Holy Sepulcher in Rome.

Mr. Budinger is survived by his wife, three daughters, three brothers, 19 grandchildren and 11 great-grandchildren.

1897   Alden Thomson Bunyan   1988

Alden (Bunny) T. Bunyan, a Fellow of the Society, died in Hartford, Connecticut, on January 8, 1988, at age ninety. Having earned his Associateship in the Actuarial Society of America in 1920 and his Fellowship in 1922, he had been a member for more than sixty-seven years.

Born in Colchester, Connecticut, on July 19, 1897, Mr. Bunyan graduated from Yale University in 1918 and immediately joined the actuarial staff of the Phoenix Mutual Life Insurance Company. He had planned to enter teaching, but the company's then actuary, Archibald A. Welch of Yale's Class of 1882, was keeping a close eye upon promising actuarial timber and no doubt helped him to change his mind. Mr. Bunyan remained with the company as a staff member, officer, and finally consulting actuary until 1974.

Mr. Bunyan earned his fame in the profession for his eminent service, perhaps over as long as a quarter-century, in editorial work on the *Transactions*. Originally this stemmed from his company post as assistant to John R. Larus, who was editor from 1936 to 1950. As Mr. Larus' successor, Mr. Bunyan moved from assistant editor to editor, continuing until 1962, after which he was elected to a three-year "appreciation" term on the Board of Governors.

Mr. Bunyan was a keen bridge player on the local and national scene and also was accomplished in drama and tennis. Active for many years in community projects, he gave his talents to the Hartford Y.M.C.A., Boy Scouts, and his church in West Hartford.

He was a true New England gentleman. His mathematical and calculating talents were prodigious, as was his ability to craft a single sentence of paragraph length with perfect syntax. Yet he remained unassuming, almost shy, and always willing to give kind and patient explanations to all.

1900 Joseph Andrew Christman 1988

Joseph A. Christman, a Fellow of the Society, died in Phoenix, Arizona, on September 18, 1988, less than a month before his eighty-eighth birthday.

Born in New York City on October 16, 1900, Mr. Christman's formal education consisted of grammar school and one year in a Brooklyn high school. He then studied accounting at the City College of New York and mathematics with the help of a tutor. He was employed outside the insurance business for nearly seven years before entering the actuarial department of Metropolitan Life Insurance Company in 1924, where he remained throughout his career. By 1929 he had qualified as a Fellow of the Actuarial Society. In his company he rose to the post of actuary in 1953, retiring in 1965.

In 1933, Mr. Christman authored, jointly with Horace R. Bassford, a paper, "Premiums and Reserves for the Accidental Death Benefits Attached to Life Insurance Policies" (*TASA*, Vol. 34, pp. 263–276). In the 1950s and 1960s he was a member, and for some time chairman, of the Society of Actuaries Committee on Disability and Double Indemnity Benefits.

In 1950 Mr. Christman rendered signal service to the profession as actuary for a committee appointed to determine the price to be paid to stockholders for mutualization of the then financially distressed Pacific Mutual Life Insurance Company. That committee's determination successfully withstood several legal challenges and was justified by subsequent company experience.

Mr. Christman is survived by his wife, Marie, five children, and several grandchildren.

Barrett N. Coates, Jr. 1988

Barrett N. Coates, Jr. died in Modesto, California, on July 14, 1988, after a short illness.

He was a Fellow of the Society, member of the American Academy of Actuaries, an Enrolled Actuary, member of the Conference of Actuaries in Public Practice, and past Associate of the Canadian Institute of Actuaries. He was also past president of the San Francisco Actuarial Club, Western Pension Conference, and the Actuarial Club of the Pacific States. He also served on the pension board of the United Church of Christ.

Mr. Coates grew up in Berkeley, California, and graduated from the University of California at Berkeley. He also studied actuarial science at the University of Manitoba under Dr. Warren. His first job was with the West

Coast Life Insurance Company in San Francisco. He joined the firm that his father had started, Coates, Herfurth and England. Later he started his own firm and soon he joined with Angus Crawford to form Coates and Crawford, Inc. The firm later became Coates, Kenney, Gavazzi and Witt, Inc. with Barrett serving as president until his retirement on April 1, 1987.

He would go out of his way to introduce prospective actuarial talent to the actuarial community. He had a talent of invoking infectious loyalty from friends and coworkers. He could explain complicated problems in terms his audience could understand.

1913   Harvey H. Conklin, Jr.   1988

Harvey H. Conklin, a 1958 Fellow of the Society, died in Westerly, Rhode Island, on June 2, 1988, at age seventy-four.

Born in Allentown, Ohio, on September 7, 1913, he graduated from Dartmouth College in 1935 and joined the actuarial division of Metropolitan Life Insurance Company in New York City. In 1960 he moved to the Life Insurance Company of Virginia, remaining there until his retirement in 1973 with the title senior vice-president and actuary. Afterwards he did some consulting work in Rhode Island.

Among Mr. Conklin's contributions to Life of Virginia was his development of a precursor of universal life, a whole life policy with renewal premiums to be adjusted in accordance with interest rate variations.

Harvey took a keen interest in development of young actuaries in the Richmond area. He arranged for weekly actuarial classes conducted by Dr. Oglesby of the University of Virginia. One of his hobbies was writing novels. He was a first-class person, well liked and respected by his colleagues.

1900   Thomas Kilburn Dodd   1988

Thomas (Tom) K. Dodd, a Fellow of the Society, died in West Hartford, Connecticut, on July 11, 1988, at age eighty-eight. The famous American actuary Amzi Dodd (1823-1913) was a cousin of his grandfather.

Born in East Orange, New Jersey, on January 20, 1900, Mr. Dodd graduated magna cum laude from Yale College in 1920. Rules of those times forced him to wait twice for educational recognition—first, to enter Yale after graduation from high school at age 15, and second, to be granted

Fellowship in the Actuarial Society in 1925 after having completed the examinations the previous year.

Mr. Dodd's insurance career was entirely in the Connecticut Mutual Life Insurance Company, which he entered in 1920 and from which he retired in 1965. After five years in the actuarial department, he had been transferred to the underwriting department, becoming supervisor of applications in 1929 and rising by 1949 to vice president, underwriting.

Under his guidance, the underwriting division was reorganized with new systems for selection, policy issue, and reinsurance. His company's favorable mortality experience resulted in great measure from his leadership.

Mr. Dodd's major professional contributions were made through the Home Office Life Underwriters Association, of which he was elected President in 1954. His favorite hobby was bridge; as a member of the Hartford Bridge Club for over thirty years he was acclaimed an expert.

He was admired and respected as a talented person and a genial companion. His mind was brilliant, remaining so to his death. Seldom did he go wrong in his carefully considered judgments. A devoted husband and father, he was married to the late Florence Marks Dodd for more than fifty years. He is survived by a son, a daughter, and five grandchildren.

1932   Francis Thomas Driscoll   1987

Francis (Frank) T. Driscoll, a Fellow of the Society, a Fellow of the Conference of Actuaries in Public Practice, and a member of the American Academy of Actuaries, died on October 31, 1987, at age fifty-five.

Born July 31, 1932, in New York City, Mr. Driscoll graduated from Yale University in 1954 and immediately joined George B. Buck Consulting Actuaries, remaining with that firm for the rest of his life, most recently as actuary and benefit consultant in the firm's law department.

He qualified as a Fellow of the Society in 1966. Among his services to the profession was as collaborator in construction of the 1974 George B. Buck Mortality Table, published that year in *The Proceedings*, Conference of Actuaries in Public Practice (Vol. XXIV, pp. 320–329).

Mr. Driscoll is remembered for the high quality of his work on highly technical problems in the pension field, for his inspiration to others, and for his ability in coping with his physical problems. He is survived by his wife, Lorraine Marie, and a daughter.

1923   Robert Donald Drisko   1987

Robert D. Drisko, a Fellow of the Society, died on April 7, 1987, in San Mateo, California, at age sixty-three.

Born in Santa Monica, California, on July 20, 1923, Mr. Drisko graduated from Stanford University in 1946 and from an actuarial science course at University of Manitoba in 1949. After two summers of employment at West Coast Life and one summer at Coates, Herfurth and England, he joined the latter company in 1951. He had originally planned to teach high school mathematics but changed his mind after discovering "actuary" listed at the top of a catalogue of 500 post-war jobs. His first full-time actuarial employment had been with Massachusetts Mutual Life.

Mr. Drisko attained his Fellowship in 1958. His specialty in consulting was the field of governmental pension systems, in which he became skilled in translating actuarial principles into lay language.

He is survived by his wife, Betty, and three children.

1912   Maurice Howard Farrant   1988

Maurice H. Farrant, a Fellow of the Society, died on May 12, 1988, at age seventy-five.

Born in Vancouver on May 21, 1912, Mr. Farrant graduated from the University of British Columbia in 1933. He then entered employment with Confederation Life Association of Toronto, where his father was an officer. He remained with that company in either its Toronto or London, England, office until 1948, except for four years, 1942 to 1946, in the Canadian Army in Canada and overseas. In 1948 he moved to the United States to become assistant actuary at Occidental Life of California.

From 1950 to 1953 Mr. Farrant was at Marsh and McLennan in Seattle as chief actuary, but he returned for another three years to his post at Occidental. Then he reentered consulting for the rest of his career, first as a partner in Coates, Herfurth and England in San Francisco, then in 1959, establishing his own firm in Vancouver. When Farrant and Company merged with The Wyatt Company in 1975, Mr. Farrant retired informally, while continuing to do some consulting for Wyatt.

Mr. Farrant qualified as Fellow of the Society of Actuaries in 1952 and was enrolled as a Fellow of the Canadian Institute of Actuaries in 1965 and a member of the American Academy of Actuaries in 1966. He is survived by his wife, Mae, and a daughter.

1903   Carl Hahn Fischer   1988

Professor Carl H. Fischer, a Fellow of the Society, died on December 21, 1988, in Ann Arbor, Michigan, at age eighty-five.

Born in Newark, New Jersey on August 22, 1903, he graduated in chemical engineering from Washington University in 1923 and received a Ph.D. degree in mathematics from the University of Iowa in 1932. His doctoral advisor, and indeed role model, was Professor Henry L. Rietz.

After three years of chemical engineering, he went into teaching at, successively, Beloit College, University of Iowa, University of Minnesota, and Wayne State University, and then at the University of Michigan from 1941 until his retirement in 1974. He was appointed professor of insurance and actuarial mathematics in 1950. He served on many university committees and was author of four books and forty-five articles on mathematics, statistics, insurance, and pensions. Assisted by his wife, Kathleen, whom he married in 1925, he prepared a series of directories of graduates of the actuarial program, most recently in 1979.

Professor Fischer qualified as a Fellow of the Society of Actuaries in 1952 and served on its Board of Governors in 1961–1962. He was a pioneer in pension actuarial work, establishing a consulting service that continues today. He was a member of an Advisory Council on Social Security and chairman of the Study of the Military Retired Pay System for the Senate Committee on Armed Services and served on other federal and state study commissions. He was a consultant on social security to the Philippines in 1956 and 1962 and to Liberia in 1977–78. In 1965 he organized an actuarial student program at the Hebrew University in Jerusalem and returned to teach there in 1967.

He served on the Ann Arbor Board of Education and was a trustee of that city's Employees Retirement System. In recent years he developed a new specialty as an expert witness in lawsuits.

He enjoyed a long and interesting actuarial career and provided wise advice to many people and groups. He is survived by his wife, Kathleen, two sons, and five grandchildren.

1905   George R. Fraser   1986

George R. Fraser, a Fellow of the Society, died on July 22, 1986, in Toronto, Ontario, at age eighty.

Born in Kincardine, Ontario, on October 23, 1905, Mr. Fraser graduated from the University of Toronto in 1928 and immediately entered the actuarial department of the Excelsior Life Insurance Company in Toronto. He served that company for forty-two years, until his retirement in 1970 from the post of vice-president and actuary. He qualified in 1949 as a Fellow of the Society of Actuaries.

He was a quiet, friendly person who always did his best in the interests of students and employees under his direction.

He is survived by his wife, Pearl.

1905   Joseph B. Glenn   1988

Joseph B. Glenn, a Fellow of the Society and of the Casualty Actuarial Society, died February 27, 1988, in Bethesda, Maryland. He was eighty-two years old.

Mr. Glenn was born on December 23, 1905, in Vincennes, Indiana. He received a degree from Indiana University in 1926 and joined the actuarial department of the Travelers Insurance Company in 1927. Mr. Glenn earned his Associateship in the Society of Actuaries in 1929 and his Fellowship in 1930.

From 1934 to 1942, Mr. Glenn was chief actuary of the Railroad Retirement Board. He volunteered for military service during World War II and was assigned to the Navy's Construction Battalion, building airstrips in the Pacific.

From 1943 to his retirement in 1975, Mr. Glenn was the chief actuary for the Department of Defense. He was an actuarial pioneer in modeling and writing computer programs. All military personnel legislation passed during this long and formative period was analyzed by Mr. Glenn. Among other things, he played a major role in the development of the Career Compensation Act of 1949, which revamped the military compensation structure to provide the pay and allowance system still used today. In addition, he acted as a consultant to the Korean government in the development of a pension system. Mr. Glenn received several prestigious awards and citations from both the Secretary of Defense and the Congress.

He is survived by his widow, Carmela, a daughter, and a grandson.

1897   George William Keith Grange   1984

Word has belatedly arrived of the death in Baldwin, New York, on December 7, 1984, of George W. K. Grange, a 1936 Associate of the Society. He was age eighty-seven.

Born in Jamaica, British West Indies, on February 6, 1897, Mr. Grange graduated from Cambridge University in 1919. After four years teaching in England's secondary schools, he joined the Ayrshire Education Authority in Scotland.

In November 1927 he came to the United States and joined the actuarial staff of Metropolitan Life Insurance Company. After three years of basic actuarial training, he became a research clerk in that company's social insurance section. In November 1937 he was temporarily employed as a senior actuarial mathematician at the Social Security Board in Washington, D.C., returning to Metropolitan Life in June 1938. In 1953 he was appointed social security consultant under Reinhard A. Hohaus, holding that position as the company's expert on social security until Mr. Hohaus retired in 1962. Although due to retire, he remained for some time in employment, while Mr. Mortimer Spiegelman was assuming Mr. Hohaus' duties in that social insurance field.

Mr. Grange contributed substantially to actuarial literature on social security. In 1937 he was joint author with Fred S. Jahn of "The Public Pension System of Sweden," (*R.A.I.A.*, Vol. 26, pp. 424–488) and in 1948 he and John H. Miller authored "Cash Benefits for Extended Disability" (*TASA*, Vol. 49, pp. 54–71). He also presented discussions and a thorough 1938 review of a survey on British public health services (*R.A.I.A.*, Vol. 27, pp. 310–316).

1915   Henry Strong Huntington, III   1987

Henry S. Huntington, III, a Fellow of the Society, died in Dedham, Massachusetts, on December 22, 1987, at age seventy-two.

Born in Watertown, New York, on February 15, 1915, Mr. Huntington graduated from Haverford College in 1936 and took a two-year actuarial science course at the University of Michigan. He then joined the actuarial staff of Lincoln National Life Insurance Company in Fort Wayne, Indiana, where he had been a summer student, continuing there from June 1938 to March 1943, when he entered upon three years in the U.S. Army Air Force Weather Service.

He then accepted employment at the John Hancock Mutual Life Insurance Company, remaining there until his retirement in late 1986 with the post of research actuary.

Mr. Huntington qualified as a Fellow of the Society of Actuaries in 1951. He was an active member, contributing several discussions and two papers, both on the subject of premiums for renewable term insurance. He was also active in the affairs of the Actuaries Club of Boston and was a charter member of the American Academy of Actuaries.

He was a genial, enthusiastic person, always a pleasure to work with.

1901 Robert James Kirton 1988

Robert J. Kirton, an eminent Fellow of the Institute of Actuaries and an Associate of the Society of Actuaries since 1950, died in England on March 7, 1988. He was in his eighty-seventh year.

Born in England on July 13, 1901, Mr. Kirton graduated from Cambridge University in 1923 and was for several years employed in the actuarial departments of insurance companies in Scotland. In 1938 he returned to England to join the Equity and Law Life Assurance Society in London, serving as general manager of that company from 1939 to 1966 and continuing on its board until 1977.

Long prominent in the affairs of the Institute of Actuaries as a member of its Council, Mr. Kirton was awarded the Institute's Silver Medal in 1966 for his exceptional services to the profession. A full account of his accomplishments appears in a memoir in the *Journal of the Institute of Actuaries* (Vol. 115, p. 553).

Mr. Kirton was a long-time friend of the profession on this side of the Atlantic. He remembered with pleasure visiting his first Actuarial Society of America meeting as far back as 1928 and was especially pleased to have proposed the toast of that Society at the formal dinner in White Sulphur Springs at the first gathering of the new Society of Actuaries in 1949.

1937   Myron Henry Margolin   1987

Myron (Mike) H. Margolin, chief executive officer of the newly formed Essex Life Insurance Company in West Orange, New Jersey, died on June 9, 1987, as a result of an automobile crash. He was 49 years old.

He was born in New York City but spent most of his life in New Jersey. Graduating from Princeton University in 1958, where he had majored in physics, he immediately started work at the Prudential, having been in that company's actuarial student training program in the summer of 1956. He qualified as a Fellow of the Society in 1963 and by 1973 had been promoted to vice-president and associate actuary at Prudential.

Mr. Margolin served the profession as chairman of the Society's Career Encouragement Committee. His intense interest in probabilities led him to submit two papers for the *Transactions*, in 1971 (Vol. 23, pp. 229–238) on credibility theory and in 1980 (Vol. 32, pp. 349–385) on the quantum interpretation of probability, which in part returned to credibility.

Mike kept much to himself but, to those who worked closely with him, was known to care greatly about people, to be an extremely devoted family man, and to be active in community projects. His reticence peaked when he left Prudential to join a group of entrepeneurs who wished to form a new insurance company to explore some new ideas. He assisted in obtaining a New Jersey license for that company, named the Essex Life Insurance Company.

Mr. Margolin is survived by his wife, three sons, and a daughter.

1908   William Craig McCarter   1988

William C. McCarter, a 1942 Fellow of the Society who had retired to Alberquerque, New Mexico, in 1972, died on May 24, 1988, at the age of seventy-nine.

Born in Duluth, Minnesota, on June 7, 1908, Mr. McCarter graduated from the University of Wisconsin in 1932. After a year of graduate study to help prepare for his actuarial examinations, he began his entire business career in 1933 with the Northwestern Mutual Life in Milwaukee. He was appointed an officer in 1943 and associate actuary in 1958.

He had become attracted to actuarial work while in high school and applied to Northwestern Mutual because of having been sold a policy in that company by Wisconsin's football coach, who was also a part-time agent.

His 1956 paper, "A New Annuity Mortality Table and a Graded Rate System for the Life Income Settlement Options" (*TSA*, Vol. 8, pp. 127–165), created considerable discussion at the time, and it is still being used by Northwestern Mutual as the basis for its life income settlement option rates, with an updated mortality table.

Undoubtedly his greatest and most satisfying achievement was his personal supervision of all aspects in the development of his company's extra ordinary life policy, which was introduced in 1968 and immediately became the company's most popular policy. It was the forerunner of the trend toward more flexible policies and enhanced the great number of advances made by all companies since that time.

The germ of this idea infected Mr. McCarter while he was doing what he liked best—attending the fall meeting of the Society and, on the free afternoon, playing golf with his actuarial friends in other companies. He, more so than many other actuaries, never let purely theoretical considerations hinder his search for the best practical and legal solutions to his research and development of new methods or products.

He married Lois Broughton in 1936 and is survived by her and their three daughters.

1900   Joseph Trevor McNeely   1988

Joseph (Bun) Trevor McNeely, an Associate of the Society, died on May 14, 1988, at the age of eighty-seven.

He attended Queens University, Kingston, Ontario, and graduated in 1921 with a B.A. in physics and chemistry. He taught mathematics for several years in high school in Windsor, Ontario, and then joined Manufacturers Life Insurance Co. in 1926, serving that company until he retired in 1966.

During his long service, he was appointed mathematician and served in several departments of the company and on the lecture staff of the Life Office Management Association. He kept a black book of company data and took pride in being able to reply to requests for information from his associates.

In retirement he continued his lifelong interest in sports and people and became a keen traveller, this leading him to take three round-the-world cruises.

His wife predeceased him in 1982. He is survived by a son.

1906   John Haynes Miller   1988

The death of John H. Miller in South Hero, Vermont, on Christmas Day 1988 represents a loss to the profession of one of its most distinguished and admired members. He was eighty-two years old.

Born in Washington, Pennsylvania, on May 29, 1906, Mr. Miller graduated in 1927 from Washington & Jefferson College of that city. After brief experience in a Pittsburgh contracting firm, he joined the actuarial staff of Metropolitan Life Insurance Company. In June 1929 he entered consulting work in the Woodward, Fondiller and Ryan firm in New York City, remaining there until after qualifying as a Fellow of the Actuarial Society in 1931. In 1938 he was admitted also to Fellowship in the Casualty Actuarial Society.

In 1934 Mr. Miller entered the service of the Monarch Life Insurance Company in Springfield, Massachusetts, becoming vice president and actuary in 1939 and vice president and senior actuary in 1957. He retired in 1966 with the rank of executive vice president.

In 1966 and 1967 he served as project director of the Future Outlook Society conducted by the Institute of Life Insurance. The foreword to its published report, *With An Eye To Tomorrow*, spoke of Mr. Miller's sparkling intellect, tireless devotion and unlimited good humor. His colleagues have well remembered his inspiring leadership; the group's prescriptions for action are summarized in the 1968 *Transactions (TSA*, Vol. 20, pp. D1–D3) and his reflections four years later in *TSA*, Vol. 24, pp. 76–78.

His first service on the Board of Governors of the Society of Actuaries was for a one-year term in 1950; in 1952 he returned for the first of two three-year terms. Elected Vice-President in 1956 and again in 1960, he served as President in 1962–1963. He was a charter Vice President of the American Academy of Actuaries in 1965, becoming President in 1967–1968.

Mr. Miller had a major role in organizing the Academy. He liked to say jocularly that he "invented the Academy"; when the organizers were wrestling with the question of just what structure would be best for the certification of actuaries and government relations in the United States, he was the one who suggested the concept of a body that would be neither subordinate to, nor would have any authority over, any of the existing actuarial bodies.

In December 1974, Mr. Miller launched his own publication, the *Disability Newsletter*, conceived as a contribution to the sound growth of long-term-disability coverages. His editorial comments, statistical summaries, and articles about past and current trends succeeded fully in giving his subscribers insights available nowhere else. He also contributed, jointly with Swiss actuary Simon Courant, three papers on disability subjects to the *Transactions*.

In 1964 he won the Harold R. Gordon Memorial Award and was named Health Insurance Man of the Year. In 1975 his work was recognized internationally as a winner of the Boleslaw Monic Fund Prize for accomplishments in insurance research. He was a familiar figure at International Congresses and contributed to their literature.

Energetic, progressive, cordial and unselfish, Mr. Miller was a delightful companion and a powerful influence for the good of the profession. Who but he would have ventured at age eighty into establishment of an organic farm in Ponce de Leon, Florida, appropriately called "The Fountain of Youth Farm"? John was also active in community projects including Goodwill Industries.

Mr. Miller's wife, Josephine, died in 1985. He is survived by four children and six grandchildren.

1923   Harry D. Morgan   1988

Harry D. Morgan, a 1959 Fellow of the Society, died on July 4, 1988. He was sixty-five years old.

A resident of Baltimore as an actuarial student, Mr. Morgan was a consulting actuary throughout his career. In 1954 he was with Eugene M. Klein and Associates in Cleveland. In 1958 he was assistant actuary at Johnson & Higgins in New York City. In February 1963 he entered the service of A. S. Hansen, Inc. in New York City, moving in 1978 to the firm's Chicago office. His post at his retirement in June 1979 was consulting principal.

After retirement, Mr. Morgan formed his own consulting firm, H. D. Morgan & Associates of Deerfield, Illinois.

1901   Bennet Bronson Murdock   1988

Bennet B. Murdock, an Associate of the Society, died on February 20, 1988. He was 87 years old.

Mr. Murdock was born January 15, 1901, at Meriden, Connecticut. He graduated from Yale College in 1924 and received his Ph.D. from Yale in 1934.

In 1934 he entered Prudential Insurance Company's actuarial training program and reached Associateship in both of the Society's predecessor bodies in 1942. His entire career was in actuarial pursuits at Prudential until his retirement in 1964.

He was an expert bridge player, a member of several Prudential championship teams. His easygoing nature, sense of humor and courtesy marked him as an outstanding gentleman.

Mr. Murdock is survived by his wife, Margaret, a son, three grandchildren, and a sister.

1940   Thomas John Norris   1988

Thomas J. Norris, a Fellow of the Society, died suddenly in Franklin, Tennessee, on July 4, 1988, at age forty-seven.

Born in Des Moines, Iowa, on August 18, 1940, Mr. Norris graduated from Iowa State University in 1965 and continued his mathematical study at the University of Colorado. After one year as mathematics instructor at Colorado School of Mines, from 1969 to 1988 he was in actuarial work, successively, at American Republic Life, Kentucky Central, Lincoln Benefit, and American General (formerly National) Life and Accident Insurance Company in Nashville, Tennessee, where his final post was senior vice president and chief actuary. He qualified as a Fellow of the Society of Actuaries in 1975.

In community affairs Mr. Norris was active in Brentwood United Methodist Church and the Nashville Area Chamber of Commerce Education Committee. He is survived by his wife, Judith, and two sons.

1914   Melvin C. Pryce   1988

Melvin C. Pryce, a Fellow in the Canadian Institute of Actuaries and the Society of Actuaries, died in London on May 4, 1988, in his seventy-fifth year.

He was born on March 12, 1914, in Windsor, Ontario. A graduate of the University of Western Ontario in honors mathematics and business, he joined the actuarial department of London Life Insurance Company in June 1936 as valuation clerk. In 1940 he began service with the Royal Canadian Air Force, where as a navigation instructor he attained the rank of squadron leader.

After his discharge in 1945, Mr. Pryce returned to London Life and proceeded to make his way through the ranks of management. In 1957 he was appointed associate actuary and an administrative officer of the company, and three years later was named actuary. In 1970 he became vice-president and general manager, and in 1972 executive vice-president. In 1973 he was elected a director of the company and in 1974 a member of the executive committee. In 1979, after 42 years of service, he retired from London Life.

He received his Fellowship in the Society of Actuaries in 1948 and was a fellow of the Canadian Institute of Actuaries. He was also very active in the Canadian Life Insurance Association (now the Canadian Life and Health Insurance Association).

Mr. Pryce was always a people person. He took a keen interest in the progress of young actuarial trainees through the examination process and was usually the first one to offer congratulations to the successful candidate. Also, he always gave high priority to the concerns of the sales staffs. He had a great understanding of people and empathy for their endeavors.

Outside of the office, he was an avid golf enthusiast, a keen bridge player, and an active member of the London Hunt and Country Club.

He is survived by his wife, Ruth, and two daughters.

1939   Anthony J. Savasta   1987

Anthony J. Savasta, an Associate of the Society since 1966, died in Melville, New York, on November 2, 1987, at age forty-seven.

Mr. Savasta was born in Brooklyn, New York, on November 22, 1939. After graduation from LeMoyne College, Syracuse, New York, in 1961 he joined the actuarial staff at New York Life. In 1964 he entered the pension consulting field as manager of A. S. Hansen in New York City.

In 1968 Mr. Savasta opened his own employee benefits consulting firm on Long Island, serving as its president until his death. He was a member of the American Academy of Actuaries and an Enrolled Actuary.

He is survived by his wife, Jane, and three children. A brother, Neil J. Savasta, is a member of the Society of Actuaries.

1953   Michael C. Schlussel   1988

Michael C. Schlussel, an Associate of the Society, died on June 22, 1988. He was 34 years old.

Mr. Schlussel was born on June 26, 1953, in Philadelphia. He was a 1975 graduate of the University of Scranton, where he received a bachelor of science degree. Shortly after his graduation, he began his actuarial career with Towers, Perrin in Philadelphia, where he remained for his entire career. He attained his Associateship in 1982. He was also an Enrolled Actuary and a member of the American Academy of Actuaries.

Mr. Schlussel was an avid sportsman with a quick wit and positive, upbeat attitude.

He is survived by his wife, Theresa, his parents, two brothers, and a sister.

1928   Edward James Seligman   1988

Edward J. Seligman, an Associate of the Society, died on January 8, 1988, at age fifty-nine.

Born in New York City on December 9, 1928, Mr. Seligman graduated from Michigan State University in 1950. After serving in the U.S. Air Force from 1951 to 1953, he gained an M.A. in mathematics from Wayne State University in 1958.

For the next nineteen years he was in industrial engineering and research, meanwhile earning his Associateship in the Society of Actuaries in 1969.

In June 1977 he joined the CNA Insurance Companies in Chicago, where he remained for ten years in statistical research until retiring in July 1987. Mr. Seligman made numerous contributions to actuarial literature in the mathematical and statistical fields in which he was expert. He served on the Committee to Recommend New Disability Tables for Valuation. That contribution, which regrettably turned out to be Mr. Seligman's last for the Society, was accorded a citation in the report of the committee (*TSA*, Vol. 37, p. 499).

1953   Phillip John Shore   1988

Phillip J. Shore, an Associate of the Society and a Fellow of the Faculty of Actuaries, died in England in January 1988, at age thirty-four.

Born in England on March 15, 1953, Mr. Shore graduated from Manchester University in 1974. He was thereupon employed at Standard Life Assurance Company in Edinburgh for three years; since then he was in the consulting actuarial field, most recently with R. Watson & Sons in Reigate, Surrey.

Mr. Shore enrolled in 1980 as an Associate of the Society of Actuaries, examinations being waived. He is survived by his wife, Lynda, and two daughters.

1912   Charles W. Southern   1983

Charles W. Southern, a Fellow of the Society, died on December 11, 1983, in Des Moines, Iowa. He was seventy-one years old.

Mr. Southern was born in September 1912 in Greenville, South Carolina. He was a graduate of Furman University and received a master's degree from the University of Michigan. He joined Bankers Life Company in 1935 in the actuarial department and spent his entire career with that company.

Mr. Southern served on the Society's Education and Examination Committee and was also president of the Actuaries' Club of Des Moines. Mr. Southern was an avid and successful competitive bridge player.

He is survived by his wife.

1895   Margaret Walker   1988

Margaret Walker, a Fellow of the Society, died in Vista, California, on April 16, 1988, at age ninety-two.

Born on December 30, 1895, in Atchison, Kansas, Miss Walker graduated from the University of Illinois in 1919. After looking at teaching, she decided that actuarial work offered greater opportunity and studied actuarial science at the State University of Iowa under Professor Henry L. Rietz. She was first employed at Central Life Assurance Company in Des Moines in 1921, then at Lincoln National Life in Fort Wayne in 1924. In 1946 she moved into fraternal actuarial work at the Royal Neighbors of America, Rock Island, Illinois, where she remained until her retirement.

She earned her Associateship in the American Institute of Actuaries in 1925 and her Fellowship in 1939.

In 1954 Miss Walker presented a discussion at a Society meeting in which she made the point, not widely accepted in those days, that because women were charged more than men for annuities, their low mortality might be taken into account in calculating their premiums for insurance.

1898   Harold Graham Walton   1986

Harold G. Walton, an Associate of the Society, died in Portland, Maine, on May 5, 1986. He was 87 years old.

Born in Bonn, Germany, on November 13, 1898, Mr. Walton came to the United States in 1912. After graduating from Kenyon College in 1920, he joined the staff of American Central Life in Indianapolis. While there he earned Associateships in the two predecessor bodies of the Society. From 1927 to 1933 he served as actuary of the Indiana State Insurance Department. Then after briefly serving as actuary of Buffalo Mutual Life, he became assistant actuary of Union Mutual Life Insurance Company in December 1935. He retired from that company with the rank of associate actuary in 1963.

Harold Walton had many avocations, being in his time an enthusiastic runner, a bowler and an avid gardener. His company colleagues remember him for his willingness to help them with problems in the fields of his knowledge and experience.

Mr. Walton is survived by his wife, a son, a daughter, five grandchildren, and a great-grandchild.

1903   Max S. Weinstein   1988

Max S. Weinstein, a Fellow of the Society, died March 12, 1988, in Albany, New York. He was eighty-four.

Born on December 7, 1903, in Brooklyn, Mr. Weinstein graduated with an engineering degree from Cooper Union in 1928. Having acquired two years experience in bookkeeping, he joined the New York Insurance Department in 1926, becoming a life company examiner in 1930. In 1945, he became the first chief actuary of the New York State Employee Retirement System, serving until his retirement in 1965. He then engaged in consulting on union pension plans.

Mr. Weinstein earned his Fellowship in 1942. He was also an Associate of the Casualty Actuarial Society.

He is survived by his wife, Evelyn, two children, and four grandchildren.

1936   Charlie Thomas Whitley   1989

Charlie T. Whitley, a 1969 Fellow of the Society, died in Winston-Salem, North Carolina, on January 14, 1989, at age fifty-two.

Born in Murfreesboro, North Carolina, on March 5, 1936, Mr. Whitley was a Phi Beta Kappa graduate of the University of North Carolina in 1960. He immediately joined Integon Life Insurance Corporation, then Security Life and Trust Company, in Winston-Salem, remaining there throughout his life and achieving the post of vice president and actuary. He became an authority on life insurance taxation.

Mr. Whitley served on the Part 10I Examination Committee in 1973–74, but his major professional contribution was to the work of the Southeastern Actuaries Club of which he was President in 1983. He was also a member of several task forces on taxation of the American Council of Life Insurance.

His service in the U.S. Army included a tour of duty in Germany. He was active in the First Baptist Church of Winston-Salem, where he was a deacon with special interest in service to young people.

He is survived by his wife, Jean, two sons, and a brother.

1906   William Shelly York   1988

William S. York, a Fellow of the Society, died in Little River, California, on March 19, 1988. He was eighty-two years old.

Born in Gordon, Nebraska, on January 30, 1906, Mr. York graduated from Harvard with an engineering degree in 1928. After four years employment as an engineer, he turned to the actuarial profession, joining the actuarial division of Metropolitan Life in May 1932. Except for service in the U.S. Navy as a lieutenant commander in World War II, his entire career until retirement in 1971 was with Metropolitan, where he became a vice-president in 1963 and a senior vice-president in 1965. He qualified as a Fellow of the

Actuarial Society of America and the American Institute of Actuaries in 1941.

Mr. York's field was largely computer work, a field in which he rendered distinguished service.

He is survived by his wife, Lucia Marguerite, and two children.

MINUTES OF THE REGIONAL MEETING

of the

SOCIETY OF ACTUARIES

HELD AT THE DISNEYLAND HOTEL
ANAHEIM, CALIFORNIA
APRIL 13–15, 1988

The meeting commenced on Wednesday, April 13, 1988 at 1:30 P.M. The following is a summary of attendance at the meeting.

SUMMARY

Fellows	540
Associates	273
Others......................	122
Total	935

The meeting convened at 1:30 P.M. in one open forum, four panel discussions, three seminar format sessions, and four workshops.

After a brief recess, the meeting reconvened at 3:30 P.M. in five panel discussions and six workshops.

After a brief recess, the meeting reconvened at 6:30 P.M. in five open workshops.

On Thursday, April 14, the meeting reconvened at 8:00 A.M. in two section meetings.

After a brief recess, the meeting reconvened at 8:45 A.M. in four panel discussions, one seminar format session, and nine workshops.

A "New Associates' Workshop" was also held at 8:45 A.M. under the sponsorship of the Committee on Professional Development.

After a brief recess, the meeting reconvened at 10:45 A.M. in four panel discussions and eight workshops.

A group luncheon was held at 12:30 P.M. for all registrants of the meeting. President Gary Corbett welcomed those attending the meeting and recognized those seated at the head table.

President Corbett reported that this special topic meeting on "Pension and Health" was cooperatively sponsored by the American Academy of Actuaries, the Conference of Actuaries in Public Practice, and the Society of Actuaries.

William David Smith, Chairperson of the Pension Section, briefly addressed the audience.

President Corbett recognized the individuals responsible for this special topic meeting: Program Committee Chairperson Peter J. Bondy and members of that committee; Chairperson William David Smith and Robert G. Utter of the Pension Section; Chairperson Howard J. Bolnick of the Health Section; and the section and committee liaison representatives and recruiters.

President Corbett recognized all the program participants—both Society members and those who were not members of the Society.

President Corbett recognized the following individuals attending this meeting from countries other than the United States and Canada: Peter Horan, Australia; and Willie R. Olivier, South Africa.

President Corbett next recognized and welcomed the new Associates and Fellows who were attending their first meeting of the Society since attainment of their present ranks.

President Corbett recognized 50-year Fellow James B. Gardiner, F.S.A., 1935.

President Corbett recognized Past President Robert J. Myers, who was attending the meeting.

President Corbett presented the report of the Secretary summarizing the nonroutine business transacted by the Board of Governors at its meeting on January 21, 1988 and by the Executive Committee at its meeting on March 8–9, 1988.

John E. O'Connor, Jr., Executive Director, made a few brief announcements.

President Corbett introduced Dr. Arthur B. Laffer, Chairman of A. B. Laffer Associates, who gave the keynote presentation on the "Laffer Curve Performance."

Following the luncheon, the meeting reconvened at 2:15 P.M. in one panel discussion, three seminar format sessions, one teaching session, and two workshops.

A dinner was held at 6:00 P.M. honoring new Fellows attending their first meeting of the Society since attainment of Fellowship. Before the dinner, brief remarks were presented by President Corbett and President-Elect Rolland. Following the dinner, Frederick W. Kilbourne addressed the audience.

On Friday, April 15, the meeting reconvened at 8:30 A.M. in one open forum, five panel discussions, and six workshops.

After a brief recess, the meeting reconvened at 10:30 A.M. in one open forum, five panel discussions, and seven workshops.

A group luncheon was held at 12:15 P.M. for all registrants of the meeting. President Corbett welcomed those attending the luncheon and recognized those seated at the head table.

William David Smith introduced Dr. Tony Alessandra, Alessandra & Associates, who gave the keynote presentation on "Relationship Strategies."

Following the luncheon, the meeting reconvened at 2:15 P.M. in one teaching session and eighteen workshops.

After a brief recess, the meeting reconvened at 3:30 P.M. in one teaching session and five workshops.

Luncheon session, open forum, panel discussion, open workshop, workshop, teaching session, and seminar format session topics, and the names of participants for this meeting are printed in the *Record*, Volume 14, Number 1.

ANTHONY T. SPANO
Secretary

MINUTES OF THE REGIONAL MEETING

of the

SOCIETY OF ACTUARIES

HELD AT THE GALT HOUSE HOTEL
LOUISVILLE, KENTUCKY
MAY 16–17, 1988

The meeting commenced on Monday, May 16, 1988 at 8:30 A.M. The following is a summary of attendance at the meeting.

SUMMARY

Fellows	352
Associates	170
Others	76
Total	598

The meeting convened at 8:30 A.M. in one open forum, two panel discussions, one seminar format session, and three workshops.

A "New Associates' Workshop" was also held at 8:30 A.M. under the sponsorship of the Committee on Professional Development.

After a brief recess, the meeting reconvened at 11:00 A.M. in three panel discussions and four workshops.

A group luncheon was held at 12:45 P.M. for all registrants of the meeting. President Gary Corbett welcomed those attending the meeting and recognized those seated at the head table.

President Corbett recognized the individuals responsible for this special topic meeting on "Product Development and Non-Traditional Marketing": Program Committee Chairperson Peter J. Bondy and members of that committee; and the liaison representatives and recruiters of the Individual Life Insurance and Annuity Product Development Section, Non-Traditional Marketing Section, Reinsurance Section, Committee on Professional Development, and Seminar Format Sessions.

President Corbett recognized all the program participants—both Society members and those who were not members of the Society.

President Corbett recognized Les W. Webb of England, who was attending this meeting from a country other than the United States and Canada.

President Corbett next recognized and welcomed the new Associates and Fellows who were attending their first meeting of the Society since attainment of their present ranks.

President Corbett recognized the following Past Presidents attending the meeting: Harold G. Ingraham, Jr. and Richard S. Robertson.

President Corbett acknowledged the authors of papers recently published in the *Transactions* April 1988 preprint and recognized one who was attending the meeting: Harry H. Panjer, "AIDS: Survival Analysis of Persons Testing HIV + ."

The Secretary presented an oral summary of nonroutine business transacted by the Board of Governors at its meeting on January 21, 1988 and by the Executive Committee at its meeting on March 8–9, 1988.

John E. O'Connor, Jr., Executive Director, made a few brief announcements.

President Corbett introduced Norman L. Phelps, Chairman and Chief Executive Officer of National Liberty Corporation, who gave the keynote presentation on "Making the Most of Your Network—Relationship Marketing."

Following the luncheon, the meeting reconvened at 2:30 P.M. in three panel discussions, two seminar format sessions, and four workshops.

A dinner was held at 7:45 P.M. honoring new Fellows attending their first meeting of the Society since attainment of Fellowship. Before the dinner, brief remarks were presented by President Corbett. Following the dinner, James C. Hickman addressed the audience.

On Tuesday, May 17, the meeting reconvened at 8:30 A.M. in one open forum, four panel discussions, one seminar format session, and four workshops.

After a brief recess, the meeting reconvened at 11:00 A.M. in one open forum, four panel discussions, one seminar format session, and five workshops.

A luncheon of the Individual Life Insurance and Annuity Product Development Section was held at 12:45 P.M. Following the luncheon, Edwin J. Gold, Chairman of the Board of PLANCO, Inc., addressed the audience.

Following lunch, the meeting reconvened at 2:30 P.M. in two seminar format sessions and one teaching session.

Luncheon session, open forum, panel discussion, workshop, teaching session, and seminar format session topics, and the names of participants for the meeting are printed in the *Record*, Volume 14, Number 2.

ANTHONY T. SPANO
Secretary

MINUTES OF THE REGIONAL MEETING
of the
SOCIETY OF ACTUARIES

HELD AT THE BOCA RATON HOTEL AND CLUB
BOCA RATON, FLORIDA
JUNE 8–10, 1988

The meeting commenced on Wednesday, June 8, 1988 at 2:00 P.M. The following is a summary of attendance at the meeting.

SUMMARY

Fellows	556
Associates	291
Others	65
Total	912

The meeting convened at 2:00 P.M. in four seminar format sessions.

On Thursday, June 9, the meeting reconvened at 8:30 A.M. in a general session with President Gary Corbett presiding.

President Corbett welcomed those attending the meeting and recognized those seated at the head table.

President Corbett recognized the individuals responsible for this special topic meeting on "Financial Reporting, Investments and Reinsurance": Program Committee Chairperson Peter J. Bondy and the members of that committee; and the liaison representatives and recruiters of the Financial Reporting Section, Health Section, Investment Section, Reinsurance Section, Committee on Professional Development, and Seminar Format Sessions.

President Corbett recognized all the program participants—both Society members and those who were not members of the Society.

President Corbett recognized the following individuals attending this meeting from countries other than the United States and Canada: John Howard Greenhalgh, England; Peter H. M. Kuys, Netherlands; Ken Magee, New Zealand; Stephen T. Meldrum, England; and John H. Taylor, Australia.

President Corbett recognized and welcomed the new Associates and Fellows who were attending their first meeting of the Society since attainment of their present ranks.

President Corbett recognized the following Past Presidents attending the meeting: John M. Bragg, Harold G. Ingraham, Jr., and Richard S. Robertson.

The Secretary presented an oral summary of nonroutine business transacted by the Board of Governors at its January 21, 1988 and May 18, 1988 meetings, and by the Executive Committee at its March 8–9, 1988 meeting.

John E. O'Connor, Jr., Executive Director, made a few brief announcements.

President Corbett introduced Gordon Pepper, Director and Senior Adviser of Midland Montagu Ltd., who gave the keynote presentation on "Behavior of Financial World Markets—A British Actuary's Perspective."

After a brief recess, the meeting reconvened at 10:30 A.M. in one open forum, three panel discussions, one seminar format session, and four workshops.

A "New Associates' Workshop" was also held at 10:30 A.M. under the sponsorship of the Committee on Professional Development.

Following lunch, the meeting reconvened at 2:30 P.M. in one open forum, six panel discussions, and two workshops.

A dinner was held at 7:45 P.M. honoring new Fellows attending their first meeting of the Society since attainment of Fellowship. Before the dinner, brief remarks were presented by President Corbett. Following the dinner, Robert D. Shapiro addressed the audience.

On Friday, June 10, the meeting reconvened at 8:30 A.M. in one open forum, three panel discussions, one teaching session, and six workshops.

After a brief recess, the meeting reconvened at 11:00 A.M. in two open forums, two panel discussions, and three workshops.

Following lunch, the meeting reconvened at 2:30 P.M. in one open forum, four panel discussions, one seminar format session, and six workshops.

General session, open forum, panel discussion, workshop, teaching session, and seminar format session topics, and the names of participants for this meeting are printed in the *Record*, Volume 14, Number 3.

ANTHONY T. SPANO
Secretary

MINUTES OF THE ANNUAL MEETING

of the

SOCIETY OF ACTUARIES

HELD AT THE BOSTON MARRIOTT HOTEL COPLEY PLACE
BOSTON, MASSACHUSETTS
OCTOBER 24–26, 1988

The meeting was called to order by President Gary Corbett on Monday, October 24, 1988 at 8:30 A.M. The following is a summary of attendance at the meeting:

SUMMARY

Fellows	1,024
Associates	219
Nonmembers	170
Exhibitors	126
Total	1,539

President Corbett introduced the Colonial Boys Fife and Drums Corps of New England for presentation of the colors and for the slide show: America the Beautiful and Canada Is.

Richard S. Robertson, Chairperson of the Committee on Elections, reported the election results of Officers and Members of the Board of Governors as follows:

President-Elect:	Allan D. Affleck
Vice-Presidents:	Barnet N. Berin
	Burton D. Jay
	Donald R. Sondergeld
Secretary:	Anthony T. Spano
Treasurer:	Michael J. Cowell
Board Members:	Nicholas Bauer
	Christopher D. Chapman
	Arnold A. Dicke
	Sam Gutterman
	Michael E. Mateja
	Daniel J. McCarthy

Following announcement of the election results, incoming President-Elect Allan D. Affleck spoke briefly.

1227

President Corbett recognized the following Past Presidents attending the meeting: Preston C. Bassett, Thomas P. Bowles, Jr., Robert H. Hoskins, Harold G. Ingraham, Jr., Barbara J. Lautzenheiser, Robin B. Leckie, Ernest J. Moorhead, Robert J. Myers, Richard S. Robertson, and Henry F. Rood.

President Corbett next recognized the individuals attending this meeting from countries other than the United States and Canada.

President Corbett recognized the individuals responsible for this meeting: Program Committee Chairperson Peter J. Bondy and members of that committee; and the liaison representatives and recruiters of the various sections and committees.

President Corbett recognized all the program participants—both Society members and those who were not members of the Society.

President Corbett recognized and welcomed the new Associates and Fellows who were attending their first meeting of the Society since attainment of their present ranks.

President Corbett next recognized 50-year Fellows Ernest J. Moorhead, F.S.A., 1938, and Henry F. Rood, F.S.A., 1937.

President Corbett advised that the Society had received word of the deaths of forty members since the last annual meeting. Those in attendance at this meeting observed a moment of silence in respect for the memory of these members. Obituaries are printed in this volume of the *Transactions*.

President Corbett announced the 1989 Annual Prize winners for the best papers published in the *Transactions* as follows: Harry H. Panjer for his paper "AIDS: Survival Analysis of Persons Testing HIV+," to be published in the *Transactions*, Volume XL, and Louis J. Lombardi for his paper "Relationships between Statutory and Generally Accepted Accounting Principles (GAAP)," to be published in the *Transactions*, Volume XL. Mr. Panjer and Mr. Lombardi accepted their awards.

President Corbett announced that the Triennial Prize winner for the period covering 1985–1988 was Jacques F. Carrieri for his paper "The Bounds of Bivariate Distributions that Limit the Value of Lost-Survivor Annuities," which was published in the *Transactions*, Volume XXXVIII. Mr. Carrieri was not present at the meeting to accept his award.

President Corbett next announced that the 1988 Halmstad Prize winner for actuarial research was Ragnar Norberg from the University of Oslo, Oslo, Norway for his paper "A Contribution to Modelling of IBNR Claims," which was published in the *Scandinavian Actuarial Journal* in 1986. Professor Norberg was not present at the meeting to accept his award.

President Corbett announced the 1988 AERF Practitioners Award winners for practical actuarial research performed during 1986 or 1987 that has not been published, as follows: Charles S. Fuhrer was awarded the top prize for his paper "A Method for the Calculation of Aggregated Stop-Loss Premiums"; honorable mention awards were presented to David L. Creswell for his paper "Required Surplus with Emphasis on C-2 Risk" and to David N. Ingram for his paper "Unreleased Capital Gains on Common Stock as Required Surplus." Messrs. Fuhrer, Creswell and Ingram accepted their awards.

John E. O'Connor, Jr., Executive Director, made a few brief announcements.

President Corbett gave his presidential address on "The Future of the Actuary/The Actuary of the Future," which is printed in this volume of the *Transactions*.

After a brief recess, the meeting reconvened at 10:30 A.M. in three open forums, five panel discussions, and eleven workshops.

A "New Associates' Workshop" was also held at 10:30 A.M. under the sponsorship of the Committee on Professional Development.

Two sections held luncheon meetings at 12:00 noon.

Following lunch, the meeting reconvened at 1:30 P.M. in three open forums, three panel discussions, one teaching session, and twelve workshops.

The Exhibit Hall was open to all registrants at various hours throughout the meeting.

A dinner was held at 7:30 P.M. honoring new Fellows attending their first meeting of the Society since attainment of Fellowship. Before the dinner, brief remarks were presented by President Corbett and President-Elect Rolland. Following the dinner, John C. Angle addressed the audience.

On Tuesday, October 25, the meeting reconvened at 7:45 A.M. in three section meetings and at 8:30 A.M. in five panel discussions, one seminar format session, one teaching session, and eight workshops.

After a brief recess, the meeting reconvened at 10:30 A.M. in one open forum, four panel discussions, and twelve workshops.

Two sections held luncheon meetings at 12:00 noon.

Following lunch, the meeting reconvened at 1:30 P.M. in three open forums, three panel discussions, and twelve workshops.

After a brief recess, the meeting reconvened at 3:45 P.M. in one workshop.

On Wednesday, October 26, the meeting reconvened at 8:15 A.M. in a general session of the American Academy of Actuaries, which was holding its annual meeting in conjunction with the Society's meeting.

President Corbett presided over the general session of the Society of Actuaries that convened at 9:00 A.M.

President Corbett introduced John G. Stoessinger, Ph.D., Director of the Advanced Institute for American Leaders, who gave the keynote address on "The United States: Its Allies and the World Economy."

The Secretary presented an oral summary of nonroutine business transacted by the Board of Governors at its October 22–23, 1988 meeting.

Treasurer Michael J. Cowell summarized the financial report, which is printed in this volume of the *Transactions*.

The gavel was passed to President-Elect Rolland. President Rolland called upon Richard S. Robertson, who presented an oil portrait of Mr. Corbett to Mr. Corbett on behalf of the Society in appreciation of his service as President.

President Rolland then spoke briefly and adjourned the general session.

After a brief recess, the meeting reconvened at 11:00 A.M. in four open forums, two panel discussions, one seminar format session, two teaching sessions, and ten workshops.

Following lunch, the meeting reconvened at 2:00 P.M. in two open forums, two panel discussions, and five workshops.

General session, open forum, panel discussion, section meeting, workshop, teaching session, and seminar format session topics, and the names of participants for the meeting are printed in the *Record*, Volume 14, Numbers 4A and 4B.

ANTHONY T. SPANO
Secretary